Baedeker

MEXICO

Hints for using the Guide

Following the tradition established by Karl Baedeker in 1844, buildings and works of art, places of natural beauty and sights of particular interest, as well as hotels and restaurants of especially high quality, are distinguished by one ★ or two ★★.

To make it easier to locate the various places listed in the "A to Z" section of the Guide, their co-ordinates are shown in red at the head of each entry: e.g., Mexico City K 8.

Coloured lines down the right-hand side of the page are an aid to finding the main heading in the Guide: blue stands for the Introduction (Nature, Culture, History, etc.), red for the "A to Z" section, and yellow indicates Practical Information.

Only a selection of hotels, restaurants and shops can be given; no reflection is implied therefore on establishments not included.

In a time of rapid change it is difficult to ensure that all the information given is entirely accurate and up-to-date, and the possibility of error can never be entirely eliminated.

Although the publishers can accept no responsibility for inaccuracies and omissions, they are constantly endeavouring to improve the quality of their Guides and are therefore always grateful for criticisms, corrections and suggestions for improvement.

Preface

This guide is one of the new generation of Baedeker guides. Illustrated throughout in colour and containing a number of specially prepared plans, they are designed to meet the needs of the modern traveller. They are quick and easy to consult, with the principal sights described in alphabetical order, and practical details and useful tips shown in the margin. The information is presented in a format that is both attractive and easy to follow. The subject of this guide is Mexico, the largest state in Central America.

The guide is in three parts. The first part gives a general account of the country, its climate, flora and fauna, population, state and constitution economy, history, famous people, pre-Columbian cultures, art and culture. A brief selection of quotations and some suggested routes lead into the second part, in which the principal places of tourist interest – towns, villages, landscapes – are described. The third part contains a variety of practical information designed to help visitors to find their way about and make the most of their stay. Baedeker Specials explain in detail the Mayan Calendar and the Aztec Stone of the Fifth Sun. Both the sights and the practical information sections are listed in alphabetical order.

Pyramid of Kukulkán Chichén Itzá

The new Baedeker guides are noted for their concentration on essentials and their convenience of use. They contain numerous specially drawn plans and colour illustrations; and at the end of the book is a large map making it easy to locate the various places described in the "A to Z" section of the guide with the help of the co-ordinates given at the head of each entry.

Contents

Nature, Culture, History
Pages 9–125

Sights from A to Z
Pages 127–541

Practical Information from A to Z
Pages 543–612

Baedeker Specials

Viva

The visitor to Mexico is hardly likely to be able to absorb the country's fascinating culture and scenic diversity on a single trip. Anyone whose sole experience of Mexico is confined to the beaches of Cancún and Acapulco, with their massive influx of tourists each year, has barely scratched the surface of this, the largest country in Central America. When visiting Mexico, always allow plenty of time – even the clocks seem to go that little bit slower here, and what doesn't get done today can most likely be fitted in tomorrow. That is probably the best maxim for anyone wishing to get to know this multifaceted land of contrasts. There will be those who choose to immerse themselves in the world of advanced pre-Colombian civilisations and surrender to the full effect of the ruins, temples and pyramids of the Olmecs, Zapotecs and Mixtecs, the Toltecs, Mayas and Aztecs. For them the reward will be a revelation of the unsurpassed riches and achievements of these peoples and their traditions which date back many thousands of years. The legacy they have left at such sites as Palenque, Chickén Itza, Teotihuacán and Monte Albán, compares favourably with the magnificent Spanish colonial buildings to be found in towns such as Guanajuato and Querétaro on the Mexican altiplano, Oaxaco in the Sierra Madre or San Cristóbal de las Casas in Chiapas. A visit to Mexico City is breathtaking in the literal sense of the word, but, in spite of the smog and pounding traffic, the special atmosphere of this city of 20 million people will hold the visitor under its sway: listen to a song from the Mariachis on the Plaza Garibaldi, take a look at the pavement artists on the Zócalo and

Cacaxtla

Magnificent wall frescos immortalise the mythical shape of old Mexico

Souvenirs

Ceramics in the market at Taxco and found in abundance throughout Mexico

Mexico

encounter in the city's museums the chequered history of the country and its artistic and cultural treasures. But those who are daunted by all this need not feel that Mexico is not the place for them. The country has plenty to offer to lovers of nature and unspoilt scenery, and to water-sports enthusiasts and sun-worshippers – whether it be the desert landscapes of the north, with their giant cacti, the parched coastland of Baja California with its picturesque bays and inlets and fascinating fauna, the stunning ravines of the Barranca del Cobra, the Chiapas rain-forest, Yucatean scrubland or Mexican altiplano. And while mountaineers can look forward to making the acquaintance of the legendary peaks of Popocatépetl and Iztaccihuatl, bathers and swimmers will find unalloyed pleasure in the countless picture-book beaches of fine sand to be found along the Pacific and Caribbean costs.

Or why not visit a restaurant and order tacos and enchilladas, mole poblano and tortillas? Or visit the colourful country markets, where it is possible to sample exotic fruits and to meet the local Indian population on equal terms, with openness and respect. If the opportunity arises, go to a fiesta, but do not let yourself be disturbed by the bizarre, yet joyful cult of the dead on All Saints' Day. If you can let yourself go and respond to this culture without inhibitions, you will receive the most generous and heartfelt of welcomes from the Mexicans, and anyone who drinks mezcal and has the courage to bite into the little worm and even swallow it, is practically an honorary Mexican. ¡Ándale pues!

The Mexican

are a people whose culture is open and respectful

Mexico City

Over 20 million people live in this huge city

Chac-mool

stands guard over many old Mexican towns and temple sites

Facts and Figures

Preface

Mexico has long been a favourite destination for holidaymakers from Canada and the United States, but it is also becoming increasingly popular with visitors from Europe, as more and more of them are prepared to put up with the long flight to get to know a country that besides sunshine, scenery, sandy beaches and clear blue seas also has a cultural heritage that is astonishingly varied and often of a breathtaking grandeur. UNESCO has in fact designated eleven world cultural heritage sites in Mexico: Mexico City's historic centre and Xochimilco, the towns of Guanajuato, Puebla, Oaxaca and Zacatecas, the archaeological sites of Teotihucán, Monte Albán, Chichén Itzá and Palenque, and the Sian Ka'an nature reserve.

Situation of Mexico in America

Anyone travelling around Mexico will undoubtedly be left with a host of striking impressions and insights into a different world. Although Mexicans are generally hospitable, there is none of the urgency or promptness that Europeans are used to. Here the visitor will experience an encounter with a distant culture, rich in tradition, but will also find people whose attitudes and ways of life are quite a culture shock as well.

Mexico is a nation in transition from developing country to industrial state, and as such is changing so rapidly that it is difficult to keep pace with its expanding infrastructure, and stay up to date

◀ *Diego Rivera: "La Gran Tenochtitlán"*

with much of the practical information (statistics, roads and mileage, accommodation). Even the official sources are often not entirely accurate.

At the same time discovery is constantly advancing knowledge of Mexico's glittering past. A single archaeological find can throw fresh light on a whole phase in its development and cause a radical rethink in the writing of history, which is why the publishers always welcome details of the latest findings.

From the tourist's point of view there is virtually no sign of any after-effects of the earthquake that devastated Mexico City and parts of the Pacific Coast on September 19th 1985.

General

Area and Geography

Map on page 9

Mexico lies between degrees of latitude 32°43′ and 14°14′N, and longitude 88°48′ and 117°7′W. It covers an area of 1,972,547sq.km/761,403sq. miles (over eight times that of Great Britain), and forms the south-western extension of the north American continent which, beyond the Isthmus of Tehuantepec, curves north-east for most of the Yucatán peninsula and south-east into the land-bridge of Central America. Bounded by 7335km/4558 miles of Pacific coastline in the west, Mexico also has 2805km/1743 miles of coastline on the Gulf of Mexico and the Caribbean in the east.

At its longest Mexico is 3170km/1970 miles from north to south and at its widest 1200km/746 miles from west to east. The Isthmus of Tehuantepec, its narrowest point, is only 225km/140 miles across. The countries on its borders are the USA in the north and Guatemala and Belize, formerly British Honduras, in the south.

Geographical areas

Mexican Plateau
(Altiplano)

The vast high plateau of northern and central Mexico is the core feature of this country of geographical and geological contrasts. Sloping gradually upward from north to south, from altitudes of 900m/2954ft to as high as 2400–3000m/7877–9846ft further south, the "altiplano" is divided into seven great broad valleys broken up by ranges of hills interspersed with canyons and gullies, and is bounded by the Sierra Madre Occidental in the west and the Sierra Madre Oriental in the east. These mighty mountain chains mean that very little rain reaches the interior, and when it does rain, mostly in the summer, the water pours into these gulches and then drains away.

Northern plateau

Much of the northern plateau, where the altitude is lower, is taken up by a series of broad, uniform bolsones – desert valleys surrounded by mountains. The largest of the landlocked valleys of this kind are the bolsones of Mapimí and San Luis Potosi, but they are drained by the tributaries flowing into the Río Bravo del Norte and the Rio Grande from the south and thence into the Gulf of Mexico. The northernmost section has a broad valley floor, at an altitude of between 900 and 1200m/2954 and 3938ft, with a scattering of lakes, sand dunes, saltflats and alluvial hillslopes. The mountains round the rim account for a further 800 to 900m/2626 to 2954ft. The ranges running from north to south, and from north-west to south-east are

Natural Regions of Mexico

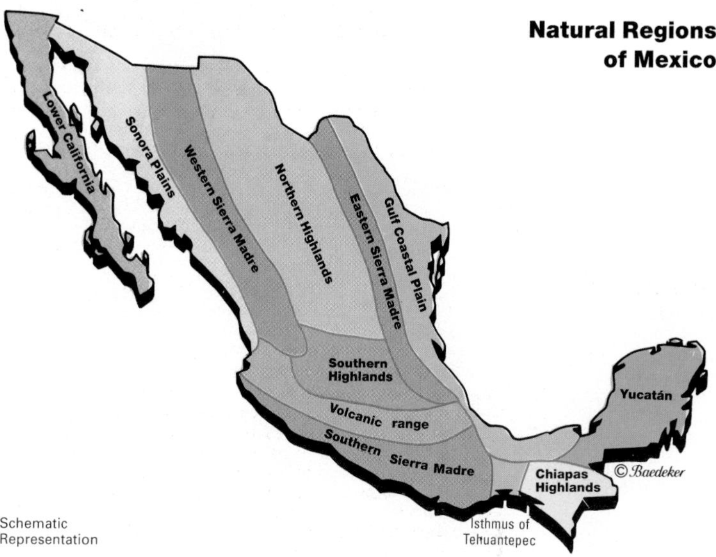

Schematic Representation

full of gold, silver, lead, zinc, mercury, oil shale, coal and iron ore, and the roads and railways cutting through them link the desert "oases" and mining towns with one another and with places and markets in the United States and in Central Mexico. The oases get their water from rivers like the Casas Grandes, Conchos, Nazas and Aguanaval which all come down from the western Sierra Madre only to lose most of their water by evaporation, seepage, etc. when they flow into the depressions. The "laguna" district around Torreón is important for the irrigation it gets from the Nazas and Aguanaval. Besides places that get their water from the river in this way there are also oases such as Ciudad Juárez and Ojiniga that have been created by the flooding of low ground.

Southern plateau

The central high plateau further south has a number of broad alluvial valley basins, those of Bajío, Toluca, México and Puebla among them, with floors composed mainly of layers of lava and ash. The valleys are separated from one another and from southern Mexico by rolling hills and jagged volcanoes. The lakes, swamps, and hot springs in these high valleys at between 1500 and 2600m/4923 and 8533ft owe their existence to the lava that has blocked any outflow. Chapala, Cuitzeo and Pátzcuaro are the best known of the lakes. This area is also the source of three of the main river systems – the Mezcala-Balsas, which rises at Puebla, the Río Lerma/Río Grande de Santiago, from west of the Mexico basin, and the Río Moctezuma/Río Pánuco from the Mexico basin itself. Already very densely populated in pre-Hispanic times, this part of Mexico includes the Bajío, one of the country's most fertile farming areas, which stretches along the Río Lerma and is mainly in the states of Michoacán and Guanajuato. For centuries agriculture has also provided subsistence for large populations in Puebla, México and Morelos.

A rural settlement in the highlands

Scenery in the volcanic belt

The principal Mountain Ranges and Rivers of Mexico

Volcano Belt (Sistema Volcánica Transversal)

South of Mexico City the volcano belt of the Cordillera Neo-Volcánica runs across the central plateau from around San Blas on the Pacific to Veracruz on the Gulf of Mexico. This range which divides the north and centre of the country from the south contains Mexico's highest mountains – Citlaltépetl (Pico de Orizaba, 5700m/18,707ft), Popocatépetl (5452m/17,893ft), Iztaccíhuatl (5286m/17,349ft), Nevado de Toluca (Cinantecátl; 4575m/15,015ft), and La Malinche (Matlalcuéyetl; 4461m/14,641ft). The southern slopes of the belt are full of fissures, the volcanic rocks eroded away by the tributaries of the Río Mezcala.

The same is true of the Sierra Mixteca, the mountain range joining the plateau to the Sierra Madre del Sur in the south.

Sierra Madre Occidental

The Sierra Madre Occidental, the western range, extends for 1100km/684 miles north-west to south-east and is about 160km/100 miles across. Most of its peaks exceed 1800m/5908ft, and the highest are over 3000m/9846ft. The big mountain chains and canyons broadly follow the line of the Mesozoic folding and older base strata. The western section has "barrancas", gorges as deep as 1500m/4923ft and that, in their grandeur, almost rival the Grand Canyon of the Colorado River in the US State of Arizona. There are only two main roads and a single railway line across the mountains, linking the high plateau with the coastal plains of Sinaloa and Sonora. The rivers which rise in the high sierras and provide the water for the oases up on the plateau are the Carmen, Conchos, Nazas and Aguanaval, while the lowlands bordering the Gulf of California get their water from the Yaqui, Mayo, Fuerte, Sinaloa and Culiacán.

Sierra Madre Oriental

A range of relatively low hills formed from the sedimentary layers left by folding runs south-east from the great bend in Río Bravo del Norte as it becomes the Rio Grande. South of Monterrey these hills develop into the impressive chain of the Sierra Madre Oriental, the eastern Sierra Madre. A late-Mesozoic formation, their peaks are generally around 2100m/6892ft, with some of them exceeding 3000m/9846ft. Many of the narrow valleys, walled in by steep cliffs, run north/south. There is only one river worth mentioning which flows down from the eastern rim of the high plateau into the Gulf of Mexico, and that is the Pánuco.

Northern Pacific Region

The northern Pacific region is made up of middle and late Tertiary parallel mountain chains and broad valleys in the State of Sonora, along with the coastal plain corridor and the Baja California peninsula, separated from mainland Mexico by the Gulf of California (or Mar de Cortés). The Sonora basins are flanked by moraine-type formations that become hilly country towards the north-east. The coast is flat and sandy, and largely unbroken, but also has lagoons and deepwater bays surrounded by rocky hills. There are very few rivers crossing the coastal plain between the Colorado in the north and the Río Sonora further south, but in the southernmost part there are fertile oases growing cotton, wheat, rice, sugar cane, fruit and vegetables. Mining, mainly for copper, occurs in the extreme north-east.

Baja California

Baja California is a narrow peninsula, averaging only 90km/56 miles across, and stretching for about 1250km/777 miles. The rock formations found here range across the Cretaceous and Tertiary periods and, particularly in the southern section, Pleistocene and Holocene volcanic and marine deposits. Crystalline mountains form the backbone of the peninsula, most of them over 1500m/4923ft and many as high as 3000m/9846ft. Besides high plateau there are broad strips of flat desert on both sides of the Sierra de Santa Clara. Both coastlines have wonderful natural bays, and at the top of the peninsula there is the delta of the Colorado River.

Gulf Coast

The coastal plain on the Gulf of Mexico gradually becomes the foothills of the Sierra Madre Oriental as it gets further south-west. The cretaceous northern and central sections have low hills, rocky outcrops seldom higher than 200m/656ft, especially in the "Huasteca" south of Tampico. The main features of the coast are its long beaches, sandbanks, marshland and lagoons. At one point in the state of Veracruz the foothills of the Sierra Madre Oriental narrow the coastal plain down to less than 15km/9 miles. The relatively flat landscape is broken up by the rocky coast and the hills around San Andrés Tuxtla.

So far as rivers and harbours are concerned, in the north it is the mighty Río Bravo del Norte, or the Rio Grande as it becomes on the American border, and the Tamesí-Pánuco which cut across the coastal plain. South and east of the port of Veracruz the Papaloapán, Coatzacoalcos, Grijalva and Usumacinta rivers all fan out into great swamps before they reach the sea. The northern part of the Gulf Coast lacks a good natural harbour, and because of the lack of shelter for anchoring ships afforded by a coastline consisting mainly of sandbanks and lagoons harbours tend to be on the rivers. Even Veracruz owes its importance as a port more to its position near the Mexican heartland than to the natural quality of its harbour.

Yucatán Peninsula

Mexico's broadest expanse of lowland is the limestone plateau of the Yucatán Peninsula, stretching for about 450km/280 miles across at its widest. Geologically this is Mexico's youngest region, its development dating from the Miocene and Pleiocene eras, the middle and end of the Tertiary period. Part of this tableland is under water, forming the Campeche Bank. Yucatán reaches its highest point in the centre of the peninsula (partly in Guatemala), but this is only around 150m/492ft. There are hardly any rivers since the rain seeps away into the porous soluble rock, creating underground caverns and "cenotes", the natural wells formed by the collapse of the overlying limestone crust. There are mangrove swamps all along the coastline, which has sandbanks and lagoons in the north and west, and coral reefs in the east.

Southern Mexico

Southern Mexico is a mountainous region measuring over 1500km/9321 miles from north-west to south-east and about 350km/217 miles across at its widest, stretching from Cabo Corrientes to the Guatemalan border and taking in the part of the country south of the volcano belt, the Gulf coastal plain and the Yucatán peninsula. It can be divided up into three parts, the Sierra Madre del Sur, the Isthmus of Tehuantepec, and the Chiapas Highlands.

Southern Sierra Madre (Sierra Madre del Sur)

The Sierra Madre del Sur is a maze of narrow mountain ridges and deep valleys. Much of the volcanic overlay deposited on the sedimentary chalk bedrock during the Mesozoic era has been worn away by erosion. Most peaks are over 2000m/6564ft, and a few exceed 3000m/9846ft. There is hardly a piece of flat land to be found anywhere. To the east the mountains drop sharply to the Isthmus of Tehuantepec, and the heart of the chain is contained by a narrow indented coastal plain in the south-west and the lowlands of the Balsa-Mezcala River system in the north. East of this depression the high plateau of the Sierra Mixteca acts as a bridge between the volcano belt and the southern Sierra Madre. Here the Pacific

A waterfall in Agua Azul near Palenque

The Pacific coast near Acapulco

coastline follows the course of the high sierras, with steep cliffs and wonderful natural bays and harbours such as Acupulco and Manzanillo. Iron ore, lead, gold and silver occur up in the mountains, which have few roads across them, and as yet no railways. This relative inaccessibility has meant that the indigenous people living here have largely managed to preserve their independent way of life.

Isthmus of Tehuantepec (Istmo de Tehuantepec)

The rolling hills of the Isthmus of Tehuantepec are topographically similar to those of the coastal plains on the Gulf of Mexico, although geologically they have more in common with the Sierra Madre del Sur in the west and the Chiapas Highlands in the east. They date from the late Pliocene and Pleistocene eras, and as gentle uplands close the gap between two major mountain regions. They have long provided a natural corridor for communications, and today carry roads, railways and pipelines. The plan to build a canal linking the Atlantic and the Pacific across the isthmus at Mexico's narrowest point (225km/140 miles) has been under consideration for centuries, but nothing has ever come of it.

Chiapas Highlands

The Chiapas Highlands already attain a height of over 1500m/4923ft only 40km/25 miles from the coast; in some parts, like the Tacaná volcano, they top the 3000m/9846ft mark. While the central plateau, the Meseta Central, mainly consisting of chalk and sandstone, dates from the Pliocene era, the Sierra Madre de Chiapas mountains were Pre-Cambrian, with the folding taking place in the Pliocene era, forming the mountain chain from Pre-Cambrian and Palezoic crystalline rock, mesozoic sedimentation and modern eruptions. Several short rivers flow down to the coastal plains, interlaced with lagoons. Between the two high mountain ranges there is a broad depression, at altitudes of between 300 and 600m/984 and 1969ft, formed mainly by the valley of the Río Grijalva.

Most of the Chiapas region is given over to farming, forest and grassland, with coffee grown on the mountain slopes. The isolation of this part of Mexico has only been ended in the past twenty years or so with the coming of better roads and a railway line along the Pacific coast.

Climate

The Tropic of Cancer cuts through Mexico just north of Mazatlán, putting it on the northern edge of the Tropics. In a country where the main single topographical feature is the high plateau climbing gradually from 1300m/4266ft in the north to 2500m/8205ft in the south, the variety of climates in individual regions is due to the combination of several basic weather patterns.

Low-lying southern areas are tropical, hot, and wet. Further north it gradually becomes dryer because of the steppes and deserts of the horse latitudes (belts of calms at northern edge of north-east trade winds).

In the east on the Atlantic coast and seaward facing slopes of the Sierra Madre Oriental, where the trade-winds blow onshore all year round, it is sultry and wet with tropical forests. The Pacific coast in the west is far dryer.

There is less precipitation further inland and in the lee of the mountains; the greater the altitude the colder it becomes. The natural vegetation and the crops that can be grown therefore alter accordingly. Mexico's Spanish conquerors devised names for these different climate zones and these are still used today.

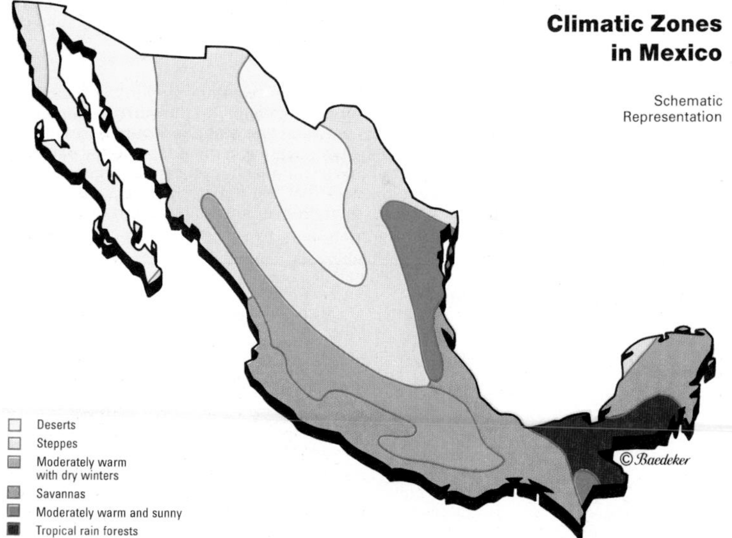

Climate

Climatic zones

The lowest zone, the Tierra Caliente or hot zone, ends at around 800m/2626ft, which is roughly the limit for growing cocoa beans. In this zone the natural vegetation in the wetter parts of southern Mexico is tropical rain forest.

The intermediate zone, the Tierra Templada or temperate zone between 800 and 1700m/2626 and 5579ft, finishes at the upper limit for growing coffee, cotton and sugar cane.

Above 1700m/5579ft comes the Tierra Fría, the cold zone. The highest volcanic peaks are snow-covered throughout the year.

Climatic Regions

Southern central high plateau: wet summers and moderate temperatures.

Northern central high plateau: wet summers and steppe climate, sub-tropical semi-desert and desert climate.

Southern Gulf Coast region with the Yucatán peninsula: ranging from constantly wet rainforest climate in the south to variably wet Savanna climates further north.

Northern Gulf Coast region: hot and wet summers and sub-tropical steppe climate.

Southern Pacific coast: tropical variably wet savanna climates.

Coastal region around the Gulf of California: sub-tropical semi-desert and desert climate.

Extreme north-west: rain in winter.

Weather Stations

The graphs on pages 20–21 show the annual monthly (J=January/D=December) precipitation and temperatures for Mexico's separate climate regions. The blue columns represent monthly precipitation in millimetre; the orange band represents the monthly temperatures in Centigrade with the figures in red. The top of the band corresponds to the average maximum temperature in the early afternoon and the bottom line stands for the average minimum temperature at night.

The figures for each of the seven weather stations, selected as being typical for their region, also apply to the surrounding area. The figures for districts between two stations would normally be somewhere between the two, bearing in mind the general patterns outlined at the start of this section, although care also needs to be taken to allow for the fact that the figures can be substantially affected by changes in altitude over a relatively short distance.

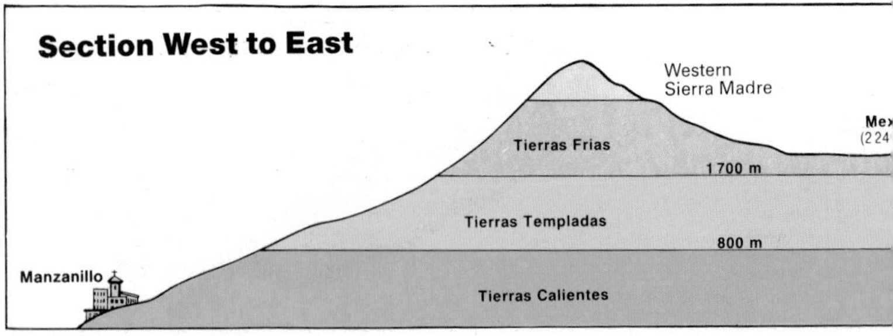

Design: Prof. Dr Wolfgang Hassenpflug

Southern central high plateau (Ciudad de México weather station)

Almost half of Mexico is above 1500m/4923ft, and Mexico City, its capital, is at 2240m/7352ft. It lies in the Tierra Fría and its high altitude means that, despite being south of the Tropic of Cancer, it does not enjoy tropical temperatures. Also since it is sheltered by mountains, it rarely gets tropical levels of rainfall or experiences high humidity.

The graph shows what the climate is like in the different months. Potential visitors can thus choose when to go or see what sort of weather can be expected for a particular month.

The broadness of the orange band is an indication of how wide the range is of the daily temperatures. As everywhere in the Tropics, temperatures vary little as between seasons, and substantially less so than in Northern Europe. Anyone who flies to Mexico from Northern Europe in mid-October, for example, will find the low night-time temperatures which they are used to and should dress accordingly.

The blue columns in the top half of the diagram show the rainfall. As in almost the whole of Mexico, most of the rain is in summer, between June and September, largely in the form of cloudbursts. For the rest of the year this part of the country is much dryer than northern Europe, and there are frequent dust storms. These form over the dried lake bed on which Mexico City stands, further worsening visibility which is already reduced by the pall of smog that hangs over the city from pollution by cars and industry. On many days it is impossible to see the snowy peak of the volcano of Popocatépetl, 5452m/17,893ft high, and 60km/37 miles away.

The high altitude has several other consequences. Atmospheric pressure is much less (below 600mm on the barometric scale). The thin air can cause breathing and circulation disorders for some people, and visitors will need three weeks to get fully acclimatised. Solar radiation is much more intense at this altitude than at lower levels and, as in the Alps for example, temperatures of 10°–15°C/50°–59°F already feel hot. Since the sun is also very high and shining almost directly overhead at midday in the southern parts of the country, protection through barrier creams and sunglasses is essential. As for the typical Mexican sombrero, no local could afford to be without it. At night the process is reversed and the heat loss is quite dramatic as the temperature drops very quickly. Sore throats are often another side-effect of the dryness of the air on the high plateau, although increasingly this can also be due to air pollution.

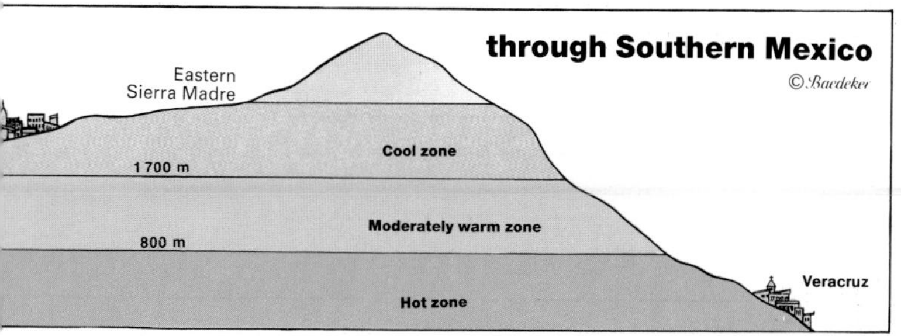

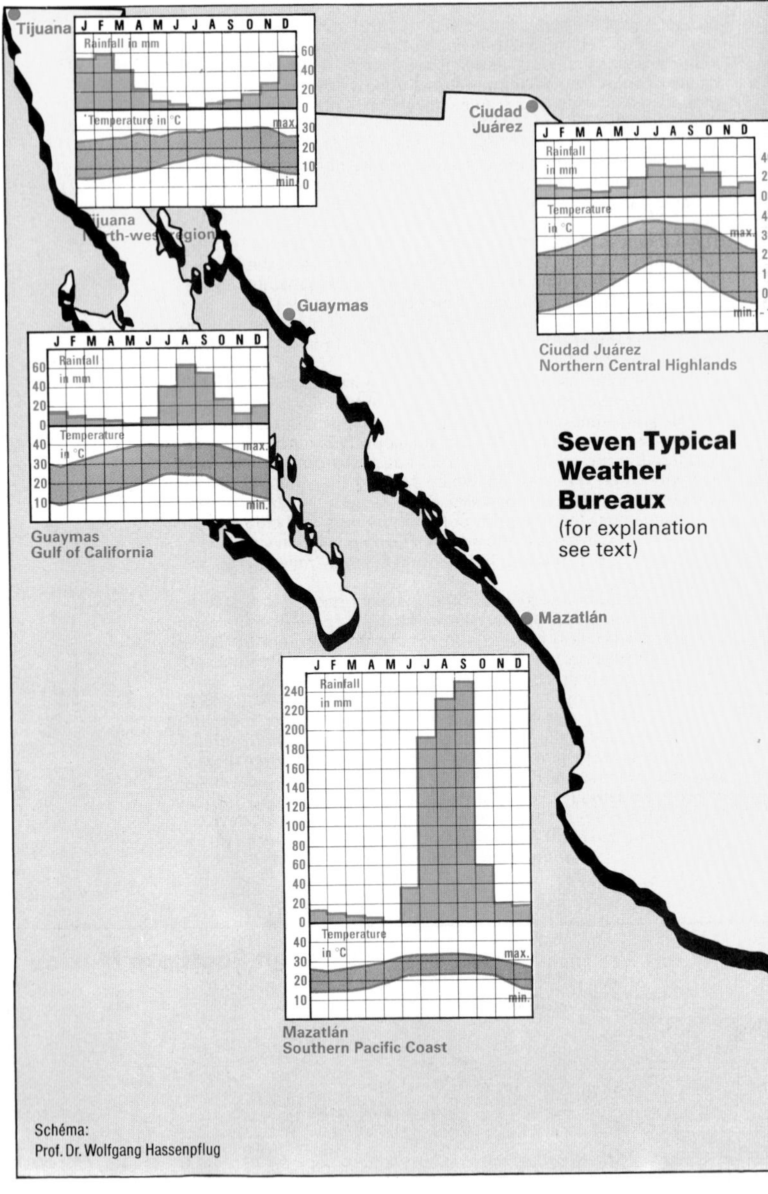
Tijuana
Ciudad Juárez
Guaymas
Mazatlán
J F M A M J J A S O N D
Rainfall in mm
Temperature in °C
max.
min.
Tijuana
North-west region
Ciudad Juárez
Northern Central Highlands
Guaymas
Gulf of California
Mazatlán
Southern Pacific Coast
Seven Typical Weather Bureaux
(for explanation see text)
Schéma:
Prof. Dr. Wolfgang Hassenpflug

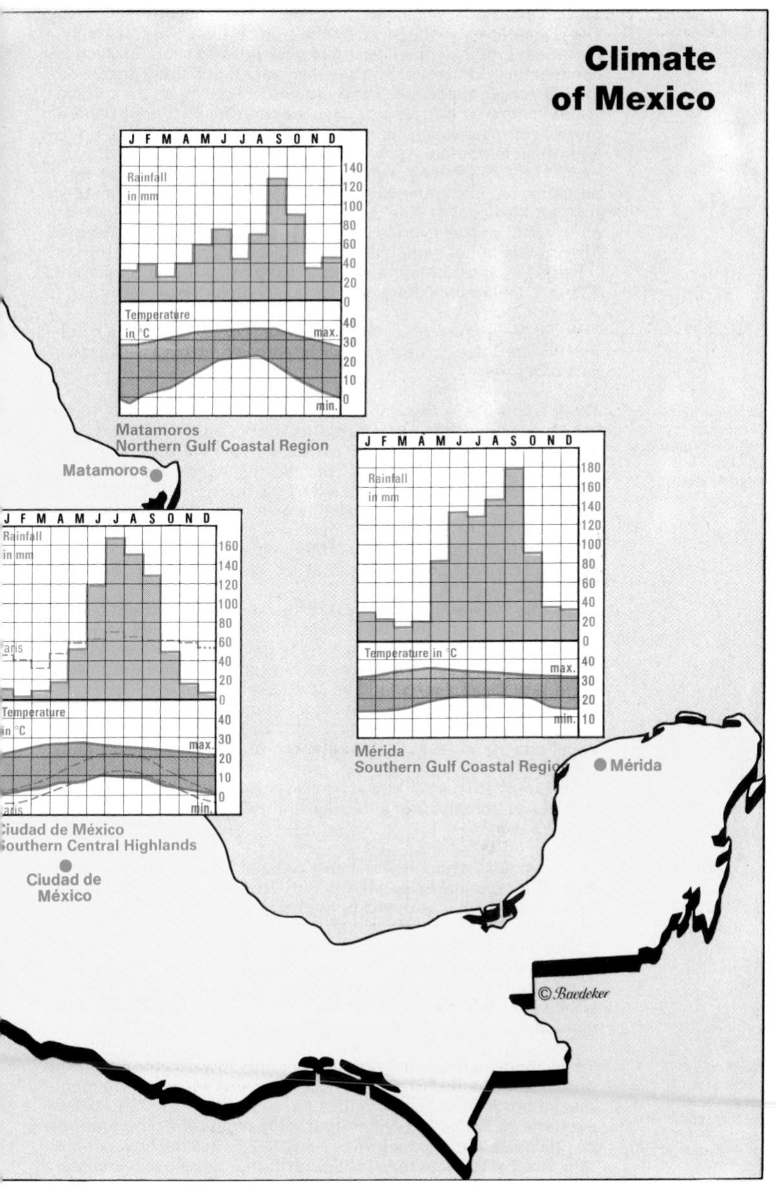

Climate of Mexico
J F M A M J J A S O N D
Rainfall in mm
Temperature in °C
max.
min.
Matamoros
Northern Gulf Coastal Region
Matamoros
Paris
Ciudad de México
Southern Central Highlands
Ciudad de México
Mérida
Southern Gulf Coastal Region
Mérida
© Baedeker

Climate

Northern central high plateau (Ciudad Juárez weather station)

Mexico's central high plateau loses height as it gets further north and is increasingly influenced by sub-tropical high pressure fronts, becoming a dry, steppe-like and basically desert climate which is continental in character. The weather station at Ciudad Juárez on the US border opposite El Paso shows just how much the climate varies compared with Mexico City. The curve in the orange band is more acute, indicating far greater differences between summer and winter temperatures. Average night-time temperatures drop to −8°C/17.6°F in January, while the summer daytime highest temperatures are just under 40°/104°F. The band is also much broader than for Mexico City. The daily range of temperature has risen to almost 30°, so that even in winter it is still as hot at midday as in Mexico City but at night it is bitterly cold.

Here, too, most of the rain falls in summer, but with a figure of 33mm/1¼in. for July there is much less than further south.

The climate in the high country between Mexico City in the south and Ciudad Juárez in the north will be somewhere between the two sets of figures.

Southern Gulf Coast and Yucatán Peninsula (Mérida weather station)

This region has a tropical climate which is hot and wet – and somewhat unhealthy – and gets drier further north in winter. Cold air fronts from the north are constantly bringing in cooling air between October and March. The rain falling on the mountain slopes west of Veracruz is boosted by the trade-winds blowing off the sea, and the figures of 1500mm/59in. for the low-lying areas rise to 4000mm/157in. at 2000m/6564ft. Here there is the whole range of features found at the different altitudes, from tropical rainforest lower down to eternal ice on the tops of the lofty volcanoes.

Mérida, the weather station, is in the drier north-western part of the Yucatán Peninsula. The heaviest rainfall is between May and October when although the maximum day temperatures, at 34°C/93°F, are about 3° less than those for May, the high humidity makes them less tolerable. As little as 10 to 30m/33ft to 99ft above the ground or the forest floor there is a cooling breeze all year round (which also drives the windmills), and this makes even a relatively small change in level such as the top of a pyramid seem quite pleasant.

The southern part of Mexico is also occasionally affected by the hurricanes from the Gulf of Mexico or the Caribbean between July and October.

The island of Cozumel off the east coast of Yucatán has the same kind of temperatures as Mérida but, like the eastern part of the peninsula which is exposed to the trade-winds, has more rainfall (1553mm/61in. a year compared to 928mm/37in. in Mérida; 200mm/8in. in July compared to 130mm/5in.; 243 and 234mm/10 and 9in. in September and October compared to 180 and 91mm/7 and 3½in.). Cozumel is a favourite with visitors, especially from the USA, who come here in winter to enjoy what for them is a summer climate.

Northern Gulf Coast (Matamoros weather station)

The climate on the Gulf Coast further north, towards the American border and the Rio Grande, differs in several respects. Although maximum daytime temperatures are still quite high (28°C/82°F in January, 36°C/96.8°F July to August), the night-time temperatures can fall in January to as low as −1°C/30.2°F. Besides the summer rain, which decreases towards the north, there is also rain in winter, brought by the "Nortes", the cold air fronts from the north, so that the climate here is mild in winter, hot in summer, and wet all year round.

Southern Pacific Coast (Mazatlán weather station)

The whole of Mexico's southern Pacific coast characteristically has high temperatures all year round and most of the rain falls in the summer, with virtually no rain for the rest of the year but plenty of sunshine and cooling sea breezes.

By comparison with Mexico City, which is higher up at almost 2500m/8200ft, the minimum night-time temperatures are greater by around 10° and maximum daytime temperatures as much as 7°. Here by the sea temperatures range much less widely than they do further inland.

Pleasant temperatures, warm seas and plenty of sun make the beaches of Acapulco, Mazatlán, etc. a great attraction for tourists from more northerly climes, especially in winter. Acapulco's temperatures are even higher than those for Mazatlán, and hardly vary throughout the year, with average highest daytime temperatures of 35°C/95°F and night-time lows of 17°C/62°F; although Acapulco's annual rainfall, at 1377mm/54in., is somewhat higher, almost all the rain falls between June and October.

Differences in altitude and whether or not a place is to leeward or windward can result in some small variations in the climate of southern Mexico, but on the whole it tends to be tropical, hot, and wet in summer.

Around the Gulf of California (Guaymas weather station)

This part of Mexico has a sub-tropical semi-desert and desert climate. In summer the Colorado Delta with Mexicali and the Sonora Desert are among the hottest places on earth. Here the sun shines on average for 10½ hours a day. The diagrams are for the weather station at Guaymas. This is on the southern edge of the region, which is not one of the hottest parts and still gets a certain amount of rain in summer. Hours of sunshine average at least eight a day. Although air-conditioning in, for example, Veracruz on the Gulf of Mexico extracts moisture, here on the Gulf of California humidity has to be added.

The climate of Baja California is particularly affected on its western edge by the cold California Current. The combination of "water cooling" and fresh breezes with strong sunshine accounts for the large number of beach resorts which have been developed on this side, especially around the southern tip of the peninsula.

Extreme North-west (Tijuana weather station)

The extreme north-west of Mexico gets the kind of rainfall in winter which is typical of the Mediterranean climate of California, the US State bordering it in the north. The Spaniards, coming from a region of winter rain to Mexico, a country of summer rain, called the wet months from June to October "Invierno" (winter) and the dry, sunny months from November to April "Verano" (summer), even though the sun was lower in the sky.

Flora and Fauna

Flora

Mexico's flora is rich and varied, and many of Europe's familiar food and plant crops, such as maize, tomatoes, and tobacco, hail from this part of the New World.

In the country's deserts and semi-deserts, which are mostly in the north-east, and Baja California, the plant species such as succulents protect themselves against drying out by their ability to store large quantities of water in their cell tissue. There are also a great many of the prickly pear types of cactus.

The vegetation is less sparse on the kind of steppe found on the high plateau of southern central Mexico, where the scrub can be temporarily transformed by a generous downpour into a lush grassland. This high country also has many kinds of cactus, as well as mesquite, yucca, agave, and sharp-thorned chaparrales. Peyotl, to give it its Indian name, which also grows here, is the mescal cactus that can produce hallucinogenic effects.

There is plenty of coniferous and deciduous woodland on the mountains around the high plateau. The trees growing on the slopes of the Western, Eastern and Southern Sierra Madre, and the volcano belt, include various evergreen and deciduous oaks, the arbor-vitae (tree of life), juniper, pines and other conifers. The ground cover is drawn from typical woodland floor species.

The evergreen tropical forest is mostly on or close to the south-western coastal strip along the Gulf of Mexico, with bamboo, mangrove and other swamp plants growing in the intertidal zone. Creepers, orchids and ephiphytic ferns festoon the trees which include swamp cypresses such as the "ahuehuetl", the Náhuatl for "old man in the water".

The usual landscape along central and southern Mexico's Pacific coast and in the north of the Yucatán peninsula is one of typical brushland, scrubby grasses dotted with low bushes and shrubs.

A banana bush

Coconut palms are a threatened species

Typical vegetation in the highlands: cacti and bushes

Mexico's tropical rainforest, which also has its share of ephiphytes and creepers, is in the south of the Yucatán peninsula and Chiapas, Tabasco and Veracruz. The forest trees include mahogany, silk-cotton and logwood, as well as sapodilla, or "chictli" in Náhuatl, from which you get the chicle of chewing gum.

Palm disease

Since 1982 the coconut palms along the coasts of the Yucatán peninsula have been dying from a disease which came from Florida and had already appeared in the early 19th c. Within a month of infection by a micro-organism carried by grasshoppers the palms drop their coconuts, within three months their fronds turn yellow and die off, and after five months all that is left is the dead trunk. A quarter of a million palms have been lost to date, bringing ruin to many of the plantations. The beaches of Cozumel, Cancún and Isla Mujeres, once fringed with palms, are mostly bare. The Mexican government is now trying to restore the stock of coconut palms by introducing new disease-resistant strains from south-east Asia.

Fauna

Mexico's fauna is equally rich and varied. Since the Pliocene age this has been the meeting place of creatures from north and south America. Wolf, coyote, black bear, and beaver have made their way here from the north to find new habitats on the high plateaux. The lowlands attracted jaguar, puma, monkeys and other south American species. In Mexico can be found ocelot, lynx, badger, otter, bandicoot, bighorn sheep, skunk, racoon, squirrel, tapir and anteater, various kinds of wild pig, deer and rodents. Bats like the

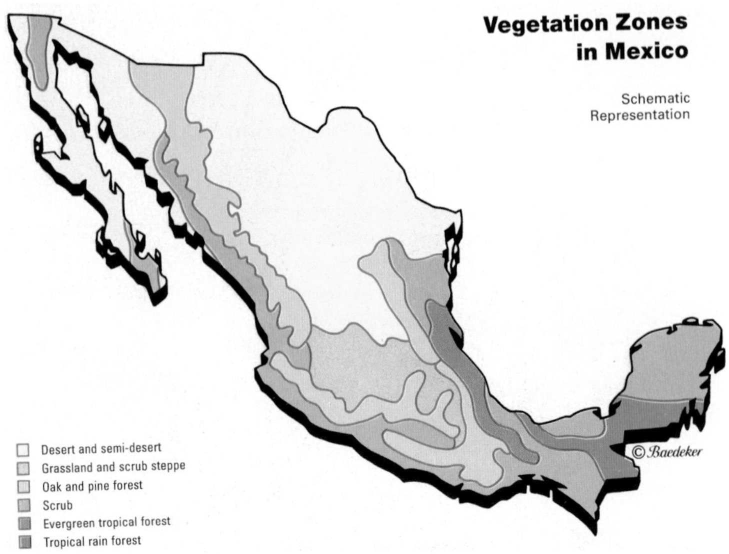

vampire bat are feared as carriers of livestock diseases and as such are subject to pest control.

Reptiles and amphibians include various kinds of lizard, among them the poisonous Gila monster in the north-west, alligators, tortoises and turtles, as well as toads and frogs. One zoological rarity is the axolotl, an aquatic, subterranean salamander which retains the larval form throughout life under natural conditions.

Poisonous snakes include various species of rattlesnake, coral snake, bushmaster and fer de lance; constrictors, such as the anaconda, which grow to enormous lengths, kill by suffocation and are non-venomous.

Birds played an important role in the the mythology of the ancient Indians because of their magical power of flight. The quetzal, whose plumage was used in the magnificent ceremonial clothing of the Indian rulers, has become very rare, as has the eagle, which appears on Mexico's coat of arms. Macaws and parrots are also of mythological significance. Other Mexican avifauna include turkey, vulture, buzzard, cormorant, pelican, toucan, egret and flamingo. Woodpeckers, wildfowl and wild geese, pigeons, gulls, hirundines and game birds are among the migrants from the north.

Mexico's spiders and stinging and biting insects can occasionally give trouble, especially the different species of gnats and mites, flies and mosquitoes. Scorpions lurk in almost every dry part of the country, and their sting can be unpleasant and dangerous. Many spiders are equally poisonous, the bird-eating spiders and black widows among them, and the red ant, *hormiga roja*, can give a very nasty nip.

A Californian sealion

Pelicans in Baja California

Butterflies abound; the loveliest of them include the admirals, monarchs, copper head bolla, malachite, peacock, morpho and calico looper.

The seas around Mexico are also rich in maritime species. On the northern Pacific coast can be seen sealions and the rare grey whale. The shallow waters hold shrimp (an important export), lobster, crabs, and flatfish. Out to sea there are perch, mackerel, sardine, tuna, bonito, barracuda, swordfish, moray eel and various species of ray and shark. Dolphins are occasionally present close inshore, especially at remote points on the Pacific coast.

Freshwater fish include trout, bass, carp and catfish.

Visitors should not buy any stuffed or prepared animals, skins or carapaces such as stuffed parrots and crocodiles, snakeskins, tortoise shells, butterflies, etc. Many of these are covered by the SITES agreement for the protection of endangered species, and it would be illegal to bring them into Europe.

See Practical Information, Protected Species.

Population

Mexico is the only country on the American continent where the greater part of the population is of mixed blood. The origins of today's population of about 93 million can be traced back to the between six and seven million original Indians, the Indígenas as they are now called, the 200,000 Spaniards who came here with the Conquistadores, and roughly the same number of negro slaves brought in during the colonial period.

In the absence of more precise figures Mexico's present population can be assumed to be predominantly mestizo. Nowadays forming 75 to 80% of the population, these were originally people of mixed blood born of Indian and Spanish parents, and who now have some African and Asian ancestry too. The Indígenas are currently 10 to 15% and the whites, mostly "criollos" from the old Spanish families, account for about 10%. Despite their small share of total population it is the whites who are still very much to the fore in politics and commerce.

Descendants of Pre-Hispanic Indians (Indígenas)

In 1870 the majority of the population was still pure-blooded Indian, and in 1921 the Indian share of the total population was still 30 to 35%.

Nowadays most of the Indígenas are concentrated in the states of the central plateau (México, Hidalgo, Puebla), the south (Guerrero, Oaxaca, Chiapas), on the Gulf Coast (Veracruz), and in the east (Yucatán Peninsula). Of the 7 to 8 million Indígenas about a quarter are reckoned to speak only an Indian tongue and no Spanish. Obviously not all the original 130 or so indigenous languages have survived, but some are still spoken in 82 Indian groups, including over 26 different Maya and Náhuatl versions, which break down into around a further 270 dialects. The most populous and best-known tribes, which to some degree still lead independent lives, include the Náhua, Otomi, Tarasco/Purépecha, Huicholes, Cora, Tarahumara, Mayo, Yaqui, Totonac, Huastec, Matlatzínca, Mazatec, Mazahua, Amuzgo, Trique, Míxtec, Zapotec, Chinantec, Tzeltal, Tzotzíl, Tajolabal, Chol and Yucatán-Maya. Some 25 of these live in their own self-governing territories.

Siesta

A bird-dealer

Despite the pride professed by the Mexican state in its pre-Hispanic heritage, the direct descendants of those Indian peoples are socially and economically on the fringes of society. The Instituto Nacional Indigenista, the national Indian institute, in its attempts at integration, is faced with the dilemma of having to try and combat the material backwardness of the rural Indian population while at the same time seeking to preserve and study their cultural heritage. In recent years some Indian groups have begun showing signs of growing self-awareness and a new consciousness of their "Indian" status. This was the background which, along with economic pressures, led to rebellion of the Tzotzil and Tzeltel on January 1st 1994.

Population trends

Despite the authorities' efforts to bring down the birthrate, Mexico's population is estimated to be growing at an annual rate of 2.3%, although the official figure is 1.9%. The 10,000 or so family planning units that have been set up since 1972 are handicapped in a country where fathering many children is seen as confirmation of a man's "machismo", and large families still have to compensate for the lack of national insurance and social security. The Church's attitude to birth control in intensely Catholic Mexico adds to the problem. Currently about 55% of all Mexicans are under 20, and average life expectancy is around 64.

Population structure

Unlike many other Latin American countries Mexico has a relatively large middle class which between 1982 and 1990 has suffered considerably under the recession. There is more of a marked contrast between the small, enormously rich, upper class, and some of those who live in abject poverty out in the countryside or who have moved into the cities and still suffer because of the

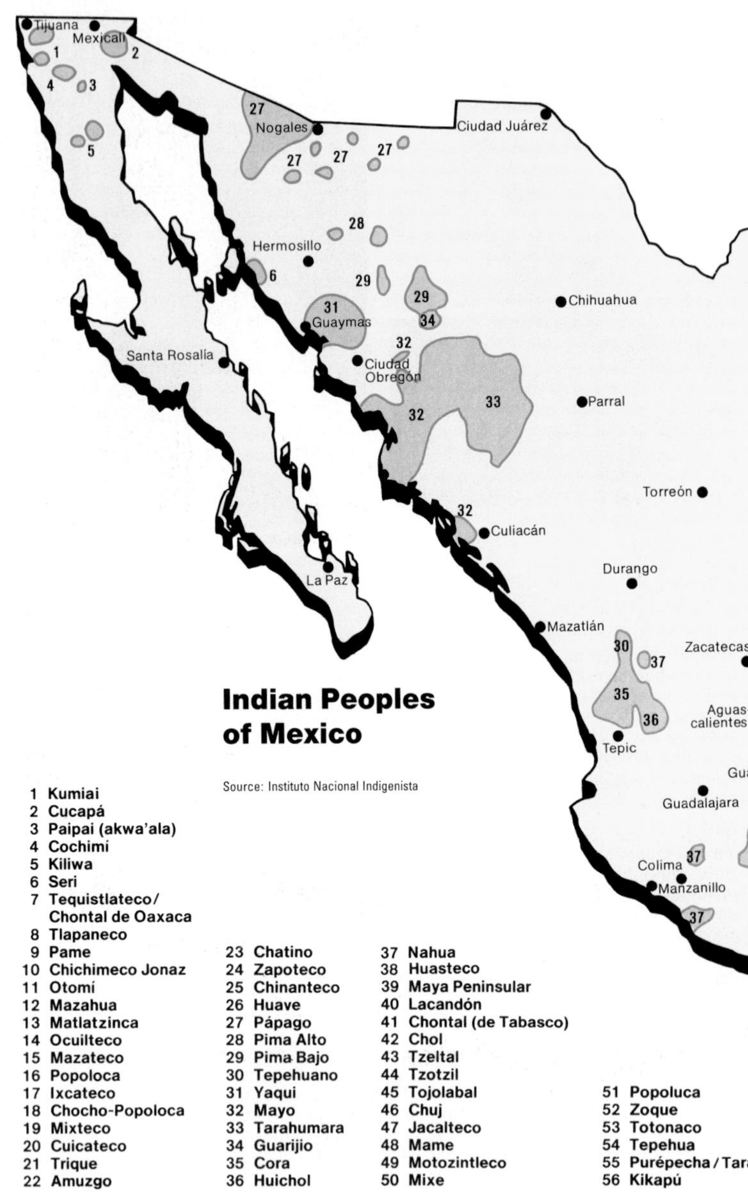
Indian Peoples of Mexico
Source: Instituto Nacional Indigenista
Tijuana
Mexicali
Nogales
Ciudad Juárez
Hermosillo
Guaymas
Chihuahua
Santa Rosalía
Ciudad Obregón
Parral
Torreón
Culiacán
La Paz
Durango
Mazatlán
Zacatecas
Aguas-calientes
Tepic
Guadalajara
Colima
Manzanillo
1 Kumiai
2 Cucapá
3 Paipai (akwa'ala)
4 Cochimí
5 Kiliwa
6 Seri
7 Tequistlateco/Chontal de Oaxaca
8 Tlapaneco
9 Pame
10 Chichimeco Jonaz
11 Otomí
12 Mazahua
13 Matlatzinca
14 Ocuilteco
15 Mazateco
16 Popoloca
17 Ixcateco
18 Chocho-Popoloca
19 Mixteco
20 Cuicateco
21 Trique
22 Amuzgo
23 Chatino
24 Zapoteco
25 Chinanteco
26 Huave
27 Pápago
28 Pima Alto
29 Pima Bajo
30 Tepehuano
31 Yaqui
32 Mayo
33 Tarahumara
34 Guarijio
35 Cora
36 Huichol
37 Nahua
38 Huasteco
39 Maya Peninsular
40 Lacandón
41 Chontal (de Tabasco)
42 Chol
43 Tzeltal
44 Tzotzil
45 Tojolabal
46 Chuj
47 Jacalteco
48 Mame
49 Motozintleco
50 Mixe
51 Popoluca
52 Zoque
53 Totonaco
54 Tepehua
55 Purépecha / Taras
56 Kikapú

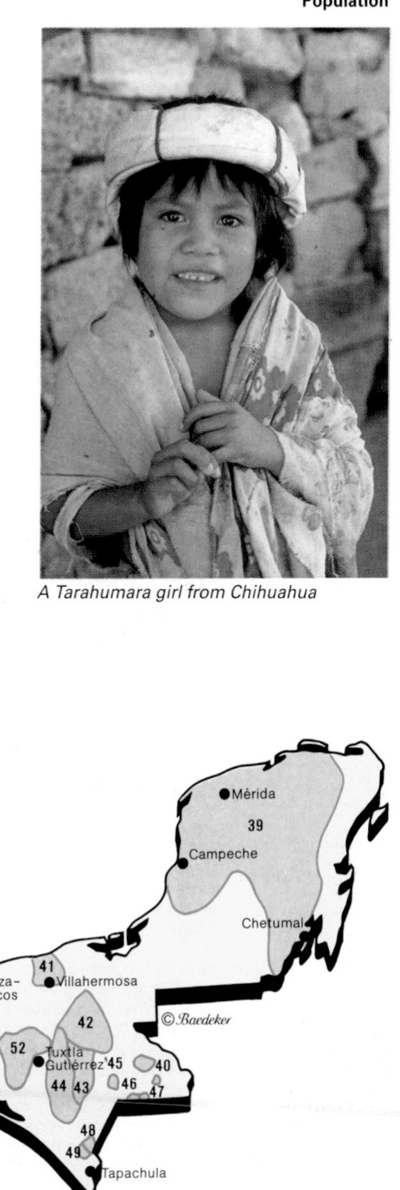

A Tarahumara girl from Chihuahua

Population Growth
in the Aztec Empire, in New Spain and Mexico

Year	Population
1519	5–6 million
1600	2 million
1810	6–6.5 million
1910	15 million
1920	14 million
1960	35 million
1980	70 million
1984	77 million[1]
1987	82.2 million[1]
1994	93 million[1]
2000	104 million[2]

[1] Estimate
[2] Projection, based on 1.9% official growth rate

uneven distribution of economic and social progress. In addition to unemployment and lack of purchasing power Mexico's biggest social problem is its inability to integrate its peasant farmers and labourers into a productive national economy – 60 to 70% of the country's population are poorly fed or undernourished.

Since it was industrial areas and the towns and cities which clearly benefited from the substantial economic progress up to 1982 there was a drift from the land of positively threatening proportions, and during the ensuing years this has continued virtually unabated. Consequently whereas not so very long ago most of Mexico's population were country dwellers, about three quarters of its people now live in the towns. On the other hand, at least 15 million people still live in more than 120,000 villages with a population of less than 3000.

Rural population

One of the declared aims of the Mexican revolutionaries with their rallying cry of "Tierra y Libertad" – Land and Freedom – was the return of the farmland of the great haciendas to the village communities. It was the 1930s, however, before the land reform took place that gave the peasants land either for collective farming ("ejidos colectivos") or for their own use ("ejidos individuales"), although ownership of the land remained with the State. At the end of 1991 the "ejido" system underwent radical liberalisation. Only a third of peasants possess a plough, while the use of tractors is still extremely rare, the hoe being the most common tool. Most farming is of a subsistence nature with only a small proportion of agricultural produce being sold in the market, the money being used for the purchases of consumer goods. Moreover these small farmers have to compete against the large agricultural companies, with the result that many give up their plot of land and go to work for the large firms on a seasonal basis, or else drift to the towns. It is estimated that as many as 700,000 a year migrate from the rural areas to Mexico City. At the same time, however, another 350,000 people leave the capital.

Urban population

About 20% of urban dwellers enjoy a modest living in relative prosperity but most of the rest live on or below the poverty line. Anyone without a permanent job hires himself out by the day or has to get casual work. Women often work in other people's homes as well or are the sole earners. Children also have to contribute to the family income in various ways such as selling chewing gum.

Indian mother and child in Chiapas

The most striking signs of poverty in the cities are the constantly expanding slums on the outskirts, the lost cities, or "ciudades perdidas" as these illegal shantytowns are called, tolerated by the authorities because of the enormous housing shortage.

Employment structure

Because of the lack of statistics it is only possible to give a rough estimate of the employment figures for the various sectors. About 30% of the labour force probably still work in farming, forestry and fishing. Industry has around 25% and services approximately 25%. The rest is taken up by the public sector (about 15%), mining and oil.

The "black" economy is also of considerable importance. The crises of the 80s and the continuing high population growth have made unemployment even more of a problem. At the end of 1993 it was calculated that out of an active population of 27 million Mexicans 17% were permanently unemployed and over 20% only found work on an occasional basis. According to the latest calculations 39% of the population is under 15. Between 900,000 and a million young people enter the labour market every year, but only a very small proportion ever find a job. Consequently an ever increasing number go to look for work in the neighbouring USA, where there are already between four and six million wetbacks or "braceros" permanently or temporarily, and usually illegally, employed. Night after night professional rings spirit groups of illegal immigrants over the Río Grande – hence the "wetbacks" – into the States where often they are picked up immediately and sent straight back, only to try again soon afterwards. Each year the "braceros" send home between 4 and 5 million dollars.

Education system

Mexico spends twice as much on education as defence. Since the Twenties compulsory school attendance and literacy campaigns

Street musicians in Mexico City

have brought illiteracy down to less than 15% – the official figure for 1990 is 12.6% of the population over 15. Children are supposed to have 6 years of "primaria", or primary school, and three years "secundaria", secondary school. However, almost half the children leave school before the end of Year 6, and in the countryside this may be as many as three-quarters. This can be due to a shortage of teachers, to the attitude of many parents, driven by poverty, who see no point in their children going to school and want them to work, and also to how much the children get to eat, since some are too chronically under-nourished to be able to attend school at all – so far the government has neglected to provide them with school milk, for example.

Mexico has a total of over 25 million schoolchildren. About 18 million are in primary education, 6 million are following three years of "preparatoria", and 1.5 million are in higher education.

The country has 32 universities, chief among them being UNAM, Universidad Nacional Autonoma Mexicana, the national independent university in Mexico City which has about 400,000 students. Very few students study technical subjects.

Religion

Mexico's population is overwhelmingly Roman Catholic (86%), with a degree of piety that can range from simply formal membership of the Church to the most fervent faith. The latter particularly applies to the Indians, who have combined their Christianity with stirring elements of their more ancient rites and beliefs. For historical reasons the government stance towards the Church tends to be somewhere between neutral and negative, although in recent years there has been some easing of the tension in relations between Church and State.

Christian fundamentalist sects from the USA have achieved considerable popularity among the Indian population in the south of the country, while in the north of Mexico there are some 600,000 Mennonites. It is estimated that the number of Protestants in Mexico is 5 million.

State and Constitution

Coat of Arms

The colours of the Mexican flag, a tricolour bearing the national coat of arms and dating back to 1821, are green for independence, white for religious purity, and red for national unity.

The coat of arms recalls the legendary founding of Tenochtitlán, the Aztec capital and now Mexico City, when the Aztecs invading from the north deemed it the will of their gods that they should found their city where they saw an eagle, its wings spread wide, perched on a cactus and with a snake in its beak.

Presidency and Constitution

Under the Constitution of February 5th 1917 the Estados Unidos Méxicanos, the United Mexican States, is a republic headed by a President and consisting of 31 states and a federal district, the Distrito Federal, containing Ciudad de México, the nation's capital Mexico City. The President, el Presidente, is the head of state and also of government, and is elected for a term of six years. He appoints his Cabinet ministers and the governor of the Federal District, who is also the mayor of the capital.

The bicameral federal legislature, the Congress (Congreso de la Unión), is composed of the Chamber of Deputies (Cámara de Diputados), which has 500 deputies, 300 of them elected by majority vote and 200 by proportional representation and up for election every 3 years, and the Senate (Cámara de Senadores), which has 64 members and elections every 6 years.

The federal states enjoy regional autonomy. Each has its own constitution and its own governor (Gobernador).

Political parties

Mexico's ruling party, and the force which is undoubtedly responsible for the modernisation of Mexican society, is the PRI, the Partido Revolucionario Institucional, the party of institutionalised revolution, which despite several changes of name has held the Presidency since it was founded in 1929. And each president has served his full term, which is something virtually unheard of in Central and South America.

The opposition parties include PAN, the Catholic-conservative party of national action, PRD, the left-wing party of revolutionary democracy, PARM, the right-wing and officially "the authentic party of the Mexican Revolution", PPS, the socialist party, PT, the workers' party, PDM, the right-wing democratic party and PVEM, the green ecology party. The FDN which appeared in the 1988 elections as an alliance of the left against the PRI, has split into two parties: the party of revolutionary democracy (PRD) and the party of national-revolutionary Cardenist Front (PFCRN). The founder of both parties is the PRI dissident, Cuauhtémoc Cardenás, son of the legendary president, Lázaro Cárdenas, and the former governor of Michoacán, who was only narrowly beaten by Carlos Salinas de Gortari in the 1988 elections and was once again the spearhead candidate of the left in the 1994 polls. In addition in 1993 many members of PAN have defected and formed the party of the Democratic Forum.

Political culture

According to author Octavia Paz, who compared the position of the Mexican President with that of a Tlaotani, Aztec leaders before the

Mexico
México

United Mexican States
Estados Unidos Méxicanos

States	Area in sq.km	Population (Est. 1992)	State Capital
1a Baja California Sur (B.C.S.)	72,465	500,000	La Paz
1b Baja California Norte (B.C.)	71,627	2,000,000	Mexicali
2 Sonora (Son.)	182,553	1,900,000	Hermosillo
3 Chihuahua (Chih.)	245,612	2,700,000	Chihuahua
4 Sinaloa (Sin.)	58,488	2,400,000	Culiacán
5 Durango (Dgo.)	123,520	1,600,000	Durango
6 Coahuila (Coah.)	150,395	2,100,000	Saltillo
7 Nuevo León (N.L.)	65,103	4,000,000	Monterrey
8 Zacatecas (Zac.)	73,454	1,300,000	Zacatecas
9 San Luis Potosí (S.L.P.)	63,231	2,000,000	San Luis Potosí
10 Tamaulipas (Tamps.)	79,602	2,400,000	Ciudad Victoria
11 Nayarit (Nay.)	27,053	850,000	Tepic
12 Aguascalientes (Ags.)	5,586	800,000	Aguascalientes

States	Area in sq.km	Population (Est. 1992)	State Capital
13 Jalisco (Jal.)	81,058	5,800,000	Guadalajara
14 Guanajuato (Gto.)	30,575	4,200,000	Guanajuato
15 Querétaro	11,480	1,200,000	Querétaro
16 Hidalgo (Hgo.)	20,870	2,000,000	Pachuca
17 Colima (Col.)	5,205	500,000	Colima
18 Michoacán (Mich.)	60,093	3,600,000	Morelia
19 México (Mex.)	21,414	11,500,000	Toluca
20 Morelos (Mor.)	4,964	1,400,000	Cuernavaca
21 Tlaxcala (Tlax.)	4,027	780,000	Tlaxcala
22 Puebla (Pue.)	33,995	4,300,000	Puebla
23 Veracruz (Ver.)	71,896	6,500,000	Jalapa
24 Guerrero (Gro.)	64,458	2,800,000	Chilpancingo
25 Oaxaca (Oax.)	94,211	3,000,000	Oaxaca
26 Chiapas (Chis.)	74,415	3,500,000	Tuxtla Gutiérrez
27 Tabasco (Tab.)	25,337	1,550,000	Villahermosa
28 Campeche (Camp.)	50,952	600,000	Campeche
29 Yucatán (Yuc.)	38,508	1,350,000	Mérida
30 Quintana Roo (Q.R.)	50,350	550,000	Chetumal
D.F. Distrito Federal (Federal District)	1,483	10,500,000	Ciudad de México
Mexican Republic	1,972,547	90,180,000	

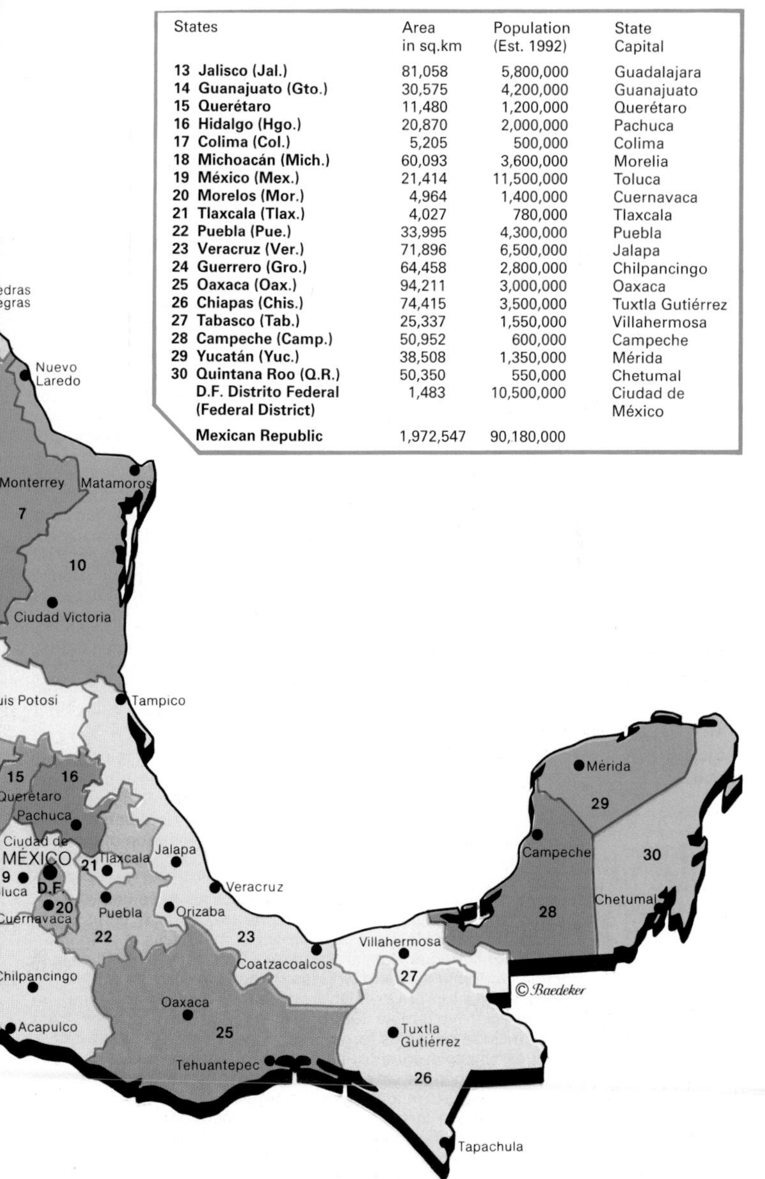

Conquistadores, "the Tlaotani embodies the continuance of rule not tied to one person. A caste of priests and bosses wields power by virtue of a fleeting incarnation: El Presidente is the Party itself". Mexico does in fact have what is probably a unique system of government. While still in office the president decides, by the tensely awaited action of "fingering" ("el dezado") him, which PRI candidate is to succeed him – and to date that candidate has never failed to be elected.

The President's power base is the PRI, and it is the President who selects the Party Chairman, officials, Senators, Deputies and State Governors, and they in turn owe their allegiance to him. Workers, peasants and soldiers form a large part of the membership, and the trade unions that belong to the party also bring in a great many votes. The PRI ensures its political dominance by a dense network of patronage and hangers-on reaching to the very furthest corners of the land – for example, when it comes to buying up the harvest the local party leaders have a monopoly.

1994 elections

On August 21st 1994 the Mexicans once again went to the polls and elected their house of representatives, senate, and, most importantly, the president to lead them into the next millennium. The turn-out for the elections was an unheard-of 77%. The polls were conducted with generally few irregularities under the watchful eye of numerous domestic and foreign observers and the actual counting of the votes was for the first time undertaken by an independent body. The result which had been widely predicted failed to materialise: the new president was the PRI candidate, Ernesto Zedillo, with 48.8%, which was, however, the lowest percentage his party had ever reached. The PAN candidate achieved 26% of the vote, while Cuauhtémoc Cárdenas of the PRD scored 16.6%. In the lower house the PRI has an absolute majority, while in the senate there is a balance of votes between the PRI on the one hand and the PAN and PRD on the other.

Foreign Policy

Mexico is a member of the United Nations, the Organisation of American States, the General Agreement on Tariffs and Trade (GATT), and the Progress Alliance, plus many other international organisations and institutions, and has a special trade agreement with the European Union.

Mexico and the USA

"Poor Mexico, so far from God and so close to the USA" is how Porfirio Diaz famously described Mexico's relationship with its northern neighbour. The country's mainly economic dependence on its American big brother continues virtually unabated and if anything has become more intense with the recession of the 80s.

A real strain on relations between the two countries comes from the problem of the Mexicans who work illegally in the States. While many American farmers and small businesses have come to depend on the cheap labour the US unions are opposed to this unfair competition. For Mexico the "wetbacks" mean less of a drain on their labour market, but at the same time they complain, with justification, that itinerant workers in the USA have no rights. The new immigration laws which came into force with the Simpson Rodino Act in November 1986, after lengthy domestic policy wrangling, include penalties for employers who take on illegal labour and an amnesty programme for illegal immigrants who since 1982 have stayed on in the United States, although most "wetbacks" are fighting shy of surrendering to the authorities.

Mexico is the largest supplier of narcotics to the USA, and according to US figures provides 70% of America's marijuana and 40% of its heroin. In addition Mexico is the principal transit country for cocaine from South America.

As a country Mexico makes considerable efforts to combat the drug dealers and those who grow the drugs, but still gets criticised by those in America who complain of a lack of willingness to co-operate on the part of the Mexican authorities. The Mexicans counter with some justification that it is the USA which provides a ready market for drugs, not Latin America.

Economy

Foreign trade

By far the most important trading partner of Mexico is the United States. About two-thirds of the imports and exports are with the USA. Mexico is, after Canada and recently ahead of Japan, the second most important country for exports from the USA. In 1992 US exports to Mexico had a total value of $40.6 billion. After the USA, Germany was Mexico's second largest trading partner.

Total exports from Mexico in 1992 (not including finishing products) amounted to $31 billion of which 62% consisted of industrial products (e.g. vehicles, motor parts, colour television apparatus and other electrical and electronic goods, leather goods, textiles), 25% oil and petroleum derivatives, 7% agricultural produce and 1.5% minerals.

Imported goods amounted in value to $51 billion and included machinery, aircraft, telecommunications equipment and soya beans. As a consequence the trading deficit of $19 billion has almost doubled since 1991. The rise in imports between 1989 and 1993 can be largely attributed to an extensive abolition of the import licence system and a radical reduction in import duty.

NAFTA

At the end of 1992 the governments of Mexico, the USA and Canada signed the North American Free Trade Agreement (NAFTA), known in Mexico as the Tratado de Libre Comercio de América del Norte (TCL), thereby creating potentially the largest consumer market in the world (370 million consumers). The scope of the treaty includes the abolition of trading restrictions, the guarantee of free competition, an enlargement of investment opportunities and the furtherance of international co-operation in the context of the GATT agreements. As a practical example of the treaty's effects the abolition on January 1st 1994 of import duties for 70% of Mexican exported goods can be cited. Indeed, with its signing of the treaty, Mexico has high hopes of becoming indissolubly linked to the all-powerful economies of its northern neighbours, although in the USA, in particular, there are fears of an exodus of jobs to Mexico, given the latter country's much lower wage structure.

Agriculture

Despite the advances made in industrialisation Mexico's economy is still very much dominated by agriculture, which employs between 25 and 30% of the work force although it only provides 7.7% (1985) of the gross domestic product (1975 11.2%). About half the total area of the country is used for agriculture (100 million ha/247 million acres), although only just on 12% is used for arable farming. The main areas under cultivation are in the southern plateau, the high country around the rim of the plateau, and the coastal plains on the Pacific and the Gulf of Mexico.

A large selection of produce in the markets

Farming land and farm products

Mexico's peasant farmers or "campesinos" form the greater part of those working on the land, generally growing crops to feed themselves and very often following the ancient Indian "milpa" system of maize, beans and fruit. The production of fruit for sale tends to be left to the hacendados and modern farm corporations. The two phases of agrarian reform in the Thirties, based on the land reforms of 1917, and again in the Seventies, took in 59% of the agricultural area and 74% of farm holdings, leaving Mexico with three main forms of farm ownership: small holdings (up to 5ha/12 acres), medium to large holdings, and the "ejido", a form of communal property where the land belongs to the state but is divided up among a group of members, the "ejidatarios", or it is farmed co-operatively. State ownership of the land is suspended so long as it is being properly farmed. The "ejido" system, one of the keystones of the revolution, was radically revised at the end of 1991 as the "ejidatorio" now has the right to sell and lease his land, not only to Mexicans but also to foreigners.

The most important crops for the domestic market are maize and wheat, then pulses, potatoes, vegetables, citrus fruit and other fruits. The farming of large parts of the country requires irrigation, and by 1992 the irrigated areas had been extended to 7 million ha/17.3 million acres. Much of this increased acreage was in the dry territory in the north. More recently the aim has been to expand the cultivable area by creating new land, especially in the tropical parts of the country. Since 1950 the amount of cultivable land is estimated to have increased by a total of about 14%.

Farm imports and exports

Nevertheless, to cover the needs of the domestic market in 1990, two billion dollars had to be spent principally for imports from the USA. In 1991 enough maize and beans were harvested in Mexico to

Processing agaves for the production of Tequila

ensure self-sufficiency. In 1992 the country suffered from too much rain which caused a decline in agricultural production including beans, maize and wheat. The bulk of these imports comes in through CONASUPO, the national foodstuffs company (Compañia Nacional de Subsistencia Populares), with the major supplier being the United States. Beans are often from South America, while oil seeds such as soya, milk and dairy products tend to be drawn from western industrialised countries.

Export crops such as coffee (the export value of which has virtually halved as a result of the drop in price in 1993/94), cotton, tomatoes, fruit, vegetables, tobacco and tequila are mostly grown on the big private farms. Over 5% of the total agricultural exports are of beer and wine. Mexico is the second largest exporter of beer to the USA. Three-quarters of the produce sold commercially comes from only about 15% of the total number of agricultural holdings. The rest are mainly concerned with feeding themselves. Exports to the USA are gaining in importance as American capital investment is ensuring that top quality products are being grown, marketed, and shipped via modern transport systems to the American market.

Meat exports have also been stepped up in recent years. The introduction of breeds of cattle resistant to tropical diseases has led to more extensive livestock and dairy farming in the tropical areas, which has also meant more meat to cover the needs of the home market.

Forestry

Mexican forestry suffers generally from poor productivity and little attempt at reafforestation. The tropical rainforests in the south, and especially Chiapas, are being plundered at an alarming rate.

Traditional fishing at Acapulco

Fishing

With more than 9000km/5600 miles of coast line Mexico should be one of the leading fishing nations of the world. Until recently elderly boats and unhelpful bureaucratic regulations hindered any improvement. In the last three years modernisation of the fleet has already brought improvement. New fishing laws are to bring further changes. Mexico's most important exports of fish are prawns, tuna, anchovies, sardines, octopus, mackerel, etc.

Mining, Petroleum and Energy Supply

Mining

With its vast mineral reserves Mexico can lay claim to being one of the most important mining countries in the world. The number of miners, however, is decreasing as a result of several mines being forced to close owing to falling world market prices. Total mineral exports of silver (the world's no. 1 producer), zinc, manganese, fluorspar, strontium, antimony, bismuth, lead and graphite, in 1993 amounted to merely 2.6% of the country's GNP.

Mineral oil

In 1993 Mexico produced 2.67 million barrels (l barrel = 159 litres) of crude oil a day and thus stood at sixth place in the world. Its assured reserves of oil amounted at the end of 1993 to 51.2 billion barrels, giving it the eighth world position. About 73% of the oil is produced by offshore wells in the Gulf of Mexico, the rest coming from the oil-fields of Veracruz, Tabasco and Chiapas. As recently as 1982 Mexico was able to earn almost $16 billion from its oil exports, a sum which amounted to as much as 74% of the total value of its exports. The sudden and dramatic fall in oil prices, coupled with the steep rise in exports from the processing industries, have meant that by 1993 this share had fallen to as little as 25%. The main market for Mexican crude oil is the United States, with 65%, the rest going to Spain, Japan, Central America and Israel. The natural gas output in 1993 was 36.8 billion cu.m per year. Mexico thus ranks among the world's top ten natural gas producers and for the first time since 1985 was in a position to export a small quantity.

Nationalisation of the oil industry

The companies which drilled for Mexico's oil riches in the first part of this century were British, Dutch and American. Although in the early Twenties Mexico was second only to the USA as a world exporter of petroleum, it had no control over its own oil. Nationalisation of the oil industry was first announced by President Lázaro Cárdenas in 1938, and the State petroleum company Petróleos Mexicanos, or PEMEX for short, was set up soon afterwards. Nationalisation of the oil industry was also the cornerstone of the country's foreign policy. Under a contractual settlement in the early Forties the government had to begin paying out compensation, and it was 1982 before Antonio Ortíz Mena, Minister of Finance at the time, handed over the final cheque to the former British owners. The nationalised PEMEX Company, which in 1988 had more than 210,000 employees, was until then not only the official "advertisement" for Mexico but was also a hyper-bureaucratic and corrupt colossus, the productivity of which, in comparison with other international companies, was the lowest in the world. The PEMEX trade-union, with its corrupt leaders who had their own political and business empire, was a "state within a state". In 1991 Salinas de Gortari ordered the army and the police to occupy the union headquarters in Tampico and to arrest the leaders. Following an explosion in April 1992 in Guadalajara, blamed on PEMEX, which officially caused casualties amounting to 200 people, 1150 houses, 450 shops and 600 vehicles, a reorganisation of the monopolist company was set in motion. Accordingly the PEMEX Holding Company was split up into four relatively automonous subsidiaries, responsible for drilling and exploration, refining, natural gas and basic petro-chemicals, as well as secondary petro-chemical production. Since 1992 foreigners can legally be involved in the latter, and since 1994 in drilling companies. The underlying weaknesses of PEMEX still remain, however: under capitalisation, lack of productivity, insufficient refining capacity and relatively high debts.

Energy supply

Energy supply is largely in the hands of the Comisión Federal de Electricidad, or CFE, the federal electricity commission. Almost 90% of all energy is generated from fossil fuels, mostly oil and natural gas (75%) as opposed to coal, and the rest from hydro-electric sources.

Mexico's only atomic energy plant, Laguna Verde at Veracruz, has had a test-phase reactor since 1987. In political terms it is a highly controversial domestic issue on two grounds: firstly, the fact that the cost for what is only 3% of total energy output has increased by 700% since the planning stage – the final price is put at 3.5 billion dollars – and, secondly, the safety aspect, especially since Chernobyl – the plant is 18km/11 miles from a still active volcano.

Industrial development

Expansion of the oil sector in the Seventies also resulted in an impressive growth in manufacturing, and at the beginning of the 90s it was employing a work force of some five million. More than

Leaving off time at VW of Mexico in Puebla

half of the sector is still concentrated around Mexico City, and in the area of Monterrey (N.L.); the other larger industrial towns are Guadalajara, Querétaro, Toluca, San Luis Potosí, Saltillo and the border towns in the north.

Petro-chemicals and heavy industry

As well as refining and a considerable petro-chemical industry, heavy industry, vehicle manufacture and in recent years the finishing of electric and electronic apparatus have developed. In 1993 steel production amounted to 9 million tonnes. Among the largest and most modern steelworks is Lázaro Cárdenas Las Truchas (Sicartsa) on the Pacific coast which at the end of 1991 was bought from the government by a private group. The Sidermex steelworks of Fundidora Monterrey, which at that time belonged to the government, was closed in 1986 as a rationalisation measure.

Automobile industry

Since 1960 the automobile industry in Mexico has played an important role. This has had a great many knock-on effects for feeder industries in sectors such as steel and rubber. With the great economic crisis, the "lost sexsenio" between 1982 and 1988 there was a severe recession in the automobile sector; some factories had to close, others concentrated on exports. Not until the year 1989 was there any real improvement. In 1992 the target of one million vehicle sales (including exports) was reached for the first time.

Other industries

Foodstuffs constitute another important industrial sector, with meat, canned fish, sugar products and drinks developing particularly well. The building of a milk-powder plant and new oil mills and the expansion of sugar processing have helped to make considerable inroads into the substantial amounts which used to be imported in this sector. Other major industries in employment terms include textiles, chemicals, mechanical engineering, graphics and printing, and precision engineering.

Foreign investment

US companies have led the way in setting up more and more subsidiaries in Mexico, transferring their labour-intensive manufacturing processes here where the legal minimum wage is one-eighth of that usually paid in the States. Nevertheless industrial productivity in Mexico in the last five years has been twice as great as that in the USA. According to available figures the hourly pay in industry in Mexico reached 2.6 dollars in 1991. Other production costs such as building land, power supply, etc. are also low compared with other countries. As a consequence foreign investment in Mexico in 1992 reached 8.33 billion dollars.

Maquiladoras

A major factor in Mexico's more recent industrial development has been the maquiladoras, the low-wage production units that have sprung up along the American border. For some time mainly American, but also Japanese and Mexican firms have been taking advantage of Mexico's low wages by having electronic and vehicle components, machines, household goods, textiles manufactured or finished here. The international firms engaged in manufacture and assembly, producing goods for export and re-export, can import plant and machinery, as well as many of their raw materials, semi-manufactures and parts, free of duty. They also benefit from other financial and fiscal privileges, particularly in the 200km/125 mile zone south of the American border. The net exports of the finishing industry, in some 2200 factories employing a work force of 540,000, realised in 1993 altogether $5.2 billion. Consequently it is Mexico's largest foreign currency earner after the oil industry. The most important places where maquiladoras are located are Ciudad Juárez, Tijuana, Mexicali, Chihuahua, Matamoros, Reynosa, Nuevo Laredo and Nogales. The Mexican job market as a whole has enjoyed a boom as a result of the maquiladoras: jobless people from all over the country have migrated to the border areas and increasingly, as a result of the NAFTA agreement, more and more similar factories are being sited away from the US border and further into the interior of the country.

Environmental pollution

Industrial expansion has severely affected the environment. A 1985 UN study of atmospheric and water pollution in Mexico City recorded figures which were 20 times those for New York City. The main culprits are road vehicles, cement works, refineries, heating plants, heavy engineering, cellulose and papermaking, and chemicals. Only 10% of the 130,000 firms causing pollution around Mexico City have any kind of environmental protection plant. The air of the capital that at one time was prized for its purity is now hopelessly polluted by the extra exhaust gases from three million cars. Children are especially badly affected, and 80% of them suffer some sort of illness as a result. The area around the port of Coatzacoalcos (Ver.) on the Gulf of Mexico is a particularly horrific example of what can happen as a result of unchecked industrial growth. The pollution of the river, the sea, and the air by pesticides and the petro-chemical industry, which has been going on, out of control, for years, has killed off a whole range of birds, fish, plants and insects, and sea turtles and migrating birds give the district a wide berth. There is a big rise in eye disorders, infectious diseases, and salmonella poisoning from the drinking water.

Acid rain is also increasingly taking its toll on the Maya cities on the Yucatán peninsula.

Tourism

Mexico is one of the world's top tourist destinations. In 1993 its 6.6 million foreign visitors brought in the equivalent of 4.1 billion US dollars, making it the leading third world country in this sector. From the start of the debt crisis in 1982 and the fall in the peso the country was generally a cheap one for visitors. Since 1989 hotel and restaurant prices have increased considerably with the result that Mexico is no longer among the cheapest holiday destinations.

Most of Mexico's tourists are from the USA. In 1992 84% of visitors hailed from the States, with other Latin American countries accounting for 7%, Canadians and Europeans around 5%. Two-thirds of all visitors travelled by air, the rest by land.

Tourism employs 2.6 million people, that is about 10% of the work force, and provides about 3% of the gross domestic product. Mexico has some 9000 hotels, providing 384,000 rooms, and from the point of view of accommodation for visitors is in the eighth position in the world.

The tourist industry has high hopes of a co-operative project with the neighbouring Central American countries of El Salvador, Honduras, Belize and Guatemala – the "Ruta Maya", which was opened in 1993. This "Maya road" is intended to make these countries' historical sites more accessible to tourists, but at the same time safeguarding them from an ecological point of view.

Debt crisis

The Root of the Problem

At the end of 1987 Mexico owed about 105 billion US dollars, almost as much as Brazil, the third world country with the largest debt. Annual interest and repayment currently amount to some 10 billion dollars, record debts that can no longer be covered by a reduced oil income. Together with the devastating earthquake in September 1985, which alone caused at least 5 billion dollars of damage, the economic crisis revealed the true root of Mexico's problems – corruption and mismanagement by the ruling party, the PRI. Despite massive investment in future projects the way forward for business is barred by the fossilised political and economic structures. The PRI, which for 59 years as the ruling party has appointed every president, minister, and provincial governor, is proving to be the millstone round the neck of the Mexican economy, two-thirds of which is run by the bureaucracy. Most of the nationalised industries and services, thanks to their unproductive working practices, have been in debt for years, and are faced above all with the problem of getting their products to be competitive in the international market.

Losses on that scale could be covered so long as Mexico's oil was still yielding enough cash. Mexico's problems began when its oil revenue started on its steady decline in the early Eighties. In 1974, when the country became an oil exporter, the prospects for lasting economic progress still appeared quite good. Foreign debt at that time was around 12.8 billion dollars, an amount that seemed manageable in the light of an annual growth in the gross national product that could exceed 8%. However, the large profits being earned from oil at that time were all too frequently being channelled into the wrong projects or seeping away in corrupt practices.

Mexico's latest major recession began in 1981 and worsened dramatically in the wake of a financial crisis the following year. In 1983 business reached its lowest point as the country experienced

A hotel complex in the tourist resort of Cancún

its worst economic decline since the great slump of the Thirties. Inflation soared to over 98% and unemployment, together with under-employment, rose to 40%. Even today 18% of Mexico's active population are long-term unemployed, and a further 35% only find work on an occasional basis. The estimated figure of 60,000 child beggars in Mexico City may not be a proven statistic, but it is certainly a very probable one.

What lay behind the great Mexican disaster of the early Eighties was the mistaken development strategy that it had been pursuing for years: the speed with which the whole economy was made dependent on oil, with its attendant waste of resources and massive rake-offs by corruption, together with a failed investment and foreign exchange policy based on the premise of a never-ending boom, caused foreign debt to soar – it mounted by almost 50 billion dollars between 1978 and 1981 – and pushed the budget deep into the red. Billions of dollars were swallowed up by inefficient state industries or squandered on palatial buildings to house an expanding army of bureaucrats. In addition, over the past ten years about 55 billion dollars, more than half the total Mexican debt, had been transferred to the United States by the private sector.

Attempted solutions

When Miguel de la Madrid became President in December 1982 Mexico was insolvent in international terms and its domestic economy was on the verge of collapse. The new President sought to rectify the mismanagement of his predecessors by adopting a better economic policy. The International Monetary Fund and the lending banks also wisely made any further payments subject to conditions that the Mexican government had to comply with. Hence, for example, de la Madrid had to bring in a series of drastic economic reforms aimed at boosting manufacturing industry and increasing the share of finished products in total exports, thus reducing the dependency on oil exports. There were changes at the top of the nationalised industries, 26 state-owned enterprises were sold off and another 150 put up for sale, including Mexicana Airlines. Several unprofitable national undertakings were closed down entirely, among them Fundidora Monterrey, an antiquated steelworks which employed 10,000 people but made a loss in 1985 of 300 million dollars.

In this way the number of state-owned undertakings was reduced between 1982 and 1986 from 409 to less than 300, with the ultimate intention of only about 200, in "strategic" sectors such as oil and petro-chemicals, energy supply and the mining of strategic raw materials, remaining in public ownership. By the end of 1986 the public sector share of industrial output had fallen to about 30%.

In 1984 Mexico was able to show a reduction of the budget deficit by about 60% and a fall in inflation to 65%. On the other hand, unemployment was on the increase and the average Mexican had experienced a grievous loss of purchasing power. However, additional government expenditure again pushed up inflation, this time to 105% by the end of 1986, and plunged the budget further into deficit. The slump in oil prices that year halved the revenue from oil exports and robbed the Treasury of 40% of its tax income.

Latest developments

Mexico was among those countries badly affected by the crisis on the international stockmarkets in October 1987. This brought with it a fresh flight of capital. In November the peso fell against the "free" US dollar, the currency of tourism, from 1700 to 2500 pesos and then recovered to a rate of 2200 pesos, which became the official rate for the dollar in trading and on the money markets. At the same time government, employers and unions made a solidarity pact aimed at the long-term reduction of inflation which stood at a record level of 159.2%. The pact contained public spending cuts, sale of nationalised industries, dismantling of subsidies, an immediate wage rise of 35% in return for a wage-freeze for two months and indexing against inflation from March 1988, plus an agreement to hold prices. By the time he left office Miguel de la Madrid had met with little success in one respect – the private sector was still fighting shy of investment on account of the high interest rates which, even in 1988, were still between 15 and 20%.

His successor, Salinas de Gortari, succeeded in July 1989 in concluding an agreement with 500 private lending banks aimed at reducing Mexico's foreign debt by 35%. This was allied with further opening up the Mexican market to foreign products, privatising unprofitable state industries, and getting rid of subsidies. After initial euphoria there has been something of a return to earth as the banks have continued to hold back and the sales of Mexican farm products have run into protectionism, mainly on the part of Japan and the USA. Debt remission has also failed to solve the main problem, the enormous domestic indebtedness at what continue to be very high interest rates.

History

Prehistory (*c.* 40,000–5000 B.C.)

As early as *c.* 50,000 B.C. a land bridge from Asia to the Americas which exists during the Pleistocene Ice Age allows people and animals to cross what is to become the Bering Strait. These "palaeo-Indian" hunters and gatherers move south and are now thought to have reached Tierra del Fuego, at the tip of South America, in about 10,000 B.C.

First traces of Man in Latin America. Hewn bones and stones have been found at El Cedral in the state of San Luis Potosí. — About 29,000 B.C.

First traces of settlement in Mexico (Tlapacoya) – a hunter and gatherer culture that barely evolves over the next 10,000 years. Animals include mammoth, giant armadillo and ancestors of bison and camel. — About 20,000 B.C.

Tepexpan Man, oldest anthropological find in Mexico. — About 10,000 B.C.

First traces of fruits of the earth in the valley of Tehuacán (gourds, avocado, chillies, cotton). — About 7000 B.C.

Archaic Period (5000–1500 B.C.)

Larger and more permanent settlements, providing the foundations for the great pre-Hispanic civilisations. Beginning of maize cultivation. — About 5000 B.C.

The first settled communities, with the development of less crude methods of cultivation and the evolution of crafts and tool-making, producing the first obsidian arrowheads and the earliest clay figurines. — About 3000 B.C.

The first Maya sites grow up at Cuello (Belize). — About 2000 B.C.

The Olmec culture is at its height. — 1200–400 B.C.

Monte Albán I — 800 B.C.

First evidence of the Maya in Mexico. — 500 B.C.

Founding of Teotihuacán — 200 B.C.

Tres Zapotes Stele C (earliest dated evidence of Olmec culture). — 31 B.C.

Classic Period (A.D. 200–900)

Mexico's great Meso-American cultures reach the peak of their development. Although they have no metal tools, and without using the wheel as a technological aid or any pack or draught animals, they achieve great feats of architecture, and create magnificent works of sculpture, ceramics, painting and other arts and crafts. Astronomy and mathematics are progressed and evolved to the very highest level.

About 400 — Beginning of the rise of the city of El Tajín.

Post-Classic Period (900–1521)

Tribes of "barbarians" from the north begin to invade central Mexico and the priests of the ruling theocracy are increasingly supplanted by the warrior caste. Human sacrifice grows in religious importance. The great cultural advance of the Classic Period grinds to a halt. The visual arts show a coarsening of style; metal-working becomes more widespread.

The Spanish Conquest marks the end of Mexico's Meso-American civilisations.

About 900 — Decline of the cities in the Mayan central area of settlement.

968 — Founding of the Toltec city of Tollan (Tula).

1000–1200 — Heyday of Chichén Itzá.

1175 — Destruction of Tollan (Tula).

About 1300 — Beginning of the Aztec invasion.

About 1350 — Founding of the Aztec capital of Tenochtitlán where Mexico City stands today.

About 1450 — End of the post-Classic Mayan culture (fall of Mayapan).

1492 — Christopher Columbus (Cristóbal Colón) discovers the New World and America.

1512 — First contacts between Spanish seafarers and the Mayans on the coast of Yucatán. Gonzalo Guerrero and the priest Jerónimo de Aguilar are left behind as captives of the Indians.

1517–18 — The Conquistadors Hernández de Córdoba and Juan de Grijalva explore the coasts of Yucatán and the Gulf of Mexico.

1519 — Hernán Cortés, aged 34, with 11 ships, 100 sailors and 508 soldiers, sails south-west out of Cuba, despite no longer having the permission of the island's Governor, Diego de Velásquez. Landing at Cozumel, off the coast of Yucatán, he frees Jerónimo de Aguilar who henceforth plays a valuable role as interpreter. Cortés sails around the Yucatán peninsula and lands on the coast at Tabasco where he skirmishes with the Maya before moving on, taking with him "La Malinche" (Malintzin; 1500–65?), the Indian maiden christened "Marina" by the Spaniards and who is to render him great service as his aide and interpreter in the time to come.

Moctezuma II receives Cortés and Malinche

Near the present city of Veracruz Cortés receives the envoys of Moctezuma II (Montezuma), the Aztec god-emperor, who have been sent to determine whether Cortés and his men are the legendary fair-skinned god-king Quetzalcóatl and his retinue returned to claim the throne.

The chiefs of many of the tribes forced to pay tribute to the Aztecs offer Cortés their support. After establishing the settlement of Villa Rica de la Vera Cruz the Spaniards advance on the Aztec capital, Tenochtitlán and conquer Cholula, where they cause a massacre among the population and destroy the temple of Quetzalcóatl. Shortly after being received as guests by Moctezuma in his capital they take him prisoner.

Pánfilo de Narváez, sent by the Governor of Cuba to arrest Cortés 1520
for his insubordination, arrives at Veracruz. Cortés leaves Pedro de Alvarado in Tenochtitlán with 80 men and hastens to the coast where he routs Narváez on May 29th at Zempoala. Returning to Tenochtitlán he finds that in his absence Pedro de Alvardo and his men have killed 200 of the Aztec nobles. In the outcry against the Spaniards that results Moctezuma is deposed and the Aztecs replace him with Cuitláhuac, who dies three months later of smallpox. He is followed by the unbending Cuauhtémoc, the "swooping eagle" as last of the Aztec emperors. Moctezuma is killed on June 27th, whether murdered by the Spaniards or by his own people is not clear to this day. On June 30th, the *noche triste* (sad night), the Spanish flee the city suffering heavy losses. Shortly afterwards Cortés vanquishes a strong Aztec fighting force at Otumba. The Spaniards then rest and recover with their allies the Tlaxcaltecs and make their preparations for their assault on Tenochtitlán.

1521 On August 13th the Spanish and their Indian allies capture Tenochtitlán and destroy it. Cuauhtémoc is taken prisoner. Three years later Cortés takes him along as a hostage on his expedition to Honduras and has him executed in 1525 on a charge of fomenting revolt.

Spanish Colonial Rule (1522–1821)

Carlos V of Spain appoints Cortés as Governor and then "Capitán General" to rule over the colony now entitled New Spain. From 1527 to 1535 the colony is governed by a powerful "Audiencia", a combination of legal and military functions. Following this, and up until the end of colonial rule, government of Spain's Mexican possessions is in the hands of the Viceroy, the King's personal representative.

The virtually complete, and often violent, conversion of the native peoples to Christianity signals the first phase of mixed race intermarriage between Iberians, Meso-Americans and Africans. European varieties of grain are cultivated and livestock farming is introduced. New Spain's silver mines become a major source of income for the mother country.

1522 Cortés has the future colonial capital city, "México" as it is to be called, built on the site of Tenochtitlán, which has been razed to the ground. Carlos V appoints Cortés Governor of New Spain.

1522–24 Cortés and his commanders manage to conquer virtually all of the Aztec empire, including Honduras and San Salvador. Franciscan monks begin arriving in Mexico, the first three in 1523 and then a further twelve in 1524, and embark on missionary work and building monasteries.

Deserving Spanish soldiers are given Indian villages and tracts of land as "encomiendas". Under their entitlement the Spanish owners are supposed not to exploit the Indians but to look after them and convert them to Christianity, but in reality this is seldom the case. Although the encomienda system is formally abolished in 1542 it continues in some form until the early 18th c.

1526 Dominican monks arrive in the colony and settle mainly in the south, among the Mixtecs and Zapotecs. They are followed by other Augustinian and Jesuit missionaries and within a decade millions of native Indians are converted to Christianity. Although they destroy the Meso-American monuments and prohibit the ancient religions, the monks study the Indian languages and chronicle the native peoples' way of life and customs. They build infirmaries and construct irrigation systems, teach the Indians European skills and farming techniques, and shield them from attack by soldiers and settlers. Chief among them are the Bishops Juan de Zumárraga, Vasco de Quiroga, Diego de Landa (although he also orders the burning of thousands of irreplaceable Maya manuscripts), and Abbot Bernardino de Sahagún, who makes some extremely important records for posterity. Bartolomé de Las Casas (1474–1566), the "apostle of the Indians", sides particularly vehemently with the native peoples and persuades Carlos V to enact laws for their protection (1542).

After 1555, when the Spanish crown gains greater authority over decision-making in the country, the rights and freedom of action of the monastic orders are increasingly curtailed, and their work is placed under the control of the bishops.

Cortés goes to Spain to defend himself against accusations of 1527
disloyalty during his governorship of Mexico. He loses his post as governor but is given the title of Marqués del Valle de Oaxac. The Audiencia – a five-man council exercising legal and administrative authority – is put in charge of ruling New Spain.

Cortés, deprived of power, returns to Mexico and undertakes a 1530
number of less successful expeditions sailing along the Pacific coast. At the same time Nuño Beltrán de Guzmán conquers several of the Pacific coastal regions, including the present state of Jalisco. Francisco de Montejo, on the other hand, is unable to secure the submission of the Maya who offer bitter resistance in Yucatán, and it is ten years before his son, bearing the same name, meets with success.

The Virgin Mary is said to have appeared to an Indian, Juan Diego, 1531
in Guadalupe on December 12th. As the dark-skinned "Nuestra Señora de Guadalupe" our Lady of Guadalupe becomes the patron saint of Mexico's Indians.

Carlos V appoints Antonio de Mendoza as New Spain's first Vice- 1535
roy. He also has administrative responsibility for the West Indies and the Philippines. On Mexican soil the Viceroy is the highest legal and administrative authority as well as acting Defender of the Faith, i.e. the Church, and supreme commander of the armed forces. Up until independence in 1821 Mexico has a total of 62 Viceroys. New Spain is divided into provinces ruled by a governor-general. Supreme authority over the new colonies remains with the king who is assisted by a Council for Colonial Affairs. The main task of Mexico's new administration is to secure the king's absolute power, run the colony's economy for the benefit of Spain, and convert and protect the native peoples. Special Indian laws are enacted to this end in 1542 but are only partly put into practice.

Expeditions in search of conquests to extend Spain's dominions 1535–65
are mounted by Conquistadors such as Ponce de León, Pánfilo de Narváez (Florida), Álvaro Nuñez Cabeza de Vaca (Texas and New Mexico), Hernán de Soto (from the Atlantic to the Mississippi) and Francisco Vázquez de Coronado (from the Gulf of Mexico to Kansas).

New Spain receives its first African slaves.

Hernán Cortés dies near Seville in Spain, a lonely and embittered 1547
man.

The first university on American soil is founded in Mexico City. 1551

Mining, especially for silver, is at its first peak.

The Santa Inquisición (Holy Inquisition), the supreme court guard- 1571
ing the orthodoxy of Catholicism, is set up in Mexico City.

The Spanish have extended their rule to cover the whole mainland About 1600
of present-day Mexico. About two thirds of the Indian population

are wiped out by disease such as smallpox, brought by the Europeans, bloody massacres, and forced labour in the fields and the mines. About 30% of the land has become the property of the Church. The haciendas, the large self-sufficient estates, are established and alongside them are the ejidos, farmlands known since pre-Hispanic times that are collectively owned by the Indian villages.

About 1650 Economic decline of New Spain with dwindling output from the silver mines.

1697 The Spanish conquer Tayasal (Petén), the last free Indian state (Itzá-Maya).

Death of Carlos II, last of the Spanish Habsburgs. The Spanish empire passes to the Bourbons whose colonial policy reforms are a mixed success.

1767 Expulsion from Mexico of the Jesuits, just as they have also been driven out of Spain.

1708–13 Indian uprisings in the Chiapas Highlands.

About 1800 New Spain reaches the limits of its expansion, and with at least 4 million sq.km/1.5 million sq. miles is the Americas' second largest country after Brazil. Its population is put at 6 million (15% Spanish, 25% mestizo, 60% Indian). The Spanish are divided into gachupines, Spaniards actually born in Spain, and criollos, or creoles, those born in the colonies, with the gachupines far outranking the criollos, especially in terms of preferential status for government office.

The ideas behind the French Revolution and the American Declaration of Independence reach New Spain and inspire the call for greater independence.

1803–04 Alexander von Humboldt travels in Mexico.

The Spanish crown seizes Church property under the Amortisation and Consolidation Law. The criollos and many of the clergy turn their back on the mother country.

1808 Napoleon's armies invade Spain and he puts his brother Joseph Bonaparte on the Spanish throne. New Spain refuses to recognise him. There is confusion as to the political consequences. A small group see this as the opportunity for independence from Spain but the majority prefer a continuation of the monarchy in the form of the deposed Spanish king, Ferdinand VII. Counting on the support of the criollos Mexico's Viceroy, José de Iturrigaray, attempts to have himself proclaimed king but is abducted to Veracruz by a body of Spaniards and thence to Spain.

1810–21 War of Independence

A group of criollos, led by Miguel Hidalgo y Costilla, an enlightened priest from Dolores, and the nationalist leader Ignacio Allende from San Miguel, head the first popular uprising, summoning their supporters on September 15th with the "Grito de Dolores", the cry to rebel against the Spanish – "Vivan las Américas, muera el mal gobierno, mueran los Gachupines!"

Country dwellers in the 19th century

After some early minor victories the revolution is put down and Hidalgo and Allende are captured and executed for rebellion. A second revolt is led by José Maria Morelos, another priest. 1811

The revolutionaries issue a declaration of independence in Chilpancingo whereby a future new constitution would enshrine the principles of unfettered popular sovereignty with universal male suffrage, establishment of Catholicism as the state religion, and the abolition of slavery, the class system, torture and royal monopolies. 1813

At the battle of Morelia the rebels are defeated by the troops of Agustín de Iturbide, the Viceroy, who has remained loyal to the king; Morelos is captured in 1815 and executed in Mexico City.

A revolution by the "Liberales" in Spain forces Ferdinand VII to adopt the 1812 Cádiz constitution, which lends added impetus to the movement for independence in New Spain. 1820

From the Achievement of Independence to the Wars of Reform and Intervention (1821–67)

Mexico's independence, wrung from the mother country by dint of fighting and confirmed in agreements between the rebels and the loyalists, is finally recognised by Spain in 1836. This first phase of Mexican independence, lasting until 1857, is marked by internal strife, fighting with the United States, and foreign interference, resulting in civil war – the "Guerra de la Reforma" – between 1858 and 1861. This follows intervention by the European powers concerned about the debts owed them by the Mexican State.

1821	General Agustín de Iturbide manages to intercede between loyalists and rebels. Now supported by the country's most powerful sources he declares Mexico independent with the "Plan de Iguala". On August 24th Iturbide and the Viceroy, Juan O'Donojú, sign the Treaty of Córdoba giving Mexico national sovereignty.
1822	The Spanish Parliament rejects the Treaty of Córdoba. Iturbide assumes control as Emperor Agustín I at the behest of the new Mexican congress.
1823	Rebellion against the government, led by Vicente Guerrero, Guadalupe Victoria, Nicolás Bravo and Antonio López de Santa Anna. Iturbide steps down and leaves the country. The monarchy is abolished and the Meso-American provinces declare their independence (United States of Central America; 1823–39).
1824	A constitution similar to that of the USA is drafted. The revolutionary leader Guadalupe Victoria is elected first President of the Republic, with Nicolás Bravo as his Vice-President. Iturbide, having returned, is court martialled and shot.
1825–28	Fort San Juan de Ulúa (Veracruz), Spain's last base in Mexico, falls to the Mexicans. The Mexican government encourages the north Americans to settle in Texas, as yet largely unpopulated. Political conflicts between the conservative centralists and the liberal federalists, together with interference by England and the USA in Mexico's domestic arrangements, hamper the government's ability to negotiate. Although the federalist Vicente Guerrero fails to win the election he is still appointed the new President.
1829	Guerrero is overthrown and flees to Acapulco but is betrayed and executed for high treason. He is succeeded by the Vice-President Anastasio Bustamante.
1832	General Antonio López de Santa Anna, who is allied with the liberals, becomes President and eventually dictator. There is growing tension between the Americans who have moved into Texas and the Mexicans there who are increasingly in the minority.
1836	Fighting breaks out between American settlers and Mexicans. Texas breaks away from Mexico. Santa Anna marches north with his troops and captures San Antonio. In the battle for the old Franciscan mission of the Alamo all the American rebels that have sought shelter there are killed, and Santa Anna's men are victorious but suffer heavy losses. A few weeks later they are defeated by American forces under General Sam Houston at the San Jacinto River and Santa Anna is taken prisoner.
1845	The United States annexes Texas, making it the 28th State of the Union.
1847	Beginning of the "war of the castes" (la guerra de las castas), the uprising of the Yuatec Maya tribes that lasts until the early 20th c.
1846–48	Following the conflict over Texas war breaks out between Mexico and the USA. Santa Anna's troops are defeated in bitter fighting.

Mexico City falls at the end of September 1847 after a last stand by young cadets ("niños héroes") in Chapultepec Castle. Santa Anna resigns as president. His successor, Herrera, signs the peace treaty of Guadalupe Hidalgo, in which Mexico cedes Texas and subsequently hands over northern California, Arizona and New Mexico to the USA for a payment of 18,250,000 dollars, thus reducing Mexico's territory by more than half.

The defeat intensifies the political tensions between Mexico's 1849–55
clerical conservatives and anti-clerical liberals. In 1853 Santa Anna returns for a two-year stint as dictator then goes into permanent exile.

The liberals under General Ignacio Comonfort and his colleagues 1856–57
Benito Juárez, Miguel Lerdo de Tejada and Melchor Ocampo take over the government and draft radical reform laws which include the abolition of privileges for the Army and the Church, repeal of the hacienda and ejido systems in favour of private ownership of land, and education being taken over by the State. The compulsory purchase of former church land and the distribution of the Indian ejidos lead to outright rejection of the legislation by the clerics and to further impoverishment of the Indians who have no sense of private property and thus suffer further deprivation.

The prolonged differences between conservatives and liberals precipitate civil war.

War of the Reform. 1858–61

Fighting breaks out during the presidency of Benito Juárez, a Zapotec from Oaxac. In the first year the conservative forces, led by the Generals Miguel Miramón, Tomás Mejía and Leonardo Márquez, are victorious. Juárez moves the liberal capital first to Guadalajara then to Veracruz. Under his reform laws he presides over the appropriation of church property without compensation, the abolition of the monastic orders, the introduction of civil marriage and the transfer of cemeteries to the State. The Church becomes entirely separate from the State.

The fortunes of war begin to favour the liberals. 1860

The liberal troops under General González Ortega enter Mexico 1861
City, followed ten days later by Juárez and his cabinet. Because of the barren state of the nation's finances the President decides to freeze the repayment of foreign debts for two years. England, France and Spain protest and decide jointly to proceed militarily against Mexico to collect their debts. In December the first allied units land at Veracruz.

European Intervention. 1862–67

Whereas the Mexican government succeeds in getting the English and Spanish forces to withdraw Napoleon III of France seizes the opportunity to press on with his aggressive foreign policy, seeking to counterbalance US expansion by creating a monarchistic alliance and once more restore French influence in the New World.

The contingent of French troops advances on Mexico City. On May 1862
5th they suffer a defeat at the hands of General Ignacio Zaragoza's

forces at Puebla but almost completely wipe out the Mexican units in the fighting that follows.

1863 The French march into Mexico City and the Juárez government flees to the north of the country. On July 10th the monarchy is proclaimed in the capital; Napoleon III and conservative Mexican politicians in exile offer the Emperor's throne to the Habsburg Archduke Ferdinand Maximilian of Austria, who only accepts the regency after a plebiscite in his favour.

1864 On May 28th Emperor Maximilian and his wife, the Belgian Princess Charlotte ("Carlota"), enter Mexico. To the disappointment of the conservatives Maximilian leaves the reform laws largely intact and attempts to improve the legal standing of the peons, and alleviate the lot of the Indians. However, the country's desperate financial straits, caused mainly by the enormous cost of the French army of intervention, make it virtually impossible for him to govern, and he also increasingly finds himself at odds with the conservatives who have invited him there, and with the French Commander, Marshal François Bazaine.

1865 By the spring the French have driven Juárez and his troops almost completely out of Mexico.

In the USA, where the northern states have won the Civil War, France's intervention is viewed as an infringement of the Monroe Doctrine and the Americans demand the immediate withdrawal of the French troops.

1866 Prussia's victory over Austria at Königgrätz and the consequent threat to France cause Napoleon III gradually to recall the army of

The execution of Maximilian I (painting by Edouard Manet)

intervention. Empress Charlotte travels to Europe in July to beg him to change his mind and to seek help from Pope Pius IX, but to no avail.

The last of the French units leave Mexico in March. Maximilian 1867
refuses to leave "his" people in the lurch and assumes command of the Mexican troops loyal to the emperor. These are not enough, however, to withstand the liberal units led by the Generals Mariano Escobedo, Ramón Corona and Porfirio Diáz. On May 15th Maximilian's small force is surrounded and he is taken prisoner. Despite much international pleading on his behalf he and his two generals Miguel Miramón and Tomás Mejía are executed on June 19th by firing squad.

The Republic Restored (1867–76)

During this period the liberals pick up their policies where they had left off before intervention by the French. The major problems facing them are the devastation caused by the war, the former soldiers now without jobs, and a growing split in their own ranks. Two main aims of the Juárez government are to revive the economy and reorganise the educational system.

Benito Juárez is confirmed as President. He tries to retain a form of 1867
the "ejidos", whereby the Indians collectively own their land, despite this being contrary to the reform laws.

The English resume building the railway line between Mexico City and Veracruz (completed 1873).

Juárez is re-elected in 1871 but dies the following year. His succes- 1871–78
sor, Sebastián Lerdo de Tejada, basically continues with Juárez' policies but with more of an emphasis on centralisation. He also initiates the change to a bicameral parliamentary system, with a House of Deputies and a Senate.

The Porfiriato (1876–1911)

This period gets its name from its autocratic President, Porfirio Díaz. It is to be Mexico's longest period free from war in the first hundred years of independence, and ushers in the country's first great wave of modernisation, with substantial economic progress, fuelled in part by foreign investment which helps to construct capital projects in industry, railways, telephone and cable communications, and more new mines.

A mestizo from a humble background, Porfirio Díaz seizes power 1876
from Lerdo and sends him into exile abroad.

After repeated breaches of the frontier with the USA by Mexican 1877
bandits and Indian gangs Díaz strengthens the border guards to prevent further forays, whereupon he receives official US recognition.

Since the Mexican constitution does not allow immediate re- 1880–84
election of the previous President Manuel González, the candidate

supported by Díaz, takes over government after a crushing election victory. While in office investment in modernisation goes beyond the bounds of the budget and in order to repay borrowings from abroad González cuts civil servants' salaries. This results in a massive increase in corruption and popular sentiment turns against the President.

1884–1911 Once re-elected Porfirio Díaz rules without a break until forced to resign. The one-time liberal politician wins over the conservatives and suppresses opposition groups, including the Indians. While the rich share in the country's economic development the lot of the poor remains more or less unchanged. The ownership of land is concentrated in fewer hands, and most of industry and mining belongs to foreigners. In 1910 Díaz stands for election one last time, promising greater political freedom. When this fails to materialise, the outbreak of revolution in 1911 forces him to resign; he dies in exile in Paris in 1915.

Mexican Revolution (1910–20)

Mexican historians term the country's history from 1910 to the present as a period of "permanent revolution". The first decade, one of "revolution and destruction" when a million Mexicans lose their lives, is the bloodiest period in the history of independent Mexico.

1910–15 The revolutionary movement is headed by Francisco Madero, the liberal son of a wealthy landowner, who allies himself with the fearsome Francisco ("Pancho") Villa, a former bandit chief. When Díaz resigns in 1911 Madero becomes President but is overthrown by an uprising under General Victoriano Huerta and executed in 1913. Huerta's dictatorial rule erupts into civil war with the constitutionalists led by Venustiano Carranza (Coahuila), Alvaro Obregón (Sonora) and Pancho Villa (Chihuahua). In the south Emiliano Zapata foments revolt among the Indian peasants who want radical land reform and whose battle cry is "tierra y libertad" – land and liberty. The USA under President Woodrow Wilson support the constitutionalists and occupies Veracruz in 1914. In July Huerta flees abroad.

Carranza allies himself with Obregón who is the first to reach the capital, now without a government, in August 1914. Villa, allied for a time with Zapata, is beaten in April 1915 by Obregón, in a battle with the heaviest losses in Mexican history, and flees to the north.

1916–20 By 1916 Carranza, who is recognised as President by the USA, has succeeded in gaining control of most of the country. Zapata alone fights on until he is gunned down in 1919. Pancho Villa invades New Mexico, resulting in an unsuccessful US punitive expedition to Mexico under General John Pershing; Villa is shot dead in 1923.

1917 A convention in Querétaro drafts a new constitution, modelled on the 1857 version, and which also abolishes the hacienda system and declares all mineral resources the property of the Mexican people. It contains sweeping measures for the protection of workers and restricts the office of President to a single term of four years. The constitution comes into force on February 5th. The political chaos continues. The USA withdraws its support from

Villa and Zapata on the presidential seat in Mexico City

Carranza because of his refusal to enter the First World War on the side of the Allies. Opposition against Carranza gathers strength within the country and in April 1920 he is assassinated. His successor is Alvaro Obregón.

Consolidation of the Revolution (1921–33)

This phase still bears the stamp of the "Caudillos", the leaders of the great revolutionary wars, and further progress is made in implementing the chief aims of the old constitution and the Revolution – the redistribution of land, a better education system, and less power for the Church.

Alvaro Obregón's Presidency sees the development of the trade union movement, more schools built and a great surge of revolutionary art (Diego Rivera, José Clementa Orozco, etc.). Estates are confiscated and reallocated as ejidos. The most important personality in the cabinet is the energetic Minister of Education, José Vasconcelos, a philosopher and author who creates the new school system and stimulates a sense of national culture. 1921–24

After being defeated at the polls Adolfo de la Huertas tries to engineer a revolt which is put down with assistance from the United States.

In an autocratic fashion President Plutarco Elías Calles presses on with Obregón's reforms. The continuing conflict with the Church results in the bloody Cristero Rebellion, which eventually drives religious life underground for years. 1924–28

An amendment of the constitution lengthens the term of the Presidency to six years and makes re-election possible provided the terms as President do not directly follow one another. This enables Obregón to win a second term, beating Vasconcelos, but he is assassinated shortly after taking office.

As Presidents Emilio Portes Gil, Pascual Ortíz Rubio, and Abelardo Rodríguez are very much under the influence of the powerful ex-president Plutarco Calles. 1929–33

Founding of the National Revolutionary Party (PNR), bringing together Mexico's main political forces. It has since provided all subsequent Mexican Presidents to the present day, despite changes in its name (since 1916 it has been the PRI) and its organisation.

The Era of Nationalism (1934–40)

The stranglehold of foreign business on major sectors of the economy is broken. Although nationalisation has its economic drawbacks it brings a greater sense of national self-confidence.

During the Presidency of Lázaro Cárdenas, the first head of state not to have come from the ranks of the revolutionary leadership, Mexico moves further towards real social reform as he helps the peasants by the redistribution of land, and the workers by reorganising the labour movement. Calles, who had originally supported Cárdenas thinking that he could influence him like the others, realises his mistake. Cárdenas starts reforming the army which had provided Calles with his support. 1934

Cárdenas eliminates the ex-president's supporters from government and administration. Calles himself is banished from the country in 1936. 1935

The Mexican assets of the American and British-owned oil companies are expropriated and become the property of the State. Nationalisation of their oil is viewed with enthusiasm by the people who see it as an important step towards economic independence. 1938

Modern Mexico (since 1940)

Mexico owes its first great economic boom since the Revolution to its favourable position in the Second World War, the pragmatic policies of Presidents Camacho and Alemán, and the absence of unrest and coups d'état. Officially the main part of the Revolution has been concluded, but carrying this out in practice appears more problematic. This outlook allows the government to deviate from the form and content of the more radical legislation, thus benefiting economic development. The infrastructure is improved but there are still problems with the distribution and cultivation of land, and with creating additional jobs for the fast-growing population.

President Manuel Avila Camacho slows down land reform, and encourages the inflow of foreign capital and the formation of private property. 1940

◀ *Emiliano Zapata, the fabled revolutionary hero*

History

1942 Mexico declares war on the Axis powers.

1946–52 Miguel Alemán Valdés becomes the first civilian to be head of state since the Revolution. Further progress is made in economic development. Agriculture and transport benefit from vast irrigation schemes and an expanding, more comprehensive road network. In 1952 Mexico becomes economically self-sufficient.

1952–64 The economic boom continues during the Presidencies of Adolfo Ruiz Cortines and Adolfo López Mateos, although growing inflation and corruption in the administration lay up problems ahead. Economic growth also continues to be unevenly distributed among the different social classes.

1964–70 During the Presidency of Gustavo Díaz Ordaz Mexico stages the Summer Olympics in 1968 and the football World Cup in 1970. When a massive rally against spending on the Olympic Games is held in Mexico City's Plaza de las Tres Culturas about 250 demonstrators are gunned down by the police (only 43 officially) and over 2000 people are arrested.

In the Treaty of Tlatelolco Latin America declares itself to be a nuclear-weapon-free zone.

1970–76 President Luís Alvarez Echeverría progresses land distribution and the decentralisation of industry. New tourist centres are created and Mexico aims to play a leading role in the Third World.

Inflationary development and the declining competitiveness of Mexican goods on the world market result in very real economic difficulties. When the economy is hit by a flight of capital on August 31st 1976 the peso is devalued by almost 50% against the US dollar.

Terrorism casts its shadow over Echeverría's domestic politics.

1976–82 José López Portillo becomes President on December 1st 1976 and sets in train anti-inflationary measures.

Rich oil reserves are discovered and by 1980 Mexico is already the world's fourth largest producer of petroleum. Oil revenues from exports soar from 500 million US dollars in 1976 to 13.3 billion dollars by 1981. With the backing of these riches the government seeks to reduce its political and economic dependence on the USA and to play a more active role itself, particularly among the countries of the Third World.

In October 1981 López Portillo presides over the North/South conference that he has initiated in Cancún.

To counter dissatisfaction with "rigged democracy" the government legalises new political parties in addition to the existing opposition groups. The electoral laws are changed so that 100 out of the 400 deputies' seats are reserved for the opposition.

The rich flow of oil revenues and the excessive level of credit offered – and accepted – from the foreign banks, stoke inflation to hitherto unheard of heights. Uneconomic investments in farming and the state undertakings, together with mismanagement and corruption, push the country into a dangerous situation where the budget deficit and foreign debt are virtually out of control. The overvalued peso and lack of confidence in the government lead to a massive flight of capital which may well have been in the order of 40 billion dollars between 1976 and 1982. In August 1982 Mexico's foreign exchange reserves reach an all-time low and the strict currency controls now introduced initially lead to a currency black market. On September 1st 1982 the President announces the nationalisation of all private banks.

López Portillo's term of office ends with the most acute political and economic crisis for 50 years.

Miguel de la Madrid Hurtado enters the Presidency on December 1st 1982. Because of the maladministration and corruption of his two predecessors he finds himself faced with a legacy of foreign debt amounting to 86 billion dollars, no foreign currency reserves, a prohibitive rate of 150 pesos to the dollar, a budget deficit of 18% of the gross national product, an inflation rate of 100%, and a demoralised population. The government immediately concludes a debt rescheduling agreement with the International Monetary Fund and the creditor banks, and gets more financial aid from the USA. Many of the savings measures imposed on the country are carried out. 1982–88

As a result Mexico again has foreign exchange reserves at its disposal and can record a fall in the budget deficit and the rate of inflation, although unemployment also goes up and purchasing power goes down.

New debt rescheduling agreements are concluded in 1984 and 1985.

Additional spending and plunging oil prices again lead to a greater budget deficit and yet another boost to inflation which by the end of 1986 reaches 105%.

In July 1986 Mexico becomes a full member of the General Agreement on Tariffs and Trade (GATT), an important step in opening up its economic policy.

The country's situation improves in the spring of 1987 thanks to an international aid programme and a new debt rescheduling agreement.

The international stock market crash in October 1987 brings a fresh flight of capital. The peso rapidly loses its value against the US dollar.

In December government, trade unions, and employers join together in a solidarity pact in order to reduce long-term inflation, which by now has reached a record 159.2%, and in fact by mid-1988 it actually declines to its lowest since 1981.

Around Christmas 1987 the governments of Mexico and the United States get together to work out a complicated new model of debt rescheduling.

By 1983 the civil war in Guatemala has driven 45,000 refugees, mainly Mayan Indians, over the border to Chiapas. They settle there and, since 1984, half in Campeche and Quintana Roo. By late 1987 about 5% of them have returned to Guatemala.

Like his predecessors Miguel de la Madrid tries to conduct a foreign policy as independent of the United States as possible. As a member of the Contadora Group Mexico works with Venezuela, Colombia and Panama to achieve a peaceful settlement of conflicts in Central America.

On September 19th 1985 Mexico City and parts of the states of Michoacán, Jalisco, Guerrero and Colima are hit by a severe earthquake (8.1 on the Richter Scale). According to the official figures it

Earthquake damage in Mexico City in September 1985

leaves over 8000 dead, more than 100,000 homeless, and causes 5 billion US dollars worth of damage, although the number of victims may well have been many more than the official total.

In May 1986 Mexico hosts football's World Cup for the second time.

At the start of his Presidency Miguel de la Madrid promises a "moral revival". Several senior officials of the previous administration are prosecuted and sentenced, although this anti-corruption campaign soon loses its momentum.

General dissatisfaction with the governing party, the PRI, leads to electoral victories in 1983 and 1984 in several cities for PAN, the conservative opposition party. However in 1985 and 1986 the PRI manages to win these cities back and also to hold on to hard-fought governors' posts. The opposition accuses the PRI of electoral fraud and there are big protest marches, especially in the states of Chihuahua, Nuevo León, Durango and Oaxca.

In the summer of 1987 Cuauhtémoc Cárdenas walks out of the PRI taking a large splinter group with him, and on July 6th 1988 he stands in the presidential and congressional elections as a candidate for the new centre-left National Democratic Front, against Carlos Salinas de Gortari of the PRI.

True to form, Salinas de Gortari is elected the new President, but at 50.36% his vote is substantially down on his predecessor, Miguel de la Madrid, who in 1982 had 71%. According to the official election results Cárdenas has 31.12% of the votes and Clouthier of PAN 17.07%. The opposition provides completely different figures and Cárdenas claims to be the real victor. Along with the other opposition parties he accuses the PRI of massive electoral fraud and vote-rigging. There is a call for "civil protest" and big anti-government demonstrations are held in Mexico City.

For the first time since 1929 the Opposition gets seats in the Senate, hitherto a PRI monopoly, but the PRI still remains the ruling party.

In September Hurricane Gilbert hits the Yucatán peninsula and causes terrible destruction. Heading north, it causes severe flooding in Monterrey and many lives are lost.

1988–94

Carlos Salinas de Gortari introduces the most radical reforms since the Revolution: state companies are increasingly privatised and import restrictions lifted in order to put pressure on domestic industries to become more productive and competitive. With the stability and growth pact (PECE) signed on January 1st 1989, both government and the two sides of industry commit themselves to budgetary discipline as well as restraint in the field of wages and prices. As a consequence inflation goes down from 51.7% (1988) to 19.7% (1989) In February 1990 a debt agreement amounting to $47.9 billion is signed with the private credit banks and underwritten by the World Bank. A change in the constitution from May 1990 opens up the possibility of privatising the banks, which were nationalised as recently as 1982. By 1992 this produces $12.5 billion which can be used to wipe out debts and for a social programme. In order to increase agricultural productivity, the "ejido" system is done away with at the end of 1991. In October 1992 the solidarity pact is extended for another year and, among other things, allows for a maximum wage rise of 9.9% – for unskilled workers amounting to a further cut in purchasing power, for skilled workers signifying a modest improvement in living standards. By contrast, in 1993, the inflation rate falls below 10% for the first time. In December 1992 the presidents of the USA and Mexico and the Canadian Prime Minister sign the NAFTA free trade agreement in San Antonio, Texas.

In tandem with the lifting of economic restrictions, considerable progress is made both in political liberalisation and in the fight against corruption. In July 1989, for the first time since 1929, an opposition politician, Ernesto Ruffo Appel of the PAN, suceeds in gaining the governorship of Baja California Norte, something which previously the PRI had always been able to prevent, notwithstanding the fact that similar opposition victories had occurred in the past. In early 1989 both the leading union officials of PEMEX and prominent investment bankers are arrested on suspicion of corruption and deception. Furthermore, corrupt police chiefs and drug traffickers are brought before the courts and sentenced. In the parliamentary and senate elections of August 1991 and PRI again emerge as winners, while the opposition has to accept large losses. In July 1992 another PAN politician is elected as governor, this time for Chihuahua, in area the largest of the Mexican federal states. In Guanajuanto the PRI governor is suspended from office because of concerted opposition pressure and is replaced by a PAN politician. The elections for governor in Michoacan are won by the PRI candidate, but this sparks off disturbances from the PRD, which cannot bring itself to accept the result.

In February 1990 the government breaches an internal political taboo by renewing restricted diplomatic relations with the Vatican, which had been broken since the Revolutionary War. Shortly afterwards the Pope pays a second visit to Mexico and the Roman Catholic Church is later officially legalised.

A gas explosion, caused by negligence on the part of those in positions of responsibility, occurs in Guadalajara in April 1992, claiming over 200 lives and causing immense damage.

History

On New Year's Day 1994 the Ejército Zapatista de Liberación Nacional (EZLN; Zapatista National Army of Liberation) occupies four towns in Chiapas. The Indian revolutionaries, who demand economic, social and political reforms, are driven out by the armed forces. At least 145 people are killed and another 20,000 flee. In March a provisional peace agreement is reached between the government and the Zapatistas.

At the end of the same month the PRI presidential candidate, Luis Donaldo Colosio, is assassinated in Tijuana. His successor, Ernesto Zedillo Ponce de Leon, gains a victory in the elections in August 1994, but his party's share of the vote (48.8%) is the lowest ever recorded.

Famous People

The following famous people were all connected in some way or other with Mexico, whether as the place of their birth or death, or because they lived or worked there.

Lázaro Cárdenas (21.5.1895–19.10.1970)

Born in Jiquilpan in Michoacán, Lázaro Cárdenas joined General Guillermo Garcia's revolutionary forces in 1913, and then the constitutionalists in 1920, where he rose to the rank of Brigade General. He was Governor of Michoacán from 1928 to 1932 and after holding a number of posts in government was elected Mexico's President in 1934. He set out to shake off the influence of the powerful ex-president Plutarco Elias Calles, actually turning his policies around. A true president of the people, he was responsible for the most extensive land reforms to date, redistributing 18 million ha./44.5 million acres of farmland to the peasants as ejidos. He also nationalised the foreign oil companies, to great popular acclaim, and strengthened the labour movement.

Frederick Catherwood (27.2.1799–September 1854)

Although born in London and only spending a few years of his life in Mexico, as an artist and draughtsman Catherwood was responsible for many drawings of the ruins left by the Maya. When accompanying the American archaeologist John Lloyd Stephens to illustrate his travels in Mexico and Central America, although weakened by malaria, he made detailed records of the ruins, stelae and glyphs still buried beneath the tangle of the rainforest. Most of his original drawings were lost in a fire. He later tried his hand as an architect and as a railroad man in South America, and worked in the mines of southern California. In 1854, on the crossing from New York to London, he was drowned when the steamer "Arctic" on which he was travelling sank in the first steamer collision in history.

Hernán Cortés (1485–2.12.1547)

When Hernán Cortés, the son of a high-born captain of infantry from Medellín in Spain, was asked by Diego de Velásquez, Governor of Cuba, to command an expedition to explore the mainland of Central America, he probably saw this as his great chance. He set out to sea on February 18th 1519 with a fleet of 11 ships and about 100 sailors and 500 soldiers. Although the ruthless conquest and destruction of the Aztec empire featured nowhere in his orders that is precisely what he achieved.

On the Gulf Coast, where Veracruz stands today, he founded the settlement of Villa Rica de la Vera Cruz. After envoys from the Aztec emperor Moctezuma II had presented them with rich gifts most of his party wanted to turn back, so Cortés burnt all of the ships but one, which was sent to Spain, and began the march inland. On November 3rd 1519 he entered Tenochtitlán where Moctezuma II allowed himself to be taken prisoner since he believed Cortés to be the returned god Quetzalcóatl. In May 1520 Cortés was temporarily forced to leave Tenochtitlán to take on the troops under Panfilo de Narváez sent after him because of his insubordination by the Governor of Cuba. Having routed them he returned to the Aztec capital only to find himself under attack from the people, enraged by the massacre of some of their nobles by the Spaniards who had been left behind. Forced to flee the city, he returned with his troops and their Indian allies over a year later to recapture it on August 13th 1521, and raze it to the ground.

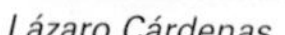

Lázaro Cárdenas

Hernán Cortés

Porfirio Díaz

In 1522 Carlos V of Spain appointed him Governor and Captain General of this colony of New Spain and in the period that followed his troops conquered nearly all the Indian states. Back in Spain from 1528 to 1530 although laden with honours the machinations of his enemies lost him his post as Governor. However, he was to continue as commander-in-chief and was made Marqués del Valle de Oaxaca. On his return to Mexico he undertook several less successful expeditions to places such as Honduras and Baja California. He returned to Spain in 1540, joined a short campaign against Algeria, and eventually died an embittered man at Castilleja de la Cuesta near Seville.

Juana Inés de la Cruz (12.11.1651–17.4.1695)

Juana Inés de la Cruz, one of the most important Spanish-speaking poets of the 17th c., was born on the Hacienda San Miguel Nepantla in what is today Estado de México. Her exceptional talent was apparent as early as the age of eight, when her grandfather already wanted to send her to university. She studied Latin in Mexico City and in 1665 arrived at the court of the Vicereine. Here too her thirst for knowledge stood out, and the Viceroy, Marques de Mancera, made her take an examination before 40 scholars, which she passed with flying colours. Two years later she entered a convent because in her own words she believed that only there could she find her redemption. While housekeeper and archivist of the convent of San Jerónimo she also devoted herself to her studies and to literature. Her writings included three religious dramas, two comedies ("Los empenos de una casa" and "Amor es más laberinto") and many love poems which are also eloquent testimony to the emotional repression and passionate feelings of the nun.

Cuauhtémoc (1496 28.2.1525)

As the successor to Cuitláhuac, who only ruled for three months, Cuauhtémoc (in Náhuatl "the swooping eagle") was the last free Aztec emperor. Like every son of the Aztec nobility he had enjoyed an excellent education, and in the defence of his people against the Conquistadors he distinguished himself by his bravery and prudence. When the Spaniards captured him on August 13th 1521 he begged Cortés for the mercy of death. Instead Cortés took him along as a hostage on his march to Honduras, and he was hanged in 1525 at Izancanac (Camp.) for alleged conspiracy.

Porifirio Díaz (15.9.1830–2.7.1915)

For more than thirty years Porfirio Díaz, the Oaxaca-born General, entirely dominated Mexican politics. Although responsible for the modernisation of the country he also set in train the great inequity in the distribution of its resources which is still current today.

Initially Díaz fought against the conservatives and on the side of Benito Juárez against the French, which left him a folk hero and the country's most powerful general. In 1871 he unexpectedly stood for the Presidency against his former colleague Juárez. Having lost he came out in open rebellion but was defeated and retired into private life. After the death of Juárez, however, he seized power by military force and henceforth ruled as a ruthless dictator, using the army to eliminate any opposition. He opened the country up to foreign investment and forged strong economic and political ties with the USA. Telephone and telegraph lines were installed, industry was built up and expanded, and large tracts of land were sold off mainly to American farm companies. Yet very few indeed of the Mexicans themselves benefited from this modernisation. The concentration of land in the hands of just a few great landowners eventually led to an uprising by the peasants under Emiliano Zapata, giving the opposition a broad base to operate from. In the end it was Díaz himself who unleashed the Revolution. Although in 1908 he had announced that he felt it was getting to be time for him to step down at the end of his term of office, in 1910 he was putting himself forward for election again. Blatant vote-rigging and the arrest of his opponent, Francisco Madero, triggered off full-blown revolution in November 1910 and Díaz finally resigned in May 1911, going via various countries to Paris, where he died in 1915.

Miguel Hidalgo y Costilla (8.5.1753–27.7.1811)

Every year on September 15th, Mexico's Independence Day, throughout the nation the "Grito de Dolores", the cry of Dolores, rings out an hour before midnight – "Mexicans, long live Mexico! Long live our Lady of Guadalupe! Long live Ferdinand!" The final phrase – "death to the Gachupines" – referring to the peninsular Spaniards, once the country's elite, is omitted these days.

This cry, sounded in the village church of Dolores north-west of Querétaro, made the parish priest, Miguel Hidalgo y Costilla, one of Mexico's national heroes. Along with the Mayor of Querétaro and his wife, and Ignacio Allende he had been part of a conspiracy to win independence from Spain. When their plot was threatened with discovery Father Hidalgo took flight then went on the attack. He had soon collected a force of thousands and with them had captured Guanajuato, Morelia and Guadalajara, leaving nothing to choose between him and his opponents for brutality and terror. At Puerto Calderón his army had to face the troops of General Calleja and was beaten. Hidalgo and the other rebel leaders tried to flee to the United States but were captured and shot at Chihuahua.

Agustín de Iturbide (27.9.1783–19.7.1824)

Mexico's first Emperor, born in Valladolid, now Morelia, initially came to the fore as a loyal officer of the Viceroy, successfully fighting the rebels demanding independence from Spain. In 1820, after the liberal constitution in the mother country had given new impetus to the Mexican independence movement he joined a conservative group which although seeking to break ties with Spain also wanted to keep a monarchy. As commander of their troops he moved against the rebel army of Vicente Guerrero, but was obviously serving his own ends since he joined with Guerrero in working out the "Plan de Iguala". This provided for equality of rights for all, and a constitutional Catholic monarchy in an independent Mexico. He managed to wrest agreement to this from the new Spanish Viceroy, Juan O'Donojú. In May 1822, however, he dissolved the

Constitutional Assembly and had himself proclaimed Emperor Agustín I. His reign was a brief one. The pressure from a fresh uprising under Santa Anna became too great and after eleven months as Emperor he was forced to flee to Italy. Congress accused him of treason. In 1824 he returned to Mexico in secret but was recognised and eventually executed.

Benito Juárez (21.3.1806–18.7.1872)

Benito Juárez was born in San Pablo Guelatao in Oaxaca, the son of Zapotec parents. He learnt to read and write at 13 and then qualified as a lawyer. In 1848 he was elected Governor of Oaxaca and was already carrying out reforms here by the end of his term of office in 1852. He escaped Santa Anna's persecution of the liberals by fleeing abroad where he met other kindred spirits. Once Santa Anna had finally departed, as Minister of Justice under President Comonfort he drafted a liberal constitution but ended up with an illiberal one. In 1858 he was finally elected President himself.

The early years of his term of office were marked by the War of the Reform which severely hampered his plans for reforms such as the abolition of church privileges, the introduction of civil marriage and state education, industrialisation and the nationalisation of church property. Having first had to contend with the conservatives, from whom he had to flee with his government to Guadalajara and Veracruz, he then came into conflict with the French after 1861 over the postponement of payment of foreign debts. He remained in the north during Maximilian I's time as Emperor, returning after the end of the Habsburg episode to resume the office of President again in 1867 and carry on with his reforms. In 1872 he died of natural causes, which was also quite remarkable in itself in the Mexico of that time.

Frida Kahlo (7.7.1910–13.7.1954)

Frida Kahlo was born in Coyoacán, the daughter of a German-Jewish father and a mestizo mother from Oaxaca. Following a serious accident at the age of 18 she was forced to spend part of her life in a wheelchair. In her pictures she expresses her suffering, her pain and fears, as well as the ups and downs of her turbulent relationship with the muralist Diego Rivera. The couple first came together in 1929 and were twice married. Both her art and the tragic story of her life have made her into an international cult figure in recent years.

Eusebio Francisco Kino (10.8.1644–15.3.1711)

This missionary and explorer, originally called Eusebius Franz Kühn, was born in Nonsberg in the Alto Adige, then South Tyrol. As a pupil of the Jesuits, whom he joined in 1665, he was trained as a mathematician and cartographer. With this training he sailed on a missionary voyage to the New World. Two expeditions under Isidro de Atondo led him to Baja California from 1683 to 1685. Father Kino then took over the mission to the Píma Indians in the Pímeria, part of the present states of Sonora, Sinaloa, Baja California and the south-west of the USA. Many mission churches date from his founding of the Jesuit mission in California. He explored and charted the desert areas on 40 expeditions, discovering the mouth of the Río Grande, pushing on to the mouth of the Río Colorado, and establishing that Baja California is a peninsula. After 24 years of missionary work and exploration he died following a brief illness in Magdalena in present-day Sonora.

Bartolomé de Las Casas (1474–31.7.1566)

Don Francisco, the father of Dominican Bartolomé de Las Casas, sailed on the "Santa María" with Christopher Columbus. Bartolomé himself studied theology and law in Salamanca then from 1502 lived in the Spanish possessions in Central America. In 1512

Miguel Hidalgo

Benito Juárez

Maximilian I

he travelled to Cuba. He was soon aware of the cruel and unjust treatment being meted out by the Spaniards towards the Indians. From 1514 he strove vigorously for their rights, in the face of countless intrigues and acts of persecution, and also made fourteen sea voyages to this end. The Grand Inquisitor bestowed on him the title of "Defensor universal de los Indios". In audiences with Ferdinand V and Carlos V he suggested how he thought the lot of the Indians could be improved. Tragically he also introduced the idea of bringing in slaves from Africa, who were physically more robust than the Indians, a suggestion that he later bitterly regretted. When his efforts proved fruitless he withdrew in 1523 to spend ten years in the Dominican monastery on Hispaniola (Cuba) where he worked on his "Apolog'etica Historia de las Indias" (Apologetic History of the Indies) and the "Historia General de las Indias" (General History of the Indies). After he had caused Spanish soldiers to desert in Nicaragua in 1539 he had to return to Spain to account for his actions. In the four years he stayed there he wrote probably his most famous work, the "Brevísima relación de la destrucción de las Indias occidentales" (Brief account of the destruction of the West Indies). He managed to persuade Carlos V to enact far-reaching new laws in 1542 to protect the Indians but these were repealed in 1545. De Las Casas was recalled to Mexico as Bishop of Chiapas where he again clashed with the colonists and again had to return to Spain. He left Mexico in 1547 and in 1550 in the famous disputation of Valladolid once more argued his views. He died in Madrid in 1566 without ever again seeing the Indians that he had sought so hard to protect. It is not known where he lies buried and there is no memorial in Spain to commemorate his achievements, but in Central America today he is still a much venerated figure.

Bartolomé de Las Casas was one of the first to recognise the intrinsic value of the Meso-American cultures. The original research that he carried out for his writings was also of inestimable importance in that, for example, it is to him that we owe our knowledge of the records that Columbus kept in his ship's log, de Las Casas having kept a copy in his archives.

José Joaquín Fernández de Lizardi (1776–1827)

José Fernández de Lizardi was the author of fables, plays, poems and translations, but above all he was an extremely prolific and critical journalist. As the editor of various journals such as "El

Pensador Mexicano" and "El Conductor Eléctrico" he campaigned fiercely in the last years of Spanish rule for independence and political freedom, above all freedom of the press. This often brought him into conflict with the law and the inquisition and he spent some time in prison. After the Spanish left he fought on against opponents of the constitution, but soon came to realise, when Iturbide became emperor, that his hopes for political freedom would not be fulfilled.

As a writer he created the typical mestizo rogue, in the tradition of the picaresque novel, with his leading character in "El Periquillo Sarmiento" (1806).

Maximilian I (6.7.1832–19.6.1867)

Maximilian von Habsburg, the youngest brother of Emperor Franz Joseph I, was born in the Palace of Schönbrunn in Vienna and pursued a military career, becoming a Commander in the Imperial Navy. In 1857 he was appointed Governor-General of Lombardo-Venezia. With the loss of this province he withdrew to Miramare Castle near Trieste.

There he received the invitation from a group of Mexican clerical conservatives to become their country's emperor. This had been suggested by Napoleon III, Emperor of France, whose troops had marched into Mexico against the republican government of Benito Juárez, and who had met Maximilian in Paris in 1856. After lengthy consideration and a plebiscite in his favour Maximilian accepted the invitation and first set foot on Mexican soil at Veracruz on May 28th 1864. To the Conservatives' dismay he left most of Juárez's reforms intact, introduced such measures as freedom of the press, and carried on with appropriation by the State of Church property. Once the French troops had also left Mexico he was virtually without support in the ongoing civil war against the republicans. He fled to Querétaro where he fell into the hands of the troops under Generals Corona and Escobedo on March 15th 1867. Together with his Generals Mejía and Miramón he was court martialled and executed by firing squad on the Cerro de las Campanas in Querétaro. His body arrived back in Vienna in December 1867.

Maximilian was married to the Belgian princess Charlotte Amalie ("Carlota"), who travelled in vain to Europe to plead for support from Napoleon III and Pope Pius IX. After her husband's death she lost her mind and ended her days in a Belgian asylum.

Moctezuma

At least two great Aztec emperors bore the name Moctezuma, or Motecuhzoma, which in Náhuatl means "the angry lord", as in the angry sky, when dark clouds veil the light of the sun.

Moctezuma I (Emperor from 1440 to 1468)

Moctezuma "Ilhuicamina" (Náhuatl for "he who shoots arrows into the heavens") built up the political entity of Tenochtitlán to become the ruling power of Central Mexico. He extended its trading far over the valley of Anáhuac, exacted tribute and taxes, and negotiated the Triple Alliance with Texcoco and Tlacopan. He was responsible for many building projects in the city of Tenochtitlán and initiated the construction of an aqueduct to carry its water supply.

Moctezuma II (Emperor from 1502 to 1520)

Moctezuma II Xocoyotzin (Náhuatl for "the younger") is probably one of history's most tragic figures. He realised too late his error in thinking that Hernán Cortés was the returned god-king Quetzalcoátl. Mexican researchers describe him as harsh, despotic, and deeply religious. During his reign Tenochtitlán's sphere of influence extended as far as the Isthmus of Panama; the city was in its

Moctezuma II

Diego Rivera

Leon Trotsky

heyday and even the Spaniards were amazed at its great size. According to Spanish sources Moctezuma II's death on June 27th 1520 was caused by a stone thrown from the crowd that he was trying to pacify from the roof of Cortés's house, but it was the Indians' belief that he was killed by the Spaniards.

José Clemente Orozco (23.11.1883–7.9.1949)

Orozco was born in Ciudad Guzmán (Jalisco) and lived for a number of years in the United States. Together with Rivera and Siqueiros he is considered one of the founders of "Muralismo". The forceful and vigorous images in his murals are often imbued with cynicism and a passionate concern for the sufferings of mankind. His principal work is the vast mural in the Cabañas Orphanage in Guadalajara.

Diego Rivera (8.12.1886–24.11.1957)

Diego Rivera, who was born in Guanajuato, is considered with Orozco and Siqueiros the founder of Mexican modern art. After first studying art at the Academy in Mexico City he spent many years in Europe, especially Paris (1911–21), where he was a friend of Modigliani and experimented with Cubism. Back in Mexico he drew on ancient Indian culture and revolutionary fervour to create "Muralismo" – murals such as those that can be seen in the National Palace and the Ministry of Education in Mexico City, that are monumental, modern, and directly aimed at the Mexican people with themes from Mexico's social and political life, highlighting the threefold unity of peasants, workers and fighters. The socialist vigour of his work was reflected in his political life and he was a leading member of the Mexican Communist Party, but was expelled in 1927 as a Trotskyite, subsequently being accepted back in 1954. His second wife was the painter Frida Kahlo.

David Álfaro Siqueiros (29.12.1896–5.1.1974)

Siqueiros, from Chihuahua, was the third member of the trio, with Orozco and Rivera, which founded Mexico's muralist art. Major works by him can be seen in the Escuela Preparatoria in Mexico City and the University of Guadalajara. Like Rivera, he was also active, from 1924 to 1930, in the leadership of the Mexican Communist Party, but unlike his fellow muralist he was a hardline Stalinist, not only in word but in deed. On May 24th 1940, three months before Trotsky was murdered, Siqueiros fired several shots at the Russian revolutionary and his wife, but missed.

John Lloyd Stephens (28.11.1805–12.10.1852)

When this cultivated American lawyer from Shrewsbury, New Jersey, heard of the discovery of ruins in Central America, he set out forthwith, as a special envoy of the United States, on two journeys between 1839 and 1842 to Mexico and Central America, taking with him the English artist Frederick Catherwood. Initially unsuccessful he eventually unearthed the ruins of walls in Honduras and bought the site for 50 dollars. Other discoveries followed, including Palenque, Chichen Itzá, Kabah, Labná and Uxmal. Without knowing it, he had stumbled upon the area settled by the Maya. He described his experiences in "Incidents of Travel in Central America, Chiapas and Yucatan", published in London in 1841, and its sequel "Incidents of Travel in Yucatan" which came out in New York in 1843. Owing in no small measure to Catherwood's outstanding illustrations, the publication of the first book unleashed a particular wave of enthusiasm, prompting the study of the Maya. In 1849 Stephens headed the building of the first trans-continental railway through the swamps of Panama, where he contracted the tropical disease which caused his death three years later.

Manuel Tolsá (24.12.1757–24.12.1816)

An architect and sculptor from Enguera in Spain, Manuel Tolsá was one of the principal figures in Mexican Neo-Classicism, a countermovement to the over-elaborate displays of the Rococo, which sought to return to the clearcut lines of antiquity. Driven by this desire Tolsá reworked many once magnificent Baroque churches on more sober lines, destroying a number of Baroque masterpieces in the process. He supervised the completion of the cathedral in Mexico City and was himself responsible for the dome. His major work is considered to be the Palacio de la Minería, with its statue of Carlos IV on horseback, in Mexico City.

Francisco Eduardo Tresguerras (13.10.1759–3.8.1883)

Tresguerras, born in Celaya, was another of the notable masters of Neo-Classicism, although he was also a poet, musician, painter, sculptor and engraver. His major buildings include the church of Nuestra Señora del Carmen in Celaya, the Teatro Alarcón in San Luis Potosí and the Ducal Palace in Guanajuato.

Leon Trotsky (7.11.1879–21.8.1940)

"Trotsky" was the name adopted as cover in 1902 by Lev Davidovich Bronstein, the Russian revolutionary born at Ianovka in the Ukraine, organiser of Russia's armed revolution and creator of the Red Army. As People's Commissar for foreign affairs he led the delegation that negotiated the Brest-Litovsk Treaty with Germany and Austria in 1918. Made Commissar for War at the outbreak of the Civil War he played a decisive role in the Bolshevik victory. His fundamental belief in "Permanent Revolution", which saw Socialism in the Soviet Union only assured once there had also been successful revolutions in the other capitalist countries, brought him into direct conflict with Stalin and his more pragmatic backing for "Socialism in One Country". The rift deepened when Trotsky saw Stalin's dictatorship as deviation from the teachings of Lenin, and in 1929 he was deported. He arrived in Mexico City in 1937 and took up life in a fortress-like house in Coyoacán with his wife and stepson. He was murdered in 1940 by Juan Ramón Mercader, a Spanish-born Stalinist agent wielding an ice-pick.

Francisco "Pancho" Villa (5.6.1878–20.7.1923)

Francisco "Pancho" Villa (born Doroteo Arango) was one of the most charismatic figures of the Mexican Revolution, but also something of a murky character, combining revolutionary and bandit.

In 1910 he joined the armed struggle against the dictator Porfirio Díaz. In September 1913 he founded the "División del Norte", the

Colossal Olmec head

Feathered snake (Teotihuacán)

trade but also included setting up colonies of craftsmen and artists. There is even a currently held view that at times such distant places as Kaminaljuyú in Guatemala (1100km/684 miles away) and settlements in the heart of the Maya country were directly controlled by Teotihuacán, although it is not known whether this involved military force or was done simply by political and commercial means. The influence of Teotihuacán and its theocracy also spread to the temples of Xochicalco, Cholula and early El Tajín, and to many places in what is now the state of Guerrero. The city fell around A.D. 750, probably with the advent of barbarian invaders.

Culture

The most striking feature of Teotihuacán is the grandeur of its architecture, extending not only to the monumental Pyramids of the Sun and Moon, the temples and palaces, but also to the dwellings of peasants and labourers. One characteristic is the "talud-tablero" principle whereby sloping support walls are visually articulated and physically stabilised by horizontal cornices, a principle that mostly in a modified form was to be taken over by other peoples. Interestingly, this great city does not appear to have had a court for the ball game.

Given the monumental nature of its architecture, sculpture in Teotihuacán faded very much into the background. Apart from the heads of plumed serpents and stone reliefs artistic endeavour tended to focus on magnificent masks, often with inlay work, and stone figurines. In pottery there were incense burners painted with brightly coloured people, cylindrical painted pots, and more figurines, of which usually only the heads remain. The fine "thin orange" ceramics found here in the form of animals and human-shaped containers were probably trade goods from Puebla or the Maya territories.

The innumerable frescos display a surprising variety of subject matter, depicting gods and animals, religious ceremonies, etc. Chief among the gods are those of maize, rain and fire, often with the faces of animals.

Maya (500 B.C.–A.D. 1450)

Origins

The origins of the Maya are also shrouded in obscurity. It was thought that this tribe first appeared around 500 B.C. in the Chiapas Highlands and Guatamala and in the Petén lowlands, but the latest research shows that there was already a sizeable Mayan centre in Cuello (Belize) around 2000 B.C. which existed until A.D. 200. A tribe which later produced the Huastecs appears to have split away as early as 2000–1500 B.C. to settle on the northern coast of the Gulf of Mexico.

Classical Maya region

The classical region of the Maya was probably already very densely populated around 1500 B.C., but it is not clear to what extent the sites at Chiapa de Corzo, Izapa, Ocós, and El Baúl were linked with the development of the Maya. Here independent civilisations, of which we still know nothing, mingled with the cultures of the Olmecs and the newly emerging Maya. Apart from the early sites in Guatemala (Nakbé, El Mirador) and Belize, the first major settlements were in Dzibilchaltún (northern Yucatán) and Petén (Guatemala), where they had been building stone temples since 500 B.C., and religious sites also appeared in Xacuná, Nakbé, El Mirador, and in Guatemala, at Uaxactún, Tikal and Kaminaljuyú, now a suburb of Guatemala City, the capital of the neighbouring state to the south.

Early Mayan influence also reached Oaxaca (Monte Albán II), followed in the Classic period by Teotihuacán, Cacaxtla and Xochi-

The Palacio in Palenque, an unusual example of Maya architecture

calco. Conversely, between 400 and 600 there were also traces of Teotihuacán's influence on the cities of the Maya.

Cultural achievements

The most significant achievements of the Maya, who had to manage without metal tools, draught and pack animals, and who used the wheel only for children's toys, date from the Classic period (900–200 B.C.), mainly in the central area of settlement. They are on show in towns and city states such as Palenque, Bonampak, Toniná, Yaxchilán and Chinkultic in the State of Chiapas, and in Guatemala, Belize and Honduras. The highest pyramid (65m) in the known Maya world to date was built in Tikal (Guatemala). Palaces, ball-courts, altars and stelae were erected according to the dictates of the calendar. The stelae are decorated with great artistry, carved with glyphs, dates, the figures of the priestly rulers, and historical scenes. Some take the form of one whole sculpture. The Maya's calendar was the most accurate of its time, and their astronomy the most highly developed. They used the zero and place value in their mathematical calculations, taking the number 20 as their base unit. The magnificence of that great period finds expression in impressive frescos (Bonampak, Cacaxtla; Tikal and Uaxactún in Guatemala), fine polychrome ceramics and jade work.

Decline

These splendid cities were already being abandoned in the 9th c. and by around 900 were quite deserted and soon swallowed up by the jungle. Up to now, it has only been possible to speculate about the reasons for this. There is a theory that the great collective religion led to internal strife and rebellion against the priestly rulers. More recent research indicates that outside pressure from invading foreign tribes also hastened their demise.

Other Mayan sites

Places in the north of the Central area such as Kohunlich and parts of southern Campeche, along the Río Bec-Stil (Hormiguero, Xpuhil,

Puuc detail in Uxmal

Maya glyphs in Palenque

Baedeker Special

The Mayan Calendar

The Maya had two different calendar systems which, with some degree of modification, can also be found in other Meso-American cultures.

The ritual calendar was based on a year of 260 days, subdivided by a series of numbers from 1 to 13 and a series of 20 day glyphs. Each day you advanced one place further along both the series of numbers and the series of glyphs, so that when the 14th glyph was reached, the series of numbers began again at one, and so on, giving each of the 260 days its own combination.

In contrast, the solar calendar was divided into 18 months, each having 20 days. In order to arrive at a year of 365 days, corresponding to the earth's orbit of the sun, five uncounted "empty" days, regarded as unlucky, were added.

The next longest period of time after the year ("Tun") was a timespan of 20 years ("Katun").

The "aeon" of the Mayan Calendar, a cycle of 52 solar years, or 18,980 days, ended when the last day of the year in the ritual calendar and the solar calendar fell on the same date.

The dates of the solar calendar were written as number or head glyphs

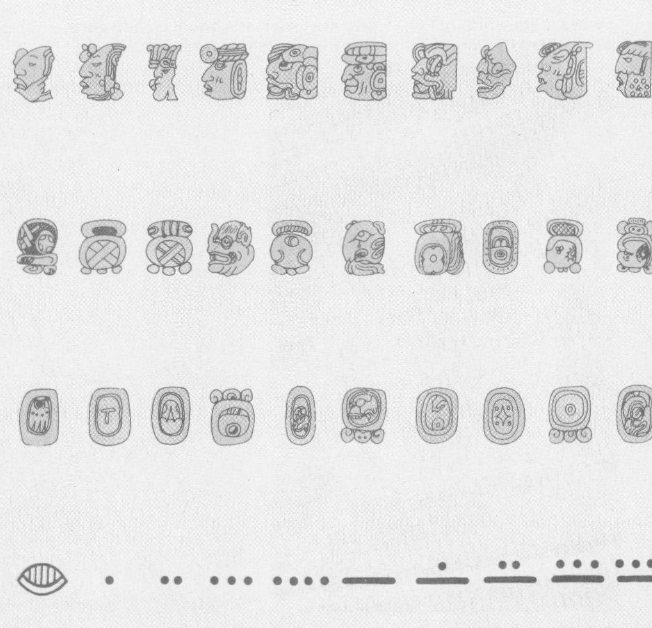

Baedeker Special

(0–19) and as 21 day glyphs and 19 month glyphs (including one for the "empty" days), which also made it possible to have one single combination and precise figures for each day of the year.

The year designation of the solar calendar was based on the date in the ritual calendar on which the beginning of each 365-day cycle fell.

The calendar was of great importance for the religion and mythology of the Maya, whose whole life centred on astronomy and astrology. Days, months and years were assigned to individual gods and each date had a definite lucky or unlucky significance, corresponding to its divine powers. The calendar always had to be consulted before important projects were undertaken, as the gods were also responsible for the different constellations.

This complex system of calculating time made it possible to deal with very long time-spans. The Maya calculated dates going back millions of years, and it seems highly likely that the world view of this civilisation included the concept of eternity.

See Aztec Calendar Stone p. 94.

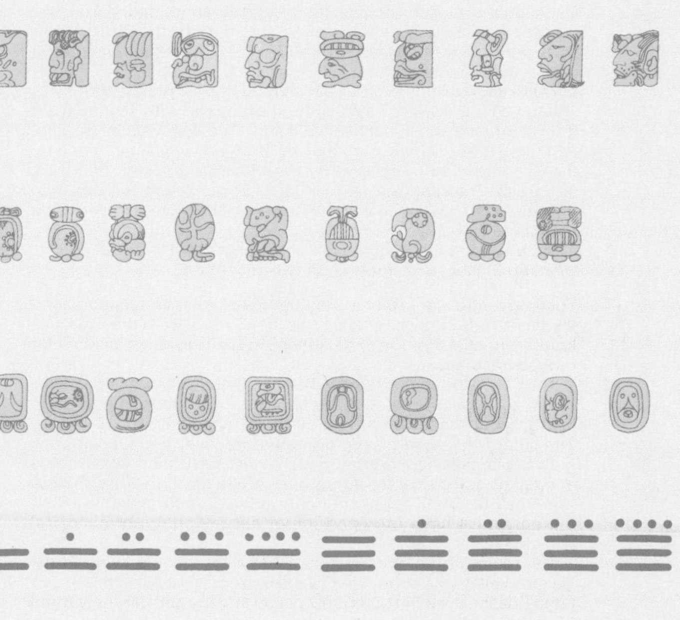

Becán, Chicaná) also experienced their golden age during the Classic period. Other styles which flourished in the northern part of Yucatatán in the late Classic period of this region, which hardly knew sculptured stelae, included the Chenes style (Hochob, Dzibilnocac) and the Puuc style (Uxmal, Kabah, Sayil, Labná). Their main features are buildings richly decorated with hundreds of small pieces of sculpture put together in complicated patterns, with the rain god Chac as the chief motif. These sites died out in the 11th and 12th c.

Impact of foreign cultures

The invasion of northern Yucatán by the Toltecs and other Mexican tribes breathed fresh life into artistic creativity. The combination of the Toltec and Maya styles is particularly obvious in Chichén Itzá, with the large stone figures of the Chac-mool and the Atlantes. The motif of the plumed serpent is more to the fore, and human sacrifice and more warriors also testify to the Mexican Influence. Chichén Itzá's heyday ended around 1200 when it was overtaken by the city of Mayapán. This last great Mayan metropolis perished around 1450, and with it two thousand years of Maya culture.

There remained quite a number of small states of no cultural significance. It took the Spanish 20 years of hard fighting before they eventually achieved the submission of the Maya of Yucatán in 1542.

Zapotecs and Mixtecs (600 B.C.–A.D. 1521)

History

The history of Monte Albán,the great religious centre in the Oaxaca Valley in southern Mexico, falls into five phases (Monte Albán I, II, III, IV and V). The stone reliefs, tombs and ceramics dating from the centuries before Christ show signs of influence by the Olmec in the early period and the Maya later on. The Zapotecs did not emerge until the beginning of the 1st c. A.D. when their distinct style began to make its mark on religious sites in the Classic period. From A.D. 300 to 600 there was a lively cultural exchange with Teotihuacán, then stagnation set in between 800 and 1000, followed by decline, and there is every indication that Monte Albán was abandoned by the Zapotecs and taken over by the Mixtecs, although only as a burial site. The Zapotecs' last capital seems to have been Zaachila. The area around Oaxaca was conquered by the Aztecs towards the end of the 15th c.

Mitla, south-east of Oaxaca, was influenced first by the Zapotecs, then the Mixtecs and another, unknown, culture.

Culture

The large, striking, sculpted clay figures of men and jaguars, and the bas-reliefs known as "Los Danzantes", date from the centuries before Christ. Attempts to decipher the hieroglyphics have so far proved unsuccessful.

The Classic period ushered in the monumental architecture influenced by Teotihuacán, and the appearance of vessels shaped in human form, mostly found in graves and representing god-priests. The cult of the dead played an important role; burial chambers, built to a cross-shaped ground plan, were decorated with frescos and reliefs and contained sumptuous grave furniture. The Mixtecs produced beautiful jewellery and multi-coloured ceramics; their hieroglyphics have provided important insights into historical knowledge.

The realm of the gods worshipped by the people living in the Oaxaca Valley was dominated by the rain god Cocijo, the maize god Pitao Cozobi, the wind god Quetzalcóatl and the god of renewal and of jewellers, Xipe Tótec.

From pre-Christian times: "Los Danzantes" in Monte Albán

El Tajín (A.D. 400–1200)

History

El Tajín, between Tampico and Veracruz near the Gulf of Mexico, was for a long time attributed to the Totonaca but they did not in fact arrive in the area until the early 13th c. when the city had already been abandoned. It is still not clear who built it. Although it has some late Olmec features and signs of influence from Teotihuacán, a number of researchers attribute the city to the Huastecs, who were members of the Mayan language group, and therefore presumably came here from the south during the Archaic or early Formative period.

Culture

El Tajín was probably at its height between 700 and 900. It developed a specific, highly localised, style of architecture, with as its most prominent feature the six-storey niche pyramid. Other typical finds include finely sculpted stone decorations known as "Yugo" (yoke), "Hacha" (axe) and "Palma" (palm), thought to be copies of wooden shields carried during ritual ball games. These ball games were of great importance in the religious life of the people of El Tajín and in the city alone 13 ball courts have been found. It is not clear whether the winner or loser was sacrificed to the gods.

Toltecs (950–1300)

Origins

The post-Classic period of the pre-Columbian civilisations began with the emergence of the Toltec city of Tollán (Tula). The Toltecs were probably originally a branch of the Náhuatl-speaking Chichimecs, "barbarian" invaders from the west, that combined with the Nonoalca from Tabasco.

Maya ornamentation (Chichén Itzá)

The Temple of the Warriors in Chichén Itzá

History

However, according to legend the Toltecs, under their ruler Ce' Acatl Topiltzin, later to be known as the god-king Quetzalcóatl ("plumed serpent"), did not found Tollán until A.D. 968. About twenty years later, the rulers are said to have left Tollán with a small group, following a dispute, and to have made their way to the Gulf Coast of Yucatán by way of Cholula. In actual fact, the imposing blend of Toltec and Mayan culture had already started around A.D. 1000, particularly in Chichén Itzá, under the god-king Kukulcán ("plumed serpent" in the Mayan tongue). Nowadays it is thought that there had already been an earlier movement of people (Toltecs?) from the Mexican plateau, who then returned (in the 9th c.?). The Toltecs, who had preserved many elements of the Classic civilisation, also exerted what was probably military and commercial influence on the northern parts of the Mexican plateau, including Teotenango and Malinalco, and further north on La Quernada, Chalchihuites and probably even Casas Grandes.

Downfall

The relatively brief heyday of the Toltecs ended in 1175 with the rapid downfall of Tula, owing to internal dissension and a new wave of Chichimec invaders. Some of the Toltecs who fled settled in Mexico's high valley (Culhuacán and also Cholula), while others moved further south down the coast to what is now Nicaragua.

Culture

In terms of style this age brought a coarser form of architecture and sculpture than in the Classic period.

Notable features of Toltec culture include great many-columned halls, the colossal 4.60m/15ft-high statues of the Atlantes, the strange reclining figure of the Chac-mool ("red jaguar"), and walls of snakes (coatepantli) and skulls (tzompantli). The reliefs of skulls and scenes of war and sacrifice reflect the warlike nature of a

Coyolxauhqui, the Aztec goddess of the moon and the night

civilisation that was represented by warrior orders of "eagles" and "jaguars". Apart from Tula itself, the finest examples of Toltec art are in the Yucatán at Chichén Itzá, which is clearly Toltec in the basic design but has been decorated by Mayan sculptors and artists. The Tollán period also provides the first examples of metalworking being brought from Guerrero.

Among the Toltec gods Quetzalcóatl in his various symbolic forms stood out in importance. Set against him was his brother Tezcatlipoca ("smoking mirror"), god of the night sky, of magicians and of punitive justice. Astral and warrior gods began to oust the gods of earth and growing things of the Classic period at a time when the priests were being forced to give way to the warriors as the ruling class.

Aztecs (1300–1521)

History

The Aztecs ("people from the land of Aztlán") were invaders from the north-west who entered the valley of Mexico on the high plateau in the 12th c. and built their capital city of Tenochtitlán (today Mexico City) on an island in Lake Texcoco in the mid-14th c. The city's founding brought with it the use of "Mexica" as a term which the Aztecs applied to themselves. Over the following 150 years they extended their dominion as far to the north and east as the coastal regions lived in by the Huastecs on the Gulf of Mexico, and to the south-west and south from Colima through Oaxaca as far as the border with present-day Guatemala. However, this was by no means an undivided empire, and beyond the heartland simply amounted to 40 provinces which had to pay tribute to the Aztecs.

Between 1519 and 1521 invasion by the Spanish and their Indian allies signalled the abrupt end of this, the last of the great Meso-American civilisations.

Culture

Aztec culture, the least artistic of the pre-Columbian civilisations, basically owed its success to its highly developed level of technological, economic and religious organisation. Usually the Aztecs adopted and evolved the ideas of their predecessors or their neighbours.

The Aztecs regarded themselves as the successors of the Toltecs, and this is also reflected in their sculpture and their architecture. They adopted the artistic techniques of their subject peoples, importing their works or employing their artists. Many of the pieces found in the Aztec heartland came from other cultures such as the Mixteca-Puebla, the Huastecs and the Purépecha (Tarascs). Most of the Aztec's great places of religion were demolished by their Spanish conquerors, who used the materials for their own buildings and left very little behind.

Excavations in Mexico City in recent years have uncovered parts of the temples for Tenochtitlán and Tlatelolco, with the high temple being discovered in Mexico City.

The most important works of art left to us by the Aztecs are great carved stones including the Calendar Stone, the stone of the Tízoc, the statue of the earth goddess Coatlícue, and the stone of the moon goddess Coyolxauhqui.

Life in the Aztec Empire

Tenochtitlán

When the Spanish Conquistadors saw Tenochtitlán, the mighty capital of the Aztec Empire, they were overwhelmed by its size, splendour and skilful planning. They found the markets particularly impressive. Even the reticent Cortés later wrote to the Emperor Charles V about Tlatelolco market: "Among us were soldiers who had travelled the world, been to Constantinople, all over Italy, even Rome, and they said they had never seen such a large, well-ordered market, and so packed with produce and people." Bernal Díaz del Castillo reported that 25,000 people visited this market daily, and that every five days a market was held that attracted forty to fifty thousand.

Tenochtitlán ("place of the cactus fruit"), and Tlatelolco, which Cortés conquered in 1473, were at that time divided into four large districts which were retained long after the Spanish conquest. However, the traditional administrative units were the smaller "Calpulli", city quarters of collectively owned land under a self-appointed chief. The centre of this lake-city, intersected by a network of canals, was connected to the shores of the lake by three large causeways. The main street to the north, starting at Tlatelolco, reached the shore at Tepeyacac, near present-day Guadalupe. The western causeway connected Tenochtitlán and Tlacopan; the southern one divided into two, with one branch leading south-westwards to Coyoacán while the other led eastwards to Iztapalapa. There were also two aqueducts, one leading from Chapultepec to the city centre, the other bringing drinking water from Coyoacán along the Iztapalapa road.

Social order

Dignitaries

Aztec society was organised along hierarchical lines, but with everyone having the possibility of advancement. Members of the highest class in the army, civil service and judiciary were addressed as Tecuhtlí ("lord", "dignitary"), a title that was also borne by the emperor. In earlier times these dignitaries were chosen on their merits, but by the time the Spanish arrived they were usually appointed by the emperor, and were mainly the heirs of their predecessors. The ruler, generally described as "emperor", bore the titles "Tlatoaní" ("speaker", i.e. leader of the "Tlatocan", the supreme council) and "Tlacatecuhtlí" ("lord of warriors", i.e. commander in chief). In Tenochtitlán the ruler was chosen by a kind of privy council. After Moctezuma I, the highest State official at the side of the emperor was the Cihuacóatl, a title derived from a goddess and meaning "snake woman". Directly below emperor and Cihuacóatl came four high dignitaries and counsellors, with next in authority the supreme council, the "Tlatocan".

Warriors

All offices and honours in the Aztec Empire were conferred for life only. There was no hereditary nobility as such; the son of a Tecuhtlí was known as Pilli ("child", "son") and initially had no claim to a title, but had to earn rank and respect by his own merits, especially in warfare. All that was easier for him was to gain access to places of higher education, the "Calmecac". Normally the upper class made up its numbers from the Macehualtin (singular: Macehualli), the commoners. A member of this class, but not a merchant, could achieve the rank of an Iyac by capturing his first enemy prisoner. If he then took part in two or three campaigns without further distinguishing himself he was obliged to give up military service and remain a Macehualli. But if he had killed or captured four enemies

Skull wall discovered in Mexico City 1982

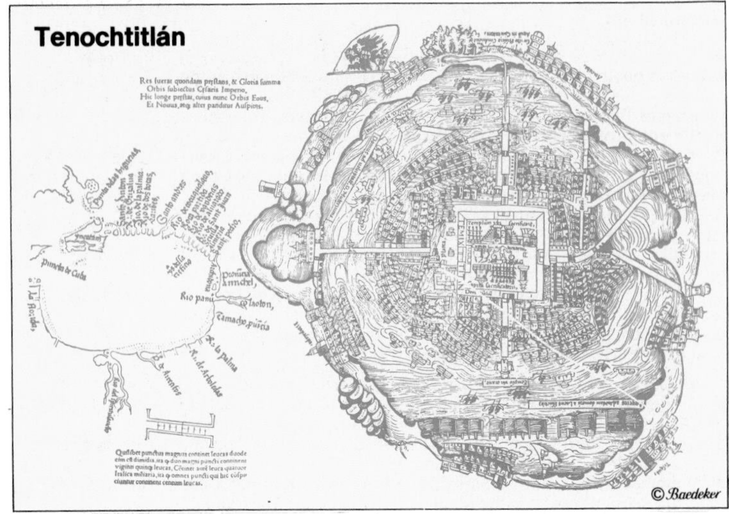

Town plan (printed in Nürnberg 1564)

he advanced to the rank of Tequia, which meant that he received a part of the tribute ("Tequitl"). Higher ranks took their names from the rough, warlike tribes of the north – "Quauhchichimecatl" (Chichimec eagle) or "Otomitl" (Otomi warrior).

Merchants

For merchants, known as "Pochteca" after Tlatelolco's famous merchant quarter of Pochtlan, their calling was hereditary. A warrior's career was closed to them, but they acted as scouts on their adventurous trading expeditions to distant parts. They often amassed considerable wealth from their monopoly of foreign trade, but were careful not to display it and thus invite the envy of the privileged priest and warrior classes.

Priests

Recruits to the priesthood, who enjoyed equal rights with warriors and civil servants, were educated in the places of higher education, the "Calmecac". At the age of twenty-two a novice who decided not to marry could acquire the honorary title of "Tlamacazqui" (priest). The priesthood was headed by two high priests, the Quetzalcóatl Tótec Tlamacazqui ("plumed serpent priest of our lord") for the cult of Huitzilopochtli, god of war and the sun, and the Quetzalcóatl Tláloc Tlamacazqui ("plumed serpent priest of Tláloc") for the cult of the rain god. There were priestesses for the female deities.

Craftsmen

Craftsmen also formed an important group of the population. The Aztecs called them "Tolteca", since it was the Toltecs who were credited with developing craft skills, or "Toltecayotl" as they were called. The most important guilds of craftsmen were the featherworkers (Amanteca) and the goldsmiths (Teocuitlahuaque); scribes, or rather picture writers (Tlacuilo), were particularly highly respected.

Slaves

There were also slaves, known as Tlatlacotin (singular: Tlacotl). Their living conditions were considerably more humane than those

A section of Diego Rivera's painting "La Gran Tenochtitlán"

for slaves in Europe. They were allowed to own property, make savings and buy their own freedom. Marriage between free people and slaves was permitted. Slaves were recruited from prisoners of war who were not sacrificed, and people could be sentenced to slavery for committing an offence. However the majority appear to have given themselves voluntarily into slavery, receiving the purchase price themselves and remaining free until it was used up, which took about a year.

Mythology

Like other Meso-American peoples the Aztecs believed that before our world there had been others which had been destroyed by cosmic forces. Our world was the fifth, which is why the famous calendar stone (see p. 94) is also known as the "Stone of the Fifth Sun". After the fourth world had been destroyed by a great flood the gods gathered in Teotihuacán. By a god's sacrifical act of self-destruction through fire, the new sun rose, but at first remained motionless. The other gods then sacrificed themselves, and their life forces transferred to the sun and set it in motion. Since the universe had now first been set in motion by sacrifice, its continued existence could only be assured by the sacrifice of something precious, namely human blood, or, in Náhuatl, "Chalchiuatl" (precious water). This concept of the cosmos is the explanation for the human sacrifice which, knowing nothing of the background, the Spaniards took for mindless cruelty.

Human sacrifice

Human sacrifice was particularly important at the end of the 52-year cycle which was the Aztec equivalent of our century. This cycle

Baedeker Special

The Stone of the Fifth Sun

The "Stone of the Fifth Sun", the original of which is in the Anthropological Museum in Mexico City, probably dates from 1479 ("13 reed"). It did not, however, serve to determine time, but as a sacrificial stone (*cuauhxicalli*) for Aztec human sacrifices.

1 Sun-god Tonatiuh, Regent of the epoch of the "Fifth Sun".

2 Symbols of past epochs; between them the points of the compass (clockwise): Jaguar Sun, Water Sun, Rain Sun and Wind Sun.

3 Ring with 20 day-signs (clockwise): Flower, Rain, Flint, Motion, Vulture, Eagle, Jaguar, Reed, Herb, Monkey, Dog, Water, Rabbit, Stag, Death, Snake, Lizard, House, Wind and Crocodile.

4 Ornamentation with the denomination of the Sun in relief: **a** Eagle's feathers; **b** Sun's rays; **c** Precious stones; **d** Drops of blood.

5 Turquoise snakes; from their gullets peer the Sun-god Tonatiuh and the Fire-god Xluhtecutli.

was determined by the sacred divinatory calendar which, as with other Meso-American peoples, was based on 13 numbers and 20 signs repeated in series. Each year bore the name of the day on which it had begun and mathematically these year names were restricted to four of the signs, each with its appropriate number. This meant it would be 52 years, or like a pack of cards, four "suits" of 13 years, making a "sheaf", before the same name and number as the first year came round again. The change from one cycle or sheaf to another was when the danger of cosmic catastrophe was particularly great, and the death of one sheaf and the birth of another was marked by the "new fire" ceremony. All fires would be extinguished throughout the country and the pyramids and temples would be stripped of their ornaments. During the night the high priests would climb to the temple on top of Uixachtecatl, the "hill of the star", overlooking the Valley of Mexico, to stargaze. When the world did not end and the stars moved on the priests would kindle the new fire in the chest of a sacrificial victim, using a wooden spindle, and its flame would then be carried throughout the land by runners with torches. And the sacred buildings would be clad with fresh decoration again.

Aztec gods and goddesses

At the heart of Aztec religion stood Huitzilopochtli ("hummingbird of the south" in Náhuatl"), god of war and symbol of the sun who, like the sun, died each night and was reborn each morning.

The other gods, most of whom had been taken from conquered peoples, included Tláloc ("Tlalli" = "earth" in Náhuatl), god of rain and of growth, Tezcatlipoca ("smoking mirror"), god of the night sky, of destruction, magic, and punitive justice, Xipe Tótec ("our lord of the oppressed"), god of natural renewal and of jewellers, Quetzalcóatl ("plumed serpent"), the many-sided god of the morning star, the wind and the forces of civilisation, Coatlícue ("woman with the snake-apron"), earth-goddess and mother of Huitzilopochtli, and her daughter Coyolxauhqui ("woman who paints bells on her face"), goddess of the moon and the night.

Warfare

Reports of earlier expeditions by the Aztecs bent on conquest show that their concept of war was quite different from that of the Europeans. There were no surprise attacks; before war was declared envoys were sent in advance to engage in protracted negotiations that constantly presented the enemy with a choice between battle and voluntary subjection. If it came to war, the aim was not to kill the enemy but to capture him. Once the high temple of the enemy city was taken, that was regarded as divine judgement; Huitzilpochtli, the Aztec's god of war, had proved himself the stronger. The fighting ceased immediately, and bargaining started on the size of the tribute. This would be set at a level which kept the economy of the subject people intact, and they were also allowed to keep their customs and traditions. This explains the Aztecs' bewilderment at the way the Spanish waged war. The Indians' tactics proved completely inappropriate against an enemy who thought that any means of destroying or totally subjugating the "heathen" was justified in the fight to conquer them.

Wars of Flowers

At the time of the Spanish conquest the Aztec kingdom had already expanded to its greatest extent. There were few new campaigns and this meant few prisoners of war for sacrifice. The ruling city states of Tenochtitlán, Texcoco and Tlacopan therefore reached an agreement with the vassal states of Tlaxcala, Huejotzingo and Cholula to have regular formalised combats for the purpose of capturing warriors to sacrifice. These combats were known as "Xochiyaótl", wars of flowers, and the people of Tlaxcala suffered particularly badly from this constant blood-bath. Their pent-up resentment caused them to ally themselves against the Aztecs with the Spanish who, but for their help, would probably not have succeeded in taking Tenochtitlán.

Codices

Apart from the records of the Conquistadors and the first monks sent out to the New World, our knowledge of Aztec life is based on original sources. These were the Codices, the most important being the Codex Mendoza, the Codex Magliabecchiano, the Codex Ríos and its parallel volume the Codex Telleriano, all of which were provided with Latin transcriptions of the pictographs and commentaries in Spanish by priests fluent in Náhuatl. Codices without such commentaries are the Codex Florentino and the Codex Nuttall.

Tradition

These commentaries were absolutely necessary since the codices were written in the form of pictographs. So, for example, to show that the emperor Moctezuma was preparing for war, the Aztec picture writer drew the seated figure of the emperor with his name glyph and weapons. This kind of writing obviously did not fully serve to express the niceties of Náhuatl literature, which excelled in rhetoric and lyric and epic poetry. Pupils training for the priesthood therefore had to learn long texts by heart, using the pictographs as an *aide memoire*.

Fortunately the monks, who were charged with teaching Christianity to the Indians after the conquest, found enough young people from the upper classes who could dictate the Náhuatl texts to them so they could write them down in Latin, or whom they could teach to write things down phonetically.

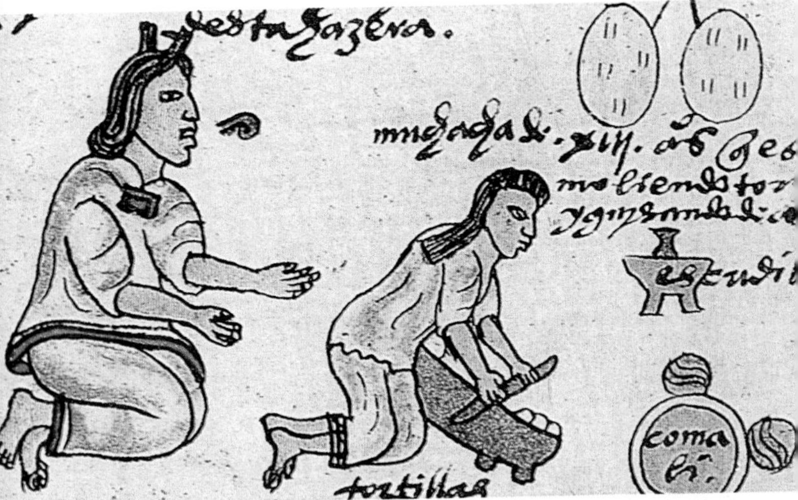

The education of Aztec girls (Codex Mendoza)

It has however been established that the Aztecs used glyphs that meant something specific also for similar sounding syllables with a different meaning. Thus the first step had already been taken towards a form of phonetic or syllabic script, and it is a matter for conjecture that they would soon have developed something of the sort if their culture had not been suppressed by the Conquistadors. The same sort of speculation could also apply to other areas. But the cultural achievements of the Meso-American peoples are quite amazing in any case, considering that basically in economic and technical terms their situation was virtually on a par with the Stone Age.

A jade mask

Magic Jade

The Indian peoples of pre-Hispanic Mexico attributed magical powers to some minerals. In fact they prized jade – quite rare there and known as Chalchihuitl or Quetzalitzli – more highly than gold, probably due in some measure to its irridescent green sheen, like the feathers of the sacred Quetzal.

Art and Culture

Painting

Pre-Columbian frescos and codices

Prior to the Spanish Conquest around 1520 Mexico's main form of painting was its frescos.

These include such major frescos as those in the Mayan temple at Bonampak and the paintings at Teotihuacán, Tepantitla, Atetelco, Cacaxtla and Cholula near Puebla, although unfortunately only a few of these ancient Indian works of art have been preserved. The red and orange tones and the gold and the famous Mayan blue of the Bonampak frescos give some idea of the advanced level of painting technique at the time of the Classic Maya culture. Finds have been made of skilfully painted ceramics as well.

This was also the period of the codex. These codices were manuscripts of picture writing made up of figures and pictograms.

Colonial art

Soon after the Spanish conquest European artists started teaching at the school founded by Franciscan monks in Mexico City. Like most painters of the time they were influenced by the Dutch school of painting. The only one to achieve significance during this period was the Flemish artist Simon Pereyns (1566–1603).

It was not until the early 17th c. that a style of colonial art developed in its own right, as can be seen from the works of Baltazar de Echave Orio (1548–1620), Baltazar de Echave Ibía (1585–1645) and Luis Juárez (1600–35). Their paintings are now principally on view in churches, monasteries and museums in Mexico City, Querétaro, Tepotzotlán, Morelia and Guadalajara. Later came José Juárez (1615–67), Baltazar de Echave Rioja (1632–82) and Pedro Ramirez (1650–78), who succeeded in combining elements of European artists as diverse as Murillo and Rubens with styles of their own. Their works can be seen in Mexico City, Texcoco, Puebla, San Miguel de Allende and Guadalajara.

Mexican Baroque

Major artists during the first phase of Mexican baroque (early 17th/late 18th c.) include Cristóbal de Villalpando (1652–1714). Juan Correa (1674–1739) and Juan Rodríguez Juárez (1675–1725), whose works show clear signs of European influence and are now mainly to be found in Mexico City, Puebla, San Miguel de Allende, Atotonilco, Tepotzotlán, Aguascalientes and Querétaro. Mexican art of the 18th c. was influenced by Correa's pupils, José María de Ibarra (1688–1756) and Míguel Cabrera (1695–1768), whose many works can chiefly be seen in museums in Mexico City, Puebla, Morelia, Tepotzotlán, San Miguel de Allende and Taxco.

Unlike Mexican architecture and the Mestizo Schools of Cuzco and Potosí in South America, Mexican painting of this period shows virtually no trace of any Indian influence.

19th century

Artists worth mentioning from the mid to late 19th c. are José Maria Estrada (1830–62), the portrait painter and representative of naïve art, and José Maria Velasco (1840–1912), the landscape artist who later taught Diego Rivera.

The provinces at this time were developing an appealing kind of folk art, of which the best examples are to be found in the many little village chapels.

In the late 19th and early 20th c. Mexican art came very much under the influence of the Impressionists, as can be seen in the landscapes of Joaquín Claussel (1866–1935) and Mateos Saldaña.

Muralismo

The next period of Mexican art, the art of monumental fresco painting, began in the 20th c. at the time of the Revolution (1910–20), when Muralismo signalled the development of an art form in its own right now considered Mexico's most distinctive contribution to modern art. The movement began with a "secessionist" exhibition in 1910, centred around Gerardo Murillo (1875–1964) who called himself Dr Atl ("water" in Náhuatl) and is better known for his landscapes than for his frescos. The works of Francisco Goitía (1884–1960) are mainly expressionist images of the fates people suffered during the Revolution. The forerunners of the new artistic movement is regarded as being José Guadalupe Posada (1851–1913), an engraver and political caricaturist.

Artists turned to the ancient folk art, which still lived on, drawing on the colours, forms and themes of pre-Columbian art to paint murals showing scenes that were didactic and ideologically aimed at a largely illiterate population, but which for the most part did not lapse into sterile "social realism". These images glorify the ancient Indian heritage and the acts of the revolution and mock the Spanish conservatives. Although these artists saw themselves as highly anti-clerical, they still did not manage to shake off their own Catholic roots. The scene was set for the spread of this new art form in the early Twenties by José Vasconcelos, the Minister for Education, who had the artists painting the walls of schools and other public buildings. Mexican artists published a manifesto in 1923 which spoke up for monumental art as opposed to work done on an easel. The three most famous Mexican artists to be known primarily as "muralists" are José Clemente Orozco, Diego Rivera and David Álfaro Siqueiros.

José Clemente Orozco

The most important of the three is probably José Clemente Orozco (1883–1949, see also Famous People). In his many works, which include drawings, engravings and paintings, he shows a harsh, cruel realism and a violence of composition. There are signs of Baroque influence on his work, although his technique and subject matter owe much to European expressionism. Yet he is a highly individual painter, unlike Rivera and Siqueiros who allowed themselves to be more strongly influenced by the various movements. His masterpiece is considered to be the painted ceiling of the Hospicio Cabañas in Guadalajara (1938–39), especially the "man in flames" in the dome. He was also responsible for the murals in the stairwell of the Government Palace in Guadalajara and the frescos for the Escuela Preparatoria Nacional and the Palacio Nacional de Bellas Artes in Mexico City.

Diego Rivera

Diego Rivera (1886–1957, see also Famous People) went through various phases as a young artist, moving from Neo-Impressionism through Fauvism to Cubism, before going on to paint his enormous murals of scenes from Mexican political and social life. He developed an extremely subtle and clear style in his fresco painting which was based on that of the Italian Renaissance, but strongly influenced in its subject matter by the art of the Maya and the Aztecs. Among his many murals those in the Palacio Nacional and the Escuela Nacional de la Agricultura in Chapingo merit special attention. The famous painting "Dream on a Sunday afternoon in Alameda Park" is in a new building in Mexico City on the Plaza de Solidaridad. Mention should also be made of his murals in the

José Clémente Orozoco: "Catharsis" (Palacio de Bellas Artes, Mexico City)

Ministry of Education, the Palacio de Bellas Artes, and the Ministry of Health in Mexico City, and the Cortés Palace in Cuernavaca.

David Álfaro Siqueiros

David Álfaro Siqueiros (1886–1974, see also Famous People) has a Baroque sense of movement in his work, but he was also influenced by Futurism, creating images of technology and machinery. Various governments commissioned him to produce his monumental and spectacular murals, most of which are to be seen on public buildings in Mexico City such as the Hospital de la Raza, the Palacio Nacional, the Palacio Nacional de Bellas Artes and the Rectoral Offices of the University; he was also responsible for the artistic form and design of the Polyforum.

Modernists

Rufino Tamayo (1899–1991), the son of Zapotec Indians, was regarded as the Grand Old Man of Mexican modern art. He combined elements of Mexican folk art with those of modern painting and Cubism in particular. Like Rivera he has promoted the idea of an "Indian Renaissance". Tamayo is a member of a group of artists which includes Carlos Mérida (1891–1984), Ricardo Martinez (born 1918), Juan Soriano (born 1920) and Pedro Coronel (1922–85). Tamaya and Mérida are also known as muralists, as are Miguel Covarrubias (1904–57), José Chávez Morado (born 1909), Juan O'Gorman (1905–82), Roberto Montenegro (1886–1968), Jorge Gonzales Camarena (1908–90), Pablo O'Higgins (1904–83) and Federico Cantú (1909–91); Tamayo's murals include those in the stair well of the Music Conservatorium in Mexico City.

Other artists, representing various movements, who have made a name in Mexico in recent decades include Frida Kahlo (1907–54, see also Famous People, 2nd wife of Diego Rivera), Manuel Rodrí-

Frida Kahlo: "Self-portrait"

Rufino Tamayo: "Watermelon eater"

guez Lozano (1896–1972), María Izquierdo (1902–55), Francisco Zuñiga (born 1913), Gunther Gerzo (born 1915), Leonora Carrington (born 1917), Rafael Coronel (born 1923), Georg Rauch (born 1924), Pedro Friedeberg (born 1937), Guillermo Rode (born 1933), José Luis Cuevas (born 1933), Francisco Toledo (born 1940), Manuel Felgueres (born 1928) and Vicente Rojo (born 1932).

Sculpture

Sculpture, like painting, was mainly used by the Maya, Aztecs and other ancient American peoples to adorn their temples; they sculpted in stone, stucco and clay, and the focus of their artistic creativity was their religion and the veneration of their gods. Temples carry figurative works, such as the famous "Los Danzantes" of Monte Albán, and geometric reliefs, in patterns often similar to those found in textiles, as in the temple city of Mitla.

Small pieces include the simpler, sculpted domestic objects as well as the more elaborate items primarily found in graves. Small female figures, thought to be fertility goddesses by many archaeologists, are particularly numerous, becoming less voluptuous and more graceful as the ideal of beauty changes. The clay sculptures, often only 20cm/8in. high, are mostly in the form of vessels. Some of the painted terracotta statuettes wear just a loin-cloth or a belt, while others are clad in grand robes. There are also differences in their posture and facial expression.

Olmecs

The Olmecs (La Venta Culture) produced incredible monumental stone sculptures. Their colossal heads, up to 3m/10ft high with broad, flattened noses and thick, negroid lips, are particularly striking.

Pre-Columbian small sculpture . . .

. . . from the Anthropological . . .

. . . National Museum in Mexico City

Aztec sculpture: a snake carved from stone

The smaller Olmec pieces are also very interesting, and they produced pieces in jade where the surface working was reduced to just a few lines.

Maya

The Maya Classic period yielded supremely accomplished works in stone and stucco. The stucco reliefs on the buildings in Palenque are particularly interesting – the Maya mixed rubber latex with plaster and water to give their stucco a hard finish which could be polished.

As the many finds from the graves on Jaina testify, the Maya also sculpted some very fine small pieces. The terracotta figurines are painted to show what priests, warriors and members of the nobility looked like. Their goldsmiths also produced wonderful masks and jewellery, and craftsmen working with feathers, which they dyed and mounted on cloth, made beautiful mosaics.

Colonial period

Spain's conquest of Mexico marked a turning-point for sculpture as it did for painting and architecture, although apart from the decoration on churches and public buildings the sculpture of Mexico's colonial period lacked an individual style of its own. One famous sculptor who came to Mexico in the early 18th c. was Jerónimo Balbás. His work included the magnificent Altar of the Kings in Mexico City Cathedral, and he also had a considerable influence on other Mexican artists. Sculpture in the late 18th and early 19th c., especially in the churches, got ever duller and less refined. One outstanding work of secular art was the bronze of "El Caballito" by Manuel Tolsá, based on an equestrian piece by Girardon. Around the mid-19th c. José Villegas de Cora, his nephew Zacrias de Cora and adopted son José Villegas based in Puebla, and Mariano Perusquía, Mariano Arce and Mariano Montenegro in Guerétaro, tried to breathe new life into sculpture. Their works can mainly be seen in museums in Puebla and Querétaro.

One characteristically Mexican form of simple but original sculpture that did evolve took the form of peasant altars and the many homely religious statuettes.

20th c.

Since the Revolution (1910–20) most of Mexico's 20th c. sculptors have been engaged in public art, often of a political nature.

As in architecture, the last thirty years have finally witnessed a generation of sculptors who are producing imaginative and independent work. Some of this can be seen in Mexico City and elsewhere throughout the country. The artists in question include Juan F. Olaguíbel (1891–1971: "Diana Cazadora" fountain with a bronze statue of Diana in Mexico City, Monumento al Rey de Coliman in Colima); Germán Cueto (1893–1975: "La Tehuana" in the Palacio Nacional de Bellas Artes in Mexico City); Ignacio Asúnsulo (1890–1965: Obregón Monument in San Angel, part of Mexico City); Rodrigo Arena Betancourt (born 1919: "Prometeus" on Mexico City's university campus); Jorge Gonzáles Camarena (1908–80: I.M.S.S. at the Paseo de la Reforma in Mexico City); Ernesto Tamariz (born 1904: Monumento a los Niños Héroes in Cuauhétemoc Park in Mexico City); Federico Canessí (1906–77: Monumento de la Bandera in Iguala); Francisco Zúñiga (born 1913: "Yucatecas en el Parque", Galería Tasende in Acapulco); Sebestián (born 1947: "La Puerta de Monterrey", in Monterrey).

Architecture

Colonial architecture

The fact that Mexico has so many examples of colonial architecture built within a relatively short timespan can be attributed to its great wealth of building materials and the vast reserves of cheap labour that the Conquistadors had at their disposal. "Tezontle", meaning "petrified hair" in Náhuatl, the porous volcanic rock mostly quarried in the central highlands, was and is a particularly versatile type of stone. Used by the Aztecs, its tone can vary from pink to dark brown and it is still apparent in most of the palaces in Mexico City. The country also has a variety of different coloured easy-to-work kinds of limestone, used for building work and generally known as "cantera".

After the Spanish conquest, beginning in 1519, many of Mexico's magnificent examples of Meso-American architecture and sculpture were destroyed or lost to posterity. During the four subsequent centuries the New World was visited by a series of European architectural styles, mainly from Spain, which often evolved into local variations.

Early church buildings

The first generation after the Spanish conquest developed a type of building which could be described as fortified medieval monastery. Churches and monasteries were often built, initially by the Franciscans, in place of Indian pyramids and temples, frequently using materials quarried from the previous structures. These early church buildings, which occasionally still showed traces of Romanesque and Gothic, also served as fortresses, with their strong walls and massive pillars. The few windows were high up and well spaced, and the plain interior would have a ribbed ceiling or barrel-vaulting. Special features of these 16th c. monasteries included the walled atrium and, unique to Mexico, the capillas posas (small processional chapels) in its four corners. Another particular form which evolved was the capilla abierta or open chapel. These were open in front and like the atrium and posas took account of the

An open chapel in Teposcoula

Chirriqueresque ornamentation Tlaxcala

Indians' dislike of enclosed religious buildings and the fact that they were often denied access to a church until they were baptised.

There are very good examples of the atrium and posas in Huejotzingo, Calpan, Izamal and Tlaxcala (San Francisco). The most interesting open chapels are in Tlalmanalco, Tepescolula, Coixtlahuaca, Tlaxcala (San Francisco), Cuitzeo, Cuernavaca (cathedral) and Actopan.

Mudéjar

Mexican buildings also contain features of the Spanish Mudéjar style, a form of Spanish Christian architecture in a purely Moslem style which gets its name from Moslems who remained in Christian Spain after the reconquest. One of its features is the "alfiz", narrow moulding forming a rectangular frame around the Moorish archway. On many 16th c. buildings, including the posas at Huejotzingo, part of the alfiz is an imitation of the cord of the Franciscan monk's habit. Other later features of Mexico's Mudéjar style are the use of "azulejos" (glazed tiles), the design of archways and ceilings and the kind of woodcarving (alfarje and artesonado).

Plateresque

The 16th c. also saw the emergence of the early form of Plateresque, which literally means "silversmith-like", from "platero", Spanish for silversmith. This kind of ornamental stonemasonry, with its lavish use of scrolling and heraldic and flower motifs stemming from the designs of Spanish silversmiths, was applied mostly to portals. Plateresque also shows the influence of the Mudéjar style as well as decorative forms of Late Gothic and Renaissance. New Spain developed a number of its own variations of Plateresque which can be summed up as follows: pure Renaissance with Italian features as in Actopan, Teposcolula and the Church of San Francisco in Morelia; Spanish Plateresque with Spanish Renaissance motifs as in the Huejotzingo posas, the Montejo House in Mérida, at Acolman and elsewhere; Colonial Plateresque, combining Spanish techniques with local interpretations, as in Tepoztlán, the side portal of Cuernavaca Cathedral and the northern entrance to Huejotzingo Church; Indian Plateresque, combining pre-Columbian craftsmanship with local interpretations, as on the main and side portals of Yuriria Church, the façade and north portal of Xochimilco parish church and the open chapel at Tlalmanalco.

Baroque

The 17th c. saw the gradual rise of Baroque. At first this took a relatively sober form as in La Soledad in Oaxaca and during this phase the main building work was carried out on the great cathedrals in Mexico City, Puebla, Morelia, Guadalajara, San Luis Potosí and Oaxaca. Convents and many parish churches were built at the same time, testimony to the growing power of the Church, now controlled directly by the Spanish Crown, as the influence of the freely-operating orders of monks and friars declined. The increasing exhuberance of Mexican Baroque and its various versions also reflect the strengthening of the position of the "criollos", Spaniards born in Mexico, as opposed to the "gachupines" who had come from mainland Spain.

Churrigueresque

Mexican Late Baroque reached its peak in the 18th c. with Churrigueresque, the style named after the Spanish architect José Benito Churriguera (1665–1723) and his brothers, who came from a family that specialised in elaborately carved retables. The Churrigueresque style in Mexico, where it is chiefly to be seen on towers, portals and altars, is characterised by boundless flights of fancy whereby, for example, as basic an architectural element as a column, still recognisable as such in the Baroque, can be so lavishly piled up and overlaid with surface ornamentation as sometimes to lose its original form. This style's main features are its "estípites", a type of pilaster tapering towards the base and much used to decorate façades and retables. New Spain's many examples of this "Super Baroque" include the façades of the Sagrario Metropolitano, the Church of La Santisima, the Casa de los Mascarones and the Altar of the Kings in the Cathedral, all in Mexico City, the Church of San Francisco Xavier in Tepotzotlán, the Ocotlán Basilica in Tlaxcala, the Church of San Sebastián y Santa Prisca in Taxco, the parish church in Dolores Hidalgo, in Church of La Valenciana in Guanajuato, the Chapel of Aránzazu in San Luis Potosí, and the Cathedral in Zacetecas.

Poblano

One particularly original variation of Mexican Baroque is Poblano, the regional style that gets its name from the town of Puebla and is typical of the area between Puebla and Tlaxcala. This combines imaginative, often Indian, stucco ornamentation with colourful azulejos and red roof-tiles. Besides Ocotlán, already mentioned elsewhere, other prime examples of this style include the churches of San Francisco de Acatepec, Santa Maria de Tonantzintla, San Bernardino de Tlaxcalcancingo, La Merced and the Rosary Chapel at Atlixco, and the Casa del Alfeñique and the chapel of San Antonio in Puebla; there is also the Casa de los Azulejos in Mexico City.

Neo-Classicism

Neo-Classicism reached Mexico from Europe in the late 18th c., and was seen as a welcome and political means of breaking away from an overpoweringly Spanish cultural heritage. This led Manuel Tolsá (1757–1816, see also Famous People), an architect and sculptor from Spain, to attempt, with mixed success, to divest the churches of their rich trappings and to make them more purely Classical. He was also responsible for "El Caballito", the magnificent statue of Emperor Charles IV on horseback. and for the plans for the Palacio de Minería in Mexico City. Another example of his work worth seeing is the dome of Mexico City Cathedral, with paintings by Rafael Jimeno y Planes.

However, the major personality involved in this new movement was the Mexican artist Francisco Eduardo Tresguerras (1750–1866, see also Famous People), famed as a poet, musician, sculptor, and engraver as well as an architect. His finest works include the church of El Carmen in Celaya, the conversion of the church of Santa Clara in Querétaro and the Ducal Palace in Guanajuato. One important Neo-Classical work, although undoubtedly rooted in Baroque, is the high altar of the Sagrario Metropolitano in Mexico City, by Pedro Patino Ixtilinque (1774–1835), an Indian pupil of Manuel Tolsás. Another major architect was José Damián Ortiz de Castro (1750–93) who was responsible for the bell towers and the final alterations to the façade of Mexico City Cathedral.

There were no significant developments in Mexican architecture in the hundred years between the winning of independence and the Revolution (1910–20) other than improvement works ordered by Emperor Maximilian, the largely Neo-Gothic achievements of Ceferino Gutiérrez (died 1896) and a few examples of Art Nouveau such as the Quinta Gameros, the former palace of justice and now the Museo Regional del Estado in Chihuahua.

Functionalism

Once the Revolution was over Mexican architects embarked on a controversial spate of public buildings, drawing on the forms of

"Towers without function" by Mathias Goeritz in Mexico City ►

The new Basilica of Guadalupe in Mexico City

modern functionalism and influenced by the Bauhaus, but it was the Fifties and Sixties before Mexico's modern architects, partly influenced by Le Corbusier and Oscar Niemeyer, started producing their most impressive buildings. The following list gives the names of some major architects and their work: Enríque de la Mora y Palomar (1907–77; Church of La Purisima in Monterrey); Juan Sordo Madeleno (1916–85; Hotel El Presidente in Acapulco); in Mexico City Garcíia José Villagrán (born 1901), Mario Pani (1911–93; Hotel Reforma, Mexico City; Colonia Satélite) and Enrique del Moral (born 1906; University campus and Water Ministry); Mathias Goeritz (1915–90; non-functional towers in the Ciudad Satélite, Seven Stations of the Cross in the Church of Santiago Tlatelolco, railings at the Hotel Camino Real in Mexico City); Felix Candela (born 1910; churches of La Milagrosa and Santa Mónica); Rafael Mijares (born 1924) and Pedro Ramírez Vázquez (born 1919; Museum of Modern Art and National Museum of Anthropology, the new Basilica of Guadalupe, Instituto Nacional de la Vivienda) and Luis Barragán (1902–85; housing; El Pedregal, Las Arboledas); also Abraham Zabludovsky (born 1925; Museo Tamayo, Mexico City; Oficinas del Gobierno, Guanajuato); Ricardo Legorreta (born 1938; Hotel Camino Real, Mexico City and in Ixtapa).

Music

Indian origins

Some elements of today's Mexican music predate the Spanish Conquest. This particularly applies to the percussion instruments used to accompany dance. Little is known of the ancient Indian music, but it clearly played an important ritual role with dancing and singing. The Aztecs, for example, had a "cuicacalli". a "house of song", where children from the age of twelve were obliged to learn music, and poems were always sung or recited to a musical accompaniment. Percussion instruments such as drums made out of terracotta, wood or tortoise-shell, rasps of notched bone or wood, and various rattles, were very important, together with pipes and conch shells, which in the case of the latter were also used to convey commands in battle. Some of these ancient instruments are still played today, mainly in the ceremonial dances of indigenous peoples such as the Seri, Yaqui, Huichol and Tzotil. Contemporary pipes are made from bone, clay or reeds, and are virtually the same as those used in pre-Hispanic times.

Folk music

Present-day Mexican folk music draws on such modern instruments as the trumpet, guitar, violin, harp and, in the south of the country, the marimba, a kind of xylophone from West Africa, with calabashes as sound boxes.

The traditional songs and melodies of the various regions are mainly a mixture of Indian and Spanish, with some Moorish, African and other European strains as well. As any tourist will realise, the Mexicans love to sing. They have a great variety of different kinds of song, too. One form particularly worth mentioning is the folk ballad called the "corrido", which acted as a news service before there were any mass media. The wandering bard often retailed the latest local gossip, but also sings of love and death and tales from history. Many of the old corridos are still enormously popular today. This kind of ballad gave rise to the "canción ranchera", a melancholy lament full of pain, rage and unrequited love, with melodies mostly derived from 19th c. Spanish songs which have been "Mexicanised". The songs of regions such as Jalisco, Veracruz, Oaxaca or Tehuantepec have an un-

Devoted musicians in Mexico City

mistakeable quality, and the folk music of the remote Tarascs (Michoacán), Yaqui and Seri-Indios (Sonora) is remarkably tuneful.

Mariachis

Mexico's best known folk music is that of the "mariachis", originally Spanish but also spiced with French and other European ingredients. The name "mariachi" probably comes from the French "mariage" since the French soldiers in Mexico mistakenly assumed that the musicians primarily played at weddings. The mariachi bands can be large or small, but usually include violins, guitars, trumpets and a singer. These wandering musicians originally came from the state of Jalisco, especially its capital Guadalajara, but nowadays they can be found in most parts of the central plateau. Dressed in their "ranchero" costumes they play lively tunes to an unmistakable rhythm. The place where the mariachi bands gather in Mexico City is the Plaza de Garibaldi, and in Guadalajara it is the Plazuela de los Mariachis, not far from the Mercade Liberdad.

Serious music

Apart from its folk music, Mexico has until quite recently looked to Europe for its music. From the colonial period onwards composers and soloists were brought in from elsewhere, and substantially influenced the local music scene. It was the early 20th c. before Mexico developed serious music of its own. Its first composer was Manuel Ponce (1886–1948) who wrote orchestral and chamber music and songs such as "Chapultepec", "Ferial", and "Estrellita", incorporating themes from popular music. Mexico's most gifted composer was probably Silvestre Revueltas (1899–1940) who before his untimely death composed works for orchestra, string quartet and ballet ("Cuauhnáhuac", "Sensemayá", "Janítzio", Magueyes", "Homenaje a Federico García Lorca"). However, the towering creative figure in Mexican music is undoubtedly Carlos Chávez (1899–1978), who was not only a composer but also a much respected conductor and musicologist. His compositions ("Concerto for piano and orchestra", "H.P.", "Sinfonía India", "Four Suns", "New Fire", the opera "El Amor Propiciado" or "Pánfilo and Lauretta") frequently draw on ancient Indian tunes and legends. Another well-known composer is Julián Carillo (1875–1965) whose music was in the thirteen-tone scale ("Preludio a Cristóbal Colón", "Tetepán"). Other major Mexican composers include José Pablo Moncayo ("Huapango"), Miguel Bernal Jiménez, Luis Sandi and Blas Galindo (d. 1993).

The best known names in light music are Tata Nacho, Agustín Lara, Guti Cárdenas and Manuel M. Ponce.

Literature

Ancient Indian Records

Although the Spanish destroyed innumerable ancient Indian records at the time of the conquest – in the mid-16th c., for example, Diego de Landa, the Bishop of Mérida, had virtually all the Mayan hieroglyphic manuscripts burnt in a huge auto-da-fé – many important documents, especially the Aztec codices, were preserved for posterity. This was primarily thanks to a number of enlightened Spanish priests, who despite their repugnance for what these codices contained recognised their worth for the cultural history of mankind (see p. 96, Codices).

Náhuatl Literature
Bernardino de Sahagún

The records of the Spanish monk Fray Bernardino de Sahagún (1500–90) are of supreme importance for research into Náhuatl writings i.e. the literature of the Aztecs and their fellow peoples. Sahagún's four major collections of source materials are "Veinte Poemas rituales" (Twenty ritual poems), "Manuscrito de los Romances de los Señores de la Nueve España" (Manuscript of the romances of the lords of New Spain), "Cantares Mexicanos" (Mexican Epics) and "Manuscrito de Cantares" (Manuscript of epic poems). Primarily heroic and religious verse, these already contain subjective, highly emotive descriptions, with something of the character of lyric poetry. The refrain is a common stylistic form, and the language is often extremely rich in metaphors and symbolism. Drama accompanied by music and dancing was very popular, often with a religious background and quite frequently including sporting contests and human sacrifice.

Netzahualcóyotl

The works of the legendary poet-king Netzahualcóyotl, translated into Spanish after the conquest, are particularly interesting. Netzahualcóyotl (1402–72), king of Texcoco, was esteemed as an extremely wise ruler, philosopher and poet, and his son Netzhualpílli (1464–1515) achieved similar importance, some of his poems being recorded by Sahagún in "Cantares Mexicanos". Tecayehuatzin, king of Huejotzingo, and Temilotzin, a warrior prince under Cuauhtémoc, the Aztecs' last emperor, were other important Náhuatl poets at the time of the conquest.

Eduard Georg Seler

In more modern times Eduard Georg Seler (1849–1922), the German Director of Mexico's International Archaeological Institute from 1910 to 1911, rendered great service to Náhuatl literature by translating a great many of the original texts, and his "Collected papers on American linguistics and archaeology" (1902–23) is a good survey of pre-Columbian literature.

Maya literature

Hardly any Maya literature has come down to us. "Rabinal Achi" was the only dramatic work to survive the Spanish conquest, giving us an insight into the Mayan Quiché culture and telling us about the Maya customs and way of life.

"Popol Vuh"

Another important work is "Popul-Vuh" (Book of the Council), which was preserved by word of mouth and was written down shortly after the conquest by a Quiché Indian in the original language but in the Roman alphabet. Its valuable information about the mythology, tradition and evolution of the various Maya peoples was translated in the early 18th c. by Fray Francisco Ximénez, a priest from Guatemala who had learnt the Maya language and several of its dialects. The Yucatecan Maya "Chilam Balam" (Book of the Jaguar Soothsayer) is a similar kind of record, a mixture of poems, soothsayings and mythology. Bishop Diego de Landa, mentioned at the outset as having been responsible for the destruction of so many priceless Maya writings, doubtless seized by remorse, later made a decisive contribution to our knowledge of the Maya with his "Relación de las Cosas de Yucatán" (Account of the affairs of Yucatán).

Conquista

The era of the Conquista and the Conquistadors was naturally also the time of the chroniclers, but it can be viewed as the birth of Mexican literature in the Spanish language as well.

Bernal Díaz del Castillo

The historic clash of Spanish and Meso-American civilisations is vividly described by Bernal Díaz del Castillo (1492–1580), Cortés' comrade-in-arms, in his "Historia verdadera de la Conquista de la Nueva España" (True history of the conquest of New Spain), an eyewitness account of Cortés' march on Mexico. Other important chroniclers of this period include Cortés himself, who left behind his own highly informative and extremely lucid, if somewhat subjective, eyewitness reports in his "Cartas de Relación" addressed to Emperor Charles V, Bartolomé de las Casas (1474–1566), Jerónimo de Mendieta (1525–1604) and Antonio de Solis (1610–86). There were also several Indian historians who wrote in Spanish, having learnt it in the monastery schools. These included Fernando de Alvarado Tezozómoc, a nephew of Moctezuma Xocoyotzin, and Fernando de Alva Ixtlixóchitl, a descendant of Netzahualcóyotl, who was responsible for the important "Historia chichimeca" (1648).

Colonial period and national uprising

Apart from its not altogether objective account of history, the colonial period was also not exactly conducive to the development of an independent freestanding form of Mexican literature. There was no escape from Spanish influence and every effort was made, often forcibly, to speed up integration. Everything had to be subjugated to the demands of Western culture and the Catholic faith.

16th and 17th centuries

However, this certainly did not prevent the emergence of some outstanding writers in the late 16th c. and in the 17th c. Juan Ruiz de Alarcón y Mendoza (1581–1639), the Mexico-born playwright who wrote mainly in Spanish, succeeded in making highly individual contributions to the character comedy genre, earning himself a name as one of its creators despite being of a disposition and way of thinking that did not suit Spanish intelligentsia of the time.

Inés de la Cruz

The nun Sor Juana Inés de la Cruz (1648–95, see Famous People) was one of the 17th c.'s most important poets writing in Spanish. Her religious dramas (e.g. "El Cetro de José" – The Sceptre of Joseph) and her comedies (e.g. "Amor es más Laberinto" – The Labyrinth of Love) were held in the highest esteem. This Mexico-born nun also wrote many love poems that some still say are "the sweetest and most tender ever to have flowed from the pen of a woman". Carlos de Sigüenza y Góngora (1645–1700) was a poet, essayist and philosopher who is regarded as an important exponent of New Spain's Baroque, attacking superstition in his "Philosophical manifesto against comets" written in 1680.

18th century

The 18th c. was marked by social commitment, the rise of scientific knowledge and the search for a national identity. Several writers took up French Neo-Classicism but this did not bear much fruit in Mexico, and José Manuel Martínez de Navarrete (1768–1809) is the only writer worth mentioning in this connection.

19th century

The early 19th c. was totally in the thrall of the independence struggle embarked on in 1810, and most of the works of this period revolved around this theme viewed from one side or the other.

José Joaquin Fernández de Lizardi

José Joaquin Fernández de Lizardi (1776–1827, see Famous People), the leading literary figure in the first quarter of the 19th c., pilloried the abuses of the colonial period in many newspaper articles, took up the cudgels for national independence, and fought for the underprivileged. In his satirical novel "El Periquillo Sarniento" (literally "The Mangy Budgie") he disguises his social critique as a picaresque account of a cheeky mestizo rogue. The realist novel in Mexico was represented by Emilio Rabasa (1858–1930; "La Bola" – Revolt, "El cuarto Poder" – The fourth power), López Portíllo y Rojas (1850–1923; "La Parcela" – The plot of land, "Los Precursores" – The precursors) and Rafael Delgado (1853–1914; "La Calandria" – The lark, "Angelina"). Heriberto Frías (1870–1925) takes up a historical theme in his novel "Tomochic" (1894) about the Tomochitec Indian uprising. A number of major writers including Manual Acuña (1849–73), Guillermo Prieto (1818–97) and Justo Sierra (1848–1912) were influenced in the late 19th c. by French and Spanish Romanticism.

Modernism

"Modernism", considered Latin America's first important contribution to world literature, rapidly evolved from the striving for renewal and as a reaction against Romanticism. Trying to appear cosmopolitan it seizes on esoteric subjects and is constantly concerned with linguistic refinement and originality.

Manuel Gutiérrez Najera

An admirer of French art and literature, Manuel Gutiérrez Najera can be regarded as the father of Mexico's modern literature, and his poems influenced generations of later poets. Other important Modernists include Amado Nervo (1870–1919), Luis G. Urbina (1864–1934) and Enrique González Martinez (1871–1952), considered to be the final representative of the movement.

Contemporary literature

Revolution and the Colonial Period as literary themes

Contemporary literature finally brought Mexico's international literary breakthrough as well. Influenced by the 1910 Revolution, these first works tended to have a topical background, often marked by elements of autobiography and a strong sense of nationalism. Mariano Azuelo (1873–1952) falls into this category. As a social critique his novel "Los de abajo" (literally "Those from below") describes the Revolution at its most uninhibited. Martín Luis Guzmán (born 1887) tackles some of the great figures of the Revolution, as in "Memorias de Pancho Villa" (Memoirs of Pancho Villa) and "La Sombra del Caudillo" (The Shadow of the Caudillo), while José Vasconcelos (1882–1959) painstakingly recreates those tempestuous times in his novels "La Tormenta" (The Storm), "Ulises criollo" (Creole Ulysses) and "El Proconsulado" (The Proconsulate).

The Twenties saw a revival of interest in the colonial period which was taken up by authors such as Artemio de Valle Arizpe (1888–1961). Gregorio López y Fuentes (born 1897), in his 1935 novel "El Indio" (The Indio), was the first to paint an extremely black picture of the tragedy of an Indian village. Many others followed suit, including Ramón Rubin with "El callado Dolor de los Tzotziles" (The silent suffering of the Tzotziles), Francisco Rojas Gonzáles and "El Diosero" (The Godmaker), and Rosario Castellanos (born 1925) in "Balun Canan" (The new guard).

Carlos Fuentes

Together with José Revueltas (1914–76), Carlos Fuentes (born 1928), who is probably Mexico's best-known novelist, and author of "La Región más transparente" (Where the Air is Clearest), "La muerte de Artemio Cruz" (The Death of Artemio Cruz), and "El gringo veijo" (The Old Gringo) cast a critical eye on Mexican society. Agustin Yañez (born 1904; "Al Filo del Agua") and Juan Rulfo (1918–86; "Pedro Páramo") provided insights into what it was like in the Mexican countryside against the background of revolutionary confusion. Juan José Arreola (born 1918) made his name with his volume of short stories "Varia Invención y Confabulario".

Octavio Paz

Mexico's greatest essayists are regarded as being Alfonso Reyes (1889–1959) and Octavio Paz (born 1914). Paz, like Fuentes, combined his literary career with the life of a diplomat, and is best known for "The Labyrinth of Solitude, The Other Mexico: Critique of the Pyramid", written after the 1968 Tlatelolco massacre, and which has been translated into many languages. He was awarded the Nobel Prize for Literature in 1990.

Mexico's major playwrights include Rodolfo Usigli (born 1905), Xavier Villaurrutia (1903–50), Salvador Novo (born 1904) and Jorge Ibargüentgoitia, who also wrote black comic thrillers. Leading roles were also played by the essayist and critic Carlos Monsiváis (born 1918: "Amor perdido", "Días de guardar", "Entrada libre") and Elena Poniatowska (born 1933: "The Strength of Silence", "Hasta no verte, Jesús mío").

Verse

Outstanding modern poets include Bernardo Ortiz de Montellano (1899–1949), Alí Chumacero (born 1918), Rosario Castellanos (born 1925), L. Guadalupe Amor (born 1920) and Jaime Sabines (born 1925).

In 1960 a number of talented young writers, among them Augusto Shelley, Jaime Labastidas, Juan Buñuelos, Oscar Olivas and Eraclio Zepedas, banded together to form "La Espiga amotinada", with the aim of reviving Mexican modern verse.

Film

The Mexican cinema has made no small contribution to establishing the cliché of the "charro", the Mexican cowboy, who's always singing, wears an enormous sombrero and struts around clanking his equally enormous silver spurs. The first film to promote this image was Fernando de Fuentes' "Allá en el Rancho Grande" in 1936 which was to usher in a wave of "Comedia Ranchera" movies that carried on until the Fifties. They were harmless comedies against a jolly country backdrop and the plot was all about kindly landowners, happy ranch-hands and hot-blooded "charros" whose only problem was with their love life. These pictures were a great success with the public and assured the Latin American market of the Forties and Fifties for the Mexican film industry. But there was also one director working during this period who, according to Gabriel Figueroa, later cameraman to Luis Buñuel, shot the "most Mexican" movies. That was Emilio Fernández who today is considered to be the pioneer of the Mexican cinema. His films include "Janitzio" (1938) about the Indians on Pátzcuaro Lake, "Flor Silvestre" and "Enamorada". They too are set on the land, which Fernández felt was the spiritual home of the Mexican, but he views his characters from a much less sentimental perspective.

The crisis in the Mexican film industry began in the late Fifties when the Ranchero comedies had run their course and Hollywood was also making inroads into the Latin American market. The only major directors were Luis Buñuel from Spain who made several of his most important films in Mexico including "Los Olvidados" (1950, The Young and the Damned), "Nazarin (1958), "El Angel Exterminador" (1962, The Exterminating Angel) and "Simón del Desierto" (1965, Simon of the Desert), and his former colleague Luis Alcoriz, who made comedies and semi-documentaries. Film-making got going again with the establishment of the University Centre for Film Studies in Mexico City in 1964 and the National Film Bank in 1970. This supervised the film studios, distribution, and cinema exhibition. Amazingly this did not result in censorship, but the birth of the new Mexican cinema with as its most important representatives Alberto Isaac, Arturo Ripstein, Felipe Cazals and Alfonso Arau, who particularly during the early Seventies produced work that was extremely impressive in form and content. Alongside the state-funded film industry there were also independent productions such as "Reed – México Insurgente", Paul Leduc's 1972 portrayal of the Mexican Revolution in 1913/14 as seen by the radical American journalist John Reed.

Since 1983 the National Film Centre has been headed by the director Alberto Isaac but even he has been unable to stop fewer and fewer films being produced, and fewer and fewer people going to the cinema, despite low ticket prices. Even smash hits from Hollywood only run for a few weeks.

The general crisis in the film industry in the 80s affected both Mexican and foreign films. Even the Hollywood blockbusters began to find less favour with Mexicans, who preferred to stay at home and watch television. From 1990 there was a small renaissance in film making by several younger directors, and this pleased both the critics and the public: Nicolás Echeverría ("Cabeza de Vaca"), María Noovaro ("Danzon"), Alfonso Arau ("Como Agua para Chocolatee"), Jaime Umberto Hermosillo ("Encuentro Inesperado"; "La Tarea Prohibida"), Francisco Athié ("Esscena de Lolo") and Alejandrom Palayo ("Miroslava"; "La Víspera"). These films were also well received abroad.

At the end of April 1993 the great comedian Mario Moreno "Cantinflas" died at the age of 82 and was buried as a folk hero. Outside Mexico he was best known for his part as Passepartout in "Around the World in Eighty Days".

Folklore

Bullfighting

Bullfighting (corrida de toros) came from Spain but has also become very firmly established in Mexico. There are bullrings (*plazas de toros*) in all the major cities, and Mexico City has the largest in the world, with seating for 80,000. The best bullfighters, the toreros, matadors, and espadas, often from Spain, appear in the high season (November to March or, in northern Mexico, in the summer) while novices, the novilleros, take on the bulls for the rest of the year. The corrida usually takes place on Sundays and public holidays at 4 o'clock in the afternoon, and is one of the very few things which begin on time in Mexico. The best seats are in the shade (*sombra*) and the cheaper ones in the sun (*sol*).

The fighting bulls (*toros bravos*) are bred on special haciendas and sent into the ring at the age of four to five after a rigorous selection procedure.

The ritual of the bullfight

The bullfight (*lidia*) is in three main parts (*tercios or suertes*). After some preliminary passes by the capeadores with their garish capes (*capa*) to tire the bull, the first main part begins, the *suerte de picar* or *suerte de varas*, when the mounted picadors allow themselves to be charged by the bull, and stab the bull's shoulder muscles with their lances (*garrocha*) as they ward off its attack. Once the bull has been worn down (*castigado*) by the stab wounds (*varas*) the second part, the *suerte de banderillas,* begins. The banderillos approach the bull armed with their banderillas, jabbing them into the bull's shoulders while skilfully averting its attack at the last moment. The usual *banderillas* are barbed stilettos, trailing glittering decorations, and 75cm/29in. long; *banderillas a cuarta* are shorter and only about 15cm/6in. long. Reticent or sleepy bulls are goaded into action by passes with the cape (*floreos*). Once the bull has three pairs of banderillas stuck in its neck this signals the start of the final phase, the *suerta suprema* or *suerte de matar.* The *espada* or matador, who has a special scarlet cape (*muleta*) and a sword (*estoque*), baits the bull with the *muleta* until finally he lures it into the right position for him to deliver the death-blow, the *estocada.* When the bull collapses, to wild applause if it has been courageous and aggressive, the *puntillero* will finish it off with a thrust to its jugular. Incompetent bullfighters are subjected to vociferous jeers and whistles from the spectators.

The gory spectacle is repeated six or eight times until darkness falls.

Cockfighting

Cockfighting (*pelea de gallos*) is widespread out in the countryside. Both of the chosen cocks have sharp steel spurs attached to their feet which they use to inflict injury on one another, and there is heavy betting on the outcome.

It is for individual visitors to decide whether they want to be spectators at events of this kind, condemned by animal protection agencies throughout the world.

Charreada

Charreadas are the Mexican equivalent of the American rodeo, and a showcase for the traditional skills of the Mexican cowboy, the charro, who rode the range on the great haciendas. They are put on by the charros themselves, most of whom are organised into associations that have their own rodeo grounds. After the opening parade, with the participants in their picturesque costumes, they show off their riding and roping skills with displays of steer wrangling, bareback riding, etc. Entertainment in the interval is provided by folk dancers and mariachi bands.

The charreadas staged in Mexico City's attractive Hipódromo de las Américas are popular with locals and visitors alike (see Practical Information, Sport).

Jai Alai (Frontón)

Jai Alai, pronounced "high-a-lie" and known as pelota in Spain, has its origins in the Basque country and like many other games was brought to Mexico by the Spanish. Probably the fastest and most dangerous of all ball games, it is played usually under cover on a long rectangular court with high walls on three sides. It is rather like squash, with a hard ball, but the players, mostly in teams of two, use long curved baskets to catch and throw the ball. A great deal of betting goes on for high stakes. The Jai Alai venue in Mexico City is the Frontón México (see Practical Information, Sport).

Frontenis is a version of Jai Alai played with tennis rackets.

Dance

Many of the traditional folk dances (*bailes folklóricos*) still performed in Mexico today have pre-Hispanic roots while others were brought here by European settlers. While the Conquistadors tried to get rid of what they saw as heathen dances, the Franciscan and Dominican missionaries tried to incorporate the songs and dances of the Indians into Catholic ritual. Hence, for example, the Aztec

A colourful Indian dance

dance symbolising the struggle between day and night, between good and evil, assumed the form of a fight between the Church and the forces of the devil. Similarly the ceremonial dances performed in honour of the Aztec earth mother Tonantzín are now danced in an almost identical form for Our Lady of Guadalupe. Traditional dances are an essential feature of the many fiestas.

Quetzal

The Nahua quetzal dance in the states of Veracruz and Puebla involves the wearing of magnificent colourful costumes and enormous round feathered headdresses.

Viejito

The Viejito, the dance of the little old men, goes back to Cortés' defeat of the Tarascans, when their ruler appeared before the conquerors in the symbolic guise of an old man to express his submission. The dancers wear masks, imitate the tired movements of greybeards, and gradually transform themselves into young men again.

Venado, Matachin

The Venado, the stag dance of the Yaqui, Mayo and Tarahumara of north-west Mexico, is supposed to bring luck in the hunt. The Matachin dance is a similar ritual, but simpler.

Penachos

The Penachos, the Zapotec feather dance performed in Oaxaca, gets its name from the feather headdress decorated with mirrors.

Sonajero

The Sonajero dancers, who also wear headdresses, are known for their use of rattles and bows and arrows. Their dance is dedicated to the symbol of the Cross and the forces of nature.

Conchero

Conchero dances are performed mainly in Central Mexico, to the accompaniment of plucked instruments made from the shells of armadillos.

Ballroom dancing

Ballroom dancing is popular and is principally based on Spanish tunes and dance-steps. These include the Jarabe Tapatio from Guadalajara, the Zandunga from Tehuantepec, the Huapango from Veracruz and the Jarana from Yucatán. The Danzón is very popular with the poor and especially in Mexico City.

Traditional dress

Only a generation ago in many parts of Mexico men still wore the charro suit, the traditional riding habit for special occasions of the cowboys and rancheros, and consisting of jacket and trousers in fine leather, with rows of silver buttons, and a ruffled shirt and broad-brimmed felt hat embroidered with gold and silver. Nowadays it is only worn as an official charro costume or by the mariachis. Women in the China-Poblana costume wear a red and green embroidered skirt over several petticoats with a white blouse and a woollen shawl (*rebozo*). Believed to have been brought over by a Chinese woman who came to Puebla from the Philippines, it is nowadays confined mostly to fancy-dress balls and folklore events.

Traditional Indian dress

By contrast, traditional Indian dress can still be seen in many places, especially away from the big cities. Some of the ancient spinning and weaving techniques are still widely in use today, and it is only the vegetable dyes which are giving way to modern synthetics. A great variety of different costumes are still to be found in the states of Oaxaca, Veracruz, Yucatán and Chiapas. It is mostly women who have kept to the traditional fashions; the men tend to wear plain white shirts and trousers held up by a woollen belt. People use poncho-style patterned sarapes to keep out the wind and the rain. In the hot areas of Yucatán on the Gulf they wear pleated shirts with many pockets (*guayaberas*). Women wear the *huipil*, a long sleeveless embroidered wool tunic, which is rather

Two elegant riders in Mexico City

similar to the *quechquémetl* of Northern and Central Mexico although this is made from two strips of cloth. The sombrero was introduced as a straw hat by the Spanish. Pre-Hispanic dress is mainly still found among the Tarahumara, Huicholes, Amuzgo, Tzotzil and Tzeltzal.

Handicrafts and folk art

In terms of quality and variety, Mexico's folk art is a match for any other country. Although here too recent years have seen a move to mass produced items of inferior quality, there is still a plentiful supply of good, imaginative handicrafts. Like much else in Mexico its folk art is a charming mix of the Mexican and the Spanish, and many places have developed their own particular style, which means there is a wide variety of arts and crafts available throughout the country (see Practical Information, Shopping and Souvenirs).

Mexico in Quotations

Richard Hakluyt (1552–1616)

The Spanyards have notice of seven cities which old men of the Indians shew them should lie towards the Northwest from Mexico. They have used and use dayly much diligence in seeking of them, but they cannot find any one of them. They say that the witchcraft of the Indians is such, that when they come by these townes they cast a mist upon them, so that they cannot see them.

The people of the countrey are of a good stature, tawny coloured, broad faced, flat nosed, and given much to drinke both wine of Spaine and also a certeine kind of wine which they make with hony of Mageuiz and roots, and other things which they use to put into the same. They call the same wine Pulco.

They are of much simplicity, and great cowards, voide of all valour, and are great witches. They use divers times to talke with the divell, to whom they do certeine sacrifices and oblations: many times they have bene taken with the same, and I have seene them most cruelly punished for that offence.

They say that they came of the linage of an olde man which came thither in a boat of wood, which they call a canoa. But they cannot tell whether it were before the flood or after, neither can they give any reason of the flood, nor from whence they came.

Mexico City

It is situated in the middest of a lake of standing water, and environed round about with the same, saving in many places, going out of the Citie, are many broad wayes through the said lake or water. This lake and Citie is environed also with great mountains roundabout, which are in compasse above thirtie leagues and the saide Citie, and lake of standing water, doeth stand in a great plaine in the middest of it.

The said Citie of Mexico hath the streetes made very broad, and right, that a man being in the high place at one ende of the street, may see at least for a good mile forward, and in all the one part of the streets in the North part of their Citie, their runneth a pretie lake of very cleare water, that every man may put into his house as much as he will, without the cost of any thing, but of the letting in. Also there is a great cave or ditch of water, that commeth through the Citie, even unto the high place, where come every morning at the break of the day twentie or thirty Canoas, or troughes of the Indians, which bring in them all maner of provision for the Citie, which is made and groweth in the Countrey, which is a very good commoditie for the inhabitants of the place.

The weather is there alwayes very temperate, the day differeth but one houre of length all the yere long. The fields and the woods are alwayes greene. The woods full of popinjays, and many other kinde of birds, that make such an harmonie of singing and crying, that any man will rejoice to heare it. In the fields are such odoriferous smels of flowers and hearbs that it giveth great content to the senses.

Principal Navigations, Voyages and Discoveries of the English Nation (Collected Works), 1598–1600

George Anson
(1697–1762)

Acapulco

The port of Acapulco is by much the securest and finest in all the northern parts of the Pacific Ocean, being, as it were, a bason surrounded by very high mountains: but the town is a most wretched place, and extremely unhealthy, for the air about it is so pent up by the hills, that it has scarcely any circulation. The place is besides destitute of fresh water, except what it brought from a considerable distance. and is in all respects so inconvenient that, except at the time of the mart, whilst the "Manila" galeon is in the port, it is almost deserted.
Voyage Round the World, 1748

George Augusta Sala
(1828–95)

Popocatapetl

The name indeed of the colossal mountain which dominates the city of Mexico is not very easy to pronounce, and it is well to adopt the mnemonic formula invented by an American traveller (was it General Grant, or the late Commodore Wyse?) "Pop the cat in the kettle". There you have Popocatapetl in the twinkling of a tongue.
America Revisited, 1882

Baedeker's
North America
(1904)

Three weeks suffice for the journey to Mexico City and back, with breaks in the most interesting places on the route and a return trip from Mexico to Orizaba, or even to Vera Cruz, Puebla and Oaxaca and back. The tour is not particularly difficult and is often undertaken by ladies; more time and trouble are necessary to visit the ruins of Yucatán and Chiapas. . . . Fairly light clothing is advisable because of the heat. A wrap or plaid is essential for the cold evenings and mornings. The visitor who would like to travel by steamer in one direction is advised to do so on the outward rather than on the return journey. The thin air of the Mexican plateaux sometimes affects the visitor.

Mexican inns are often primitive and their cleanliness leaves much to be desired. . . . The place of chambermaids is often taken by "Mozos" or boys. Small tips are customary and effective. Soap and matches will not be found in the bedrooms. Wine and foreign beers are expensive, local beer and pulque are cheap.
North America. The United States together with an Excursion to Mexico – Handbook for Travellers (second edition), 1904

D. H. Lawrence
(1885–1930)

Yes, U.S.A., you do put a strain on the nerves. Mexico puts a strain on the temper. Choose which you prefer. Mine's the latter. I'd rather be in a temper than pulled taut.

The old people had a marvellous feeling for snakes and fangs down here in Mexico. And after all, Mexico is only the sort of solar plexus of North America. The great paleface overlay hasn't gone into the soil half an inch. . . . It's a queer continent. The anthropologist may make what prettiness they like out of the myths. But come here, and you'll see that the gods bite . . . it seems to me Mexico exasperates, whereas the U.S.A. puts an unbearable tension on one. Because here in Mexico the fangs are still obvious. Everybody knows the gods are going to bite within the next five minutes.
Laughing Horse, 1923

Suggested Routes

Mexico is so vast that it would be impractical to suggest routes taking in the whole country. The following suggestions are for routes within Mexico that take in several of its most important sights and regions and are mostly planned as round trips. They can also be undertaken by bus using Mexican bus companies.

The suggested routes do not include every destination mentioned in the guide, but places and areas which are covered in the A to Z section under a main heading are printed in **bold**. Most of the places, scenic areas and archaeological sites described, whether under main headings or in the surroundings, can be found in the index at the end of the guide.

Most of the routes are on the federal roads (MEX . . .). The distances in brackets included in the route headings are in round figures and only apply to the direct route. The distances for detours or alternatives of any length are given separately.

There are further suggestions for routes in the A to Z section under Acapulco, Baja California, Barranca del Cobre, Campeche (city), Cancún, Lake Catemaco, Chetumal, Chiapas (state), Durango (city), Morelos, Oaxaca (state) and Pachuca.

1. Mexico City to Taxco and back via Cuernavaca (about 300km/190 miles)

Head south from **Mexico City** on the MEX 95 (or the MEX 95 D motorway) to get to colonial **Cuernavaca**, capital city of the state of **Morelos**. Still heading south, 25km/15 miles beyond Cuernavaca turn west on the road to Miacatlán, then make a detour north to see the interesting ruins at **Xochichalco** from a number of different pre-Columbian cultures. From Miacatlán carry on south again to the border with **México** state and Cacahuamilpa (surroundings of **Taxco**, see entry), which is worth a visit for its beautiful underground caverns. The furthest point of the round tour is reached at the delightful old town of **Taxco**. Return to **Mexico City** on either the MEX 95 D motorway which saves time, or on the MEX 95.

Detour (52km/32 miles)

It is worth making the trip from **Cuernavaca** east to Tepoztlán (see **Morelos**) to visit its fortress-like Dominican ex-convent.

Alternative

As an alternative to the round trip it is possible to continue on the MEX 95 from **Taxco** to Mexico's famous resort of **Acapulco** on the Pacific coast.

2. Mexico City to Uruapan via Lake Pátzcuaro (about 300km/190 miles)

Take the MEX 15 west out of **Mexico City**. **Toluca**, famous for its market, is the first stop then just past the town a road branches north to the pre-Columbian site at Calixtlahuaca. Back on the MEX 15 there is a winding stretch through the Sierra Madre Occidental to **Morelia** on the Río Grande de Morelia and capital city of the state of **Michoacán**. From there continue on the MEX 15 to Quiroga, the starting point for the scenic trip south along the shore of **Lake Pátzcuaro**, via **Tzintzuntzan**, with its Tarascan temple pyramids, and Pátzcuaro itself where a boat trip can be made to the island of Janitzio. From Pátzcuaro take MEX 14 west to **Uruapan**, town of fruit and flowers, and a base for visiting the lava fields and volcano of Paricutín.

Detour (40km/25 miles)

The MEX 120 south out of Pátzcuaro leads to the little town of Santa Clara del Cobre which is famous for its copper craftwork.

3. Mexico City to Veracruz and back via Puebla (about 740km/460 miles)

The first stop on this round trip to the Gulf of Mexico after heading east out of **Mexico City** on the MEX 150 D motorway or the MEX 150 is **Puebla**. The MEX 150 passes through **Huejotzingo** and **Cholula** first (see detour). The route continues on the MEX 150 D, past Mexico's highest mountain, the Pico de Orizaba (Citlaltépetl), to **Orizaba** followed shortly, via Fortín de las Flores with its lovely gardens, by **Cordóba**. Back on the MEX 150 this takes us to **Veracruz**, Mexico's most important port, and the Gulf Coast. Heading north along the coast for a short stretch of the MEX 180 the route then turns off west onto the MEX 140 to **Jalapa**, where a visit to the Anthropological Museum should be made. Turning south the route leaves the MEX 140 at Zacatepec to go west again via Huamantla to **Tlaxcala** on the eastern slopes of the Sierra Madre. The archaeological site of **Cacaxtla** is just south-west of Tlaxcala, and from there take the MEX 150 back to **Mexico City**.

Alternative (900km/560 miles)

Follow the above route to **Veracruz** and continue north, but instead of turning west take the MEX 180 up the coast to Papantla and nearby **El Tajín** with its strange niched pyramid. At Poza Rica take the MEX 130 to the south west. At Teopancingo either turn south on the MEX 119 and return via Apizaco to **Tlaxcala** and the original route, or remain on the MEX 130 and turn off south-west 8km/5 miles beyond Tulancingo (see **Hidalgo**) to return to **Mexico City** by way of the magnificent ruins of **Teotihuacán**, for which plenty of time should be allowed.

Alternative

Instead of turning south-west after Tulacingo continue to **Pachuca** which is the starting-point for a drive through beautiful mountain scenery taking in several 16th c. Augustinian convents (see A to Z, Pachuca).

Detours

Puebla is a good base for a trip to two of Mexico's mighty volcanoes, **Popocatépetl** and **Iztaccíhuatl**, taking in **Cholula**, one of ancient Mexico's great cities, with the world's largest pyramid.

Another trip out of **Puebla**, this time on the MEX 190 to Atlixco, is the 20km/12-mile run to **Acatepec** which like nearby Tonantzintla has a fine church in the Poblano style.

From **Veracruz** on the MEX 180 continue through José Cardel, without branching west on the MEX 140 to **Jalapa**, to reach Zempoala and the ruins of the ancient Totonac capital.

4. Mexico City to San Miguel de Allende via Tula and Querétaro (about 420km/260 miles)

The first stopping point, just outside the Distrito Federal, on this northbound route out of **Mexico City**, is **Tepozotlán** where a stop should be made to see the magnificent interior of its convent church. Carry on north on the MEX 57 D and then turn right off the motorway to get to the great Toltec site of **Tula** (Tollán). The quickest way forward is to rejoin the MEX 57 and stay on it as far as 28km/17 miles beyond the historically important city of **Querétaro** before taking the MEX 111 west to **San Miguel de Allende**, a lovely well-preserved colonial town.

5. San Miguel de Allende to Zacatecas and back (about 750km/465 miles)

Take the MEX 111 north out of **San Miguel de Allende** then turn west at Dolores Hidalgo, where Mexico's independence movement began, onto the MEX 110 and the picturesque city of **Guanajuato**, followed by Silao. Here take the MEX 45 north-west via **León** to the state capital **Aguascalientes**. Continue to **Zacatecas**, another scenic silver city and with a wonderful Baroque cathedral, then turn east on the MEX 45, followed by the MEX 49, towards the old silver city of **San Luis Potosí**. From here head south on the MEX 57 before turning west on the MEX 111 back to **San Miguel de Allende**.

Detours

From **Zacatecas** it is a 55km/35-mile drive south to the pre-Columbian religious site of the Quemada or Chicomoztóc Ruins. About 20km/12 miles east of **San Luis Potosí** it is possible to visit the ghost silver town of Cerro San Pedro. The hot springs of Gogorrón and Lourdes are good places to relax on the way back to **San Miguel de Allende**.

6. Round trip in the southern part of the Gulf of California
(about 950km/590 miles)

This tour provides an opportunity for visitors to see something of **Baja California** without having to cross into the United States, but that does mean having to take two 7–8 hour crossings by car ferry.

The tour sets out from **Guaymas** (also accessible by plane) where swimming at nearby San Carlos is a pleasant way to relax before taking the car ferry across the Gulf of California to the port of Santa Rosalía in the southern part of **Baja California**. Take the MEX 1 (Carretera Transpeninsular) south via La Paz to **Cabo San Lucas** (see description of route in the A to Z section, Baja California), where the MEX 9 turns back to La Paz. From January to early March grey whales may be seen on their breeding grounds in the Bahia Magdalena. From La Paz there is a car ferry back to the mainland at Los Mochis in the state of **Sinaloa**.

Alternative
(1300km/810 miles)

It is also possible to start this tour at La Mochis and drive north on the MEX 15 through a vast irrigated area to Navojoa, where there is a detour east of 106km/65 miles to the old silver mining town and national conservation site of Alamos (see **Guaymas**). Back on the main road continue north through land settled by the Mayo and the Yaqui to reach **Guaymas** and the car ferry.

7. Around Oaxaca

The charming city of **Oaxaca** is a good base for trips to the interesting towns and archaeological sites within a 50km/30 mile radius. These include **Monte Albán**, **Mitla**, **Yagul**, Dainzú, Santa María del Tule, Tlacochahuaya, Teotitlán, Tlacolula and Cuilapan.

8. Villahermosa to San Cristóbal de Las Casas and back
(about 530km/330 miles)

This route, mostly in the state of **Chiapas**, starts from **Villahermosa**, where a visit should be made to the La Venta Museum Park before taking the MEX 186 east as far as the MEX 199, which then runs south to **Palenque** and its great Maya ruined city. Continue on this road, skirting the beautiful cascades of Agua Azul, to Ocosingo and **San Cristóbal de Las Casas**. Take the MEX 190 heading west to **Tuxtla Gutiérrez** and the nearby Sumidero Canyon. To return to **Villahermosa** retrace a short stretch of the MEX 190 before turning north on the MEX 195.

Detour (about 300km/190 miles)

The Maya site of **Bonampak**, famous for its frescos, can be reached along the gravel road from **Palenque** or it is possible to fly there in a light plane. The ruined city of **Yaxchilan**, which is also deep in the jungle and possible even more impressive, can be reached by air or by river.

9. Mérida to the Maya sites further south (about 250km/155 miles)

The MEX 261 and the Puuc route south from **Mérida**, the interesting and agreeable capital of the **Yucatán**, is the best way to explore several of the most important Maya sites, all of which are quite close to one another.

The first stop is at the magnificent ruins of **Uxmal**, followed quite shortly by **Kabah**, with its impressive arch, and then, after leaving the MEX 261 and turning east, by **Sayil** and **Labná**, which also has a great arch. The route continues via the Loltún Caves to Oxkutzcab (detour to Maní), where it meets the MEX 184 and turns north-west as far as Muna. Here it rejoins the MEX 261 to return to **Mérida**.

This route also takes in a number of other less important sites.

10. Mérida to the Caribbean via Chichén Itzá (about 470km/290 miles)

This route also starts from **Mérida**, this time heading east on the MEX 180 to what is probably the most important of all the Maya sites, **Chichén Itzá**. It continues from here via Valladolid to the state of **Quintana Roo** and the Caribbean resort of **Cancún**. There are beautiful beaches around here and all along the MEX 307 which runs south down the coast via the resort of **Akumal** and **Xel-há Lagoon** to the Maya ruins of **Tulum**.

Detours

From **Cancún** regular ferry services run to **Isla Mujeres** and to the larger Caribbean island of **Cozumel**, which can also be reached by car ferry from Puerto Morelos on the MEX 307.

From **Tulum** it is a 54km/33-mile trip to **Cobá**, a vast Maya city, largely still unexcavated and deep in the jungle. From here a road goes via Nuevo Xcan (45km/28 miles) to Valladolid (a total of 115km/71 miles) where the main route is rejoined.

Mexico from A to Z

Acapulco

K 9

State: Guerrero (Gro.)
Altitude: 2m/6½ft
Population: 1,100,000
Telephone code: 91 74

Access

By air from Mexico City (hourly flights) and other Mexican or US airports; by bus from Mexico City (journey time approximately 5 hours); by car on the spectacular but expensive Autopista del Sol (MEX 95) from Mexico City (journey time 3½ hours, about 380km/236 miles). Travelling by bus the return journey should be booked immediately on arrival in Acapulco.

Location

Acapulco is situated on Mexico's Pacific coast, at the foot of the Sierra Madre del Sur a good 400km/250 miles south of Mexico City.

★★ Resort

The sun-blessed seaside resort, famous the world over, lies on the shores of the Bahía de Acapulco, a large crescent-shaped bay. Blue seas, white beaches, green hills and steep rocky cliffs combine to make it a scenic paradise set around a fine natural harbour. Despite having become overrun by tourists in recent years Acapulco is still worth visiting, several pleasant spots near by offering escape from the worst of the crowds.

History

Some settlement of the Acapulco region (Náhuatl: "place where the grasses were disturbed") almost certainly occurred in the early period, though no mention is made of a town here until after the Aztec conquest at the end of the 15th c. (There is a suggestion however that Peruvian seafarers visited this part of the coast even earlier.) Arriving in 1521 the Spanish conquistador Gil Gonzales Ávila was presumably the first European to discover the bay. Later Acapulco served as a supply base for expeditions heading north up the Pacific coast or down towards South America. By the end of the 16th c. it had become a home port for ships trading with the Philippines, China and India, as well as with South America. From the latter came silver and gold, and from the former mainly silk, porcelain and spices. In its turn the viceroyalty of New Spain shipped out silver, textiles and cocoa, goods brought in from abroad being transported overland via a road the Spanish built to Mexico City and thence to the gulf port of Veracruz for onward passage to Europe. In the 17th and 18th centuries the sea lanes out of Acapulco, as elsewhere, were prey to pirates. Then at the end of the 18th c. the fortunes of the port declined as new trade routes were opened from the Philippines through the Indian Ocean and around the Cape of Good Hope to Spain. When Mexico gained its independence Acapulco's status was further reduced, a process halted only when the highway to Mexico City was constructed in 1927. However, the city's real resurgence began after the Second World War when American tourists first "discovered" Acapulco.

◀ *A colonial church in Guanajuato*

Sights

Scenic beauty and luxury hotels apart, Acapulco has little of particular interest to offer.

★Fort San Diego (history museum)

Fort San Diego (Fuerte San Diego), originally erected between 1615 and 1617, was rebuilt in 1776 following an earthquake. Its main function was to defend the port against piracy. The fort is now the city's historical museum (Museo Histórico de Acapulco) with collections of documents and other items relating to the Conquest, the history of the fort itself, and Acapulco's trade with Asia. There is also a section devoted to the history of piracy in the Pacific.

The Moorish-Byzantine-style cathedral gracing Acapulco's main square (Zócalo) dates from the 1930s. In the east of the city there is a culture and congress centre (Centro Cultural y de Convenciones) with conference halls, theatres, displays of folk crafts (items for sale also) and a small archaeological museum. Tourist activity is concentrated along the Avenida Costera Miguel Alemán where most of the big hotels, restaurants, night-clubs and shops are located.

Beaches

There are more than 20 beaches in or close to Acapulco. Caleta and Caletilla, both very popular with the Mexicans especially in the morn-

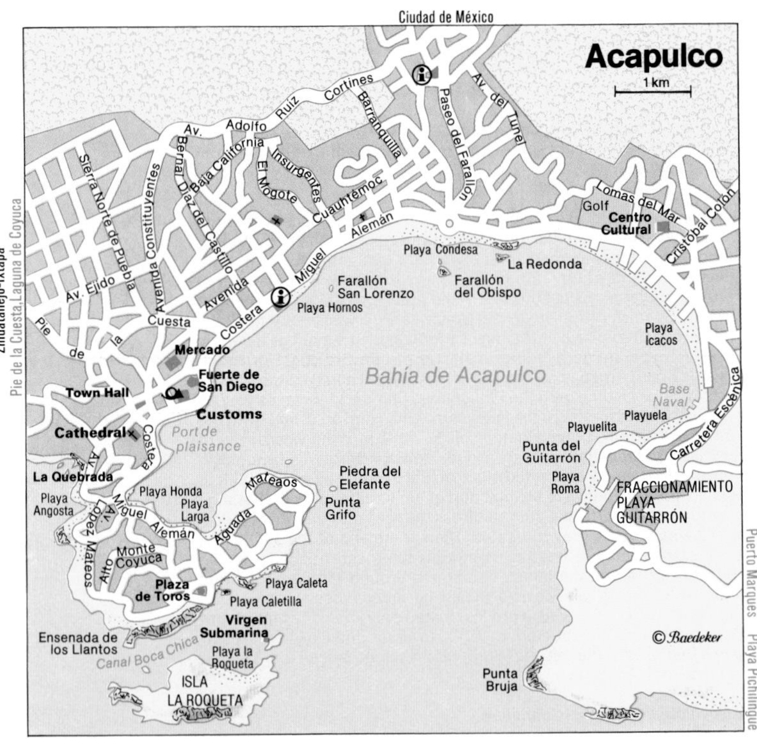

The Bay of Acapulco on the Pacific Ocean

ings, are known for their calm waters and fascinating submarine life (glass bottom boats). From Playa Caletilla boats make the short crossing to the island of La Roqueta where the beach of the same name has been transformed into a most attractive nature reserve. Visible in the water just to the north-east of the island (in a depth of about 2m/6½ft) stands the "Virgin Submarina", a bronze statue of the Virgin of Guadalupe. Playa Hornos and Playa Hornitos are particular afternoon favourites, as too is Playa Condesa to the east (the latter, being especially fashionable at the moment, is lively in the evenings as well). The calm waters of the delightful bay near the fishing village of Puerto Marqués, 13km/8 miles east of Acapulco, usually attract a morning crowd to the beach (likewise called Puerto Marqués). The lovely Revolcadero beach (about a kilometre further on) is less crowded but, being open to the Pacific, the surf tends to be heavy and the currents strong. Surfing competitions are held there every year. About 12km/7½ miles north-west of Acapulco is a little place called Pie de la Cuesta, situated on a sandy spit between the beach (heavy surf and currents) and the freshwater Laguna de Coyuca. At sunset the dunes offer a superb panorama, while the lights of Acapulco make an equally impressive sight at night. The Laguna de Coyuca is a natural Eden, with dense tropical vegetation, freshwater fish and exotic birds. There are boat trips on the lagoon from Pie de la Cuesta. There are other beaches deserving of mention, including La Angosta, Honda, Manzanillo, Redonda and Icacos.

★Laguna de Coyuca

★Quebrada divers

Early afternoon (1pm) and in the evening (7.15, 8.15, 9.15 and 10.30pm) the famous "clavidistas", the divers of Quebrada, can be seen performing their feats of daring. Having offered their prayers to a statue of the Madonna, they leap from 40m/130ft up on the Quebrada cliffs into the waves surging back and forth over the rocks below. After dark floodlights illuminate the divers, some of whom carry torches as they hurl

A hotel complex made for relaxation

Quebrada diving

themselves into the depths. The nearby "El Mirador" hotel boasts a notable restaurant, "La Perla", opened in 1949 by the Swiss musician Teddy Stauffer who first publicised the delights of Acapulco in Europe.

On most evenings also the voladores – Totonac Indians from Papantla, close to the archaeological site at El Tajín (see entry) – provide yet another extraordinary spectacle with their danza del volador, a ritual flying act with its origins in an ancient fertility myth.

Coastal drive from Acapulco to Puerto Escondido

View

The drive follows the MEX 200 into the Costa Chica, the coastal region to the east of Acapulco. Once having left the built-up area behind, the Carretera Escénica affords a superb view of the Bahía de Acapulco. Skirting the bay at Puerto Marqués, beyond which a short stop can be made at the picturesque Laguna Tres Palos, the road then enters a little known area lying between the Sierra Madre del Sur and the Pacific. This is an interesting countryside dotted with small towns – San Marcos (about 80km/50 miles), Cruz Grande (about 120km/75 miles), San Luis Acatlán (turn off, about 27km/17 miles), Ometepec (turn off, about 16km/10 miles), Cuajinicuilapa (about 234km/145 miles), Montecillos (turn off, 17km/10½ miles), Punto Maldonado (turn off, about 14km/9 miles) – and well worth exploring on account of its tropical vegetation and many rivers, lagoons and rock formations. The inhabitants in some parts are the descendents of runaway slaves, though most are now integrated into the local Indian communities. At the end of the last century a German American called Johann Schmidt set himself up as the self-appointed ruler of the region until he was eventually "deposed" in the upheavals of the 1910 revolution.

Over the Oaxaca state border lies Pinotepa Nacional (about 284km/176 miles; population: 60,000), about 6km/4 miles before which the MEX 125 branches off for the Mixteca Alta convent route (see Oaxaca, State). From Pinotepa Nacional, the MEX 200 continues for roughly another 145km/90 miles to the seaside resort of Puerto Escondido (see entry).

Acatepec

K 8

State: Puebla (Pue.)
Altitude: 2200m/7220ft
Population: 3500

Access

From Puebla (see entry), via the Oaxaca road (MEX 190; about 16km/10 miles) in the direction of Atlixco.

Location

Acatepec, only a small place, is situated some 120km/75 miles south-east of Mexico City and about 16km/10 miles west of Puebla.

Its church, San Francisco de Acatepec, is one of the finest examples of regional High Baroque in Mexico.

History

Not very much is known about the history of the church. It is presumed to have been constructed about 1730, the tiles (azulejos) being specially designed for it and manufactured in Puebla. Part of the interior was destroyed by fire in the late 1930s. The subsequent restoration work, carried out by well-intentioned local craftsmen, unfortunately fails to live up to the original 18th c. splendour. That such superb churches are to be found in even the smallest towns and villages in the area let alone the larger ones is a tribute to the Spanish who so successfully harnessed the unique artistry and craftmanship of the local Indian population.

★San Francisco de Acatepec

Façade

Access to the church is through an impressive Neo-Mudéjar-style arch, beyond which stands the triply-articulated, azulejos and brick clad façade. Framed by an irregular arch the portal is flanked on either side by three unequally spaced Corinthian pillars with a statue occupying the niche between. Above, on the mid-section of the façade, estípites (pilasters in the form of an upturned truncated pyramid, a notable feature of the Churriguera style) take the place of the columns, while an emblem of St Francis embellishes the large central window. The outermost pilasters of this section continue upwards in whorls or volutes, the overall effect being that of a gable. A statue of St Francis adorns the star-shaped upper niche above which, at the highest point, stands a sculpture symbolising the Trinity.

The corners of the right-hand tower comprise Salomonic (twisted) columns with ornamental bands of blue and yellow azulejos. Somewhat unusually, the left-hand tower is set at an angle to the façade.

Interior

The interior of the church contains a wealth of stucco-work and wood carving, all painted in a profusion of colours and gilded in the Poblano style typical of the 18th c. Of particular interest is an oldish altar-piece (17th c.) with statues finished in the estofado technique – gilding first, then overpainted – and almost lost amidst a welter of gilded Salomonic columns and other ornamentation. Note too the exceedingly intricate and sumptuously ornate door to the baptistery. Greater sobriety prevails in the remainder of the interior, Indian influence being less in evidence here than in Santa María de Tonantzintla (see below).

San Francisco de Acatepec

Surroundings

Barely a kilometre to the west lies the village of Tonantzintla (2200m/7220ft; population: 4000; fiesta: August 15th, Día de la Asunción de la Virgen María). Whereas in the case of San Francisco de Acatepec it is the façade which is the masterpiece of the Poblano style, here in Santa María de Tonantzintla the same variant of the Baroque finds supreme expression in the interior. In contrast the doubly-articulated façade of the church, kept predominantly red but with blue and white tile ornamentation as well as sculptures, is comparatively plain. The "extravagantly Baroque" interior of the church is quite unique, its breathtaking colouring and its mix of Indian and European elements being the work of anonymous local artists and craftsmen. Decoration embodying the mystic predilection for fruit, flowers and birds so characteristic of the pre-Columbian period, interwoven with Christian motifs, covers every available inch. Outstanding among the many features of interest are, in the choir, the orchestra of Indian musicians and stucco-work scenes with reliefs of Jesus, the Virgin Mary and St Christopher, and in the mid-section of the nave the picture of St Francis and sculptures of St James and St Anthony. High in the dome a bevy of cherubim appear to float earthwards from a flower in a

★★Santa María de Tonantzintla

Interior

Dome

sea of foliage. The pulpit arch exhibits some remarkable stucco-work – crowned devils spewing forth fruit, and ornamental atlantes.

Not far from the church stands a state-owned observatory (built in 1942) equipped with a Schmidt telescope. Inside are frescos by Miguel Prieto.

Tlaxcalancingo

The village of Tlaxcalancingo (2200m/7220ft; population: 6000) lies on the way back from Acatepec to Puebla, about 4km/2½ miles from Acatepec along the MEX 190. On the right stands another fine example of Poblano Baroque, the 18th c. church of San Bernardino, its magnificent façade with curved gable being completely clad in tiles and red brick. On its left side the church is crowned by an elegant tower, the dome and cap also being tiled.

San Bernardino

From Tlaxcalancingo it is only 6km/4 miles back to Puebla (see entry).

Acolman de Netzahualcóyotl — K 8

State: México (Mex.)
Altitude: 2215m/7270ft
Population: 5000

Access from Mexico City

By bus from Terminal Indios Verdes; by car on the MEX 85 then, after about 40km/25 miles (10km/6 miles before Teotihuacán), MEX 85D;

Location

The magnificent San Agustín de Acolman, an archetypal 16th c. New Spanish fortified convent founded by Augustinian monks, is located on a plateau north-east of Mexico City. Although the overall impression is Iberian Gothic, the façade of the convent church provides an outstanding example of the Renaissance-influenced Plateresque style.

History

The fortress-like appearance of the Acolman convent (Náhuatl: "encircled by water") testifies to the unsettled times immediately following the Conquest. The foundation stone was laid as early as 1539, but construction of the existing church began only around the middle of the 16th c., the façade dating from 1560. Even when the actual convent building was completed in 1571, parts of the church were still unfinished. By 1580 the convent was occupied by 24 monks, nineteen devoting themselves to their studies while five engaged in converting the Indians. The convent building was badly damaged by floods in the 19th c. and again in the 1930s.

★Fortified convent

In the 16th c. great importance was generally attached to the design of the entrance façade, reflected here at Acolman by its pure Plateresque style. The finely decorated arch is flanked on either side by twin classical Italian Renaissance pilasters between which are statues of saints under splendidly ornate baldachins. This type of arrangement is almost unknown elsewhere in Mexico. Above the cornice are three niches embellished with sculptures while, higher still, the choir window, similar in style to the portal, displays the richly decorated Augustinian arms on its gable. To the left of the window can be seen the royal arms of Castile and Léon and to the right those of Acolman. A simple bell tower (espadaña) crowns the crenellated façade. A plain arched balcony on the right of the main façade forms an open pulpit the inside of which is ornamented with frescos.

Arch

The fortified Convent of Acolman

Interior, cloisters, posas

The nave of the church measures 57×12.5m/187×41ft. Only one of the altars dates from the period of the convent's foundation, the others having been added in the 17th and 18th centuries. Frescos in grey, black and ochre, painted in about 1600, decorate the end of the nave and also the cloisters. The design of the cloisters suggests the work of more than one architect. Integrated into the church is a typical Mexican "open chapel" (atrium), built to accommodate the vast numbers of baptised Indians. The processional chapels (*posas*) bore the brunt of the flooding, though one has now been restored.

Stone cross

Outside the present atrium stands a superb carved stone cross with, in the centre, the face of the suffering Christ. The arms and upright bear the symbols of the Stations of the Cross as well as floral ornamentation. Many of the details, such as the skull at the foot of the cross, are executed with remarkable simplicity.

Convent museum

The convent has a small museum.

Surroundings

Tepexpan

In 1949 a human skeleton estimated to be 11,000 years old was found at Tepexpan, 4km/2½ miles south-west of Acolman. Among the exhibits in the small museum is a mammoth dating from the same period, together with stone implements likewise unearthed during excavations near by.

The fascinating ruined city of Teotihuacán (see entry) is another 10km/6 miles from Acolman.

Actopan K 7

State: Hidalgo (Hgo.)
Altitude: 2050m/6728ft. Population: 52,000

Access

By car on the MEX 85 from Mexico City, then via Pachuca (MEX 45; 92km/57 miles), about 130km/80 miles in all.

Location

The small Otomí Indian town of Actopan lies north of Mexico City. Its convent is a supreme example of the fortified ecclesiastical architecture typical of 16th c. New Spain.

History

The convent, an Augustinian foundation, was established in the village of Actopan (Náhuatl: "place of fertile land") in 1548. It was designed by a self-taught architect Pater Andrés de Mata and built with the assistance of Juan Mica Actopan and Pedro Izcuitloapilco, the local Indian chief. The church was dedicated to San Nicolás Tolentino.

★Fortified convent

Convent church

The beautiful Renaissance façade with its Plateresque elements is rendered all the more special by the originality with which the decoration around the inner portal is repeated on a larger scale on the outside. Adorning the façade on either hand are a pair of Corinthian columns, the smaller being surmounted by a scalloped fan with ornamental panels and the outer supporting a cornice with decorative frieze, above which is the window of the choir. In addition to the crenellations, stylised sentry-boxes serve further to enhance the fortress-like appearance of the building. The massive square tower shows Moorish influence.

The nave, its Gothic vaulting rising to more than 24m/78ft in height, terminates in an angular apse. The interior furnishings are now predominantly Neo-Classical having undergone alteration several times.

Font

The sacristy contains a particularly fine font and a statue of St John the Baptist.

★Bóveda de Actopan (Open Chapel)

A fortification wall extending left from the church surrounds the old cemetery, at the end of which stands the Bóveda de Actopan ("Actopan Vault") or Open Chapel. It comprises a large, boldly curved arch, and walls covered with mosaic decoration (those on the sides illustrating various biblical and historical themes).

Convent
★★Renaissance frescos

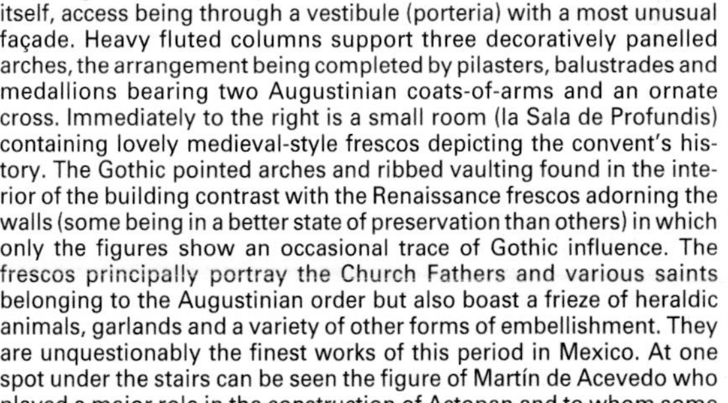

To the right of the church portal can be seen the entrance to the convent itself, access being through a vestibule (porteria) with a most unusual façade. Heavy fluted columns support three decoratively panelled arches, the arrangement being completed by pilasters, balustrades and medallions bearing two Augustinian coats-of-arms and an ornate cross. Immediately to the right is a small room (la Sala de Profundis) containing lovely medieval-style frescos depicting the convent's history. The Gothic pointed arches and ribbed vaulting found in the interior of the building contrast with the Renaissance frescos adorning the walls (some being in a better state of preservation than others) in which only the figures show an occasional trace of Gothic influence. The frescos principally portray the Church Fathers and various saints belonging to the Augustinian order but also boast a frieze of heraldic animals, garlands and a variety of other forms of embellishment. They are unquestionably the finest works of this period in Mexico. At one spot under the stairs can be seen the figure of Martín de Acevedo who played a major role in the construction of Actopan and to whom some of the frescos are attributed. He is pictured in the company of two Indian noblemen. Also noteworthy are the design and furnishings of the refectory, especially the frescos on the barrel vaulting, and the polygonal pulpit.

A small building near the convent has been turned into an Otomí folk museum. Items of religious interest are also exhibited from time to time in the former parochial office. The vast atrium, which once measured 290×180m/950×590ft but now lies almost entirely in ruins, is reputed to have held as many as 40,000 to 50,000 worshippers at a time.

Surroundings

Ixmiquilpan

Ixmiquilpan (1750m/5743ft; population: 35,000; market day: Monday), about 45km/28 miles north-west of Actopan, was the Otomí Indian capital in pre-Columbian times. It has an interesting Augustinian convent dating from between 1550 and 1554, built, like the convent at Actopán, by Pater Andrés de Mata. The church, dedicated to San Miguel Arcángel (the Archangel Michael), has a lovely façade in the Plateresque variant of the Renaissance style, with Corinthian columns and a panel-embellished border around the arch. Some unusual frescos, presumed to be by an Indian artist, were discovered in the church and convent building in 1960. They depict scenes of battle between Indian warriors and figures from Classical mythology. Also worth seeing are the church of El Carmen, which has a Churrigueresqui façade and Baroque retablo, and two bridges dating from the colonial period. Local handicrafts include miniature musical instruments, decorated mirrors and combs and embroidered blouses and bags.

Thermal baths

There are several thermal baths in the near vicinity, including one at Tzindijeh, 2km/1¼ miles from Tasquillo.

Barranca de Tonaltongo

Barranca de Tonaltongo, a picturesque gorge with attractive waterfalls and rich subtropical vegetation, is located some 45km/28 miles to the north-east.

Zimapán

About 40km/25 miles along the MEX 85 to the north-west of Ixmiquilpan lies the old mining town of Zimapán (1950m/6400ft; population: 8000; fiestas: June 24th, San Juan Bautista; market days: Saturday and Sunday). It has an interesting 17th c. parish church with Baroque façade and Neo-Classical retablo.

After Zimapán, MEX 85 continues northwards through delightful mountain scenery to Tamazunchale (see Tampico, Surroundings).

Aguascalientes (State)

Abbreviation: Ags.
Capital: Aguascalientes
Area: 5486sq.km/2117sq. miles
Official population 1990: 719,200 (1994 estimate: 900,000)

Location and topography

Aguascalientes, bordered to the north, west and east by Zacatecas and to the south by Jalisco, is one of Mexico's smallest states. Averaging 1800m/5900ft above sea level it forms part of the central Mexican highlands, hugging in the west the foothills of the Sierra Madre. Its

Mexico
United Mexican States
Estados Unidos Mexicanos

Aguascalientes

numerous small rivers and one large one make it an unusually fertile region by Mexican standards. Almost all the population are of Spanish descent.

History

In pre-Columbian times Aguascalientes was the territory of the semi-nomadic Chichimecs (a disparaging name meaning "descended from dogs", used by more civilised tribes to refer to hunter-gatherers generally, rather than to any particular group or race). From the 8th c. onwards these relatively primitive peoples, whose languages were of the Náhuatl family, made repeated incursions into the central Mexican highlands. Chichimec raids were certainly responsible for the destruction in 1168 of the Toltec capital Tollan (see Tula), and the Aztecs, who first made their appearance in the 13th c., were originally of Chichimec extraction. Although most invasions ended in absorbtion into the already established cultures, the area which is now Aguascalientes remained largely uninfluenced by the principal centres of civilisation in the Mexican highlands or La Quemada.

The first Spaniard to arrive in the region was Pedro de Alvarado, one of Hernán Cortés' henchmen, in 1522. It took several decades for the conquest to be completed and the Indians either killed or driven into the mountains – as a result of which the Spanish had to establish their colonies and build their cities without the assistance of forced labour. During the colonial period the inhabitants, especially the people of the capital, were exceptionally active politically and culturally, hence later playing a leading role in the War of Independence (1810–21). Until 1789 Aguascalientes was part of the province of Nueva Galicia, afterwards being annexed to Zacatecas and only becoming a state of the Mexican Republic in its own right in 1857. Situated as it was in the very heart of the country, during the Mexican Revolution (1910–20) Aguascalientes was the scene of a bitter struggle between the opposing sides.

Economy

In the fertile valleys the main crops apart from cereals are maize, fruit – including grapes for wine – and vegetables. Livestock is farmed extensively on the plateau (including the breeding of horses and fighting bulls). There are numerous mines producing gold, silver, copper, lead and antimony. Textiles, leather and ceramics, tobacco refining and brandy distilling provide other sources of income. Tourists are attracted to Aguascalientes mainly by the much-acclaimed thermal baths and the capital's annual spring festival (Feria de San Marcos).

Aguascalientes (Town) H 7

State: Aguascalientes (Ags.)
Altitude: 1889m/6700ft
Population: 520,000
Telephone code: 91 49

Access from Mexico City

By rail a journey of about 14 hours; by bus about 9 hours; by car on the MEX 57 as far as Querétaro, then MEX 45 via Salamanca.

Location

This most agreeable of colonial cities located at the heart of Mexico is very Spanish in atmosphere. The climate is exceptionally pleasant and Aguascalientes lies surrounded by orchards, vineyards, and haciendas where fighting bulls are reared. Renowned for its pottery, embroideries and woven goods, it has also long been famous for its Feria de San Marcos, the colourful spring festival which has inspired many a folk song.

History

It took the invading Spaniards until 1575, and then only at the end of a hard-fought campaign against the semi-nomadic native population, before they were able to establish a town here, bestowing on it the melodious-sounding name of Nuestra Señora de la Asunción de las Aguas Calientes (the latter part, meaning "warm waters", reflecting the numerous thermal springs near by). For a long time it was little more than an outpost against hostile Indian tribes. When in 1857 a state of the Republic was created under the same name, Aguascalientes became the capital. As a major rail junction it was hotly contested during the years of revolution (1910–20), passing repeatedly from one side to the other.

Sights

"La Ciudad Perforada"

Aguascalientes is also known as La Ciudad Perforada – "the perforated city" – on account of the labyrinth of passages extending beneath it. These catacombs, carved from the rock by pre-colonial Indians of unknown origin, are not at present open to the public.

Thermal springs

It is for its thermal springs, found both in the city and the countryside around, that Aguascalientes is best known and most valued however. The healing qualities of the springs attract many Mexican and foreign visitors.

Palacio de Gobierno

Gracing the city's main square (Zócalo or Plaza Principal) are the 17th c. Palacio Municipal (town hall) and the 18th c. Palacio de Gobierno (government building), formerly the Palais des Marqués de Guadalupe. The inner courtyard of the superb Baroque palace is decorated with murals by Rivera's pupil Osvaldo Barra depicting the agriculture and industry of Aguascalientes State.

Instituto Cultural

In the Instituto Cultural, Zaragoza 505, can be seen pictures by Saturnino Herrán (1887–1918) and Gabriel Fernández Ledesma (1900–83), both born in the state.

Aguascalientes: the Cathedral

Churches

As well as the 18th c. cathedral the city has a number of other important ecclesiastical buildings. These include the church of San Marcos, in which can be seen a painting "The Adoration of the Magi" by José Alzíbar, the church of El Encino, endowed with a black Christ and pictures by Andrés Lopés, the church of San Antonio, built this century in the Neo-Byzantine-style, and the Convento de San Diego where there are a number of very interesting paintings.

Museums

Opposite San Antonio stands the Museo de la Ciudad (City Museum) housing a fine art collection. The Museo Posada in the Jardín del Encino (attached to the church of that name) comprises an exhibition of prints and drawings by Juan Guadalupe Posada (1852–1913). A native of Aguascalientes, he became famous for his socio-political caricatures. Other drawings by the same artist explore the topic of death, again through the medium of caricature. Among items of interest in the Instituto Cultural (Zaragoza 45) are pictures by Saturnino Herrán (1887–1918) and Gabriel Fernández Ledesma (1900–83), both of whom were from Aguascalientes (state).

Feria de San Marcos

The major tourist attraction of Aguascalientes is the Feria de San Marcos which has been celebrated every April and May since 1604. Held in honour of the city's patron saint, the festival features bull and cock fighting, charreadas, serenades, firework displays and a great deal more.

A visit to a nearby hacienda where fighting bulls are reared can be strongly recommended to any aficionados.

Akumal Q 7

State: Quintana Roo (Q.R.)
Altitude: sea level

Access

By bus or car: 106km/67 miles from Cancún city centre (see entry) via the MEX 307; 36km/22 miles from Playa del Carmen; 25km/15½ miles from Tulum (see entry).

Akumal

Location

★Bathing

Akumal, a small settlement with a hotel complex and club lies on a crescent-shaped bay with a snowy-white, palmed-fringed beach 15km/9 miles long. Akumal is one of the most attractive, and by European standards one of the best developed, places for bathing on the east coast of the Yucatán peninsula.

History

Akumal, originally a small Maya settlement (the name being Maya for turtle) only really became known about 25 years ago when CEDAM, a marine archaeology research and conservation organisation commenced activities there, later making the bay its headquarters. Since then, in the course of its many expeditions, CEDAM has uncovered several Mayan sites both above and below water and has raised a number of old Spanish wrecks. In conjunction with the US National Geographic Society and the Instituto Nacional de Arqueología e Historia (INAH), CEDAM has also carried out exploratory dives in the Sacred Cenote at Chichén Itzá.

What to do and see

Akumal provides plenty of opportunity for watersports, fishing and excursions. In addition, not far off the beach it is possible to look down through the clear, relatively shallow water and spot wreckage (cannon, anchors, chests, etc.) some of which dates from the 16th and 17th centuries. The little museum housing finds brought up from the seabed has now been moved to Xel-há (see entry).

Surroundings

Numerous Mayan ruins, water holes (cenotes) and tranquil little bays are found along the coast north and south of the resort. The geology of the Yucatán peninsula is such that most of the cenotes and lagoons in the otherwise almost dry limestone plateau have subterranean links with the sea. In the little bays and the lagoons situated close to the shoreline, freshwater and seawater meet, giving rise not only to a "mixed" underwater fauna but also to a unique visual effect which can be observed by anyone snorkelling or diving. Small fissures occur even in the seabed, from which freshwater flowing through underground channels spews out into the ocean.

Yal-ku lagoon

About 2km/1¼ miles north of Akumal lies the pretty Yal-ku lagoon (Maya: "son of the god"), excellent for swimming and snorkelling.

Chakalal lagoon

Another 12km/7½ miles to the north, a track on the right leads off the MEX 307 to the attractively situated Chakalal lagoon and to an interesting Mayan temple. About 5km/3 miles further on along MEX 307 there is a second turn off, leading to the beach and the Mayan ruins of Pamuul (as yet largely undisturbed).

★Xcaret

11km/7 miles further on still, an unsurfaced road branches off to Xcaret. Developed as an "eco-archaeological park" this has become a popular tourist spot. Its attractions include swimming in underground rivers and cenotes, or in the bay, a superb aquarium, dolphin shows, as well as "Xcaret by Night" entertainment. Several partially exposed Mayan temples are also found in the vicinity. Some 18km/11 miles south of Xcaret is the new development of Puerto Aventuras, with hotels, villas, golf and an attractive deep-water marina which can accommodate large luxury yachts.

Another 6km/3¾ miles north lies the little harbour town of Playa del Carmen (see Cancún).

Alamos

See Guaymas

Amecameca de Juárez K 8

State: México (Mex.)
Altitude: 2468m/8099ft
Population: 50,000

Access from Mexico City

By rail about 2½ hours journey time; by bus approximately 1½ to 2 hours; by car on the MEX 190 to the Chalco exit, then on MEX 110 (60km/37 miles in all).

from Cuautla

From Cuautla: via the MEX 115 (44km/27 miles).

Location

The small town of Amecameca is situated south-east of Mexico City at the foot of the twin snow-clad volcanoes of Popocatépetl and Iztaccíhuatl (see Popocatépetl/Iztaccíhuatl). Its dramatic location in a barren but impressive mountain landscape, and the presence of some interesting examples of colonial art and architecture, make Amecameca an excellent base for sightseeing excursions and mountain walking.

History

In the Late Classic period, Amecameca (Náhuatl: "many water holes") was second only to Chalco in what was a powerful league of city-states. The Aztecs conquered Amecameca in 1464, enabling them finally to defeat their arch adversaries the Chalca one year later.

The Spaniards under Hernán Cortés passed by the town in 1519 en route to Tenochtitlán. The area was missionised very early on by the Franciscans.

Sights

Sacromonte

On Ash Wednesday, at the same time as a bustling, atmospheric market is held at its foot, huge numbers of pilgrims and tourists make the journey to Sacromonte ("Holy Mountain") rising 150m/492ft above the town. A Way of the Cross marked out by brightly tiled stations ascends the hill to a little church containing a picture of Christ to which miraculous powers are attributed. The tiny shrine was erected in honour of Martín de Valencia, a cave-dwelling recluse who was among the first Franciscan patres in New Spain. Above it, on what was previously the Indian cult site of Teteoinán, stands another chapel, dedicated to the Virgin of Guadalupe.

View

The hill offers a superb panorama over the Valley of Mexico and the mountains around, a scene dominated by the snow-covered Popocatépetl and Iztaccíhuatl.

Dominican monastery

The convent church on Amecameca's main square has a fine Baroque altar. In the 16th c. Dominican monastery itself there is a well preserved cloister.

Surroundings

Tlalmanalco

Situated 10km/6¼ miles north-west is the small town of Tlalmanalco (Náhuatl: "on the plain"; population: 25,000) which boasts a Franciscan friary built in 1525. In the cloister, reached through the vestibule, sections of fresco still survive. Behind its fine Renaissance façade the late 16th c. church of San Luis Obispo contains a beautiful Baroque altar and some paintings. The Open Chapel, built between 1559 and 1564 but only partly preserved, is rather special. With its very ornate pillars and arches it is one of the loveliest examples of the Spanish-Plateresque style to have been executed by Indian craftsmen.

★ Open Chapel

Chalco

Tlalmanalco is no more than 12km/7½ miles from Chalco (Náhuatl: "many months"; 2270m/7450ft; population: 50,000), once the capital of a powerful Nahua tribe which for more than a century vied for supremacy in the Valley of Mexico with the cities of Atzcapotzalco and Tenochtitlán. It was because of this ancient feud that the Chalcas chose to assist the Spanish in subjugating the Tenochtitlán Mexica during the Conquest.

A network of canals links the town with the "floating gardens" of Xochimilco (see Mexico City). Chalco's only building of historical interest is a 16th c. Franciscan friary; the façade of the monastery church was altered in the Baroque style during the 18th c.

Tlapacoya

About 10km/6¼ miles north-west of Chalco, near the village Ayotla, lies the Tlapacoya archaeological site, investigation of which has thrown new light on early pre-Columbian history. A six-storey pyramid, probably constructed between the 6th and 4th c. B.C., and numerous graves with figurines dating back to 1200 B.C., indicate an early Olmec culture. Other remains found here have been scientifically dated to about 23000 B.C., the earliest evidence yet of human presence in Mexico.

Heading south from Amecameca, a turn off after 2km/1¼ miles goes to Paso de Cortés and Tlamacas, as well as to La Joya at the foot of the Popocatépetl-Iztaccíhuatl massif.

Ozumba de Aizate

Continuing along the MEX 115 for 10km/6¼ miles in the direction of Cuautla, the small town of Ozumba de Aizate (population: 20,000) is reached. The 16th c. Franciscan friary is adorned with interesting frescos depicting Hernán Cortés receiving the first group of twelve Franciscan monks to arrive in New Spain (in 1524). The monastery church of Concepción Immaculata, with its Baroque altar and Open Chapel, underwent some rebuilding in the 18th c. Located near Ozumba de Aizate are the Salto de Chimal waterfall and the little town of Chimalhuacán with its lovely gardens.

Atotonilco

See Miguel Allende

Atotonilco el Grande

See Pachuca

Baja California / Lower California A–D 1–6

Baja California Norte (State)

Abbrevation: B.C.
Capital: Mexicali
Area: 71,627sq.km/27,650sq. miles
Official population 1990: 1,661,000 (1994 estimate: 2,600,000)

Baja California Sur (State)

Abbreviation: B.C.S.
Capital: La Paz
Area: 72,465sq.km/27,970sq. miles
Official population 1990: 317,800 (1994 estimate: 600,000)

Access

By air from Mexico City and other Mexican airports to Tijuana, La Paz, Mexicali and Los Cabos (see entries); by ferry see Practical Information, Ferries; by rail Mexico City to Mexicali (journey time approximately 60 hours); by bus from Mexico City (about 44 hours). From the USA by air, coach (Greyhound) and car.

Location and topography

The 1250km/776 mile-long, 90km/50½ mile-wide Baja California (Lower California) peninsula, comprising two States, is bounded to the north by California USA, to the west by the Pacific Ocean and to the east by the Gulf of California, the border between Baja California Norte and Baja California Sur being the 28th parallel. The peninsula is a hot, arid region with mountain ranges and a deeply indented coastline.

The principal mountain chain, the Sierra de San Pedro Mártir, runs north–south, reaching 3080m/10,108ft at its highest point, the Cerro de la Encantada. The Río Colorado, flowing into the north-west corner of the Gulf of California, divides Baja California Norte from Sonora State. Completion of the Carretera Transpeninsular in 1974 opened up Baja California by providing a direct road link between the north and the south. As a result, with the exception of a few mission stations, little that could be called typically Mexican now survives. Proximity to the USA, and the consequent influx of North American tourists, has meant that the towns and villages in particular have become largely Americanised. The attraction for the tourist lies more in the desert flora (cacti), the impressive silhouettes of the bare, mountainous regions,

An idyllic bay in Baja California

and the seemingly endless coastline with its alternating sandy beaches, rocks and lagoons. One or two crowded tourist centres apart, Baja California comprises a generally barren and empty landscape.

The indigenous Indians, the Cucapá, Kiliwa, Paipai, Cochimí and Ki-nai, are today reduced in number to no more than 1000.

Fauna

Baja California has an extremely varied wildlife. Puma, coyote, fox, red deer, hare, wild duck, wild geese and many varieties of sea bird inhabit the peninsula, while grey whales (whale-watching in the bay of San Ignacio December to February), sealions, seals, swordfish, dolphins, barracuda and tuna flourish in the waters around the coast.

Archaeological sites

There is little of archaeological interest in Baja California apart from a few rock paintings such as those at San Borjita, San Ignacio and Calimalí. One or two archaeological finds have also been made in caves in Caguama, Metate Comondú and on the Isla de Cedros.

History

Archaeologists have found traces of pre-Columbian settlements dating back to about 7500 B.C. Almost nothing is known however about the relatively unsophisticated culture of the early Indian tribes who lived on the peninsula.

In 1535 Hernán Cortés landed in the vicinity of La Paz, searching for the Amazon paradise of legend, ruled by the black queen Calafia. The Spaniards who followed after him met with strong resistance from the Indians and were unable to gain a foothold. Disillusioned, they christened the area "California" after the queen they had failed to find. It was only later, with the arrival in 1697 of the Jesuit missionaries Francisco Eusebio Kino, Juan María de Salvatierra and Juan de Ugarte, that a part of the region was successfully colonised. After the expulsion of the Jesuits in 1767, Franciscan friars assumed the missionary role before they in turn were replaced in 1772 by the Dominicans. In 1804 Lower

California was separated from California. In 1847–48, while at war with the USA, the peninsula was occupied by American troops. The division of the region into northern and southern territories took place in 1931. Baja California Norte and Baja California Sur became fully-fledged states in 1952 and 1974 respectively.

Economy

In addition to a sizeable tourist industry, which in recent years has expanded considerably as a result of extensive developments taking place at the southern tip of the peninsula, the cultivation of fruit, cotton, maize, wheat, alfalfa and vegetables figures large in the economy of those areas with artificial irrigation. Important industries include the processing of agrarian and fish products, as well as gold, copper, iron, silver and salt mining. Although fishing is capable of providing a good source of income, Mexico presently lacks both a sufficiently large fleet and the facilities for processing the catch.

Places to visit

Tijuana (see entry) apart, Tecate, Mexicalí and San Felipe, all of which lie off the Carretera Transpeninsular, are among the more interesting places to visit in Baja California Norte (for all three, see Tijuana).

The Carretera Transpeninsular from Tijuana to Cabo San Lucas

The MEX 1 (la Carretera Transpeninsular), running for 1700km/1056 miles along the whole length of the peninsula, starts on its way south from Baja California's biggest city, Tijuana (see entry) on the US border.

Ensenada

After El Rosarito, 30km/18½ miles to the south, the next town of any interest is Ensenada (another 80km/50 miles; population: 260,000). This popular tourist resort (watersports, deep-sea fishing) extends along the beautiful bay of Todos los Santos, discovered by the Portuguese navigator Rodríguez Cabrillo in 1542. Following the division of the peninsula into northern and southern territories, Ensenada was capital of the North from 1888 until 1910, when Mexicali took its place. After tourism the city lives primarily from fishing and its deep-water harbour. It is also the home of Mexico's biggest winery, the "Bodegas Santo Tomás".

"La Bufadora"

16km/10 miles south of Ensenada, near Maneadera, take the road which branches off north-west to the headland of Cabo Punta la Banda (22km/13½ miles) where "La Bufadora" (from "bufar" = to snort) provides a natural spectacle not uncommon on the Pacific coast. Seawater, gushing with enormous force through a blow-hole in the rocks, emits a great roar as it is hurled up to 20m/66ft into the air.

Returning to the highway, continue for approximately 175km/109 miles to San Quintín. Places of interest along the way include several old mission stations such as Santo Tomás, San Vicente and Vicente Guerrero as well as the Cochimí

San Quintín

Indian settlements of La Huerta and San Miguel. San Quintín itself, a farming and fishing community set in a fertile valley on the shores of a shallow Pacific bay (Bahia de San Quintín), has some superb white sandy beaches.

The road proceeds south to El Rosario where it leaves the coast and heads inland. In addition to El Rosario several other mission stations lie along this particular stretch, among them being San Fernando, San Augustín and Cataviña, the latter located in magnificent rocky surroundings.

The Force of Nature: roaring spray in Baja California

Bahía de los Ángeles

Next the route runs through Laguna Chapala and then on for another 50km/31 miles to where a turn off on the left leads east to the beautiful Bahía de los Ángeles (angling).

State border

Return to the MEX 1 and continue south via Rosarito. Shortly before Guerrero Negro a 40m/130ft-high steel eagle (Monumento Aguila) marks the 28th parallel, the border between Baja California Norte and Baja California Sur as well as the boundary between two time zones – the Hora del Pacífico in the north and Hora de las Montanas (+ 1 hour) in the south. Near Guerrero Negro are some of the most extensive salt deposits in the world, formed by evaporation.

★★Grey whales

Every year from the end of December to March, the quiet waters of the lagoons in the Bahía Sebastián Vizcaíno (Laguna Scammon, Laguna Ojo de Liebre) and the more accessible Laguna San Ignacio to the south of the Sierro Vizcaíno, are the scene of a unique spectacle when schools of grey whales (Spanish: "ballena gris") arrive to mate and to give birth to their young. The whales can be observed from a number of points in or near Guerrero Negro. About 3km/2 miles south of the town a road marked with grey whale signs branches off to the Parque Natural de la Ballena Gris (National Park. N.B. Opportunities for whale-watching from boats are nowadays rather severely restricted).

In autumn the grey whales (*eschrichtius gibbosus*), weighing up to 25 tonnes and between 10 and 15m/33 and 49ft in length, begin their long journey south from the Arctic waters of the Bering Sea. With a gestation period of thirteen months, pregnant grey whales give birth at the same time as others are congregating together to mate. The act of mating involves two males and one female, the dominant male of the pair coupling with the female, the other helping her to maintain a suitable position. Having been all but exterminated by commercial whaling, the grey whale was made a protected species in 1947.

San Ignacio

★Jesuit church

From Guerrero Negro the road heads inland, continuing for about 126km/78 miles to the pretty town of San Ignacio. In the Jesuit church, begun in 1728 and completed in 1786 by Juan Crisóstomo Gómez, the town possesses one of the best preserved colonial churches in Baja California. For anyone with an interest in cave paintings the excursion from San Ignacio to the Cueva de la Cuesta del Palmerito, three to four hours distant, can be highly recommended. Expert guides explain about the large paintings of people and animals the origin and age of which have yet to be investigated. There are other caves in the area but anyone thinking of visiting them will need to have not only a guide but several days available and the appropriate clothing and equipment.

Driving towards the coast the still active volcano of Las Tres Virgenes (2180m/7154ft) can be seen on the left.

Santa Rosalía

Some 74km/46 miles beyond San Ignacio lies the small port of Santa Rosalía (population: 25,000), founded only in the mid 19th c. The church of Santa Rosalía, built by a French company which used to own the local copper mines, was constructed from imported pre-fabricated galvanised sections designed, it seems, by Gustave Eiffel (of Eiffel Tower fame). Also worth seeing here are the anthropological museum in the Casa de Cultura and, on the northern exit from the town, a mining museum with an old train used for transporting ore. Santa Rosalía is linked by ferry with Guaymas (Son.).

San Borjita caves

Leaving Santa Rosalía, drive south for another 40km/25 miles before turning off to the right for the Hacienda Baltasar. From here follow the track which makes its way across country for some 22km/13½ miles to the large San Borjita cave, its walls painted with colourful hunting and battle scenes. (The trip should only be attempted with a 4-wheel drive vehicle and the last 2 to 3km/1 to 2 miles have to be covered on foot.) A number of other caves, with similar though somewhat less impressive paintings, are found in the surrounding area (e.g. La Trinidad, San José de los Arce, El Coyote and La Esperanza).

Mulegé

The next reasonably sized community on the MEX 1 is the small Gulf of California town of Mulegé (population: 15,000). Its Jesuit mission, Santa Rosalía de Mulegé (1705), is a replica of the famous prison at Cananea (Son.), immortalised in folk song and ballad as the prison without bars (or locked doors). A pleasant walk leads through the date palm groves alongside the river. There are several beaches at Mulegé and the fishing is good.

★ Bahía Concepción

Against a backcloth of delightful coastal scenery, the Bahía Concepción, 10km/6 miles beyond Mulegé, has several exceptionally attractive beaches including Punta Arena, Santiapac, El Coyote, El Requesón and Los Muertos.

Loreto

From Mulegé the road makes its way for another 135km/84 miles to picturesque Loreto (population: 30,000; fiesta: September 8th, Día de Nuestra Señora de Loreto), founded by the Jesuits in 1697 – when the now restored mission church was built. This makes Loreto the oldest Spanish settlement on the peninsula, the foothold from which Lower California was first explored and converted to Christianity (aspects of its history which are well documented in the mission museum). Between 1776 and 1830 the town was also the capital of Lower California. Today this Gulf of California resort makes a particularly good base for trips to the offshore islands and for deep-sea fishing and diving.

San Francisco Javier

With a 4-wheel drive vehicle available it is possible to make a detour from Loreto over the 40km/25 miles of generally bad roads to San

Cave-painting in San Borjita

San Francisco Javier

Francisco Javier, to see the well preserved mission church there. Dedicated to San Francisco Javier, it was built in the first half of the 18th c. and has a lovely Baroque façade and gilded high altar.

Set amid superb natural scenery 26km/16 miles south of Loreto lies the expanding new seaside resort of Puerto Escondido.

About 40km/25 miles beyond Loreto the road turns inland once more, crossing the sierras to the small town of Villa Insurgentes (80km/50 miles). From here another road branches off to Puerto A. López Mateos, on the shores of the large Bahía de Magdalena on the Pacific coast. As at Sebastián Vizcaíno, many grey whales winter in the bay, mating and giving birth to their young. The small harbour town of Puerto San Carlos further south, best reached by the road west from Ciudad Constitución (55km/34 miles), is also conveniently placed for whale-watching by boat. Large numbers of sealions live on the Isla de Santa Margarita on the west side of the bay.

Rejoin the Carretera Transpeninsular at Ciudad Constitutión for the 210km/130 mile drive to La Paz (see entry).

From La Paz the MEX 1 runs via San Pedro and the old mining town of El Triunfo to the fishing village and seaside resort of Los Barriles (104km/65 miles), 6km/4 miles beyond which lies Buenavista, popular particularly with yachtsmen and anglers. Forking right off the MEX 1 about 26km/16 miles south of La Paz leads alternatively to Todos Santos and Cabo San Lucas (see entry).

San José del Cabo

From Buenavista the route continues via Miraflores, a former Pericúe Indian settlement now famous for its leather-work, to San José del Cabo (75km/47 miles; population: 40,000; fiesta: March 19th, Día de San José). This old, former fishing village and mission has today become an important agricultural centre for the region as well as a centre for the sizeable holiday area extending north as far as Buenavista and served by the new Los Cabos international airport. There are several good beaches along this stretch of coast – some of them exposed, with big surf – and some good fishing. The Casa de Cultura has a small museum and library. South of San José del Cabo there are a number of good places for surfing.

35km/22 miles or so further on, the most southerly point of the Carretera Transpeninsular is reached at Cabo San Lucas (see entry).

Barranca del Cobre — D/E 3/4

State: Chihuahua (Chih.)

Access

By car: from Chihuahua (city, see entry) to Cuauhtémoc (104km/65 miles), then on asphalted roads via La Junta (152km/94 miles) to Creel.

By rail: from Chihuahua to Los Mochis or vice versa (653km/406 miles). It is also possible to fly in by light aircraft.

The scenic splendours of the Tarahumara canyons can be explored by car, horse, mule or on foot, using one of the little towns along the railway line such as Creel or Divisadero, as a base. The approximately thirteen-hour train ride from Chihuahua to Los Mochis aboard the "Ferrocarril de Chihuahua al Pacífico" is a quite unforgettable experience. The journey can be broken to allow for excursions and stopovers of various durations.

★★Location

The Barranca del Cobre (Copper Canyon) comprises a dozen or so large gorges in the Sierra Madre Occidental in north-west Mexico. This rugged and deeply fissured mountain range is also called the Sierra Tarahumara after the area's indigenous Indian inhabitants.

History

In pre-Columbian times the Sierra was populated by semi-nomadic Indians who can be regarded as the ancestors of the present-day Tarahumaras. Stone built remains and huge storage containers dating back as far as 1000 B.C. have been found in the region's caves. Early in the 17th c. Jesuit missionaries discovered the area while prospecting for copper, christening it Barranca del Cobre (Copper Canyon). The Tarahumara Indians occupied this rugged, impassable terrain only after being driven off the high plateaux by the introduction of large-scale land ownership. The Spanish found silver, gold, opals and other minerals in the gorges. Although plans for a railway linking Texas (USA) and northern Mexico with the Pacific were drawn up as early as 1903, the exceptionally ambitious project, involving the construction of this particular stretch of track, was only completed between 1953 and 1961.

★★By rail from Chihuahua to Los Mochis

Tickets for the journey can only be purchased in the morning and reservations should be made in plenty of time. Notice is required of any intended breaks or stopovers. Much the best option is to take the "Vista Tren", equipped with especially large windows to allow maximum enjoyment of the scenery. Leaving Chihuahua at 7am it arrives in Divisadero at about 1.40pm and in Los Mochis at about 8.45pm. The ordinary 2nd class train leaves at 6am and takes four to five hours longer. The "Autovia" (car train) goes only as far as Creel, departing at 8.25am and arriving at 1.25pm. Travellers should be warned that lengthy delays can sometimes occur.

Reservations:
Ferrocarril de Chihuahua al Pacífico,
AP 46, Mendez 24a,
Chihuahua (Chih.),
México 31030,
Tel: (91 14) 12 22 24

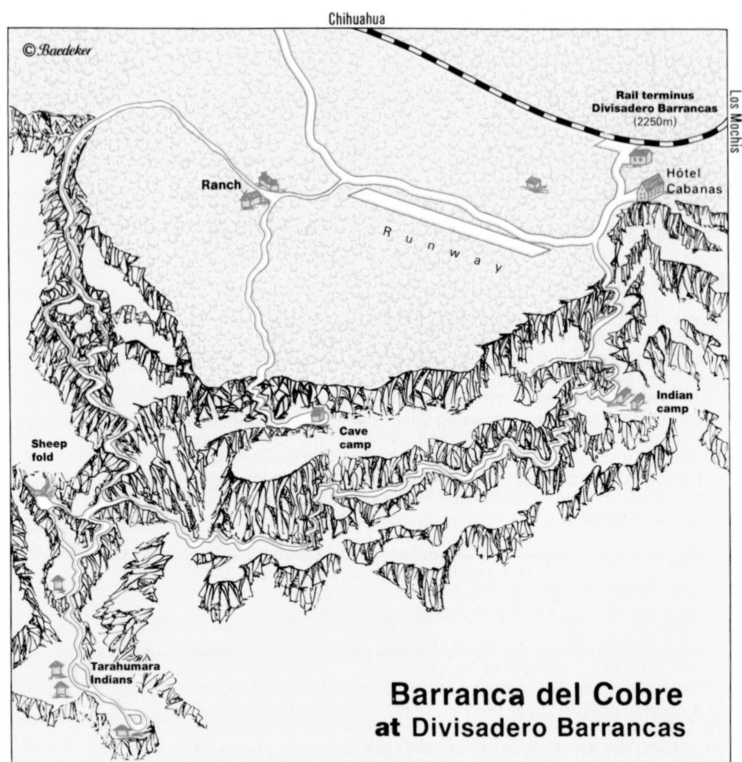

N.B.

If the train does happen to run late, darkness may fall prior to reaching some of the most interesting stretches of scenery, e.g. between Creel and Los Mochis. The journey can also be made the other way. As an alternative a round trip can be made from Chihuahua to Creel and back by car.

The track, climbing to a height of almost 2500m/8200ft above sea level, passes through 86 tunnels and crosses 39 bridges, traversing a variety of landscapes from cacti dotted plateaux, coniferous forest-clad hills and mountains and bizarre rock formations and ravines to lushly vegetated slopes, sub-tropical plantations and groves of palm trees and bamboo. The huge cañons between Creel and Los Mochis are anything up to 1200m/3940ft deep and 1500m/4900ft wide, easily rivalling the more famous Grand Canyon in Arizona. While the tops are often bare or conifer covered (snow covered in winter), lush tropical vegetation (citrus fruit and banana trees) festoons the cañon bottoms. The major gorges are Batopilas, Sinforosa, Tararécura, Chinipas, Candameña and Río San Miguel.

Stations

Creel

The little town of Creel (2345m/7700ft; population: 15,000) makes its living from the timber industry. Creel makes a good base for exploring not just the immediate vicinity but further afield as well (though these longer excursions will require extra time). Cuzárare, 21km/13 miles to the south, boasts an interesting 18th c. Jesuit mission church decorated with Indian paintings.

Waterfall

Other attractions near by include Indian cave paintings and a delightful waterfall which can be reached either on foot or by 4-wheel drive vehicle. Worthwhile detours can be made to Basíhuare and Humira (52km/32 miles) and the mining town of La Bufa, as well as to Batopilas and the San Ignacio mission. Rocheáchic, Norogáchic and Guachóchic are among Tarahumara settlements in the area.

★ Basaseáchic waterfalls

Creel also provides an opportunity to visit the magnificent Baseaseáchic falls, the highest in Mexico, plummeting down more than 300m/984ft. They are reached via San Juanito (31km/19 miles), from where an unsurfaced road goes through Yoquivo to the Parque Nacional Cascadas (about 135km/84 miles).

Divisadero

★★ Panorama

At Divisadero (2250m/7384ft) the train stops for quarter of an hour to enable photographs to be taken. Situated on the watershed between the Atlantic and Pacific Oceans it affords particularly spectacular views of the grandiose scenery of the del Cobre, Urique and Tararécura gorges.

Cerocahui

The children from the village of Cerocahui (12km/7½ miles from Bahuichivo railway station; population: 600; courtesy bus for hotel guests) still have lessons in the old Jesuit mission school dating from the late 17th c.

Beyond Bahuichivo the line begins its zigzag descent to the Pacific coast.

Cuzárare Waterfall

Tarahumara Indians

The Barranca del Cobre, extending over 60,000sq.km/23,160sq. miles mainly in Chihuahua State, is the domain of the 50,000 Tarahumara Indians, or Rarámuri ("runners") as they call themselves. They belong to the large Uto-Aztecan group of languages and are most closely related to the Pima (see Hermosillo). Generally speaking little is known about their history apart from the fact that, prior to the Conquest, they were spread over large parts of Chihuahua. Centuries of bitter conflict with Whites and mestizos, continuing even into the 20th c., drove them to take refuge in the inaccessible Sierra Madre Occidental. Here they have to some extent been able to preserve their identity and independence. The first modern European explorer to visit the Barrancas was the Norwegian Carl Lumholtz in about 1900. He began researching into the people and their culture.

In addition to places already mentioned, Bocoyna, Carichic, Guazápares and Guanacevi are also Tarahumara villages. Each community elects a council of three responsible for its administration. In winter many of the Indians move to the shelter of caves in the canyon bottoms. The men, who grow their hair long, wear a white or red headband, a simple poncho and a form of loincloth. The women dress in a sack-like tunic and full woollen skirt secured by a belt.

As well as hunting, the menfolk engage in a little farming and cattle rearing. Craftwork ranges from clay censers, wickerwork, and wooden masks depicting men or animals to handwoven belts and wool blankets.

Religion

Although notionally the vast majority of Tarahumara are Christian, in practice the old Indian religion retains its hold. The Sun and the Moon are the principal deities. Like the Huicholes (see Nayarit) the Tarahumara hold the peyoti cactus sacred, enjoyment of its intoxicating effect

Refuge for the Tarahumara Indians: Barranca del Cobre

being the privilege of elders and medicine men. The souls of the dead are believed to return with the power to transform humans into animals; whenever someone dies a secret ceremony is held to placate their soul. Christian festivals celebrated by the Tarahumara include Holy Week, Corpus Christi, All Saints and Christmas. Their best known tribal dances are the "Moors and Christians", "Matachines" and the Peyote dance. Running races held every year are a major event in the Tarahumara calendar. Individual races can take several days, covering distances of more than 200km/125 miles. The contestants often push a wooden ball ahead of them with their foot.

Bonampak

O 9

State: Chiapas (Chis.)
Altitude: 360m/1180ft

Access

By air taxi from Villahermosa, Palenque, San Cristóbal de las Casas, Tuxtla Gutiérrez (see entries) and Tenosique.

Although a road of sorts covers the approximately 150km/93 miles from Palenque to Bonampak (via Río Chancalá, San Javier, Lacan-há, and Frontera Echeverría), it is often impassable and until improved should not be attempted without a 4-wheel drive vehicle. Day trips are organised from Palenque.

Location

The ruined Mayan city of Bonampak stands surrounded by dense rain forest on a hill near the Río Lacan-há in east Chiapas. Although relatively small and of no great architectural significance, its discovery in 1946 caused a sensation throughout the world on account of the wall paintings found in one of the buildings. These murals constitute an unrivalled source of information and insight into Mayan life and mythology.

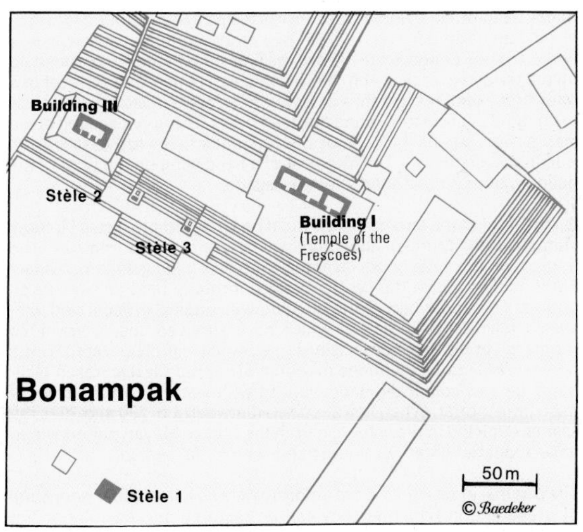

History

The city, christened Bonampak (Mayan: "painted wall") by S. G. Morley, the expert on Mayan culture, belongs to the Classic period of Mayan civilisation (A.D. 300–900) which had its heyday here between A.D. 650 and 800. Although the site has not been fully excavated, the evidence points clearly to Bonampak's having been of only secondary religious and political importance in comparison with the major Mayan centres in the area (Palenque and Yaxchilán in Chiapas and Piedras Negras in Guatemala). In the Bonampak frescos the glyph (character) representing the Yaxchilán emblem appears in association with one of the principal female figures, from which archaeologists conclude that the Bonampak temples were subordinate to those of Yaxchilán. This view was recently reinforced when hieroglyphs were deciphered recording the victory in A.D. 729 of the Yaxchilán ruler "Jaguar Shield" over Ah-chuen of Bonampak. As well as being the most extensive, the murals are, from an artistic point of view, unquestionably the finest in Meso-America. Precisely why they should adorn so relatively unimportant a site as Bonampak will probably never be explained.

The ruins were first discovered in February 1946 by the Americans Charles H. Frey and John Bourne, though the temple with the murals was not found and photographed until three months later by Giles G. Healy. When exposed the frescos were in an outstanding state of preservation, the damp having deposited a protective film of lime over the paint. The Carnegie Institute immediately commissioned Antonio Tejeda to copy them. Following the discovery, Bonampak and its surroundings became the focus of several scientific expeditions while also attracting large numbers of adventure-seeking travellers intrigued by news of the sensational finds.

Visiting the ★ruins

The principal buildings are situated on stone terracing at the foot of a natural mound. In front of the mound is an open rectangular space measuring some 90 × 110m/98 × 120yd, at the centre of which stands Stela 1, about 6m/20ft high and ornately carved with the figure of the ruler Chaan-muan. The stela, reconstructed from its shattered remains, has a date deciphered as A.D. 785. Two other prominent stelae, Nos. 2 and 3, are positioned at the head of the first short flight of steps leading up the terracing. Stela 2 (left) has a particularly finely carved relief of a ruler-figure with two persons of lesser importance in attendance. Note the magnificent costumes and the head-dress. The upper section of the stela carries glyphs. More steps then continue to the top terrace, with Building III on the left. The fragment of a head lying on the floor of the building once embellished a temple façade.

Stela 1

Stela 2

Temple of the Murals

On the right of the terrace stands Building I, the Templo de las Pinturas (Temple of the Murals), now protected by a corrugated iron roof. The lintels over the three doors resemble those of Building 44 in Yaxchilán. Three niches above the central cornice formerly held seated stucco figures. The upper part of the building was originally decorated with stucco reliefs, hardly any of which have survived. Inside are three rooms, all of the same dimensions, their walls entirely covered by the now world-famous paintings executed using the Classic fresco technique i.e. raw colour pigments applied with water on a thick layer of fresh lime mortar. When first executed (between A.D. 790 and 792), the scenes depicted in these murals from the Classic Mayan period would have appeared brightly coloured and sharply delineated.

N.B.

The original in situ frescos are unfortunately now in a rather poor state of preservation (whether they can be restored successfully or not

Bonampak: Relief on Stele 1

Painting in Room 2

remains to be seen). In consequence the rooms are quite often closed to the public. The reproductions in the National Anthropological Museum in Mexico City (see entry) are however excellent and offer visitors a thoroughly worthwhile alternative.

★★ Murals

Room 1

On the left is a scene portraying some kind of ceremony, the participating dignitaries being decked out in white capes and shells (symbols of Earth and the Underworld). The halachuinic ("real man" = ruler of the city-state), identified in this case as Chaan-muan, sits on a slightly raised podium, flanked by two female figures. To one side is a servant, the halachuinic's child in his arms. Three lesser chieftains are also seen, surrounded by numerous attendants. These three chiefs appear again in the centre of the lower section of the mural, this time wearing typical, large, quetzal feather head-dresses.

To their left, in addition to two figures holding sunshades, are a group of musicians whose instruments include drums, trumpets, pipes, rattles and tortoise-shells. Moving among the ranks of musicians are six grotesquely masked characters representing the Crocodile, Crab, Earth, Fertility and Maize gods (the other is yet to be identified). The figures on the right, also holding sunshades, are the audience.

Room 2

The battle scenes, showing bedecked, lance-wielding warriors attacking unclothed, unarmed adversaries, are dated August 2nd A.D. 792. They are thought to depict Bonampak warriors on a surprise raid of the kind commonly carried out in those days with the purpose of capturing prisoners for sacrifice.

Another picture shows the captives being paraded before the halachuinic. Chaan-muan, dressed in jaguar waistcoat and gaiters and adorned with jade and quetzal feathers, stands on a podium surrounded by other chiefs and officials. Seated or lying prone on the ground in front of and below him are the almost naked captives, some with blood dripping from their fingers. A decapitated head rests on a mat of large leaves.

Room 3

These murals record the preparations for a feast. The chief, in the company of three women, is shown in the process of performing a sacrifice, piercing the sacrificial victim's tongue with a sharp thorn. An attendant hands him more thorns while between the two men stands a vessel for collecting the blood. Ten officials, some dressed in white capes, talk animatedly together. Below them are a further nine seated figures who also appear to be in some way involved.

In another scene higher up twelve men are shown carrying a small figure with grotesque features, possibly the Earth god.

Taking up most of the wall area of the room is the final scene portraying dancers and a human sacrifice. Three principal dancers stand on the top two steps of a pyramid, seven more dancers appearing lower down. All are exceptionally finely costumed, their quetzal head-dresses being particularly magnificent. Assistants untie the hands and feet of a naked figure who has apparently already been sacrificed.

To the left of this central scene stand four dignitaries in head-dresses, probably participants in the blood-taking ceremony. A further eight figures appear on the right, some with musical instruments, others carrying sunshades.

Surroundings

Lacandones

The Río Lacan-há countryside in the vicinity of the ruins is home to the only surviving groups of Lacandón Maya (Yucatecan Maya: "Ah acantun" = "those who erect the stones") who, until recently, were the last descendants of the Maya to remain largely untouched by civilisation. Historians can only speculate about their origins. The now fast disappearing tribe, once numbering thousands, are believed to be remnants of a Mayan people who migrated here from southern Yucatán in the early 18th c., somehow contriving to avoid contact with the Spaniards. They lived a mainly nomadic existence in the rain forest named after them (the Selva Lacandona), engaging in only rudimentary forms of agriculture around their temporary encampments.

The Lacandones, of whom at most 400 are alive today, call themselves Caribs, their settlements being known consequently as "caribals". Most are found in Lacan-há (Maya: "on snake river"), Na-há ("big water") and Mensäbäk ("powder maker"). They wear their hair to the shoulder and dress traditionally in a calf-length, white, sack-like garment. Not very long ago these isolated forest Indians still lived by the bow and arrow, celebrating their ancient rituals in the decaying ruins of the temples built by their forefathers. In recent years they have been overwhelmed by a spate of missionaries, ethnologists and tourists, forfeiting much of their self-sufficiency and independence in the process.

Cabo San Lucas — E 6

State: Baja California Sur (B.C.S.)
Altitude: sea level
Population: 25,000
Telephone code: 91 684

Access

By car or bus on the Carretera Transpeninsular (MEX 1) from Tijuana (see entry) via Ensenada, Mulegé, Loreto, La Paz and San José del

Camping on the beach at Cabo San Lucas

Cabo; by ferry from Puerto Vallarta (see entry); service at present out of operation.

By air internal Mexican and international flights to San José del Cabo (86km/53 miles to the north-east).

Location

The former fishing community and now fast expanding modern holiday centre of Cabo San Lucas lies surrounded by a landscape in which virtually nothing grows, at the southern tip of the Lower Californian peninsula. Spectacular rock formations, varied beaches, an ocean teeming with fish and an excellent tourist infrastructure attract increasing numbers of holidaymakers, mainly from the USA, and keen deep-sea anglers in particular.

★Seaside resort

Having grown up in an isolated setting at the southern end of the 1700km/1056 mile-long Carretera Transpeninsular (See Baja California), Cabo San Lucas comprises just a harbour and a number of houses, shops, restaurants and hotels. It is a really excellent centre for all forms of watersports. Boats run trips to El Arco, a rock arch hollowed out by the sea at the point where the Gulf of California and Pacific Ocean meet. The beaches and bays on either side of the headland (El Médano, Amor, Sol, Santa María, Colorado, etc.) are individually very distinctive, characterised by their varied types of sand and rock. While some have calm waters, others are pounded by huge breakers; fish abound everywhere. Among the many enticing diving grounds within easy reach near by perhaps the most fascinating are those around the extraordinary submarine "sand cascade". At another site nodules of manganese litter the seabed.

★El Arco

Cascade of sand

Surroundings

More pleasant beaches and interesting coastal scenery can be found by driving north along Road 19 towards Todos Santos (70km/43 miles). Beyond Todos Santos (fruit and vegetable growing, Jesuit mission church built in 1734) the road continues to San Pedro and La Paz (80km/50 miles; see entry).

About 40km/25 miles north-east of Cabo San Lucas is the little port of San José del Cabo (see Baja California).

Cacahuamilpa Caves

See Taxco

Cacaxtla

K 8

State: Tlaxcala (Tlax.)

Access

By car from Mexico City (MEX 150 or 190 D) or from Tlaxcala (city) by the MEX 136 via San Martín Texmelucan (Cacaxtla 5km/3 miles).

Location

The intriguing Cacaxtla (Náhuatl: "trader's back-pack frame") archaeological zone lies just under 20km/12½ miles south-west of Tlaxcala, near the village of San Miguel del Milagro. In 1975 the ruins caused a sensation overnight when grave robbers excavating a tunnel came across some pre-Hispanic wall paintings and told the authorities of their discovery.

History

This site, like those at Xochichalco and El Tajín, appears to owe its existence to the folk migrations linked to the decline of Teotihuanán. Experts suggest that between A.D. 650 and 850 the Puebla valley and Cacaxtla with it was controlled by the Xicalanc Olmecs, a people of ill-defined origin from the southern Gulf coast (distinct however from the pre-Classic Olmecs). Cacaxtla's heyday is presumed to have been between A.D. 700 and 900. The frescos, so impressive and so difficult to classify, were executed sometime in the 9th c. The paintings show strong Mayan and final phase Teotihuacán influence, the latter finding expression mainly in the modified Talud-Tablero style (sloping and upright walls) and the motifs and glyphs bordering the murals. Whether the frescos were the work of small groups of artists from the central Mayan area living in Cacaxtla or of Xicalanca Olmecs influenced by the Maya remains unknown.

Visiting the ★ruins

Opening times

The site is open Tues.–Sun. 10am–5pm; the murals, however, can only be viewed between 10am and 1pm, after which the building is closed to protect the paintings from the damaging effects of sunlight. The archaeological zone known as "Los Cerritos" is now for the most part roofed over. The little museum at the entrance contains mainly ceramics.

Mound B

The tour of the site starts at Montículo B (Mound B) which consists of the partially exposed base of a three-storey pyramid.

"Great Base"

Across from Mound B, on the opposite side of a dip, stands the Gran Basamento or "Great Base", an enormous terraced complex on which

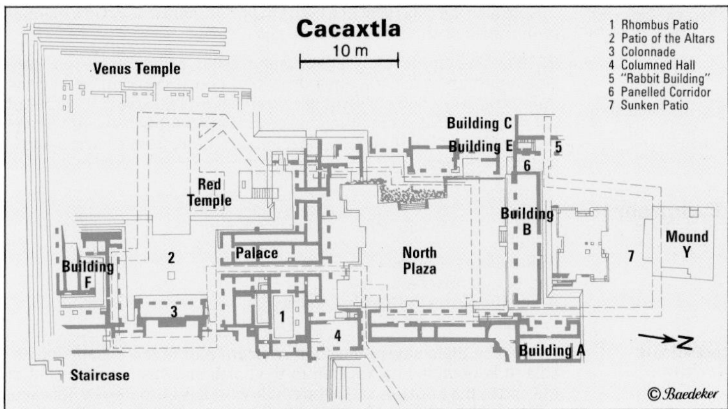

can be seen a large number of structures of various ages including palaces, colonnades, platforms, patios and altars. A glass screen protects paintings adorning the steps of the Red Temple, so-called on account of its predominantly red colouring.

"The Battle"

The sloping walls of Edificio B (Building B) on the north side of the Gran Basamento are also adorned with colourful murals, in this case two wall paintings known as "The Battle". They depict a bloody encounter between Jaguar warriors (the victors) and Bird men (the vanquished). Two huge figures, dressed in the style of the Mexican highlands but wearing tall Mayan-type sandals, stand in the centre of the battlefield surveying the scene. The deformed heads, long Roman noses and pectorals (breastplates) are all further indications of Mayan influence. Whether these battle scenes represent a real or only a mythological struggle – perhaps in the latter case between night (Jaguar) and day (Bird) – remains unclear. The skeletons of children, burned and mutilated, found beneath the floor, suggest a cycle of mass human sacrifice.

Building of the Paintings

The jewel in Cacaxtla's crown however is Edificio A or Edificio de las Pinturas (Building A or Building of the Paintings), situated in the north-east of the site. Adorning the interior are five colourful wall paintings, almost certainly consisting for the most part of symbolic representations of Quetzalcóatl and Tlaloc.

The fresco in the north colonnade shows a life-size figure in the guise of a jaguar, with a broad ceremonial staff from which drops of water fall on a serpent in the jaguar's fur. Note the glyph "9 Reptile Eye" with the typical Teotihuacán-style dot-and-dash numeral.

The mural adjacent to the door also depicts a figure in jaguar costume, in this case holding a Tlaloc vessel and a serpent. The head-dress and cross-fret motif are typically Mayan.

In the painting by the south entrance the magnificent winged figure, shown standing on a serpent and holding an exceptionally large ceremonial staff ending in a stylised serpent's head, is portrayed in the Classic Mayan manner. The glyphs of the dot-and-dash numeral 13 and the hand- and footprints higher up on the left are typical Teotihuacán elements.

The figure on the door jamb at the south entrance clearly has some connection with the sea, the octopus head-dress and large shell held in its hand being suggestive of a Mayan Shell god from the Gulf coast.

Note also the clay relief of a figure in profile, here framed in a manner reminiscent of similar reliefs at El Tajín.

In 1987 several more pre-Columbian frescos were discovered, considerably older than the ones described above. Most unusually the figures portrayed do not symbolise animals. The uncovering in 1990 of yet more buildings containing frescos may yet throw new light on the history of what is still largely unexplored territory from an archaeological point of view.

Campeche (State)

Abbreviation: Camp.
Capital: Campeche
Area: 50,952sq.km/19,667sq. miles
Population: 535,200

Location and topography

Campeche State covers the south-western part of the Yucatán peninsula. It is bounded by Yucatán to the north and east and the Gulf of Mexico to the north-west. To the south-west it is bordered by Tabasco, to the south by Guatemala and to the south-east by Quintana Roo. It lies on a low Yucatán limestone plateau rising to hills in the north. The northern half is relatively dry, the people having to rely on underground lakes and watercourses for their water supply. The south and east in contrast experience heavy precipitation supporting the growth of lush rain forest. The rivers in the south flow into the Laguna de Términos. Along the Gulf coast are many lovely beaches but also belts of swampland. Campeche's population is made up mainly of Maya and mestizos.

Fauna

Even today Campeche's bush country and rain forest boast a rich and varied fauna, jaguar, ocelot, tapir, wild pig, armadillo and deer being

just some of the mammals found. Birdlife includes pheasant, wild duck, wild turkey, herons, flamingoes and many different kinds of parrot, while alligators, tortoises, iguanas and boa constrictors are among the various reptile species seen. As regards marine life the coastal waters of Campeche are some of the most abundantly stocked in Mexico, harbouring tuna, barracuda, shark, mackerel, swordfish, schnapper, dolphin and numerous crustacea such as crabs, prawns and many kinds of shellfish.

Mayan ruins

The most important of the Mayan ruins in Campeche State are at Edzná (see entry), Hochob, Dzibilnocac, El Tabasqueño (for these latter two, see under Campeche, City), Xcalunkin, Calakmul, Hormiguero, Becán, Chicaná, Xpuhil (see Chetumal) and Río Bec.

Jaína

Jaína is even more special. In olden times this little limestone island off the north coast of Campeche was a major burial site which, judging by the disproportionately few buildings found (compared with the number and richness of the graves), must have served as a cemetery for the Mayan nobility of the entire Puuc region. The unique hollow clay figurines with arrows on their backs, beautifully modelled and painted, are recognised as the finest ceramics produced in the pre-Columbian period. Although a special permit is required to visit the island, a great many finds from the site are displayed not only in the Mayan section of the National Archaeological Museum in Mexico City (see entry) but also in the Archaeological Museum at Campeche (city) (see entry).

History

Like other parts of the Yucatán peninsula Campeche boasted a large number of centres of Mayan Classic culture (A.D. 300–900). Archaeological finds show that some of these sites were probably already settled in the pre-Classic period (300 B.C.–A.D. 300). Comparatively little is known however about later pre-Columbian Indian history in the period between A.D. 1000 and 1500. During this time many towns on the Gulf coast must have been involved in trade between central and southern Mexico and the north and east Yucatán peninsula.

The first European to make an appearance here was Hernández de Córdoba who, in 1517, landed on the coast near present-day Champotón. A brief and bloody encounter with the native Indians saw the Spaniards repulsed, Córdoba himself dying later of the wounds he received. Although both Juan de Grijalva in 1518 and Hernán Cortés in 1519 established temporary footholds in Campeche, it was another 20 years before Francisco de Montejo succeeded in colonising at least some part of the area. Throughout the colonial period, and also for the first three decades of the Mexican Republic, Campeche remained incorported in Yucatán. It became a state in its own right in 1863.

Economy

Largely cut off from the rest of the country until about 30 years ago, the contribution of Campeche to the Mexican economy was always relatively small. Only its precious woods were of any great significance, in particular the blue or Campeche logwood (used in dye making) and the sapodilla tree (*Achras sapota*, the source of chicle used in the manufacture of chewing gum). A growing fishing industry, heavily backed by the state, and the discovery of offshore oil have today given a new impetus to economic development while at the same time bringing environmental problems in their wake. Agriculture and cattle rearing also receive state support. The highly interesting archaeological sites, excellent beaches and rich opportunities for angling should bring a considerable boost to tourism in the near future.

Campeche (City) O 8

State: Campeche (Camp.)
Altitude: 16m/52ft
Population: 220,000
Telephone code: 91 981

Access from Mexico City

By air in about 1½ hours; by rail a 32 hour journey via Coatzacoalcos (16 hours); by bus in about 17 hours.

Location

Campeche, capital of the Mexican state of that name, is situated on the Gulf of Mexico, on the west side of the Yucatán peninsula. The city is a mixture of ancient and modern, romantic relics of the colonial period mingling with the modern districts which have arisen in recent years. The current oil boom has unfortunately blighted both the city and the countryside around.

History

The first European to land here was the Spanish conquistador Hernández de Córdoba in 1517. The settlement from which the city later grew was founded by Francisco de Montejo the Younger ("El Mozo") in October 1540. As the 16th c. progressed Campeche (from the Mayan Ah-kin-pech, "place of the snake and the tick") developed into the principal port on the Yucatán peninsula. In both 16th and 17th centuries it suffered repeated attack by pirates, of which the assaults by William Park (1697), Diego El Mulato (1631), Laurent van Graff ("Lorencillo", 1672 and 1685) and L'Olonois ("El Olonés) were the most devastating. Over and over again sections of the town were destroyed and its people decimated (the many underground passages in which the women and children took refuge can still be seen today). Eventually, between 1686 and 1704, a defensive wall 2.5km/1½ miles long, 2.5m/8ft wide and up to 8m/26ft high, together with eight forts, was built around the town, finally rendering it safe from further pirate attack. In 1777 Charles III of Spain granted Campeche full civic status. In 1807 a cyclone destroyed many of its buildings. In 1867 the city became the capital of the Republic's new state of Campeche.

Sights

Cathedral

The cathedral church of La Concepción stands on the Plaza Principal (Plaza de Independencia) which is also graced by beautiful old colonial houses. The cathedral was begun in 1540 but only completed in 1705. It has a plain Baroque façade.

Mansión Carbajal

This magnificent villa (Calle 10 No. 584) houses a sizeable exhibition of craftwork, including work for sale.

Baluarte de la Soledad

Situated not far from the plaza is one of the bastions (baluartes) of the still largely intact city wall. The fort, known as the Baluarte de la Soledad, now houses the local history museum (Museo de Historia) with pictures and drawings chronicling Campeche's history, also a collection of weaponry and, in a special room, 22 Mayan sculptures.

On leaving the museum, turn right into Calle 8 and proceed past the Puerta de Mar (city gate) and the modern government building (the Palacio de Gobierno, also known as the Edificio de Poderes) to the Cámara de Diputados, the State parliament. Between the latter two buildings and the road along the waterfront lies an artificial lake surrounded by modern buildings, one of which is a theatre.

Fuerte San Carlos

Calle 8 leads to Fuerte San Carlos, one of the oldest and best preserved of the city's ancient bastions, now occupied by a craft centre.

A fort in Campeche

Regional Museum

A new Museo Regional (Regional Museum) has been established in the Casa del Teniente del Rey near the Puerta de Tierra. It houses archaeological finds related to the history of Campeche. They include grave goods from Calakmul, among them a superb mosaic mask.

Church and monastery of San Francisco

Situated at the intersection of Calle 59 and Calle 18, the 16th c. church of San Francisco contains five carved wooden altars painted in vermilion and white. The San Francisco monastery, somewhat further north on Miguel Alemán (Malecón) quay, is thought to stand on the site where, in 1517, the first Christian mass was held on Mexican soil. Here also Hernán Cortés' grandson Jerónimo, born in 1562, is believed to have been christened. The font is still in use.

Market

Much the best time to visit the market (mercado) is during the fiesta. Souvenirs on sale include "jipis" (Panama-style hats) and handcrafted items made from tortoise-shell, seashells and hardwoods.

Fuerte de San Miguel

A detour from the coast road on the southern outskirts of the city leads to the Fuerte de San Miguel, attractively situated overlooking Campeche. Access to the bastion – still furnished with its old cannon – is by way of a drawbridge.

★Archaeological museum

The interior houses a small but very interesting archaeological museum (Museo de Arqueología) with artefacts from a wide range of Mayan cultures. Especially noteworthy are the terracotta figurines from Jaína and the museum's excellent synoptic presentation of pre-Columbian civilisations.

A drive along the coast to Villahermosa

Head south on the MEX 180, driving through the small fishing communities of Lerma (8km/5 miles) and Seybaplaya (33km/20 miles) to Champotón (population: 41,000; about 65km/40 miles from Campeche).

Champotón

In the pre-hispanic period the port of Champotón lay at the heart of an area of extensive Indian settlement forming the cultural interface between Guatemala, Yucatán and central Mexico. It is more than likely that Toltec culture was intermixed here with that of Mayan tribes living under Toltec domination, tribes who after the 10th c. migrated east to be absorbed by the Maya already living there. According to old chronicles – not altogether reliable – both the Itzá and Xiú tribes were at different times temporarily settled in the area. The town today is predominantly a fishing port. It makes a convenient base for deep-sea angling expeditions and for excursions into the interior.

Isla del Carmen

Beyond Champotón continue for another 105km/65 miles to the little Isla Aguada where a 3400m/3700yd-long road bridge called the "Puente de Unidad" crosses to the Isla del Carmen. This latter, once called Isla de Tris and resembling an enormous sandbank, is lapped on its northern side by the waters of the Bahía de Campeche and to the south by the Laguna de Términos, a large freshwater lake fed by several rivers. Between 1558 and 1717 Isla del Carmen was a pirate's lair from which buccaneers set out to raid the Spanish ports along the Gulf of Mexico. On the south-west tip of the 40km/25 mile-long island lies Ciudad del Carmen (population: 100,000; fiesta: July 15th–31st, celebrating the expulsion of the pirates in 1717).

The town (its patron saint is the Virgin of Mount Carmel) was given its name by Alfonso Felipe de Andrade, the man responsible for driving out the pirates in 1717. Today Cuidad del Carmen boasts a thriving prawn fishing industry and has for some years been the major terminal for oil exports from the Gulf of Mexico. The cathedral of La Virgen del Carmen is noteworthy for its stained glass windows in particular. The small archaeological museum in the Liceo Carmelita is chiefly devoted to Mayan ceramics.

Xicalango

From Ciudad del Carmen cross by ferry to the small mainland fishing village of El Zacatal, a few kilometres beyond which the road passes the lighthouse at Xicalango. In pre-Columbian times Xicalango played an important role in trade between central Mexico and Yucatán. When Hernán Cortés sailed away from here, having called in on his way to Veracruz, he took with him an Indian woman of noble birth who became known as "La Malinche", later his interpreter and advisor as well as lover during his conquest of Mexico.

About 30km/18½ miles beyond Xicalango take the ferry across the Río San Pedro y Pablo (bridge under construction) before continuing for a further 24km/15 miles to Frontera. Here a new bridge spans the Río Grijalva at the start of the final 75km/47 mile drive to Villahermosa (see entry).

North from Campeche to Mérida

Hecelchakán

Leaving Campeche by the MEX 180 (shown on some maps as MEX 261), drive north via Tenabo to the little town of Hecelchakán (56km/35 miles) with its Franciscan church dating from 1620 and Museo Arqueólogico del Camino Real. The latter has a fine collection of clay figurines from Jaína island. Stelae and lintels found during excavations in the area are also displayed on the museum patio.

There are numerous archaeological sites around Hecelchakán, two of which, Kocha and Xcalumkin (Holactún), deserve particular mention.

Becal

Continue to Calkiní (25km/15½ miles) and then Becal (32km/20 miles), both larger towns, the latter having a reputation for "jipi"-making. Before being put on sale these light-weight tropical hats are left to "mature" in dank store-rooms under the ubiquitous patios.

Maxcanú (see Uxmal) is 30km/18½ miles beyond Becal, and Mérida (see entry) another 95km/59 miles beyond that.

East from Campeche via Hopelchén to Mérida

Once again leave Campeche on the MEX 180, this time driving east for about 43km/27 miles, through Chencoyí, to join the MEX 261 at Cayal – the road branching off south leads to the archaeological zone at Edzná (see entry). Hopelchén (Mayan: "five wells"), about another 42km/26 miles east of Cayal, has a 16th c. fortified church.

Chenes culture

From Hopelchén anyone with an interest in archaeology should make a detour south into the region noted for sites emanating from the so-called Chenes culture (A.D. 550–830; the name derives from the recurring "-chén" ending meaning well).

In the Late Classic period, Mayan building in the Yucatán peninsula developed into three differing though related styles – Puuc architecture (see Uxmal) in the north-west, Río Bec architecture (see Chetumal) in the south, and, north of Río Bec, the architecture of the Chenes. Although all three styles have much in common, Chenes architecture differs from Puuc in that the façades of the buildings are completely clad in stucco and rough-hewn stone. Entrances have the form of monster jaws and the corners of the buildings are decorated with masks of the prominent-nosed deity Chac. Examples of the Chenes style can be seen on archaeological sites at Dzenkabtún, El Tabasqueño and Dzibalchén (San Pedro), 20km/12½ miles south of Hopelchén.

Hochob

Access to the Classic Chenes-style Mayan site of Hochob (Mayan: "place where the maize is picked"), 13km/8 miles south-west of Dzibalchén, is by field track from Chenkoh, passable only in the dry season. The most notable of the various buildings set around the central plaza is a well-preserved triple-chambered temple on the north side, the remains of the middle section being capped by a towering roof-comb. The entrance is framed by the jaws of a huge mask while stylised serpent motifs embellish the remainder of the façade. A reconstruction can be seen in the National Anthropological Museum in Mexico City.

Dzibilnocac

From Dzibalchén another track runs for almost 20km/12½ miles to Iturbide, near which lies the Dzibilnocac archaeological zone, one of the largest in the Chenes area. The main temple at Dzibilnocac (Mayan: "Painted buildings") has a similar façade to the principal temple at Hochob.

★Grutas Xtacumbil-xunan

Returning to Hopelchén follow the MEX 261 north for 33km/20½ miles to Bolonchén (Mayan: "nine wells") de Rejón. From here a track leads to the nearby Grutas Xtacumbil-xunan (Mayan: "hidden woman"), a vast system of limestone caves the full extent of which is impossible to gauge. Stalactites, stalagmites and cenotes abound. According to legend a beautiful mestiza abandoned herself to life as a recluse in these dark caves following an unhappy love affair.

Kichmool and Itzimté

Situated a short distance from Bolonchén are the ruined temples of Kichmool and Itzimté, two archaeological sites where the architecture is a mixture of the Chenes and Puuc styles.

About 24km/15 miles north of Bolonchén and some 150km/93 miles after leaving Campeche the road crosses the state border into Yucatán. From here there is a choice of two routes to Mérida. The first goes via Kabah (8km/5 miles; see entry), Uxmal (31km/19 miles; see entry) and Muna (46km/28 miles) direct to the "White City" as Mérida is known. The other, branching off to the right after 3km/2 miles, makes a detour via Sayil (6km/3¾ miles; see entry), Xlapak (10km/6 miles; see Sayil, Surroundings), Labná (14km/9 miles), Loltún (32km/20 miles; see

Labná, Surroundings), Oxhutzcab (41km/25 miles) and Tikul (58km/36 miles) before rejoining the first route at Muna (79km/49 miles) for the final lap of the journey to Mérida (138km/86 miles).

Cancún Q 7

State: Quintana Roo (Q.R.)
Altitude: sea level
Population: 200,000
Telephone code: 91 988

Access

By air internal flights from Mexico City (about 2 hours), Mérida and Monterrey; international flights from various US and European airports including Zürich, London and Paris; by bus from Mexico City (about 24 hours).

Location

★Holiday centre

Situated on a 21km/13 mile-long, 400m/440yd-wide, L-shaped island off the north coast of Yucatán, Cancún is a purpose-built luxury resort with an excellent tourist infrastructure. Having been built up from virtually nothing in little more than a decade, the large holiday centre lies fringed by glorious white sand beaches and coral banks, its reputation further enhanced by an equable subtropical climate relatively free from rain. The tourist area is linked by causeway to the mainland on which the modern city of Cancún now stands. In recent years the palm trees on the Yucatán coast have been severely reduced in number by a disease which made its appearance during the last century.

History

Originally occupied by an old Mayan settlement, this lovely subtropical location first came to the notice of two explorers, Stephens and Catherwood, in 1843, being given the name Can-cune (Mayan: "pot at the end of the rainbow"). By the time the project to build a new city was mooted in 1970, only about 100 Maya still lived here, eking out a livelihood from fishing and gathering chicle. The site was computer-selected as the most favourable for an international holiday centre, to be built as a joint

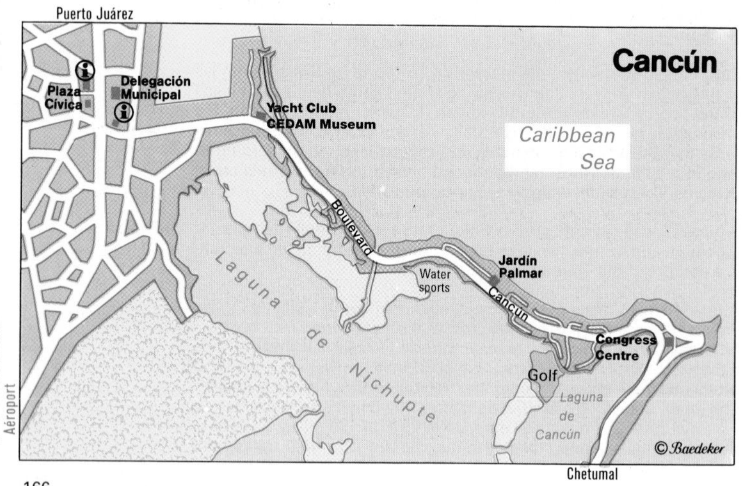

venture between the Mexican government and private enterprise. Construction proceeded to a systematic plan and was completed just a few years ago. In 1992 the 18,000 hotel bed resort (projected to rise to 26,000) was Mexico's biggest foreign currency earner, its more than 2 million holidaymakers accounting for 12% of total revenue. In September 1988 hurricane "Gilbert" had wreaked considerable havoc here.

Tourist attractions

Cancún, test-tube city

The still infant city of Cancún (Ciudad de Cancún), conceived, as it were, in a test-tube, complete with all facilities such as shops, restaurants and hotels, has virtually no sights to speak of. Unfortunately during the season it becomes very crowded and noisy.

The resort

The actual holiday resort is situated immediately offshore on Cancún island, linked to the mainland by causeway. It comprises a delightful strip of coast lined with big luxury hotels. From Punta Cancún to Punta Nizuc a narrow spit of land separates the sheltered Laguna Nichupte from the open waters of the Caribbean while, at the north end, the Boulevard Cancún runs along the shores of the Bahía de Mujeres. In the bay lies the lovely Isla Mujeres.

Archaeological museum

In addition to holiday homes, private houses and large modern hotels, the resort boasts a convention centre (Centro de Convenciones) with a 2500-seat auditorium used for cultural events as well, performances by the Ballet Folklórico for example. Also housed in the convention centre building is an archaeological museum (Museo de Arqeología), with photo-montages, plans and artefacts relating to Mayan culture. There are two shopping precincts in the immediate vicinity.

CEDAM Museum

Mexico's underwater exploration club CEDAM has its own museum, located near the Bahía Complex on the Paseo Kukulkán. Finds recovered on underwater expeditions, etc. are among the items exhibited.

Beaches

A series of beaches – de las Perlas, Juventud, Linda, Langosta, Tortugas, Caracol and Chac-mool – extend alongside the Boulevard Cancún and the Paseo Kukulkán all the way from the city boundary. Tortugas, Caracol and Chac-mool are the most popular. Laid out beside the 7.5km/4½ mile Paseo Kukulkán is an 18-hole public golf course known as Pok-ta-Pok.

There is a hydrofoil service from the resort (pier at the Centro de Convenciones) to Cozumel (island) and the Isla Mujeres (see entries).

Mayan sites

Between Punta Cancún and Punta Nizuc a number of interesting Mayan ruins have been found, mostly Puuc in style. They are usually referred to collectively as the El Rey ruins though occasionally heard called Pinturas, San Miguel, Yamilum, Pok-ta-poc or El Conchero. Most consist of stumps of pyramids with temples built on them, some with rounded corners. In addition, more than 50 tombs have been discovered.

Along the coast from Cancún to Playa del Carmen

Leaving Cancún, drive south on the MEX 307, past Cancún Airport (15km/9 miles) to the little harbour of Puerto Morelos (37km/23 miles) from where passenger and car ferries cross to Cozumel (see entry).

Punta Beté

Next continue for another 25km/15½ miles to Punta Beté where good accommodation is available close to the beach and where diving equipment can be hired.

Cancún: white sands and crystal-clear water

Playa del Carmen

10km/6 miles further on lies Playa del Carmen, another small port from which ferries run to and from Cozumel. The town has a pretty beach but has suffered from too rapid growth in past years. There are good facilities for diving and deep-sea fishing.

Akumal, Xel-há and Tulum (see entries) are 37km/23 miles, 44km/27 miles and 62km/38 miles respectively from Playa del Carmen.

Casas Grandes

See Chihuahua (State)

Lake Catemaco (Laguna de Catemaco) M 8

State: Veracruz (Ver.)

Access

By bus from Veracruz (see entry), changing buses at San Andrés Tuxtla; by car from Veracruz (about 155km/96 miles) or Minatitlán (about 120km/75 miles), both via the MEX 180.

Location

Surrounded by mountains of volcanic origin, Lake Catemaco lies just off the Veracruz–Coatzacoalcos road (MEX 180), some 10km/6 miles south-east of San Andrés Tuxtla and roughly 35km/22 miles from the Gulf coast. One of Mexico's most beautiful lakes, it is 16km/9 miles long with an area of 130sq.km/50sq. miles. There are two islands, Ténapi and Agaltepec.

★Scenery

Insulated from the hot and humid coastal lowlands of the Gulf by the Sierra de los Tuxtlas, Catemaco enjoys a pleasantly equable climate. Together with its European-style landscape, this once prompted Alexander von Humboldt to call the area "the Switzerland of Veracruz" (Suíza Veracruzana). The extinct San Martín volcano, visible in the near distance, is, at 1850m/6071ft, the highest peak. Catemaco is blessed by Mexican standards with an abundance of water, evidenced by the flow of the Río Cuetzalapa and the Eyipantla waterfall, setting of many a jungle film (41m/135ft high; 8km/5 miles south of San Andrés Tuxtla). On the volcanic slopes of San Martín east of Acayucan, Popoluca Indian villages can still be found, home to tribes such as the Mecayapan and Soteapan whose languages are distinct from those of the Náhuatl family.

Catemaco

The principal town on the lake, also called Catemaco (370m/1215ft; population: 42,000), lies on the north-west shore, its inhabitants making a living mainly from fishing and tourism. The church of the Virgen del Carmen (feast day: July 16th), situated on the plaza, is a popular place of pilgrimage, as is evident from the many votive offerings left at the portal. Catemaco also has a reputation for its "curanderos" (healers) and "brujos" (medicine men) who, with their supposedly miraculous powers, still wield considerable influence over some elements of the population. The tropical forests around Catemaco are in any case famous for their many species of medicinal plant.

Isla Tanaxpilo

The excursion by boat to the Isla Tanaxpilo or Isla de Changos (Monkey Island) rarely disappoints. A colony of Macaques originally introduced from Thailand live on the island under the aegis of a biological institute and keep visitors amply amused.

Laguna de Catemaco

Montepío

From Catemaco a road makes its way north to the fishing village of Montepío, some 40km/25 miles distant. It winds past steep mountain slopes covered with luxuriant vegetation, picturesque lagoons and attractive beaches – of which Jicacal and Escondida are the most delightful.

Catemaco to Veracruz

San Andrés Tuxtla

West of Catemaco, the MEX 180 runs for 15km/9 miles to San Andrés Tuxtla (370m/1215ft; population: 60,000), an old colonial town nestling in a basin-shaped valley encircled by volcanic hills (it was known in pre-Hispanic times as "Zacoalcos", a Náhuatl name meaning "enclosed space"). The churches of San José and Santa Rosa are both worth visiting. In 1902 a 20cm/8in.-high jade Olmec figurine of a priest, subsequently found to date from A.D. 162, was discovered in the vicinity. Today the so-called "Tuxtla statuette" can be seen in Washington DC (USA). San Andrés is an important cigar manufacturing centre; the "Teamo" factory is well worth visiting.

Laguna Encantada

A short distance from the town (about 5km/3 miles over a poor track inaccessible by car) lies a legend-rich crater lake called the Laguna Encantada ("Enchanted Lake"). The water level paradoxically falls in the rainy season, recovering again in the dry. From time to time volcanic activity heats the water up to such an extent that all the fish in the lake die. The stocks miraculously replenish themselves as soon as it cools down.

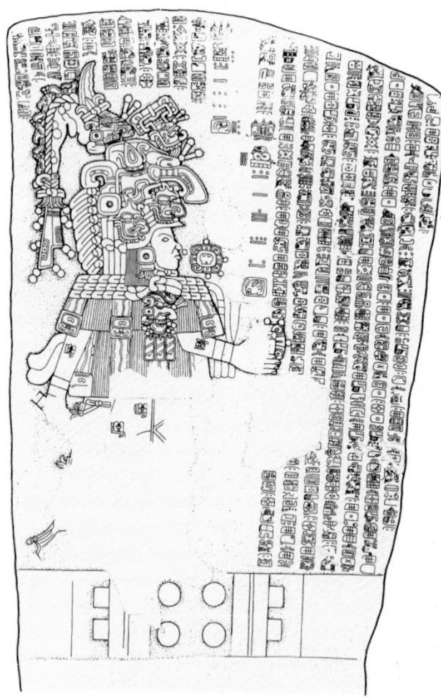

The Mojarra Stela

Santiago Tuxtla

Continue along the MEX 180, driving north-west for about 10km/6 miles to Santiago Tuxtla (360m/1180ft; population: 51,000; fiestas: July 24th, San Juan, and July 23rd–25th, Santiago Apóstol). The town straddles the Río Tuxtla on the edge of the tropical forest. Adorning the plaza is a typical Olmec colossal head. Other Olmec artefacts, including some fine stone carvings from the Olmec sites at Tres Zapotes and Nestepe, can be seen displayed in the small Tuxteco Museum.

Tres Zapotes

The huge basalt heads recovered from Tres Zapotes included two which turned out to be the second earliest New World artefacts to bear a date, in this case 32 B.C. In the early days of excavation most of the finds from the site were distributed around several different museums, but for some time now Tres Zapotes has had its own excellent collection (24km/15 miles from Santiago Tuxtla via Villa Isla). The large stone sculptures, which include (Monument A) the first colossal head ever found, will prove absorbing to anyone interested in Olmec culture. Equally fascinating are three stelae, Stela A, very ancient but not yet definitively dated, Stela B, and the upper portion of the famous Stela C which was only uncovered in 1972. The lower part of the stela, bearing the date in dot-and-dash numerals, is now in the National Anthropological Museum in Mexico City (see entry). There is very little left worth seeing at the excavation site itself.

In 1986 a 4-ton basalt sculpture known today as the Mojarra Stela ("La Mojarra Stela") was discovered on the marshy banks of the Rio Acula west of Tres Zapotes. On the top and sides of this immensely important find were carved 22 rows of hitherto unknown glyphs, 465 in all, together with the figure of a ruler whose name has since been deciphered as "lord of the mountain harvest". He, it is thought, may have reigned during the period covered by the text (21.5.143–13.7.156). The script, unravelled by philologists and dubbed "Epi-Olmecic", is essentially a Mixe-Zoque-Mayan language (a modified form of which is still spoken by some 150,000 Indians) reminiscent of the glyphs on the "Tuxtla statuette". Its discovery showed that, contrary to prevailing assumptions, an older system of writing was in existence before the emergence of Mayan script, pre-dating the latter by between 100 and 150 years and continuing in use among the successors of the Olmecs.

Alvarado

From Santiago Tuxtla carry on north-westwards for another 70km/43 miles to Alvarado (population: 35,000) on the Gulf coast. The town is built on a sandy spit separating the Laguna de Alvarado from the Gulf of Mexico.

Cerro de las Mesas

About 40km/25 miles beyond Alvarado, serious students of archaeology should leave the MEX 180, driving through El Callejón in the direction of Tlalixcoyán to visit the archaeological zone at Cerro de la Mesas ("Hill of Altars"), located between the villages of Piedras Negras and Ignacio de la Llave on the flood plain of the Río Blanco. This very extensive site is dotted with hundreds of artificial mounds, many still to be excavated. Digs carried out in the 1940s by the US Bureau of American Ethnology and the National Geographic Society uncovered a whole series of small pyramids, temple platforms, altars, stone carvings and stelae (the oldest dated A.D. 206) as well as ceramics and 782 elaborately worked items of jade. The finds were all distributed among various museums in Mexico and the USA, so a visit to the site is of little interest to those lacking a specialist background.

El Zapotal

The El Zapotal archaeological zone near by was discovered only recently. Finds, including life-size terracotta figures dating from A.D. 600–900, can be seen displayed in the Anthropological Museum at Jalapa (see entry).

Veracruz (see entry) is 70km/43 miles or so north-west of Alvarado, still on the MEX 180.

Catemaco to Villahermosa

Acayucan (160m/525ft; population: 37,000), about 80km/58 miles south-east of Catemaco on the MEX 180, is a major road junction where the MEX 185 branches off southwards, crossing the Isthmus of Tehuantepec to Juchitán (195km/121 miles), Tehuantepec (220km/137 miles; see entry) and Santa Cruz (235km/146 miles).

Minatitlán

Beyond Acayucan, the MEX 180 turns north-eastwards towards Minatitlán (65m/113ft; population: 180,000) which lies just off the road some 40km/25 miles distant. Exploitation of oil and sulphur deposits has transformed the town in recent years into a busy industrial centre.

San Lorenzo Tenochtitlán

Located on the Río Chiquito 45km/28 miles or so south of Minatitlán (and somewhat difficult of access) is the San Lorenzo Tenochtitlán archaeological zone, site of the earliest known centre of Olmec culture on the Gulf coast (it flourished between 1400 and 1200 B.C.). Here numerous ritually mutilated stone images were found. Originally connected in some way with the death of a ruler of the time, they had later been buried, presumably when the culture went into decline. Artefacts from San Lorenzo can be seen in several Mexican museums, but particularly those in Jalapa and Villahermosa (see entries).

Coatzacoalcos

Beyond Minatitlán a motorway, carried across the Río Coatzacoalcos by a magnificent bridge, provides speedy access to Coatzacoalcos (5m/16ft; population: 400,000), a major industrial city and port 25km/15½ miles to the north-east. Here too the oil boom has brought massive expansion, including development of a huge petro-chemicals complex. A terrible price has however been exacted, with air, soil and water pollution reaching catastrophic levels. The once thriving fishing and farming economies have today all but disapppeared.

La Venta

From Coatzacoalcos continue south-east for 40km/25 miles to where the MEX 180 crosses the Río Tonalá and with it the state boundary into Tabasco State. Some 4.5km/2¾ miles further on a road branches off north-west to the little town of La Venta (5km/3 miles), situated in an oil-rich region of swampland. On the outskirts of the town is an Olmec archaeological site, also known as La Venta. The first excavations were undertaken here in the 1920s by Frans Blom and Oliver La Farge of the University of Tulane, their pioneering research being followed up some fifteen years later by M. W. Stirling. The site turned out to be almost certainly that of the principal Olmec political and religious centre (which is why the Olmec period is often referred to as the La Venta culture). The influence of this first advanced Meso-American civilisation spread from the Gulf coast into central Mexico (e.g. Tlatilco, Tlapacoya and Chalcatzingo), across to the west coast (Guerrero) and south to El Salvador, leaving its mark on the early phases of Monte Albán culture and Mayan civilisation. The Olmec people themselves remain an enigma, known only through the magnificent works of art bequeathed to posterity, some of the most important of which were found here. Although La Venta's heydey was between 800 and 500 B.C., it is known to have been still inhabited at the beginning of the Christian era. In addition to the great temple pyramid made of argillaceous clay, now overgrown but once standing more than 32m/105ft high, archaeologists uncovered four of the famous basalt colossal heads, also stone altars and stelae, ceramics and figures in jade some of which can be seen in a recently opened museum. Virtually all finds from the site connected with the mysterious Olmec culture are now in museums, principally the La Venta Open Air Museum in Villahermosa (see entry).

Celaya — I 7

State: Guanajuato (Gto.)
Altitude: 1800m/5900ft
Population: 220,000
Telephone code: 91 461

Access from Mexico City

By rail in about 6½ hours; by bus in about 3½ hours; by car on the MEX 57, about 270km/168 miles.

Location

The busy town of Celaya lies north-west of Mexico City in a fertile valley basin known as Bajío. Although not exactly favoured by its location, the town has attractive parks and squares as well as some fine examples of Baroque and Neo-Classical architecture.

History

Founded in 1570 by sixteen families from the Basque country, Celaya (Basque: "zalaya" = "lowland") was granted full civic status in the mid 17th c. Its most famous son, Francisco Eduardo Tresguerras (1759–1833), was a man of many parts, an architect, artist and poet of distinction. Like most of Guanajuato's cities, Celaya played a leading role in the Mexican War of Independence (1810–21) and it was here in 1915, during the Revolution, that the bloodiest battle in Mexican history was fought, in which the future president, Alvaro Obregón, finally succeeding in defeating Francisco ("Pancho") Villa.

Sights

The main, arcade-surrounded square (Plaza Principal, Jardín) has recently been embellished with a new town hall (Palacio Municipal).

The nearby Plaza de Armas contains three buildings of note, Francisco Eduardo Tresguerras's monument to Mexican Independence (Monumento a la Independencia) and two churches, the Iglesia de la Tercer Orden (Church of the Third Order) and Iglesia de la Cruz (Church of the Cross).

The façade, towers and high altar of the 17th c. church of San Francisco, on the corner of Miguel Doblado and Guadalupe Victoria streets, are also examples of Tresguerras's work, he having been responsible for their redesign.

★Nuestra Señora del Carmen

The highly versatile Tresguerras's real masterpiece, however, is the church of Nuestra Señora del Carmen, built between 1803 and 1807. Despite its size the Neo-Classical building captivates through its sheer grace and harmony. Note in particular the main dome by Tresguerras, also the sculptures, altar-pieces and frescos, all likewise by his hand. The finest of his murals are those in the Capilla del Juicio (Chapel of the Last Judgment). In addition to their principal theme, the frescos portray the raising of Lazarus from the dead and the burial of Tobias. Tresguerras also designed the unusual bridge which crosses the Río Laja a short distance from the city.

Surroundings

Yuriria
★Augustinian monastery

About 70km/43 miles south of Celaya (via MEX 51 to Salvatierra) the little Tarascan town of Yuriria (formerly Yuririapúndara; 1733m/5688ft; population: 40,000; fiesta: January 3rd, Día de la Preciosa) lies on the shores of Salvatierra's crater lake. It boasts an extremely handsome Augustinian monastery, built between 1556 and 1567 by Padres Diego Chávez y Alvarado (a relative of the conquistador Pedro Diego Chávez) and Pedro del Toro. For many years this cross between a priory and a fortress was a refuge for monks and local converts to Christianity from the frequent attacks by hostile Indians. Most unusually for the 16th c., the transept of the church is built in the manner of the earlier medieval Gothic tradition. The exterior is distinguished by a solid tower with open bell-cage, crenellated roof and massive flying buttresses. The main façade, clearly copied from the Spanish-Plateresque façade of Acolman (see entry), is an inspired example of imaginative Indian adaptation of the Plateresque style, the latter's strong lines being softened here by a complicated pattern of flowers and foliage. At the side of the tower stand statues of St Peter and St Paul. The side elevation with the doorway takes the form of a scaled-down version of the main façade, with a statue of St Nicolás, the patron saint of the province,

Tower of Yurina Convent

above the cornice. The interior of the church was partially damaged by fire in the 19th c. and later restored. The monastery's superb two-storey cloister with its magnificent flight of steps consists of a series of Gothic arcades. Pre-Hispanic artefacts and 17th and 18th c. colonial period paintings and sculptures are displayed in four rooms.

Yuriria is only 30km/18½ miles or so from the small town of Cuitzeo (see Morelia, Surroundings).

Apaseo el Alto

Apaseo el Alto, about 25km/15½ miles south-east of Celaya, is widely known for its blown glass and fine wood carvings.

Cempoala (Zempoala)

See Veracruz (City)

Lake Chapala (Laguna de Chapala) H 7

State: Jalisco (Jal.)

Access

By bus or car from Guadalajara (about 55km/34 miles).

Location

The Laguna de Chapala, the largest expanse of inland water in Mexico, is situated some 55km/34 miles south-east of Guadalajara. The greater part of the lake, 82km/51 miles long and an average of 28km/17 miles

Sunset over the Laguna de Chapala

wide, lies in Jalisco State, only the south-eastern portion being in Michoacán. There are three islands, Chapala (Alacranes), Mezcala (Presidio) and Maltarana.

Scenery

With its pleasant climate and delightful setting in a circle of low, sparsely vegetated hills, the Laguna has attracted a great many American and Canadian expatriates, most of whom have taken up residence on the north-west shore. Although the water can occasionally become very polluted, making swimming impossible, a rich variety of watersports can usually be enjoyed. Carp (*carpa*), mojarra, catfish (*bagre*) and whitefish (*pescado blanco*) are among the edible fish found in the lake.

The principal towns on the lake are:

Chapala

Chapala (Náhuatl: "lapping waves"; 1500m/4920ft; population: 40,000) and, adjoining it, Chula Vista (which have the largest expatriate population).

Ajijic

Ajijic (1500m/4920ft; population: 25,000), a fishing village/artist colony generally brimming with US tourists. It has some widely reputed thermal baths and a small archaeological museum. Local craftwork includes handwoven fabrics and embroidery.

Jocotepec

Jocotepec (1444m/4740ft; population: 45,000; fiesta: January 14th and 15th, Fiesta de los Dulces Nombres), another delightful fishing village also with a small artist colony. It was founded in 1528 and enjoys a reputation for its white sarapes (blankets).

Chetumal

P 8

State: Quintana Roo (Q.R.)
Altitude: sea level
Population: 180,000
Telephone code: 91 983

Access

By bus from Mexico City in about 22 hours.

Location

Chetumal, capital of Quintana Roo, is situated at the southern extremity of the Yucatán peninsula's east coast, at the mouth of the Río Hondo which forms the frontier with Belize (formerly British Honduras). Improvements in transport and communications together with the establishment of a free port have brought a marked upturn in the fortunes of this modest harbour town.

History

Chetumal, formerly called Chactemal (Mayan: "place where the redwood grows") has had a long and eventful history. For centuries it was the hub of Mayan maritime activity, boat building included. Gerónimo de Aguilar and Gonzalo Guerrero, the first Spaniards to arrive, did so inadvertently in 1512 as the result of shipwreck. At first enslaved by their Mayan captors, Aguilar was later freed by Cortés to whom he rendered invaluable service as an interpreter, while Guerrero married a Mayan princess and for a long time successfully fought the Spanish invaders. The Spanish chapter of Chetumal's history really only began much later, in 1898, when the town proper was founded by Captain Othón P. Blanco (alias Payo Obispo, a name he later discarded). The principal purpose was to help suppress the smuggling of arms and munitions destined for the rebellious Indians during the "Caste Wars". In the early years the collection of timber houses grew up more or less haphazardly, the townsfolk living as best they could from farming and fishing. In 1954 however Chetumal was almost completely destroyed by a cyclone. Mexico's federal government stepped in to rebuild the city, since when it has developed into the major centre of trade and commerce on the east coast of the Yucatán peninsula.

Free port

Apart from its one or two old timber houses, modern Chetumal has little to distinguish it. Mexicans nevertheless flock here in numbers, taking advantage of the free port to buy goods brought in from Panama. Recently also tourism has been expanding, exploiting Chetumal's potential as a base for excursions to the numerous archaeological sites in the vicinity and also the attractive coastal lagoons and reefs.

Surroundings

★Laguna Bacalar

Laguna Bacalar, reached via the MEX 307, lies 35km/22 miles north-west of Chetumal. The calm, shallow waters of the 56km/35 mile-long freshwater lake are ideal for a wide variety of watersports and also fishing, while the shores are dotted with Mayan ruins and the remains of old Spanish settlements. In the small town of Bacalar at the southern end of the lagoon (interesting fiesta: August 13th–16th, San Joaquín), the Fuerte de San Felipean, a Spanish fort built in the early 18th c., now houses the local history museum. The Cenote Azul, 3km/2 miles outside the town, is only 200m/220yd across but 70m/229ft deep (bathing; fish and game restaurant).

Bahía de Chetumal

Bahía de Chetumal provides further opportunities for excellent fishing. On its east side the bay is enclosed by a tongue of land, towards the south end of which the fishing village of Xcalac (reached by a poor road from Majahual) looks out over the Caribbean. Xcalac is a good centre for deep-sea angling and diving. The Chinchorro Bank, part of a huge coral reef, lies some miles offshore.

Felipe Carrillo Puerto

Situated on the MEX 307 at the intersection of several roads 153km/95 miles north of Chetumal, Felipe Carrillo Puerto (30m/98ft; population: 31,000) was, as Chan Santa Cruz ("Little Holy Cross"), the centre of the cult of the "Speaking Cross", the Indian movement that was the driving force behind the "Caste Wars" of 1847–1901. At the time, Chan Santa Cruz was also temporarily the capital of the independent Mayan state of Yucatán.

The remains of the original temple ("Oratorio") of the "Speaking Cross" can be seen on the north-west corner of Calle 60 y 69, while photographs and documents relating to the "Caste Wars" – as well as to the town's history in general – are displayed in the museum ("Santuario de la Cruz Parlante"). The large church built for the cult in 1858 stands on the main square. It was here that the "voice" of the Cross – in reality of course a concealed human voice – spoke to the Indians, guiding their destiny.

Chetumal to Villahermosa via Francisco Escárcega

The MEX 186 cuts across the virtually uninhabited south of Yucatán, an area of mainly jungle and open savannah. At Francisco Villa, 58km/36 miles west of Chetumal, a detour leads south for 9km/5½ miles to the Mayan site at Kohunlich (see entry).

The false towers of the Maya palace at Xpuhil

★ Xpuhil

Beyond Francisco Villa the road continues west for another 60km/37 miles to Xpuhil (Mayan: "place of the cattails"), just a short distance over the border into Campeche. The archaeological zone is on the right, not far from the road. The excavations have been identified as Mayan Late Classic (A.D. 800–900) though Xpuhil and other neighbouring sites are thought to have been occupied from much earlier. The principal building is a palace-like structure embellished with three towers, all of which are purely decorative and otherwise functionless (note incidentally how features of the two lateral towers are reversed on the central one). The general design simulates that of the temple pyramids at Petén (Guatemala), but at Xpuhil the towers are solid and the steps too narrow and steep to climb. Originally, monster masks, probably stylised representations of cats, would have decorated the façades above the doorways (bits of masks can still be seen on the lateral towers of the palace-like structure today). This distinctive combination of "false" towers and façades decorated in a similar manner to the Chenes culture, is known as the Río Bec style.

Río Bec style

Hormiguero

There is another large Mayan archaeological site about 15km/9 miles away at Hormiguero, accessible from Xpuhil by bus (or even on foot).

★ Becán

More Mayan ruins in the same Río Bec style are found at Becán (Mayan "moat"), only 4km/2½ miles further on on the right, again not far from the road. They include palaces with the typical "false" (in this case, twin) towers, a pyramid (originally crowned with a temple), altars and a ball court. The site was enclosed within a man-made moat or ditch, begun in the Classic period but never completed.

Structures I–IV, dating for the most part from the final phase of building (A.D. 550–830) stand grouped around the first plaza. Structure IV (north side) with its huge external staircase – one of the widest seen anywhere in the Mayan world – is perhaps the most interesting on the site. Some relief sculptures still survive intact on the south facing walls of the upper building. On the north side are several chambers and terraces, their numerous doorways framed with decorative stonework in the shape of, for instance, inset panels and step masks.

The twin towered Structure VIII on the south side of the adjacent Central Plaza has a small entrance leading into several interconnecting rooms. Structure IX on the north side, still to be excavated, is Becán's tallest, rising some 32m/105ft into the air. The great majority of the many buildings on the site, including Structure IX, are still wholly or partially hidden beneath a blanket of subtropical vegetation.

★Chicanná

2km/1¼ miles further along the highway is a turn off leading to the Chicanná (Mayan: "house of the serpent jaw") archaeological zone, about five minutes' drive from the road. The site comprises several buildings scattered over a wide area. Many of the ornately embellished façades are either well preserved or recently restored, making Chicanná especially suitable for studying the Río Bec style. The remarkable Structure II on the east side of the main plaza features a very characteristic monster mask dominating the façade, its open jaws framing the doorway. Equally typically, the entire central façade (i.e. including the lower part right down to the level of the terrace), is decorated with stylised motifs. Note also the stacked masks of the prominently-nosed Rain god Chac on the corners of the temple. Unfortunately virtually nothing remains of the once highly ornate roof-comb. Other buildings on the site sport the again typical, purely decorative, lateral towers.

More Mayan sites

Between the three archaeological zones mentioned and the Guatemalan frontier to the south, lie as many as 20 Mayan sites. Access is by means of poor tracks, in some cases passable only during the dry season (December to April). Among the most important are: Calakmul, site of 103 stelae and after which the 7500sq.km./2900sq. mile Calakmul biosphere reserve is named; Rio Bec, which has given its name in turn to the area's predominant architectural style; Multún; and La Muñeca.

Some 273km/170 miles after leaving Chetumal, and 146km/90 miles beyond the Chicanná turn off, the MEX 186 converges with the MEX 261 (coming from Campeche and Champotón) at Francisco Escárcega. Continue on the MEX 186, crossing the Río Usumacinta after about 150km/93 miles. At Catazaja, 32km/20 miles further on, branch left for a detour to Palenque (see entry) 33km/20½ miles away to the south.

Returning to Catazaja follow the MEX 186 west again for the final 116km/72 miles to Villahermosa (see entry), crossing the Río Grijalva just before reaching the town.

Chiapas (State)

Abbreviation: Chis.
Capital: Tuxtla Gutiérrez
Area: 74,415sq.km/28,725sq. miles
Official population 1990: 3,210,500 (1994 estimate: 3,300,000)

Location and topography

Chiapas, the south-easternmost state in Mexico, extends westward almost as far as the Isthmus of Tehuantepec, sharing its border with Oaxaca and Veracruz. To the north it abuts Tabasco and Campeche, the boundary running through the hot and humid lowlands of the Río Grijalva valley. Eastward lies the frontier with Guatemala, the mid-section of which is formed by the Río Usumacinta winding its way through impenetrable rain forest. Further south, high ground in the

Chiapas

shape of the craggy foothills of the Sierra Madre del Sur dominates the landscape on both sides of the frontier. Though the average altitude is only about 1500m/4900ft, individual peaks such as Tacaná rise well above the 3000m/9800ft mark. As it approaches the Pacific, the Sierra drops sharply away to the coast.

Indigenous Indian peoples

Marginal area that it is, Chiapas until very recently remained largely unaffected by the modernisation processes at work in the more central regions of Mexico. As a result the rural culture of tribes belonging to the Mayan family of languages (e.g. the Zoque, Tzotzil, Tzeltal, Chol and the Lacandon Indians, whose customs and traditions are very varied) has survived rather better here than in most other parts of the country.

Archaeological sites

The most important pre-Columbian Mayan sites in Chiapas are found at Chiapa de Corzo (Lagartero), Toniná (see San Cristóbal, Surroundings), Chinkultic (see Montebello Lakes), Bonampak, Yaxchilán, Palenque (see entries) and Izapa.

History

In the early period this area was probably settled first by Olmec tribes, replaced in pre-Classic times by the Maya whose culture experienced its heydey between A.D. 300 and 900. Later abandoning their great cities, the Maya then became dispersed in numerous small settlements, most of which, by the end of the 15th c., were forced to pay tribute to the Aztecs. The Spanish arrived in Chiapas in 1524. Some hard fighting took place before they succeeded in subjugating what is now south-east Mexico.

In 1544 Bartolomé de Las Casas was appointed Bishop of Chiapas. He brought Spanish enslavement of the Indians to a halt and, through his influence at court, won a measure of legal protection for the indigenous peoples of the newly conquered areas of Spanish America. Although his endeavours achieved only limited success, he is still revered today as a champion of the Indian cause. From 1543, right up to Mexican Independence in 1822, Chiapas was governed by the Spanish administration in Guatemala. Both during the colonial period and following Independence there were repeated Indian uprisings against the authorities, the last being staged by the Tzotzil and Tzeltal tribes in 1911. On January 1st 1994 the self-styled "Zapatist National Liberation Army" (Ejercito Zapatista de Liberación National, "EZLN") occupied San Cristóbal de las Casas, Altamirano, Ocosingo and Las Margaritas. It took the deployment of a large number of troops to drive the rebellious peasant farmers, most of them again from those same two tribes, the Tzeltal and Tzotzil, back into the mountains, and then only after a violent struggle.

Economy

Traditional forms of agriculture apart, exploitation of tropical woods (including chicle, the raw material for chewing gum), salt mining and coffee and cocoa cultivation all make major contributions to the economy. In recent years gold, silver and copper mining, and oil extraction in particular, have seen rapid expansion. Tourism too has experienced a strong upturn.

Drive along the Gulf of Tehuantepec

Tonalá

To join the coast road (MEX 200), fork right off the main Oaxaca–Tuxtla–Gutiérrez highway (MEX 190) at San Pedro Tepanatepec and head for Arriaga (44km/27 miles). Tonalá, 23km/14 miles further on (population: 50,000), is a small town with a modest archaeological museum, located in an area of lush subtropical vegetation. From here a turn-off leads south for 17km/10½ miles to the fishing port of Puerto Arista, near which is an archaeological zone with ruins reflecting early Aztec influence.

Tapachula

Beyond Tonalá, the MEX 200 runs south-east for 221km/137 miles along the Pacific coast, through Huixtla, to Tapachula (150m/490ft; population: 190,000), attractively situated at the foot of an extinct volcano, the 4093m/13,433ft-high Tonaná. Tapachula is the commercial hub of a region in which high-lying coffee plantations are very much in evidence playing a significant economic role. Finds from the Chiapas area, mainly from Tonalá and Izapa, are displayed in the city's Museo Arqueológico de Soconusco. There is also a zoo.

Izapa

The archaeological zone at Izapa, scarcely 11km/7 miles east of Tapachula, encompasses the remains of what was once the largest centre of pre-Hispanic culture on the Pacific coast of Meso-America. This ancient temple city was a site of major importance from as early as about 1500 B.C. right up to A.D. 900, i.e. from the early formative period through to the end of the Classic era. Quite apart from its numerous artificial earth mounds, temple platforms, inner courtyards and ball court, what makes the 4sq.km/1½sq. mile Izapa archaeological zone so special are the 50 or more carved stone monuments, the majority dating from as early as 300–50 B.C. Many show clear Olmec influence while others have features characteristic of the transition to the Mayan style. Some of the stelae for example bear bas-reliefs portraying an unusual "long lipped" god. Unquestionably the most important among these finds is Stela 5, carved with ancient deities and a tree of life, probably a representation of the myth of creation.

The road cuts through the archaeological zone, dividing it into two sectors. About 600m/650yd away to the right in the southern sector, the Grupo Central comprises an overgrown earth mound and ceremonial plaza containing a number of stelae and altars, including Stela 5. The Grupo del León is similar in arrangement, the most important item in this case being Monument 2 depicting a jaguar with a human figure in its jaws. The northern sector on the left hand side of the road incorporates a dozen or so pyramidal platforms, an overgrown earth mound, the ball court and various stelae and altars, including the remains of Stela 60 and the ornate Stela 67. Fragments of further stelae are exhibited in the museum in Tapachula.

Puerto Madero

27km/17 miles south of Tapachula lies the small harbour town of Puerto Madero, a popular holiday resort. The Guatemalan frontier can be crossed at either Puente Talismán or Ciudad Hidalgo, 18km/11 miles and 20km/12 miles beyond Tapachula respectively.

The railway line from Salina Cruz via Tehuantepec to Guatemala runs roughly parallel with the coast road.

Chichén Itzá — P 7

State: Yucatán (Yuc.)
Altitude: 10m/33ft

Access

By bus or car via the MEX 180 from Mérida (1½–2½ hours; 116km/72 miles) or Valladolid (1 hour; 42km/26 miles). An air taxi service is also available.

Location

Chichén Itzá, 116km/72 miles east of Mérida, is one of Mexico's largest and best restored archaeological zones. With only the briefest of interruptions it was a sacred Mayan site for over 700 years, and in the 11th and 12th centuries A.D. was the political and religious capital of a renascent Mayan empire under Toltec rule. Today Chichén Itzá is a UNESCO-designated world cultural heritage site.

History

Chichén Itzá (Mayan: "near the well of the Itzá") was probably founded around A.D. 450 by Mayan tribes migrating from the south. Experts assume that the site continued in occupation beyond the end of the Mayan Classic era (around A.D. 900), in contrast to those in central and southern Mayan regions (Campeche, Chiapas, Guatemala, Honduras) which, up to that time, had been of far greater importance. The most recent research suggests that tribes from the central Mexican highlands had already penetrated eastward into this part of Yucatán as early as the 7th or 8th centuries, mingling with the resident Maya before perhaps returning whence they came a century or two later – which would explain the strong Mayan elements to be found at Tula. Archaeologists had previously believed that the Toltecs first made the 1200km/745 mile journey from Tollán (present-day Tula) to north Yucatán in about A.D. 1000, at which time they established themselves at Chichén Itzá (or Uucil-abnal, Mayan: "seven bushes", as it was then known). According to old Nahua chronicles these latter migrants were led by the legendary Prince Ce Ácatl Topiltzín, called, as were several Toltec rulers, Quetzalcóatl, or Kukulkán (Náhuatl and Mayan: "plumed serpent"). He is said to have been driven out of Tula for being too peaceable.

In the following two centuries the merging of these two advanced civilisations, the Toltec and the Mayan, resulted in a post-Classic renaissance of Mayan architecture. With Toltec influence dominant throughout this golden age, Chichén Itzá's buildings, despite many Mayan features, show a remarkable similarity to those of the old Toltec capital of Tollán. Unfortunately this chapter of Chichén Itzá's history remains rather obscure. Mayan records, such as the Books of Chilan

Chichen Itzá: the Nuns' Building (drawing by Catherwood 1841/42)

Balam, the "Jaguar Prophet" (records which in many respects are at variance with the Nahua chronicles), speak of a three-fold alliance (the Mayapán League) being forged between Chichén Itzá, Uxmal and Mayapán, persisting from 1007 until 1194. Modern research throws doubt on this however, since Uxmal was already abandoned in the 11th c. and Mayapán is believed to have been founded only in the 13th c. The evidence relating to Chichén Itzá's demise is also somewhat contradictory. The site appears to have been abandoned in about A.D. 1250, following, it is thought, a second migration of Itzá Maya, the tribe, long influenced by the culture of the central highlands, to whom Chichén Itzá owes its name. This second invasion again took place under a leader called Kukulkán (or Quetzalcóatl), the link with Toltec tradition being thus preserved. Soon afterwards the Itzá seem to have dispersed. Some of the tribe, led by the Cocom family, founded Mayapán, from where they continued to control the north of the Yucatán peninsula until about 1450. Chichén Itzá apparently played no significant role at this time, building having to all intents and purposes ceased and a large part of the site lying abandoned.

At the time of the Spanish Conquest in 1533 Chichén Itzá was virtually uninhabited, though it remained a frequently visited place of pilgrimage. Bishop Diego de Landa journeyed there in 1566, describing some of the buildings. In 1841 and 1842 the American John Stephens investigated the ruins, followed in 1876 by the French archaeologist Le Plongeon. After that came the Briton Maudslay, and then the Austrian Maler, before, in 1885, Edward Thompson, the US consul in Mérida, opportunistically acquired the entire site. Between 1904 and 1907, on behalf of the Peabody Museum, he commissioned divers to search the Holy Cenote for sacrificial treasure. During the 1920s an outstanding contribution was made to the excavation and restoration of Chichén Itzá by the American Sylvanus Morley. Later, in the 1960s, further

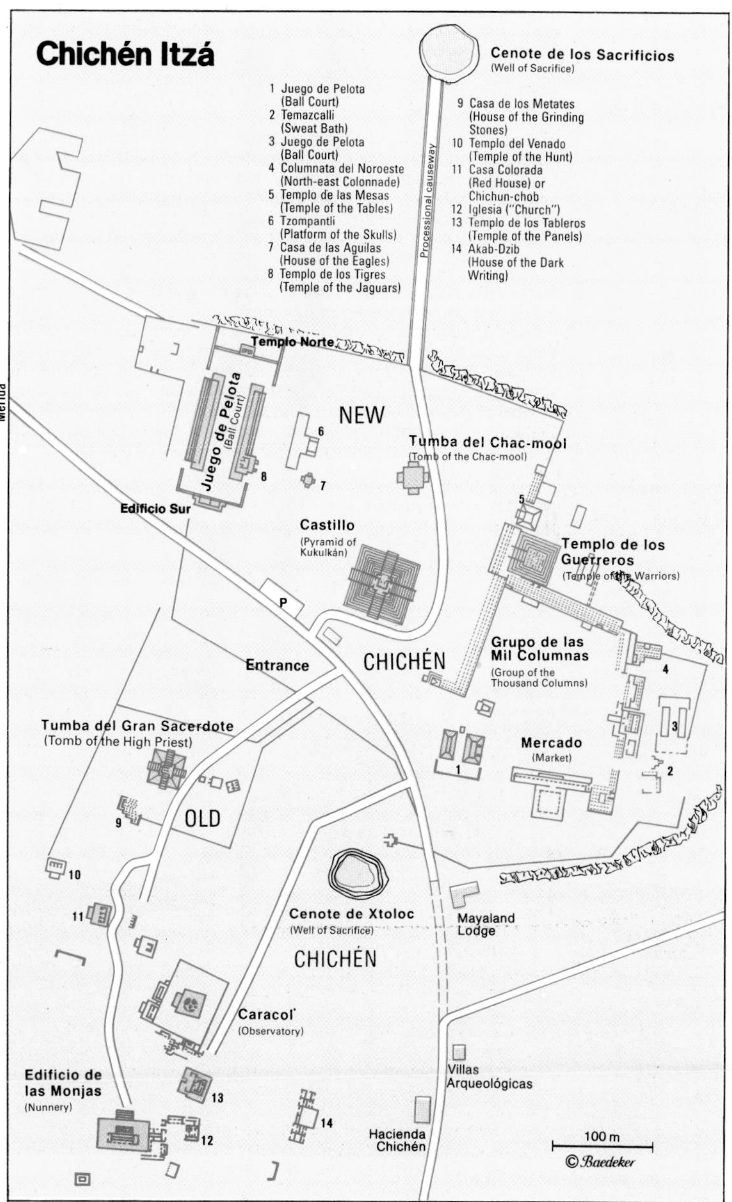
Chichén Itzá
Cenote de los Sacrificios
(Well of Sacrifice)
1 Juego de Pelota (Ball Court)
2 Temazcalli (Sweat Bath)
3 Juego de Pelota (Ball Court)
4 Columnata del Noroeste (North-east Colonnade)
5 Templo de las Mesas (Temple of the Tables)
6 Tzompantli (Platform of the Skulls)
7 Casa de las Aguilas (House of the Eagles)
8 Templo de los Tigres (Temple of the Jaguars)
9 Casa de los Metates (House of the Grinding Stones)
10 Templo del Venado (Temple of the Hunt)
11 Casa Colorada (Red House) or Chichun-chob
12 Iglesia ("Church")
13 Templo de los Tableros (Temple of the Panels)
14 Akab-Dzib (House of the Dark Writing)
Processional causeway
Templo Norte
Mérida
Juego de Pelota
(Ball Court)
NEW
Tumba del Chac-mool
(Tomb of the Chac-mool)
Edificio Sur
Castillo
(Pyramid of Kukulkán)
Templo de los Guerreros
(Temple of the Warriors)
P
Entrance
CHICHÉN
Grupo de las Mil Columnas
(Group of the Thousand Columns)
Tumba del Gran Sacerdote
(Tomb of the High Priest)
Mercado
(Market)
OLD
Cenote de Xtoloc
(Well of Sacrifice)
Mayaland Lodge
CHICHÉN
Caracol
(Observatory)
Edificio de las Monjas
(Nunnery)
Villas Arqueológicas
Hacienda Chichén
100 m
© Baedeker
Puerto Juárez,Cancún

investigations were carried out mainly by the National Geographic Society of America and the Mexican Institute of Anthropology and History (I.N.A.H.).

Visiting the ★★ruins

The archaeological zone covers an area of almost 8sq.km/3sq. miles. Here, as at virtually all pre-Columbian sites, only some of the buildings have been excavated, the majority still lying concealed beneath a luxuriant blanket of vegetation. The frequently misleading names by which the buildings are known were bestowed on them either by early Spanish sources or various archaeologists. The historic Mayan names have for the most part been lost or forgotten.

Northern group

Toltec influence at Chichén Itzá is principally seen in the buildings making up the northern group. The inappropriately named chac-mool (Mayan: "red jaguar"), a reclining figure holding a sacrificial vessel, head turned to one side, usually positioned at the entrance to a temple, is typically Toltec, as are the so-called atlantes, stone carvings, often of warriors, supporting a temple roof or altar. Note too the ever-recurring symbol of the plumed serpent (Mayan: "Kukulkán") which displaces the Mayan Rain god Chac, and the scenes of battles and sacrifices which appear far more often than is usual in Classic Maya art.

★★El Castillo (Pyramid of Kukulkán)

The structure known as El Castillo, also called the Pyramid of Kukulkán, dominates this part of the site. As is the case with most pre-Columbian buildings, it is positioned in accordance with strict astronomical-astrological rules.

The 30m/98ft-high, four-sided pyramid, excellently restored, impresses with its classic simplicity. The nine-tiered terracing and four

El Castillo (Pyramid of Kukulkán)

Temple of the Warriors and Group of the Thousand Columns

stairways, one on each side, symbolise the nine heavens and four points of the compass. Each stairway has 91 steps, a total of 364, the platform at the top being the 365th, the whole corresponding therefore to the number of days in a year. Large serpent heads adorn the foot of the main stairway which rises steeply, at an angle of 45°, to the upper platform on which the actual Temple of Kukulkán stands. The climb to the top of the steps is rewarded with a superb view over the entire site. A pair of typical Toltec serpent columns flank the temple's main entrance. During the restoration of El Castillo workers discovered a pure Mayan-style temple hidden away inside, crowning an older pyramid over which the later one lies superimposed. At its entrance were a stone chac-mool and a throne in the shape of a red-painted stone jaguar, its coat inlaid with jade. A passage leading into the interior of the pyramid now gives access to these hidden rooms (open: 11.30am–1pm and 4–5pm).

View

★ Snake phenomenon

At the equinoxes (March 21st and September 21st/22nd) the Kukulkán Pyramid becomes the scene of a spectacular shadow show. On these two afternoons the setting sun, falling on the corners of El Castillo's nine terraces, casts an undulating shadow onto the west-facing wall of the north staircase. Running all the way down the edge as far as the great snake's head at the foot, the effect is of a huge serpent slithering earthwards from the top of the pyramid, a dramatic symbol of Kukulkán's descent heralding the sowing season or the ending of the rains.

★ Temple of the Warriors

On a step platform east of El Castillo stands the Temple of the Warriors (Templo de los Guerreros). This magnificent structure comprising several spacious, columned halls is unmistakeably a larger version of the Temple of the Morning Star at Tula. Several rows of square pillars

Chac-mool guards the Warrior Temple

guard the foot of the stairway, at the top of which squats a chac-mool. The main temple entrance is again flanked by two massive serpent columns, heads on the ground, tails, originally carrying the lintel, pointing to the sky. Behind them four atlantes support a large stone altar. Here too archaeologists discovered the remains of an earlier, smaller Temple of the Warriors concealed inside the pyramid.

Group of the Thousand Columns

Adjoining the Temple of the Warriors on its south side is the Hall of the Thousand Columns (Grupo de las Mil Columnas), the original purpose of which remains something of a mystery. It may have served as an indoor market or place of assembly. Near by are a small ball court (Juego de Pelota), the so-called Mercado (Market) and a steam bath (Temazcalli), of which the vestibule, the bath itself and the heating room can still be seen.

Tomb of Chac-mool

A hundred metres or so north of El Castillo lies the so-called Tomb of Chac-mool (Tumba del Chac-mool). Here, more than 100 years ago, Le Plongeon found a stone figure which he christened Chac-mool. The structure is also known as the Venus Platform, having interesting reliefs featuring both Kukulkán's symbol and that of the Morning Star.

★Holy Cenote

Further north still, a 6m/20ft-wide causeway runs for 300m/330yd to the large sacred cenote (Cenote Sagrado or Cenote de los Sacrificios; Chen-ku), the existence of which was probably the reason for the Maya settling here in the first place. The almost perfectly round, natural water hole has a diameter of 60m/197ft, its sides plunging 24m/79ft to the surface of the water below. The greatest depth yet recorded is 82m/269ft.

From the 7th c. onwards until after the Spanish Conquest the cenote was a place of sacrifice and pilgrimage, a sweat bath at the water's edge

Holy Cenote

probably having a ritual function. In times of drought precious objects and live human sacrifices were thrown into the water as offerings to the gods, in particular the Rain god Chac. Between 1904 and 1907 Bowditch and Thompson made several exploratory dives, finding 50 human skeletons together with numerous artefacts of ceramic, stone, gold, copper, jade and obsidian. Further exploration in the 1960s, carried out at greater depths, brought to light another 4000 such objects together with others made of copal (resin), rubber and wooden dolls and human and animal bones. Examination of the skeletons revealed the majority of sacrificial victims to have been men and children, rather than the beautiful young virgins of popular myth.

Tzompantli

Returning from the cenote, a large square platform called Tzompantli (Náhuatl: "wall of skulls") can be seen on the right of the plaza. This served as a base for the stakes on which the decapitated heads of human sacrifices were impaled. Reliefs consisting of rows of skulls decorate the sides.

House of the Eagles

Next to Tzompantli stands a smaller platform known as the House of the Eagles (Casa de los Aguilas). Stone serpents embellish the stairway. The walls are adorned with reliefs of eagles and jaguars – symbols of the two orders of Toltec warrior – holding human hearts in their claws.

★★Ball court

Like almost all Mayan cities, Chichén Itzá had several arenas used for the ritual ball game. Seven such ball courts have been found on the site to date. The one at the north-west end of the great plaza is the most impressive so far discovered anywhere in Meso-America.

Along the sides of the playing area – almost 146m/160yd in length and about 37m/40yd wide – run vertical walls 8.5m/29ft high. Fixed in the centre of each wall is a heavy stone ring with serpent ornamentation, positioned 7.25m/24ft above the ground. The game involved hitting a hard rubber ball through the stone rings using only the elbow, knee or hip. The ball, representing the sun, was probably not allowed to touch the ground, otherwise its symbolic "course" would be interrupted. The losers of the game are thought to have been ritually sacrificed (reliefs on panels decorating the bases of walls show players suffering decapitation).

Some experts believe that the small temples at either end – the Edifico Sur and the Templo Norte – were dedicated to the gods of Sun and Moon.

Temple of the Jaguars

The Temple of the Jaguars (Templo de los Tigres) occupies a platform built into the south-east wall of the ball court. The lower shrine, facing onto the great plaza, contains a carved stone jaguar, presumably an altar. The upper temple, reached by a steep stairway at the side, looks westwards onto the ball court. As in the Temple of the Warriors, serpent columns flank the entrance. The façade is enhanced by several friezes, the majority of which depict jaguars. Still visible inside are murals, apparently of a battle between the Maya and the Toltec (open: 10–11am and 3–4pm).

Southern group

The southern group of buildings, comprising what is known as Old Chichén (Chichén Viejo), is reached by crossing the former Mérida to Puerto Juárez road, now disused. On the other side, to the right of the path, rises the Tomb of of the High Priest (Tumba del Gran Sacerdote), a ruined pyramid 10m/33ft high. When excavated the structure was found to contain seven tombs and some valuable artefacts.

Tomb of the High Priest

★Caracol (Obervatory)

A short distance away on the left lies one of the most interesting of all the buildings at Chichén Itzá, the Caracol ("Snail"), thought to have been an observatory. Inside the circular building, which stands on a two-tier platform, a passageway winds upwards in a gently ascending spiral. Narrow slits in the walls are so positioned as to allow the sun's rays to penetrate the centre of the building for just a few seconds twice a year, a simple but reliable method used by Mayan priests to accurately determine the time. The observatory embodies stylistic elements clearly deriving from the central highlands in addition to its Mayan Classic features.

Nunnery

The path continues south beyond the Caracol to an edifice which the Spanish misleadingly christened the Nunnery (Edificio de las Monjas). The elaborately ornamented structure and subsidiary buildings are executed in the Mayan Chenes style, virtually every inch of the façades being decorated with symbols of the Mayan Rain god Chac. The so-called "Church" ("Iglesia") is a particularly fine example of Puuc architecture, an early style in which the façades are decorated with geometric patterns and animals as well as Chac masks. In this instance a crab, an armadillo, a snail and a tortoise, the creatures which in Mayan mythology support the heavens, can be seen between the masks.

"Church"

Other buildings

Other buildings of interest in the southern sector include the Temple of the Panels (Templo de los Tableros) with reliefs of Toltec warriors and jaguars; the Akab D'zib (Mayan: "obscure writing"; Building of the Unknown Writing), so named because of the as yet undeciphered characters above the door of the second room; the Temple of the Window Lintel (Templo de los Dinteles); the Red House (Casa Colorada or Chichan-chob), predominantly in the Puuc style; the so-called "Dates Group" (Grupo de las Fechas), with a phallic temple, mainly Toltec in style; another ball court (Juego de Pelota); and the Cenote Xtoloc, almost certainly a reservoir. An attractively-designed museum houses sculptures and ceramics.

Surroundings

★Balankanché

Balankanché ("throne of the Jaguar Priest"), 5km/3 miles east of the excavation zone on the Valladolid and Puerto Juárez road (MEX 180), is a fascinating cult and burial site in a stalactitic limestone cave discovered quite by accident in 1959. It had evidently lain undisturbed for many centuries, its entrance blocked with rough hewn stone. The cave is almost certainly part of an extensive labyrinth of underground caverns and waterways yet to be investigated. Artificial lighting has been installed allowing the visitor to see the numerous clay dishes and jars, "metates" (stones for grinding maize), copal burners and other objects still lying where the priests using the site left them. Many items are decorated with the mask of the Toltec-Aztec Rain god Tláloc, suggesting that the cave was an exclusively Toltec burial place. The focal point of the cave is a chamber containing an altar and a limestone formation reminiscent of the sacred Mayan ceiba tree. A narrow passageway leads to a deeper-lying stalactitic chamber, at the end of which crystal-clear water surrounds another altar also dedicated to the Rain god Tláloc. Tiny shrimps and blind fish live in the pool.

Valladolid

Valladolid (population: 60,000), the second largest city in Yucatán, is situated 42km/26 miles east of Chichén Itzá. Its church of San Bernardino, founded by the Franciscans in 1552, is one of the few colonial buildings to survive the civil war which caused such havoc in the first half of the last century. The Cis-ha and Zac-hi cenotes are well worth visiting, a gangway leading down to the water's edge some 45m/147ft below (bathing possible). On the right some 5km/3 miles before Valladolid is the 20m/66ft-deep Cenote Dzitnup, a really delightful spot with warm, cobalt blue water.

Tizimín

From Valladolid, the MEX 295 makes its way north for 52km/32 miles to the small town of Tizimín. Here, from December 30th to January 6th, a major festival is held in honour of the Three Kings, celebrated with much pomp and ceremony.

Río Lagartos

★Flamingo breeding colony

A further 52km/32 miles to the north the little seaside town of Río Lagartos (Nefertiti) lies amid delightful scenery. 16km/10 miles away, at Las Coloradas on the estuary of the Río Lagartos, there is a large breeding colony of pink and red flamingos and colonies of other protected birds (boat trips cater for sightseers). Further east still, Chiquila boasts what for Yucatán is a rare source of pure sulphur. West of Río Lagartos is the fishing village of San Felipe.

From Valladolid a new road runs via Nuevo X-can to Cobá (see entry).

Chihuahua (State)

Abbreviation: Chih.
Capital: Chihuahua
Area: 245,612sq.km/94,806sq. miles
Official population 1990: 2,441,900 (1994 estimate: 2,800,000)

Location and topography

Chihuahua is the largest as well as one of the richest states in Mexico. It borders the USA (New Mexico and Texas) to the north and north-east, Coahuila to the east, Durango to the south, and Sinaloa and Sonora to the west. The frontier with Texas is constituted by the Río Bravo del Norte (Río Grande del Norte) into which Chihuahua's principal river, the Río Conchos, flows. The greater part of the state comprises a high plateau with an altitude between 1200 and 2400m/3940 and 7875ft

Mexico
United Mexican States
Estados Unidos Mexicanos

Chihuahua

Federal State
Estados

1a Baja California Sur
1b Baja California Norte
2 Sonora
3 Chihuahua
4 Sinaloa
5 Durango
6 Coahuila
7 Nuevo León
8 Zacatecas
9 San Luis Potosí
10 Tamaulipas
11 Nayarit
12 Aguascalientes
13 Jalisco
14 Guanajuato
15 Querétaro
16 Hidalgo
17 Colima
18 Michoacán
19 México
20 Morelos
21 Tlaxcala
22 Puebla
23 Veracruz
24 Guerrero
25 Oaxaca
26 Chiapas
27 Tabasco
28 Campeche
29 Yucatán
30 Quintana Roo

D.F. Distrito Federal (Federal District)

above sea level. In the west the land rises to merge with the deeply fissured mountain chains of the Sierra Madre Occidental. Chihuahua's population is mainly composed of mestizos and Whites, the Indian tribes – the Guarijio in the west, the Tarahumara in the mountainous south-west, and the Tepehuano in the south – having retreated into outlying areas following the Conquest.

Pre-Columbian sites

Apart from the Casas Grandes archaeological zone, Chihuahua's principal pre-Columbian sites are found around Pacheco (El Willy and Cueva de la Olla) and Ciudad Madera (Huaynopa, Vallecito and Cuarenta Casas), and in the Sierra Tarahumara (Arroyo de Guaynopa). Most consist of cliff or cave dwellings proper and are frequently difficult to reach.

History

The region is known to have had a long pre-Columbian history, the details of which, though, remain largely obscure. What can be said with certainty is that the main cultural influence on the area was from the north, in particular from what is now the south-western USA. Any impact from central Mexico came relatively late and was limited in extent. Casas Grandes is known to have been a site of major cultural importance for over 700 years.

In the period immediately before the Conquest, the Nahua peoples inhabiting Chihuahua were driven back by tribes from the north, such as the Apaches. By this time the Tarahumara were probably already the dominant group.

The first Spaniard, Álvaro Núñez Cabeza de Vaca, arrived in the area in 1528. Although the 16th c. Spanish prospectors were quick to find sources of valuable ore, few of their settlements were able to withstand the unceasing attacks by Indians. Even well into the last century, the Comanches from Texas in particular were notorious for their frequent raids into Chihuahua, incursions which saw them rampaging as far

Casas Grandes: Ruined town

south as Zacatecas. In the colonial period Chihuahua and Durango together formed part of the province of Nueva Vizcaya. Chihuahua was separated from Durango in 1823 and became a fully-fledged state the following year. From the time of Mexican Independence onwards, the history of the state and its capital are closely intertwined.

Economy

Cattle rearing (mainly beef) is by far the most important sector of Chihuahua's economy. In those areas with artificial irrigation, cereals, cotton, beans, alfalfa, fruit and vegetables are grown. Mining (iron, antimony, gold, silver, copper, lead and coal) also makes a significant contribution, as too does forestry. Refining is one of the fastest growing activities.

Places of interest

Apart from the state capital Chihuahua (see entry), the three neighbouring towns of Cuauhtémoc, Ciudad Camargo and Hidalgo del Parral, and the magnificent Barranca del Cobre (see entry), places of interest in Chihuahua are comparatively few.

★Casas Grandes

The most remarkable of all the pre-Columbian ruins in northern Mexico is found on the outskirts of "old" Casas Grandes, a small town 8km/5 miles south of the "new", modern, agricultural town of Nuevo Casas Grandes (about 335km/208 miles north-west of Chihuahua; 1600m/5251ft; population: 80,000). The site, also known as Casas Grandes (Paquimé; Náhuatl: "big town"), shows affinities with the cultures of the area now encompassed by the south-western USA, the influence of Meso-America on northern Mexico having been relatively small.

Narrow house entrance, Casas Grandes

Casas Grandes is classed as one of the so-called oasis cultures, the most notable of which are Casa Grande (Arizona), Mesa Verde (Colorado) and Pueblo Bonito (New Mexico). Little has come down to us about its builders or their times. Probably first settled from the north between the 7th and 8th centuries A.D., Casas Grandes experienced an initial flowering about A.D. 1000. More recent finds suggest that in the 12th and 13th centuries it came somewhat more under the influence of the central Mexican highlands, though later indications point to renewed ties with the north, principally the Anasazi culture. The significance of the Tarahumara, Pima and Apache cultures for the history of Casas Grandes remains uncertain. Some historians believe that the Apaches were responsible for Paquimé's demise, probably in around 1340 when the town was burned down and abandoned. Remains of pottery workshops and others for producing artefacts in turquoise and shell, suggest that Casas Grandes must have been an important centre for both manufacture and trade. Parrot feathers from captive birds are believed to have been bartered for turquoise from the north.

Semi-subterranean dwellings, very old pottery, and underground cult chambers called kivas, all dating from the early period, have been uncovered in the archaeological zone. Finds from the middle period include remains of multi-storeyed adobe houses, stairways and irrigation channels. In addition to Anasazi pottery, Toltec Mexican-style buildings (ball courts, platforms, remains of pyramids), some decorated with Quetzalcóatl motifs, have been discovered dating from the late period. Some items found are displayed in a small museum located between the archaeological site and the old town.

Today a considerable area of the valley is farmed by descendents of Mormons who fled the USA a century ago when polygamy was banned.

Cuidad Juárez

Cuidad Juárez (1144m/3755ft; population: 1,100,000; fiestas: December 4th, Día de Santa Bárbara; December 5th–12th, celebration of the city's foundation; August 10th–12th, cotton fair; air, bus and rail connections with Mexico City) is situated 336km/209 miles north-west of Nuevo Casas Grandes on the US frontier. It lies on the south bank of the Río Grande, directly opposite El Paso (Texas). Originally called Paso del Norte, in 1888 the city was renamed in honour of Benito Juárez who, in 1865 and 1866 at the time of the War of Intervention, had his headquarters here. During the Mexican Revolution (1910–21) it was used as a base by the revolutionary hero and bandit leader Francisco ("Pancho") Villa. Today Cuidad Juárez is an important agricultural processing and distribution centre ("maquiladoras").

Among places of interest in the city are the mid 17th c. Guadalupe mission church and the recently built cultural centre (Centro Cultural). The latter incorporates a museum of history and archaeology (ceramics from Casas Grandes, memorabilia from the Mexican Revolution) and displays of folk art.

Chihuahua (City) F 3

State: Chihuahua (Chih.)
Altitude: 1330m/4365ft
Population: 600,000
Telephone code: 91 14

Access from Mexico City

By air (about 2–3 hours), rail (about 30 hours) or bus (about 21 hours).

Location

Chihuahua, capital of the large Mexican state of that name, is attractively located in a valley open to the north but otherwise enclosed on three sides by chains of hills emanating from the Sierra Madre Occidental. Once primarily a mining town, it is now a lively commercial and industrial centre.

History

In pre-Columbian times as well as later, Apaches from Arizona and Comanches from Texas made frequent incursions south, roaming the region.

Early Spanish attempts at settlement and missionising came to nothing, but in 1709 Antonio de Deza y Ulloa successfully founded a community which he christened San Francisco de Cuéllar; the name was changed to San Felipe El Real de Chihuahua (Tarahumara: "dry place") in 1718. Discoveries of rich deposits of silver made Chihuahua prosperous, though constant attacks by Indians impeded its development. In 1811, after being taken prisoner by troops of the Spanish Crown, Pater Miguel Hidalgo y Costilla, father of Mexico's independence, was executed in Chihuahua along with several comrades-in-arms. Both during the war with the USA (1846–48) and during the War of Intervention (1862–66), US forces temporarily occupied the city. Benito Juárez also made Chihuahua his base for a time. The riots at the end of 1910, which followed President Porfirio Díaz's re-election and presaged the Revolution, had their roots in the city. In northern Mexico the revolt was led by Abraham Gonzáles and the charismatic ringleader Francisco ("Pancho") Villa. In 1913, having occupied Chihuahua with his "Divisíon del Norte", Villa set up his headquarters here.

Sights

★ Cathedral

The cathedral of St Francis of Assisi, gracing the Plaza de la Constitución, was built between 1717 and 1826. With its Baroque façade

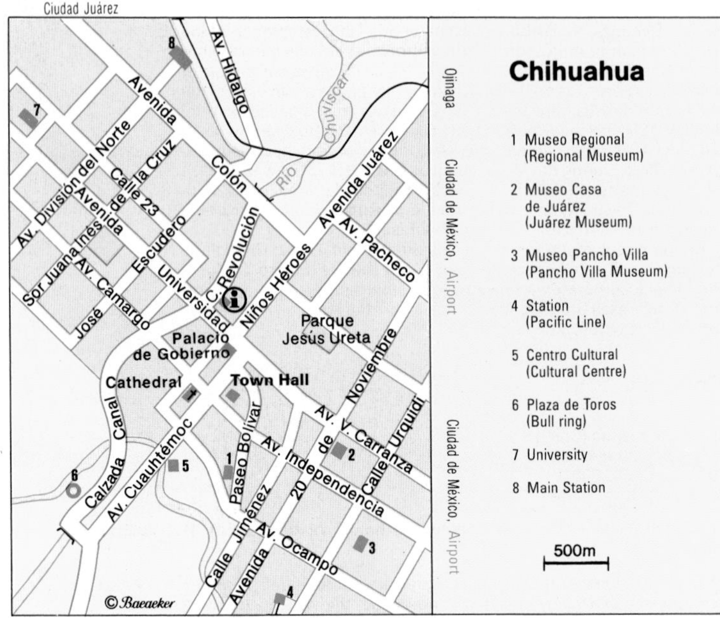

embellished with statues of the twelve apostles there is no more impressive ecclesiastical building in northern Mexico.

Palacio de Gobierno

The Government Palace (Palacio de Gobierno), a short distance away on the Plaza Hidalgo, was originally a Jesuit college but rebuilt in the 19th c. It was here in 1811 that Pater Hidalgo and his principal collaborators were first held prisoner and then executed. Their heads were afterwards impaled and put on public display in Guanajuato. Also to be seen on the Plaza Hidalgo is the Federal Palace (Palacio Federal) where Hidalgo was detained during his trial.

San Francisco

His remains were interred in the church of San Francisco (1721–41) on the Calle Libertad until removed for reburial in Mexico City in 1823.

Museo Regional

★Quinta Gameros

The Chihuahua State Regional Museum (Museo Regional del Estado) is located at Paseo Bolivar 401 (on the corner of Calle 4a). This lovely mansion, called Quinta Gameros, was built between 1907 and 1910 and is one of the finest examples of art nouveau in Mexico. It contains rooms with art nouveau furniture, archaeological exhibits, mainly from Casas Grandes (Paquimé), photographs of and chattels belonging to the strong local Mennonite community, and photographs and documents relating to the history of Chihuahua generally.

★Museum of the Revolution

The Museo Histórico de la Revolución (Museum of the Revolution, also known as the "Pancho Villa Museum"), occupying Quinta Luz, the

Chihuahua: the Cathedral ►

house where Villa once lived at Calle 10 Norte No. 3014, began as a museum run by the revolutionary leader's family. It is now the responsibility of the Mexican army. In addition to Villa's death mask there is a large collection of memorabilia of the famous bandit and popular hero. This includes weapons, photographs, uniforms, flags, documents and the car in which he was driving when shot.

More museums

The Museo Casa de Juárez (Ave. Juárez y Calle 3a) has documents, photographs and newspaper cuttings relating to Benito Juárez's stay in the city and the 1857 Constitution, as well as furniture from the period. Items on display at the Centro Cultural de Chihuahua, housed in a beautiful 19th c. Spanish building at Aldama 430, include pottery from Casas Grandes. Among the other buildings of note are two churches, Santa Rita (1731) and Guadalupe (1826), and the now disused, 5583m/6108yd-long aqueduct (1754–1864).

"Perritos Chihuahuenses"

The tiny hairless Chihuahua dogs ("perritos Chihuahuenses"), which weigh just 600 to 1200g/1½ to 2½lbs and have a body temperature of 40°C/104°F, can sometimes be found on sale at the Sunday market. The breed probably originated in Europe or Africa rather than in Chihuahua.

Surroundings

A number of reservoirs close to the city (Presa Francisco Madero, Las Vírgenes, Chuviscar) offer bathing and fishing.

Some of the old silver mines (Santa Eulalia or Aquiles Serdán) are also worth a visit.

Cuauhtémoc

The countryside around Cuauhtémoc (2100m/6892ft; population: 42,000; fiesta: June 13th, Día de San Antonio), 105km/65 miles west of Chihuahua, is home to Chihuahua's 50,000 strong Mennonite community. Most still speak "Plattdeutsch", a Low German dialect, and make a living from arable farming and cattle rearing.

Mennonites

Founded in the 16th c. by the Dutch reformer Menno Simons, the sect first established communities in Switzerland, Germany and the Netherlands. At the beginning of the 18th c. some Mennonites, forced out of their Frisian homes, made their way to southern Russia by way of Danzig (Gdansk). There too they soon found their privileges – religious freedom, their own schools and exemption from military service – curtailed, as a result of which they emigrated to the USA and Canada. In 1921 Canada required the Mennonite community to participate in the State school system. Once more a number of groups felt forced to move on, this time to a new home in Chihuahua where they set up model farming communities. Measures introduced by the Mexican government in 1976 caused some of the stricter members of the sect to uproot themselves yet again, this time seeking refuge in Texas. The Mennonites still living around Cuauhtémoc are not "Conservadores" (who, for instance, reject electricity as the work of the devil). Although highly conservative in dress – the men wear blue dungarees and the women high-necked dresses, with straw hats trimmed with ribbons over their headscarves – they have accepted the benefits of electricity, cars and tractors. Their villages of simple, spotlessly clean houses are called "campos" and have no names, only a number. Best known among their agricultural products are butter, cheese, ham and apples. The local newspaper is published in German.

La Junta

47km/29 miles west of Cuauhtémoc (MEX 16), La Junta stands at the gateway to the Barranca del Cobre (see entry), access to which is either by train or via a good new road.

★Basaseachic Falls

The Basaseachic Falls at Ocampo are reached by continuing westwards from La Junta in the direction of Yepáchic, the road being asphalted to begin with but later unsurfaced. Set in superb wooded mountain scenery the waterfall is the highest in Mexico, plunging 310m/1017ft into a gorge on the Basaseachic River.

Also from La Junta a reasonable dirt road runs the 132km/82 miles to the small town of Creel which makes a good base for exploring the Barranca del Cobre (see entry).

Ciudad Camargo

Cuidad Camargo, a little town about 150km/93 miles south-east of Chihuahua on the MEX 45, is noted for the curative powers of its three nearby thermal springs, Ojo de Jabalí, Ojo Caliente and Ojo Salado. Also only a short distance away is the Boquilla reservoir.

Hidalgo del Parral

Beyond Ciudad Camargo, the MEX 45 continues first south and then west for 150km/93 miles to the mining town of Hidalgo del Parral (1660m/5500ft; population: 85,000). The town has a number of noteworthy buildings including the parish church, built in 1710, with a Chirrigueresque altar; the church of El Rayo, also 18th c., a popular place of pilgrimage among the Indians (note the Churrigueresque retablo); and the 20th c. church of La Fátima, built of locally-mined lumps of ore. It was in Parral in 1923 that Pancho Villa was ambushed and gunned down in his car. A plaque and a small museum commemorate the event.

Chilpancingo de los Bravos — K 9

State: Guerrero (Gro.)
Altitude: 1360m/4463ft
Population: 180,000
Telephone code: 91 747

Access

From Mexico City by bus (approximately 4½ hours) or car (MEX 95, about 300km/186 miles).

Location

Chilpancingo de los Bravos, capital of Guerrero State, is situated in a valley on the slopes of the Sierra Madre del Sur. The city itself has little in the way of tourist attractions but its location at a junction on the Cuernavaca to Acapulco road makes it an excellent base from which to explore the still largely undisturbed mountainous regions both near at hand and further afield.

History

Since ancient times the area around Chilpancingo (Náhuatl: "place of the wasps") has been the home of a succession of Indian tribes, the Olmecs being the first to leave any traces. In the colonial period its role as a staging post for east-bound merchandise, en route to the central highlands, gave the town its chief raison d'être. In 1813 Chilpancingo's prestige increased when it became the venue for the first Mexican National Congress, chaired by José María Morelos. The soubriquet "de los Bravos" was acquired in 1825, being recognition for the outstanding contribution of the three Bravo brothers to the cause of Mexican independence. Today the city is a centre for the agriculture and forestry in the surrounding area.

Places of interest

Pride of place must go to the Museo Regional with archaeological finds mainly from Guerrero. Of the rest, only the Government Palace (Palacio de Gobierno; frescos illustrating Mexican history), the parish church, and the zoological garden are at all noteworthy.

Surroundings

The road running east to Chilapa and Tlapa has no links with major through routes, leaving the vast area stretching south to the Pacific coast one of the remotest and least known in Mexico.

Chilapa

Chilapa (population: 21,000; fiesta: June 3rd–4th, dancing; Sunday market), 56km/35 miles east of Chilpancingo, was at one time the state capital. It has a modern cathedral and a 16th c. Augustinian monastery.

★ Oxtotitlán Caves

Cave paintings

7km/4 miles north of Chilapa lies the village of Acatlán near to where the Oxtotitlán Caves were discovered as recently as 1968. The two 30m/98ft-deep stalactitic caves, reached after about 45 minutes up-hill walking, contain paintings which have been dated to between 900 and 700 B.C. The motifs suggest Olmec origin. Pictures include a male figure seated on a jaguar throne, stylised jaguar heads and children's faces.

Tlapa

Tlapa, about 66km/41 miles further on, is a Tlapanec settlement with a 16th c. Augustinian monastery. The Tlapanecs probably migrated here in the 9th c. from the south-west of what is now the USA.

Olinalá

Lacquerwork

Roughly half-way (34km/21 miles) along the final stretch of road between Atliztac and Tlapa, a side turning branches left to Olinalá, 35km/22 miles to the north. This little place is famous for its lacquerwork, the lacquer being applied both to wood and to a gourd-like rind using a process which dates back to pre-Hispanic times. (Olinalá lacquerwork is found on sale in shops and markets in many reasonably-sized towns.)

★ Juxtlahuaca Caves

Leaving Chilpancingo via the MEX 95, drive south for 9km/5½ miles to Petaquillas where a side road on the left leads to Colotlipa (a further

Juxlahuaca: cave painting of a jaguar

38km/24 miles). The Juxtlahuaca Caves are situated another 7km/4 miles to the north. Although known about since at least the 1930s, the limestone caves were explored for the first time only in 1966 when they were found to contain 3000-year old wall paintings, skeletal remains and pottery. The paintings, at distances of 1050m/1150yd and 1150m/1260yd from the entrance, again have Olmec themes (depicting Olmec-style chiefs, jaguars, and snakes in shades of black, red, yellow and green).

Chinkultic

See Montebello Lakes

Cholula — K 8

State: Puebla (Pue.)
Altitude: 2150m/7056ft
Population: 40,000

Access

By bus from Mexico City (Terminal del Oriente; about 1½ hours) or Puebla (about 20 minutes); by car motorway from Mexico City to Puebla (126km/78 miles), then a further 12km/7½ miles.

Location

Occupying the same plateau as Puebla 12km/7½ miles away, Cholula was once one of the leading religious, economic and political centres of old Mexico. Today very little of its former splendour remains apart from a gigantic earth mound concealing, if scale is anything to go by, the world's largest pyramid. From the vantage point of the top, now crowned with a church, the eye travels over the towers and domes of numerous other Spanish-built churches and monasteries which, following the Conquest, were erected over the ancient pyramids and temples. Cholula is often said to have 365 churches but in fact there are rather fewer.

History

No one knows who the early inhabitants were, i.e. the people responsible for building Cholula (actually "Atchalollan", Náhuatl: "place where the water rises") in the first place. However there was definitely a major settlement on the site by between 400 and 300 B.C. Around the beginning of the Christian era the influence of the great Classic Teotihuacán culture first seems to have made itself felt, holding sway for 500 years. This shows itself chiefly in the "talud-tablero" structure of Cholula's pyramidal platforms – sloping sections ("taluds") alternating with vertical rectilinear panels ("tableros") with borders, the overall effect being one of long horizontal lines. Early ceramic finds further confirm this initial chronology.

The city's central geographical position relative to a number of later pre-Columbian civilisations then saw Cholula responding stylistically to both the Monte Albán IIIb and El Tajín cultures. In the 7th c. the Xicalanca Olmec people – not to be confused with the pre-Classic Olmecs – took over the Puebla valley, retaining their hold until driven out in about 850. Shortly before 1000 the legendary god-king Quetzalcóatl (Ce Ácati Topiltzin) is reputed to have spent some considerable time here following his expulsion from Tula. After the fall of Tula in 1175 B.C. the Toltecs and Chichimecs moved into the Cholula area, eventually forcing the city's rulers to flee to the Gulf coast.

At about this time also the influence of yet another culture, the Mixtec, already to some degree noticeable, became much more marked, giving rise to the Mixtec-Puebla culture, the outstanding achievement of which was the development of glazed polychrome ceramics. Although occupied from time to time by neighbouring powers (the Huejotzingo, for instance in 1359, and the Aztecs a century later), as a cult site Cholula remained relatively undisturbed throughout the latter part of its long pre-Hispanic history.

Together with their Tlaxcaltec allies, the Spanish conquerors under Cortés arrived in Cholula in 1519, at which time they estimated its population to be 100,000. On the pretext of a suspected ambush they brutally attacked the city and its inhabitants, unleashing a blood-bath in which between 3000 and 6000 people are thought to have been killed. They also destroyed the main temple dedicated to Quetzalcóatl. By the time the great plague epidemic of 1544–46 had finished reaping its grim harvest, Cholula's splendour had already passed into history.

The excavation of the huge pyramid was begun in 1931 under the direction of José Reygadas Vérti, his work being continued by Ignacio Marquina on behalf of the Instituto Nacional de Antropología e Historia (I.N.A.H.). Investigation remains in progress today.

Sights

★Temple pyramid

Cholula's great temple pyramid was dedicated to Quetzalcóatl, pale-skinned, bearded god of the wind who was also identified with Venus, the Morning and Evening Star. In the mythology of the peoples of Meso-America it was he who, representing the forces of technology and civilisation, brought them knowledge of the arts, sciences and agriculture.

The pyramid, almost completely buried beneath a layer of soil and vegetation, is the largest such structure in the world. Measuring 425m/1400ft along each side at the base, it once stood over 62m/200ft high and occupied an area of some 17ha/42 acres. Over a period of about 1500 years it was enlarged on seven occasions by a process of superimposition, until the total interior area amounted to some 3.4 million sq.m/4 million sq.yd. Up to now reconstruction has been confined to a section of the west side. Exploratory work so far carried out, involving excavation of almost 9km/5½ miles of passageways, has revealed not only the remains of platforms, living quarters, temple walls and patios but also a curious stairway and interesting frescos.

Mural

Teotihuacán-style butterflies and grasshoppers decorate the walls together with a magnificent, colourful mural (about A.D. 200), 150m/164ft-long, depicting figures drinking (known as the "Drunkards" mural).

Some idea of the true scale of the huge pyramid complex can be had from the model in the little museum facing the entrance.

Nuestra Señora de los Remedios

Following the Conquest, finding that the indigenous population remained faithful to the cult of Quetzalcóatl and their other deities, the Spanish erected churches over the ancient temples or on the sites. On the razed summit of the main pyramid at Cholula they constructed the church of Nuestra Señora de los Remedios ("Virgin of the Eternal Redemption"). A collapse in 1666 meant that building work had to be restarted, continuing into the 18th c. The church was extensively damaged again in 1884, this time by an earthquake, afterwards being rebuilt in the Neo-Classical style. A statue of the Madonna, preserved behind glass above the altar, is said to have been given to the Franciscans by Cortés.

View

The church affords a magnificent view over the city.

Cholula: Temple Pyramid and Nostra Señora de los Remedios

San Gabriel Monastery

Also to be found surrounded by the ruins of this ancient cult site is the vast San Gabriel monastery, built by the Franciscans in 1549. Note in particular the large atrium, the Plateresque portal, the massive doors and the Gothic arches. The Capilla Real ("Royal Chapel"), modelled architecturally on the great mosque in Córdoba (Spain), dates from the mid 16th c. Renovated in the 17th c. the huge building comprises seven aisles surmounted by 49 cupolas, opening onto a spacious atrium with three prettily ornamented posas (processional chapels).

★Capilla Real

Other churches deserving mention in Cholula are San Andrés, San Miguel Tianguistengo, Guadalupe, Santiago Mixquitla and San Miguelito.

The city is also the site of the University of the Americas, opened in 1970.

Surroundings

Acatapec (see entry), Tonantzintla and Tlaxcalancingo (see Acatapec, Surroundings) are just a few kilometres south of Cholula. Huejotzingo (see entry) is about the same distance to the north-west, with Calpan (see Huejotzingo, Surroundings) a little way beyond.

Citlaltépetl (Pico de Orizaba)

See Puebla (City)

Ciudad del Carmen

See Campeche (City)

Ciudad de México

See Mexico City

Ciudad Juárez

See Chihuahua (State)

Ciudad Obregón

See Guaymas

Ciudad Victoria

See Tamaulipas

Coahuila de Zaragoza (State)

Abbreviation: Coah.
Capital: Saltillo
Area: 150,395sq.km/58,052sq. miles
Oficial population 1990: 1,972,000 (1994 estimate: 2,200,000)

Location and topography

Coahuila, Mexico's third largest state after Chihuahua and Sonora, shares its borders with the USA (Texas) to the north, Chihuahua and Durango to the west, Zacatecas to the south and Nuevo León to the east. It consists mainly of a vast uneven plateau crossed by several mountain chains. The climate is predominantly hot and dry and the soil infertile, except in those valleys which are artificially irrigated (at considerable cost).

History

Álvaro Nuñez Cabeza de Vaca, the first European to reach the area – at the time inhabitated mainly by nomadic tribes – did so after an eight year trek on foot. The first reasonably-sized settlement in Coahuila (Náhuatl: "featherless serpent"), was established in 1575 by Francisco de Urdiñola on the site of present-day Saltillo. To provide protection against hostile Indians, Urdiñola brought some of Spain's Mexican allies the Tlaxcaltecs with him. Unlike other tribes they were accorded substantial privileges. From this initial outpost the Spaniards slowly pressed further north into what is now the USA.

From Mexican Independence until the hiving off of the Texan territories in 1836, Coahuila and Texas formed a single state, with Monclova or Saltillo as its capital. At that time, and also subsequently, unrest verging on civil war brought the Mexicans under General Antonio López de Santa Ana into conflict with Americans led by Zachary Taylor, culminating eventually in outright war against the United States. In 1857 Coahuila was amalgamated with Nuevo León, only becoming an independent state in 1868. In 1863 Benito Juárez, fleeing from French Interventionist troops, temporarily set up his headquarters in Saltillo.

Economy

The state, blessed with good transport links, boasts a relatively stable economy based principally on steel production, a substantial mining

Mexico
United Mexican States
Estados Unidos Mexicanos

Coahuila

industry (silver, lead, coal, copper, iron), an increasingly important agricultural processing industry, and many branches of agriculture as such including cultivation of maize, wheat, beans, cotton, sugar cane and wine. Livestock farming also contributes significantly.

Places of interest

Saltillo

The Coahuila state capital is Saltillo (1550m/5087ft; population: 350,000; fiestas August 8th, Santo Cristo de la Capilla; August 13th, fair) where the lovely Churrigueresque Baroque cathedral of Santiago, gracing the main square, was constructed between 1746 and 1801. Noteworthy too are the 16th c. church of San Esteban (1592) and the picturesque Plaza Alameda. Saltillo is also famous for its woollen industry (sarapes) and its university (summer courses for foreigners).

Torreón

Torreón (1137m/3732ft; population: 450,000), situated in the far southwest of the state, is Coahuila's largest city, an industrial centre which grew up at the intersection of several major transport routes. Scarcely a hundred years old, the city has little of tourist interest apart from the Museo Regional de la Laguna (Parque Carranza) which houses archaeological finds from the area. The surrounding countryside is exceedingly dry but rendered exceptionally fertile, by artifical irrigation. Wheat and cotton are the principal crops though others are also grown. Processing of minerals, wheat and wine are major industries.

Monclova

Monclova (600m/1970ft; population: 180,000), also an industrial city of considerable importance, is the site of one of Mexico's largest iron and steelworks. The Museo Biblioteca Pape (Blvd. Constitución 505 Sur) has several interesting collections including pictures and graphics by modern Mexican painters, pre-Columbian artefacts, coins and antiquarian books.

Coahuila's other main towns are Piedras Negras, near Eagle Pass (a US frontier crossing point); Parras, northern Mexico's oldest town, known for its vineyards (Museo del Vino at kilometre 18 on Paila to Parras road); and Sabinas, not far from the Don Martín reservoir.

Coatzacoalcos

See Lake Catemaco

Cobá Q 7

State: Quintana Roo (Q.R.)
Altitude: 8m/26ft

Access

By bus from Cancún (about 2½ hours), Tulum (about 1 hour) or Valladolid (about 2 hours); by car from Cancún via the MEX 307, branching off 2km/1¼ miles south of Tulum (128km/79 miles) onto a good road heading north (Cobá 42km/26 miles); alternatively via the MEX 180 to Nuevo Xcan (85km/53 miles), there turning off to the south (Cobá 45km/28 miles).

Location

Cobá, one of the biggest Mayan sites in Mexico encompassing a number of groups of ruins, lies close to several small lakes in dense Quintana Roo bush country. Blessed by Yucatán standards with an abundance of water, this now almost completely overgrown ancient cult site and settlement was inhabited for a very long period from the early Classic period to the late 15th c.

History

Recent research suggests that Cobá (Mayan: "water moved by the wind") experienced its heydey in the Mayan Classic period (A.D. 600–900) though some of the buildings have been shown to date from the post-Classic era (A.D. 900–1450). It was still occupied when the Spanish arrived in the country but they were evidently unaware of its existence.

The site was rediscovered in 1891 by the Austrian Teobald Maler. Between 1926 and 1929 excavations were carried out for the Carnegie Institute by leading scholars, initially by the Briton Dr Thomas Gann and afterwards by the American and British archaeologists Sylvanus G. Morley, J. Eric Thompson and H. D. Pollock. Since 1973 research at Cobá has been undertaken by the Mexicans themselves.

Visiting the ★ruins

N.B.

Ample time is needed for a visit, both because the site covers a very large area and because the scenery is so beautiful. Some of the excavated pyramids, temples and stelae have yet to be named, others are identified only by numbers or letters assigned to them by archaeologists. The network of paths is also subject to frequent change.

Within the vast area of the site, estimated to be at least 70sq.km/27sq. miles, researchers have so far identified 45 local thoroughfares and connecting roads as well as more than 6000 buildings and other structures. A total of 32 stelae from the Mayan Classic period have already been found, most of them decorated with reliefs. Although the earliest date so far recorded (on Stela 6) is A.D. 613, the architecture of a number of buildings is strongly reminiscent of the Guatemalan Petén, suggesting construction during the Early Classic era (A.D. 300–600). Cobá's

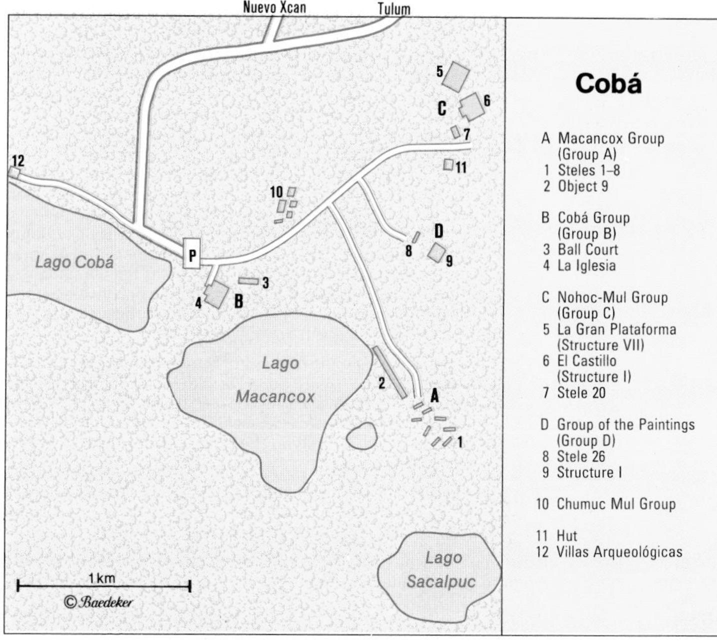

special status as a major metropolis is further indicated by the large number of sacbeob (plural of sacbé = white road) uncovered. These causeways, surfaced with limestone mortar flattened by heavy rolling, form an extensive network linking the centre with outlying districts. Quite exceptionally some of the raised roadways are as much as 10m/33ft wide, and one runs for almost 100km/62 miles to Yaxuná, an ancient cult site south-west of Chichén Itzá where, in the early 1990s, two graves were discovered dating from between A.D. 300 and 315 and unexpectedly revealing the influence of Teotihuacán. The road system in the vicinity of Cobá constitutes the most elaborate found anywhere in Meso-America.

Sacbeob

Cobá Group

"La Iglesia"

To the right on entering the archaeological zone stands a row of buildings known as the Grupo de Cobá (Cobá Group or Group B) among which is the large, partially restored, 24m/79ft-high pyramid called the "Church" ("Iglesia"). Measuring 40m/131ft along its east/west axis and 50m/164ft north to south, it has nine terraces, all with rounded corners. A wall above the seventh terrace supports the upper platform on which stands a small temple. The view from the top, a panorama of the Cobá area with its many pyramids, temples and lakes, is outstanding.

Stela 11

Just in front of the stairway leading up to the "Church" there is a stone block (Stela 11) about 1.40m/4½ft high and 90cm/35in. across, inscribed on one side with a large number of glyphs now unfortunately no longer legible. To the left of the pyramid lie a small group of other buildings in one of which there is a chamber with corbel vaulting.

Ball court

Close to the "Church", but identified rather more easily from the road, are the remains of a ball court (Juego de Pelota).

Nohoch-Mul Group

★El Castillo (pyramid)

Follow the track as it bears north-eastwards to the Nohoch-Mul Group (Mayan: "big hill"), also known as Group C. The principal pyramid (Structure I), called El Castillo, rises to a platform 42m/138ft above the ground, making it the highest accessible Old Indian structure in the Yucatán peninsula. From the base, measuring 55×60m/180×197ft, a 12m/39ft-wide external stairway of 120 steps mounts six terraces to the upper platform. Many of the steps are carved with shell motifs. Entry to the little temple atop the pyramid, in front of which stands a small altar, is by way of two narrow flights of steps 1m/3¼ft wide. The pyramid itself is Mayan Classic but the temple crowning it is in the style of Tulum and dates from considerably later, probably the 14th or 15th c. All three of the square-shaped niches in the upper frieze of the temple contained figures of the so-called "Descending God", though only two now survive. The single doorway leads into a room with corbel vaulting. The view from the top is once again magnificent.

Stela 20

Also on the same plaza are the remains of Structure X, a platform with rounded corners, and the superb Stela 20, dated A.D. 780. The relief on the stela depicts a sumptuously arrayed ruler, each foot resting on the back of a slave shown on hands and knees. The ceremonial staff held at an angle is typical of the Cobá style. The sides and the upper part of the stela are inscribed with glyphs.

La Gran Plataforma

North of El Castillo lies La Gran Plataforma (Structure VII), the largest in volume of all the buildings at Cobá with a base measuring 110×125m/361×410ft and height of more than 30m/98ft.

Group of Paintings

Returning along the track towards the site entrance, veer left a little way along to the so-called Group of Paintings (Grupo de las Pinturas or

The El Castillo Pyramid dominates the Nohoch-Mul Group

Grupo D). The main building is a pyramid (Structure I) crowned by a small temple with doors facing east and west and a main portal on the north side divided in two by a column. The lintel over the portal and the three horizontal stone ledges above it all show clear traces of the original painting. The post-Classic frescos portray various numbers and deities. There is a splendid view of the El Castillo pyramid through the east door.

In the centre of the group stands Structure IV with its stela (No. 26), the latter with typical reliefs in the Cobá style.

Macanxoc Group

On the way back from the Grupo de las Pinturas take the path which runs off leftwards after a short distance to the Macanxoc Group (Group A) situated between Lakes Macanxoc and Sacalpuc. Lacking any major structures but linked to the great 20m/66ft-wide Sacbe 9, this now very overgrown area was presumably a ceremonial site of some kind. Eight stelae have so far been discovered, of which Nos. 1, 4 and 6 are in a relatively good state of preservation. These oblate stone pillars, 3m/10ft high and 1.5m/5ft across, are carved with reliefs of rulers and Mayan inscriptions in glyphic form. Stela 1 is unusual in being one of a small number of Mayan monuments bearing four different dates: 29. 1. 653, 29. 6. 672, 28. 8. 682 and 21. 12. 2011. Of these, the first three probably refer to real events while the last looks ahead to the start of a winter far in the future. With a total of 313 glyphs on its four sides, this stela is exceptionally heavily inscribed. Apart from the stelae the Macanxoc Group also includes several circular altars hewn from a single block of stone.

There are plenty of other interesting ruins in Cobá. Which to visit is a matter best decided on the spot since it will depend on their state of restoration and/or accessibility at the time.

Colima (State)

Abbreviation: Col.
Capital: Colima
Area: 5205sq.km/2009sq. miles
Official population 1990: 428,500 (1994 estimate: 550,000)

Location and topography

The small Pacific coast state of Colima borders on Jalisco in the north and north-west and Michoacán in the east. Most of the state is covered by a flat coastal plain, merging in the north-east into the foothills of the Sierra Madre where the rock is of tectonic origin. The Islas Revilla Gigedo (Sorocco, San Benedicto, Roca Partida and Clarión) are also part of Colima. The population includes Nahua Indians as well as descendents of the Spanish and mestizos.

Archaeological sites

The archaeological sites in Colima are principally burial grounds, the most interesting of which are El Chanal, Los Ortices and Periquillos.

History

Little or nothing is known about the early peoples to whom Colima and neighbouring regions are indebted for their Old Indian art. Until more is discovered about their true identity, they are simply referred to as the Teca. They were most probably Nahua tribes who settled the area at various times during the Late and post-Classic period.

On the basis of numerous grave finds, including well-preserved examples of the unusually naturalistic and attractive ceramic art of the region, historians have tentatively proposed a chronology of cultural phases. Of these, the Classic era, known as the Los Ortices/Las Ánimas (about A.D. 200 to 850), was, artistically speaking, the most fertile,

developing in parallel with the corresponding phase in Teotihuacán. The next phase, called the Armería/Colima, lasted from about A.D. 850 to 1250. It thus overlaps with the early post-Classic period and is marked by Toltec influence. The final, or Periquillo, phase (A.D. 1250–1521) coincided with the so-called Chimalhuacán Alliance to which four cultural groups, including the indigenous Colimán (Náhuatl: "conquered by our grandfathers"), belonged. This confederation came under attack from the Purépecha (Tarascans) in the second half of the 15th c. Cajitlán (Náhuatl: "place where pottery is made"), believed to have been founded in the 11th c. and which later became an important city in the region, probably stood on the site now occupied by Tecomán.

Just a year after the collapse of Tenochtitlán (1521), the first Spanish invaders arrived in the area of present-day Colima led by Gonzalo de Sandoval and Juan Álvarez Chico. It was left however to Francisco Cortés de San Buenaventura, a nephew of Hernán Cortés, to complete the initial conquest. During the colonial period Colima was part of the province of Nueva Galicia, administered from Guadalajara. In 1792 Miguel Hidalgo, father of Mexican Independence, was priest in charge of the parish of Colima. For a time Colima was part of Michoacán State, then an independent territory, before becoming a federal state in its own right in 1867.

Economy

Sugar cane, rice, maize, copra and coffee are the main crops, with livestock farming widely practised in higher-lying areas. Mineral extraction is chiefly of copper, lead, iron and salt. Forestry, fishing and tourism are also important. The Revilla Gigedos islands produce sulphur, guano, timber, fruit, sheep and fish.

Principal towns

Apart from the capital Colima (see entry) and the port cum holiday resort of Manzanillo (see entry), the only fairly large towns of note are

Colima: terracotta model of temple . . . *. . . and terracotta dogs*

Armería (near Manzanillo) and Tecomán (80m/262ft; population: 53,000; fiestas: 2 February, Día de la Candelaria, 12 December, Día de Nuestra Señora de Guadalupe).

Colima (City) H 8

State: Colima (Col.)
Altitude: 508m/1667ft
Population: 250,000
Telephone code: 91 331

Access from Mexico City

By rail via Guadalajara (see entry) in about 17 hours (4 hours from Guadalajara); by bus via Guadalajara in about 13 hours (3½ hours from Guadalajara); by car on the MEX 54 from Guadalajara (265km/165 miles) via Ciudad Guzmán.

Location and "townscape"

Colima, capital of Colima State, extends across the slopes of a fertile valley watered by two rivers. With its views of two magnificent mountain peaks, its simple colonial architecture, its luxuriant gardens and air of tranquillity, the city is a most delightful place.

History

The area around Colima almost certainly has a long pre-Columbian history, although next to nothing is known about the early inhabitants. Arriving in 1522 the Spanish under Gonzalo de Sandoval found an Indian settlement already in place, and established a town called San Sebastián de Caballeros next to it. Over the years, mainly in the 18th c. but again in recent decades, it has grown into a flourishing centre where the livestock, timber and agricultural produce of the ranches and haciendas in the countryside around is processed and marketed.

Sights

Museums

The city is well worth visiting just to see the Museum of Western Cultures (Museo de las Culturas de Occidente; Calz. Galván y Ejército Nacional). It is principally devoted to archaeological finds from the Colima culture burial sites.

The Museo de Arte y Cultura Popular (or Museo Maria Teresa Pomar; corner of Calle 27 Septiembre/Manuel Gallardo Zamora) has a collection of regional costumes and musical instruments from all over Mexico, also a complete bakehouse for making the very typical "pan dulce".

Pre-Hispanic ceramicware, baskets, furniture and dancers' masks can be seen at the Museo de Historia de Colima (Portal Morelos 1).

Buildings

In addition to the Government Palace (Palacio de Gobierno) and the cathedral, the churches of San José, Fátima and El Sagrado Corazón all deserve mention.

Surroundings

Tampuchamay

The hotel at Tampuchamay (turn off for Los Azmoles 12km–7½ miles south of Colima; after 5km/3 miles take the Los Ortices road) has an open-air museum with numerous sculptures; at the burial sites themselves, bones and fragments of pottery can sometimes still be seen in situ. Various species of bat and other coelenterates inhabit the Gruta de Tampuchamay.

Comalá

Situated about 10km/6 miles north of Colima, the attractive small town of Comalá is the centre of the local crafts industry (furniture, paintings and wrought ironwork). Comalá is also the location of an unusual magnetic phenomenon. Take a taxi from the main square; the driver will turn off his engine and the vehicle will be drawn uphill as if by magic.

★Nevado de Colima and ★Volcán de Colima

Some 40km/25 miles north of Colima, across the state boundary in Jalisco, tower the peaks of Nevado de Colima (4339m/14,240ft) and Volcán de Colima (3838m/12,596ft). The former, also called Zapotépetl ("mountain of the zapote tree), is the seventh highest mountain in Mexico. The Volcán de Colima, known as the "Volcano of Fire" (Volcán de Fuego; crater 1800m/1869yd in diameter and 250m/820ft deep) erupted several times between 1957 and 1975 causing considerable damage. A very poor track off to the left a short distance before the little town of Atenquique (timber factory), leads to the volcano and also the Parque Nacional de Volcán de Fuego 27km/17 miles further on. In its present condition the track is only negotiable, when at all, using a 4-wheel drive vehicle. A little way beyond Atenquique a poorish country road/field track likewise branches off left for 37km/23 miles to the Parque Nacional de Nevado de Colima, to which another track beginning 2km/1¼ miles before Ciudad Guzmán (leading to Albergue La Joya and the Canal 13 radio station) also gives access. Once again neither route should be attempted without a cross-country vehicle.

N.B.

These tracks are heavily used by timber transporters.

Córdoba

L 8

State: Veracruz (Ver.)
Altitude: 920m/3019ft. Population: 200,000
Telephone code: 91 271

Access from Mexico City

By rail in about 7 hours; by bus in about 5 hours; by car via the MEX 150 (about 305km/189 miles).

Location

Picturesque Córdoba lies amidst the lush greenery of the valley of the Río Seco, at the eastern end of the Orizaba–Córdoba section of the still incomplete motorway from Mexico City to Veracruz (the other completed section being Mexico City–Puebla). Tropical fruit is cultivated in the lower-lying areas bordering the hot coastal plain, while coffee and tobacco are grown at middle altitudes. Higher up still, many of the mountain slopes are covered with cedar forest and nut groves.

History

Córdoba (named after the Andalusian city and old Moorish capital) was founded by the Spanish in 1618. It was here on August 24th 1821 that the Treaty of Córdoba, agreed between General Agustín de Iturbide (who later had himself crowned Emperor of Mexico) and the last Spanish viceroy Juan O'Donojú, was signed giving recognition to Mexico's independence. It was some years, however, before the treaty was accepted in Spain.

Sights

Zócalo

A strong Andalusian-Moorish influence is still evident in many of the houses, especially the ancient, solid wooden doors, heavily barred windows and wooden balconies. Two buildings of particular note stand on the arcaded main square (or zócalo), the neo-Classical-style Town Hall (Palacio Municipal) and, at the edge of the square, the Hotel Zevallos, the latter being of historical interest as the place where the Treaty of Córdoba was concluded. Another historic landmark is the Casa Quemada ("burnt house") on the corner of Calle 7 and Avenida 5, where a small group of Mexican rebels fought to the death with Spanish forces at the outbreak of the War of Independence.

Museum

Pride of place in the city's small museum (Museo de la Ciudad de Córdoba, Calle 3 No. 303) is given to the relics of the Totonac culture and a copy of the Treaty of Córdoba.

Market

The Mercado Juárez, the market between Calle 7 and Avenida 8, well repays a visit. It draws large numbers of people from all over the area, particularly at weekends.

Surroundings

★Fortín de las Flores

Fortín de las Flores ("fort of flowers"; 1010m/3315ft; population: 60,000; fiesta: April 15th–17th, flower festival), 6km/3¾ miles west of the city on the MEX 150, was the site of a Spanish stronghold in colonial times. Today the town's equable climate and abundance of subtropical and temperate flowering plants, make it an exceptionally pleasant place to stay. The superb main plaza, on which stand the town hall and public library, comprises two equal-sized gardens separated by a narrow thoroughfare. Fortín de las Flores is surrounded by coffee plantations covering the high mountain slopes, while in the lower-lying areas subtropical fruit such as mangoes, oranges, bananas, pineapples and papayas thrive. On clear days, especially early in the morning, there is a fine view of Mexico's highest summit (5700m/18,707ft), the snow-clad Pico de Orizaba (Citlaltépetl = "mountain of the star"; see Puebla, Surroundings). A visit to a nearby hacienda or to the Sunday market make interesting outings.

View of Pico de Orizaba

The area around Córdoba and Fortín de las Flores has the heaviest rainfall in all Mexico. From May to September long periods of torrential downpour can be expected, becoming less torrential but hardly any shorter from October until late December. The period from January to May is usually dry.

Cozumel

Q 7

State: Quintana Roo (Q.R.)
Area: about 500sq.km/193sq. miles
Population: 70,000
Telephone code: 91 987

Access

By air from Mexico City in about 2½ hours, Mérida (see entry) in about 40 minutes, Cancún (see entry) in about 15 minutes; also from other Mexican and US airports; by ferry from Playa del Carmen (passenger ferry) in about 1 hour or Puerto Aventuras (car ferry) in about 2 hours (see Practical Information, Ferries). A hovercraft service operates from Cancún.

Location

★Resort and
★diving ground

45km/28 miles long and 18km/11 miles across at its widest, Cozumel, one of the largest Mexican islands, lies 20km/12½ miles off the north-east coast of the Yucatán peninsula. The flat terrain is covered for the most part with dense green scrub, while around the shores magnificent white sand beaches contrast vividly with the blue-green sea. Because the seabed consists of very fine white coral sand, the water is crystal clear.

The island, an excellent diving ground, was first opened up to tourism in the late 1950s.

History

Cozumel, known to the Maya as Ah-cuzamil ("land of the swallows"), was apparently a site of major significance during the Mayan post-Classic period, particularly between A.D. 1000 and 1200. As the most easterly of all the Mayan sites, the island was almost certainly a sanctuary associated with worship of the rising sun. Old records also suggest that it was from Cozumel that several Mayan tribes, including the Itzá, set off on their migrations across the mainland. In addition the island was undoubtedly an important place of pilgrimage dedicated to the goddess of fertility Ix-chel, patroness of birth, medicine and the art of weaving. As Moon goddess and wife of the Sun god Itzamná (the supreme deity), Ix-chel occupied a central place in Yucatán Mayan mythology. Mayan women were especially fervent in their veneration of such sites.

The first Spaniard to discover the island was Juan de Grijalva in 1518, followed in 1519 by Hernán Cortés and in 1527 by Francisco de Montejo. The latter aimed to use it as a base from which to take control of the entire Yucatán. When Cortés landed, there were some 40,000 people living on the island.

In the 17th, 18th and 19th centuries. Cozumel served primarily as a refuge for pirates and smugglers, including Henry Morgan, Laurent de Graff, Long John Silver and Jean Lafitte. In the second half of the 19th c. many refugees from the "Caste Wars" fled the mainland to Cozumel. During the Second World War the old town of San Miguel was bulldozed to make way for a US airforce base.

In September 1988 hurricane "Gilbert" swept over Cozumel at 370kph/230mph, causing severe damage to everything in its path.

Sights

San Miguel de Cozumel

In addition to a small marine aquarium, San Miguel de Cozumel, the island's "capital" on the north-west side, has an interesting museum,

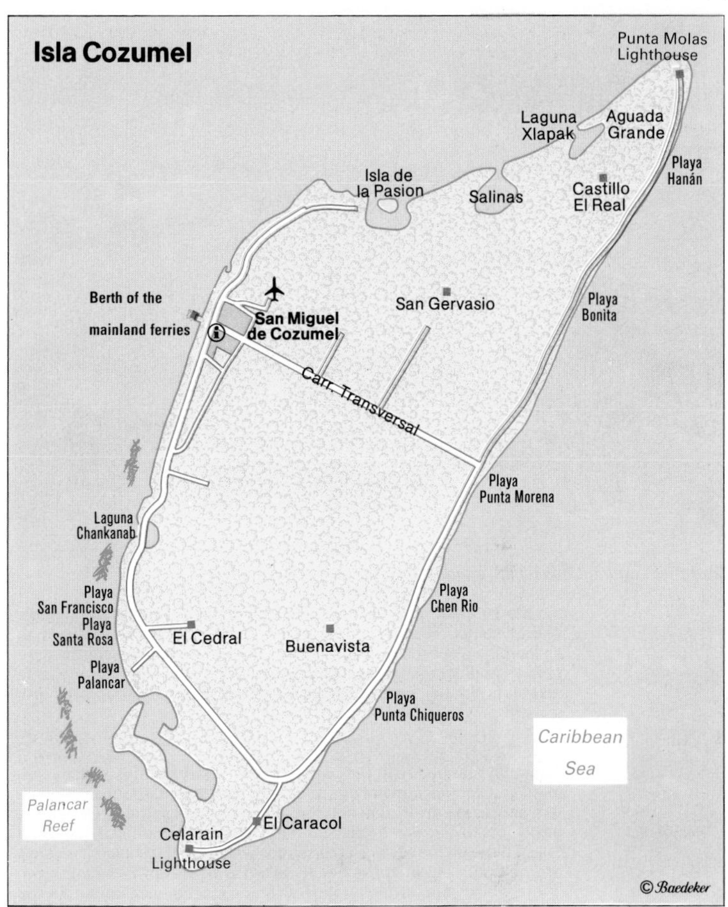

the Museo de la Isla (Avda. Rafael E. Melgar/C. 6 Norte). Exhibits reflect the island's geography and history, as well as the fascinating world beneath the sea.

★ Beaches

Among the most popular and attractive of Cozumel's beaches are the Playas San Juan and Pilar (north-west) and the Playas San Francisco, Santa Rosa and Palancar (south-west). On the east side, open to the Caribbean, are the Playas Encantada, Hanan, Bonita, Punta Morena, Chen Río and Chiqueros.

N.B.

Under certain conditions the heavy swell and strong currents can prove dangerous.

Laguna Chankanab

The Laguna Chankanab (Mayan: "little sea"), a small freshwater lake situated 7km/4½ miles south of San Miguel de Cozumel and linked to

Cozumel: Laguna Chankanab, an ideal lake for snorkelling

the sea by underground channels, is particularly popular for outings. The crystal-clear water, home to a variety of creatures, make it an enchanting place to swim and snorkel. Recent years have seen a nature reserve and botanic garden established beside the lagoon. (A wildlife reserve is also being set up on the Isla de la Pasión, off Cozumel's north coast.)

Diving ground

Although marine life in the waters around Cozumel has already suffered considerably (mainly from over-fishing with harpoons), snorkellers and scuba-divers can still find much to interest them. One of the best spots to dive is the Palancar reef, rising from depths of 80m/262ft to just beneath the surface at the south-west end of the island, where a bronze figure of Christ has been erected underwater, 17m/56ft down. There is also good diving on the San Francisco, Paraíso, Columbia and Maracaibo reefs and the Santa Rosa Wall.

★ Palancar reef

Mayan sites

More than 30 small Mayan sites have been found on the island, of which only a handful have been investigated and still fewer have undergone any restoration. Although most of the unexplored ruins are of no great architectural interest, some are delightfully situated, hidden away in the jungle. The most important of the sites is San Gervasio, about 16km/10 miles from San Miguel de Cozumel and accessible by vehicle. Its temple of Ix-chel was the chief focus of the island's religious life and the centre to which pilgrims were drawn. Near by are more ruins at Santa Rita. Other sites include Santa Pilar in the north and Castillo Real to the north-east, the latter boasting Cozumel's largest Mayan structure. There are also Mayan remains in the south-east of the island at Buenavista and in the south at El Caracol, near the lighthouse.

Cuauhtémoc

See Chihuahua (City)

Cuautla K 8

State: Morelos (Mor.)
Altitude: 1280m/4200ft. Population: 150,000
Telephone code: 91 735

Access from Mexico City

By rail in about 3½ hours; by bus in about 2 hours; by car via the MEX 115 (about 100km/62 miles).

Location

Cuautla, long known about and much valued because of its thermal springs, lies in a part of the country blessed with a subtropical climate and correspondingly luxuriant vegetation. Located at the intersection of several cross-country routes, the town makes a good base for excursions to places of interest in the surrounding area, the main attraction being the many convents (see Morelos) within reach.

History

Cuautla (Náhuatl: "Cuauhtlán" = "place of the eagle") was already well known for its healing waters in pre-Columbian times, and in the early 17th c. became a fashionable spa for prosperous Spaniards.

In 1812, during the Mexican War of Independence, a battle was fought here between rebel forces led by José María Morelos and troops of the Spanish Crown. Emiliano Zapata, leader of the indomitable peasants' revolt during the Mexican Revolution (1910–20), came from Anenecuilco, 6km/3¾ miles to the south.

Sights

Little from the colonial period survives in the town, though the two best-known churches, San Díego and Santíago, both date from the 17th c. Memorabilia from the time of the War of Independence are displayed in the Casa de Morelos.

Therapeutic baths

Agua Hedionda (Spanish: "stinking water", on the east side of the town), Agua Linda, Casasano and El Almeal are the principal therapeutic baths in and around Cuautla, most being hot sulphur springs.

Surroundings

Zacualpan de Amilpas

A road branching north off MEX 160, about 20km/12½ miles from Cuautla in the direction of Puebla, leads to Zacualpan de Amilpas (8km/5 miles). This delightful village boasts an Augustinian convent complete with fortified church dating from the 16th c. In the corners of the atrium are two posas (processional chapels). Note also the frescos in the cloister (restored in the 19th c.). The pretty spa of Atotonilco is about 8km/5 miles to the south.

Atotonilco

Tepalcingo
★Shrine of Jesús Nazareno

Some 7km/4½ miles further on lies the small town of Tepalcingo (population: 16,000). One of its six churches, the Shrine of Jesús Nazareno (1759–89), is an outstanding example of Mexican-Indian Baroque. The richly sculpted façade contrasts with those of other Baroque and Churrigueresque buildings in the province in lacking the usual estípites (pilasters) and Salomonic columns. It is carved almost in the manner of an altarpiece with scenes from the New Testament interpreted through Indian eyes. Inside, note the altarpieces (*c.* 1800) posing as paintings. They are ascribed to Juan de Sáenz.

On the third Friday of Lent Topalcingo witnesses the climax of a major pilgrimage together with a feria involving much merrymaking.

Chalcatzingo

To get to Chalcatzingo, take the road south off the MEX 160 not far from Amayuca, then, after 2km/1¼ miles, branch left for the village 4km/2½ miles further on. The façade of the pretty colonial church of San Mateo has naïve sculptures and ornamentation showing Indian influence.

Cerro de la Cantera and Cerro Delgado

★Rock reliefs

At Cerro de la Cantera and Cerro Delgado, two pre-Hispanic archaeological sites 2km/1¼ miles beyond Chalcatzingo, reliefs hewn in the rock are among the most important of their kind. Judging from the motifs the people responsible for the carvings must either have been Olmec or at least within the Olmec sphere of influence. Recent investigation dates the heyday of the sites as between 1100 and 550 B.C. with the finest of the reliefs probably dating from between 700 and 500 B.C. The most interesting is Petroglyph 1 ("El Rey"), an almost 3m/10ft-high relief of a richly-arrayed figure seated in a cave (or possibly in monster jaguar jaws). Maize plants sprout at the edge of the "jaws" while above are clouds making rain. Petroglyph 2 shows a bearded captive menaced by two Olmec warriors, Petroglyph 4 has jaguars attacking reclining figures, and in Petroglyph 5 a strange snake coils round another reclining human figure (possibly an early allusion to the Quetzalcóatl cult). Complex III, at the foot of the hillside, comprises a number of platforms and altars.

Las Pilas

The Las Pilas archaeological site lies 3km/2 miles west of Chalcatzingo.

Cuernavaca K 8

State: Morelos (Mor.)
Altitude: 1540m/5054ft
Population: 800,000
Telephone code: 91 731

Access

From Mexico City: by bus (about 1½ hours) or car via the MEX 95 (75km/47 miles).

Location

★Old colonial atmosphere

Cuernavaca, state capital of Morelos, lies barely an hour's drive south of Mexico City. Its mild subtropical climate, myriads of brightly-coloured flowers and city centre full of old colonial charm make it a popular place of escape for people from the capital, adding to the large proportion of its residents who are retired. Recently however, creeping industrialisation and ever greater numbers of visitors have tended to mar the city's once rather intimate atmosphere.

History

Cuernavaca (Náhuatl: Cuauhnáhuac = "near the trees") has a long Old Indian history, believed to date back to the Olmecs. From about A.D. 1200 it was the capital of the Tlahuica (Náhuatl: "people of the earth") who were subjugated by the Aztecs under Itzcóatl early in the 15th c. Even before that there is some suggestion of an association – most likely simply mythical – between the Aztec chief Huitzilíhuitl and Miahuaxihuitl, daughter of the ruler of Cuernavaca, a man famous for his supernatural powers. The future mighty Aztec ruler Moctezuma I was allegedly born out of this relationship. Right up until the Spanish Conquest the Aztecs maintained magnificent summer residences in Cuernavaca.

The Spaniards under Hernán Cortés seized and sacked Cuauhnáhuac in 1521. After the Emperor Charles V deprived him of his political power, Cortés stayed on in the city for a long while as Count of Cuerna-

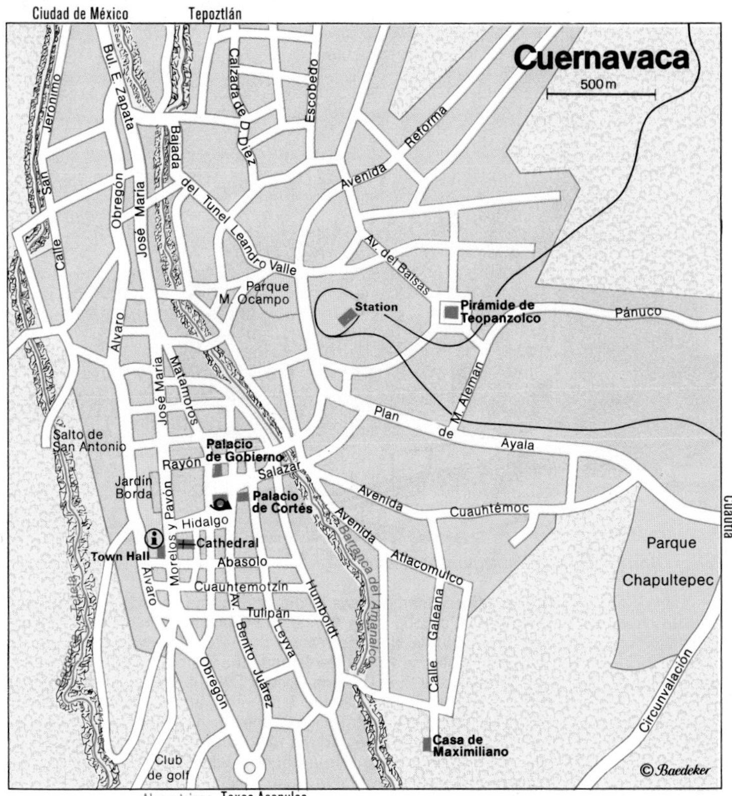

vaca, before finally returning to Spain in 1540. In the colonial period the Spanish upper class greatly enjoyed visiting Cuernavaca, and the Emperor Maximilian and his wife Charlotte took up residence there on several occasions during their short reign (1864–67). In the course of the Mexican Revolution (1910–20), the rebellious peasantry led by Emiliano Zapata – who, with his cry of "Tierra y Libertad" (Land and Liberty), demanded redistribution of the huge landed estates – razed many haciendas in the surrounding area.

From 1936 to 1938 the English author Malcolm Lowry (1909–57) lived in Cuernavaca at Calle Humboldt 15. Using its old name he made the city the setting of his novel "Under the Volcano", published in 1947.

Sights

★ Palacio Cortés

Situated not far from the Plaza Principal (Zócalo or Plaza Morelos), the Palacio Cortés, begun in about 1530 but later altered several times, was once Cortés' residence and administrative headquarters. The first floor

Palacio Cortés, housing the regional Museum

loggias offer splendid views of the city and its environs. The Palacio now houses, among other things, the Cuauhnáhuac regional history museum, documenting the history of the Cuernavaca area. Among many items of interest are the famous murals by Diego Rivera, commissioned by the then US ambassador Dwight Morrow, father-in-law of the transatlantic flyer Charles Lindbergh, and painted in 1929 and 1930. They depict scenes from the Conquest, the history of Cuernavaca, the War of Independence and the Mexican Revolution. The image of Emiliano Zapata leading Hernán Cortés' white horse symbolises the people's re-appropriation of the land.

★ Regional history museum

★ Cathedral

The cathedral, located on the corner of Hidalgo and Morelos streets, began life as a Franciscan friary, founded by Hernán Cortés in 1529. Work started on the fortress-like complex in 1533. The side portal of the church has a fine colonial-Plateresque façade with, above the gable, the symbols of a crown, cross, skull and bones framed by an alfiz.

Interior

During restoration of the cathedral interior in the 1950s, some early murals were uncovered depicting the departure of 24 Mexican Franciscan friars, embarking at the start of their missionary journey to Japan, and their subsequent martyrdom on the cross in 1597. Among them was Mexico's only saint, San Felipe de Jesús.

Chapel of the Third Order

The Chapel of the Third Order, at the rear of the monastery building, has a very typical Mexican Baroque façade, embellished with a small figure representing Hernán Cortés. Like the chapel's lovely carved wooden altar (1735), the façade shows strong Indian influence.

Open Chapel

Adjoining the cathedral stands the spacious Open Chapel, its vaulting supported on three arches. Two buttresses reinforce the central

Colourful market in Cuernavaca

columns. Remains of murals showing the lineage of the Franciscan order can be seen in the cloister.

Every Sunday a folk mass is celebrated in the cathedral to the accompaniment of mariachi music. Mariachi players also perform there on Sunday and Wednesday evenings.

Jardín Borda

The Jardín Borda (Borda Garden), diagonally opposite the cathedral, was laid out in the second half of the 18th c. by José de la Borda, the so-called "silver king" from the mining town of Taxco. The park, restored most recently in 1987, contains terraced gardens, ponds, fountains and an open-air theatre. During their brief reign (1864–67) it was used by the Emperor Maximilian and his wife Charlotte for garden parties. The Casa de Maximiliano (restored 1960) in the Calle Galeana was the imperial couple's summer residence.

Museo Casa Robert Brady

Formerly a private house, the Casa Robert Brady (C. Netzahualcóyotl 4) now contains 1300 works of art including items from the pre-Columbian and colonial periods, pictures by Frida Kahlo and Rufino Tamayo, and examples of American, African and Asian art.

Museo Taller

The Museo Taller occupies Calle Venus 7. Here, together with his companion Angélica Arenal, the artist David Álfaro Siqueiros spent the last nine years of his life. On display are unfinished murals, photographs and other memorabilia.

Casa Olinda

Be sure to make the short journey (1½km/1 miles) south from the city centre to visit the Casa Olinda (also known as the Casa del Olvido) in the one-time village and now suburb of Alcapatzingo. The house, still enjoying a tranquil almost rural setting, was built by Emperor Maximilian as a pied-à-terre to be shared with "India Bonita", his Indian mistress. Today the park contains a herb museum (Museo de la Herbolaría).

Salto de San Antón

Salto de San Antón, a waterfall in picturesque surroundings with a 30m/98ft-high cascade, can be seen on the western edge of the city.

Teopanzolco

Teopanzolco (Náhuatl: "abandoned temple"), a pre-Columbian site dating from late post-Classic period (1250–1521), is located on the north-east outskirts of the city, near the railway station. It was discovered only in 1910 when, following fighting between government troops and Zapata-led rebels, traces of a wall were left uncovered by an exploding shell. The complex, a last relic of the old capital of Tlahuica and typically Aztec in style, comprises two pyramids of different age, superimposed one upon the other. A double external stairway ascends to the top of the pyramid where the remains of walls belonging to two temples (to Huitzilopochtli and Tláloc) can still be seen. Embedded in the walls are primitive animal heads, worked in stone and at one time stucco-covered. Smaller pyramids were dedicated to Ehécatl (the god of wind) and Tezcatlipoca ("smoking mirror").

Surroundings

Tequesquitengo crater lake

About 50km/31 miles south of Cuernavaca the Tequesquitengo crater lake and, on the east shore, the village of Tequesquitengo itself (914m/3000ft; population: 7000) lie surrounded by lush subtropical vegetation. A whole range of watersports are catered for on the lake.

Tlaquiltenango

16km/10 miles north-east of Tequesquitengo the village of Tlaquiltenango boasts a monastery founded by the Franciscans in around 1530 but taken over by the Dominicans 40 years later. Note in particular the atrium and posas (processional chapels), also the side portal with a colonial-Plateresque façade similar to that of Cuernavaca Cathedral.

Xochichalco

Roughly 35km/22 miles south-west of Cuernavaca are found the ruins of Xochicalco (see entry), a site which at various times came under the influence of several different pre-Columbian cultures.

Monasteries

In the eastern part of Morelos (see entry) there are a number of towns and villages of interest, in particular on account of their monasteries.

Culiacán

See Sinaloa (State)

Distrito Federal / Federal District

Abbreviation: D.F.
Area: 1483sq.km/572sq. miles
Population 1990: 8,235,700 (1994 estimate: 10,600,000)

Location

Like the US Federal District of Columbia, the Distrito Federal was established around the nation's capital as a means of preserving the independence of central government from individual states (its administration is the direct responsibility of the Mexican president). The Distrito occupies the south-east corner of the Valley of Mexico, with the Estado de México (see entry) encircling it on three sides and

Distrito Federal

the Estado de Morelos (see entry) on its southern edge. It is bounded naturally by the Sierra de Guadalupe in the north, the foothills of the volcano belt – called the Sierra Nevada on account of the permanent snow-cover on 5000m/16,410ft-high Popcatépetl and Iztaccíhuatl (see entries) – in the east, the Las Cruces mountains in the west, and in the south, guarded by the rounded summits of Cerro Ajusco and Cerro Cuautzín, the Tres Marías Pass near the high Tres Marías. The population consists chiefly of mestizos, Creoles and local Nahua Indians whose numbers have been swelled by Indian migrants from elsewhere. There is also a substantial foreign community.

Archaeological sites

The two most interesting archaeological sites, Cuicuilco and Copilco, are close to "University City", campus of Mexico City's National University. They lie on the southern edge of the Pedregal lava field which covers most of the northern part of the Distrito Federal. The ruins date from the pre-Classic or in some cases the Archaic period. In contrast, after systematic destruction by the conquistadors, little has survived from the golden age of the Aztec empire, such few remains as there are being of no great importance. They are seen to best advantage in the excavations on the corner of Argentina and Guatemala streets, not far from the Zócala, and in the reconstructions on the Plaza de las Tres Culturas in Tlatelolco (see Mexico City).

History

As the El Arbolillo, Ticomán, Zacatenco, Cuicuilco and Copilco archaeological sites testify, the first cultivators had already settled the Valley of Mexico (or Anáhuac Valley) in the pre-Classic (early formative and middle formative) era between 1500 and 800 B.C. Tlatilco (1300–800 B.C.), adjacent to what is now the Distrito Federal, was an important settlement within the Olmec sphere of influence.

Classic period

At times during the Classic period (A.D. 300–900) the area came under the sway of Teotihuacán. After the collapse of Toltec Tollán (Tula) in the second half of the 13th c., various tribes began to migrate into the Anáhuac Valley. A number of small city-states emerged, the most important of which were those of the Otomí-speaking Tepanecs at Atzcapotzalco (Náhuatl: "place of the ant hill"), the Acolhua at Coatlichán, the Chichimecs (Náhuatl: "descended from dogs", i.e. barbaric tribes) at Tenayuca and later Texcoco, and the Toltecs at Culhuacán (Náhuatl: "place of the grandfather").

The Aztecs

It was however the Náhuatl-speaking Aztecs (also known as the Tenocha or Mexica) who were destined to dominate this central valley, together with other sizeable areas of what is now Mexico, during the final 150 years leading up to the Spanish Conquest. They are believed to have abandoned their as yet unidentified island home at Aztlán (or Aztatlán; Náhuatl: "place of the heron", probably in a lagoon somewhere on the north-west coast of Mexico) in about A.D. 1111. Led by their god-king Huitzilopochtli (Náhuatl: "humming bird of the south"), they came via Chicomoztoc (Náhuatl: "seven caves"), origin, so legend has it, of all the migrant 12th c. Náhuatl-speaking peoples, into the Valley of Mexico. The warlike tribe, by this time calling themselves the Mexica, arrived at Chapultepec (Náhuatl: "grasshopper hill") in 1299. Reduced at first to servitude by the Tepanecs, they fled to Culhuacán. Driven out once more, in 1345 they founded Tenochtitlán (Náhuatl: "place of the cactus fruit") on an island in Lake Texcoco. Legend has it that Huitzilopochtli bade the tribe make their home where they came across an eagle perched on a cactus devouring a snake. The eagle symbolised the sun and thus Huitzilopochtli also, while the red cactus fruit represent the human heart, consumed by the sun (this same Aztec emblem survives today on the Mexican flag). Led by their High Priest Ténoch and claiming to be the successors of the great Toltecs whose cultural inheritance they usurped, in a short time the arrogant Mexica had transformed the inhospitable swampy island into an economically self-sufficient domain. This they did with the aid of chinampas (artificial islands used for cultivation; see Xochimilco near Mexico City). In 1358 a second city, Tlatelolco (Náhuatl: "earth mound"), was established on a neighbouring island. For a long time it was in rivalry with Tenochtitlán before being annexed by the greater power. Afterwards it assumed an important role as the commercial capital of the Aztec empire.

The accession in 1372 of the ruler Acamapichtli (Náhuatl: "handful of reeds"), a Toltec prince from Culhuacán, marked the emergence of an Aztec dynasty, numbering eleven rulers in all, which was to last until the Spaniards captured Tecochtitlán in 1521. In Tlatelolco in contrast, the Mexica installed a Tepanec prince as founder of the ruling house. In the course of the next 150 years, aided by a succession of dynastic marriages, alliances and numerous wars, the Mexica emerged as the dominant power in the Anáhuac Valley (see Texcoco), at the same time extending their hegemony to cover much of present-day Mexico as far south almost as Guatemala. Under their belligerent rulers, Moctezuma I (Náhuatl: angry Lord", 1440–68), Axayácatl ("water face", 1468–81) and Ahuizotl ("ghostly water face", 1486–1502) especially, Aztec armies were able to subdue huge areas of what are now the states of México, Hidalgo, Morelos, Guerrero, Veracruz, Puebla, Oaxaca and Chiapas, forcing the inhabitants to pay them tribute. Only the Purépecha (Tarascan) empire in Michoacán and the states of Tlaxcala and Meztitlán proved strong enough to resist conquest and retain their independence. In 1502 Moctezuma II took the throne, the last of the Aztec dynasty to wield absolute power and destined to face, in Hernán Cortés, an even more powerful adversary. The subject peoples, vanquished in war and intimidated by threats, faced burdensome taxes imposed on them by Tenochtitlán, mainly in the form of tradable commodities, slaves and military service. Aztec garrisons, permanently stationed at strategic points, special tax collectors, and itinerant merchants ensured contracts were kept and that Náhuatl, then the lingua franca of Meso-America, spread. But in 1517 the first Spaniard, Francisco Hernández de Córdoba, landed on the coast of the Yucatán peninsula, and in 1519 Hernán Cortés alighted on Mexican soil. Their arrival spelled the end of the Aztec empire, its collapse being largely attributed by the rulers to rebellion on the part of the oppressed indigenous peoples.

Moctezuma's immediate successor in the by now threatened Tenochtitlán was his brother Cuitláhuac (Náhuatl: "protector of the empire"). Having ruled for only four months he died in an epidemic however, his nephew Cuauhtémoc ("falling eagle") then assuming the throne. Taken captive after the Mexica's final defeat at the hands of the Spanish, Cuauhtémoc was hanged in 1525.

The Federal District itself was created by a decree of President Guadalupe Victoria in 1824. Its history, both during the colonial period and subsequently, is one and the same with the history of the Mexican Republic and its capital.

Economy

More than 50% of Mexico's entire industrial capacity is located in the Distrito Federal, a situation which even a deliberate policy of decentralisation such as has been instituted in recent years can do little to alter. The main sectors represented are iron and steel, construction, vehicles, textiles, paper, chemicals, glass and ceramics, machinery, electrical appliances and food. In addition to central government and the head offices of a great many administrative departments, major banks and insurance companies also have their headquarters in Mexico City. The capital is the nerve centre of all the principal rail and air routes, and the hub of numerous bus and coach services. Being the country's major internal marketplace as well as the source of most of its consumer goods, the District is also Mexico's leading centre of commerce. The numerous sights in the city and its environs, combined with a good infrastructure, mean that tourism is now another important element in the local economy.

Such a vast concentration of industry is inevitably accompanied by serious environmental problems, especially in Mexico City (see entry). The highland air of the Distrito Federal, once widely acclaimed as exceptionally clear and healthy, has today deteriorated into an almost unendurable smog which seldom dissipates.

Dolores Hidalgo

See San Miguel de Allende

Durango (State)

Abbreviation: Dgo.
Capital: Durango
Area: 123,520sq.km/47,678sq. miles
Official population 1990: 1,349,400 (1994 estimate: 1,650,000)

Location and topography

The large, sparsely populated state of Durango borders on Chihuahua in the north, Sinaloa in the west, Nayarit in the south, and Zacatecas and Coahuila in the east. Extending as far as the western slopes of the Sierra Madre, it consists primarily of dry plateaux covered with lava rock and deeply fissured by ravines. Its inhabitants are mestizos and Creoles, with Tepehuano Indians still living in remote areas.

Mexico
United Mexican States
Estados Unidos Mexicanos

Durango

Federal State
Estados

1a Baja California Sur
1b Baja California Norte
2 Sonora
3 Chihuahua
4 Sinaloa
5 Durango
6 Coahuila
7 Nuevo León
8 Zacatecas
9 San Luis Potosí
10 Tamaulipas
11 Nayarit
12 Aguascalientes
13 Jalisco
14 Guanajuato
15 Querétaro
16 Hidalgo
17 Colima
18 Michoacán
19 México
20 Morelos
21 Tlaxcala
22 Puebla
23 Veracruz
24 Guerrero
25 Oaxaca
26 Chiapas
27 Tabasco
28 Campeche
29 Yucatán
30 Quintana Roo

D.F. Distrito Federal (Federal District)

© Baedeker

History

The region now making up the state was populated in pre-Hispanic times by semi-nomadic tribes, in particular the Tepehuano and Acaxe.

The first Spaniard to penetrate the area is thought to have been the conquistador Ginés Vásquez del Mercado, who arrived in 1551 to search for precious metals. He was followed by a Basque, Francisco de Ibarra, who established the first settlements, among which were Nombre de Dios (1555) and Durango (1563). A state of almost permanent war with the Indians lasted until 1616 when the Tepehuano finally suffered decisive defeat. Even then Indian uprisings were still common right up until the late 19th c. Prior to becoming separate federal states in 1823, Durango and Chihuahua together made up the province of Nueva Vizcaya.

Economy

Durango has great mineral wealth including gold, silver, copper, iron, zinc, sulphur and antimony. In fertile areas watered by rivers or artificially irrigated, agricultural products such as cotton, maize, tobacco, sugar cane and vegetables are grown. Livestock rearing and agricultural processing also play a part in the economy. Tourism is not yet particularly important.

Places of interest

Gómez Palacio

Apart from the state capital Durango (see entry), only Gómez Palacio (population: 138,000) is of much economic significance. Situated on the border with Coahuila (see entry) close to Torréon, it is a centre of commerce generally and agricultural processing in particular. A cotton and wine fair is held annually in late summer but the city has little of interest to the tourist.

Bermejillo

Around the little town of Bermejillo (population: 12,000; 45km/28 miles north of Gómez Palacio on the MEX 49), fossil fish and snails are found. Once treated they are then offered for sale.

★Puente Ojuela

From Bermejillo the MEX 30 heads west towards Mapimí. Some 20km/12½ miles along it, a narrow road branches off left to the Puente Ojuela Mine (7km/4 miles) located in an unusual and bizarre landscape. A swaying, rickety wooden bridge over a gorge is only one of several curious sights at this part abandoned, part still worked mine where they prospect for silver, lead and manganese.

Mapimí

The old mining town of Mapimí (Tepehuano: "stone over the hill"; 1360m/4463ft; population: 15,000) is situated 23km/14 miles west of Bermejillo. The nearby Sierra del Rosario is famous for its weird rock formations and the so-called "Red Caves", their colour produced by iron oxide.

"Zone of Silence"

About 145km/90 miles north of Bermejillo lie the villages of San José del Centro and Mohóvano, reached via Ceballos (MEX 49). Between them stretches a region known as the "Zone of Silence" ("Zona del Silencio") where strong electro-magnetic fields created by the massive iron oxide deposits make any radio or television reception impossible. Another remarkable feature of this exceptionally dry region (average annual precipitation 250mm/10in.) is that about 35% more of the sun's rays are absorbed here than in comparable places. Unusual mutations have also been identifed in both plants and animals. The area is the focus of on-going research by an international group of scientists.

Durango (City) G 5

State: Durango (Dgo.)
Altitude: 1890m/6200ft. Population: 500,000
Telephone code: 91 181

Access from Mexico City

By rail via Felipe Pescador in about 26 hours; by bus: in about 17 hours.

Location

Situated on an eastern spur of the Sierra Madre Occidental the city of Durango (de Victoria) overlooks the very attractive and fertile Guadiana valley. It has a dry pleasant climate and an unmistakable Old Spanish air. Durango is an important commercial and industrial centre, involved mainly in processing local products.

History

The first settlement, unofficially called San Juan de Analco, was founded here in 1556 by Pater Diego de la Cadena. In 1563 it was officially named Durango by Francisco de Ibarra and Alonso Pacheco, but even as late as the 18th c. it was still generally known as Villa de Guadiana. As a far-flung Spanish outpost frequented mainly by prospectors the town was long prone to attack by Indians, the Tepehuano especially. Peace was eventually secured in the 17th c. Durango's elevation to bishopric brought a considerable flowering culturally, but in the 19th c. the city suffered through economic stagnation. It is only in recent decades that prosperity has returned.

Sights

The tranquil city has few architectural highlights to lure the tourist. The fine cathedral on the main square (Zócalo) was built between 1695 and 1777 and so reflects the development of Mexican Baroque in that period. Of interest too are the Baroque Jesuit church of Sagrario and the Casa del Conde de Suchil, the latter being not only the one-time residence of the Count of Suchil but the local headquarters of the Inquisition as well.

Cerro del Mercado

The 200m/656ft-high Cerro del Mercado, a hill to the north of the city, consists almost entirely of iron ore (haematite). Although this was well-known to the 16th c. conquistadors, mining only began in 1828. Recently more than 300 tonnes a day have been extracted, despite which reserves are estimated to be sufficient for another 100 years.

Museums

As well as archaeological and ethnographic exhibits, the Museo de Antropología e Historia "El Aguacate" (Victoria 100 Sur) has collections of art from the colonial period and folk art. A large avocado tree stands in the garden. Another museum, the Colección de Minería (Casa del Cuerno), is primarily devoted to minerals, including gold, silver and other metals. There is also a gigantic mammoth tooth.

Surroundings

Thermal baths

The city makes a good base for visiting the several thermal baths in the vicinity. These have a high iron and sulphur content and include e.g. Navacoyan and El Saltito.

Reservoirs

Not far from Durango are a number of reservoirs catering for water-sports and fishing (Garabito, La Tinaja, Guadalupe Victoria, Peña del Aguila, etc.).

"Wild West" towns

Film fans should head for one of the many locations near by used for shooting westerns. They are found beside the MEX 45 northbound, near the 12 kilometre mark, and incorporate part of the village of Chupadores. Villa del Oeste is another screen set, with a saloon, church and cemetery.

★Drive to Mazatlán

The 320km/199 mile drive on the MEX 40 from Durango via El Salto to Mazatlán (see entry) passes through magnificent scenery. Some stretches of the route, winding through rugged mountain country, are very tortuous and it is advisable to enquire about road conditions before setting out. The journey can also be made part way by train, as far as El Salto.

Dzibilchaltún P 7

State: Yucatán (Yuc.). Altitude: 12m/39ft

Access

By bus from Mérida (see entry) to the Dzibilchaltún turn off where taxis wait; by car on the MEX 261, turning right after 15km/9 miles.

Location

Situated just off the Progreso road only 17km/10½ miles north of Mérida, the Dzibilchaltún archaeological site lay neglected for a long time because of its less than spectacular buildings. It is only really in the last 20 years or so that archaeologists have come to recognise Dzibilchaltún as having been one of the largest pre-Columbian cities on the Yucatán peninsula as well as one of the longest occupied.

History

Sporadic investigation in the 1940s had already shown the site to be an area of extensive and very ancient settlement. In 1956 Tulane University and the US National Geographic Society began a new phase of excavation under the direction of E. Wyllys Andrews IV. It was established that Dzibilchaltún (Mayan: "where the flat stones are inscribed") had been inhabited since at least 600 B.C. and covered an area of more than 50sq.km/19sq. miles. Taking into account the more than 8000 buildings recorded, Dzibilchaltún has proved to be one of the largest, most ancient and perhaps the longest settled Old Indian city not only in Yucatán but in the whole of Mexico. It is even possible that a community existed here during the Archaic period, i.e. prior to 1500 B.C. The city is known, furthermore, to have still been inhabited when the Spanish first arrived. Historians now believe Dzibilchaltún to have had major religious significance as a place of pilgrimage, as well as being a politically important metropolis. The population during the city's golden age is thought to have exceeded 40,000.

Many of the buildings so far uncovered date from the pre-Classic era (3rd to 1st c. B.C.), though some have had more recent structures superimposed on them (e.g. in the late Classic, A.D. 600–900). A considerable number of dated stelae have also been found, the first such stelae to be discovered in this area – as opposed to in the southern central Mayan region (Chiapas, Tabasco, Guatemala, Honduras). They included one with the relatively early date of A.D. 327. All the evidence points to a very early Mayan civilisation having developed independently here in the Yucatán. Such a finding conflicts with previous assumptions that Mayan culture in the more northern areas post-dated and was derivative from that of the southern central region, which later flourished in the Classic period (A.D. 300–900).

The Spaniards destroyed the ancient buildings and, using the rubble, erected a chapel in the centre of the site. For a long time thereafter the ruins continued to be treated as a convenient source of stone.

Visiting the ruins

Dzibilchaltún encompasses a number of ceremonial centres, linked at one time by sacbeob ("white roads"). Only a few of the structures on the vast site have been sufficiently restored to warrant visiting.

★Temple of the Seven Dolls

The building known as the Temple of the Seven Dolls (Templo de las Siete Muñecas) or Building 1 sub, is most unusual.

Radio carbon tests on remains of timber have established that the temple dates back to the 7th c. A.D. It differs from all other known examples of Mayan architecture not only in its simplicity of style but also in having a square ground-plan and a window either side of the entrance. No such apertures have previously been found in any Mayan building. The temple roof-comb also departs from the traditional style, consisting as it does of a pyramid-like stump. This perhaps suggests an early form of roof-comb, possibly reflecting adjustment of the internal vaulting to the square ground-plan. Seven primitive clay figures were found inside, these being the so-called "dolls" which give the building its name. The temple, with flights of steps leading up to it on all four sides, stands, together with a number of other smaller structures, on a rectangular platform measuring some 250×90m/820×295ft.

Central Group

Building 38, one of the Central Group situated near the entrance to the archaeological zone, still retains some of its ornamentation. Remnants of some fairly early murals can also just be discerned.

Cenote Xlacah

Xlacah (Mayan: old city), the sacred cenote located at the heart of Dzibilchaltún, was clearly of great religious significance. Exploratory dives have so far yielded no less than 30,000 archaeological finds, among them clay vessels, ceramic figures, jewellery and some skeletal remains. Indications are that the sacred pool, about 30m/98ft across and thought to be 45m/148ft deep, was not generally used for human sacrifices. Today it offers the chance of a welcome dip.

Open Chapel

Standing close to the cenote, in the centre of what was the main plaza, are the remains of a large "open chapel", erected by the Spanish at the

Dzibilchaltún: Temple of the Seven Dolls

end of the 16th c. Its size and position are confirmation that Dzibilchaltún still boasted a sizeable population even at the beginning of the colonial period.

Other structures in the Central Group include the Palacio and the Templo del Pedestal.

Museum

The small museum at the entrance to the site contains stelae, carvings, bones and ceramics. Many of the exhibits were recovered from the cenote. Plans are afoot to build a large museum of the Maya people, embracing all the peninsula's outstanding cultures.

Edzná O 8

State: Campeche (Camp.)
Altitude: sea level

Access

By bus from Campeche (see entry); by car from Campeche follow the route signposted "Mérida via Ruinas", driving east on the MEX 180 and then 261 through Chencoyl (42km/26 miles) to Cayal where turn south on the MEX 261 for a further 19km/12 miles.

Location

The excavation site at Edzná is located on the edge of an area known to archaeologists as the "Chenes" region, the name deriving from the "-chén" ending (meaning "well") characteristic of many of its place-names. This Mayan site lies in a large scrub-covered valley partly under cultivation, enclosed to the north and east by a chain of low hills.

History

Recent excavation and research has shown Edzná (Mayan: "house of grimaces") to have been settled as long ago as 400 B.C. The city's heyday, however, was undoubtedly during the Mayan Classic period. Stelae uncovered bear dates ranging from A.D. 435 to 810. No post-Classic development (i.e. post A.D. 1000) has yet been recorded.

In the 1920s the American Sylvanus Morley and the Mexican Enrique Juan Palacios both completed important work on the site, in particular involving the deciphering of glyphs. Further research was undertaken in the 1940s by the Mexican archaeologists Alberto Ruz l'Huillier and Raúl Pavón Abreu, the latter continuing with restoration work into the 1950s and 60s. Most recently excavations have been carried out by the New World Archeological Foundation and scientists from the Instituto Nacional de Antropología e Historia. Between 1986 and 1989 the latter in particular were active here under the direction of Pavón Nabreu and Luis Meller Camara. Guatamalan refugees helped with the excavations assisted by funds from the UN.

Visiting the ★ ruins

The Edzná archaeological zone covers an area of about 6sq.km/ 2¼sq. miles. Most of the structures remain unexcavated or have become overgrown again after the original investigations. As occurs frequently in old Mayan architecture, some buildings have had others superimposed – in some cases several times – making them extremely difficult to date. As far as sightseeing is concerned, priority should be given to the structures grouped around the Plaza Central, in the middle of which stands a square altar with a small altarpiece known as "La Picota" on its west side.

★ Five-Storeyed Building

The east side of the plaza is dominated by Edzná's most interesting easily accessible monument, El Edificio de los Cinco Pisos (Five-

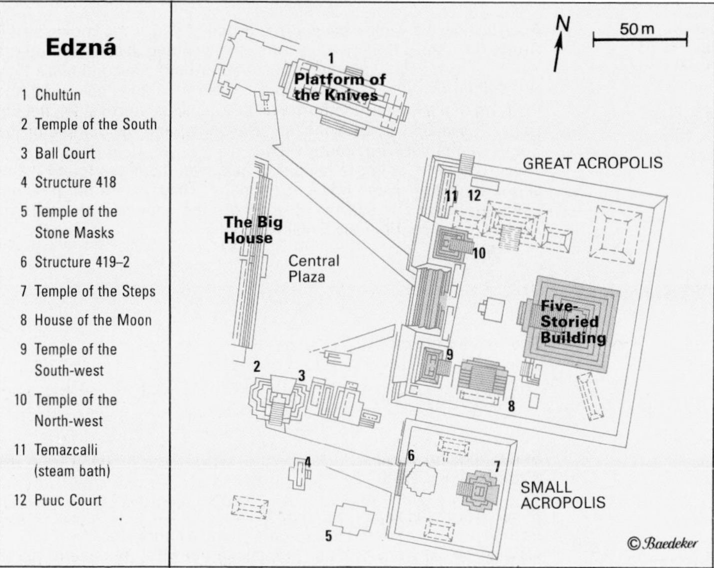

Storeyed Building). From the almost square base, measuring 60×58m/197×190ft, an external "flying" stairway mounts the pyramid's four lower tiers, each 4.6m/15ft in height. The fifth storey consists of a 5m/16½ft-tall temple building crowned by a 6m/19ft roof-comb. The top of the comb reaches 31m/102ft above the ground.

The four, chambered, lower storeys are thought to have been priests' quarters, the temple with its altar comprising the actual shrine. The lowest storey is adorned with masonry columns reminiscent of the Río Bec style, while the fourth in contrast boasts the kind of monolithic columns with capitals commonly found in the Puuc region. On the first floor, a passageway with corbel vaulting leading inwards from underneath the stairway gives access to the inner chamber.

This impressive structure perfectly illustrates the rather austere style of building typical of Edzná, with plain cornices and unadorned façades. The contrast with the architecture of the Classic Chenes or Puuc sites is very marked. Only the roof-comb could be described as at all ornate, being richly embellished with stucco figures.

House of the Moon

On the south side of the plaza stands the restored House of the Moon (Casa de la Luna; Mayan: "Paal u'ná"). Flanked either side by six terraces, the wide external stairway ascends to the temple remains on the top.

Temples of the South-west and the North-west

Occupying the south-west corner of the plaza is the appropriately named Temple of the South-west (Temple del Suroeste) consisting of a rectilinear platform from which sloping walls, reminiscent of Petén architecture, rise to an upper terrace with temple ruins. The Temple of the North-west (Templo del Nordeste) occupies the other corner on the west side.

Sweat bath

Adjoining the latter is a building which was originally a sweat bath ("temazcalli").

Gruppo del Centro Ceremonial

Also deserving mention are another group of structures known as the Grupo del Centro Ceremonial, some still awaiting excavation, others reverting to being overgrown. Clustered around a second plaza they include the so-called Great Acropolis (Gran Acrópolis; east side), the Platform of the Knives (Platforma de los Cuchillos; north side), the Big House (Casa Grande or Nohol'na; west side) and the Temple of the South (Templo del Sur; south side).

Because parts of Edzná lay below sea level the Maya found themselves forced to install efficient drainage. They solved the problem using an ingenious system of underground channels and cisterns located to the south of the Great Acropolis.

El Sumidero

See Tuxtla Gutiérrez

El Tajín L 7

State: Veracruz (Ver.)
Altitude: 298m/978ft

Access

By air to Poza Rica and from there by car (about 15km/9 miles); by bus from Veracruz (see entry) to Papantla (about 4 hours), then by local bus service; by car from Mexico City, taking the MEX 85 towards Teoti-

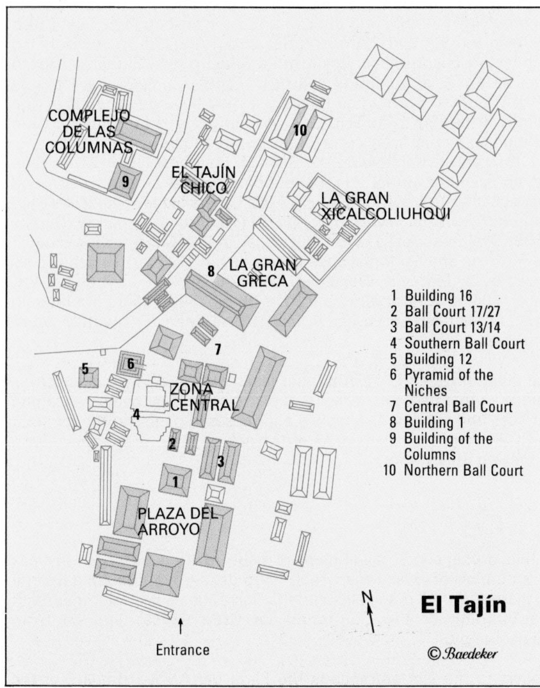

huancán, then the MEX 130 and 132 (the "Vanilla Route") via Tulancingo and Poza Rica to El Tajin (about 300km/186 miles in all); from Veracruz, the MEX 180 via Nautla and Papantla (about 240km/149 miles).

Location

The ruined city of El Tajín lies surrounded by vanilla plantations in a hilly region where the warm, moist climate clothes everything in tropical green. The archaeological zone covers some 11sq.km/4¼sq. miles, 40% of which has been excavated in recent years. The city, with a population in its heyday of about 50,000 people, is one of the most important pre-Columbiann sites in Mexico.

History

For a long time the Totonacs were believed to have built El Tajín (Totonac: "lightning"), a view based largely on the fact that they inhabited the area at the time of the Spanish Conquest. The great city had however already been abandoned for at least 300 years before the Spanish arrived. It may originally have been a late Olmec or proto-Mayan settlement, set up in collaboration with the Huastecs. When founded, in around A.D. 200, its builders were evidently much influenced by Teotihuancán. It took until about A.D. 600 before an independent culture evolved. El Tajín's own influence then began to spread, in time being felt even in Teotihuancán. The city reached the peak of its development between A.D. 700 and 900.

The first major buildings, including the Pyramid of the Niches, date from the 4th and 5th centuries. There followed two phases of new building and superimposition of new structures on old, the first in El Tajín between the 6th and 8th centuries, the second in El Tajín Chico between the 9th and 12th centuries. From the 12th c. onwards the architecture becomes manifestly more Toltec in style. El Tajín ceased to exist as a city and cultural centre in about A.D. 1200, evidence of destruction and burning suggesting it may have been razed by the Toltecs. In the 15th c. the Totonacs inhabiting this part of Veracruz were subjugated by the Aztecs and forced to pay tribute.

In the centuries following the Spanish Conquest (1519–21) El Tajín initially failed to attract much attention. The first person to visit and describe the site was Diego Ruiz in 1785. Others to report later were the German Alexander von Humboldt (1811) and the Austrian W. Dupaix (1836). Systematic excavation only began in 1934 under the direction of the Mexican archaeologist José García Payón. His work was then continued by S. Jeffrey K. Wilkersen. Excavations carried out by I.N.A.H. since 1984 have uncovered a further 36 buildings; there are now, in total, 48 well-preserved buildings to be seen. Excavation work continues.

Style

The style in which El Tajín is built (seen also at e.g. Yohualichán) is unique to this particular area; it is characterised by heavily receding cornices and window-like niches and recessed panels in the pyramid walls. Buildings were painted red, black or blue, occasionally with murals on the exterior.

Visiting the ★ ruins

Lay-out of the site

El Tajín proper and El Tajín Chico are made up of several different areas on a number of levels: the Grupo Plaza del Arroyo; the Zona Central (with the Pyramid of the Niches); the Complejo de las Columnas (with the Building of the Columns); La Gran Greca; and La Gran Xicalcoiunqhui.

Plaza del Arroyo

Closest to the site entrance is the Plaza del Arroyo (Square of the Stream), surrounded by recently excavated pyramids. The finest of these structures, Edificio 16, was evidently over-built three times. Behind it two new ball courts (17/27 and 13/14) have been uncovered.

Pantheon of the ball game

Seventeen ball courts of various different shapes (T-shaped, double T-shaped, I-shaped) show El Tajín to have been a pantheon of the ball game which, originating on the Gulf coast, was taken up extensively throughout Meso-America. Though regional variations developed in the rules and players' clothing, the game's ritual significance as depicted on the walls of the two ball courts referred to above and also the Southern Ball Court, remained unchanged – the reconciliation of good and evil, day and night, life and death and the duality of Quetzalcóatl and Tezcatlipoca (Venus and moon). In the case of the 60m/197ft-long, 10m/33ft-wide Southern Ball Court, the ends of the side walls are decorated with exceptionally interesting rectangular panels in bas-relief, with borders top and bottom in stylised snake motifs.

★ Southern Ball Court

The four panels themselves depict: the dedication of a young warrior in the presence of gods or priests; a priest holding a ball player over a sacrificial stone while another thrusts an obsidian dagger into his breast; two ball players in conversation, one carrying a "yugo" (see below) the other a "palma", being watched by deities one of whom is masked; the dedication of a warrior reclining on a bench, probably to the god of the ball game, Tlachtli, symbolised by a sunbird hovering above. The Pulque cult, preparations for which are also illustrated, seems to have been an important element in the El Tajín ball game. A distinctive feature of the game in the Gulf region, and El Tajín in particular, was the use of so-called yokes ("yugos"), axes ("hachas") and palms ("palmas"). The only examples found are carved in stone, replicas, it is thought, of the wooden equipment used in the ball game itself. The stone yokes are horseshoe-shaped and ornately carved, weighing up to 30kg/66lb; the axes are thin, hatchet-shaped stone blades, often pierced and usually decorated with human faces; the palms are triangular wedges, finely worked, used as some sort of protective cushioning for the yokes. These stone carvings represent some of the most elaborately worked artefacts produced in the pre-Columbian period.

★★Pyramid of the Niches

Near the Pyramid of the Niches in the Zona Central stand Monuments II, III and IV. Monument II and the adjoining Monument V are of particular interest. The remarkable Pyramid of the Niches (Pirámide de los Nichos) rises to a height of 25m/82ft on its square base, the sides of which are 35m/115ft in length; the pyramid was dedicated to the Rain or Wind god.

Construction of the seven-storeyed pyramid (seven counting the temple at the top) began in the 4th c. and was probably completed in the 7th c. As is often the case with Old Indian buildings, it was superimposed on an older pyramid already there.

Each storey of the building is embellished on all four sides with a row of relatively shallow niches, square in shape and surrounded by a projecting stone "frame". The niches total 365 in all, symbolising the days of the year. At first it was thought they were intended to house figures, but archaeologists now believe their purpose was simply decorative. At one time the entire structure was clad in polychrome stucco, even the niches being painted in bright colours. The intention may perhaps have been to create a mystical effect using the interplay of

Pyramid of the Niches

light and shade. Up either side of the 10m/33ft-wide stairway run broad alfardas (lateral balustrades) with a decorative stone mosaic of meandering fret design. The centre-line of the stairway is interrupted by five platforms, regularly spaced, each having three smaller niches. The stairway was a later, and almost certainly purely functional, addition.

From the plaza a track runs northwards to the Plaza El Tajín Chico in the least ancient part of the city. Here the architecture is rather more Mayan in character, with roof-combs, columned entrances and corbel vaulting.

★Building of the Columns

The Complejo de las Columnas, the highest section of the site, is dominated by the extraordinary Building of the Columns (Edificio de las Columnas or Palacio del Gobierno) standing on a mound 45m/147ft in height and in part artificially raised. Glyphs discovered here recount the history of a ruler known as "13 rabbits", who probably lived in the 10th c. Once again niches are a major feature of the building, in this case decorated with meandering motifs. The cornices are so constructed as to appear to defy the laws of gravity. Equally astonishing is the fact that the solidly built stairway was apparently added purely for decoration, access to the upper chambers being by ladder. The creators of the building certainly possessed some unique skills, covering the roof, for example, with slabs made from a cement completely unknown elsewhere in Meso-America.

At the base of the structure can be seen the stumps of several huge columns 1.20m/4ft in diameter. These were once part of a gallery running along the front of the building. The stumps are covered with bas-reliefs depicting warriors and priests, human sacrifices and hieroglyphs. Panels with cross-shaped reliefs embellish the east side of the upper storey. From the top of the building a magnificent view unfolds of the entire area.

Remainder of the site

Lower down from the Building of the Columns stands Building I where polychrome paintings of zoomorphic deities were recently discovered. Below the steps is the Central Ball Court, with six panels depicting among others the deities Tláloc, Quetzalcóatl and Macuilxochiti. To the north of the ball court rises "La Gran Greca", a platform of dimensions unique in Meso-America which served as a base for several buildings. Further north again can be seen "La Gran Xicalcoiunqhui" (Nahuátl: "great stepped meander"), a huge serpentine wall associated with Quetzalcóatl.

Museum

A hall near the site entrance serves as a museum where excavated finds are put on display. On Sunday mornings the "voladores" perform their flying act at the car park.

Surroundings

Papantla

Papantla (290m/952ft; population: 90,000; fiestas: New Year, Corpus Christi, Fiesta de Vainilla beginning of June, All Saints), 15km/9 miles south-east of El Tajín, is an attractive town set in hilly country carpeted with dense tropical forest. Spread out all around are the most extensive vanilla plantations in America.

★Voladores

However Papantla's fame rests chiefly on the "voladores", whose flying act is traditionally performed here on major holidays (in particular during the eight day Feast of Corpus Christi). The origins of the ceremony can be traced back to a ritual drama based on the mythological story of the new maize, pre-Hispanic interpretations of which sur-

Voladores performing their act

vive in hieroglyphic form. A musician sits playing on a small platform at the top of a tall mast, from which four "flyers" ("tocotines"), secured by a rope to a revolving frame at the masthead, glide earthwards head first. As they circle the pole the ropes progressively unwind until they reach the ground. Although associated principally with the Totonacs, the tradition survives among the Huastecs and Otomís as well. The Chorti in Honduras and the Quiché in Guatemala also perform similar flying acts.

Tecolutla

40km/25 miles south of Papantla, on the MEX 180, Tecolutla (population: 30,000) is a family resort with a flat sandy beach, set in an area of lush subtropical vegetation. It is popular with the Mexicans.

Castillo de Teayo

19km/12 miles north-west of El Tajín lies the industrial town of Pozo Rica (60m/197ft; population 224,000), 15km/9 miles north of which in the direction of Tihuatián a road branches off to Teayo (Huastec: "in the stone tortoise"; a further 22km/13½ miles). The main plaza of the village is dominated by the excellently restored Castillo de Teayo Pyramid, a triple-tiered structure almost 13m/43ft high, on the upper terrace of which are the remains of a rectangular temple. Stone carvings discovered near by, mainly of Aztec origin, can be seen displayed in a small museum. Similar sculptures are found in the vicinity of Zapotitlán and La Cruz. Until recently archaeologists assumed that the pyramid was constructed by the Aztecs in the 15th c., serving as their base in the Totonac region. Now it is thought to have been erected at least four centuries earlier, probably by Toltenacs from Tula. Tunnelling work is planned which is expected to reveal a Huastec core. The countryside around the pyramid was not generally settled until 1870. The villagers used materials from part of the Old Indian structure to build their homes.

Tuxpan

The port of Tuxpan (population: 135,000) lies on a river, 58km/36 miles north of Poza Rica and 10km/6 miles inland from the coast. Famous for its splendid sea and river fishing, it is also the venue of popular angling competitions held every year in late June/early July.

Ensanada

See Baja California

Guadalajara H 7

State: Jalisco (Jal.)
Altitude: 1552m/5092ft
Population: 4,100,000
Telephone code: 91 3

Access from Mexico City

By air about one hour; by rail about 13 hours; by bus about 9½ hours; by car 572km/350 miles on the MEX 57 and MEX 90 via Querétaro (see entry).

Location

Guadalajara, Mexico's second largest city, lies on a low hill in the fertile high valley of Atemajac and enjoys an equable subtropical climate. As a result of its long period of isolation from the Mexican capital it has been able, as the chief town of Jalisco state, to preserve the independent character of a town conscious of its own traditions with something of a European atmosphere. The Tapatíos, as the people of Guadalajara call themselves, have contrived, thanks to their prosperity and their artistic sense, to create an attractive city of broad avenues, carefully-tended parks and trim light-coloured buildings. However, the drive for modernisation of recent years and the rapid population growth have tended slightly to detract from the friendly and comfortable atmosphere of Guadalajara.

★ Cityscape

Folklore Centre

Guadalajara is not only a centre of "mariachi" music but also a stronghold of "charreadas" (the Mexican version of the rodeo) and the popular folk dance, the "Jarabe Tapatío" – three things which to the foreigner express the very essence of Mexican folk traditions.

History

The old Indian history of Guadalajara in pre-Columbian times reflected that of Jalisco (see entry) and neighbouring regions. The first temporary settlements founded by the Spanish conquistadors in this region were abandoned between 1530 and 1542, but in the latter year Pérez de la Torre founded Guadalajara (named after the Spanish town of that name) on its present site. In 1560 it became capital of the province of Nueva Galicia. Its distance from Mexico City and its isolated situation preserved Guadalajara from any major setbacks during the wars of the 19th and 20th c. Notable events in the history of the town include Miguel Hidalgo's declaration on the abolition of slavery in 1810, the defeat of Hidalgo and Allende by Spanish forces in 1811 and the occupation by French troops between 1863 and 1866. Guadalajara was not connected with Mexico City by rail until the end of the 19th c. On April 22nd 1992 a violent explosion in the city's sewers killed more than 200 people.

Sights

The central feature of Guadalajara is a magnificent group of four squares arranged in the form of a cross, with the city's principal public buildings set around them.

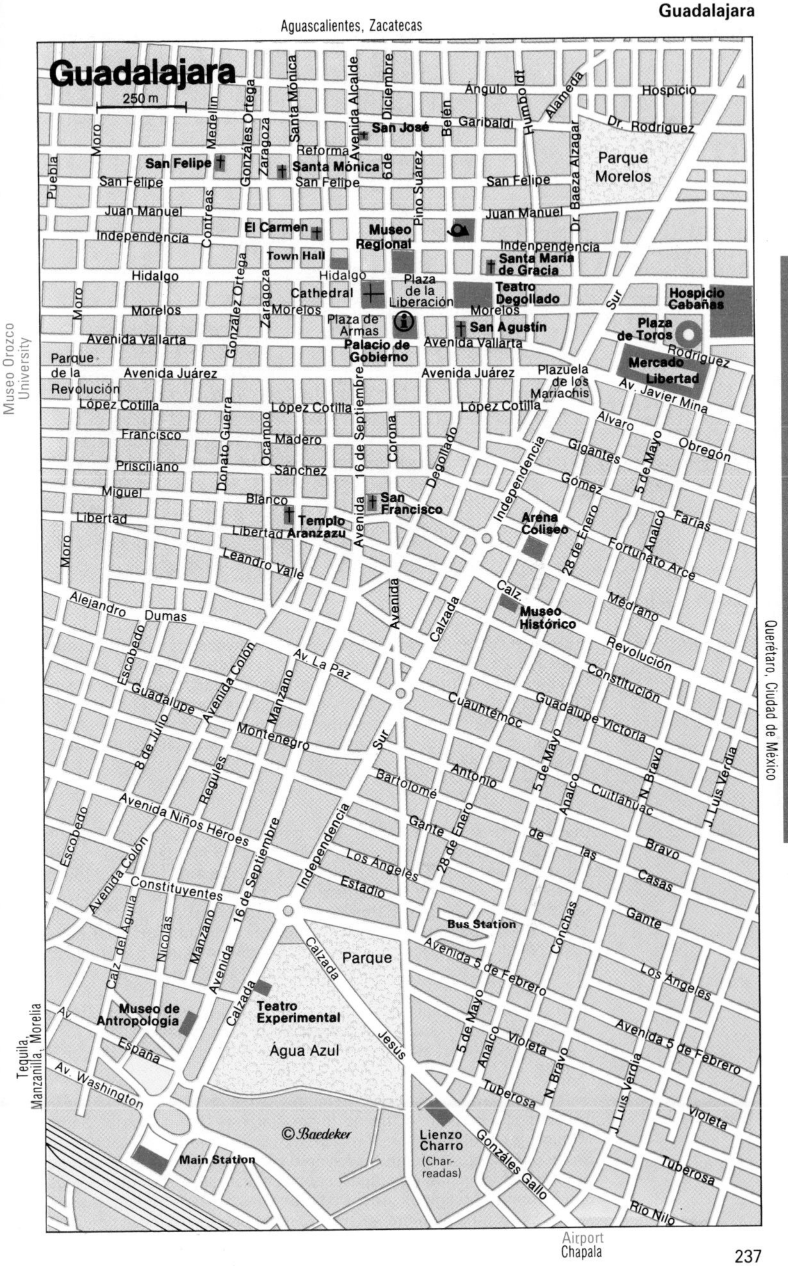
Aguascalientes, Zacatecas
Guadalajara
250 m
Puebla
Moro
Medellín
Gonzáles Ortega
Zaragoza
Santa Mónica
Avenida Alcalde
6 de Diciembre
Belén
Humboldt
Alameda
Ángulo
Garibaldi
Hospicio
Dr. Rodríguez
San José
Reforma
San Felipe
Santa Mónica
San Felipe
Pino Suárez
San Felipe
Dr. Baeza Alzagar
Parque Morelos
Juan Manuel
Contreas
Independencia
El Carmen
Museo Regional
Juan Manuel
Indenpendencia
Town Hall
Santa María de Gracia
Hidalgo
Hidalgo
Plaza de la Liberación
Teatro Degollado
Sur
Hospicio Cabañas
Moro
Morelos
González Ortega
Zaragoza
Cathedral
Morelos
Morelos
Plaza de Armas
San Agustín
Plaza de Toros
Avenida Vallarta
Palacio de Gobierno
Avenida Vallarta
Rodríguez
Mercado Libertad
Parque de la Revolución
Avenida Juárez
Avenida Juárez
Plazuela de los Mariachis
Av. Javier Mina
López Cotilla
López Cotilla
López Cotilla
Alvaro
Obregón
Francisco
Donato Guerra
Ocampo
Madero
16 de Septiembre
Corona
Degollado
Independencia
Gigantes
5 de Mayo
Prisciliano
Sánchez
Gómez
Miguel
Blanco
San Francisco
Arena Coliseo
Farías
Libertad
Templo Aranzazu
Libertad
Avenida
28 de Enero
Analco
Fortunato Arce
Moro
Leandro Valle
Calz.
Médrano
Alejandro
Dumas
Avenida
Calzada
Museo Histórico
Revolución
Escobedo
Avenida Colón
Av. La Paz
Constitución
Guadalupe
Manzano
Cuauhtémoc
Guadalupe Victoria
8 de Julio
Montenegro
Sur
5 de Mayo
N. Bravo
J. Luis Verdia
Regules
Bartolomé
Antonio
Analco
Cuitláhuac
Avenida Niños Héroes
Gante
de
Escobedo
Independencia
28 de Enero
las
Bravo
16 de Septiembre
Los Ángeles
Casas
Avenida Colón
Estadio
Constituyentes
Conchas
Gante
Calz del Aguila
Nicolás
Manzano
Avenida
Bus Station
Calzada
Parque
Avenida 5 de Febrero
Los Ángeles
Calzada
Teatro Experimental
Museo de Antropología
Av.
Água Azul
Jesus
5 de Mayo
Avenida 5 de Febrero
España
Analco
Violeta
N. Bravo
J. Luis Verdia
Av. Washington
Tuberosa
Violeta
©Baedeker
Lienzo Charro (Charreadas)
Gonzáles Gallo
Main Station
Tuberosa
Rio Nilo
Museo Orozco University
Querétaro, Ciudad de México
Tequila, Manzanilla, Morelia
Airport Chapala

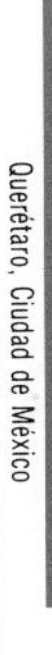

Cathedral and Plaza de los Laureles

Government Palace

In the finest of the four squares, the Plaza de Armas, stands the Government Palace (Palacio de Gobierno, 1643–1774), a splendid Baroque building with columns with zigzag ornamentation, large volutes and Churrigueresque "estípites" (pilasters). On the staircase and in one of the council chambers can be seen murals depicting Hidalgo in the War of Independence 1936–39, and heroes of the three great Mexican wars, 1948–49, by the famous fresco-painter José Clemente Orozco, a native of Jalisco.

Cathedral

On the north side of the Plaza de Armas, with its façade fronting the Plaza de los Laureles to the west (with its large fountain), stands the Cathedral and the Sagrario. Built between 1558 and 1616 and much altered in later periods, the Cathedral is basically Baroque but shows a remarkable mingling of different styles (naïve Gothic, neo-Classical, etc.) In the chapels and the Sagrario hang pictures attributed to Cristóbal de Villalpando, Miguel Cabrera and Murillo. A painting ascribed to Murillo – the Assumption of the Virgin Mary – hangs over the doorway of the sacristy.

To the north it joins the Plaza de los Hombres with its columned rotunda erected in honour of some famous sons of Jalisco.

To the north-west stands the modern Colonial-style Town Hall built in 1952.

★Santa Mónica

Three blocks farther to the north-west stands the church of Santa Mónica, built in the first half of the 17th c. The Baroque façade, with Salomonic twisted columns, is covered with rich and intricately-carved ornamentaion, including grapes, cobs of maize, angels, double eagles and symbols of religious orders. At the corner an early and impressive statue of St Christopher looks down on the passing traffic.

Other Baroque churches in Guadalajara include San Francisco (17th c.), San Felipe Neri (17th c.), Aránzazu (17th–18th c.: Churrigueresque retablos), San Juan de Dios (18th c.) and San Agustin (16th–17th c.).

Casa Jaliscense de la Culturas Indigenas

Opened in 1993, the attractive "House of Jalisco Native Culture" (Marsella Sur 75) displays mainly Huichol Indian artefacts including thread pictures, masks and costumes.

Regional Museum

In a former Jesuit seminary in the Plaza de la Rotunda, to the north of the Cathedral, stands the Museo Regional de Guadalajara. This museum covers a wide range, including the archaeology of the western states and west coast, ethnography (Huicholes, Cora Indians), paintings (colonial art of the 17th–19th c., European painters of the 16th–19th c., modern Mexican pictures and frescos), religious objects, historical collections and palaeontology.

Palacio de Justicia

To the right of the Regional Museum can be seen the Palace of Justice, a building which began life as the first monastery in Guadalajara (1588).

Teatro Degollado

To the south-east of the Museum, in the Plaza de la Liberación, stands the mid-19th c. Teatro Degollado (formerly Teatro Alarcón), a large Neo-Classical building with frescos by Gerardo Suárez in the dome showing scenes from Dante's "Divine Comedy".

Hospicio Cabañas

Four blocks east of the Theatre, by way of the newly-laid pedestrian zone known as the Plaza Tapatío, the Hospicio Cabañas, a Neo-Classical orphanage built by Manuel Tolsá at the beginning of the 19th c., boasts no fewer than twenty-three patios.

★★Orozco frescos

In a former chapel can be seen what are probably José Clemente Orozco's finest frescos; painted in 1938–39, they portray the Four

José Clemente Orozco

Frescos by Orozco in Hospicio Cabañas

Elements, Art and Science, the Conquest and the Four Riders of the Apocalypse. The high point is the fresco of Mankind in Flames ("Hombre del Fuego") in the dome. Various rooms around the patios house exhibitions devoted to Orozco's works.

Mercado Libertad

A little way from the Hospicio Cabañas, to the south of Plaza de Toros, is the huge Market Hall (Mercado Libertad) where, in addition to the usual wares, regional costumes and pottery, paper flowers, musical instruments and live birds are offered for sale.

Plazuela de los Mariarchis

Between Avenida Javier Mina and Calle Obregón lies the Plazuela de los Mariachis, a lane where mariachi orchestras demonstrate their skill and are available for hire.

Parque Agua Azul

From here the Calzada Independencia leads south-west to the beautiful Parque Agua Azul, around which will be found the Casa de las Artesanías, where folk arts are exhibited and on sale, a small Anthropological Museum, an open-air theatre (Teatro Experimental), a bird park, a flower market and the House of Culture.

Orozco Museum

In Avenida Vallarta to the west, at Av. Aceves 27 just past the Triumphal Arch, stands the former home and studio of the painter José Clemente Orozco (1883–1949), now the Orozco Museum with many paintings and drawings by the artist. Other frescos by Orozco, including scenes from Dante's "Inferno", can be seen in the auditorium of the University in Avenida Vallarta. Behind the University will be found the Templo Expiatorio, begun in 1897 and still unfinished.

Zoo

On the Calzada Independencía Norte/Av. Flores Magón, 6km/4 miles north of the city centre, the grounds of Guadalajara's completely renovated zoo overlook the Santiago Gorge.

Surroundings

★San Pedro Tlaquepaque

Some 6km/4 miles south-east of the city centre lies the suburb of San Pedro Tlaquepaque, with a small Ceramic Museum (Independencia 237) and shops selling ceramics, glass, papier-mâché work and antiques. This was a great pottery centre even before the Conquest, and still is today.

Tonalá

Tonalá, 7km/4½ miles further on, is also noted for its fine pottery, in characteristic patterns and a variety of forms. It too has a Ceramic Museum (Constitución 4; market Thur./Sat.). In pre-Columbian times Tonalá was capital of the state of Tonalán.

Zapopan

8km/5 miles north-west of the city centre lies Zapopan, an old Indian settlement, now also a suburb of Guadalajara. It is widely famed for its 17th c. Baroque Franciscan church dedicated to the city's patroness, the Virgin of Zapopan. During the summer the statue is set up in various churches in the city in turn, and on October 4th it is brought back to Zapopan in an impressive procession of dancers, charros and mariachi orchestras. In the museum adjoining the church art and craftwork by Huichol Indians from the Jalisco and Nayarit mountains is exhibited and sold.

50km/30 miles south-east of Guadalajara lies Laguna de Chapala, or Chapala Lake (see entry), with a number of picturesque little places around its shores which are popular with summer holidaymakers.

Guanajuato (State)

Abbreviation: Gto.
Capital: Guanajuato
Area: 30,575sq.km/11,805sq. miles
Official population 1990: 3,982,600 (1994 estimate: 4,250,000)

Location and Topography

Guanajuato, the heartland of Mexico during the colonial period, is bounded on the north by the state of San Luis Potosí, in the west by Jalisco, on the south by Michoacán and on the east by Querétaro. Predominantly mountainous, with fertile valleys and plains, it is part of the Bajío, the granary of the central Mexican plateau. In addition to its capital, Guanajuato, the state boasts several handsome colonial towns which together with its beautiful scenery and numerous health resorts make it a popular tourist region. The population includes Indians of the Otomí and Chichimeco-Jonaz tribes as well as Tarascans.

Archaeological Sites

There are some smallish archaeological sites in Ibarilla near León, Agua Espinoza near Dolores Hidalgo, Cañada de la Virgen near San Miguel de Allende and Oduña near Comonfort.

History

At an early stage the Otomí mingled with the Chichimecs in this region; then in the 15th c. Tarascans (Purépecha) and Aztecs (Mexica) moved in and eventually became dominant. After the fall of the Aztec empire the first Spaniards, led by Nuño Beltrán de Guzmán, arrived *c.* 1526 in what is now the state of Guanajuato (Tarascan: "Cuanax-huato", "hilly place of the frogs"). Simultaneously with the first discoveries of minerals, areas of fertile land were granted to Spanish settlers as ecomiendas. The subsequent history of the region during the colonial period and after Independence is substantially that of the larger towns in the state. Until 1824 Guanajuato was joined with Querétaro as an administrative unit under Spanish control.

Economy

The state has a well-developed system of communications by road and rail. Guanajuato once had the most productive silver-mines in the world, now largely worked out. Other minerals worked include gold, tin, lead, copper, mercury and opals. Industry is mainly concerned with the processing of wheat, cotton, sheep's wool and alcohol; there are also some smelting works and pottery production. León is the shoe manufacturing centre of Mexico. In the fertile southern part of the state productive agriculture (maize, wheat, tobacco) and livestock-farming both contribute to the economy. The area around Irapuato is one of the largest strawberry-growing regions in the world. Tourism now also plays an important part in the economy.

Places of Interest

In addition to the capital, Guanajuato (see below), the state has numerous other places of interest to the tourist, including San Miguel de Allende together with Atotonilco and Dolores Hidalgo, Celaya, Yuriria (a suburb of Celaya), Salamanca, Irapuato (a suburb of Salamanca) and León (see entries).

Guanajuato (Town) I 7

State: Guanajuato (Gto.)
Altitude: 2050m/6725ft
Population: 95,000
Telephone code: 91 473

Access from Mexico City

By rail about 8½ hours to Irapuato; change there for Guanajuato, a journey which takes a further 1½ hours (there is no direct line); by bus in about 5½ hours; by car on the MEX 57 and MEX 45 (370km/230 miles).

Location

Guanajuato, capital of the state of the same name, extends along a narrow valley and up the lower slopes of the bare hills on either side. The trim houses, often painted in bright colours, the narrow streets and lanes, the snug little squares and the old colonial buildings give the town a charm all of its own.

★★Townscape

Its rich cultural life combines with the visual attractions of the townscape to make Guanajuato one of the most popular tourist centres in Mexico.

History

In pre-Columbian times the region was occupied by Tarascans, who called the settlement here "Cuanax-huato", or "hilly place of the frogs". Between 1526 and 1529 the region was conquered and settled by the Spaniards, led by Nuño Beltrán de Guzmán. By the middle of the 16th c. the first silver-mines were opened up, establishing the prosperity of the town. In 1557 it was granted the name of Santa Fé y Real de Minas de Quanaxhuato, and in 1741 was granted a municipal charter.

Shortly after the declaration of Mexican independence in 1810 Ignacio de Allende succeeded temporarily in occupying the town after Juan José de los Reyes Martínez, known as El Pípila (the "Turkeycock"), had blown up the entrance to the Spanish fort of Alhóndiga de Granaditas and compelled the garrison to surrender, but the town was soon afterwards retaken by royalist forces under General Félix M. Calleja. In 1811 the severed heads of the leaders of the fight for independence – Hidalgo, Allende, Jiménez and Aldama – were hung at the corners of the Alhóndiga de Granaditas, remaining there until Mexico achieved independence in 1821. During the Guerra de la Reforma (1857–60)

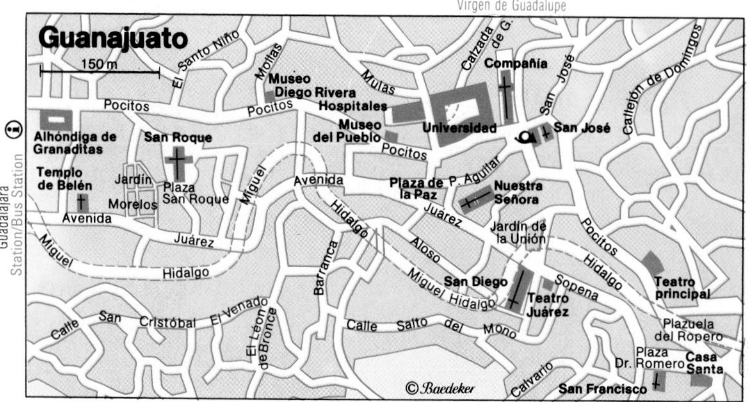

Guanajuato was capital of the republic for a month at the beginning of 1858. During the dictatorship of Porfirio Díaz (1876–1911) foreign capital flowed into the mines, and the town enjoyed a great surge of prosperity, during which many public buildings such as the Teatro Juárez, the Mercado Hidalgo and the Palacio Legislativo were erected. Guanajuato, with its Festival and University, is now a centre of intellectual life.

Sights

Teatro Juárez

A tour of the town usually starts in the pretty little main square, the Jardín de la Unión or Zócalo, with the Teatro Juárez, an opera-house in Neo-Classical style with Doric columns, which was opened in 1903 having taken thirty years to complete.

★San Diego

Beside the opera-house stands the elegant church of San Diego, altered during the 17th and 18th c., with its Churrigueresque façade.

Museo Iconográfico Del Quijote

The Museo Iconográfico Del Quijote, Manuel Doblado 1, is of especial interest to admirers of Cervantes.

Nuestra Señora de Guanajuato

From here Avenida Benito Juárez leads to the Plaza de la Paz (Peace Square) in which, to the right, stands the Baroque Basilica of Nuestro Señora de Guanajuato, formerly the parish church.

★Statue of the Virgin

This church, originally 17th c. but much altered thereafter, houses the much revered statue of the Virgin of Guanajuato, a carved wooden figure on a silver base which is believed to date from the 7th c. and was presented to Guanajuato by King Philip II of Spain in 1557.

Casa Rul y Valenciana

Also in the Plaza de la Paz stands the Casa Rul y Valenciana, a Neo-Classical mansion built by Francisco Eduardo Tresguerras at the end of the 18th c. for the Conde de Rul, a wealthy mine-owner. The German naturalist and geographer Alexander von Humboldt stayed here for a short time in 1803.

★Plazuelas

On either side of Avenida Juárez will be found a number of picturesque little squares or (plazuelas). Off the Plazuela de los Angeles, to the left,

Nusetra Señora de Guanajuato, with the University in the background

opens the Callejón del Beso (Kissing Lane), so called because it is only 68cm/2ft 3in wide, allowing a loving couple to kiss from windows on opposite sides. Farther along, on the left, stands the Mercado Hidalgo, a market hall opened in 1910.

Templo de Belén

Opposite the market a street leads to the Templo de Belén (Bethlehem), a church begun in 1773, with a Churrigueresque façade.

Alhóndiga de Granaditas

A little way north stands the Alhóndiga de Granaditas, built in 1799 and originally a granary. Thereafter it was used as a prison and a fort, the gate of which was blown up by "El Pípila", Guanajuato's folk hero. It now houses the Museum of Mexican Independence (Museo de la Independencia Mexicana), which contains archaeological and ethnological material as well as historical relics and silver-mining souvenirs. On the staircase are murals by José Chávez Morado (1955–66) depicting scenes from the fight for independence, the revolutionary wars and folk tradition. At the corners of the Alhóndiga can be seen the hooks on which the heads of the executed freedom fighters were displayed in iron cages for ten years.

Museo Diego Rivera

In Calle de los Pocitos, at the corner of Calle Mollas, lies the birthplace of the famous mural painter Diego Rivera (1886–1957), now a museum devoted to the artist and his work.

To the south-west in the Plaza San Roque will be found the Baroque church of the same name. This square forms a picturesque setting for performances – given annually by the University, primarily during the Cervantes Festival in October – of the "Entremeses Cervantinos" ("Cervantine Interludes"), one-act plays by the great Miguel de Cervantes Saavedra (1547–1616), famous Spanish author of "Don Quixote". At the end of 1987 the Spanish prime minister Felipe González opened the Don Quijote Museum.

Cervantes Festival

Municipal Museum

At the end of Calle de los Pocitos, in the former residence of the Marqués de Rayas, is the Municipal Museum (Museo del Pueblo de Guanajuato), which houses temporary exhibitions including works by the artist José Chavez Morado and other painters as well as collections of folk-art.

University

To the north of the Museum the main building of the University (rebuilt in 1955) is approached by an impressive flight of steps. The University is built of white stone in a colonial style showing Moorish influence which fits very naturally into the townscape of Guanajuato.

La Compañía

On the east side of the University towers the massive bulk of the church of La Compañía, a Jesuit foundation of 1747. The façade is in Churrigueresque style, the mighty dome Neo-Classical. The church contains two pictures by the great Mexican painter Miguel Cabrera. On the way back to the main square we pass the Plazuela del Barratillo, with its pretty fountain presented to the town by the Emperor Maximilian.

Avenida Miguel Hidalgo

It is worth driving along Avenida Miguel Hidalgo – which follows the line of the old river bed, running underground for part of the way – into the Carretera Panorámica, from which there are magnificent views of the town and surroundings. Along this road to the south-west stands a Monument to El Pípila.

Iglesia de Cata

The Carretera Panorámica leads north to the Iglesia de Cata (Iglesia del Señor de Villaseca) on the Calle Mineral de Cata. Built in the first quarter of the 18th c., this church has a fine Churrigueresque façade.

Also worth seeing are the churches of San Francisco, Guadalupe and Pardo, which has the façade of the old church of San Juan Rayas.

Entrance to the Cathedral

The Baroque Church of La Valenciana

★ Mummy Museum

The Calzada de Tepetapa leads past the station, in the direction of Guadalajara, to the Municipal Cemetery (Panteón Municipal), which adjoins a macabre Mummy Museum (Museo de las Monias). Here, in a crypt, mummified bodies of men, women and children, all of them deceased within the last 120 years, are displayed in glass cases, their excellent state of preservation apparently being due to mineral salts contained in the soil of the cemetery.

Surroundings

Marfil

4km/2½ miles further on towards Silao lies the township of Marfil, an old silver-mining town in which some of the old houses have been restored and re-occupied by new owners, including foreigners. The gardens and old chapel of the Hacienda San Gabriel are worth a visit.

Cerro del Cubilete

16km/10 miles beyond this on the road to Silao a side road branches off on the right to the Cerro del Cubilete (2700m/8860ft), on which stands a conspicuous statue of Christ the King (El Cristo Rey), almost 23m/75ft high. Sculpted by Fidias Elzondo and Carlos Olvera between 1922 and 1929, the statue is much visited by pilgrims and day-trippers and affords a superb panoramic view of the Baijo and the forest-covered hills of Tarascan territory. The Cerro del Cubilete is regarded as the geographical centre of Mexico.

★ Church of la Valenciana

5km/3 miles from Guanajuato on the Dolores Hidalgo road stands the church of La Valenciana or San Cayetano, built by the Conde de Valenciana. Antonio Obregón y Alcocer, owner of the famous silver-mine of La Valenciana (see below).

The church, built in pink cantera stone and consecrated in 1788, represents the great final period of the Mexican "Ultra-Baroque". It has only one of the intended two towers, the other not having been built. The façade is in late Churrigueresque style, while the windows along the sides have Neo-Mudéjar arches. Particularly attractive is the side doorway into the church from the garden, with an elaborately stuccoed and decorated scallop-shell and a statue of St Joseph.

The church contains three splendid Churriguresque retablos, partly gilded and partly polychrome. Note also the fine intarsia work of ivory and precious woods on the pulpit. Another striking feature is the doorway into the sacristy, with a carved stone lambrequin above the Mudéjar arch. The arches are particularly elegant, with their bands of intricate ornamentation in tezontle stone.

La Valenciana silver-mine

Near the church lies the interesting La Valenciana silver-mine, now reopened. It was discovered in 1766 by Antonio Obregón y Alcocer, a miner who became a mine-owner and Conde de Valenciana. It rapidly became the most productive mine in the world, employing up to 3300 miners in shafts penetrating to a depth of 500m/1650ft. Some of the old buildings have fallen into ruin or disappeared altogether, but visitors can still see the pyramid-shaped walls over which Indian workers hauled the ropes bringing up baskets of ore.

Guaymas **D 4**

State: Sonora (Son.)
Altitude: 8m/26ft
Population: 150,000
Telephone code: 91 622

Access

By air from La Paz, Tijuana, Guadalajara and Tucson (Arizona); by rail from Mexico City to Empalme rail station in about 34 hours; by bus from Mexico City via Guadalajara in about 31 hours; from the USA via Tijuana or Nogales.

Location and ★Topography

The port of Guaymas lies in a quiet bay in the Mar de Cortés, a section of the Gulf of California rich in fish. The bay is surrounded by impressive hilly country. A ridge of high ground divides the port area from the popular bathing beaches in the bays of Bacochibampo and San Carlos.

History

The first Spaniards explored the bay in 1535 and named it Guaima after a tribe of Seri Indians. About 1700 Father Francisco Eusebio Kino founded the mission station of San José de Guaymas near the present harbour, but the little township of Guaymas de Zaragoza was not established until 1769. As a port shipping large quantities of precious metals from the hinterland Guaymas frequently attracted the attention of pirates and adventurers and also the intervention of foreign countries. In 1847–48, during the war with the United States, it was occupied by US troops; and six years later a French expedition under Comte Gaston Raousset de Boulbon tried to seize Guaymas in order to found a private colony in Sonora – an attempt which failed and ended in the capture and shooting of the count. In 1865, during the War of Intervention, the town was occupied by French troops. Its later history ran in tandem with that of the state of Sonora.

Sights

The town has few features of great tourist interest, apart from the church of San Fernando, the offices of the Banco de Sonora and the Town Hall (Palacio Municipal).

Water sports

It is, however, a very popular holiday resort on account of the facilities it offers for water sports of all kinds, especially deep-sea fishing (sailfish, fanfish, swordfish, etc.). Among the most popular beaches are Miramar, San Francisco, San Carlos Lalo and Catch 22.

The islands of San Nicolás, Santa Catalina and San Pedro offer good diving facilities and the opportunity to observe birds and sea-lions.

Surroundings

San Carlos

The village of San Carlos (population 5000) lies 20km/12½ miles from Guaymas. In recent years a tourist centre has been developed, aimed especially at those interested in fishing and diving.

San José de Guaymas

Some 10km/6 miles north of Guaymas, the village of San José de Guaymas has an 18th c. Jesuit pilgrimage church.

★Selva Encantada

35km/21½ miles north of Guaymas stretches the Selva Encantada ("Enchanted Forest"), a huge cactus grove which is the nesting-place of many parrots.

★Rock-paintings near la Pintada

Access to La Pintada is by way of the MEX 15 towards Hermosillo (see entry). After 80km/50 miles a track leads off to the right to La Pintada, a further 6km/4 miles. From here it is a 20-minute climb up to some interesting rock-paintings on the walls of a gorge. Painted mainly in shades of black, ochre and red, they portray dancing, hunting and boating scenes as well as animal and heraldic symbols attributed to the Seri Indians.

Ferry to Baja California

There is a ferry service from Guaymas to Santa Rosalia on the peninsula of Baja California (see entry and also Practical Information, Ferries).

Yaqui Indians

South-east of Guaymas, along the lower course of the Rio Yaqui between Ciudad Obgregón and the Gulf of Mexico, lie several villages now occupied by Yaqui Indians, a tribe numbering over 15,000 which belongs to the large Uto-Aztec language family. The origins of this once warlike people, never completely subjugated by the Spaniards, are buried in obscurity, but until the middle of the 19th c. they were widely scattered over the state of Sonora. At the turn of the century numbers of rebellious Yaquis were deported to Yucatán by the Mexican government, but later almost all of them returned. In 1927 there was another Yaqui rising against the government, which ended with the death of their last war leader, Luis Matuz. The Yaquis are now mainly occupied in farming, hunting and fishing.

Religion

The religious practices of the Yaquis are a mixture of Indian and Catholic elements. An important part is played in their social structure by various "fraternities", particularly that of the magicians and soothsayers, who on the one hand are medicine-men able to drive out evil spirits and on the other take part in religious festivals. Most social and religious rites involve dances, the best known of which is the Stag Dance ("danza del venado"). To the Yaqui and the related Mayo tribe the stag is sacred as the incantation of the forces of Good.

Music

Features of Yaqui music, especially its rhythms, have been used in symphonic works by modern Mexican composers, including Carlos Chávez.

Festivals

Among the principal festivals celebrated by the Yaquis are Holy Week, June 24th (Día de San Juan Bautista), October 4th (Día de San Francisco) and Christmas Week.

The self-government of the village communities and the region of which they form part is based on both Indian and Jesuit models.

The dress of the men differs very little from that of other countryfolk in Sonora, but they frequently carry knives, pistols or ammunition pouches on their leather belts. The women wear brightly-coloured cotton blouses, skirts and rebozos (shawls), the ends of which hang down over their backs; their long hair is decked with coloured ribbons.

The most notable products of Yaqui folk art are the beautifully made wood and paper masks, usually representing animals, which are worn in the old folk dances.

Ciudad Obregón

About 130km/80 miles south-east of Guaymas lies the modern town of Ciudad Obregón (alt. 70m/230ft; population 291,000), which until 1924 was known as Cajeme, after a Yaqui chieftain. It is an important centre for the processing of the agricultural produce of the surrounding area. The creation of the Alvaro-Obregón reservoir has made possible the cultivation of corn, cotton, alfalfa, rice and other crops.

Navojoa

68km/42 miles south-east lies Navojoa (alt. 36m/118ft; population 83,000), a rapidly growing modern town which is the centre of an agricultural region made productive by irrigation and growing cotton, fruit and vegetables.

Mayo Indians

Around Alamos, Navojoa, Etchojoa and Huatabampo and in the villages of Tesila, Guasave and San Miguel Zapotitlán in Sonora state, and around the towns of El Fuerte, San Blas and Los Mochis in Sinaloa extends the large area of settlement of the Mayo Indians, a tribe belonging to the Uto-Aztec language family and related to the Yaquis which still numbers some 28,000. As with most of the Indian peoples of this region, very little is known about their origin. Probably they arrived in the area between A.D. 100 and 1300 during the great migration of the Nahua peoples. Their first encounters with the Spanish conquistadors took place between 1530 and 1540, but this warlike tribe was not pacified until about 1700, when they were evangelised by a Jesuit mission under the celebrated explorer Father Eusebio Francisco Kino. There were serious uprisings by Mayo and Yaqui Indians at the end of the 18th c. against the Spaniards and during the 19th c. against the Mexican government, but about 1900 the Mayo gave up the struggle and turned to farming.

Religion

As with other Indian tribes in this region, Mayo religious beliefs are a mingling of ancient Indian and Catholic practices, with the latter predominating. Like the Yaquis, they have a Stag Dance ("danza del venado") as well as another dance known as the "Pascola". The principal religious festivals in which dancing plays a part are May 3rd (Día de la Santa Cruz), June 24th (Día de San Juan Bautista) and October 4th (Día de San Francisco).

The traditional self-government system of the Mayo Indians based on the village community, with village headmen and tribal chiefs, is now gradually breaking up. Mayo dress is now very much the same as that of their non-Indian neighbours.

Álamos

Inland, 53km/33 miles east of Navojoa, lies the old mining town of Álamos (alt. 410m/1345ft; population 20,000). The Festival of the Conception of the Virgin Mary is celebrated on December 8th, and the town is now protected as a national monument. After the discovery of gold and silver here in 1680 the town grew rapidly and 100 years later had a population of over 30,000. Its decline began with the fall in silver prices, and thereafter raids by the warlike Mayo Indians and the turmoil of the revolutionary wars reduced it to a mere ghost town. Then after the Second World War a group of artists from the United States settled in Álamos and began to restore some of the old buildings. The Casa de los Tesoros and the Palacio Almada are now hotels. Other features of

Álamos: Plaza de Armas

interest include the parish church, the House of Mexican Folk Art and the pottery centre of La Uvulama. In recent years many retired people from the USA have come to Álamos, building houses in an "Americanised" version of the colonial style.

Guerrero (State)

Abbreviation: Gro.
Capital: Chilpancingo
Area: 64,458sq.km/24,887sq. miles
Official population 1990: 2,620,600 (1994 estimate: 2,900,000)

Location and Topography

The state of Guerrero is bounded on the north by the states of México and Morelos, on the north-west by Michoacán, on the north-east and east by Puebla and Oaxaca and on the south and west by the Pacific. It lies on both sides of the Sierra Madre del Sur and is thus one of the most mountainous and unspoiled regions in Mexico, although a series of major tourist resorts have developed along its coast. Apart from the great river system of the Río Balsas and the Río Papagayo it has a number of smaller rivers flowing into the Pacific.

Guerrero is mainly inhabitated by mestizos and various Indian tribes including the Nahua, Tlapanecs, Mixtecs and Chatino; in the south-east there are still some descendants of negro slaves.

Archaeological sites

A large number of archaeological sites have been discovered in the state, but they have either not been excavated or are of relatively little interest. Among them are Los Monos, Mommoxtli, Ixcateopan and Xochipala.

The caves of Juxtlahuaca and Oxtotitlán (pre-Columbian wall-paintings – see Chilpancingo) are well worth a visit.

History

The region was probably already settled in the Archaic period. The first archaeological remains were left by the mysterious Olmecs, who came to this area *c.* 1000 B.C. from the Gulf coast by way of the central highlands, probably seeking jade, and left traces of their presence in the form of rock paintings and terracotta and jade figures. Practically nothing is known of the people who created the Mezcala style (stylised geometric figures carved in various kinds of stone). In this region Olmec and Teotihuacán styles have evidently fused to produce a new artistic whole. Figurines and masks in pure Teotihuacán style have also, however, been found in Guerrero. The later development of metal-working in central Mexico is attributed to possible influences from Peru, Colombia and Costa Rica, passing by way of Guerrero. In the post-Classic period (950–1521) the predominant cultural influences were those of the Mixtecs and later the Aztecs, who conquered part of Guerrero in the mid 15th c.

Between 1522 and 1532 the Spanish conquistadors, under Cristóbal de Olid, Gonzalo de Sandoval and Hurtado de Mendoza, conquered parts of Guerrero and advanced to the coast. During the colonial period the important route from the Pacific port of Acapulco to Mexico City and on to the Gulf of Mexico passed through Guerrero. The state of Guerrero was established in 1849 and named after Vicente Guerrero, one of the leading fighters for Mexican independence and the second President of the Republic.

Economy

In addition to mining for silver, gold, mercury, lead, tin, zinc and sulphur, the main elements in the economy of Guerrero are agriculture (sugar-cane, cotton, coffee, tobacco, vanilla and corn) and forestry (hardwood and rubber). Tourism also makes a major contribution, the great tourist centres being Taxco, Acapulco and Zihuatanejo-Ixtapa.

Places of Interest

In addition to the capital, Chilpancingo and the major tourist centres of Taxco, Acapulco and Zihuatanejo-Ixtapa (see entries), there is also the town of Iguala. Agustin Iturbide promulgated the "Iguala Plan" which laid the foundations for the practical achievement of Mexican independence.

Hermosillo D 3

State: Sonora (Son.)
Altitude: 537m/1762ft
Population: 500,000
Telephone code: 91 62

Access

By air from Mexico City in about 2 hours, also flights from other Mexican airports; by rail from Mexico City via Guadalajara and Ciudad Obregón in about 38 hours; by bus from Mexico City via Guadalajara in about 35 hours; from the USA via Tijuana or Nogales.

Location

Hermosillo, capital of the state of Sonora, is located on the shores of a lake at the confluence of the Río Sonora and Río Zanjón, surrounded by fertile fruit orchards, market gardens and arable land. More recently refining industries (maquiladoras) have established themselves here. Few old colonial buildings survive, since the town has developed rapidly in recent years and has largely been modernised. The stretch of coast opposite the Isla Tiburón attracts many visitors with its agreeable winter climate.

History

The first Spaniards arrived in this region in 1531 and encountered stiff resistance from the warlike nomadic Indian tribes. It was not until 1742 that the first fortified settlement was established here by Agustin de Vildósola under the name of El Real Presidio de la Santisima Trinidad de Pitic. In 1828 the town was given its present name in honour of General José María Gonzáles Hermosillo, a hero of the War of Independence. In 1879 Hermosillo finally became the capital of Sonora state, having previously been its provisional capital.

Sights

The town has few buildings of tourist interest. Notable features are the 19th c. Neo-Classical Cathedral, the Government Palace (Palacio de Gobierno, also 19th c.), the Madero Park and the Mirador, an outlook tower on the Cerro de la Campagne. At the northern exit onto the MEX 15 to Nogales stands the equestrian statue of the Jesuit missionary Eusebio Francisco Kino.

Museo Regional de Historia

On the campus of the modern University will be found the Museo Regional de Historia de Sonora, which contains archaeological material from Sonora and ethnological collections illustrating local Indian cultures (Seri, Pima, Opata, Yaqui). Particularly notable is a mummified body thought to be at least 10,000 years old, found in a cave near the village of Yécora.

Palaeontological Museum

The Palaeontological Museum, housed in the former gaol near the Cerro de la Campaña (Bell Hill), boasts a collection of, among other things, 19th c. weaponry and traditional Yaqui Indian dance costumes.

Surroundings

Bahía Kino

Some 115km/72 miles west of Hermosillo lies a beautiful bay, the Bahía Kino, with the fishing village of Viejo Kino and the tourist resort of Nuevo Kino, with facilities for many kinds of water sports. The names commemorate the famous Jesuit missionary and explorer Eusebio Francisco Kino (1644–1711), who established more than 25 missions in Sonora at the end of the 17th and beginning of the 18th c. and thus helped to open up the region. It was the Austrian-born Kino who proved that Baja California was not an island but a peninsula. A visit is recommended to the Museo Regional in Calle Puerto Peñasco in Nuevo Kino, where Seri Indian handicrafts are exhibited.

Punta Chueca

15km/9 miles north of Viejo and Nuevo Kino lies the little township of Punta Chueca, which boasts a particularly beautiful beach and is a popular meeting place for Seri Indians.

Isla Tiburón

The Isla Tiburón (Island of Sharks), lying just off the coast of Sonora in the Mar de Cortés (Gulf of California), is over 50km/30 miles long and up to 30km/20 miles wide, making it Mexico's largest island. Discovered by Fernando de Alarcón in 1540, it was for a long time inhabited by Seri Indians, but since 1976 it has been an uninhabited nature reserve, with rich animal and plant life, which can be visited only with special permission.

Seri Indians

The Seri Indians, now dying out and numbering fewer than 500, are still semi-nomadic hunters, fishermen and food-gatherers. Practically nothing is known about the origin of these tall Indians, whose language belongs to the Sioux group. They once lived on the island of Tiburón but were resettled by the Mexican navy on the strip of mainland opposite.

Religion

Although they were converted to Christianity by the Jesuits they still worship the sun, the moon and various animal demons. Their ceremonies, which usually involve dancing, are intended to ensure success in hunting and fishing, and they also attach importance to girls' puberty rituals.

They recognise women as having great authority, but in times of crisis they elect a hunter as their leader. Nowadays only the women paint their faces in bright colours on special occasions; their jewellery is mostly made from shells, bones and seeds. Their traditional crafts are confined to elaborately woven baskets and carved ironwood, which they sell at weekends in Nuevo Kino.

Pima Indians

East of Hermosilla, around the settlements of Ures, El Novillo, Sahuaripa, Yeecora and Maycoba on the slopes of the Sierra Madre Occidental, live the Pima Indians, some 1500 in number. The Pima, whose language belongs to the Uto-Aztec family and is thus similar to Náhuatl, originally lived a nomadic life in Sonora and Arizona. Towards the end of the 17th c. they were pacified with the help of the Jesuits, and thereafter they fought with the Spaniards against the Seri and their traditional enemies the Comanches. They now live mainly by farming and rearing cattle. Their principal fiesta is October 4th (Día de San Francisco).

Ópata Indians

North-east of Hermosillo, between the Río Sonora and Río Bavispe, live the Opata Indians, now numbering only about 300. They also belong to the Uto-Aztec family, being related to the Pima and Tarahumara, and are believed to be descended from the Aztecs. They now live mainly by farming and breeding silkworms.

Religion

Although they, too, were converted by the Jesuits at the end of the 17th c., they still preserve many ancient Indian rituals and believe in a kind of transmigration of souls. Their dances represent battles with the Apaches and their first encounters with the Spaniards. Like the Tarahumara, they go in for long-distance races and contests of skill.

Some 140km/90 miles south of Hermosilla lies the port of Guaymas (see entry).

Hidalgo (State)

Abbreviation: Hgo.
Capital: Pachuca
Area: 20,870sq.km/8058sq. miles
Official population 1990: 1,888,400 (1994 estimate: 2,050,000)

Location and Topography

The state of Hidalgo, most of which lies in the central Mexican highlands, is bounded on the north by the states of San Luis Potosí and Veracruz, on the west by Querétaro, on the south by México state and Tlaxcala, and on the east by Puebla. The northern and eastern parts of the state are very mountainous, while to the south and west lies a relatively flat plateau. The population consists of whites, mestizos and a considerable proportion of Indians – Otomí, Nahua and Huastecs.

Archaeological sites

In addition to the great Toltec site of Tula (see entry) Hidalgo has a number of archaeological sites of lesser importance at Tepeapulco, Tepeyahualco and Huapacalco.

History

In pre-Columbian times the Hidalgo area was mainly under the influence of Teotihuacán and to a lesser degre El Tajín cultures during the Classic period. Later the city of Tula (Tollán) became the centre of the

splendid Toltec culture (A.D. 968–1175). The Otomí and Huastecs, who settled here after the departure of the Toltecs, fell under the dominance of the Aztecs in the second half of the 15th c. The history of Hidalgo during the colonial period was for the most part that of its capital, Pachuca. Under the Republic it was part of México state until 1869, when it became an independent state under the name of the hero of Mexican independence, Miguel Hidalgo y Costilla (1753–1811).

Economy

In terms of mineral resources Hidalgo is one of the richest states in Mexico, with mines yielding silver, gold, mercury, copper, iron, lead, zinc and antimony. Its agriculture and forestry produce wheat, coffee, agaves, tobacco, mahogany and ebony. In the south of the state is a considerable concentration of industry (textiles, cement, goods wagons, motor vehicles, machinery). Hidalgo also boasts a large oil refinery. Tourism is making an increasing contribution to the economy.

Places of Interest

Places of interest in Hidalgo include the archaeological sites already mentioned, the state capital of Pachuca (see entry), Actopán (see entry), Ixmiquilpan and Zimapán (see Actopán, Surroundings) and Tepejí del Río (see Tula, Surrroundings). The places listed below are also worth visiting.

Tulacingo

Tulacingo (2200m/7200ft; population 72,000) celebrates the Día de Nuestra Señora de los Angeles on August 2nd. It is an industrial and agricultural centre noted for the production of sarapes and apple juice. Near the town lies the archaeological site of Huapacalco.

Huichapan

Huichapan (2100m/6900ft; population 19,000) holds its fiestas on March 19th (Día del Señor San José) and September 21st (Día de San

Mateo). Sunday is market day. The 16th c. parish church has an Indian-Plateresque doorway, a stone cross and a Baroque tower.

★Augustinian convents at Epazoyucan and Singuilucan

To get to Epazoyucan take the MEX 130 towards Tulancingo and after 17km/10½ miles turn right near El Ocote. The town has a 16th c. Augustinian convent with an atrium with a stone cross, Spanish-Plateresque posas (processional chapels) and open chapels, and a church with a Renaissance façade. There are some interesting frescos, some multicoloured, in the cloister, baptistry and sacristy.

Access to Singuilcan is by way of a further road which branches to the right off the MEX 130 12km/7½ miles from El Ocote. It also has an Augustinian convent of 1540 with a Plateresque doorway and interesting cloister, a Baroque church with 18th c. retablos, and a Franciscan friary of 1527. Note the frescos in the cloister and the 16th c. Indian carved stone cross.

Hidalgo del Parral

See Chihuahua (Town)

Huejotzingo (Huexotzingo) K 8

State: Puebla (Pue.)
Altitude: 2304m/7559ft
Population: 65,000

Access

By car on the MEX 190, 106km/66 miles from Mexico City, 26km/16 miles from Puebla and 14km/9 miles from Cholula. Local buses.

Location

Huejotzingo lies amid fruit plantations at the foot of the snow-capped volcano of Iztaccíhuatl (5286m/17,343ft). The old pre-Columbian town of Huexotzingo played a leading role in this area during the late Post-Classic period. Today Huejotzingo is noted as a centre of manufacture of apple juice and sarapes.

History

Huejotzingo first made its appearance in Indian history in the 14th c. A.D., when Náhuatl-speaking nomads from the north (Chichimecs) settled in this area. Thereafter they built up an independent state which for a time dominated the rival states of Cholula and Tlaxcala. In the second half of the 15th c. they came into conflict with the Aztecs (Mexica) and the neighbouring town of Tlaxcala, and took part in the "Flower Wars", the purpose of which was not to win territory but to capture prisoners for sacrifice to the gods. After suffering defeat at the hands of the Tlaxcalans Huejotzingo finally, in 1518, entered into an alliance with them against the Aztecs of Tenochtitlán.

When the Spaniards under Hernán Cortés came to Huejotzingo in 1519 on their way to Tenochtitlán the people of the town (which then had a population of 40,000) gave them assistance, as did the Tlaxcalans. Recognising the importance of Huejotzingo as an Indian centre, the Spaniards built one of their earliest and most imposing convents just outside the old town.

★Convent of San Francisco

The Convent of San Francisco de Huejotzingo, built by Father Juan de Alameda and Toribio de Alcazar between 1529 and 1570, is one of the oldest and finest in New Spain.

Posa (processional chapel)

Danza de los Viejitos

Atrium

★ posas

On the way to the convent we first come to the atrium, which is entered by a broad flight of steps and a doorway with three Plateresque arches. In the middle stands a carved stone cross, and at the four corners are posas (processional chapels) which are among the finest of the kind in Mexico; with their pyramidal roofs and their pattern of ornamentation they are in the Spanish-Plateresque tradition. Note the arms of the Franciscan order and the alfiz (hood-mould framing a doorway), here usually in the form of a Franciscan rope-girdle – a characteristic of the Mudéjar style.

Fortified church

The façade of the typical fortified church is decorated in Spanish-Plateresque style with columns and symbols of the order. The framing of the north doorway (now walled-up) is a fine example of colonial-Plateresque: here again the doorway arch is enclosed by an alfiz and the exuberantly but harmoniously ornamented façade bears the arms of the Franciscans. The triangular merlons, with openings, of the battlements are found only at Huejotzingo.

Interior

★ Retablo

In the spacious nave of the church, with its magnificent Gothic ribbed vaulting, will be seen a large four-part retablo decorated with fourteen statues (1586), another fine example of the Plateresque tradition. Its seven oil paintings are by the Flemish artist Simón Pereyns, who came to New Spain in 1566. Some remains of the frescos which once covered the walls can still be seen. The wall at the entrance to the sacristy has Mudéjar ornamentation.

Convent building

The convent is entered through a door on the right-hand side of the church. In the porch is the Trinity Chapel, adjoining which is the cloister. The friezes in the corridors and cells are in Renaissance style. The interesting frescos include representations of the Immaculate Conception, the arrival of the first twelve Franciscans in New Spain in 1524 (Sala de Profundis) and scenes from the life of St Francis.

San Diego

A smaller church in Huejotzingo is that of San Diego (16th c.) with a richly carved early 17th c. sacristy roof, a font with Franciscan symbols, and ornamentation on the façade similar to that at Calpan (see below).

Surroundings

★Franciscan friary of Calpan

10km/6 miles from Huejotzingo on an unsurfaced road lies Calpan (Náhuatl for "in the houses"), now also known as San Andrés Calpan, which boasts another interesting Franciscan friary founded in 1548. The simple Plateresque façade of the church has sculptured decoration, including representations of agave plants. In the interior will be found a triumphal arch decorated with the Franciscan rope-girdle. At the corners of the atrium stand four fine posas richly decorated with sculpture in the form of flowers, geometric patterns, the Annunciation, the Last Judgment, Franciscan symbols, etc.

Isla Mujeres — Q 7

State: Quintana Roo (Q.R.)
Population: 20,000
Telephone code: 91 987

Access

By ferry from Puerto Juárez and from Punta Sam (see Practical Information, Ferries); by bus from Mérida or Chetumal (see entries) to both these ports; by hydrofoil from Cancún (see entry).

Location
★Seaside resort

The Isla Mujeres (Island of Women), 8km/5 miles long and up to 2km/1¼ miles across, lies in the Caribbean off the coast of the Yucatán peninsula. It offers the visitor beautiful beaches of white sand fringed by coconut palms, lagoons of crystal-clear water and coral reefs with an abundance of fish.

History

Little is known of the island's history in pre-Conquest days. The Mayas have left traces of their presence in remains of buildings, some of which date from the 8th and 9th c. A.D. Most of the temples that have been found are thought to have been dedicated to Ixchel, goddess of the moon and fertility.

The island was discovered in 1517 – two years before Cortés landed in Mexico – by a Spanish expedition under Francisco Hernández de Córdoba, who named it "Island of Women" after the large number of terracotta female figurines which he and his men found in the Maya ruins. In later periods the Isla Mujeres, like most of the Caribbean islands, was a pirates' and smugglers' lair. It is only within the last twenty years or so that tourism has come to the island and turned a sleepy fishing settlement into a popular holiday resort. Unlike the neighbouring island of Cozumel and the modern seaside resort of Cancún, Isla Mujeres has remained relatively unspoiled and not too crowded. In order to promote its trade the island has been made a free port.

Sights

Beaches and coral reefs

The island's main attractions lie on and in the sea and are readily accessible on foot, by bicycle or by moped. The best bathing place is the Playa Cocteros ("Los Cocos") on the north-west side of the island;

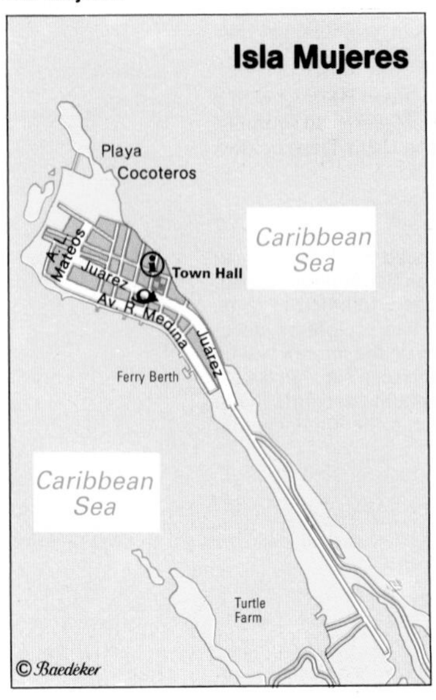

Isla Mujeres: a coral diver

and at the northern tip begin the coral reefs which provide such splendid opportunities for snorkellers. The east coast, on the Caribbean, also boasts some beautiful beaches and reefs, such as Playa Ponchol, but strong currents make bathing hazardous.

★El Garrafón

At the south end of the island lies a charming bay, El Garrafón (the "Carafe"), which can be reached by road or by boat. In this statutorily protected underwater area countless tropical fish, denizens of the coral reef, can be observed. At one spot in the bay can be seen, just under the water, a huge shoal of fish which, extraordinarily, has remained almost in the same place for many years and is unique.

Los Manchones
★Caves of the Sleeping Sharks

Farther out lies a reef known as Los Manchones which attracts many diving enthusiasts. For experienced scuba divers a boat trip can be arranged to the Caves of the Sleeping Sharks, 20–30m/65–100ft under water, which were discovered in the late 1960s by a local fisherman and became widely known through television films.

On the way to El Garrafón those interested in animals might care to visit the turtle farm and the marine biology station in the centre of the island. In the latter fish and amphibians are displayed and there are regular performances by dolphins, sea-lions and sea-elephants.

Hacienda Mundaca

An experience of a unique kind is provided by a visit to the Hacienda Mundaca, with the remains of the house and garden of the 19th c. Basque pirate and slave-dealer Antonio de Mundaca.

Maya ruins

The most interesting Maya remains on the Isla Mujeres lie beyond the lighthouse on the southern tip of the island. Damaged by Hurricane Gilbert in 1988, they are believed to have served as an observatory dedicated to the goddess Ixchel. From here there is a magnificent view of the Caribbean Sea and Cancún (see entry).

Surroundings

Isla Contoy

There is an interesting day trip by boat to the Isla Contoy (Mayan: "conto"=pelican), a bird sanctuary some 20km/12½ miles to the north of Isla Mujeres; 6km/4miles long and on average 200m/220yd wide, it is a bird sanctuary under statutory protection. Over 70 species of birds have been observed, including flamingos, frigate birds, pelicans, ducks, spoonbills, cormorants and other species.

Isla Holbox

In the waters between Cabo Catoche and Isla Holbox live marlin, shark, sailfish, barracuda, sea bass and mackerel. The island of Holbox can be reached by car and boat from the mainland – take the side road to Chiquilá off the main MEX 180 Valladolid–Puerto Juárez road (about 90km/56 miles), and then by boat.

Ixtaccíhuatl

See Popacatépetl/Iztaccihuatl

Ixtapa

See Zihuatanejo-Ixtapa

Izamal P 7

State: Yucatán (Yuc.)
Altitude: 13m/43ft
Population: 45,000

Access

By rail from Mérida (see entry) in about 1½ hours; by road from Mérida on the MEX 180 to the turn-off near Kantunil (68km/42 miles), from where it is a further 26km/16 miles.

Location
★Townscape

Izamal, one of the most interesting places in Yucatán but still hardly discovered by tourists, lies only 26km/16 miles north of the MEX 180 from Mérida to Chichén Itzá. With its remains of Maya pyramids and temples and its 16th c. Franciscan churches and convents it provides a dramatic illustration of the encounter between pre-Columbian and Spanish cultures.

History

Although Izamal ("City of Hills" in Maya) has been the subject of little archaeological investigation, it is believed to have reached its peak in the Maya Classic period (A.D. 300–900). According to legend, it was founded by Itzamná ("Dew from Heaven"), later revered as a sky god. After his death his body is said to have been divided into three parts, which were then buried under the three hills of Izamal. On these hills were built three huge temples, the principal one being known as Kinich-kakmó ("Sun-Bird with the Fiery Face"). Izamal then became a place of pilgrimage frequented by worshippers of the sun god Kinich-kakmó and the sky god Itzamnea, from all over the country. Together with other sacred sites such as Cozumel and above all Chichén Itzá, Izamal later developed, perhaps under the rule of the legendary ItzEa ("May-anised" Toltecs or "Toltecised" Mayas), into an important political centre.

The chronicles tell of the abduction by Chac-xibchac, ruler of Chichén Itzá, of the betrothed wife of Ah-ulil, ruler of Izamal, and of the subsequent war which ended in the expulsion of the population of Chichén

Itzá about A.D 1200. This war seems also, however, to have initiated the political decline of Izamal. At the same time began the rise of Mayapán, the last stage in the development of Maya civilisation.

Izamal's importance as a place of pilgrimage led the Spaniards to take strong measures when they captured it about 1540. They at once pulled down most of the pyramids and used the stone to construct their own religious buildings.

Sights

★Convent of San Antonio de Padua

From the main square of the town the houses of which are painted white and yellow, a broad flight of steps leads up to the Franciscan Convent of San Antonio de Padua, built by Juan de Mérida between 1553 and 1561. The huge atrium, with an area of some 8000sq.m/ 9500sq.yd, is surrounded by an arcade of 75 arches. It is said to be exceeded in size only by St Peter's Square in Rome.

Convent church

The church, with its very plain façade, is a typical example of the fortress-like churches built by the Franciscans in the 16th c. The horse-shoe-shaped arch above the arcade dates from the 19th c. On the walls of the nave hang oil-paintings of archbishops of Mérida. The original altar of the Virgin of Izamal, patroness of Yucatán, which came from Guatemala, was destroyed by fire in 1829; the present altar, a skilful copy, has ten niches, most of which contain effigies of saints. In the convent courtyard is an old Indian sun-stone.

The atrium, church and convent are built on the foundations of the large Maya temple of Popol-chac, which the Spaniards called the "Castle of the Kings" (Castillo de los Reyes).

Convent of San Antonio de Padua, seen from the atrium

Maya pyramids

Most of the twelve pyramids which originally stood here were destroyed either by the Spaniards or by natural causes. The three principal pyramids were known by the names of Itza-matul, Kab-ul and Kinich-kakmó, only the last of which, dedicated to the sun god, still conveys some impression of its original imposing bulk. One of the largest pyramids in Mexico, it is notable for the steepness of the staircase leading up to the summit. From the top there are superb panoramic views of the town and surrounding area.

Surroundings

Returning to the MEX 180 at Kantunil and proceeding east in the direction of Chichén Itzá and Valladolid, it is a further 26km/16 miles to Libre Unión, from which a road leads south to Yaxcabá. 3km/2 miles down this road a side road branches off to the beautiful Cenote Xtojil, 1km/¾ mile away. 16km/9 miles beyond the turning lies Yaxcabá, which has an interesting parish church with an unusual façade and three towers. Also in the village will be found a cenote, into which the local people threw their weapons, jewellery and money to save them from looting during the 19th c. "Caste War"; most of the objects were later recovered.

Iztaccíhuatl

See Popocatépetl/Iztaccíhuatl

Jalapa (Xalapa) L 8

State: Veracruz (Ver.)
Altitude: 1420m/4659ft
Population: 400,000
Telephone code: 91 281

Access

By rail from Mexico City in about 8½ hours, from Veracruz in about 4 hours; by bus from Mexico City and Veracruz; by car from Mexico City 315km/196 miles on the MEX 140, from Veracruz about 120km/75 miles on the MEX 180/140.

Location

Jalapa, capital of Veracruz state, is built on a number of hills in a garden-like region at the foot of the Cerro de Macuiltepec. It is surrounded by high mountains, with the Cofre de Perote (Nauhcampatépetl) towering above the others, and to the south can be seen the Pico de Orizaba (Citlaltépetl), Mexico's highest mountain. This situation gives the region an abundant rainfall and at times heavy cloud cover, promoting a luxuriant growth of vegetation. Jalapa has modern districts as well as old colonial parts of the town, and also has a university.

History

When Cortés passed through Jalapa (Náhuatl name "Xallaapan", or "river in the sand") in 1519 on his way to Tenochtitlán it was a flourishing Indian settlement under Aztec influence. After the Conquest Spaniards settled here in large numbers. During the colonial period Jalapa was famed for its important annual fair, at which goods brought from Spain by the returning "silver ships" were sold. Lying 120km/75 miles from Veracruz and 300km/185 miles from Mexico City, it later became a staging point on the mailcoach route.

Townscape

Narrow streets and alleyways, their gaily coloured houses and luxuriant gardens dating from the Spanish period, contrast strikingly with the

Museum Jalapa: Clay figure

Agave plantation in Julisco

wide avenues of the newer districts. There are few colonial buildings of note, the most interesting being the huge late 18th c. cathedral situated diagonally opposite the Parque Juarez. Across on the other side of the park stands the pale-coloured government building.

★★Museum of Anthropology

In the north-west of the town, on the Mexico City road, lies the impressive Museum of Anthropology (Museo de Antropologia de la Universidad Jalapa), the most important and attractively laid-out museum of its kind in the country matched only by the Museum of Anthropology in Mexico City. Three atria and six other rooms are linked by a large orientation hall equipped with information boards, models and items for comparison. The 3000 exhibits on display are mainly from the pre-Columbian cultures of the Gulf region, including the Olmecs, Huastecs, Remoyadas and Totonacs.

In the grounds stand several basalt Olmec colossal heads, brought from San Lorenzo where they were found (the large Olmec sculptures discovered at La Venta can be seen in the open-air museum at Villahermosa, see entry). Of those here at Jalapa, Head No. 8 particularly stands out; in contrast to the others its lips are slightly parted and it has avoided ritual mutilation. Other impressive Olmec stone sculptures include not only altars and stelae but also life-sized terracotta figures dating from A.D. 600–900 which were found as recently as 1986 in El Zapotal, west of Alvarado. In all, 22 of these previously unrecorded and richly ornamented figures were found; they were probably dedicated to the goddess Cihuatéotl, the patroness of women who died in childbirth.

The museum also houses the largest collection of cult objects connected with ball games, such as yokes, axes and palms as well as the "laughing faces", terracotta sculptures from the Remoyadas culture from the central Gulf region. Recent additions include parts of a multi-coloured mural from Las Higueras (A.D. 600–900), once probably a satellite town of the grat El Tajin. There are also collections of ethnological material on the Indian tribes of the region.

For some time now the curator of the museum has been Brigido Lara, known around the world as a maker of perfect reproductions of old Indian figures. He had sold these to dealers as copies, but they then sold them on to the large museums as the genuine article.

Surroundings

★Jardin Lecuona

7km/4½ miles north-west on the MEX 140 Puebla road lies the garden city of Banderilla with the beautiful Jardin Lecuona, a botanic garden with more than 200 species of orchids alone.

Perote

53km/33 miles further on lies the town of Perote (2400m/7875ft; population 40,000), at the foot of the volcano known as Cofre ("coffer, chest") de Perote (Nauhcampatépetl for "square mountain"; 4282m/14,049ft). On the outskirts of the town stands the forbidding Fort San Carlos de Perote, built in the 18th c. to control bandits and rebels and later used as a prison.

Coatapec

16km/10 mile south of Jalapa lies Coatapec, an old Indian village surrounded by tropical forests with abundant plant life of interest to the botanically minded. The coffee plantation enjoys the reputation of producing the best coffee in Mexico.

★El Lencero

12km/7 miles from Jalapa on the Veracruz road is the great hacienda known as El Lencero, built by a comrade-in-arms of Cortés. The drive leading up to it is roofed over with large trees. Parts of the buildings and gardens were recently restored in the correct style and now accurately reflect the 450-year history of the Mexican hacienda.

Jalisco (State)

Abbreviation: Jal.
Capital: Guadalajara
Area: 81,058sq.km/31,297sq. miles
Official population 1990: 5,302,700 (1994 estimate: 5,900,000)

Location and Topography

The state of Jalisco is bounded on the north by Zacatecas and Aguascalientes, on the west by Nayarit and the Pacific, on the south by Colima and Michoacán and on the east by Guanajuato. It is a region of varied scenery, with an extensive high plateau, ranges of hills in the Sierra Madre Occidental, deep gorges, numerous lakes and a coastal region of luxuriant vegetation. The mountains, many of them volcanic, rise to their highest points in the south, with the Nevado de Colima (4339m/14,240ft) and the Volcán de Colima (3838m/12,596ft). The population is made up of whites, mestizos and a considerable proportion of Indians, mainly Nahua, Huicholes and Purépacha (Tarascans).

Archaeological sites

A number of pre-Columbian sites have been identified, many of them merely cemeteries. They include those at Ixtepete, Teuchtitlán, Etzatlán, Tuxacuesco and Ameca.

History

The pre-Columbian history of Jalisco (Náhuatl: "place in front of the sand") began in the Pre-Classic period and continued in the Classic. Since very little is known of the peoples who created these cultures they are referred to simply as the "cultures of the West" (Occidente).

Mexico
United Mexican States
Estados Unidos Mexicanos

Jalisco

Federal State
Estados

1a Baja California Sur
1b Baja California Norte
2 Sonora
3 Chihuahua
4 Sinaloa
5 Durango
6 Coahuila
7 Nuevo León
8 Zacatecas
9 San Luis Potosí
10 Tamaulipas
11 Nayarit
12 Aguascalientes
13 Jalisco
14 Guanajuato
15 Querétaro
16 Hidalgo
17 Colima
18 Michoacán
19 México
20 Morelos
21 Tlaxcala
22 Puebla
23 Veracruz
24 Guerrero
25 Oaxaca
26 Chiapas
27 Tabasco
28 Campeche
29 Yucatán
30 Quintana Roo

D.F. Distrito Federal (Federal District)

Their most notable products are the life-like terracotta figures, named Jalisco, Colima and Nayarit, after the states. During the Post-Classic period there grew up in this region a number of Indian states, including Coliman, Zapotlán, Xalisco and Tollan, which were conquered in the second half of the 15th c. by the Purépecha (Tarascans) under their king, Tzitic Pandácuaro.

The first of the Spanish conquistadors to arrive in this area, in 1525, was Francisco Cortés de San Buenaventura, who encountered the Chimalhuacanes, then dominant over the other local tribes. It was left to the notorious Nuño Beltrán de Guzmán, however, to conquer the greater part of the region between 1530 and 1535. After the dismissal and arrest of Guzmán, Pérez de la Torre was made governor of the province of Nueva Galicia, to which Aguascalientes and Zacatecas also belonged until 1789. In subsequent years there was bitter fighting between the Spaniards and rebellious Indians, who entrenched themselves in the old strongholds (peñoles) originally built by the Tarascans. After the pacification of the area and the discovery of minerals the state, with its capital at Guadalajara, became independent and prosperous. In 1889 Jalisco gave up part of its coastal territory, including the town of Tepic, and this developed into the state of Nayarit. The bloody Cristero War (1926–29) started in the region of Los Altos in north-eastern Jalisco. During this struggle Catholic peasants rebelled against the the oppression of the church by Presidents Plutarco Elías Calles and Emilio Portes Gil.

Economy

The state has a richly productive agriculture, including maize, beans, wheat, sugar-cane, cotton, agaves, rice, indigo and tobacco. The coastal regions grow rubber and copra, and there is also much livestock-farming. Minerals worked include gold, silver, cinnabar, copper and semi-precious stones. Industry, mainly in Guadalajara, produces textiles, leather goods, chemicals, tobacco, glass, ceramics, cement and drinks. The growing tourist trade is centred on Guadalajara, the area around the Laguna de Chapala and the beach resorts on the Pacific.

Places of Interest

In addition to Guadalajara (see entry), the region around the Laguna de Chapala (see entry) and the seaside resorts of Puerto Valllarta (see entry), Barra de Navidad and Playa de Tenacatita (both in the Surroundings of Manzanillo – see entry), the following towns are also of interest:

Tequila

Tequila (the Náhuatl name for a drink made from mezcal: alt. 1218m/3996ft; pop. 35,000; fiestas: May 2nd, Día de la Santa Cruz; December 12th, Día de la Virgen de Guadalupe), with the beautiful church of San Francisco, is a centre of tequila and mezcal production. These potent liqueurs are made from the fermented juice of the mezcal agave or maguey. The distilleries in the town, which can be visited, obtain their supplies from the large agave plantations in the surrounding area.

Ciudad Guzmán (formerly Zapotlán: 1507m/4944ft; population 112,000; fiesta: October 22nd–25th, Día del Señor San José). The town boasts a small archaeological museum which also contains pictures by José Clemente Orozco. It is a good base for climbing the Nevado de Colima and the Volcán de Colima (see Colima, Town).

San Juan de los Lagos

San Juan de los Lagos (1864m/6116ft; population 57,000; fiestas February 2nd Día de la Candelaria, or Candlemas, and December 8th, Día de la Inmaculada Concepción).

★Pilgrimages

The miracle-working statue of the Virgen de la Candelaria in the parish church draws thousands of pilgrims from all over Mexico, especially at the beginning of February, and the pilgrimages are the occasion of great fiestas, with mariachis, dancing, bullfights, cockfights, etc. The town is also noted for its embroidery and its horse market, held between November 2nd and December 13th.

Kabah P 7

State: Yucatán (Yuc.)
Altitude: 25m/82ft

Access

By bus from Campeche and Mérida (see entries); by car from Campeche on the MEX 261, about 120km/75 miles, from Mérida on the MEX 261 about 130km/80 miles, from Uxmal (see entry) about 20km/12½ miles.

Location

Having previously been somewhat neglected by archaeologists, investigation of Kabah resumed in 1990. A visit to the site is highly recommended, situated as it is right beside the Mérida–Campeche road just 20km/12½ miles south of Uxmal (see entry). An additional attraction is that, since 1993, the 1000ha/2470 acre site has been a designated conservation area (Parque Estatal). Although the buildings so far excavated at Kabah are in the traditional Puuc style, they have revealed unusual features which are attributed to Chenes influence.

History

Little is known of the history of Kabah. It seems to have been a dependency of the great city of Uxmal, with which it is linked by a sacbé, one of the Maya "white roads" used mostly for ceremonial purposes. In the mid 19th c. the site was explored by the indefatigable John Lloyd Stephens and Frederick Catherwood, but the first systematic digs were carried out by Teobert Maler towards the end of the century. These and later excavations have shown that the principal buildings on the site date from the 9th c., also that Kabah was abandoned in about 1200.

Visit to the ★Ruins

★Palace of the Masks

In the southern part of the site, east of the road, lies the Palace of the Masks (Templo de las Máscaras, or codz-poop, "rolled-up mat"). The Maya name comes from the trunk-like nose of the rain-god Chac, resembling a rolled-up mat, here used as a staircase.

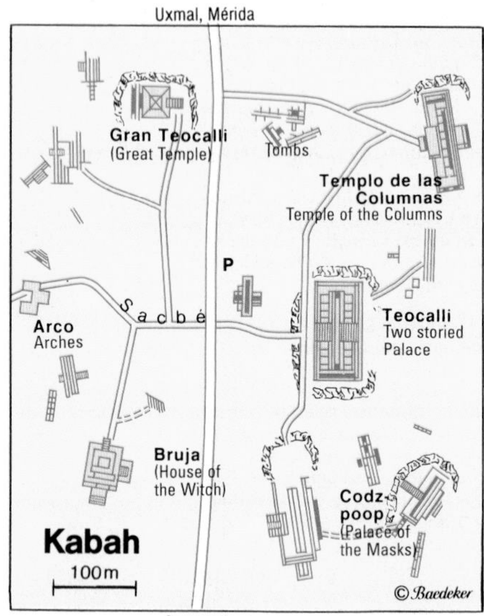

The Temple, 45m/150ft long and 6m/20ft high, stands on a low platform, the front of which is decorated with a horizontal row of stylised masks. The palace is unique in Puuc architecture in having the façade as well as the main structure covered with decoration – a feature attributed to the influence of the Chenes style. Above a richly ornamented sill is a continuous row of masks with huge trunk-like noses now mostly broken off; above this can be seen a cornice decorated with geometrical patterns, and above this again are three further continuous rows of Chac masks. Little is left of the roof-comb, once 3m/10ft high, with its rectangular apertures. Bizarre and overloaded with decoration as the façade may appear, with more than 250 masks, the technical mastery which it displays is no less astonishing.

Palace

A little way north of the Palace of the Masks stands the Teocalli, or Palace (Palacio). This two-storey building, the lower storey of which is destroyed, shows a plain and unadorned style of architecture which is in striking contrast to the over-decorated façade of the Codz-poop. The decoration here consists mainly of panels of close-set columns between two projecting mouldings.

Temple of the Columns

Near the Teocalli stands the much-ruined Temple of the Columns (Templo de las Columnas), which shows some affinity to the Governor's Palace at Uxmal (see entry).

★Arch of Kabah

West of the road stands the fine Arch of Kabah (Arco de Kabah), a notable example of the corbelled or "false" arch so typical of Maya architecture, formed by allowing each successive course of stone on either side of the opening to project over the one below until they meet at the top. This undecorated arch was presumably the entrance to the main cult centre, and there was probably a sacbé ("white road") leading through the arch to Uxmal. These Maya ceremonial highways, constructed of limestone with a cement surface, stood between 0·50m/1½ft and 2·50m/8ft above the ground and were an average of 4·50m/15ft wide.

Kabah: Palace of the Masks

Kabah Arch: an example of a "false" arch

In the western part of Kabah will be found a largely unexcavated area containing the Great Temple (Gran Teocalli), the Western Quadrangle (Cuadrángulo del Oeste) and the Temple of the Lintels (Templo de los Dinteles).

Surroundings
Mul-chic

Near Santa Elena, some 5km/3 miles north of Kabah, lies the small archaeological site of Mul-chic. The largest building here is the restored six-storey Pyramid with steps on the outside, which was built over a temple with a vaulted roof and roof-comb. The wall-paintings discovered inside are now scarcely visible.

See Recommended Routes, No. 9

Kohunlich (Kohunrich) P 8

State: Quintana Roo (Q.R.)
Altitude: 85m/279ft

Access

By car from Chetumal 58km/36 miles on the MEX 186 to Francisco Villa, then take the road on the left (9km/6 miles to the site).

The excavated area in the centre of the Maya site of Kohunlich lies amid primeval tropical forest, but in spite of its isolated situation it is one of the best maintained excavation sites in Mexico. This little known site of the early Classic period is easily acessible, and is well worth visiting for its beautiful setting as well as its archaeological interest.

History

The name Kohunlich is a garbled version of the English name "Cohoon Ridge"; the Spanish name is Aserradero ("sawmill").

Little is known of the early history of the site, or of the neighbouring Río Bec area. Kohunlich was undoubtedly occupied for several centuries before the beginning of the Christian era and continued in occupation until the 13th c., i.e. from the Formative to the Post-Classic period. Its heyday as a religious and political centre lay between A.D. 400 and 700; basically, therefore, it is a site of the early Maya Classic period.

The site was first recorded by the US archaeologist R. E. Merwin in the course of an archaeological survey of southern Campeche in 1912. The real discovery of the site, however, came in 1968, when plunderers were caught in the act of stealing the large masks on the Temple of the Masks. Since then exemplary excavation and restoration work has been carried out by Mexican archaeologists under the direction of Victor Segovia.

Visit to the ★Ruins

The area so far explored at Kohunlich covers more than 2sq.km/¾sq. mile. The earlier occupants of the site levelled and consolidated almost half the total area, using and extending natural ditches and depressions to channel rainwater into collecting basins for use during the dry period.

Plaza of the Stelae

East Building

The large Plaza of the Stelae (Plaza de las Estelas) is named after the four monolithic stelae which were found in the East Building (Edificio Oriente) and are now set on either side of the staircase. The East Building, like the three others around the square, dates from the 8th c. A.D., It is 60m/200ft long, with nine tiers leading up to a temple on the summit. Of the original three doors only the middle one, the main entrance, survives.

The South Building (Edificio Sur) is 87m/285ft in length and boasts a very long staircase formed of nine unusually broad steps.

South Building

The West Building (Edificio Poniente), almost 50m/165ft long, has a short side staircase of five steps which leads through a small passage to the front platform, evidently intended to serve as a stage for ceremonies.

West Building

The North Building (Edificio Norte), 70m/230ft long, has a staircase leading to another plaza on the west side of the building, which gives access to a patio 10m/33ft above ground level, with an area of 2500sq.m/3000sq.yd.

North Building

The Ball Court (Juego de Pelota) has a wall 33m/110ft long, with no stone rings. It is similar in structure to the ball courts of Copán in the Honduras and Becán in Campeche state.

Ball Court

The most interesting structure at Kohunlich, unique of its kind in Maya territory, is the Pyramid of the Masks (Pirámide de los Mascarones). Flanking the staircase are eight large stucco masks, originally found by tomb robbers, which are still in situ but are now protected from the weather by roofs.

★Pyramid of the Masks

The Pyramid and the masks date from the 5th c. A.D. Within the upper part of the pyramid, on different levels, were found four tomb chambers which had been looted by tomb-robbers. The six masks, all different, are about 1·60m/5ft 3in. high and appear to represent the sun god. Their tall headresses portray a mythological creature with eyes of spiral form. Some of the eyes bear the glyph "chuen", representing the trolkin, the Maya ritual year of 260 days. As was usual with Maya nobles, the noses are ornamented with rings. The teeth originally had an L-shaped inlay, now barely visible, representing the glyph "ik" (wind). Interestingly, the feline-like mouths, with the twirling moustaches of the rain god, display Olmec characteristics. All the masks have ear-rings and ear-plugs, the sides of which are formed by snakes, perhaps representing rain. Traces of red paint are still discernible.

About twenty years ago one of the masks was stolen and, after being hardened with artificial resin, was cut into small pieces and smuggled into the USA. There it was put together again and offered to a New York museum for a considerable sum. The museum informed the Mexican government, which was then able to recover the mask. It can now be seen in the National Museum of Anthropology in Mexico City.

A little way below the excavated area lies a picturesque little lagoon.

Archaeological enthusiasts will wish to visit the sites of Xpuhil, Becán and Chicanná, some 62km/40 miles west on the MEX 186 (see Chetumal).

Surroundings

Labná

P 7

State: Yucatán (Yuc.)
Altitude: 28m/92ft

By bus from Mérida (see entry); by car on the MEX 261: about 5km/3 miles south of Kabah (see entry) a new road leads to Labná via Sayil (15km/9 miles).

Access

Labná – buried, like the neighbouring sites of Sayil and Xlapak, amid dense tropical vegetation – is an important Maya centre, the full extent of which has not yet been explored. It offers classical examples of the Puuc architectural style.

Location

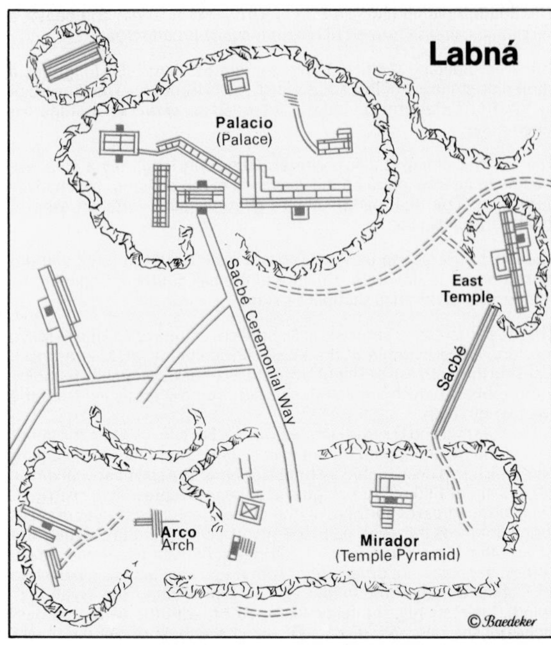

History

As with Sayil and Xlapak, little is known of the history of this interesting site. The few datings that have been established indicate that the principal structures at Labná ("broken houses" in the Maya tongue) were built in the 9th c. A.D., in the Maya Late Classic period. Here, as at most Maya sites, we owe the first account of the remains to John L. Stephens and Frederick Catherwood, who visited Labná in the mid 19th c. The large numbers of chultunes (cisterns), over sixty of which were found, suggest that the town had a considerable population.

In recent years the Carnegie Institute and various Mexican institutions have done excellent restoration work at Labná as well as the neighbouring sites of Sayil and Xlapak.

Visit to the ★Ruins

Palace

The group of structures in the northern part of the site known as the Palace (Palacio) is one of the largest temple precincts in Puuc territory. The group, haphazard and asymmetrical in layout, has a total length of almost 135m/445ft east to west and stands on a terrace 167m/550ft long. In front of it lies a huge plaza, crossed by the remains of a sacbee (ceremonial way). The façade of the eastern range is decorated with groups of three clustered columns, bands of geometrical ornamentation and nose masks. At the south-east corner, above a cluster of three columns, can be seen an unusual Chac mask with a snake's jaws, wide open, disgorging a human head. The trunk-like nose is curled up over the forehead. Here one of the two "year glyphs" so far recorded at Labná was found.

Labná: the Arch and Viewing Tower

The façades of the other parts of the palace are, with one or two exceptions, in simpler form. On the upper level is a rainwater-collecting basin, linked with a chultun (cistern) in front of the group.

East Building

130m/140yd south-east of the palace stands the East Building. Although also palace-like in construction it is decorated in simpler fashion. L-shaped and containing several rooms, it stands on a terrace. The only definite ornamentaion is the row of small pillars with a simple frieze on the upper façade.

Lookout tower

The southern group of structures is dominated by a pyramid (not yet properly restored) topped by a temple known as the Mirador ("Lookout"). Above the two restored platforms and the temple rears the imposing roof-comb, like a free-standing façade. We know from Stephen's account that it was originally decorated with a large seated figure in brightly painted stucco. The projecting stones on the front of the roof-comb provide a base for the stucco. The only surviving remnant of decoration on the temple is the lower half of a figure at the south-west corner of the building.

★Arch of Labná

The best-known feature of the site is the magnificent Arch of Labná (Arco de Labná), south-west of the Mirador.

Since the Mayas were ignorant of the true arch they used the corbelled or "false arch" formed by the overlapping of successive courses of stone and topped by a cover-slab. The richly decorated Arch of Labná, which is 3m/10ft deep and has an interior height of 5m/16ft, is flanked by two small chambers with entrances on the north-west side. The frieze along the front of the arch, with mosaic patterns reminiscent of those at Uxmal (see entry), is framed by projecting sills. Above the entrances to the two lateral chambers are representations in high relief

Arco de Labná: the front . . .

of two typical Maya huts, with thatched roofs in feather patterns; originally there were probably figures at the doors of the huts. On the stepped roof of the higher middle section the remains of the open roof-comb can still be seen.

The rear of the arch is much plainer. Above a sill with similar decoration to that on the front of the arch is a striking frieze with a meander pattern against a background of clustered columns.

Surroundings

★Lol-tún Caves

About 20km/12 miles north of Labná via Cooperativa on the road to Oxcutzcab are the Lol-tún Caves ("Grutas de Lol-tún"); the name means "stone flower" in Maya.

Flat relief

On the outside rock wall near the Nahkab entrance to the cave can be seen a larger-than-life flat relief figure of a richly-ornamented Maya warrior with a spear in his right hand. Experts have not yet been able to decipher a row of vertical glyphs above and to the left of the figure, but there is little doubt that they are among the oldest Maya inscriptions yet found. The relief has now been dated at 300 to 100 B.C. The interesting stalactitic caves contain remnants of wall-paintings and rock-drawings as well as the "Stone Head of Lol-tún". The caves were probably inhabited as long ago as 2500 B.C. Pottery dating from 1200 to 600 B.C. has been found, as well as some from the Maya Classic period and later. It is assumed that the caves were also used as places of refuge from the Spanish conquistadors. There are conducted tours of the caves at certain times of the day.

Maní

From Oxkutzcab, only 7km/5 miles beyond Lol-tún, it is worth making a detour to the little town of Maní, 10km/6 miles to the north.

. . . the rear, with remains of wall painting

Historically this was a place of some importance. About A.D. 1450, after the destruction of Mayapán, the Xiú tribe, coming from the Uxmal area, founded the town, prophetically calling it Maní ("it is all over" in Maya). The subsequent period, until the arrival of the Spaniards, saw the decline of the great Maya civilisation and the disintegration of the Maya empire into some twenty warring city states, the most important of which was the Xiú city of Maní. The fall of the Maya empire facilitated the Spanish conquest of the country. The last ruler of Maní, Titul-Xiú, surrendered to the conqueror of Yucatán, Francisco de Montejo, in 1542 and became a convert to Christianity.

In 1562 the main square of Maní was the scene of the great auto-da-fé in which Bishop Diego de Landa burned all known Maya manuscripts as works of the devil, with the sole exception of three codices.

The imposing church of San Miguel was founded by the Franciscans. Maní also has a cenote (sacrificial well) which is the subject of many legends.

★ **Chacmultún**

Those interested in archaeology would do well to make a further detour from Oxkutzcab to the seldom visited but most impressive Maya site of Chacmultún. Proceed 18km/11 miles south-east to Tekax, then turn right on an unsurfaced road to Kancab (7km/4½ miles), from where it is a further 3km/2 miles to the site.

Chacmultún group

Chacmultún (Maya for "hill of red stone") consists of three groups. The first is the west group (Chacmultún). Building 3 consists of several rooms in which remains of wall-paintings have been found. Building 1 has a central flight of steps and columned entrances; it is positioned on a high terraced plateau and has clustered columns on its upper façade. A well-preserved hut-like niche is reminiscent of Labná architecture. In one of the relatively large rooms six projecting foot-shaped stones are of particular interest. Building 2 boasts an unusual flight of steps surrounded by vaulted rooms.

Cabalpak group

It is more than 200m/220yd back along the path to the Cabalpak group (Maya for "lower terrace"). The major building in this group is No. 5; the ground floor of the multi-storied structure consists of twelve rooms some of which still have their console arches intact. More clustered columns can be seen near the top of the façade. Access to the upper, overgrown floors is by way of a path to the right.

Xetpol group

The path through the site continues for a further 500m/550yd to the Xetpol group on higher ground. On the hill stands the partially-restored Building 4 with five entrances in its middle section. Some wall-paintings can still be made out in the central room. Above this building a further structure with a projecting terrace provides a fine view over these ruins surrounded by relatively unspoiled natural woodland.

Lago de Pátzcuaro

See Pátzcuaro Lake

Laguna de Catemaco

See Catemaco Lake

Laguna de Chapala

See Chapala Lake

Lagunas de Montebello

See Montebello Lakes

La Paz D 5

State: Baja California Sur (B.C.S.)
Altitude: 13m/43ft
Population: 190,000
Telephone code: 91 682

Access

By air from Mexico City in about 1½–2 hours, and from other Mexican and US airports; by ferry from Los Mochis (Topolobampo) in 8 hours, from Mazatlán (see entry) in 16 hours (see Practical Information, Ferries); by bus from Tijuana (see entry) in about 22 hours.

Location

La Paz, capital of the state of Baja California Sur, lies in the bay of the same name on the Mar de Cortés (Gulf of California). A few years ago just a quiet old-world fishing port known only to fishermen, it has now grown into a sizeable town, mainly owing to the construction of the new north–south route, the Carretera Transpeninsular (MEX 1). In spite of this hectic growth La Paz has managed to preserve something of the restful atmosphere of earlier days.

History

Before the Conquest the southern part of Baja California was inhabited by Indian tribes, including the Pericúe, Cochimí and Guaicura, who at first gave the Spaniards a friendly reception but later tried to prevent the first attempts at settlement. Hernán Cortés is said to have been the first Spaniard to set foot on the peninsula, near the site of present-day La Paz, in 1535. At the end of the 16th c. the region around La Paz became a refuge for pirates, including the legendary Sir Francis Drake. The Jesuit mission established here in 1720 had to be abandoned in 1745 because of shortage of water and illness, and a permanent settlement was not established until 1800.

In 1830 La Paz became capital of the southern territory of Baja California. In 1847–48, during the war with the United States, it was occupied by US troops. In 1853 an American adventurer named William Walker seized the harbour in an unsuccessful bid to set up an independent state. La Paz was for a long time a centre of pearl-fishing (black and pink pearls) but this industry is of liitle importance today. The town's principal sources of revenue are tourism, fishing, commerce and a developing processing industry.

Tourist Attractions

Being a comparatively young town it has few features of tourist interest, apart from the parish church (19th c.), the Government Palace (Palacio de Gobierno, 20th c.), the House of Folk Art, the Anthropological and Historical Museum, the shell market and the harbour promenade (Malecón). La Paz is however an excellent base for deep-sea fishing and diving expeditions and trips to the many beautiful beaches in the surrounding area. It has also acquired importance as a free port.

Beaches

Among the many beaches near La Paz, some close to the town and others rather farther away, are Playa Sur to the south, Centenario to the west and Costa Baja, Eréndira, Pichilingue, El Tecolote and Puerto Balandra to the north and north-east; near Las Cruzes are El Saltito, El Palo, Los Muertos and El Rosarito.

Excursions

There are boat excursions to the offshore islands such as Espiritu Santo, La Partida and Islotes, where visitors can observe sealions and various species of birds, There are also good facilities for diving and fishing.

From Los Planes there is a trip to Punta Arenas Las Ventanas and Ensenada de los Muertos, with some fine bathing beaches.

Taking the MEX 1, the Carretera Transpeninsular (see Baja California), it is 215km/134 miles to Cabo San Lucas (see entry) by way of San José del Cabo or 150km/93 miles by way of Todos Santos.

La Venta

See Catemaco Lake

León de los Aldamas I 7

State: Guanajuato (Gto.)
Altitude: 1884m/6181ft
Population: 970,000
Telephone code: 91 47

Access from Mexico City

By rail in about 9 hours; by bus in about 5¾ hours; by car 380km/236 miles on the MEX 57.

Location

León lies on the banks of the Río Turbio in a fertile valley with an equable climate. It is the largest town and principal industrial centre of the state of Guanajuato, producing mainly leather goods (shoes, saddles, etc.), textiles, soap and steel products. It is surrounded by a rich wheat-growing region.

History

In pre-Columbian times the population of this area was a mixture of Otomi Indians and the nomadic tribes from the north known as Chichimecs. In the second half of the 15th c. these were displaced by Tarascans and Aztecs. The Spaniards established their first settlement here in 1552, and this was followed in 1576 by the official foundation of a town, which received its municipal charter in 1836. The words "de los Aldamas" were then added to its name in honour of Juan Aldama, one of the prominent figures, together with Miguel Hidalgo and Ignacio Allende, in the struggle for Mexican independence between 1810 and 1821.

Thereafter the town developed rapidly, but suffered several times from severe flooding, as in 1888, when much of it was destroyed. It is now protected by a dyke.

Sights

Although León is now predominantly a modern industrial city it has a number of handsome colonial buildings. The main square (Zócalo) with the 18th c. Baroque Cathedral is surrounded by arcades.

The Town Hall (Palacio Municipal) boasts a richly carved façade. A notable 20th c. church is the Neo-Gothic Templo Expiatorio, which has more than twenty altars and numerous crypts which served as hiding-places during the Cristero War (1926–29).

Also of interest are the Market and the Ciudad Deportiva (City of Sport).

Comanjilla

17km/10½ miles along the MEX 45 to the south a road branches off to the left, and 10km/6 miles down this road lies the spa of Comanjilla together with a health farm.

Malinalco K 8

State: México (Mex.)
Altitude: 1750m/5742ft
Population: 35,000

Access

By bus from Mexico City or Toluca (see entry) to Chalma, and thence by group taxi; by car from Mexico City it is 44km/27 miles on the MEX 95D to Tres Marías, then turn right and proceed via the Lagunas de Zempoala (14km/8½ miles) and Chalma (40km/25 miles) to Malinalco (11km/7 miles); from Toluca take the MEX 55 south as far as 13km/8 miles past Tenango, and then turn left to Malinalco (27km/17 miles). From the town of Malinalco to the ruins is a steep climb taking 30 minutes.

Location

The archaeological site of Malinalco lies on the Cerro de los Idolos ("Hill of Idols"), 220m/720ft above the village of the same name, in a region of green forests and rugged rock formations. This Aztec cult site is unique in having one of the very few rock-cut pre-Columbian structures in Meso-America.

History

Finds of pottery in Teotihuacán style indicate that the site was occupied in the early Classic period. Later it appears to have been under the influence of the Toltecs. In the 12th c. A.D. one of the Nahua tribes moving from Aztlán to the Anáhuac valley settled in Malinalco (Náhuatl: "place of the manilalli herb"). The town was taken from the Matlatzinca by the Aztecs (Mexica) under Axaycatl in 1476, and the building of the main cult structures probably began 25 years later.

When the Spaniards, led by Andrés de Tapia, captured Malinalco in 1521 the ceremonial centre was not yet complete. Augustinian missionaries established themselves here in 1537.

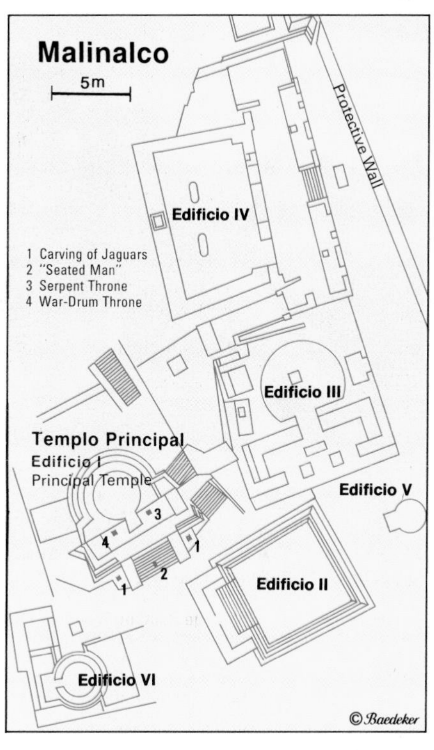

Visit to the ★ Ruins

At the south-west corner of a group of buildings on a narrow platform cut into the hillside lies Building VI (Edificio VI), the construction of which was interrupted by the Spanish conquest.

Immediately north of this will be found Building I (Edificio I), the Templo Principal. Entirely hewn from the rock, this temple was originally faced with a thin coating of coloured stucco. As the House of the Eagle (Cuauhcalli), symbolising the sun, it was used for the initiation of members of the religious military orders, the Eagle Knights and the Jaguar Knights.

The staircase is flanked by the remains of carved jaguars: in the middle can be seen the damaged figure of a standard-bearer. The Temple which stands on the platform is now protected by a palm-leaf roof. The entrance to the circular shrine is carved in low relief to resemble the jaws of a snake, on either side of which stand a serpent-throne and a war-drum throne. The temple-chamber, 6m/20ft in diameter, contains three figures of sacred animals hewn from the native rock; to the left and right are eagles and in the middle, to the rear, a jaguar. In the centre of the semicircle rests the carved representation of an eagle's skin, and behind this is a cavity in which the hearts of sacrificial victims were probably deposited.

Building III

North-east of the House of the Eagle and to the north of Building II lies Building III, consisting of an antechamber and a round chamber containing an altar hollowed out of the rock. This was probably a tzincalli, a temple in which the "messenger of the Sun" – a warrior killed in battle or sacrificed by the enemies of the Aztecs – was cremated and "deified". The Aztecs believed that the souls of warriors killed in this way became stars. In the ante-chamber can be seen the remains of interesting frescos, probably depicting warriors who had already been transformed into stars.

House of the Eagle, cut into the rock

Building IV

The large Building IV, partly hewn from rock and adjoining Building III to the north, is believed to have been a Temple of the Sun. A remarkable wooden drum (tlapanhuéhuetl), with finely carved figures and glyphs of the eagle and jaguar associated with the "messenger of the Sun", was found here; it is now in the museum in Tenango.

Village of Malinalco

The village of Malinalco boasts the interesting church of San Salvador belonging to an Augustinian convent, with a plain 16th c. Renaissance doorway and early frescos on the rear wall on the right through the entrance. Between January 6th and 8th dances are held in the convent's atrium in honour of the Magi.

Surroundings

Chalma

12km/7 miles east lies the village of Chalma, one of Mexico's principal places of pilgrimage. In pre-Columbian times a statue of Otzoctéotl, the god of caves, was worshipped here, and when this was destroyed by Augustinian monks in 1533 and replaced by a large crucifix, popular devotion was transferred to this new object.

The church, built in 1684, in which the Christ of Chalma (El Señor de Chalma) is now worshipped, attracts many thousands of pilgrims on the great feast-days, especially on the first Friday in Lent, at Ascension and on San Augustin's Day (August 28th). On these occasions there is a fascinating mixture of Catholic and ancient Indian rituals, including ceremonies, processions, dances and purifying baths.

Lagunas de Zempoala

40km/25 miles north-east of Chalma lie the seven Lagunas de Zempoala, in a magnificent setting reminiscent of the Alps.

Tenancingo

15km/9½ miles west of Malinalco lies Tenancingo (Náhuatl for "place of little walls"; 2040m/6693ft; population 40,000; fiestas May 15th, Día de

San Isidro Labrador; October 4th, Día de San Francisco; December 8th, Día de la Inmaculada Concepción. The town has an 18th c. Carmelite convent, the Convento del Santo Desierto de Tenancingo, and is noted for its wooden furniture and rebozos (shawls).

Ixtapán de la Sal

33km/21 miles south of Tenancingo on the MEX 55 is the spa town of Ixtapán de la Sal (1900m/6234ft; population 40,000; Sunday market; fiesta on second Friday in Lent, Día del Señor de la Misericordia). This attractively situated resort attracts many visitors with its radioactive mineral springs and the facilities it offers for a variety of sports.

Grutas de la Estrella

14km/9 miles south of Ixtapán lie the Grutas de la Estrella, caves which have been opened up since 1976 and are thought to link up with those at Cacahuamilpa (see Taxco, Surroundings); to date, however, the connecting passage has not been discovered.

Manzanillo — H 8

State: Colima (Col.)
Altitude: sea-level
Population: 145,000
Telephone code: 91 333

Access from Mexico City

By air in about one hour; by rail via Guadalajara (see entry; 12 hours) to Manzanillo (8 hours; however, there is no direct connection in Guadalajara, so there is a waiting time); by bus in about 19 hours; by car about 940km/580 miles via Guadalajara and about 840km/520 miles via Morelia ad Zamora.

Location

Manzanillo lies on a peninsula at the southern end of two curving bays, the Bahía de Santiago and Bahía de Manzanillo, surrounded by luxuriant jungle and by banana and coconut plantations. It is an important Pacific port, but has also developed into a popular holiday resort in recent years, thanks to its extensive beaches and the excellent deep-sea fishing.

History

Near the site of Manzanillo there stood in pre-Columbian times the settlement of Tzaiahua (Náhuatl, "where cloth is laid out to dry"), at one time capital of the Indian state of Coliman. It has been suggested that during this period the port was already engaged in trade with Peru, Ecuador and Colombia. In 1526 Cortés and his Spaniards reached Tzalahua, and soon afterwards founded a settlement here, Santiago de Buena Esperanza. From here they sailed along the coast as far as the Gulf of California. After 1560 the Spanish vessels which sailed to east Asia (e.g. for the conquest of the Philippines) were built and fitted out here. It is only within recent years, however, that the building of roads and railways and the establishment of air services have enabled Manzanillo to develop to its present size.

Tourist Attractions

Fishing

Anglers are superbly catered for (sea-raven, catfish, mojarra, sea bass, snapper, etc.), together with excellent deep-sea fishing (sailfish, fanfish, bonito, etc.).

Beaches

Manzanillo has a whole range of fine beaches on the open sea. To the south lie the Playa de Campos and Playa de Ventanas (waves and currents); in the Bahía de Manzanillo in the north-west the beaches of

Rompeolas, San Pedrito (near the town: popular), Las Brisas, Playa Azul, Salagua and Las Hadas (with a well-designed holiday centre); in the Bahía de Santiago are La Audencia, Santiago Olas Altas, Playa de Miramar and La Boquita; past the Juluapán peninsula lies the Playa de Oro.

Surroundings

Laguna de Cuyutlán

South-east of the town lies the Laguna de Cuyutlán, with interesting animal and plant life.

"Green Waves"

From the lagoon it is 24km/15 miles via Armería to the resort of Cuyutlán. The coastal region between there and Boca de Pascuales 8km/5 miles south-west of Tecomán is known for the "green waves", high waves coming in from the Pacific which sometimes appear green as a result of the presence of fluorescent marine organisms.

Barra de Navidad

The popular seaside resort of Barra de Navidad in Jalisco state (population 30,000) lies 65km/40 miles along the MEX 200 past the airport. It was from this former fishing-port that Captain Miguel López de Legazpi set out in 1564 to cross the Pacific to the Philippines, where he established the first Spanish settlement and thus started the Spanish colonisation of Asia.

As the MEX 200 continues towards Puerto Vallarta (see entry) several beautiful beaches (e.g. Blanca and Chamela) and resorts such as Melaque and San Patricio, adjoin one another. Special mention should be made of Playa Tenacatita (country track after 39km/24 miles) and the Bahía Careyes (turn off after 53km/33 miles).

Matamoros

See Tamaulipas

Matehuala

See San Luis Potosi (State)

Mazatlán F 6

State: Sinaloa (Sin.)
Altitude: sea-level. Population: 410,000
Telephone code: 91 69

Access from Mexico City

By air about 1½ hours (also flights from other Mexican and US airports); by rail in about 23 hours; by bus in about 17 hours.

Location

Mazatlán lies on a natural bay on a projecting tongue of land just to the south of the Tropic of Cancer. It is the major Mexican commercial and fishing port on the Pacific, with the world's largest shrimping fleet, and in recent years has become a very popular beach resort.

History

Mazatlán (Náhuatl: "Place of the Deer") was an area of Indian settlement long before the Conquest. The Spaniards, led by Hernando de

Bazán, arrived here in 1576, but it was 1806 before the town was founded. Mazatlán and the surrounding area had previously been exposed to frequent pirate raids, and at times served as a buccaneers' lair. The foundations of the town's subsequent development were laid in the mid 19th c. by German settlers, who improved the harbour in order to facilitate the export of their agricultural produce and the import of farming equipment.

Tourist Attractions

There are few buildings in Mazatlán which can be described as outstanding. Features of interest, however, include the lighthouse (El Faro), towering 154m/505ft, and the historic Teatro Angela Peralta, a pretty building named after a famous diva, victim of a cholera epidemic in 1863. Other attractions include the "Death Divers" who launch themselves into the sea from the Mirador, the Cerro del Vigia with its observatory, from where pirates once kept watch, and the Cerro del Neveria, also a look-out point, which gets its name from the tunnels in the mountain used for storage of ice for refrigerating fish.

★ Aquarium

The well-equipped Aquarium, together with the zoo and small botanical gardens, is the largest of its kind in Mexico. Shells from seas all over the world are displayed in the "Seashell City" Museum. The massive Monumento al Pescador reminds the visitor of Mazatlán's fishing tradition.

Water sports

The main attractions for visitors are the excellent facilities for all kinds of water sports, chief among them being deep-sea fishing (sailfish, fanfish, shark, swordfish, tarpon, etc.). Among the most popular beaches, to the north of the town, are Olas Noltas, Norte Camarón, Las Gaviotas, Sábalo, Los Cerritos and El Delfín.

Excursions

Also very popular are trips to the offshore islands, some of them used as nesting places by large numbers of birds. Boats ply from the hotels on the "Zona Dorada" to Isla Pájaros and Isla Venados, and from the ferry terminal to Isla de la Piedra.

View over Mazatlán

Copala

From Mazatlán the MEX 15 heads south to Villa Unión. Here the Durango road branches off, first passing through Concordia with its charming 18th c. parish church, then continuing to the picturesque old mining town of Copala where narrow alleyways, colourful house façades and wrought-iron balconies evoke a Mexico of times past.

Ferry link to Baja California

There is a daily ferry service between Mazatlán and La Paz (see entry), capital of Baja California Sur (see Practical Information, Ferries).

Mérida P 7

State: Yucatán (Yuc.)
Altitude: 8m/26ft
Population: 610,000
Telephone code: 91 99

Access from Mexico City

By air in about 1½ hours (also flights from other Mexican and US airports); by rail in about 37 hours (often considerably longer); by bus in 24–28 hours.

Location

Mérida, capital of the state of Yucatán, lies at the north end of a plateau of porous limestone which is well suited to the cultivation of a type of agave-yielding henequen (sisal) fibre. Before the development of man-made fibres the henequen industry brought prosperity to the town, whose trade connections linked it with Europe and particularly with France.

★Ciudad blanca

During this period it became known as the "ciudad blanca", the "white city", since the people of Mérida liked to dress in white and took pride in keeping their town trim and clean. Thanks to its warm and humid climate this attractive town is gay with flowers, and life goes at a leisurely pace.

History

The town was founded on January 6th 1542 by the conquistador Francisco Montejo, known as "El Mozo" (the "Boy") to distinguish him from his father, "El Adelantado" (the "Governor"). After bitter fighting with the Maya tribes the younger Montejo succeeded in conquering most of Yucatán within the following four years. Mérida was built on the site of the Maya town of Tihó, using material from the demolished temples. In the year in which it was founded the last Maya ruler of the area, Titul-Xiú, cacique or chief of Maní, surrendered to the Spaniards. A prominent role in the history of Mexico was played by the second bishop of Mérida, Diego de Landa, who tried with all the means at his disposal to eradicate the old Indian culture – burning, for example, a great number of irreplaceable Maya manuscripts written in hieroglyphics. He did, however, write a valuable "Relación de las Cosas de Yucatán", an account of the conquest of Yucatán and the civilisation of the Mayas as seen through Spanish eyes. He died in Mérida in 1579. In 1648 Mérida and Yucatán were ravaged by an epidemic of yellow fever brought by negro slaves from Africa.

During the struggle for independence from Spain Mérida and Yucatán, owing to their remoteness, played little part. There were, however, movements aimed at securing the independence of Yucatán from Mexico. In the second half of the 19th c. Yucatán was the scene of a ruthless civil war (Caste War) when the Maya tribes rebelled against Mexican rule. The peninsula was not finally pacified until the early years of the 20th c.

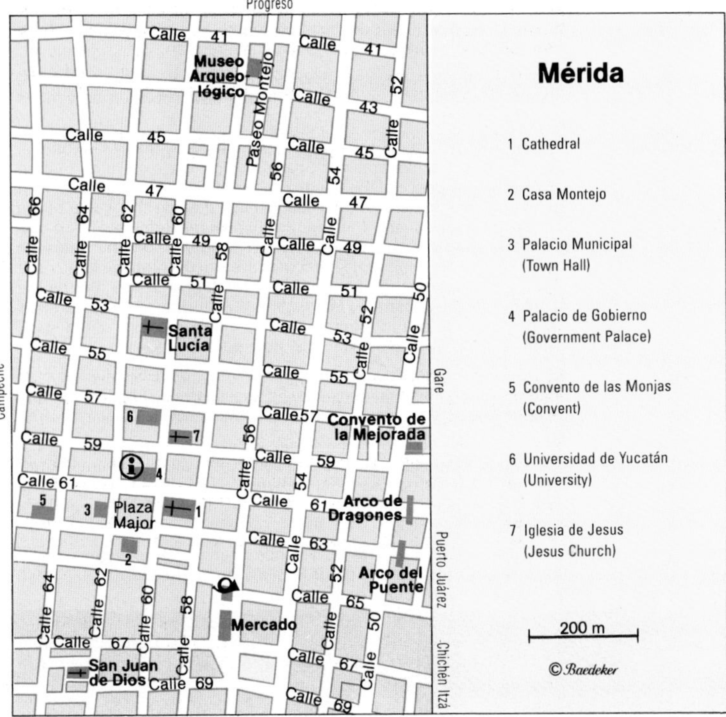

Sights

Finding your way

Unlike most other Mexican towns, Mérida has a regular layout with the streets running at right angles to one another. The streets have numbers instead of names, those running from north to south having even numbers and those going from east to west odd numbers.

Plaza Mayor

The Plaza Mayor (Plaza de la Independencia) is the commercial and cultural hub of Mérida. It is surrounded by some of the town's most important buildings.

Cathedral

On the east side of the square, occupying the site of an earlier Maya temple, stands the Cathedral, built by Pedro de Aulestia and Miguel de Auguero between 1561 and 1598. The largest church in the Yucatán peninsula, its façade shows few architectural features of particular merit.

Above a doorway in the interior hangs a picture of the Maya ruler of Maní, Titul-Kiú, visiting the conquistador Francisco Montejo in Tihó. To the left of the high altar is the Chapel of the Christ of the Blisters (Capilla del Cristo de las Ampollas), with a 16th c. Indian woodcarving. According to legend this was made from the wood of a tree which the Indians once saw burning all night long without leaving any traces of the fire. The statue originally stood in a church at Ichmul which was burned down, and after the fire it was found black and covered with blisters. It has been in the Cathedral since 1645, and is the subject of special veneration at the beginning of October every year.

Archbishop's Palace

Near the Cathedral, but now separated from it by an intervening street, stands the Archbishop's Palace, which is now occupied by various government offices.

★Casa Montejo

The south side of the Plaza Mayor is dominated by the Casa Montejo, one of the finest examples of Spanish colonial architecture, built in 1549 as the residence of the Montejo family. Originally this palace, with its magnificent Plateresque façade, extended along the whole of the south side of the square. The large and handsome rooms are laid out as a museum around two patios and furnished with antique furniture imported from Europe. Note the coat of arms of the Montejo family and the stone sculptures of conquistadors standing with one foot on the bowed head of a conquered Maya. Until 1978 the house was still owned by descendants of the Montejo family; it now belongs to the state. There is a branch of a bank on the ground floor.

Town Hall

Opposite the Cathedral stands the Town Hall (Palacio Municipal), a 16th c. building with colonnades and a clock-tower. It was from here that the town-crier gave news of the independence of Yucatán in 1821.

Government Palace

At the north-east corner of the square is the Government Palace (Palacio de Gobierno), built in 1892 and decorated with interesting murals painted by the Campeche artist Fernando Castro Pacheco in 1971–74. From the balcony there is a fine view of the Plaza Mayor and the Cathedral.

Convento de las Monjas

One block west of the Town Hall stands a handsome conventual building, a relic of the Convento de las Monjas, founded at the end of the 16th c. The viewing tower dates from 1633.

Government Palace in Mérida

Church of Jesus

In the Parque Cepeda Peraza (or Parque Hidalgo), one block north of the Plaza Mayor on Calle 80, stands the Church of Jesus or Church of the Third Order (Iglesia de la Tercera Orden), a favourite church for weddings. On the left of the high altar will be seen an altarpiece of carved and gilded wood in the Plateresque style. The park also serves as a "taxi-rank" for Mérida's calesas (horse-drawn coaches).

Pinacoteca Gamboa Guzmán

Near the church, with its entrance on Calle 59, the Pinacoteca Gamboa Guzmán displays 19th and 20th c. paintings, mainly portraits and religious subjects, as well as pictures by the artist Gamboa Guzmán.

Churches

The Emita de Santa Isabel church, at the corner of Calles 66 and 77, is notable mainly for the surrounding gardens with their Maya statues. The hermitage was once much frequented by travellers to and from Campeche, who prayed here for a safe journey or gave thanks on their return. Another church of historical interest is that of Santa Lucía, at the corner of Calles 60 and 55; it was originally built by the Spaniards for the exclusive use of their negro and mulatto slaves. Concerts are held in the evenings every week (usually on Thursdays) in the Parque Santa Lucia.

Paseo Montejo

During Mérida's heyday at the beginning of the 20th c. the Paseo Montejo was laid out on the model of the Paris boulevards. It passes through a select residential district and is flanked by a large number of monuments, the most striking of which is the Monumento a la Patria (Monument to the Fatherland), constructed between 1946 and 1957 by the Columbian sculptor Rómulo Rozo. The principal sections portray Mexico's history and important personalities in the Maya style.

★ Museum of Archaeology and History

At the corner of Paseo Montejo and Calle 43 the former government building known as the Palacio del General Cantón now houses the Museum of Anthropology and History (Museo de Arqueología e Historía). This imposing 19th c. building contains a fine collection of material mostly from the halcyon days of the Maya civilisation, although the other advanced cultures of pre-Columbian Mexico are also well represented. The highlights of the collections are the sacrificial gifts retrieved from the cenotes at Chichén Itzá (see entry). There are also reproductions of the sketches of the Maya sites drawn by Frederick Catherwood and the photographs taken by Teobert Maler at the turn of the century. There is another archaeological museum on the corner of Av. Iztáes and Calle 59.

University

The University of Yucatàn, originally a Jesuit boys' school dating from 1618, stands on the corner of Calles 57 and 60. It offers summer courses for visitors in a number of subjects, including Spanish and archaeology.

Museo Regional de Arte Popular

Textiles and costumes, pottery, jewellery, toys and musical instruments are exhibited in the Museo Regional de Arte Popular ("La Mejorada") at No. 441 Calle 59. Regional folk art of good quality is offered for sale near by (No. 513 Calle 63, a restored monastery building).

★ Mercado Municipal

This Municipal Market, south of the Plaza Mayor, is well worth a visit. The main products on sale here include articles made from sisal (hammocks, panama hats, bags, carpets, sandals) together with huipiles (Maya-style dresses with brightly coloured embroidery around the neck) for women, and guayabera (shirts) for men.

Surroundings

Mérida is a good base for excursions to most of the archaeological sites in Yucatán, such as Chichén Itzá, Uxmal, Dzibilchaltún, Kabah, Izamal (see entries) and others.

Hacienda Yaxcopoli

Situated 35km/22 miles south of Mérida on the Uxmal road, and now a museum, the vast and reasonably well-preserved Hacienda Yaxcopoli offers an insight into life on a sisal (henequén) farm in the 19th c.

Progreso

It is 35km/22 miles from Mérida to Progreso, Yucatán's principal port, with a pier 2km/1¼ miles long.

Arrecifes Alacranes

130km/80 miles north of Progreso in the Gulf of Mexico lie the Arrecifes Alacranes ("Scorpion Reef"), a semi-circular collection of islands, sand-banks and reefs around a lagoon. Rich in submarine life and with a number of sunken wrecks, these are popular with experienced skin-divers. Access to the reef is by charter boat from Progreso.

Beach resorts

To the east of Progreso, near Chicxulub, are the summer resorts traditionally favoured by the people of Mérida. Also very popular are the beaches west of Progreso, with the little ports of Yucalpetén and Chelem. In addition to bungalow hotels there are also furnished houses available at very reasonable rents between September and June. It must be admitted, however, that this coast does not compare with those on the Caribbean side of Yucatán.

Sisal

52km/32 miles west of Mérida on a good road passing through Huncumá, lies Sisal, the major port in Yucatán when sisal production was at its peak. Visitors can see the house where the Mexican Empress Charlotte Amalie ("Carlota") spent the night in 1865 before embarking for Europe in an attempt to obtain support for her husband.

Celestún

This pretty fishing port lies 92km/57 miles west of Mérida by a large, green lagoon. The inhabitants obtain their living from fishing, growing coconuts and salt extraction. The lagoon itself is a national park area, where numerous water-birds such as pelicans, flamingos, herons, cormorants and ducks can be observed. There are, however, plans afoot to build a large port here which will be accessible to international shipping.

South-east of Mérida lie a number of small places, some with interesting churches and convents of the colonial period (see Yucatán). This excursion should be combined with a visit to the once important city of Mayapán, 48km/30 miles south of Mérida.

Mayapán

The Maya chronicles tell contradictory stories about the origin and development of Mayapán. It seems probable that the Itzá (who are now believed to have been a "Toltecised" Chontal-Maya people from Tabasco) came to Yucatán about 1200, resettled the abandoned site of Chichén Itzá and finally founded Mayapán ("Banner of the Maya"). Thereafter for almost 200 years Mayapán, under the Cocom dynasty, was the predominant power in Yucatán. Its end came around 1450 when the town was destroyed during a rising by the Xiú tribe, who had previously been settled at Uxmal. This led to the final collapse of the Maya civilisation, when the empire broke up into some 20 unimportant petty states.

In its heyday the town covered an area of about 6·5sq.km/2½sq. miles, with some 3500 buildings, and was surrounded by a strong town wall. Its architecture was never on a par with that of Chichen Itzá and has only partially been excavated and restored.

On the right side lies first the "House of the Elders", followed by the Tzompantli (Maya for "Wall of Skulls"). The columned palace somewhat to the left still possesses a large stone-mask and two figures. The dominant building, however, is the Castillo (Pyramid of Kukulkán), with a fine view over the beech forest which surrounds the site. To the east of the Castillo a path leads left to a low structure, impressively decorated with masks of the rain-god Chac in the purest Puuc style, a style which flourished at least 300 years earlier.

Mexicali

See Tijuana

México (State)

Abbreviation: Mex.
Capital: Toluca
Area: 21,414sq.km/8268sq. miles
Official population 1990: 9,185,800 (1994 estimate: 11,600,000)

Location and Topography

The state of México (Estado de México) – not to be confused with the name of the country or with the Federal District which contains Mexico City – is bounded on the north by the states of Hidalgo and Querétaro, on the west by Michoacán, on the south by Guerrero and Morelos and on the east by Puebla and Tlaxcala, and encloses the Federal District on three sides. The eastern half of the state is hilly, the western part flat. Although in process of marked industrial development, México has much beautiful scenery – snow-capped mountains, lakes and forests – and there are a number of national parks within its boundaries. It also boasts many works of colonial art and architecture and many

México

archaeological sites. In addition to whites and mestizos its population includes several Indian tribes, including the Otomí, Matlatzinca, Ocuilteca and Nahua.

Archaeological Sites

The state is unusually rich in pre-Columbian sites, the most important of which are individually entered in this guide and include Teotihuacán, Tepexpan (see Acolman, Surroundings), Texcotzingo, Huexotla, San Miguel Coatlinchán (all under Texcoco, Surroundings), Tlapacoya (see Amecameca, Surroundings), Tenayuca, Santa Cecilia Acatitlán (see Tenayuca, Surroundings), Calixtlahuaca, Teotenango (for both see Toluca, Surroundings), Tepozteco (see Morelos) and Malinalco.

Places of interest

In addition to these major archaeological sites – at some of which examples of colonial art and architecture can also be seen – the main places of interest in México state are Toluca (the capital), Tepotzotlán, Acolman, Texcoco and Amecameca (see entries).

History

The history of human settlement and culture in the state of México goes back a long way, as the finds at Tepexpan and Tlapacoya have shown. On the whole its historical development has been the same as that of Mexico City and the principal towns within the state. As part of the Viceroyalty of New Spain and later as the Intendencia de México, with Mexico City as its capital, that state had a considerably larger area than it has now. It was given its present boundaries only after Mexico became independent.

Economy

The state's chief forms of industry are cement manufacture, metal processing and vehicle assembly. The principal agricultural crops include wheat, maize, agaves, sugar-cane, coffee, fruit and vegetables; dairy farming also flourishes. Substantial contributions are made to the economy by forestry and tourism.

Mexico City/Ciudad de México K 8

Distrito Federal (D.F.)
Altitude: 2240m/7349ft
Population (with suburbs): 20 million (1994 estimate)
Telephone code: 91 5

Access

There are flights to "Benito Juárez" International Airport from all the major European and many United States airports.

★★Capital of Mexico

Mexico City (Ciudad de México), capital of the country and seat of the central government, lies at an altitude of over 2200m/7300ft in the Valley of Mexico or Valley of Anáhuac, a high valley surrounded by mighty mountain ranges. Owing to the city's high altitude it has an equable climate which suits visitors from more northerly regions, and its situation is breathtaking, seeming to lie at the foot of two magnificent snow-covered volcanoes rising to over 5000m/16,000ft, Popocatépetl and Iztaccíhuatl. The city preserves countless reminders of its past of more than 650 years, though pre-Columbian art and architecture exist almost solely in isolated fragments and museum reproductions, since the conquistadors built the nucleus of their new town on the ruins of the old Aztec metropolis of Tenochtitlán which they had destroyed. Against this, however, there are many churches and palaces of the colonial period, mainly in the Baroque style; and modern Mexican architecture is represented by numbers of fine buildings, particularly those of the 1950s and 1960s.

The city area extends for more than 40km/25 miles from north to south and for an average of 25km/15 miles from east to west. The Federal District (Distrito Federal; see entry), which is headed by a Regente directly responsible to the President, was created to establish the capital as a separate administrative unit but is no longer adequate to contain the city's northward growth, so that its new industrial suburbs extend into the neighbouring state of México.

Population growth

The city's rate of growth, primarily due to the influx of population from the agricultural regions to the north with their harsh climate, is enormous. The present population of Mexico City is estimated at almost 20 million (some estimates are as high as 26 million), making it the most populous city in the world. This over-population, combined with the increasing growth of industry – which, however, fails to produce enough jobs for those who need them – creates serious economic and social difficulties. The number of those seeking their fortune in the capital and being forced to live as "paracaidistas" (parachute-jumpers) and spend the nights huddled-up in the streets of the "cardboard city" district in the east of the capital, is estimated at about 2000 per day.

Environmental problems

IMECA (Mexico City air quality)

1–100: satisfactory

100–200: mostly tolerable

200–300: barely tolerable

over 500: dangerous

Traffic problems have been eased somewhat by the construction of the Metro and intersection-free roads such as the Anillo Periférico, a highway round the city, but conditions are still chaotic at peak periods. The number of vehicles on the city's roads is estimated at about 3.5 million. In addition to the motor car, environmentalists place much of the blame for the 11,000 tons of particles to which the inhabitants of Mexico City are exposed every day, on the 35,000 industrial concerns operating in Mexico's high-altitude valley. Many of these are located in the one and only outlet from the Anáhuac Valley, which might otherwise provide a source of much-needed fresh air. Instead, vast quantities of only partly filtered factory emissions blow across the city, contributing to a truly appalling state of affairs. The valley's once crystal-clear mountain air has been replaced by a bell-shaped cloud of pollutants, usually blotting out the view of the city's magnificent mountain backdrop while at the same time giving rise to streaming eyes and respiratory problems. Newspapers publish reports on air quality using the so-called IMECA index (on a scale from 1 to 500).

The federal government is now attempting to address the problem. Mexico spends 1% of GDP on environmental protection, and the NAFTA Agreement incorporates measures against air and water pollution. Since the late 1980s a programme called "Un Dia sin Auto" – "A

Population Growth
of Mexico City including suburbs

Year	Population
1910	0.8 million
1930	1 million
1950	3 million
1960	5 million
1970	7.5 million
1980	12 million
1994	20 million
2000	25 million[1]

[1] Projection, based on 2.4% official growth rate, plus 350,000 new immigrants per annum

Panorama of Mexico City with the snow-covered Iztaccihuatl . . .

day without the car" – has been in operation (applying to tourists and hire cars as well). PEMEX is making lead-free petrol more widely available, and catalytic converters are compulsory on new cars. Environmentally damaging industries are being forced to shut down temporarily (and in some cases even permanently), while others have agreed to relocate. Mexico City is built on unstable ground. The marshy subsoil means that the city sinks about 20cm/8in. every year. Many buildings, such as the Palacio de Bellas Artes, lean at an angle. It was the Spaniards who first made a start on draining the ancient city of Tenochtitlán, surrounded as it was by lakes and pierced by canals. Today only the dried-up beds of these lakes remain. As the springs no longer meet demands for drinking-water a third of the water supply has to be pumped into the high-lying city at considerable cost in terms of energy. At the same time many parts of the city are considerably lower than the level of the drains and sewer systems, so that their waste has to be pumped away. If the pumps were to fail large areas of the city would be flooded with sewage.

Despite conditions which leave much to be desired, and notwithstanding the areas of nondescript, uniform new housing (which promptly collapsed during the earthquake) and wretched slum districts on the outskirts, Mexico City nevertheless holds an abundance of fascination for the visitor – the style and dignity of the Paseo de la Reforma, the art treasures in its many museums, the numerous parks with their magnificent old trees, the secluded little nooks and corners with their old Spanish atmosphere which can be found only a few hundred yards from the noisy swirl of the city traffic. As a major traffic

. . . and Popocatépetl

centre it is also an ideal setting-out point for excursions elsewhere in the country.

History

Tenochtitlán

The pre-Columbian history of the area around Mexico City centres mainly on the Náhuatl-speaking Aztecs or Mexica, who in 1345 founded their capital of Tenochtitlán (Náhuatl: "place of the cactus fruit") on a swampy island in Lake Texcoco, which until the Spanish conquest covered the eastern part of the present city area. Clustered around the capital were a number of other, originally independent, towns occupied by other Chichimec peoples including the Tenayuca, Texcoco (Alcolhua tribe), Chalco (Chalca tribe), Tlatelolco, Coyoacán, Tlacopán (now Tacuba, a Tepaneca tribe), Atzcapotzalco (Tepaneca tribe), Xochimilco (Xochimilca tribe, one of the Toltec Chichimecs) and Culhaucán (Colhua-Toltec tribe). Three great causeways and an aquaduct linked the island city, which was criss-crossed by numerous canals, with the mainland. In the centre of the city stood the massive principal pyramid, with two temples dedicated to the war and sun-god Huitzilopochtli and the rain-god Tláloc. The ceremonial precinct (Teocalli), surrounded by the "Serpent Wall" (Coatepantli), also contained the temples of other important gods (Tezcatlipoca, Xochiquetzal, Quetzalcóatl, Cihuacóatl). The remains of all these magnificent buildings lie under the present Zócalo (Plaza de la Constitución) and the immediately surrounding area, and parts of these have been brought to light over the years.

Smog over Mexico City

Outside the cult centre lay the royal palaces, the residential areas with their market squares and smaller groups of temples.

Tlatelolco

The older town of Tlatelolco, the rival and later the ally of Tenochtitlán, also boasted a pyramid similar to that of Tenayuca on which the remains of temples dedicated to the gods Tláloc and Quetzalcóatl were found. Tlatelolco's importance, however, was chiefly as the principal trading centre of the Aztec empire. The site of pre-Cortesian Tlatelolco is now covered by the La Languilla market, the church of Santiago, the Foreign Ministry and modern apartment buildings; some remains have been unearthed in the Square of the Three Cultures. On the lake around the two towns were the artificial islands (chinampas) which provided areas of cultivable land. Relics of this method of cultivation can still be seen in the "floating gardens" of Xochimilco. No doubt similar methods were employed on the lakes of Chalco to the south and Xaltocán and Tzompanco (now Zumpango) to the north.

Spanish conquest

On November 8th 1519 Hernán Cortés with his small force of Spaniards and more numerous Tlaxcalan allies set foot for the first time in the Aztec capital, which at that time must have covered an area of 12 to 15sq.km/4½ to 6sq. miles with a population of 200,000 to 300,000, making it the world's third largest city after London and Peking. After the imprisonment of the Aztec ruler, Moctezuma II Xocoyotzín, in his own palace and his violent death, Cortés was driven out of Tenochtitlán by the Mexica under their new ruler Cuitláhuac (Náhuatl, "guardian of the kingdom"); during their flight on what came to be known as the "Noche Triste" ("Sad Night", June 30th 1520), the Spaniards lost more than half their strength as well as their booty. After reorganising their forces, securing reinforcements in the form of native auxiliaries and building thirteen brigantines to control the shores of the lake, the

Mexico City: Model of the temple quarter of Tenochtitlán

Spaniards laid siege to Tenochtitlán in May 1521; and on August 13th, after the capture of the last Aztec ruler Cuauhtémoc, the city was compelled to surrender. Thereafter its buildings were razed to the ground and its canals filled in with rubble.

Capital city of the province of New Spain

In 1522 the Spaniards began to build a new town, to which they gave the name of Méjico, on the ruins of the Aztec temples, using material from the demolished buildings, including the detested "idolatrous temples". In 1523 the town was granted its municipal coat-of-arms. In 1535 Franciscan friars established in Santiago Tlatelolco the Colegio de Santa Cruz, later to achieve wide reputation, in which the children of the Aztec nobility were educated. In the same year the Viceroyalty of New Spain, in which Mexico played a leading part, was created. By 1537 the population of the town had risen again to some 100,000 Indians and 2000 Spaniards. Now capital of New Spain, it became in 1546 the see of an archbishop, with Juan de Zumárraga as the first incumbent. In 1551 the first university on the American continent was founded here. During the Indian uprisings of 1692 several public buildings were devastated by fire, including the viceregal palace, which had originally been Cortés' residence. During the war of independence (1810–21) the supporters of independence were unable to dislodge the royal forces who held the capital, and it was only when Agustin de Iturbide joined the movement that the garrison was finally obliged to surrender in 1821.

Imperial residence and capital of the Republic

After Iturbide's episodic "empire" there was a long struggle for power between Liberals and Conservatives and between supporters of the "centralist" and federal systems. During the war between Mexico and the United States (1846–48) the town was occupied for a time by US troops. In 1863 French troops captured the capital, and from 1864 to 1867 the Archduke Maximilian reigned as emperor from Chapultepec

Castle. During this period the city's finest boulevard, the Paseo de la Reforma, was laid out. After the defeat of the French invaders and the shooting of Maximilian at Querétaro, the dispossessed President Benito Juárez returned to the city.

During the dictatorship of Porfirio Díaz (1876–1911) Mexico City was modernised in a style which owed much to foreign and particularly to French influence, and there was a period of intense building activity. During the following decade Mexico was racked by bloody conflicts between the various revolutionary leaders – Francisco Madero, Victoriano Huerta, Alvaro Obregón, Francisco "Pancho" Villa, Emiliano Zapata – and it was only in the post-revolutionary years that the city could again begin to forge ahead. In 1930 the population reached the one million mark.

Latest developments

During and after the Second World War the modernisation and industrialisation of Mexico City made great strides, and there still seems no end to the influx of people from the poorer rural areas and a resultant "population explosion". Today some 50% of the country's industry is concentrated in the capital, together with 70% of banking and 50% of all other commercial firms. In 1968 the Summer Olympics were held in the city, only to be preceded by a demonstration on the Square of the Three Cultures in which 250 people died.

Official figures indicate that almost 10,000 people died in the earthquake of September 19th 1985; in addition, 100,000 were rendered homeless and enormous damage was done which changed the face of the city completely. New concrete buildings in particular failed to withstand the shocks.

Sightseeing in Mexico City

Getting your bearings

Mexico City is divided into sixteen main administrative units called Delegaciones or wards, with names such as Alvaro Obregón, Benito Juárez, Cuauhtémoc, Coyoacán, Atzcapotzalco, Xochimilco, etc. The wards are in turn subdivided into 240 Colonias or neighbourhoods, often with street names of a particular type. e.g., named after well-known rivers, philosophers, European cities, etc. Many streets in different neighbourhoods have the same names; for example, there are more than 100 named after Emiliano Zapata. It is therefore important to know the name of the district or neighbourhood as well as just the name of the street when quoting addresses or seeking directions.

Although Mexico City, like all Spanish colonial towns, was originally laid out on a regular "grid" plan, the city's frenetic pace of development has wrought such havoc with the system that visitors may sometimes have difficulty in getting their bearings. In general the avenidas (avenues) run from east to west and the calles (streets) from north to south, but there are a number of other designations such as bulevar (boulevard), calzada (originally a causeway), callejón (lane), prolongacíon (extension), eje vial (expressway) and urban motorway. Only the largest and most important thoroughfares retain the same name throughout their length; these include the great north–south axis, the Avenida de los Insurgentes, and the Paseo de la Reforma stretching from north-east to west. Another important north–south connection is formed by Calzada Vallejo, Avenida Lázaro Cárdenas (formerly San Juan de Letrán), Calzada Niño Perdido and Avenida Universidad, and a second east–west axis is provided by the Avenidas Chapultepec, Dr Río de la Loza and Fray Servando Teresa de Mier. There is also a ring road (circuito interior, partly of motorway standard) formed by the Calzada Melchor Ocampo, Avenida Río Consulado, Bulevar Puerto Aéreo and Viaducto Miguel Alemán. On the south side this ring is supplemented by Avenida Río Churubusco which, like the Viaducto, joins the outer ring road, the Anillo Periférico, the south-eastern section of which is not yet complete.

Centro Histórico

In 1980 the government declared an area of 15sq.km/6sq. miles, containing 1436 buildings typifying the architecture of the 16th to 19th c., as the Centro Histórico de la Ciudad (Historic City Centre), and classified it as an historical monument. The area is bounded by the streets of Abraham González and Paseo de la Reforma in the west, by Calle Anfora in the east, by Bartolomé de las Casas in the north and by José María Izazaga in the south. A number of important buildings have been restored in recent years. In September 1987, as a further measure, a part of this zone was made traffic-free.

Sightseeing programme

Those spending several days in Mexico City are advised to start by visiting the sights around the Zócalo (main square), taking in mainly the Cathedral and the adjoining Sagrario, the National Palace and the new Museo del Templo Mayor in the archaeological zone; this will easily fill the first day. The second day could be employed seeing the sights around Alameda Park and the adjoining Avenida Juárez, with the Palacio de Bellas Artes, Torre Latinoamericana, Casa de los Azulejos, Iglesia de San Francisco and much more. Peace and quiet away from the noise of the city can be found in the Bosque de Chapultepec with its botanical gardens, zoo and the Castillo de Chapultepec. The highlight must surely be a visit to the National Museum of Anthropology, and a whole day should be set aside for this if possible; nor should the Museo de Arte Moderno (Museum of Modern Art) be overlooked. Lively night-life can be enjoyed in the Plaza de Garibaldi, where mariachi bands play. Those able to stay longer in the capital are recommended to visit the more outlying districts, with perhaps a stroll through Coyoacán with its Frida Kahlo Museum and Museo León Trotsky, a visit to the Ciudad Universitaria, a boat trip in the "floating gardens" of Xoccimilco and a visit to the Basilica of Guadalupe. Mexico City also has many other places of interest to suit all tastes.

Transport

Because of the chaotic traffic conditions and heavy smog visitors are strongly advised against renting a car for their own use.

Metro
(Map see page 593)

The main and cheapest form of transport is the eight-line Metro by which most of the major sights can be easily reached. The underground network covers a total of 170km/106 miles of track and is used by 4,500,000 people every day. Directions are easily followed with the help of signs using both words and symbols, and most stations also have an information desk. Hand luggage may be taken on the Metro, and it is best to avoid using it during the rush hours (prior to 10am and after 4pm), when the crush is unbelievable. At those times parts of the platforms are reserved for women and children and the trains have "ladies only" compartments. Ladies are strongly advised against travelling on the Metro alone at night, for obvious reasons.

City buses

There are over 60 bus routes, but their use is recommended only for those who speak Spanish well and have a good sense of direction. Route 76 from the Zócalo via the Paseo de la Reforma to the Bosque de Chapultepec is quite popular with tourists, however, and in consequence with pickpockets too, so anyone using it should carry as little of value as possible and keep a sharp look-out.

Peseros

There are several kinds of taxis in Mexico City.

The old peseros have been replaced by 22-seater VW mini-buses. Known as "colectivos" or "peseros" still they ply on fixed routes, with

Métro
(Plan of Metro: see Practical Information, Railways)

1 Sagrario Metropolitano
2 Museo de Arte Religioso
3 Monte de Piedad
4 Templo Mayor
5 Primer Edificio de la Universidad
6 Casa del Arzobispado
7 Santa Teresa la Antigua
8 Primera Imprenta de América
9 Mayorzago de Guerrero
10 Mayorzago de Guerrero
11 Santa Inés
12 Casa del Siglo XVII
13 Casa de los Marqueses del Apartado
14 La Enseñanza Antigua
15 Colegio Nacional
16 Antigua Aduana
17 Biblioteca Iberoamericana
18 Secretaría de Educacion Pública
19 Santo Domingo
20 Escuela Nacional Preparatoria
21 Anfiteatro Bolivar
22 Hemeroteca Nacional
23 Colegio de San Pedro y San Pablo
24 Iglesia de Loreto
25 Santa Teresa la Nueva
26 Museo Juárez
27 Antigua Casa de Moneda
28 Academia de San Carlos
29 La Santísima
30 Departamento del Distrito Federal
31 Suprema Corte de Justicia
32 San Bernardo
33 Casa de Don Juan Manuel
34 Casa de los Condes de la Cortina
35 Museo de la Ciudad de México
36 Iglesia de Valvanera
37 Convento de la Merced
38 Hospital de Jesús Nazareno
39 San Pablo el Viejo
40 San Pablo el Nuevo
41 Mercado de la Merced
42 Concepción Tlaxcoaque
43 Santa Cruz Acatlán
44 La Profesa
45 Casa de los Azulejos
46 Palacio de Minería
47 Museo Nacional del Arte und 'El Caballito' (Monumento a Carlos IV)
48 Cámara de Senadores
49 Cámara de Deputados

Mexico City/Ciudad de México

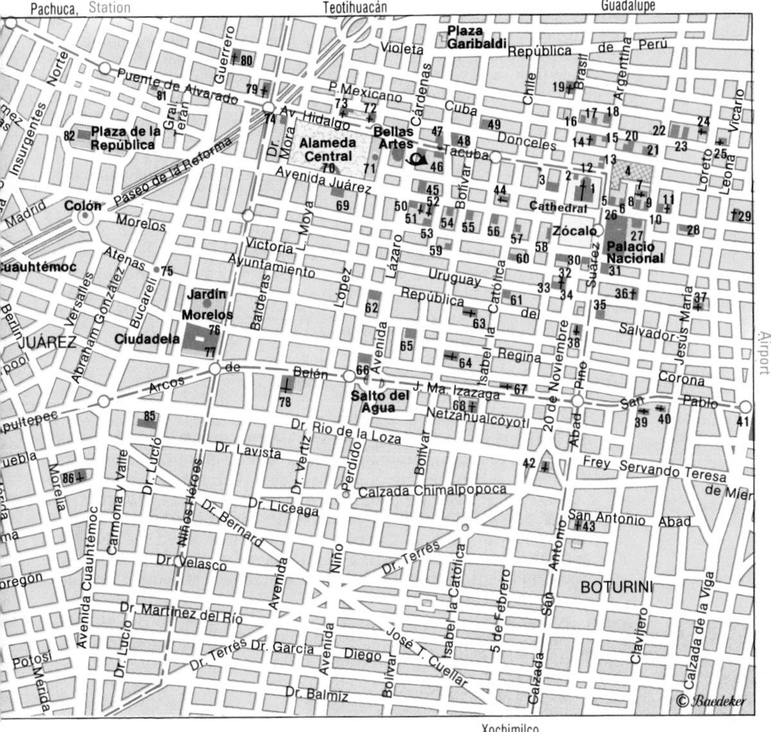

50 Torre Latinoamericana
51 San Francisco
52 San Felipe de Jesús
53 Claustro de San Francisco el Grande
54 Palacio de Iturbide
55 Casa de Don José de la Borda
56 Casa del Marques de Prado Alegre
57 Casa de los Condes de Miravalle
58 Portales de Mercaderes
59 Colegio de Niñas
60 Casa de los Condes de San Mateo de Valparaíso
61 Biblioteca Nacional
62 Mercado de Curiosidades
63 San Felipe Neri
64 Iglesia de Regina
65 Colegio de las Vizcaínas
66 Mercado San Juan
67 San Jerónimo (Claustro de Sor Juana)
68 Capilla de Monserrat
69 Museo de Artes e Industrias Pouplares
70 Hemiciclo Juárez
71 Monumento a Beethoven
72 Santa Veracruz
73 San Juan de Dios
74 Museo Pinacoteca Virreinal
75 Reloj Chino
76 Exposicíon de Artesanías
77 Escuela de Artesanías
78 Templo de Belén
79 San Hipólito
80 San Fernando
81 Palacio de Buenavista (Museo de San Carlos)
82 Monumento a la Revolucíon
83 Monumento a la Madre
84 Librería Benjamin Franklin
85 Arena México
86 Iglesia de Romita
87 Sagrada Familia
88 Restos del Acueducto Azteca
89 Monumento a Venustiano Carranza
90 Diana Cazadora
91 Monumento a Simón Bolivar
92 Deportivo Chapultepec
93 Monolito Chalchiuhtlícue
94 Casa del Lago
95 Monumento a los Niños Heroes
96 Baño de Moctezuma
97 Galería de Hostoria
98 Fuente de Netzahualcóyotl
99 Monumento a Madero

fares according to zone (from 1 peso at the time of going to press). Tourists are advised to take only those operating in central areas.

Taxis

The yellow and white or green "taxis libres", often Volkswagen "Beetles", ply freely and pick up passengers on request. Insist on the meter being set and describe your destination exactly, as otherwise the driver cannot be expected to know where you mean in a city which has so many streets with the same name in different districts.

Red "taxis de sitio", or radio taxis, have fixed ranks from where they can be hailed.

"Turismos" wait in front of the major hotels; these are mainly large limousines with no meters and are correspondingly expensive. Visitors should be sure to agree the fare in advance.

A sort of bicycle taxi, known as "bici-taxis", can take you from one point to another, or on a short tour, within the old historic centre, for a flat rate.

Transport to and from the airport by taxi is at a fixed fare.

★National Palace

Metro Station
Zócalo (Line 2)

Opening Times
Tues.–Sun.
9am–6pm

The whole of the east side of the main square (Zócalo) is occupied by the National Palace (Palacio Nacional), with a façade over 200m/650ft long. Built of reddish tezontle stone, it is the official residence of the President and houses various government offices. Originally built by Cortés on the razed site of Moctezuma II's "New Palace", it was the seat of the Spanish viceroys during the colonial period and thereafter that of the President of the Republic. Much altered and enlarged over the years and partly destroyed during the 1692 uprising, it is one of the oldest and finest buildings in the city. The third storey was added in the 1920s, under the rule of President Calles.

The National Palace

Freedom Bell

Above the large central doorway, surmounted by the Mexican coat-of-arms, hangs the Freedom Bell, rung by Miguel Hidalgo at Dolores on September 15th 1810 at the start of the War of Independence. Every year on September 15th the bell is rung by the President at 11pm and the "Grito de Dolores" is repeated from the balcony.

The National Palace boasts a large number of handsome rooms laid out around fourteen courtyards, only some of which are open to visitors. From the arcaded Grand Courtyard a staircase leads up to the first floor.

★★ Rivera Frescos

The most notable feature of this courtyard is the fresco on the staircase and first floor by the muralist Diego Rivera, "Historia y Perspectiva de México" (History and Perspective of Mexico). Covering a total area of 450sq.m/540sq.yd, and painted between 1926 and 1945, it depicts the history of Mexico from Indian times to the period after the revolution. In portraying this wide span of historical events and their principal actors Rivera gives expression to his own very "Indian" social and political attitudes; this is shown perhaps most clearly of all in the picture "La Lucha de Clases" (The Class Struggle) at the foot of the staircase. In the gallery on the first floor can be seen "La Gran Tenochtitlán", another of Rivera's famous murals.

Museo Benito Juárez

Opening Times
Mon.–Fri.
10am–6pm

The rooms once occupied by Benito Juárez off the northern inner courtyard are open to visitors. Some of his furniture and personal belongings can be seen in the room in which he died in 1872. Also open to the public are some large halls and the parliamentary chamber in which the Reform Constitution of 1857 was drawn up. The latter and the Constitution of 1917 are on display.

The National Palace also houses the main State Archives, with many interesting historical documents, and the Biblioteca Miguel Lerdo de Tejada, one of the largest and most important libraries in the country.

★ Cathedral

Metro Station
Zócalo (Line 2)

The Cathedral, which dominates the square on the north side as the National Palace does on the east, is one of the oldest and largest churches in the western hemisphere. It stands on the south-western part of the old Azrec temple precinct, once occupied by the Wall of Skulls (Tzompantli) and the Temple of Xipe Tótec. The original building, begun in 1525, was later partly demolished and partly rebuilt; the present structure dates from 1563, although the definitive plans were prepared at the end of the 16th c. and the beginning of the 17th by the architects Claudio de Arciniega, Juan Gómez de Mora and Alonso Pérez de Castañeda. Although the construction of this massive building of basalt and grey sandstone extended over more than 250 years and thus shows a mingling of various styles, it nevertheless achieves a notably harmonious effect. In spite of the two openwork towers in Neo-Classical style and certain other features, the façade creates a predominantly Baroque impression with its massive volutes and pairs of twisted columns. The bell-towers, by José Damián Ortiz de Castro, were completed in 1793, the statues (attributed to Manuel Tolsá) of Faith, Hope and Charity on the clock-tower were done in 1813. The bells are unusual in their method of hanging and vary greatly in size; one of them, known as "Guadalupe", weighs no less than 5600kg/5½ tonnes.

Interior

The Cathedral, with a main nave and two lateral aisles on either side, is 118m/387ft long, 54m/177ft wide and 55m/180ft high. There are fourteen subsidiary altars as well as the high altar. Like the exterior, the

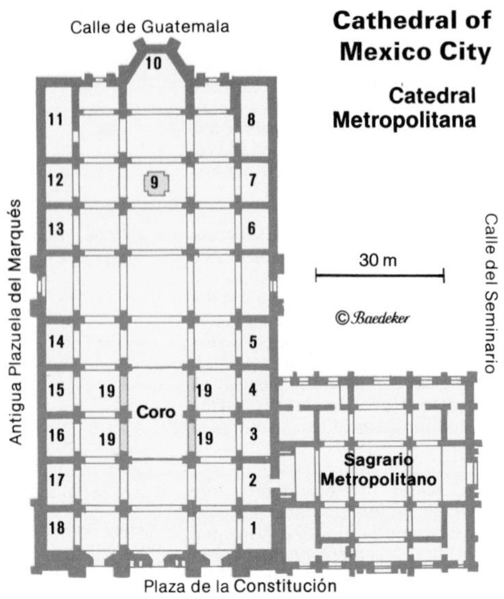

interior shows a mingling of all the different styles and fashions prevailing during the colonial period. Its great glory is the richly carved Altar of the Kings (Altar de los Reyes, 1718–39) behind the high altar, with a retablo by Jerónimo de Balbás, a sculptor of the Churrigueresque school from Seville. The retablo, which follows the form of the apse, has paintings by Juan Rodriguez, including an Adoration of the Kings ("La Adoración de los Reyes") and an Assumption ("Asunción de María"), to which the Cathedral is dedicated. The chapel west of the high altar contains the mortal remains of the Mexican Emperor Agustin de Iturbide. In the third chapel on the left from the main doorway note the statue of the "Señor del Cacao", which dates prior to the original church and to which the Indians offered their contribution towards the cost of building the Cathedral in the form of cocoa-beans. The other chapels and side altars contain some notable pictures, mainly of the Baroque period.

Choir

The very fine carved cedarwood choir-stalls (by Juan de Rojas, 1696) were destroyed by fire in 1967 and have since been restored.

At the south end of the choir, opposite the main entrance, stands the Altar de Perdón (Altar of Mercy), the Churrigueresque retablo of which (by Jerónimo de Balbás) with a painting of the Virgin by Simón Pereyns (1568), was also damaged in the 1967 fire; it has since been restored.

★ Sacristy

In the Sacristy, which has 16th c. Gothic groined vaulting, hang pictures painted about 1665 by Cristóbal de Villalpando ("Immaculate Conception", "Triumph of the Church") and Juan Correa ("Coronation of the Virgin", "St Michael and the Dragon", "Entry into Jerusalem").

Crypt

In the Crypt can be seen the tombs of most of the archbishops of Mexico City, among them Juan de Zumárraga, the great teacher of the Indians and the first incumbent of the see.

Cathedral and Sagrario Metropolitano

Adjoining the Cathedral is a Museum of Religious Art containing many precious church artefacts.

★Museum of Religious Art

This parish church, quite independent of the Cathedral, adjoins it on the east. Built to the design of Lorenzo Rodriguez and conscecrated in 1768, the Sagrario is one of the finest examples of Mexican Churrigueresque.

★Sagrario Metropolitano

On the façade geometric ornamentation predominates in the form of the pilasters known as estípites. The harmonious transition from the high central part of the façade to the lower side elements is contrived with consummate skill.

Façade

A particularly notable feature of the interior is the high altar (1829) by Pedro Patiño Ixtolinque, an Indian pupil of Manuel Tolsá who is also credited with the altar in the chapel of the Virgen Dolorosa. Part of the interior was destroyed by fire and earthquake in the 18th c. Here, as in many other buildings in Mexico City, the foundations are sinking on one side as a result of the settlement of the subsoil of the drained lake.

On the east side of the Sagrario various craftsmen tender their services, with their tools spread out before them – like the musicians on the Plaza Garibaldi.

★★Templo Mayor

Behind the Cathedral, at the corner of Calles Argentina and Guatemala, lie remains of the Temple Precinct of Tenochtitlán which were discovered some years ago and left in situ. In February 1978 workers building the Metro found a carved stone, a round disc 3·25m/nearly 11ft in diameter and weighing 8500kg/8½ tons, finely sculpted with a relief of the beheaded and dismembered goddess Coyolxauhqui (see Sacrificial Stone, below).

★Excavation site

Metro Station
Zócalo (Line 2)

Opening Times
Tues.–Sun.
9am–5pm

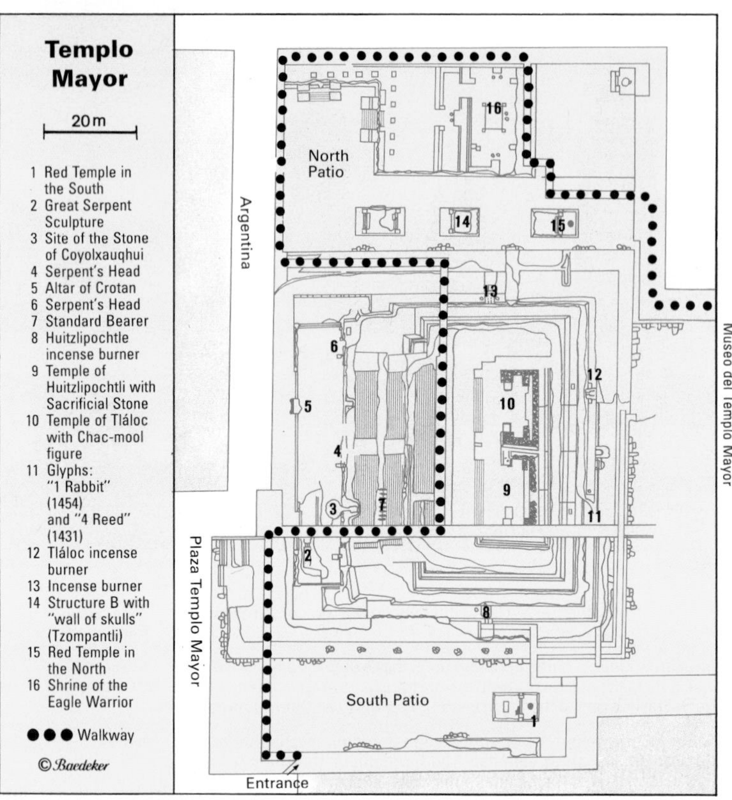

This find stimulated other excavations. Until then it had been assumed that the Gran Teocalli, the principal pyramid of Tenochtitlán, lay buried under the Zócalo, but these latest excavations showed the religious and political centre of the Aztec kingdom to have been here, further to the north-east. This temple pyramid had been the dominant building of the holy precinct; on the top, pointing south, stood the temple to Huitzlipochtli, god of war, and to the north that of Tláloc, the god of rain. Together these symbolised the chief Aztec deities of war and death, life and water.

The excavation work, which necessitated the demolition of a whole block of flats, began at the main front of the pyramid with its double staircase, roughly on the line of the east side of Calle Argentina. It was discovered that this side of the pyramid had been built over no less than eleven times, while on the other sides there were only five rebuildings. Nothing has survived of the two temples, dedicated respectively to Tláloc and Huitzilopochtli, which originally stood on the top of the pyramid.

In the fifth layer from the top, however, was found the summit platform of an earlier pyramid with well-preserved temple walls. In front of the left-hand temple, dedicated to Tláloc, stood a figure of Chac-mool, still preserving most of its vividly-coloured painting. From the height of the walls and the material used it is deduced that these temples were probably erected before the Aztecs gained control of the Aneahuac valley in 1428. There may well be even older temples at lower levels, but it seems improbable that these will be brought to light.

Buried between different building levels were found the skulls of sacrificial victims and numerous vessels containing votive offerings. An interesting feature is the fact that only a fraction of the objects found, which numbered more than seven thousand, were of Aztec origin, most of them coming from the territories of other Indian peoples. Probably these represent tributes from the Aztecs' subject peoples, offered to the gods before the completion of a new pyramid.

A walkway through the site leads past the precinct of the aristocratic "winged warriors", where remains of their residences, decorated with multi-coloured reliefs, have been unearthed.

★★ Museo del Templo Mayor

Opening Times
Tues.–Sun.
9am–5pm

As the National Museum of Anthropolgy has no more room to accommodate the numerous finds it was decided to build a new museum close to the excavation site. Pedro Ramírez Vázquez, who had designed the National Museum of Anthropology, was asked to draw up the plans. The new museum was opened on October 12th 1987, the anniversary of the discovery of America by Columbus. The front of the museum is fully glazed, allowing a view over the excavation site. On four floors around a central courtyard are eight exhibition halls, an auditorium and a library, covering a total floor area of 1700sq.m/ 18,300sq.ft. The majority of the exhibits are displayed on open stands rather than behind glass. Information is provided (in Spanish translation only) in the form of wordings from various Aztec manuscripts.

At the entrance to the museum stands a Tzompantli ("wall of skulls"), which originally formed part of the northern section of the site. In the centre of the courtyard a model shows what the Temple Precinct of Tenochtitlán looked like before the Spanish conquistadors arrived.

★ Sacrificial Stone

The most impressive exhibit is the Sacrificial Stone carved with a relief of the moon goddess Coyolxauhqui (Náhuatl, "she who decorates her face with bells"). It depicts a naked female form from which the head, arms and legs have been severed. Legend has it that she, together with 400 of her disciples, was killed and dismembered on the Hill of Serpents of Coatepec near Tula (see Tollán) by her brother Huitzilopochtli, the god of war, because she sought the blood of her mother, the earth-goddess Coatlicue and objected to human sacrifice. Huitzilopochtli devoured the hearts of the slain. Copil, the son of Coyolxauhqui, attempted to avenge her death but he, too, was slain by Huitzilopochtli and his heart thrown into Lake Texcoco; from it is said to have sprung the "eagle cactus", which the Aztecs believed was a sign from the gods of a good place in which to build a settlement.

Visitors can view the Stone in two ways, either from the ground floor, in which it lies flat in front of the main windows, or from the floor above through a hole in the ceiling. The latter view shows the purpose of the stone more clearly; it stood at the foot of the pyramid below the Temple of Huitzilopochtli, and the priests standing above would have slain the prisoners and then – after ripping out the hearts – would have thrown the corpses down onto the Stone of Coyolxauhqui.

South Wing

The museum is divided into a South Wing and a North Wing, to correspond with the position of the two temples on the pyramid. The South Wing is reserved for the god of war, Huitzilopochtli. The first room shows the migration of the Aztecs until they arrived in the Valley of

The seven "Standard-bearers", as they were found

Anáhuac. The theme of the second room is war and sacrifices to appease the gods, while the third room deals with the Aztec toll system and trade. Finally, in the fourth room can be seen some of the major monoliths discovered on the site. The staircase is flanked by two life-size stone statues of "winged warriors" with stylised eagle wings, which originally stood in the aristocratic warrior precinct. Note the statue of Xiuhtecutli, the god of fire. A special find were the eight "standard-bearers" from the altar of the Temple of Huitzilopochtli, some of which still bore traces of colouring and pieces of obsidian and shells to imitate eyes. So far their function has not been discovered. It is assumed that they date from the third building period (1431), and that when the pyramid was being built over for the fourth time they were laid down on the steps and covered up to protect them from damage.

★"Standard-bearers"

North Wing

The four rooms of the North Wing are devoted to Tláloc the rain-god, who appears again and again at various stages of building. One room displays the skeletons of sacrificed animals, such as crocodiles, eagles, pumas, jaguars and sharks. Another room portrays various aspects of Aztec life and religion, including birth, upbringing and their vision of the Universe. The last room deals with the Conquest, concentrating on the arrival of the Spaniards and the demise of the Aztecs.

Around the Zócalo

★★Zócalo

The central feature of Mexico City is the Zócalo (Plaza de la Constitución), where Mexico's first Constitution was proclaimed in 1813. Measuring some 240m/260yd each way, it is one of the largest squares in the world. The Spaniards began to lay out the square immediately after the conquest of Tenochtitlán, with its northern half overlying the southern part of the demolished Aztec temple precinct, the Teocalli. In the early colonial period the square served a variety of purposes – as a bullfighting arena, a market and a place of public execution, among other things. Today the square is one large empty space, which is used for festivals, parades and demonstrations. A huge flag is hoisted every morning. In the Metro station below the square models are on display illustrating the city's development. Dominating the square are the National Palace and the Cathedral, with the Templo Mayor site behind it. The Majestic Hotel roof terrace offers a fine view over the square.

Old and New Town Halls

On the south side of the square, at the end of Avenida 20 de Noviembre, on the left stands the Old Town Hall (Palacio del Ayuntamiento), a building of the colonial period which was altered *c.* 1700, and on the right the New Town Hall. Both of these now house Federal District offices.

Nearby, at Avenida 16 de Septiembre 82, the foyer of the Gran Hotel de la Ciudad de México is well worth a look, furnished as it is in genuine and nostalgic late 19th c. style. The glass roof designed by Tiffany in Art Nouveau style is particularly noteworthy.

Merchants' Arcades

The west side of the square is taken up with the Portales de los Mercadores, or Merchants' Arcades, where goods have been offered for sale ever since Cortés' day.

Monte de Piedad (Pawnshop)

West of the Cathedral stands a much altered building of the colonial period, now occupied by the Monte de Piedad ("Mountain of Compassion"), the state pawnshop. Now the largest in Latin America, it was founded in 1775 by Pedro Tomero de Terreros and moved into its present home in 1850.

Unredeemed articles are sold off at monthly auctions.

Museo José Luis Cuevas

This museum at Academia 13, esq. Moneda, is named after the artist but exhibits not only his work but also that of other modern painters. The prints of world-famous artists are notable.

Calle Moneda

Archbishop's Palace

From the north-east corner of the Zócalo, Calle Moneda leads off to the east. Going along this street, on the left at the corner of Calle Licenciado Verdad, can be seen the Baroque Archbishop's Palace (Palacio del Arzobispado). On the other side of this cross street stands a building in which Viceroy Antonio de Mendoza set up the first printing office in New Spain in 1536.

Antigua Casa Moneda (Museo de las Culturas

On the right, at Calle Moneda 13, stands the Antigua Casa de la Moneda, a building with an attractive patio which housed the Government Mint from 1734 onwards. It now contains the Museum of the Cultures (Museo de las Culturas), with works of art and applied art from all over the world.

Museo Cuevas

As well as works by Cuevas himself, and other modern painters, the Museo José Luis Cuevas (C. Academia 13) also features a collection of graphic art by well-known international figures.

Academia de San Carlos

One block farther on, on the right-hand side beyond Calle Academia, will be seen the Academia de San Carlos, once the country's major art school. This building, which was altered in the 19th c., now houses reproductions of European sculpture of the Classical period.

★Iglesia de La Santisima Façade

In the continuation of Calle Moneda, Calle Emiliano Zapata, stands the church of La Santisima on the left. Its façade, built between 1755 and 1789, is one of the finest in the city; the first stage in its construction is attributed to Lorenzo Rodriguez, the architect of the Sagrario Metropolitano. A notable feature is the bell-tower in the form of a papal tiara.

Nuestra Señora de Loreto

To the north-west, reached by way of Calle Loreto, lies the Plaza Loreta, on which stands the church of Nuestra Señora de Loreto, one of the most interesting Neo-Classical churches in Mexico, built by Ignacio de Castera and José Agustin Paz between 1809 and 1816. Notable features include the elegant dome, the large windows between the buttresses and, in the sacristy, a reproduction of the Santa Casa de Loreto, with fine pictures of the colonial period by Miguel Cabrera and other artists. It says much for the solidity of the church's structure that it shows no significant damage, although on account of the unstable subsoil the east end, built of heavy stone, has sunk quite considerably while the west end, in the lighter volcanic tezontle, has subsided very little.

Escuela Nacional Preparatoria

Two blocks west, at Calle Ildelfonso 43, will be found a Baroque building, erected in 1749 as a Jesuit college, which now houses the Gabino Barreda Escuela Nacional Preparatoria, the most famous of Mexico's state secondary schools, and an office of the UNAM University.

★ Frescos

The school is noted particularly for the frescos on the walls of the patio and staircase by Fermin Revueltas, Ramón Alva de la Canal, Fernando Leal, Jean Charlot, David Alfaro Siqueiros and José Clemente Orozco, who were invited in 1921 by the then Minister of Education José Vasconcelos to decorate the school. This marked the birth of Muralismo, the world-famous school of Mexican wall-painting. The finest of the murals here are those painted by Oroczo between 1922 and 1927, which combine spiritual and religious themes with the revolutionary history of Mexico.

★ Baroque Choir-stalls

In the great hall of the school, known as "El Generalito", are the choir-stalls, recovered after a fire, of the former Augustinian church which later housed the National Library. The carving of these stalls, which are of walnut wood, is among the finest of its kind, depicting scenes from the Old and New Testaments; it was the work of Salvador de Ocampo, son of the great Indian sculptor Tomás Xuárez, and dates from 1701–02.

Antiteatro Bolivar

The Antiteatro Bolivar at Calle Justo Sierra 16 also belongs to the school; the wall-painting of "The Creation" was the first example of the fresco technique as employed by Diego Rivera.

Ministry of Education

To the north-west, in Calle República Argentina between Calles Venezuela and L. G. Obregón, will be found the Ministry of Education (Secretaría de Educación Pública), on the site of the mid 17th c. Convent of the Incarnation. The Baroque church which formerly belonged to the convent now houses the Ibero-American Library (Biblioteca Iberoamericana).

★ Murals

Covering a total area of 1600sq.m/17,200sq.ft, the Ministry building is decorated with magnificent murals, mainly by Diego Rivera but also by Amado de la Cueva, Juan O'Gorman, Carlos Mérida and others. Rivera's frescos, mostly concerned with the life and work of the Indians, were done between 1923 and 1928 and reflect the spirit of social criticism prevalent at that time and to which he subscribed. In the publications section of the Ministry visitors can obtain books and informative material about the land and people of Mexico.

★ **Plaza de Santo Domingo**

One block north, to the west of Avenida República de Brasil, lies the Plaza de Santa Domingo, a square of the colonial period which has preserved much of its Spanish atmosphere. Under the arches on one side of the square sit the public letter-writers (evangelistas), offering their services to illiterate customers. On the edge of the square, at Calle Cuba 95, a tablet records that the Indian women known as Malinche, or Doña María, who was Cortés' interpreter, adviser and mistress, lived in the house in 1527 with her husband, Juan de Jaramillo.

In the square stand two monuments – a seated figure of Josefa Ortiz de Domínguez, known as "La Corregidora", one of the heroines of the fight for independence and after whom the square was formerly named Jardín de la Corregidora; and, in front of the church, a statue of Manuel Carmon y Valle, a well-known doctor and dean of the medical faculty.

Iglesia de Santo Domingo

On the north side of the square stands the handsome Baroque church of Santo Domingo, the only remnant of a once powerful Dominican convent. The present building, in red tezontle, dates from the first half of the 18th c. and is notable for its elegant azulejo-decorated tower, harmonious façade, two Churrigueresque retablos and Neo-Classical high altar by Manuel Tolsá.

Escuela Nacional de Medicina (Museum of Medical History)

The east side of the square, at the corner of Calles Brasil and Venezuela, is the site of an 18th c. palace now housing the museum of medical history and known as the Antigua Escuela Nacional de Medicine. During the colonial period the building was used as a prison by the Inquisition, the highest court of judgment in matters of faith (although it had no authority over the Indians). The Inquisition was introduced into New Spain in 1571 and remained active until 1815.

★ Iglesia de La Enseñanza Antigua

In Calle Justo Sierra, one block south in the direction of the Cathedral, stands the church of La Enseñanza Antigua, a Baroque conventual church built by Francisco Guerrero y Torres in the second half of the 18th c. The interior is notable for its magnificent Churrigueresque retablos and pictures of the Mexican colonial school.

Acequia Real

On returning to the Zócalo and passing the National Palace to Calle Corregidora, the visitor will see a reconstructed canal, the Acequia Real. It is a remnant of the canals which once flowed through Mexico City and on which small boats conveyed goods to outlying villages.

Supreme Court

The south-east corner of the Zócalo is taken up with the building of the Supreme Court of Justice (Suprema Corte de Justicia), erected in 1929 in colonial style on the site of an 18th c. market building. The staircase is decorated with two murals by José Clemente Orozco.

Between the Alameda and the Zócalo

Metro Station
Bellas Artes (Line 2)

Torre Latinoamericana

The 177m/580ft high, 44-storey Torre Latinoamericana at the corner of Avenida Madero and Lázaro Cárdenas, to the south of the Metro station, is second only in height to the more recently built Hotel de México. The viewing terrace on the 42nd floor affords a magnificent view over the city. The serious earthquake of September 1985 made the tower sway considerably, but thanks to its floating "hydrolastic" foundations it remained undamaged.

San Francisco

Avenida Francisco I leads south from the Torre Latinoamericana, and on the right-hand side of the street stands first of all the church of San Francisco, with a handsome Churrigueresque doorway of the early 18th c. This is a remnant of a large convent founded by Cortés in 1524 which was destroyed by the Reform government in 1856. The remains of Cortés are said to have lain in this church from 1629 to 1794.

SEGUROS
LATINOAMERICANA

Casa de los Azulejos

Opposite the church is the Casa de los Azulejos (House of Tiles), originally built in 1596 and decorated by the Conde del Valle de Orizaba 150 years later with blue and white tiles from Puebla. In 1925 José Clemente Orozco painted murals on the walls of the staircase. The building is now a shop and café belonging to the Sanborn chain, where Emiliano Zapata and Pancho Villa breakfasted together on arrival in Mexico City. This meeting is marked by a photo which hangs on the wall of the café.

★ Palacio de Iturbide

Beyond this, on the right, will be found the Palacio de Iturbide, now owned by the Banco Nacional de México. This excellently restored 18th c. Baroque palace was designed by Francisco Guerrero y Torres in 1780 and until 1823 was the residence of Agustin de Iturbide, later to become the first Emperor of Mexico. The bank arranges exhibitions from time to time in the inner courtyard.

Museo del Zapato

This highly original museum (Museo del Zapato), recently opened above a large shoe shop at Calle Bolivar No. 27, boasts a collection of more than 7500 items of footwear, old and new.

Iglesia de La Profesa

On the left-hand side of the street, at the corner of Madero and Isabel la Católica, stands the fine Baroque church of La Profesa (1720), once part of a Jesuit convent. The high altar is by Manuel Tolsá.

★ Museo de la Ciudad de México

Opening Times
Tues.–Sun.
9am–7.30pm

Farther south, at the corner of Isabel la Católica and Uruguay, is a former Augustinian church which housed the National Library until it was moved to the University City.

Going east along the next cross street, Avenida República de Salvador, and crossing Avenida Pino Suárez, the visitor will come to the Museum of Mexico City (Museo de la Ciudad de México). at Pino Suárez 30, in the imposing former Palacio de los Condes de Santiago de Calimaya. This has an interesting collection of documents, photos, furniture and other material on the history of the city from prehistoric times to the present day. Notable items include a model of the Teocalli, the cult centre of ancient Tenochtitlán, and another of the city as it is today. At the corner of the building note the serpent's head stone taken from the wall of the Templo Mayor.

Mercado de la Merced

Some blocks (cuadras) farther east along Avenida del Salvador stands the Mercado de la Merced, a modern market hall designed by Enrique de la Mora y Palmor. Until recently it was the city's largest food market, but this has now moved to Iztalapa and less market business is done here now.

★ Convento de la Merced

It is also worth looking in at the 17th c. Convent of La Merced (rebuilt in 1834), at the corner of Uruguay and Jesús María. The fine cloister shows a pleasant mingling of styles, including in particular Mudéjar.

Capilla Manzanares

Farther along Avenida Uruguay stands the Capilla Manzanares, primarily frequented by market folk, with its beautiful 18th c. Churrigueresque façade.

Hospital e Iglesia Jesús Nazareno

Opposite the Museum will be seen the 17th c. Baroque church of Jesús Nazareno, with frescos by Orozco (1944) in the dome. It was either here or at the church of Santa Cruz Acatlán that Cortés is said to have met the Aztec ruler Moctezuma II for the first time on November 8th 1519. The body of Cortés, who died at Seville in 1547, now rests in the Jesús Nazareno church. The Hospital La Purísima Concepción adjoining the

◀ *Torre Laitinoamericana*

church, the first of its kind in America, was founded by Cortés in 1524 and was until recently still managed by his descendants.

In the Pino Suárez Metro station, to the south, stands a circular Aztec pyramid which was excavated here.

Convento San Jerónimo

From the Metro station Calle San Jerónimo leads west to the former Convent of San Jerónimo on the square of the same name (No. 47). The great poetess and painter Juana Inés de la Cruz (1651–95) lived and worked here, and her remains were recently discovered in the church. The museum, with its library, film-shows and excavated finds, which is now housed in the building is named after her.

Museo de la Charrería

One block south on Isabel La Católica lies Avenida José María de Izazaga in which, near the Isabel la Católica underground station, stands the little church of Nuestra Señora de Monserrat. This former convent now houses the Charro Museum (Museo de la Charrería), with exhibits relating to all aspects of horses and equine sports, including traditional Charro costumes and the saddle used by the revolutionary leader "Pancho" Villa.

★Colegio de las Vizcainas

Returning to Calle San Jerónimo and going west along this street we come, just before Avenida Lázaro Cárdenas and on Callejon San Ignacio, to the Colegio de las Vizcainas or Colegio de San Ignacio. This is a Baroque structure built by Miguel José de Quiera between 1734 and 1786 as a Basque girls' school. It boasts a very beautiful Churrigueresque chapel which, like the north front, is attributed to Lorenzo Rodríguez. There is a small religious museum which is open to the public at certain times only.

La Purísima

At the west end of Calle Izazaga, on Avenida Lázaro Cárdenas, stands the mid 18th c. church of La Purísima, with a richly-decorated doorway. In the square in front of the church can be seen the Salto de Agua fountain, the original of which, dating from colonial times, was removed over sixty years ago to Tepotzotlán.

★Mercado San Juan

North-west of the square, at the junction of Lopez and Ayuntamiento, lies the Mercado San Juan, one of the city's oldest and largest markets for foodstuffs, flowers, household articles and folk-art.

Bellas Artes and Alameda

★Palacio de Bellas Artes

Metro Station
Bellas Artes
(Line 2)

On Avenida Lázaro Cárdenas, east of Alameda park, towers the massive marble building of the Palacio de Bellas Artes (Palace of Fine Arts). Commissioned during the presidency of the dictator Porfirio Díaz and designed mainly by the Italian architect Adamo Boari, it clearly shows Art Nouveau and Art Deco influences. Although begun in 1900 it was not completed until 1934. The weight of the heavy Carrara marble has caused it to sink more than 4m/13ft into the ground, in spite of attempts to lighten it by removing part of the facing of the dome. During construction work in front of the palace in 1993/94, no fewer than 2000 pre-Hispanic items, including 700 examples of Aztec ceramic ware, were uncovered, together with 200 graves dating from the colonial period, and the remains of the 17th c. Santa Isabel convent. The headquarters since 1946 of the Instituto Nacional de Bellas Artes, the palace now serves primarily as an opera-house and concert hall.

Teatro de Bellas Artes

★Tiffany glass curtain

The great hall, known as the Teatro de Bellas Artes, can seat an audience of 3500. The stage has a glass-mosaic curtain weighing 22 tonnes, designed by Dr Atl (Gerardo Murillo) and made by Tiffany's of New York. It depicts, with carefully contrived lighting effects, the landscape

Palacio de Bella Arts, gradually sinking into the ground

of the Valley of Mexico with the two mighty volcanoes of Popocatépetl and Iztaccihuatl.

The famous Ballet Folklórico performs in the theatre three times a week.

★ Museo de Artes Plásticas

Opening Times
Mon.–Sat.
10am–5.30pm
Sun. 10am–2pm

The same building houses the Museum of Art (Museo de Artes Plásticas), which is notable for its collection of works by Mexican artists of the 19th and 20th c. It also has rooms for periodic special exhibitions and a number of lecture and concert halls. On the second and third floors can be seen murals by the leading Mexican exponents of this genre. In the corridors on the second floor hang two large works by Rufino Tamayo, "The Birth of our Nationality" and "Mexico Today". On the third floor can be seen a painting by Diego Rivera, "Man at the Turning-Point" (1934), a copy of that done for the Rockefeller Center in New York which was painted over because of its Marxist trend. There is also an interesting series of frescos by David Álfaro Siqueiros depicting Democracy and the last Aztec ruler Cuauhtémoc, done in the then new technique using a spray-gun. The work entitled "Catharsis" by José Clemente Orozco was painted in 1934.

Museo Nacional de Arte e Industrias Populares

South of Alameda Park Avenida Benito Juárez links the Paseo de la Reforma with Avenida Lázaro Cárdenas; to the east of the Palacio de Bellas Artes – where there are many elegant shops selling silver, leather goods and folk art, etc., as well as offices, hotels and restaurants – the avenue takes the name of Francisco I. Madero. At No. 44, in the former Corpus Christi church (with murals by Miguel Covarrubias), is the Museum of Folk Arts and Crafts (Museo de Artes e Industrias Populares) where, under the management of the Mexican Indian Institute INI, products of the different regions of Mexico are displayed and on sale. Handicrafts can also be bought in the state-run FONART shop at No. 89 (further shops at Calle Londres 136/Zona Rosa, Avda. de la Paz/San Angel, Patriotismo 691/Mixcoac).

★Rivera painting

The famous painting by Diego Rivera, "Dream of a Sunday Afternoon in Alameda Park" (1947–48) was in the foyer of the Hotel del Prado (Juárez 70) when the building was destroyed in the September 1985 earthquake. Fortunately it was salvaged and is now in the Museo Mural Diego Rivera on the Plaza de Solidaridad. This square was laid out after the earthquake on the site of some destroyed buildings, close to Alameda Park. In his mural the artist caricatured some of Mexico's historical figures whom he regarded as enemies of his people. There was a scandal when it was finished, because Rivera had entitled it "Dios no existe" (God does not exist). For years the picture remained covered up until in 1958, with a great flourish of publicity, the artist painted over the offending words.

Parque Alameda Central

Metro Stations
Bellas Artes (Line 2)
Hidalgo (Lines 2, 3)

Bounded on the south by Avenida Juárez and on the north by Avenida Hidalgo, the Parque Alameda Central, a shady and beautifully kept park with fine old trees, benches, numerous fountains and pieces of sculpture, was originally laid out in 1592 and in pre-Columbian times had been a market place (tianguis). In the early colonial period it was also used as a drill-ground and as a place of execution for heretics condemned by the Inquisition. Always crowded with visitors and hawkers, the park is at its busiest and gayest at Christmas, when it is illuminated and decorated and becomes a popular amusement park.

Hemiciclo Juárez

In the park stands a semicircular memorial to the reforming President Benito Juárez (1806–72); known as the Hemiciclo Juárez, it was erected in 1910 and unveiled by Porfírio Díaz. Between the seated statue stand two female forms symbolising Justice and Glory. On September 18th every year the President inspects a parade at this spot.

Beethoven Memorial

On the east side of the square, opposite the Palacio de Bellas Artes, stands a Beethoven Memorial, with a death-mask of the composer, donated by the local German community.

North-west of Bellas Artes

Metro Stations
Bellas Artes (Line 2)
Hidalgo (Lines 2, 3)

Iglesia de La Santa Veracruz

On the far side of Avenida Hidalgo, which bounds Alameda Park on the north, lies the little Plaza Morelos (Plaza 2 de Abril or Plazuela de San Juan de Dios), in which stand two churches. The church of La Santa Veracruz, on the east side of the square, occupies the site of an earlier mid 16th c. church; the present building with its beautiful Churrigueresque main door was consecrated in 1764. The once richly decorated interior has suffered from the attentions of robbers, but still proudly displays a fine crucifix on the high altar which was presented to the church by Charles V. The famous architect and sculptor Manuel Tolsá is buried in the atrium.

San Juan de Dios

On the other side of the square stands the church of San Juan de Dios, built in 1727. It boasts an interesting façade in the form of a huge niche with a conch-like top and several statues in smaller niches around those of the saints. Adjoining the church is a former hospital in which craft goods are now offered for sale.

★Museo Franz Mayer

Situated close to the church of San Juan de Dios, at Avenida Hidalgo 45, since 1986, the Museo Franz Mayer exhibits both European and Mexican applied art, and is the only museum in Mexico to do so.

At the west end of the Alameda the Pinacoteca Virreinal (Viceregal Picture Gallery) is housed in the old conventual church of San Diego, built between 1594 and 1621. The pictures displayed in the church, the chapels and the cloister are by leading artists of the colonial period (16th–19th c.), including Simón Pereyns, Baltazar de Echave Orio, Cristóbal de Villalpando, Juan Rodríguez Juárez, José María de Ibarra, Miguel Cabrera and José María Tresguerras.

★Pinacoteca Virreinal

Opening Times
Tues.–Sun.
9am–5pm

The Avenido Hidalgo leads west into the Paseo de la Reforma. Just beyond the intersection, on the right, stands the church of San Hipólito – a massive early 17th c. edifice with a Baroque façade – dedicated to Mexico City's patron saint.

Iglesia de San Hipólito

Two blocks farther west, to the right, lies the Plaza San Fernando, on the north side of which will be seen the church of San Fernando, a mid-18th c. building with a relatively plain Baroque front. In the churchyard are the graves of famous Mexicans, including Benito Juárez.

Iglesia de San Fernando

Two blocks west of the Plaza San Fernando, at the corner of Calle Puente Alvarado (No. 50, on the left), stands the Neo-Classical Palacio de Buenavista, an early 19th c. building by Manuel Tolsá. In 1865 the Emperor Maximilian presented the palace to Marshal Bazaine, commander of the French troops in Mexico. Today it houses the Museo San Carlos, named after King Carlos III of Spain, who unveiled the first paintings. On display is a fine collection of works by Mexican and European artists which formerly hung in the Academia San Carlos, including some by Titian, Tintoretto, Goya and El Greco.

★Museo San Carlos

Opening Times
Tues.–Sun.
10am–5pm

North-east of Bellas Artes

To the east of the Palacio de Bellas Artes, at the intersection of Avenida Lázaro Cárdenas and Calle Tacuba, is the Head Post Office (Correo Mayor, Dirección General de Correos), a building in Neo-Renaissance style with Gothic features (1902–8), designed by Adami Boari, architect of the Palacio de Bellas Artes. On the upper floors will be found a Postal Museum (Museo Postal). There is a special counter for the sale of commemorative stamps.

Metro Stations
Bellas Artes, Allende (Line 2)

Head Post Office and Postal Museum

West of the Post Office, fronting on to Calle Tacuba, stands the Palacio de Minería, built *c.* 1800 by Manuel Tolsá in the French-influenced Neo-Classical style of the period. Until 1954 it housed the College of Mining Engineers.

Palacio de Minería

In front of the palace stands the famous bronze equestrian statue of Charles IV of Spain, popularly known as "El Caballito" (the "Little Horse"); also by Manuel Tolsá, it was modelled on a statue by the French sculptor Girardon. The statue originally stood on the Zócalo, but after independence it was moved to various places in the city before finally ending up at its present site.

"El Caballito"

The imposing building opposite, at Calle Tacuba 8, built in the early 1900s by the Italian architect Silvio Contri, housed the offices of the Ministry of Transport and Public Works for a number of years. Since 1982 it has contained the new Museo Nacional de Arte, with two floors of 22 rooms in all displaying exhibits ranging from Maya sculptures to religious items from the Spanish colonial period and 19th c. landscape paintings through to contemporary art.

★Museo Nacional de Arte

Opening Times
Tues.–Sun.
10am–6pm

To the north-west of the Palacio de Minería lie the buildings occupied by the two houses of the Mexican Parliament – at the corner of Calles

Parliament Building

Donceles and Xicoténcatl, the Cámara de Senadores (Senate), with murals by Jorge González Camarena on the staircase; and at the corner of Donceles (north side) and Calle Allende the Cámara de Diputados (House of Representatives).

Convent of the Conception

Two blocks north-east, on the north side of Calle Belisario Domínguez, lies the Plaza de la Concepción, with an octagonal chapel in the centre. Here, too, stands the Convent of the Conception, the first nunnery to be built in the town and founded by Bishop Juan de Zumárraga in 1540. The building has been added to down the centuries, and now displays a whole range of styles from early Baroque to the Neo-Classicism of the 19th c.

★ Plaza Garibaldi

Two blocks farther north, between Calles Montero, Ecuador, Allende and Santa María la Redonda, opens up the picturesque Plaza Garibaldi, which can be reached direct from the Palacio de Bellas Artes by way of the northward continuation of Avenida Lázaro Cárdenas. The square is surrounded by cafés and restaurants much favoured by tourists, and in these and in the square itself groups of musicians play folk music. Most of these groups are "mariachis" from Jalisco, dressed in Charro costume and playing trumpets, violins, guitars and the guitarrón or bass guitar. However, there are usually also other groups from Veracruz – in white costumes with straw hats, and playing harps and small guitars – as well as from other regions. Payment is expected for each song, but it is also possible to arrange for a longer performance (bargaining required!) or to hire a group for a private party. Visitors are warned to beware of pickpockets and the like, especially at night when the square is usually crowded.

Mercado de la Lagunilla

A short distance east, on the north side of the Calle República de Honduras, lies the Mercado de la Lagunilla. Now that most of the stalls are in a modern market hall this has lost much of its old and colourful "flea-market" atmosphere. On Sundays, however, "antiques" (rarely genuine!) are on sale.

Mercado de Tepito

A few blocks to the north-east, around Calle de Toltecas, is the Mercado de Tepito where, around the modern market hall, second-hand articles (some smuggled!) are offered at very reasonable prices.

Tlatelolco

Metro Station
Tlatelolco (Line 3)

To the west of the Tepito market, reached by taxi direct from the city centre by way of Paseo de la Reforma and thence to the north, stretches the district of Tlatelolco. It was here that the large housing scheme known as the Conjunto Urbano Nonoalco-Tlatelolco, covering an area of almost 1,000,000sq.m/250 acres was built, only to suffer serious damage in the 1985 earthquake, when one block of flats collapsed completely, burying hundreds underneath. Many of the buildings are now unsafe and standing empty.

★ Square of the Three Cultures

The central feature and principal sight of this quarter is the Square of the Three Cultures (Plaza de las Tres Culturas or Plaza Santiago de Tlatelolco).

The Plaza occupies roughly the same site as the main square of the pre-Columbian town of Tlatelolco, Tenochtitlán's great rival until 1473, when the Aztecs captured the town and killed its ruler by hurling him from the principal pyramid. However, Tlatelolco still remained the most important trading town in the region with a market which, according to the accounts of the conquistadors, was visited by 60,000 people

Square of the Three Cultures

every day. During the siege of Tenochtitlán by the Spaniards in 1521 Tlatelolco was the scene of the last desperate stand by the Aztecs. This event is remembered by means of a memorial tablet bearing the words "On 13 August 1521 Tlatelolco, so heroically defended by Cuauhtémoc, finally fell into the hands of Hernán Cortés. It was neither a triumph nor a defeat; it was the painful moment of birth of the Mexico of today, of a race of mestizos".

The square was designed by Mario Pani and completed in 1964. It takes its name from the fascinating juxtaposition of buildings from three different periods – Aztec pyramids and temples, a Spanish conventual church and modern tower blocks. In 1968 the police fired on a crowd which was demonstrating in the square and, according to unofficial estimates, killed some 250 people. In 1985 and 1986 it was covered with tents to provide shelter for the many who had been rendered homeless by the earthquake.

Aztec ruins

In addition to the principal pyramid which shows fourteen superimposed structures, the Aztec remains include other pyramids, platforms, staircases, walls and altars and a "tzompantli" ("wall of skulls"). On one of the subsidiary pyramids can be seen some fine reliefs of Aztec calendar signs.

★Santiago de Tlatelolco

In the centre of the park-like square stands the church of Santiago de Tlatelolco, in unadorned Baroque style. The present church (rather unhappily restored) was built at the beginning of the 17th c. on the site of a small chapel of 1535 belonging to the Franciscan convent of Santiago. Adjoining the church is one of the old conventual buildings, formerly the Colegio Imperial de Santa Cruz, in which the Franciscans taught the gifted sons of the Aztec nobility. One of the most notable teachers was Bernardino de Sahagún, the great chronicler of the history of New Spain.

Foreign Ministry

The south-west side of the square is taken up by the modern office block of the Foreign Ministry (Secretaría de Relaciones Exteriores). The construction of this and of the street entailed the destruction of the pryramid of Quetzalcóatl and of part of another cult building.

★Paseo d la Reforma

Metro Stations
Hidalgo (Lines 2, 3)
Chapultepec (Line 1)

Bus
Several stops along the Boulevard
Bus
Several stops along the Boulevard

The Paseo de la Reforma, the principal east–west traffic artery of Mexico City, extends for a total distance of 15km/9 miles from Tlatelolco to the residential district of Las Lomas ("The Hills") on the city's western boundary. The principal section, however, is the stretch from the intersection with Avenido Benito Juárez to Chapultepec Park. This boulevard is 60m/200ft wide, with six to eight traffic lanes, a green strip in the middle, busts of famous men (mainly heroes of the wars of independence, etc.) along the sides and large roundabouts (glorietas) at the intersections, with monuments or groups of trees. The patrician houses of the colonial period which once flanked the street have almost completely disappeared, to be replaced by tall modern blocks containing offices, hotels, restaurants, cinemas and shops. This magnificent avenue was originally laid out during the reign of the Emperor Maximilian to provide a direct link between his residence in Chapultepec Castle and the official seat of government on the Zócalo. It takes its present name from the reforming laws promulgated by Maximilian's antagonist Benito Juárez in 1861; it was previously known as the Calzador del Emperador ("Avenue of the Emperor") and Paseo de los Hombres Ilustres ("Promenade of Famous Men").

Columbus Monument

Going south-west down the Paseo de la Reforma from Avenida Juárez to the first intersection, the Glorieta de Cristóbal Colón, the visitor will

Paseo de la Reforma, with the Columbus Monument

see the Columbus Monument by the French sculptor Charles Cordier, erected in 1877. On the base of the statue are the figures of four of the monks who played a leading part in the settlement of Mexico and the integration of the Indians: Juan Pérez de Marchena, Diego de Deza, Pedro de Gante and Bartolomé de Las Casas.

Monumento a la Revolución

From the intersection Calle Ignacio Ramirez, to the right, leads north to the Plaza de la República, with the huge Monumento a la Revolución, commemorating the 1910 Revolution. This was formed from an unfinished building originally commissioned by Porfirio Díaz to house law-courts. The columns of the dome=shaped structure contain the remains of the revolutionary leaders Francisco I. Madero, Venustiano Carranza, Francisco "Pancho" Villa, Lázaro Cárdenas and Plutarco Elías Calles. Since 1986 the ground floor has housed the Museo de la Revolución.

Ciudadela

To the south-east of the Glorieta de Cristóbal Colón, by way of Avenidas Versailles and Atenas, stands the Citadel (Ciudadela), a Neo-Classical building completed in 1907 in which the independence leader José María Morelos was confined before his execution. It now houses the National Institute of Handicrafts (Instituto Nacional de Artesanía), with a school for the training of craftsmen, an exhibition of articles for sale and a library, the Biblioteca México.

Cuauhtémoc Memorial

In the centre of the next glorieta (roundabout) continuing south-west on the Paseo de la Reforma stands a statue of Cuauhtémoc, the last Aztec ruler. Here the Paseo is crossed by the 26km/16 mile long Avenida de los Insurgentes, the city's main north–south axis.

Zona Rosa

Beyond the intersection, to the south of the Paseo, lies the district known as the Zona Rosa ("Pink Zone") or Colonia Juárez, which is bounded on the south by the Avenida Chapultepec. In this area, in which the streets are named after European cities, there is a great concentration of hotels, restaurants, cafés, night spots, art galleries and elegant shops.

Wax Museum

At Calle Londres 6 will be found the Wax Museum (Museo de Cera) and Chamber of Absurdities ("Aunque Usted no le crea"/"You'll never believe it"); on the same street between Calles Amberes and Florencia lies a market for clothes and craftwork; and at Calle Londres 136 is a FONART (state-owned) shop selling folk-art.

Independence Monument

The next-but-one glorieta is dominated by the Independence Monument (Monumento a la Independencia), known as "El Angel" from the figure of a winged goddess of victory which stands on top of a tall column. This memorial, too, was a gift from the dictator Díaz on the occasion of the century of Mexican independence in 1910. At the foot of the 36m/118ft column will be seen statues to the heroes of the movement for independence, such as Miguel Hidalgo, Guerrero and Morelos. The foundations of the column were made very deep to prevent it from sinking into the swampy subsoil. However, because the surrounding land sinks about 20cm/8in. every year the monument "grows" in a most curious fashion, so that a new step has to be added to its base nearly every year.

I.M.S.S.

Behind the next roundabout, on the left, stands the Institute of Social Security (Instituto Mexicano del Seguro Social, I.M.S.S.). The entrance is decorated with relief carving and sculpture by Jorge González Camarena, and the interior displays frescos by Camarena and Federico Cantú.

"El Angel", the Independence Monument

Further to the left, on the edge of Chapultepec Park, is the Ministry of Health (Secretaría de Salubridad), which boasts frescos and stained glass by Diego Rivera in some of its rooms. To the right, in a small triangular garden, stands the Diana Fountain with a statue to the goddess of hunting (Fuente de Diana Cazadora), nearby a monument to Venustiano Carranza and, beyond this, at the entrance to the park, a statue of Simón Bolívar, the hero of South American independence.

★Chapultepec Park

Metro Station
Chapultepec (Line 1)

Bus
Several stops on the Paseo de Reforma which runs through the park

The Bosque de Chapultepec (Náhuatl, "hill of the grasshoppers") is Mexico City's principal park and, with an area of 4sq.km/2½sq. miles, its largest. It was once a stronghold of the Toltecs, and the Toltec ruler, Huémec, is said to have hanged himself here in 1177 after fleeing from Tula. In 1200 the Aztecs (Mexica) settled on the hill after their long wanderings but were driven away again twenty years later by neighbouring tribes. Legend has it that the park was originally laid out in the first half of the 15th c. by Netzahualcóyotl, the poet king of Texcoco. As the power of Tenochtitlán increased the hill became a summer residence of the Aztec rulers, and water from the springs here was conveyed to the temple precinct in the capital by means of an aqueduct, remains of which can still be seen in Avenida Chapultepec between its junctions with Calles Praga and Warsovia. Portraits of the Aztec rulers were carved from the rock on the slopes of the hill, and remnants of these can still be seen on the eastern slope.

Leisure park

The park still preserves numbers of fine old trees, the most imposing being some massive specimens of cedars and ahuehuetes (swamp cypresses, Náhuatl for "old man of the water"). Lakes, sports facilities,

Boating on the Lago Antiguo

botanic garden, zoo, museums and castle attract crowds of city-dwellers, especially at weekends, to walk, ride, picnic or enjoy the wide range of entertainments available here, such as concerts, theatre, childrens' programmes, etc.

Southern section

The major part of the park lies south of Paseo de la Reforma.

★Museo de Arte Moderno

On the east side, to the left of Paseo de la Reforma, stands the important Museum of Modern Art (Museo de Arte Moderno), designed by Rafael Mijares and Pedro Ramírez Vázquez and opened in 1964. Apart from a retrospective look at Mexican art before and during the colonial period, the museum is notable primarily for its collection of pictures and sculpture by Mexican artists of the 19th and 20th c. There are also periodic special exhibitions of work by Mexican and foreign artists.

Opening Times
Tues.–Sun.
10am–6pm

Monumento a los Niños Héroes

Just south of the museum can be seen the Monumento a los Niños Héroes (Monument to the Young Heroes), a semicircular structure of six columns decorated with fountains. It commemorates the last stand by the six young cadets in Chapultepec Castle during the siege by US forces in 1847. The sculpture shows a mother holding her dying soldier son in her arms, surrounded by six marble columns with bronze torches representing the six cadets.

On the top of a hill in the south-east corner of the park towers Chapultepec Castle (Castillo de Chapultepec), access to which is on foot, by bus or by lift.

Chapultepec Castle was built at the end of the 18th c. by the Spanish Viceroy Conde de Gálvez, as a summer residence, on a site once occupied by Aztec buildings and later by a Spanish hermitage. In 1841 it became a military academy, which six years later was to be the last

Mexican stronghold against US troops. Maximilian and Charlotte made the castle their residence and carried out various alterations in 1864–65. The dictator Porfirio Díaz also used it as a summer residence from 1884 onwards.

★ Museo Nacional de Historia

Opening Times
Tues.–Sun. 9am–5pm

In 1944 Chapultepec Castle finally became the National History Museum (Museo Nacional de Historia). The Museum's nineteen rooms contain, in addition to a collection of pre-Columbian material and reproductions of old manuscripts, a vast range of exhibits illustrating the history of Mexico since the Spanish conquest. These include arms and armour, documents, maps and plans of the Conquest period and its immediate aftermath; furniture, ceramics, clothing, jewellery and coins from three centuries; relics and souvenirs of the struggle for independence and the revolutionary wars; portraits of leading figures in Mexican history; frescos by Orozco, Siqueiros and O'Gorman, and a number of state carriages, including those used by Benito Juárez and the Emperor Maximilian. The apartments occupied by Maximilian and Charlotte, decorated in Neo-Classical style, contain the furniture which they brought from Europe.

From the castle there is a superb view of the city on a fine day.

Galería de Historia

The road down from the castle leads past the round, white building of the Galería de Historia (Gallery of History), where showcases depicting Mexican history from the time of the independence struggles (1810–21) up to the present day may be studied. Entrance to the gallery is on the upper floor, with a spiral passage leading down to the lower floor.

Lago Antiguo

North of the Castle lies Lago Antiguo, a lake divided into two by the Gran Avenida. On its west bank stands the Casa del Lago ("House on the Lake"), now belonging to the University and used for certain courses and cultural events.

Zoo and Botanic Garden

Auditorio Nacional

Between the lake and Calzada Molino on its west bank lie the Zoo (Parque Zoológico), the only zoo outside China in which giant pandas have successfully been bred, and the excellent Botanic Garden (Jardín Botánico). In the newer part of the park is the Auditorio Nacional, a huge hall with accommodation for 15,000 spectators, which is used for cultural events, sporting contests and so on.

Fuente de Netzahualcóyotl

South-west of the lake lies the Fountain of Netzahualcóyotl (Fuente de Netzahualcóyotl), commemorating the ruler of Texcoco who also made a name for himself as a poet and philosopher.

Los Pinos

The Calzado Molino cuts through the park from north to south and thence to Los Pinos ("The Pine Trees"), the official residence of the presidents of Mexico.

Nueve Bosque de Chapultepec

West of this road and of the Anillo Periférico stretches the newest part of Chapultepec Park together with the artficial lake known as Lago del Nuevo Bosque. South of this will be found the Fuente Lerma, a fountain with a basin containing an underwater mosaic by Diego Rivera.

A little to the east lies the Amusement Park, with a big dipper, and further to the south-west the modern Museum of Natural History (Museo de Historia Natural), the Museum of Technology (Museo Tecnológico) and a cemetery, the Panteón de Dolores.

★ Museo del Niño

Just outside the park, on the Avda. Constituyentes, are the very new, highly original, Pápalote Museo del Niño (No. 268), a high-tec children's museum to which adults are admitted only if accompanied by a child, and a lienzo charro in which Mexican rodeos (charreadas) are regularly held (No. 500).

Lienzo Charro

Just east of the National Museum of Anthropology, at the corner of Paseo de la Reforma and Calzada Gandhi, lies the Museo Rufino Tamayao, named after Rufino Tamayo (1900–91), one of Mexico's most famous painters. Designed by Abraham Zabludovsky and Teodore González with a most unusual interior, the building was officially opened in 1981. In addition to his own works it also displays Tamayo's own collection of several hundred works by contemporary artists, including prints, paintings, sculptures, wall-hangings, etc.

North section
Museo Rufino Tamayo

In the residential quarter (colonia) north of the National Museum of Anthropology the visitor will find a museum known as the Museo Sala de Arte Público David Álfaro Siqueiros, named after the artist of that name. In the house which formerly belonged to the Siqueiros family pictures, drawings, photographs and documents by this famous mural painter and member of the Communist Party are on display.

Museo Siqueiros

An impressive building of red marble near the Hotel Presidente Chapultepec on Calle Campos Eliseos houses the new Centro Cultural de Arte Contemporáneo belonging to the television company Televisa. The museum displays pre-Spanish art as well as contemporary Mexican and foreign painting and photography.

Centro Cultural de Arte Contemporáneo

★★National Museum of Anthropology

The National Museum of Anthropology, one of the most important of its kind in the world, is to be found in the northern section of Chapultepec Park. At the entrance stands a huge monolithic figure hitherto identified as the rain god Tláloc but in fact, according to the latest theories, more probably his sister, the water-goddess Chalchiuhtlicue (Náhuatl, "she of the jade-rock"). This colossal unfinished figure, weighing 167 tonnes, was found near San Miguel Coatlinchán (see Texcoco, Surroundings) and transported to its present site with the greatest difficulty.

The Museum was designed by Pedro Ramírez Vázquez and built in 1963–64. A strikingly successful example of contemporary architecture and of notably harmonious effect, it is one of the world's finest museums, with its old Indian art treasures magnificently displayed.

A notable feature is the Central Patio, part of which is roofed over by a kind of gigantic stone umbrella, sculpted by José Chávez Morado and borne on a column 11m/36ft high. From the top a continuous curtain of water falls into the basin below, symbolising the eternal cycle of life.

Metro Station
Chapultepec (Line 1)

Bus
Museo de Antropologia stop on Paseo de la Reforma

Opening Times
Tues.–Sat. 9am–7pm
Sun. 10am–6pm

Guided Tours

The Museum is divided into two completely separate sections dealing with different aspects. On the ground floor twelve rooms provide an introduction to anthropology and display archaeological finds from extinct Indian cultures, while the upper floor documents the life-styles of contemporary Indian inhabitants of Mexico. Each room is devoted to one centre of culture or group of people.

During the night on Christmas Day 1985 thieves managed to break into the Museum and stole 173 extremely valuable items, including many of the burial objects from Palenque (see entry). During a drugs raid in June 1989 most of these pieces were recovered and are once again on view.

Arrangement of the collection

In the Entrance Hall the museum shop (salón de venta) on the left sells books, guides, catalogues and reproductions of pre-Columbian

Ground Floor
Entrance Hall

UPPER FLOOR

I Introduction to Ethnology
II Sala Cora Huichel
III Sala Purépecha (Tarascans)
IV Sala Otomi-Pame (Toluca valley, Querétaro)
V Sala de Puebla (Otami, Tepehua, Totonacs, Nahua)
VI Sala de Oaxaca (Zapotecs, Mixtecs)
VII Sala Totonaca y Huasteca
VIII Sala Maya (Highlands)
IX Sala Maya (Lowlands)
X Sala del Norte (Seri, Talahumara)
XI "Indigenisimo" (measures to promote Indian development)

GROUND FLOOR

I Sala del Resumen (films, etc.)
II Temporary exhibitions
III Auditorium
IV Most recent excavations
V Introduction to Anthropology
VI Cultures of Meso-America
VII Sala de Prehistoria (Prehistory)
VIII Sala del Periodo Preclásico (pre-Classic or Formative epoch)
IX Sala de Teotihuacán
X Sala de Tula (Toltec Classic period)
XI Sala Méxica (Aztec Post-Classic period)
XII Sala de Oxaca (Zapotec-Mixtec culture)
XIII Sala de las Culturas del Golfo de México (Culture of the Gulf Coast)
XIV Sala Maya
XV Sala de las Culturas del Norte (Cultures of northern Mexico)
XVI Sala de las Culturas del Occidente (Cultures of western Mexico)
XVII Sala de Venta (Museum shop)
XVIII Monolith Chalchiuhticue

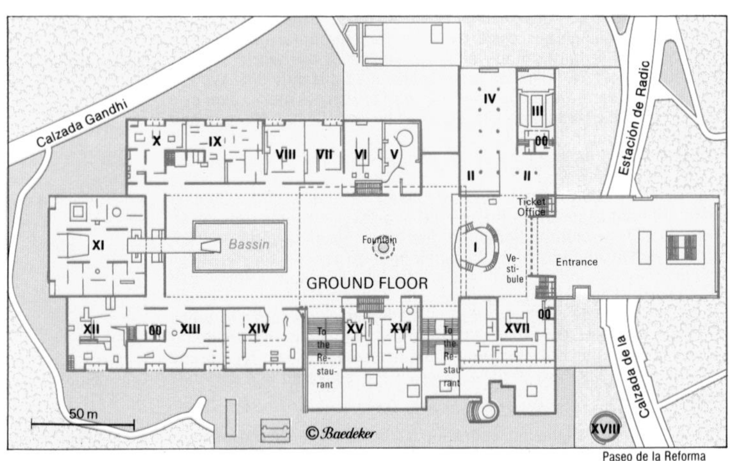

Paseo de la Reforma

Monolith of Chalchiuhlicue

A realistic Aztec head

objects. In the Sala de Resúmen (Orientation Room) in the centre of the Entrance Hall films and slides on the Museum and its collections are shown. On the right-hand wall is a mural by Rufino Tamayo, depicting a feathered serpent and a jaguar, the two central symbols of the ancient Indian gods. On that side, too, begins the anti-clockwise tour of the Museum, commencing with rooms in which temporary special exhibitions devoted to various aspects of pre-Columbian cultures are held.

Introduction to Anthropology

In this room the visitor is given a brief introduction to the study of mankind and allied subjects by means of models, dioramas, maps and drawings.

Cultures of Meso-America

This room covers the basic lives of the peoples of Meso-America, including hunting, weapons, animals hunted, the development of agricultural, population situation, rites (including burial customs and festivals) and cultural achievements in the fields of music, numerology, the calendar, writing, medicine, architecture and painting.

Sala de Prehistoria

The early history of human settlement in America begins with the arrival of Asiatic tribes by way of the Bering Strait. Other subjects covered include the development of the hunting and collecting cultures, with fossils of humans and animals, and the first attempts at agriculture on the Anáhuac plateau.

Sala del Período Preclásico

The pre-Classic or Formative period (1400–300 B.C.) is illustrated by means of exhibits showing developments in the fields of ceramics and other skills, including in particular some especially good examples of statues from Tlatilco, such as the female figures known as the "mujer bonita", the "Acrobat Vase" in the shape of a man in a grotesquely contorted pose, and a model of the pyramid at Cuicuilco (see later).

Sala de Teotihuacán

The four phases of the culture of the plateau of Teotihuacán (200 B.C.–A.D. 700; see entry) are illustrated by examples of artistic techniques of various kinds, particularly in the field of ceramics. Note particularly the sculptures of various deities, including Xipe Tótec (from Tlamimiloplan), Chalchiuhtlicue and Huehuetéotl. A section of the Quetzalcoátl Temple from Teotihuacán has been restored in its original colourings and decoration. There is also a reconstruction of the fresco "Paradise of Tláloc", showing the souls of warriors and drowning men frollicking together.

Sala de Tula

The outstanding example of the culture of the Toltecs from Tula (see Tollán) is one of the 4m/13ft high figures of Atlas. Other examples from the classical Toltec period (A.D. 700–1200) include stelae, Chac-mool sculptures and a warrior's head set with mother-of-pearl mosaic.

Sala México

★★Stone of the Fifth Sun

This section describes the Aztec culture from the coming of the Chichimecs through to the fall of Tenochtitlán. This room contains the highlight of the collection, the "Stone of the Fifth Sun", also wrongly described as the "Calendar Stone". Other notable exhibits include the Tizoc Stone, manuscripts, maps and sculptures, including those of Coatlicue and Xochipilli (Náhuatl, "lord of the flowers"), god of love, dancing and poetry. A mural by Miguel Covarrubias, a model of the temple precincts and a diorama of Tlatelolco market give some idea of the size and splendour of ancient Tenochtitlán. Moctezuma's headdress made of quetzal feathers is in fact only a reproduction; the original is housed in the ethnological museum in Vienna, where it arrived by a somewhat circuitous route. It was presented, together with a plumed shield and ritual fan, to the emperor Charles V who, in 1524, made a gift of them to his brother Ferdinand, the future Ferdinand I. In due course he gave them to his son, the archduke Ferdinand II, for

The "Stone of the Fifth Sun"

inclusion in the latter's art collection in Schloss Ambras in the Tyrol. From there they went to Vienna in 1806.

Sala de Oaxaca

The centre of the Zapotec-Mixtec culture (600 B.C.–c. A.D. 1500) was Monte Albán (see entry), whence came most of the ceramic and gold objects exhibited. Also displayed is a reproduction of Grave 7 from Monte Albán. Two of the showpieces of the collection – the mask of the god of bats, carved from green stone, and the Yanhuitlean breastplate of gold and turquoise – were stolen in the robbery of Christmas 1985.

Sala de las Culturas del Golfo de México

Here can be seen colossal Olmec sculptures standing in the open, Huastec stelae and painted ceramics, hachas (lit. axes; ceremonial objects), yugos and palmas (yokes and palms; stone objects probably connected with a ritual ball game of some kind) from El Tajín (see entry), all representative of Indian cultures from the Gulf of Mexico.

Sala Maya

The thieves of Christmas 1985 took a third of their booty from the Maya Room alone, a sign of how attractive this department is. A large proportion of the burial objects from Palenque (see entry), including a mask in jade mosaic, and various objects in gold, mother-of-pearl, turquoise and coral from the sacrificial well at Chichen Itzá (see entry) were recovered in 1989. Note the reproduction of the famous Palenque gravestone, the open-air reconstruction of the Temple at Bonampak (see entry) with its famous wall-paintings, stucco heads and stelae, as well as the particularly beautiful ceramics from the island of Jaína and some fine stonework fron Chichén Itzá.

Sala de las Culturas de Norte

The cultures of the Indians from Northern Mexico are represented by burial objects, everyday utensils, ceramics and various finds from Casas Grandes (see Chihuahua, State) and La Quemada.

Sala de las Culturas de Occidente

Fine terracotta figures from Jalisco, Nayarit and Colima give a picture of daily life in the period before the arrival of the Spaniards. There is also some Tarascan material.

Upper Floor

The ethnological collections on the Upper Floor are so arranged that the cultures of the descendants of various extinct peoples are positioned directly above those which they superseded. The collections include costumes, utensils and dwellings of the Indians still living in Mexico today.

Commencing from the right, the room providing an Introduction to Ethnology is followed by the Sala Cora-Huichol, Sala Purépecha (Tarascans), Sal Otomí-Pame (Toluca valley, Querétaro) and Sala de Puebla (Otomí, Tepehua, Totonacs, Nahua). Opposite these will be found the Sala de Oaxaca (Zapotecs, Mixtecs), Sala Totonaca y Huasteca, two rooms dealing with the Maya (Highlands and Lowlands) and Sala del Norte (Seri, Tarahumara). Finally, there is the "Indigenismo" room, dealing with measures to promote Indian development, together with selected craft products.

National Library of Anthropology

The Museum also houses the National Library of Anthropology, founded by Lucas Alamean in 1831 and developed by the Emperor Maximilian; it now has more than 300,000 volumes.

A few years ago the State School of Anthropology was moved to the Isidro Favela housing estate at Periférico Sur y Zapote. In 1983 the museum opened a new section containing workshops, exhibitions and gardens.

The Northern Outskirts

Access

These sights lie north of the motorway ring-road (Avenida Río Consulado and Calzado Melchor Ocampo); the best way to get there is by Metro (Lines 3, 5 and 6) or by taxi.

★The Basilicas of Guadalupe

Location
about 6km/4 miles north of the Zócalo

Metro Station
Basilica (Line 3)

Atahualpa Memorial

When travelling by taxi the pilgrimage churches of Guadalupe can be reached by either of two routes.

The Paseo de la Reforma initially leads north to its junction with Avenida Matamoros. On the roundabout stands a statue of the last Inca of Peru, Atahualpa, brought here from the Peruvian town of Cuzco in exchange for a figure of the penultimate Aztec ruler Cuitláhuac which now stands in the Plaza de Armas in Cuzco. In the Tlatelolco district of the city the road continues to the Glorieta de Peralvillo, from where the Calzada de Guadalupe and Calzada de los Misterios lead direct to the pilgrimage site.

Monumento a la Raza

The westerly route leads from Buenavista station (Estación Central) along Avenida Insurgentes Norte to a busy traffic junction, where Calzado Vallejo (leading to Tenayuca; see entry), Avenid Rio Consulado and Insurgentes Norte all meet. On the roundabout stands the massive pyramidal Monumento a la Raza, a monument to the mingling of the European and Indian races built in 1964 by a team of sculptors under the direction of Luis Lelo de Larrea. Every year on October 12th, the date on which Columbus discovered the New World, the Día de la Raza is celebrated here. Nearby stands the Hospital de la Raza, with frescos by David Siqueiros and Diego Rivera.

Rancho Grande

"Indios Verdes"

At the end of Insurgentes Norte, on the left, lies the Rancho Grande (Lienzo Grande), where charreadas (the Mexican equivalent of the rodeo) are held regularly. A short distance beyond this stand two bronze statues, one on each side of the road, known as the Indios Verdes ("Green Indians") – the Aztec rulers Itzcóatl (1426–40) and Ahuítzotl (1486–1502). The road then continues to the Glorieta Lindavista roundabout, with Calle Montevideo on the right leading to the pilgrimage site.

Old Basilica

The Old Basilica of Nuestra Señora de Guadalupe was built in 1709 on the site of an earlier 16th c. church and several times altered since. The exterior is unremarkable, but the interior (now closed for safety reasons) is impressive, with its wide nave and the contrast between the white marble and the gilded ornamentation; it made an even deeper impression on the observer when it was thronged with pilgrims, imbued with the profound native piety of the ordinary Mexican.

New Basilica

When this church sank ever deeper into the swampy subsoil and became dangerous it was replaced by the New Basilica, a modern structure of concrete and marble which was designed by Pedro Ramírez Vázquez, architect of the National Museum of Anthropology, and consecrated in 1976. The spacious interior, which apart from the figure of the Virgin of Guadalupe contains no statues or pictures, can accommodate a congregation of 20,000. An unusual feature is a "four-lane" conveyor-belt behind the high altar which automatically and smoothly conveys worshippers – many of them kneeling – past the statue of the Virgin.

Legend of the Virgin

According to legend the Virgin Mary appeared on December 9th 1531 to Juan Diego, a baptised Aztec, in the form of a dark-skinned Indian woman who charged him to ask the bishop to have a chapel built for her on a particular spot. Bishop Juan de Zumárraga did not believe the story and asked for proof. Thereupon the Virgin appeared to Juan Diego a second time on December 12th and caused roses to bloom on a bare hilltop, although it was then the season of drought. Juan Diego plucked the roses and took them to the bishop, but when he opened the folds of the cloak in which he had been carrying them it was seen to bear an image of the Virgin surrounded by a radiant halo. This, it is

Basilica of Guadalupe

believed, is the miracle-working Image of the Virgin of Guadalupe which now hangs above the high altar in the New Basilica. Bishop de Zumárraga caused a shrine to be built on the Hill of Tepeyac, on the site of an earlier Aztec temple of the earth-mother Tonantzin. Soon the church and the Image of the Virgin began to attract large numbers of pilgrims; and even the Indians, who had been disillusioned with Christianity by the cruelties of the colonial regime, became more willing to accept the Christian faith. After being venerated for centuries as the patroness of the Indians and mestizos, the Virgin of Guadalupe was invoked in the struggle for Mexican independence, and in 1810 Miguel Hidalgo inscribed her image on the banner of the insurgents.

Pilgrimage site

The Basilica is visited by many thousands of pilgrims throughout the year, but on December 12th, the anniversary of the Virgin's second apparition, the square in front of the church as well as the building itself is filled to overflowing. The colourfully garbed dancers and mimes who are everywhere to be seen help to create an atmosphere of a great popular fiesta. The Virgin of Guadalupe is venerated by all classes of the Mexican population, and in addition draws pilgrims from many other countries in Latin America. These manifestations of popular faith have been called the "culto guadalupano", and it is a notable fact that many of its aspects lie outside the bounds of Catholic dogma and frequently show affinities with pre-Christian myths.

Capillo del Pocito

Near the old Basilica stands the late 18th c. Capilla del Pocito (Chapel of the Spring), designed by Francisco de guerrero y Torres; the dome is faced with azulejos. Bubbling out of a rock inside the chapel is a spring credited with healing powers, and the faithful come here to fill their bottles with its water.

Capuchin church

An old Capuchin church now houses a Museum of Religious Art, which displays treasures from the old Basilica and large numbers of votive offerings, mainly of silver.

Capilla del Tepeyac

On the Hill of Tepeyac, from which there are fine views of the surrounding area on a fine day, stands the Capilla del Tepeyac, with frescos by Fernando Leal depicting the miracle. It was built in the 18th c. on the spot where the Virgin is said to have appeared to Juan Diego.

North of Chapultepec

Fuente de Petróleos

At the north-west end of Chapultepec Park the Paseo de la Reforma passes the Fuente de Petróleos, a fountain erected to commemorate the nationalisation of foreign oil companies in 1938.

The Paseo now crosses the Anillo Periférico and turns south-west to pass through the elegant residential district of Lomas de Chapultepec.

The Annillo Periférico continues north-westward to become Bulevar Avila Camacho; on the left lies the Hipódromo de las Américas, a racetrack which can accommodate 60,000 spectators, followed by the Olympic Sports centre (Centro Olímpico Mexicano). Beyond this, on the right, is the El Toreo bullring, with seating for 35,000 spectators (reconstruction in progress).

Tacuba

Location
5km/3 miles north-west of the Zócalo

Metro Station
Cuitlahuac (Line 2)

"Arbol de la Noche Triste"

To the right of Avenida Manuel Avila Camacho extends the district of Tacuba, formerly Tlacopan, which in pre-Columbian times was capital of the Tepanec kingdom for three generations until the defeat of the Tepanecs by other Nahua tribes in 1428. The victorious cities of Tenochtitlán, Texcoco and Tlacopan then formed a triple alliance which lasted until the Mexica established their predominant authority. In the middle of Tacuba near the Cuitlahuac Metro station (Calle Campos Elíseos y Jorge Eliot) stands the Arbol de la Noche Triste ("Tree of the Sad Night"), recently damaged by fire, an ahuehuete (swamp cypress) under which Cortés is said to have lamented his defeat of June 30th 1520 when the Aztecs drove him and his troops temporarily out of Tehochtitlán.

★House of Masks

At No. 71 Avenida Ribera de San Cosme, which begins in Tacuba and leads to the centre, stands the House of Masks (Casa de los Mascarones), with the finest Churrigueresque façade on any secular building in the city.

La Virgen de los Remedios

Location
13km/8 miles north-west of the Zócalo

Bus
from Tacuba Metro Station (Line 2)

2km/1¼ miles north of the El Toreo bullring the Avenida Manuel Avila Camacho joins the Avenida 16 de Septiembre. Going left along this and continuing along Calle de los Remedios the visitor will see the church of La Virgen de los Remedios, consecrated in 1629 and a place of pilgrimage in which a statue of the Virgin brought from Spain by the conquistadors is venerated. During the struggles for independence (1810–21) the royalist troops carried flags bearing the image of this Virgin of Perpetual Succour, while the victorious Mexicans fought under the banner of the Virgin of Guadalupe. There is an annual fiesta in honour of the Virgen de los Remedios on September 8th.

★Functionless Towers

Returning to the main road, the MEX 57, and going north away from the city we come, at the entrance to the new suburb known as the Ciudad Satellite, to the Goeritz or Functionless Towers (1957) – five coloured prismatic obelisks of different heights which represent an interesting attempt by the Danzig artist and architect Mathias Goeritz to combine sculpture and architecture.

The Southern Outskirts

South of the Viaducto Miguel Alemán lie the districts of Mixcoac, Coyoacán, San Angel, San jerónimo, El Pedregal, Tlalpan and Xochimilco. The best way to travel to these districts and places of interest is again by underground (Lines 1, 2 and 3) or by taxi.

Access

A large number of buses to the southern outskirts depart from the Insurgentes Metro station (Line 1).

Along the Insurgentes Sur

About 3km/2 miles from its junction with the Paseo de la Reforma, on the right of Avenida Insurgentes Sur, lies the Parque de la Lama with the as yet uncompleted Hotel de México, the city's tallest building.

Parque de la Lama

In the hotel grounds, on Calle Filadelfia, stands the very modern Polyforum Siqueiros, a twelve-sided mushroom-like edifice built in 1965–69 and designed by José David Siqueiros (1886–1974), who was also responsible for the "plastic" mural, "The March of Mankind", in the large egg-shaped hall inside. Regular son et lumière shows are given in this hall which emphasise the effect of this painting which covers an area of 2400sq.m/26,000sq.ft. The building also includes a theatre, conference and exhibition halls and sale-rooms for arts and crafts.

★Polyforum Siqueiros

3km/2 miles further south lies Ciudad de los Deportes ("City of Sport"), with a football stadium accommodating 65,000 spectators and Plaza México, the largest bullring in the world, with 60,000 seats.

Ciudad de los Deportes

★Coyoacán

Location
10km/6 miles south-west of the Zócalo

Metro Stations
Coyoacán, Viveros, Quevedo (Line 3) General Anaya (Line 2)

From Insurgentes Sur the taxi will turn left into Río Churubusco and then right along Avenida Universidad into the district of Coyoacán (Náhuatl, "town of the coyotes"), which has preserved much of the tranquil atmosphere of colonial times. At the corner of Avenida Universidad and Calle Francisco Sosa, a few minutes from the Viveros and Quevedo underground stations, stand the modern church of El Altillo ("The Hillock") and the little 18th c. Baroque Capilla de San Antonio (Panzacola). Calle Francisco Sosa, lined by handsome 17th and 18th c. houses, leads to the main square, Plaza Hidalgo, in which will be seen the church of San Juan Bautista, built by Dominicans in 1538. Very typical of the style of the period, it boasts a fine, richly carved doorway on the side leading into the atrium which has Indian decoration. On the left inside will be found the interesting High Baroque Capilla de Santísima.

★Calle Francisco Sosa

San Juan Bautista

At Hidalgo 289 is the National Museum of Popular Culture (Museo Nacional de Culturas Populares), in which (somewhat unusually for museums of this kind) the exhibits are more than just that – they make things come alive and bring the visitor into close contact with the living traditions of the various Mexican ethnic groups.

Museo Nacional de Culturas Populares

Proceeding north from the square, Avenida Centenario leads to Calle Londres. At Londres 247, on the corner of Calle Allende, the Frida Kahlo Museum is well worth a visit. This little blue house was the birthplace of the painter Frida Kahlo (1910–54), who was confined to a wheelchair and lived here with her husband Diego Rivera from 1929 until her death. The rooms have been left just as they were during her lifetime. Leon Trotsky stayed in the house as a guest after his arrival in Mexico in 1937. In addition to personal mementoes and works by Frida and her husband the museum contains pictures and sculptures by 18th and

★Frida Kahlo Museum

Opening Times
Tues.–Sun.
10am–2pm
and 3–5pm

19th c. Mexican artists, as well as pre-Columbian objects and examples of Mexican folk-art from Frida Kahlo's private collection.

★Leon Trotsky Museum

Opening Times
Tues.–Sun.
10am–5pm

At the corner of Calles Viena and Morelos stands the Leon Trotsky Museum. In this house, which he had converted into a veritable fortress, Trotsky lived in exile until he was murdered with an ice-pick on August 20th 1940 by Ramón Mercader, an agent of Joseph Stalin. Today visitors are guided through the rooms by members of the Trotskyite Partido Revolucionario de los Trabajadores (Workers' Revolutionary Party). Trotsky's study is just as it was on the day he was killed, with his broken spectacles still lying on the desk. The walls of the simply-furnished bedroom show bullet-holes from an earlier attack by Stalinists in which the painter David Álfaro Siqueiros was involved. There is a tablet by the entrance in memory of Trotsky's bodyguard who was also shot. The great revolutionary and his wife are buried in the garden (tomb by Juan O'Gorman).

★Museo Nacional de las Intervenciones

Opening Times
daily 9am–9pm

The Museo Nacional de las Intervenciones on Calle 20 de Agosto, a few minutes' walk from the General Anaya underground station (Line 20, is housed in the former Franciscan friary of Churubusco. Opened in 1981, the museum boasts a remarkable collection of photos, weapons, pictures, flags and historical documents which provide an interesting if somewhat subjective portrayal of Mexico's wars against invading armies – the struggles for independence between 1810 and 1821 with subsequent Spanish intervention, the war with the United States 1846–48, the French Wars of Intervention of 1838 and 1861–67, and finally the revolutionary period during which US troops invaded Mexico. The situation of the museum is very relevant to the exhibits, because it was on this very spot in 1847 that the Battle of Churubusco took place, when the Mexicans under General Anaya found themselves outnumbered and were decisively defeated by US troops under General Winfield Scott.

Centro National para los Artes

In the autumn of 1994 the National Centre for the Arts opened on land formerly occupied by the Churubusco film studios. Designed by six leading Mexican architects, the Centre houses institutes and academies representing a variety of art forms.

★Anahuacalli (Diego Rivera Museum)

Opening Times
Tues.–Sun.
10am–2pm
and 3–5pm

A somewhat longer but most rewarding taxi-ride will take the visitor further south via Avenida División del Norte for some 3km/2 miles and thence along Calle del Museo, to the right. In the House of Anáhuac ("Anahuacalli"), a pyramid-like structure based on a Maya grave and designed by the artist himself, Diego Rivera laid out his own collection of pre-Columbian material, some 200 objects – primarily ceramics – of various Western cultures and Aztec stone sculptures. A reconstruction of his studio gives visitors an insight into the artist's career.

Aztec Stadium

Avenida División del Norte now enters Calzada Tlalpan, which leads to the famous Aztec Stadium (Estadio Azteca) which was built in 1986 for the 1968 Olympic Games and also hosted the Soccer World Cup Finals in 1970 and 1986. It has seating for 115,000 spectators.

Villa Obregón

Location 10km/
6 miles south-west of the Zócalo

Metro Station
Quevedo (Line 3)

Continuing south on Insurgentes Sur from its junction with Río Mixcoac and Río Churubusco we see on the right the modern Teatro de los Insurgentes, a circular building with a mosaic by Diego Rivera on the façade depicting the history of the Mexican theatre. To the right stretches the district of Tlacopac.

The Insurgentes Sur continues south to the district of Villa Obregón, passing on the left the Álvaro Obregón Monument which commemorates the revolutionary hero and President, murdered here in 1928. The sculpture and relief carving on this massive granite memorial are by Ignacio Asúnsolo. A macabre showpiece to be found in the memorial is a glass container in which is preserved in spirit Obregón's hand and arm which he lost during the revolutionary struggles.

Álvaro Obregón Monument

The eastern part of the district, to the right of Insurgentes Sur, is known as San Ángel. One block west of the Obregón monument, on the corner of Avenidas Revolución and La Paz, is the Museo Colonial del Carmel. It is housed in a former Carmelite convent (1617) dedicated to the martyr, San Angelo, from whom the little town takes its name. Notable features of the building, which is richly decorated with azulejos, include the Virgen del Carmen in Talavera mosaics, a de caña figure of Christ, paintings by Cristóbal de Villalpando and some valuable religious objects. The patio has a beautiful tiled fountain, and in the crypt, which contains a number of mummified bodies, nobles and nuns lay buried. The sacristy boasts a beautiful panelled ceiling and some fine colonial furniture.

★ San Ángel

Museo Colonial del Carmen

A little way to the west lies the picturesque Plaza San Jacinto, where the Bazar Sábado is held on Saturdays. In a 17th c. building in the square is a shop selling traditional handicraft articles as well as modern art.

Plaza San Jacinto

Buildings 5 and 15 on the north side of the square house the Museo Casa del Risco ("House of the Cliff"); this is an 18th c. palace with valuable antiques and an interesting two-tier fountain faced with tiles and ceramics. Paintings on display are 14th–18th c. from Europe and Mexico. Historically the square is of some importance, for it was here that in 1847, during the war between Mexico and the United States, sixteen Irish deserters from the US army who had fought on the Mexican side were captured and hanged.

Museo Casa del Risco

In 1929 Juan O'Gorman erected a purpose-built house at the corner of what are now Calles Altavista and Rivera (Palmas), where Diego Rivera stayed from time to time between 1933 and 1957. Today it contains the Museo Estudio Diego Rivera, where visitors can study the artist's life with the aid of personal documents, clothing, furniture, pictures, drawings and photographs.

Museo Estudio Diego Rivera

Another museum in the San Ángel quarter is the Museum of Art (Museo de Arte) on Calle Alvar y Carmen T. de Carillo Gil, in which are exibited works by the great muralists as well as those by some lesser-known contemporary Mexican artists such as Gunther Gerzo and Wolfgang Paalen.

Museo de Arte

From San Ángel the Calzada del Desierto de los Leones leads to the Desierto de los Leones National Park, some 25km/15 miles away. At an altitude of some 3000m/9800ft, this magnificent expanse of coniferous forest surrounding a beautiful 17th c. Carmelite convent is a popular resort of the people of Mexico City.

Excursion to the Desierto de los Leones National Park

Copilco

The Insurgentes Sur continues south from Villa Obregón to the district of Copilco, lying on the fringes of El Pedregal, a vast sheet of lava 6–8m/20–25ft thick covering an area of some 40sq.km/15sq. miles. The lava was deposited mainly around 30 B.C. and A.D. 300 following eruptions of the Xitle volcano (3120m/10,237ft). On this site University City and the residential quarter of Pedregal de San Ángel to the west were built, using the local lava in the construction of many of the buildings. Excavation has revealed evidence of a culture which was brought to an abrupt end by the eruption of the volcano.

Excavation site

Taking Avenida Copilco, which leads east off Insurgentes Sur, and turning left into Calle Victoria, the visitor will see the offices of the National Institute of Anthropology and History (No. 110), which administers the excavation site. Here, under a 3m/10ft thick layer of lava, were found a number of graves containing skeletons, stone implements, pottery and figurines, some of them dating from the Archaic period (before 1500 B.C.).

★Ciudad Universitaria

Location
12km/7½ miles south-west of the Zócalo

Metro station
Universidad (Line 3)

The district of Ciudad Universitaria (University City) lies south of Copilco, with Avenida Insurgentes Sur running through it. Begun during the presidency of Miguel Alemán it covers an area of 3sq.km/1sq. mile and consists of more than 80 buildings housing some 350,000 students. The complex was primarily planned by José García Villagrán, Mario Pani and Enrique del Moral, and some 150 architects were involved in the work.

★Rector's Office
★Central Library

Among the principal buildings, many of them decorated with old Indian symbols, are the Rector's Office, with its harmonious alternation of horizontal and vertical features including frescos by Siqueiros, and the Central Library, with its windowless ten-storey book stack, the façade of which has a mosaic in natural stone by Juan O'Gorman which is the largest anywhere in the world, the four panels each measuring 1200sq.m/12,920sq.ft. The Auditorium of the Science Faculty has a glass mosaic by José Chávez Morado, and the Faculty of Medicine a mural by Francisco Eppens Huelguera. The extensive sports facilities include a large swimming pool, football and baseball pitches, tennis and jai alai courts. To the south of the main University buildings is a concert hall seating 2500, the Sala de Netzahualcóyotl.

Ciudad Universitaria: Rector's Office, with frescos by Siqueiros

Tower of the Central Library

Olympic Stadium

On the west side of Insurgentes Sur the Olympic Stadium, decorated with coloured stone reliefs by Diego Rivera, can seat more than 80,000 spectators. Like some other buildings on the University campus, it incorporates features taken from pre-Columbian architecture.

Botanic Garden

Near the University, to the right, lies the University Botanic Garden.

Cuicuilco

Location
15km/9½ miles west of the Zócalo

About 3·5km/2 miles south of the Olympic Stadium and immediately beyond the underpass below the Anillo Periférico, a road branches off on the left to the archaeological site of Cuicuilco (Náhuatl: "place of singing and dancing").

Probably first established by a farming community of the Formative period (900–700 B.C., Cuicuilco enjoyed its heyday between 500 and 200 B.C., when it must have played a dominant role in the region and had a population of some 20,000. As its rival town of Teotihuacán grew in importance, however, Cuicuilco became less so, and the site was finally abandoned before the final eruption of the Xitle volcano *c.* 50 B.C.; presumably the inhabitants moved to Teotihuacán (see entry) and Tlapacoya (see Amecameca, Surroundings).

Circular Pyramid

The Circular Pyramid, erected between 600 and 400 B.C. and today 18m/60ft high, has a diameter of 112m/365ft, and since the eruption of Xitle has been covered and surrounded by lava. During the difficult process of excavation part of the structure was destroyed, and the restoration is of doubtful authenticity. The pyramid seems originally to have been an artificial earth mound, which was subsequently built over on several occasions. The primitive fortress-like style of the pyramid reflects the very beginnings of pre-Columbian monumental religious architecture.

The pyramid consists of five circular tiers of decreasing size, ending in a platform with the remains of an altar. There were probably two staircases leading up to the top of the pyramid, originally 27m/90ft high.

In addition to the principal pyramid excavations have brought to light a further one which could be even older, together with the remains of a horseshoe-shaped altar covered in stones from the river and – to the right of the main entrance to the principal pyramid – a chamber built of stone slabs showing signs of having been painted red. Large numbers of figurines, jewellery and everyday objects of terracotta and stone have also been unearthed. The central deity of Cuicuilco seems to have been the old fire-god Huehuetéotl, who would naturally be associated with the active volcanoes in the surrounding area.

Museum

The museum contains finds, mainly terracottas, from the pre-Classic period which are associated with Cuicuilco.

★ Tlalpan

To the south of the site lies the attractive suburb of Tlalpan (Náhuatl, "footprint of man"), a quiet residential area which is also a popular weekend resort. Between 1827 and 1830 it was the capital of México state. It boasts a number of fine colonial buildings, including the 16th c. church of San Agustín de las Cuevas and the 18th c. Casa Chata, which once housed the infamous Inquisition and is now a restaurant.

From Tlalpan the Anillo Periférico Sur leads to Xochimilco, with its "floating gardens" (see below).

★ Xochimilco

Location
20km/12½ miles south-east of the Zócalo

Metro Station
Tasqueña (Line 2); thence by tram, bus or group taxi

The little town of Xochimilco (Náhuatl, "place of the flower-fields"), on the southern outskirts of Mexico City on the far side of the Anillo Periférico Sur, with a population which still includes many Nahua Indians, was probably founded at the end of the 12th c. by Toltec refugees from Tula. In the 13th c. a Náhuatl-speaking nomadic tribe related to the Aztecs settled here; they later became known as Chinampanecs owing to the "chinampa" system of cultivation which they practised.

★ Floating gardens

Under this system the crops were planted on small rafts covered with mud and water plants and held together by a retaining screen of interwoven reeds, which eventually became anchored to the lake bottom by the growth of roots.The abundance of water and the fertilising effect of the mud enabled these "floating gardens" to produce up to seven crops a year, ensuring a plentiful food supply for Tenochtitlán.

Around 1430 Xochimilco was conquered by the Aztecs, saw bitter fighting during the Conquest (1521) and was finally burned down by the Spaniards.

This is still an important flower and vegetable-growing region. Little remains of the former lagoon. In the 1970s and 1980s the region suffered from lack of water and from pollution, but – with help from UNO – further waterways have now been opened up and an ecological park covering 3000ha/7500 acres is being laid out. The "floating gardens" are now once again a favourite place for week-end outings with both the locals and tourists, who can sail along these waterways on brightly-painted and flower-decked boats known as "trajineras", accompanied by other boats selling food, drinks and handmade articles or bearing bands of mariachi musicians. Xochimilco has now been declared a world cultural heritage site by UNESCO.

In the "Floating Gardens" of Xochimilco ▶

★San Bernadino

In Xochimilco itself the parish church of San Bernadino is worth a visit. The present church, on the site of an earlier Franciscan foundation (1535), was probably built about 1590, and is thus one of the oldest in the country. Note the Indian-Plateresque façade of the main door, a rare 16th c. Renaissance retablo, the 17th c. choir-stalls and a crucifix with a figure of Christ formed from maize stems in a typically Indian technique ("de caña"). There is also an interesting Saturday market.

Michoacán (State)

Abbreviation: Mich. Capital: Morelia
Area: 60,093sq.km/23,202sq. miles.
Official population 1990: 3,548,000 (1994 estimate: 3,650,000)

Location and Topography

Michoacán is bordered on the north by the states of Guanajuato and Jalisco, on the west by Jalisco and Colima, on the south by the Pacific Ocean and Guerrero and on the east by the Estado de México and Querétaro. The lakes and volcanoes of the high plateaux are in strong contrast to the subtropical valleys with their rivers, waterfalls and ravines, and the undisturbed white beaches, all of which contribute to the particularly attractive landscape found here. The highest point of the mainly-forested Michoacán mountains is Pico de Tancítaro (3850m/12,636ft). The rivers Lerma, Tepalcatepec and Balsas flow into the Pacific Ocean. Michoacán is mainly populated by mestizos and Indians from the Tarascan (Purépecha) tribe as well as a smaller number of Nahua Indians.

Archaeological Sites

Several pre-Columbian, predominantly Tarascan sites are to be found in the state of Michoacán. These include Tzintzuntzan (see entry), Ihuatzio (see Tzintzuntzan), Zacapu (see Lake Pátzcuaro), Tingambato and Los Alzati (see Morelia) and Tres Cerritos.

History

Present-day Michoacán (Náhuatl: "place of the fishermen") was probably first settled in the 11th and 12th c. by Indians from the north-west. It later became known as Purépecha and following the Spanish Conquista was called Tarasken. Michoacán's old-Indian and colonial history has close ties with its capital Morelia and the towns of Pátzcuaro and Tzintzuntzan.

Inhabitants of Michoacán such as Ignacio López Rayón, Gerdis Bocanegra and José María Morelos played important parts in Mexico's War of Independence (1810–21). Morelos is also linked to the convening of the first legislative assembly and the publication of the constitution in Apatzingán on October 22nd 1814. Michoacán became a state of the Mexican republic in December 1821. Melchor Ocampo (1814–61), liberal co-author of the radical reform laws of 1859 under the presidency of Benito Juárez, was also a native of the state. The Mexican president General Lázaro Cárdenas (1895–1970), who dispossessed the foreign oil companies during his term in office (1934–40), came from Jiquilpan.

Economy

The cultivation of grain, vegetables, fruit and coffee plays an essential role in the economy, while forestry, cattle breeding and especially mining (gold, silver, lead, copper and iron ore) are also of importance. Hydro-electricity generation and the steel industry have recently developed rapidly. Trade, traditional crafts and tourism are additional mainstays of the economy. Communications have been greatly improved during the past decades. Lázaro Cárdenas is now one of Mexico's busiest ports.

Places of Interest

In addition to the well-known places of interest and their surroundings, such as Morelia (see entry), Lake Pátcuaro (see entry), Tzintzuntzan (see entry) and Uruapan (see entry), the following towns in the state of Michoacán should also be mentioned:

Zamora de Hidalgo (1600m/5152ft; population 123,000) with its 19th c. Neo-Classical cathedral; Apatzingán de la Constitución (680m/2232ft; population 79,000), home of the Museo de la Casa de la Constitución; Lázaro Cárdenas (population 290,000), a modern industrial port with a large steelworks and petro-chemical and fertiliser industries; La Piedad Cavadas (population 69,000); Jiquilpan de Juárez (1645m/542ft; population 29,000) with the San Francisco Church (17th c. portal), the Bibliothek Gabino Ortíz featuring murals by José Clemente Orozco and the Casa Museo del General Lázaro Cárdenas; Playa Azul (at sea-level; population 14,000), a fishing village and popular seaside resort. A few miles north, a coast road, in parts very winding, passes lonely beaches and picturesque bays via Tecomán on the way to Manzanillo (see entry).

Mitla L 9

State: Oaxaca (Oax.)
Altitude: 1480m/4857ft
Population: 20,000

Access

By bus from Oaxaca about 1 hour; by car from Oaxaca on the MEX 190 eastwards via El Tule, after 38km/24 miles turn off left to Mitla, 4km/2½ miles away.

Location

The ruined site of Mitla, situated on the edge of the village of the same name, is one of Mexico's most famous archaeological attractions.

★ Stone ornamentation

Although the site, like its architecture, appears fairly unimposing, the elaborate stone ornamentation is unsurpassed in the art history of Meso-America.

History

The mountains around what became known as Mitla were already settled around 6000 B.C., as can be concluded from cave finds. As the area around Oaxaca saw a constant shift in population, the prehistory of Mitla (Náhuatl: Mictlán = "place of the dead") proves difficult to unravel. Zapotec influences certainly dominated the Classical period, i.e. during the Monte Albán III a and III b (A.D. 100–800) phases. After A.D. 900 the influence of the Mixtecs (Náhuatl: "those from the land of the clouds") is evident. These people, who lived mainly in north Oaxaca and who were under attack from the Toltecs from Tollán (Tula) between the 10th and the 12th c., slowly migrated south into the Zapotec kingdom. Through war and marriage the Mixtecs were able, until the arrival of the Spanish, to seize about three-quarters of the approximately 200 important places ruled by the Zapotecs and by other peoples. It is thought that the Mixtecs exercised considerable influence over Mitla between A.D. 900–1500. However, stylistic elements which are neither Mixtec nor Zapotec date from the important period of the 10th and 11th c. and it remains impossible to know who contributed to the development of these interesting sites. The 14th c. ceramics found at Mitla are almost wholly Mixtec in origin. In 1494 the Aztecs, who were advancing towards Oaxaca, managed to capture the town.

When the Spanish came to Mitla in 1521 the town was inhabited mainly by Zapotecs. By 1576 the Spaniard Diego García de Palacio was

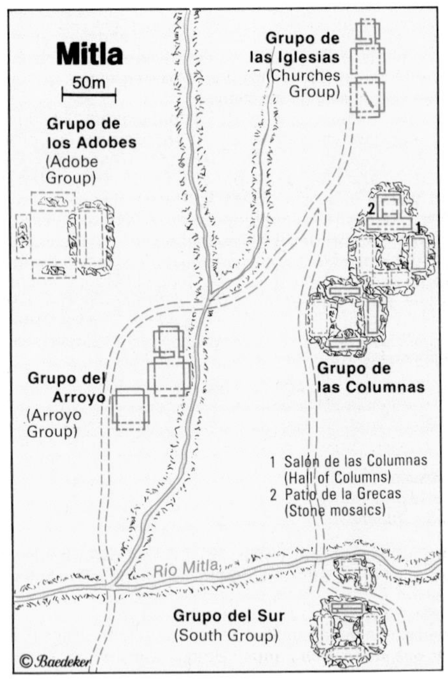

already reporting on Mitla. He was followed by Francisco de Burgoa, who recorded his impressions in 1679. Other chroniclers included Alexander von Humboldt, Guillermo Dupaix and Eduard Seler.

Visit to the ruins

The archaeological area includes five important groups of buildings and a large number of houses and tombs around these groups.

★Grupo de las Columnas

The most important complex, the Grupo de las Columnas (Group of Columns), is in the eastern part of the site. The palace-style construction comprises two square patios meeting at one corner. The inner courtyards are each surrounded by three large rooms.

Salón de las Columnas

An altar stands in the middle of the first patio which measures 45m/148ft×36m/118ft. Steps lead on the northern side to a platform via which the Salón de las Columnas (Hall of Columns) is entered through three doors. This room (38m/125ft×7m/23ft), once roofed, has six round porphyry columns 4.20m/13¾ft tall and almost 1m/3ft in diameter.

★Patio de las Grecas

A narrow low-roofed passage leads to a small inner courtyard, called the Patio de las Grecas, surrounded by long narrow rooms. The high priest Uija-táo (Náhuatl: "he who sees everything"), who was at the same time the region's most important judge, is supposed to have lived here.

The walls of the courtyard and of the rooms are decorated with stone mosaic-work typical of Mitla. These mosaic walls were created by

Mitla: typical stone ornamentation in the Patio de las Grecas

covering the walls with a layer of mortar into which precisely-squared stones were set in clear patterns. All of the extremely elaborate designs are geometric – human and mythological portrayals were not found in Mitla – and can be seen in no fewer than fourteen variations. Diagonal and interlaced bands alternate with gradual meanders, zigzag friezes and other ornamentation "á la grecque". Their appearance alters through the play of light and shadow. It is thought that the different forms symbolise religious ideas such as those of the feathered serpent or of the sky and the earth. It is estimated that more than 100,000 precisely-cut mosaic stones were used in the decoration of this construction.

Also typical of the architecture of Mitla are the impressive expertly-hewn square stone blocks which served as lintels and posts.

The installation of these stone blocks, which measure up to 8m/26ft long and weigh 23 tonnes, must have been an enormous achievement for people who were without the use of the wheel and who had neither pack nor draught animals.

Patio de las Cruces

The Patio de las Cruces (Patio of the Crosses) adjoins the Patio de las Grecas on its south side and is itself bordered to the east by a building with a magnificent colonnaded entrance, also hewn from heavy square stone blocks.

Burial Chambers

In front of this is an underground cross-shaped burial chamber. This is also decorated with meander mosaics for which larger stone slabs were used. This well-preserved tomb was found plundered, as were a number of others in Mitla. The tomb, also cruxiform, situated on the north side was borne by a column called the Columna de la Muerte (Column of Death). Visitors embrace this column and measure how much of it they cannot reach. This is said to indicate how long they have left to live.

Grupo de las Iglesias

The Churches Group (Grupo de las Iglesias), located to the north, is named after the Iglesia de San Pablo and was built by the conquering Spanish in the middle of the old-Indian walls. The ground plan of this site resembles that of the group of columns but on a smaller scale. A patio and part of the buildings surrounding it fell victim to the construction work. The northern patio was partially retained; this and a small courtyard on the north side have mosaics on their walls and in the chambers. Here can also be found the remains of a frieze with murals. These once decorated most of the site's door beams. They had been kept in the style of the Mixtec pictographic writing systems, the most famous of which are the Codex Vindobonensis (Mexicanus 1) and the Codex Becker (Kaziken manuscript). They are preserved in the Austrian National Library and the ethnological museum in Vienna respectively.

Other groups of buildings

On the other side of the Rio Mitla lie the Grupo del Sur (Southern Group) and to the west the Grupo del Arroyo (Bach Group) as well as the Grupo de los Adobes (Group of the Clay Bricks) which have not yet been completely excavated and restored.

Frissell Museum

Frissell Museum (Museo Frissell de Arte Zapoteca) is situated near the village square. It exhibits the largest collection of pre-Hispanic ceramics from the Oaxaca Valley.

Surroundings

An interesting cruciform burial chamber was found in the Hacienda Xaaga a few miles south of the ruins. It is embellished with meander ornamentation and retains some of its original painting.

Grupo de las Iglesias, built on the Indian remains

Monte Albán L 9

State: Oaxaca (Oax.). Altitude: 2000m/6564ft

Access

By bus from Oaxaca (see entry) about ½ an hour; by car from Oaxaca approximately 10km/6 miles in a south-westerly direction.

Location

The settlement of Monte Albán covers an area of 40sq.km/15½sq. miles. It once extended across several mountains and served various peoples for almost 2500 years as a place of worship. The centre of the ruins, rising on a man-made platform 400m/1313ft above the subtropical valley of Oaxaca, is possibly Meso-America's most impressive pre-Columbian site.

History

Monte Albán I

By about 6000 B.C. there had already been sporadic settlements in the Oaxaca valley. After the decline of San José Mogote, which had until then been the valley's most important place, Monte Albán was probably founded in the seventh century B.C. In its heyday some 35,000 people inhabited the heartland which covered an area of 6·5sq.km/2½sq. miles.

The first calendar signs, mainly day-symbols from the 260-day calendar (tzolkin) hewn in stone, were probably earlier. Whether the first settlers and builders of the place of worship were Zapotecs remains unknown. The Monte Albán I period (600–200 B.C.) is in any case characterised by Olmec artistic features. Between 500 and 400 B.C. a town-like settlement evolved, from which simple tombs containing ceramics have survived as have hewn stone blocks with bas-reliefs of human figures and 260-day calendars.

Monte Albán: The central and eastern groups, seen from the South Platform

Monte Albán II

In the Monte Albán II period (200 B.C.–A.D. 100) the pre-Classical influence of the Maya from the south became evident. Better-quality ceramics, a completion of the calendar and large Cyclopean buildings became the style.

Monte Albán III

Going into decline at the same time as the Zapotecs emerged, the ensuing phases, called Monte Albán III a (until about A.D. 400) and Monte Albán III b (until about A.D. 800), are seen as a cultural heyday. This epoch was characterised by the construction of the most important buildings in the Talud Tablero style (vertical panels alternating with sloping walls) and elaborate burial chambers with beautiful frescos and clay funeral urns in a wealth of forms. In the first half of this period stylistic elements of the advanced civilisation of Teotihuacán, which radiated from the central plateau, became apparent. Towards the end of this period the cultural influence of the Mixtecs can be detected.

Monte Albán IV

The decline began with the onset of the Monte Albán IV phase (A.D. 800–1200). No new buildings were constructed; the magnificent site began to decay, while towns such as Lambityeco, Yagul, Mitla and Zaachila were founded or extended. Monte Albán appears to have continued only to serve as a burial site for the Zapotecs and later primarily for the Mixtecs. The artistic form of ceramics and the shape and furnishing of burial chambers became simpler.

Monte Albán V

The Monte Albán V phase, the last before the Spanish conquest, was essentially determined by the Mixtecs, who built numerous tombs or cleaned out existing ones and used them again.

The Aztecs, who built a military base in 1486 on the site of the present-day town of Oaxaca, influenced the development of Monte Albán little more than the Spanish who arrived in 1521. Serious studies of Monte Albán did not take place until the 19th c. and were mainly carried out by Desiré Charnay, Eduard Seler and W. H. Holmes. During the 20th c. the Mexican archaeologists Alfonso Caso and Ignacio Bernal were at the forefront of pioneering work achieved here. They were followed by Ernesto Gonzáles Licón and Marcus Winter, among others. Monte Albán was also declared a world cultural heritage site by UNESCO.

Visit to the ★★ruins

Gran Plaza

The Gran Plaza (Grand Square) measures 200m/656ft×300m/985ft and forms the centre of the archaeological ruins. The plateau was created partly by removal of soil and partly by incorporating rocks, which were difficult to move, into the constructions as in the north platform, the south platform and the group of buildings G, H, I. This led to these buildings not standing exactly central and the large open steps belonging to each platform not lying exactly opposite one another. To conceal this lack of symmetry the Zapotecs constructed two more small build-

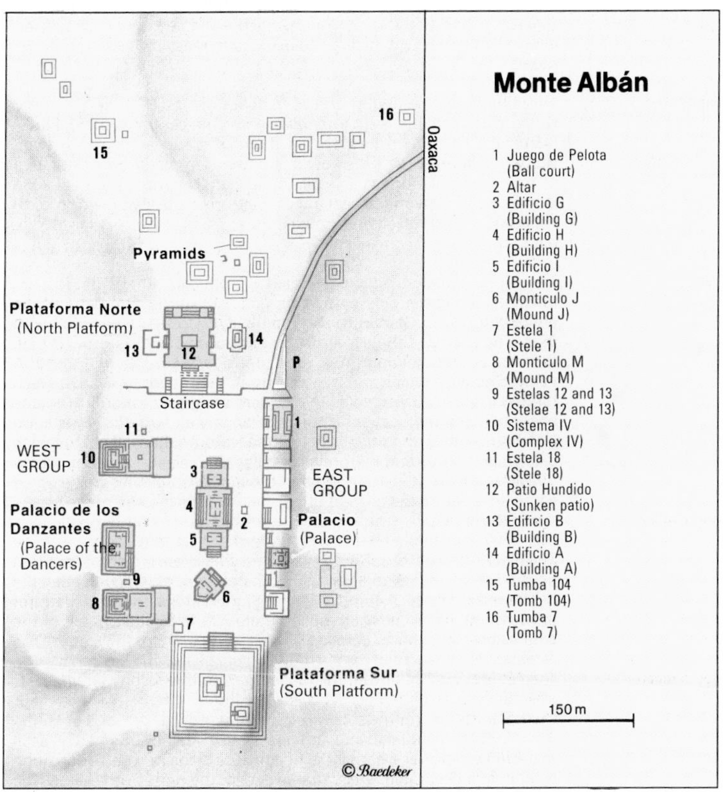

ings during period III. They stand in front of buildings M and IV and are separated by patios. As in all pre-Columbian architecture almost all of the buildings here were built over up to six times. The walls of the buildings were also covered with multi-coloured stucco.

East group
Ball Court

The Juego de Pelota (ball court), an area used for the ball game, can be found immediately to the left of the car park, i.e. on the east side of the Gran Plaza. Like all ball courts found in and around Oaxaca the stone rings, which would have served as "goals", were missing here. This area was last built over during phase III b.

Pyramid

Of all the adjoining structures built in the style typical of Monte Albán III the first pyramid is of most importance. It contains an internal flight of steps leading to the very top of the building. From here an underground tunnel passes below the Gran Plaza to the middle group (G, H, I). This enabled priests to reach the Gran Plaza unseen.

Palace

The next important construction in this group also has a wide stairway and is called the Palacio (Palace). On its upper platform only ruins of the walls of the rooms once probably inhabited by priests remain. Below the inner courtyard was found a cruciform tomb dating from the Monte Albán IV phase. Between the Palace and the Middle Row can be seen an integral altar, within which an unusual jade mask of the bat god was found.

Middle Row

Three buildings belonging to the Middle Row (G, H, I) form a group which was probably used to house altars. The central construction H (45m/148ft×30m/98ft) has a wide flight of steps leading to a twin-sectioned temple. A little lower are two temple rooms with two columns in front of them. The pair of flanked constructions G and I are almost identical: temples rest on two platforms, the lower with vertical walls, the upper with slanted ones; the steps lead to the north and to the south.

★ Hill J

The fourth isolated building is called Monticulo J (Hill J). This interesting site is the only one which does not fit the symmetry of the entire complex, as it stands at an angle of 45° to the remaining buildings. The shape of the construction is also unusual; its ground plan resembles an arrowhead with the steps forming the blunt end. A vaulted tunnel, which crosses the front part, leads upwards. Such tunnels in Meso-American buildings were designed primarily to enable observation of the heavens, though strangely enough the sky is completely invisible from this tunnel. Stone slabs on the walls of the wide side show figures and hieroglyphics recording clearly successful conquests of towns. It is assumed that most of this building was erected some time before the birth of Christ, i.e. towards the end of the Monte Albán II period.

South Platform

★ View

The Plataforma del Sur (South Platform), which borders the Gran Plaza on the south side, is an enormous construction, of which only a little has been excavated. A 40m/131ft-long flight of steps leads to a platform from where, particularly at sunset, there is a marvellous view of the whole complex. This is extolled as the "symphony of the steps". The remarkable Stelae 5 and 6 were found on the platform. They can now be seen in Mexico City's National Museum of Anthropology.

★ Stela 1

On the north-west corner of this structure stands Stela 1, one of Monte Albán's best-maintained and artistically most valuable. Seated on a hill to the left is a jaguar wearing the head-dress of the rain god Cocijo who is holding a decorated lance. Above and on the right-hand side can be seen rows of glyphs. Other stelae found here were taken to the National Museum of Anthropology in Mexico City.

West Group

Hill M

Monticulo M (Mound M) is located in the south-west corner of the Gran Plaza. A square site, it comprises two buildings separated by a patio with a small altar. A traditional central flight of steps leads via two floors with four slanting walls to the upper platform where the remains of four columns, which once formed part of the temple's façade, can be seen. The building in front was constructed during period III to correct the symmetry. On the north side of the main construction stand reproductions of stelae 12 and 13. The originals are in the National Museum of Anthropology in Mexico City. They are covered with number glyphs and are evidently associated with the adjoining Palazio de los Danzantes (Building of the Dancers).

★ Palazio de los Danzantes

The Building of the Dancers is without doubt the most interesting part of the ruins. Its altar dates from the 6th/5th c. B.C. which corresponds to the Monte Albán 1 phase. The core of the original building was built over several times. Today a two-storey construction (30m/98½ft × 60m/197ft) dating from the III a and III b phases can be seen.

★★ Danzantes

The most important elements are the stone slabs, once used to decorate a 3m/10ft-tall terrace wall, which depict reliefs of figures, the Danzantes. Today they are displayed in several groups. The features and the glyphs are very similar to those of the Olmecs (La Venta culture) from the coast of the Gulf of Mexico. It is evident that the inhabitants of Monte Albán already used a system of script, numbers and a calendar in early days. It used to be thought that the strangely-contorted figures were surprised dancers, or perhaps tortured slaves. Experts now believe, however, that the glyphs around the figures indicate that they

Monte Albán: the famous "Danzantes"

represent important personalities. Recently several of these stone slabs have been taken to museums and replaced by polyester reproductions. A complete exchange is planned to protect the originals from the effects of bad weather.

Complex IV

Further to the north stands Complex IV (Sistema IV) which is extremely similar to Hill M.

Stela 18

On the north side of the building is the badly weathered Stela 18 thought to date from the Monte Albán II phase. It is the only stela still in existence from that time and may have been erected at about the same time as the original construction of System IV, which was built from heavy stone blocks in the cyclopean style of this epoch. Between the building and the north platform lies a flat site with chambers and several tombs.

North Platform

A 38m/125ft-wide stairway leads to the impressive 12m/39ft-high Plataforma del Norte (North Platform) which covers an area of 250m/820ft×200m/656ft. Each side of the stairway was flanked by a cult chamber decorated with hieroglyphs and figures, and containing a tomb.

Stela 9

Stela 9 stood opposite the western chamber. Covered on all four sides by reliefs, it is considered the most important find of its kind and is now kept in Mexico City's National Museum of Anthropology. On the platform can be seen the ruins of 2m/6½ft-thick columns in two rows. These once carried the weight of the enormous roof of the hall.

Patio Hundido

Steps lead down into the Patio Hundido (sunken courtyard) in the middle of which stands an altar. This once finely-sculpted rectangle served as a base for Stela 10, which has also been taken to Mexico City.

The west group, seen from the South Platform

Buildings A and B

Edificio B (Building B) stands to the left of the North Platform. Its poorly-preserved superstructure is possibly the most recent building at Monte Albán and is attributed to the Mixtecs. To the right of the platform stands Edificio A (Building A), an earlier pyramid, of which only the wall base and the flight of stairs have survived.

Several unexcavated ruins of various types lie to the north of the main platform.

Tombs
★Tomb 104

A path leads north-west to Tumba 104 (Tomb 104), the most magnificent of those discovered in Monte Albán. It dates from about A.D. 500. Above the elaborate façade of the entrance is a niche containing a clay urn shaped like a seated person with the headdress of the rain god Cocijo. The door between the tomb and the ante-room consists of a huge stone slab covered with hieroglyphs. All three sides of the burial chamber are decorated with coloured frescos. On the right-hand side can be recognised the figure of Titao Cazobi, the Zapotecs' corn god, who is wearing a large headdress composed of a serpent and feathers. The central picture above a niche on the back wall depicts the head of an unknown red deity with an arched headdress, the "5 turquoise" glyph and the opening of heaven. On the left-hand wall can be seen a figure with features of an old man holding a copal sack and decorated on the waist, neck and head. This is probably meant to be the god Xipe Tótec, who for the Zapotecs, Mixtecs and Aztecs was the god of renewal, of jewellers and of the maltreated. In the burial chamber were found the remains of an adult male with a large urn depicting the same deity as that portrayed on the back wall; four smaller urns were found next to this.

Tomb 172

Tomb 172 lies beneath the mound of Tomb 104. The skeleton and the objects buried in this tomb can be seen here in the condition in which they were found.

Tomb 7

The famous Tumba 7 (Tomb 7), discovered in 1932 by Alfonso Caso, lies north-east of the Gran Plaza but somewhat away from the real cult centre to the right of the approach road. The discovery of the tomb was an archaeological sensation: this burial chamber, built by the Zapotecs during the III period, held the largest treasure trove hitherto found in Meso-America. The ante-room contained Zapotec receptacles and burial urns; the Mixtecs buried the mortal remains of nobles here later, probably around the middle of the 14th c. Almost 500 elaborately-worked gold, silver, jade, turquoise, rock crystal and alabaster objects buried by the Mixtecs were discovered. They are now kept in the Oaxaca (see entry) Regional Museum (Santo Domingo monastery).

Tomb 105

Tomb 105 should also be seen. Situated on Plumaje Hill it has a magnificent entrance door and interesting murals.

Museum

It is worth visiting the small museum near the car park. It mainly exhibits ceramics and stone statues and documents the excavation work.

Lagunas de Montebello (Montebello Lagoons) O 9

State: Chiapas (Chis.)
Altitude: 1500m/4923ft downwards

Access

By bus or by group taxi from Comitán de Dominguez; by car on the MEX 190 (Panamericana) from San Cristóbal de Las Casas (see entry) for 103km/64 miles to Comitán de Dominguez, from there a further

16km/10 miles to La Trinitaria, turn left here and continue for another 40km/25 miles to Montebello Lagoons National Park.

A road, asphalted only at the start, crosses the national park. Tracks across fields, some more passable than others, lead to individual lagoons.

Location

The group of small and medium-sized lagoons, known collectively as the Lagunas de Montebello and thought to number more than 100, extends inwards from the beginning of the national park (6700ha/16,556 acres) eastwards as far as Guatemala and to the Selva Lacandona. These inshore waters of varying hues extend across terraced landscape mainly planted with pine forests and still largely unspoiled. As well as the lagoons there are a number of large swallow-holes, grottoes and waterfalls, adding to the scenic attractions of this region.

★Landscape

Lagos de Colores

Visitors should take a guide with them as this extensive and broken ground can prove difficult to explore alone. One group of lagoons is called the Lagos de Colores (Coloured Lakes) because they appear in the most diverse tones from emerald green to midnight blue. This phenomenon is caused by the angle of the sun, the depth of the lakes and by the combined nature of the land and the water. The lakes and their surroundings consequently bear such fine-sounding names as La Encantada (Enchanted Lagoon), Ensueño (Dream), Esmeralda (Emerald), Bosque Azul (Blue Forest) and Agua Tinta (Coloured Water).

Arco de San Rafael

Near a small settlement lies the remarkable Arco de San Rafael (Arc of San Rafael), a natural chalk bridge through which the Rio Comitán flows into a cave where it seems to disappear.

Lago Tziscao

Lago Tziscao lies 10km/6 miles to the east and is one of the largest of the accessible lagoons. It forms the border with Guatemala and at present offers the only accommodation in the area (Albergue and camp site). The road is being extended to the east.

Surroundings

Chinkultic

After 32km/20 miles along the turn-off from MEX 190 to the Montebello Lagoons a 2km/1 mile-long unmade road across fields leads left to Chinkultic. This ruined site on the rocky escarpment of a forest-covered mountain (1600m/5251ft) is surrounded by a charming landscape of lakes and pastures. It is remarkable that a cenote also exists here far from the Yucatan karst area.

Chinkultic (Maya: "cave of steps") was inhabited from about the beginning of the Christian era until the 13th c. Its heyday occurred during the Maya Classic period (A.D. 300–900). The first to visit this Maya site was the German archaeologist Eduard Seler in 1895. It was explored by the Dane Frans Blom and the American Oliver La Farge around 1925; during the 1960s Stephan F. de Borhegyl and Gareth W. Lowe led the excavations. Recently many exposed sites have become overgrown again. More than 200 mounds in this area, varying in size, still hold Maya constructions. Of the six main groups only a few remain visible.

Ball Court

A large Juego de Pelota (ball court) extends into Group C on the west side. It measures 54m/177ft×25m/82ft. On its west side are three sculpted stelae; a total of nineteen stelae with relief carvings of figures and glyphs have so far been found at Chinkultic.

El Mirador

Not to be missed is Group A, in the north-west, with the exposed Temple 1 or El Mirador at the top of an approximately 40m/131ft-tall pyramid. It stands on a terrace from which rise four platforms. The wide steps leading to the pyramid are now once more overgrown with scrub.

Agua Azul

The picturesque turquoise blue cenote Agua Azul lies about 50m/164ft below the temple. As it was assumed that, as in the case of the cenote of Chichen Itzá, human sacrifices and gifts had been thrown in here, archaeologists dived for such objects. The murky layer of silt lying immediately below the surface of the water rendered these attempts useless. The cenote was then drained into neighbouring Lake Chanujabab and excavation work uncovered various ceramics.

In addition to interesting stelae and elaborate incense burners, a stone disc, with a diameter of 55cm/21½in., weighing 78kg/172lb and dated A.D. 590, was found nearby. This valuable object, used as a marker stone for the game of pelota, shows a pelota player with an elaborate feather headdress and ritual games equipment surrounded by a band of glyphs. The stone is now in the National Museum of Anthropology in Mexico City.

Monterrey 15

State: Nuevo León (N. L.)
Altitude: 538m/1766ft
Population: 2,800,000
Dialling code: 91 83

Access from Mexico City

By air 1½–2 hours; by rail about 16 hours; by bus in approximately 12 hours.

Location

Monterrey, an industrial town, lies in Santa Catarina Valley and is dominated by the curiously-jagged Cerro de la Silla (Saddle Mountain, 1740m/5711ft) and the Cerro de la Mitra (Mitre Mountain, 2380m/7811ft). The capital of the state of Nuevo León, Monterrey is Mexico's third-largest town after Mexico City and Guadalajara and the country's second-largest industrial centre. Although it has developed into a modern city the old-Spanish atmosphere can still be found in its narrow alleys, flat-roofed houses and picturesque patios. The climate is hot and dry in summer, damp and cold in winter. Monterrey is a totally Spanish town with no evidence of Indian influence.

History

The area around Monterrey has no pre-Columbian history; unfortunately, the nomads who roamed the region left little trace of themselves.

The first Spaniards arrived here in 1584 under Luis Carvajal de la Cueva and established the outpost of Ojos de Santa Lucia against the Indians; it was not until eleven years later, however, that twelve Spanish families led by Diego de Montemayor finally settled here and called the place Ciudad de Nuestra Señora de Monterrey after the then viceroy the Count of Monterrey. The isolated settlement, which could only boast 258 inhabitants in 1775, often had to defend itself against attacks by the nomadic Indians. During the war between Mexico and the USA it was occupied by American troops in 1846 and again in 1864 during the War of Intervention by French troops. Not until 1882, when the rail link between Laredo and Monterrey was established, did the town experience an upswing which has continued undiminished ever since.

In September 1988, as a result of Hurricane Gilbert which swept across the town, rainfall was so heavy that the Santa Catarina river

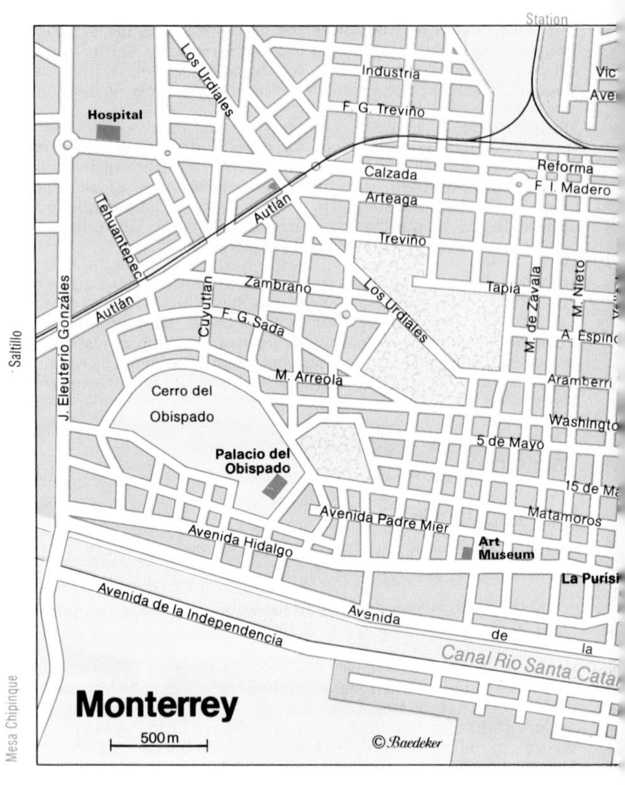

burst its banks; the resulting floods carried away four fully-occupied buses in their wake. More than 200 people probably drowned at this time. The flooding also caused some damage to the town.

Economy

Thanks to its excellent communications Monterrey has become a major centre of heavy industry and it is also an important producer of consumer goods; its principal products include glass, cement, synthetic materials, foodstuffs and beer. In its Instituto Tecnológico Monterrey possesses one of the largest and best technological universities in Latin America.

Sights

As Monterrey only became of particular importance one hundred years ago it offers little in the way of colonial art. Nevertheless, the lively town and its surroundings have attracted many tourists, mainly from the USA.

5 Plaza Zaragoza 6 Cathedral 7 Palacio Municipal 8 Shopping Street

Plaza Cinco de Mayo

The Plaza Cinco de Mayo, with the statue of Benito Juárez in the middle, lies in the centre of the town and forms the northern section of the Gran Plaza. The sandstone Palacio de Gobierno (Government Palace) stands in the square. It is worth viewing the colonial patio and the fresco-decorated state apartments displaying a small historical exhibition, which includes the guns used by the firing squad which shot Emperor Maximilian and his generals in 1867. The modern Palacio Federal lies diagonally opposite. Its tower offers a fine view across the town and its surroundings.

★ Gran Plaza (Macro Plaza)

Opened in 1984 the Gran Plaza extends between the Palacio de Gobierno and the modern new town hall situated to the south. This 40ha/99 acre complex is five times larger than the Zócalo in Mexico City. At the Palacio de Gobierno the Esplanada de los Héroes (Heroes' Esplanade) leads past memorials to Miguel Hidalgo, José Maria Morelos, Benito Juárez and Mariano Escobedo. The waters of the impressive 60m/197ft×30m/98½ft Fuente de la Vida (Neptune Fountain) pour over three levels between bronze sculptures by Luis Sanginio. The single-

Monterrey: Plaza Cinco de Mayo, the Government Palace and the Palacio Federal

towered cathedral on the west side of the square was begun in 1603 and completed in 1851. Opposite, on the east side, stands the remarkable 76m/249ft-tall monument by Luis Barragán from whose Point of the Night a laser beam is directed up into the sky. The equestrian statue of General Zaragoza and the memorial to the city's founder Diego de Montemayor are in the centre of the southern part of the Gran Plaza. Rufino Tamayo's sculpture called "Homage to the Sun" occupies a position near the Palacio Municipal (town hall) which adjoins the square.

★ Museo de Arto Contemporáneo

The grandiose Museum of Contemporary Art (MARCO), designed by Ricardo Legorreta, was opened in 1991. It stands on Gran Plaza, Zuazo and Ocampo. As well as some excellent temporary exhibitions there is a permanent exhibition of modern paintings.

★ Iglesia La Purisima

To the west of the square, at the junction of Avda. Padre Mier and C. Serafin Peña, stands La Purísima Church, one of the best examples of modern sacral architecture in Mexico. It was constructed by Enrique de la Mora y Palomar.

Cerro del Obispado

The Calle Padre Mier ends further west on the hill called Cerro del Obispado or Chepe Vera which is crowned by the Obispado (Bishops' Palace). The palace, dating from the end of the 18th c., served later at different times as a fortress and a hospital. In 1913 the notorious bandit and revolutionary hero Francisco "Pancho" Villa took refuge here.

Museo Regional

Today the building houses the Museo Regional de Nuevo León (Regional Museum) which features exhibits relating to the economic and cultural development of the region. Of note is the chapel with its beautiful Churrigueresque façade and the printing press on which

The Neptune Fountain, with the Cathedral and Steel Monument in the background

Pater Servando Teresa de Mier produced pamphlets in the Mexican War of Independence (1810–21) against Spanish rule and two rifles with which Emperor Maximilian and his two generals were said to have been shot in Quertaro.

Technological University

The modern Instituto Tecnológico (Technological University) contains an enormous library which possesses a large stock of books about 16th c. Mexican history and a 2000-volume collection of various editions of Don Quixote. The library is decorated with a mural by Jorge Camarena.

Cuauhtémoc Brewery (Museo Monterrey)

The old brewing room of the much-visited Cuauhtémoc Brewery (Av. Universidad 2202 Nte.), one of the country's largest, houses the Museo Monterrey. It mainly displays paintings by 20th c. Latin-American artists. The brewery garden contains a baseball museum (Salón de la Fama del Beisbol).

Other sights

Other recommended sights include the Espíritu Santo Church, an asymmetric modern building by Armando Rauize with a large wall mosaic, the Casa de la Cultura (House of Culture, Colón 400 Ote.), a glass museum (C. Zaragoza/Magallanes) and an Oldtimer (vintage car) museum in the Del Valle suburb (C. Rio Suchiata y Vasconcelos).

Surroundings

Centro Cultural Alfa

Leave the town southwards in the direction of the Club de Golf along Avenida Mesa Chipinque to reach the part of town called San Pedro Garza García. Here the Centro Cultural Alfa exhibits pre-Spanish finds, paintings by Mexican artists, folk art, shells and minerals. A planetarium built like an upturned cylinder offers insights into the world of astronomy.

Mesa Chipinque

After San Pedro Garza García the road leads upwards to the Mesa Chipinque, a forested mountain ridge, from which a marvellous view of Monterrey and its surroundings can be enjoyed.

Cascadas Cola de Caballo

By following the MEX 85 in the direction of Ciudad Victoria southwards to the Villa de Santiago (36km/22 miles), a turn-off is reached which leads to the Cascadas Cola de Caballo ("Horse Tail Falls"), an impressive 30m/98ft-high waterfall, which is, however, often dried up.

Cañon de la Huasteca

About 18km/11 miles along the MEX 40 in the direction of Saltillo a road to the left comes to the Cañon de la Huasteca, an almost vertical ravine 300m/985ft deep surrounded by bizarre rock formations.

★ Grutas de García

The Grutas de García, one of the country's largest and most beautiful cave systems, is reached by following the same main road for another 6km/4 miles, then taking a right-hand turn and continuing for a further 24km/15 miles. The entrance to the caves is reached by taking a cableway.

Morelia I 8

State: Michoacán (Mich.)
Altitude: 1950m/6400ft
Population: 710,000
Dialling code: 91 451

Access from Mexico City

By air about 45 minutes; by rail approximately 10 hours; by bus about 6½ hours; by car 309km/192 miles along the MEX 15 via Toluca (see entry).

Location

Morelia, the magnificent captal of the state of Michoacán, lies on the right bank of the Rio Grande de Morelia within an extensive fertile hollow between Mexico City and Guadalajara, Mexico's two largest cities.

★ Townscape

Morelia retains the character of a distinguished Spanish colonial town.

History

During the pre-Columbian period the Morelia region was settled by a tribe of Matlatzinca who had retreated before the Aztec advance into this Tarascan-ruled (Purépecha) region in the mid 15th c.

Soon after the Conquista the first Spaniards, led by Cristóbel de Olid, came to the area and conquered the Tarascans. In the Spanish chronicle of the settlement the first entry concerns the establishment of a convent by the Franciscan friar Father Juan de San Miguel in 1537. Founded in 1541, Morelia was first named Valladolid on the orders of the first viceroy of New Spain Antonio de Mendoza. By 1547 Valladolid had gained its municipal charter. In competition with "Indian" Pátzcuaro, where Bishop Vasco de Quiroga had his seat of office, "Spanish" Valladolid finally became the see of a bishop in 1570, and in 1582 it became Michoacán's capital in place of Pátcuaro. During the 17th and 18th c. Morelia developed into a trading centre for the agriculture of the surrounding area. In the Mexican War of Independence (1810–21) the town was for a time the operational base of the freedom fighter Miguel Hidalgo y Costilla. In 1828, after independence had been won, it was named Morelia in honour of another of the freedom fighters Father José Maria Morelos y Pavón (1765–1815), who was a native of the town. Inheriting the cultural traditions of Spain, Morelia eventually became one of Mexico's leading intellectual centres thanks largely to its university.

Morelia Cathedral

Sights

★Cathedral

The beautiful main square (Plaza de los Mártires or Zócalo) is lined on three sides by arcades. The east side is completely dominated by the magnificent cathedral which is built in pinkish-brown trachyte. Construction began in 1640 and continued until more than a century later. Despite this length of time the cathedral's style, predominantly strictly Baroque, has remained completely unified. The azulejo-decorated dome of the church is striking. The interior, which was partly refurbished at the end of the 19th c., contains several notable features: the Neo-Classical retablos, the silver font, a crucifix by Manuel Tolsá, the imposing organ built in Germany in 1903, and a number of paintings in the chancel and the sacristy which are attributed to the leading painters of the first half of the 18th c., Juan Rodríguez Juárez, José Maria de Ibarra and Miguel Cabrera. An Indian "de caña" figure of Christ, wearing a golden crown donated by the Spanish king Philip II, is also kept in the sacristy.

Government Palace

Opposite the cathedral, on the other side of the Avenida Madero Oriente, stands the Baroque Palacio de Gobierno (Government Palace) built between 1732 and 1770 with an interesting patio. The enormous murals by the native artist Alfredo Zalce are remarkable. They depict the history of independence, the reforms, and Mexico's revolution.

Regional Museum

The Museo Regional de Michoacán (Regional Museum, Av. Allende 305) is housed in a mid-18th c. Baroque building on the corner of Allende Street and Abasolo Street. It contains pre-Columbian exhibits as well as paintings, weapons, implements and furniture from the colonial period. The stairwells are decorated with frescos by Alfredo Zalce and Federico Cantú.

Town Hall

To the left of the museum is the Palacio Municipal (town hall), a Neo-Classical building, dating from the end of the 18th c.

Colegio de San Nicolás

The Colegio de San Nicolás is reached by following Calle Galeana northwards and crossing the Avenida Madero Poniente. The original building dates from 1580 and became home to the school founded in Pátzcuara in 1540; after the Santa Cruz de Tlatelolco school (1537) it is the oldest on the American continent. It now belongs to the University of Morelia. The courtyard with fine Baroque arcades is noteworthy.

Palacio de Clavijero and Iglesia de la Compañía with ★library

On the opposite side of the road stands the massive Clavijero Palace, named after Francisco Javier de Clavijero, a Jesuit teacher. Part of the complex is the Iglesia de la Compañía, a Jesuit church built between 1660 and 1681. It now houses the Biblioteca Pública (Public Library). On sale at the Mercado de Dulches ("Sweet Market") are not only sweets but also handcrafted articles.

Santa Rosa de la Lima

Cross Calle Santiago Tapia to an attractive little square where stands the Church of Santa Rosa de Lima. This building, begun at the end of the 16th c., has a double portal showing Renaissance influences, while the upper façade and the gilded and painted retablos are dominated by the Baroque style in its Churrigueresque form. A conservatoire, the oldest college of music in America, adjoins the church.

Museo del Estado

Diagonally opposite is the Museo del Estado (State Museum) opened in 1986. It is housed in La Casa de la Emperatriz (House of the Empress, Guillermo Prieto 176) where the wife of Emperor Agustin de Iturbide, Doña Ana Huarte, spent her youth. It displays many exhibits, including pre-Columbian pieces and Indian costumes, a valuable collection of precious stones and minerals, a pharmacy and other objects and documents connected with the history of Michoacán.

Museo del Arte Colonial

The Museo del Arte Colonial (Museum of Colonial Art) is situated in Av. Benito Juárez, which crosses the Santiago Tapia a little further to the east. On display are paintings, sculptures, incunabula and other art objects from the colonial period.

Casa de la Cultura

The Casa de la Cultura (House of Culture) is to be found further north on the corner of Humboldt and Fray Juan de San Miguel near the del Carmen Church (early 17th c.). In addition to archaeological objects, beautiful masks and statues of Christ from all over Mexico can also be seen here.

Iglesia de San Francisco

The church of St Francis, built around 1540 and thus the town's oldest sacral building, stands behind the Plaza Valladolid. Of note is the entrance façade, built in the Renaissance style with Plateresque elements. The bell-tower has a small dome covered with azulejos.

★Palacio de las Artesanías

The convent, formerly adjoining the church, now houses the Palacio de las Artesanías, which displays and sells excellent pieces of regional folk art, such as lacquerware and copperware, wood carvings, ceramics and embroidery.

Morelos museums

Two buildings in Morelia's old town are now dedicated to the memory of the hero of independence Jose María Morelos; these are the house where he was born (Casa Natal de Morelos) on the corner of Corregidora y García Obeso, which displays letters and other memorabilia, and the Museo Morelos, the real Morelos museum, housed in his later home (Av. Morelos 323). Here can be seen his weapons, uniform, priest's robes and documents. A library and an auditorium adjoin the museum.

Aqueduct

The aqueduct to the east of the town centre is a distinctive local landmark. Built between 1785 and 1789 it measures 1600m/5251ft in length and is borne on 253 arches.

Other sights include the churches of San Agustin, Guadalupe and Santa Catalina, the Museo de Arte Contemporáneo (Museum of Contemporary Art) in the attractive Park Cuauhtémoc, and the new planetarium, the largest and most modern of its type in Mexico.

Surroundings

Cuitzeo Augustinian convent

An approximately 35km/22 mile journey northwards along the MEX 43 leads across Lake Cuitzeo, which is almost dried up, and on to the small town of Cuitzeo (1883m/6180ft, population 17,000). This former fishing village proves a popular destination because of its Augustinian convent built in 1551. The church which belongs to it has a beautifully ornamented façade in a predominantly Spanish-Plateresque style. Above the portal can be seen a pierced heart, the emblem of the Augustinian order. The double eagle of the Casa Austria is sculpted into the columns which flank it. The tower was built at the beginning of the 17th c. The defensive character of the church and the convent, with its once much larger atrium, is evident. The remains of a fresco depicting the Last Judgment can be seen on the left at the beginning of the portico. The Open Chapel is integrated into the third arch of the portico.

From Cuitzeo it is a further 30km/19 miles to Yuríria (see Celaya, Surroundings).

Pátzcuaro

By leaving Morelia in the direction of Uruapan the town of Pátzcuaro is reached after 58km/36 miles. Pátzcuaro is a good base for excursions to the interesting places around Lake Pátzcuaro (see entry), including the archaeological ruins at Tzintzuntzan (see entry).

Mil Cumbres

The MEX 15 leads eastwards (Toluca, Mexico City) across several passes, more than 3000m/9846ft high, for 70km/43 miles to Mil Cumbres ("Thousand Peaks"). From here there is a unique panorama across the forest-covered mountain chain of the Sierra Madre Occidental.

Ciudad Hidalgo

Ciudad Hidalgo (2360m/7746ft, population 80,000) is reached after about a further 30km/19 miles. The parish church, which belongs to a 16th c. Franciscan convent, has a Plateresque façade. A gravel road turns off to the left 2km/1 mile before the town to Los Azufres National Park 25km/16 miles away. The park contains magnificent coniferous woods, lakes and sulphur springs.

★ San José Purúa

Continuing in the direction of Titácuaro it is 19km/12 miles to the town of Tuxpan. After Tuxpan a turning on the right leads in about 8km/5 miles to San José Purúa (1689m/5543ft, population 35,000). This picturesque spa lies within tropical vegetation on the edge of a deep ravine.

Los Alzati

After returning along the MEX 15 for 6km/4 miles a track leading across fields is reached. Follow this for 4km/2½ miles to arrive at the old Indian ruins of Los Alzati (Camaji). It is attributed to the Matlatzinca of the late Classic period (A.D. 700–900) and comprises an impressive several-storeyed complex of pyramids of which only a small part has been uncovered. As well as platforms stones chiselled with cult signs can be seen.

Angangueo

San Felipe de Alzati is reached another 2km/1 miles along the MEX 15. From here a road on the left goes via Ocampo to the small mining town of Angangueo (2268m/7444ft; Purépecha: "at the entrance to the cave") some 24km/15 miles away. Organised tours depart from here to the Santuario de la Mariposa Monarco, one of the rare wintering areas of the monarch butterfly and the only one officially accessible to visitors.

★★ Monarch butterfly

Millions of these butterflies (*Danaus Plexippus*) fly here every November from Canada and North America and leave this more than 3000m/9846ft-high coniferous forest the following April. The butterflies cover up to 140km/87 miles a day on their long flights. This and two other wintering areas, in Michoacán and in the Estado de México, were discovered by American scientists in 1975 but not made public until ten years later. In recent years deforestation, too many tourists (1992: 12,000) and the very cold winter of 1992 have all resulted in a considerable fall in the numbers of the butterflies. The official figure is now given as 35 million and so, in the interests of the species, visitors may like to think twice before intruding into this area.

From San Felipe de Alzati it is 9km/6 miles more to Zitácuaro, from there a further 97km/60 miles to Toluca (see entry) and another 70km/43 miles to Mexico City (see entry).

Morelos (State)

Abbreviation: Mor.
Capital: Cuernavaca
Area: 4964sq.km/1916sq. miles
Official population 1990: 1,195,000 (1994 estimate: 1,430,000)

Location and Topography

Morelos, Mexico's smallest state after Tlaxcala, is bordered on the north by the Distrito Federal (Federal District) and the Estado de México, on the west also by the Estado de México and by Guerrero, and on the south-east by Puebla. Situated on the southern slope of the Mexican central plateau, the state is surrounded by forested mountain ranges and lush river valleys with numerous waterfalls. Thanks to its proximity to Mexico City and its good communications Morelos is one of Mexico's most popular tourist and vacation areas. As well as mestizos there are closed communities of Nahua Indians in many parts of the state.

Archaeological Ruins

Of the old-Indian ruins within the state of Morelos those at Xochicalco (see entry), Tepozteco, Chalcatzingo (see Cuautla, Surroundings) and Teopanzolco (see Cuernavaca) are the most imporant.

History

Numerous finds (Chalcatzingo, Gualupita, La Juana, San Pablo) indicate that this area had already been settled, or at least strongly influenced, by Olmecs in around 1200 B.C. During the Classic period Morelos lay predominantly in the sphere of influence of the Teotihuacán. Following this Xochicalco played a considerable role to which the strong influence of the Toltecs was later added. During the 11th or 12th c. the Náhuatl-speaking Tlahuicas (descendants of the Chichimecs), who had been driven from the Anáhuac valley, came into the area. In the first half of the 15th c. the Aztecs gained control and exacted tribute from the population.

In 1520 the Spanish, led by Gonzalo de Sandoval, had conquered parts of the region, while Hernán Cortés took present-day Cuernavaca in 1521 after bitter conflicts. In 1529 Cortés was granted extensive estates by Charles V and until 1540 he resided mainly in Cuernavaca.

The first sugar-cane plantation in New Spain was established in Tlaltenango with black slaves introduced as workers who, in the course

of time, became assimilated into the Indian population. Some places in the state, including Cuautla, played an important part in the Mexican War of Independence (1810–21). After the war the state of Morelos was named after the freedom fighter José Maria Morelos. During the Mexican Revolution (1910–20) Morelos was the scene of the peasants' uprising led by Emiliano Zapata who managed to keep parts of the state under his control until he was murdered in an ambush near Cuautla in 1919.

Economy

Morelos is primarily a flourishing agricultural region, mainly producing sugar, rice, maize, coffee, wheat, fruit and vegetables. The existing mineral resources (silver, vermillion, iron, lead, gold, petroleum and coal) are still worked on a small scale. Tourism plays an important role.

The Morelos Convent Route

As well as the capital Cuernavaca (see entry) and the attractive health and seaside resorts, the historically-interesting convents in the area should not be missed. These mainly 16th c. Dominican and Augustinian buildings were, in accordance with the policy of the Spanish conquerors, mostly constructed in important Indian centres.

★ Tepoztlán

About 80km/50 miles south of Mexico City and 26km/16 miles east of Cuernavaca lies the picturesque little town of Tepoztlán (Náhuatl: "place of the axe"; 1701m/5583ft; population 35,000; fiestas; Carnival Thursday; November 1st and 2nd, All Saints' Day, All Souls' Day; markets: Sunday and Wednesday). An important Dominican convent is in the town, above which rise bizarre cliff-like rock formations.

Dominican Convent

This fortress-like sacral building dates from between 1559 and 1588 and was probably designed by the Spanish architect Francisco Becerra.

Convent churches in Atlatlahuacán . . .

. . . and Yecapixtla

Interesting Capillas Posas (procession chapels) with gables and Gothic fluted vaults stand in the corners of the atrium. Their workmanship, however, cannot be compared with that of Huejotzingo (see entry) and Calpan. To the right in front of the remains of an open chapel can be seen a 16th c. stone cross.

Convent Church

The convent church of Nuestra Señora de la Asunción has a marvellous doorway, a fine example of the colonial-Plateresque style. The sculpture, executed with consummate skill, has representations of the Virgin Mary between two saints, and medallions with the sun, the moon, planets and the Dominican Cross. Sculptures of angels, which once held inscription tablets, are fixed above the front gable. On the left-hand side of the portico are two chapels with beautiful Gothic groined vaulting, but otherwise in traditional Renaissance style. Remains of frescos have been preserved both in the chapels and in the Posas. The rustic cloister is reached through the single-aisled church.

From the first floor of the loggia on the north-west corner of the convent there is a marvellous view of the surrounding mountains.

The small archaeological museum behind the convent complex exhibits pre-Hispanic finds from the area.

Tepozteco

The Tepozteco ruins are found on a steep rocky height 500m/1641ft above the town itself. Here the Tlahuicas built a 20m/66ft-tall temple-pyramid in honour of Tepoztécatl, their god of the harvest and of pulque (pulque is a fermented drink prepared from the sap of the maguey, an agave plant). The temple can be reached via a steep footpath in about an hour; the view from the top is remarkable. Two flights of steps lead to the pyramid's first section, a third to the second section and the entrance to a small shrine. Within the pyramid are columns with figures and abstract drawings. Calendar symbols are on the walls and the stone floor, as well as symbols for pulque, water, war and blood.

Nearby are more old-Indian ruins.

Yautepec

Yautepec (population 10,000; fiesta: first Friday in Lent, Entierro del Malhumor = Grave of the Bad Mood) lies about 15km/9 miles south of Tepoztlán. The fortress-like Dominican convent was founded in the mid-16th c. by Lorenzo de la Asunción. An open chapel, an atrium cross and ruins of a small processional chapel (posa) can also be seen.

Oaxtepec

Approximately 20km/12 miles to the west is Cocoyoc, from which a side-road leads in 4km/2 miles to the spa of Oaxtepec (1085m/3561ft; population 12,000). This village has been converted recently into a centre of state social tourism. In pre-Spanish times the Aztec ruler Moctezuma I is supposed to have had a summer palace here.

In the village there is another Dominican convent dating from the first half of the 16th c. which now houses a school and, occasionally, an exhibition of archaeological finds from the state of Morelos. Compared with other monasteries this one is of minor importance. Charming naïve pictures of saints and monks, and frescos showing Mudéjar influence can be seen in the cloister. The fortified church with its Gothic groined vaulting is divided into five parts by large columns and double arches.

★Tlayacapan

Approximately 10km/6 miles further to the north lies Tlayacapan (Náhuatl: "in the first hills"; 1634m/5363ft) situated in a particularly attractive hilly setting. The Church of San Juan Bautista with its Augustinian convent was one of the first to be founded by the order in this area, where the native Indians defended themselves particularly doggedly against the Spanish invaders.

Unusually the convent is on the south side and not, as was customary, on the north side of the church which stands at the end of the spacious atrium. It has a simple façade which is topped by an Espadaña with five oriel windows. A portico to the left of the church leads to the cloister, the Gothic arcades of which are of multi-coloured stone. The cloister is adjoined by the "Sala de Profundis" in which can be seen 16th c. frescos depicting scenes of the Way of the Cross and figures of saints. Within the refectory a small exhibition room has archaeological pieces, historical documents and mummies.

Totolapan

The village of Totolapan lies about 10km/6 miles to the north-west. Its Augustinian convent was founded in 1534 by Jorge de Avila, but was not actually built until later. The large atrium with a posa (processional chapel) lies in front of the fortified church. The convent, which has a simple cloister, contains the remains of 16th c. frescos.

★Atlatlahuacan

Atlatlahuacan is situated approximately 6km/4 miles south-west of Totolapan. The Augustinian convent was built between 1570 and 1600. Two remarkable posas stand in the large atrium. The church has a simple façade and an open bell-tower. To the left can be seen an open chapel standing in front of a tall tower which was built later. The cloister vaulting is painted with frescos.

Yecapixtla

Yecapixtla (Náhautl: "where the weak wind blows"; population 20,000; fiestas: Easter Sunday; April 25th, Dia de San Marcos; May 3rd, Dia de la Santa Cruz; last Thursday in October, Tianguis) is reached via two junctions and after about 10km/6 miles. The All Saints' market is remarkable. Indians buy burial gifts for the Dia de los Muertos here, and coloured candles in commemoration of the dead are sold: black for the graves of married people and adults, blue for those of young people, green for those of children and white for those of young girls.

★ San Juan Bautista

A hermitage of Franciscans of 1525 in an Indian settlement was replaced in 1535 by the Church of San Juan Bautista with an Augustinian convent, founded in 1535 by Father Jorge de Avila. This fortified construction has more Gothic features than any other 16th c. convents in New Spain. In the atrium there is a cross and relatively simple posas decorated with pinnacles.

The convent church has a marvellous plain façade with battlements flanked by buttresses which merge into the watch-towers. The main portal is embellished with typical colonial-Plateresque ornamentation, medallions cherubs, niches, Tritons and flowers. Below the gable can be seen the coat of arms of the Augustinian order (a heart pierced by arrows) and the five stigmata of St Francis of Assisi. The choir window is in the shape of a Gothic rosette. Within the church the Gothic groined vaulting above the altar, the 16th c. pulpit chiselled from stone, and the painting of the ceiling and of the walls below the chancel are especially fine. The cloister is simple and solid.

Ocuituco

About 20km/12½ miles further east is the village of Ocuituco with the first Augustinian convent of New Spain begun here in 1534. A 16th c. stone cross stands in the atrium, while in the Church of Santiago can be seen the remains of frescos. Of note in the convent are the hexagonal 16th c. fountain with animal sculptures and the remains of frescos.

Nayarit (State)

Abbreviation: Nay.
Capital: Tepic
Area: 27,053sq.km/10,445sq. miles
Official population 1990: 824,600 (1994 estimate: 870,000)

Location and Topography

The state of Nayarit, which lies on the Pacific coast, is bounded on the north by Durango and Sinaloa, and on the south and east by Jalisco. The island group Tres Marías (María Magdalena, María Madre, María Cleofas) lie approximately 100km/62 miles offshore. The Sierra Madre Occidental rises steeply from a thin coastal strip and divides the landscape into deep ravines and narrow valleys. The coastal area comprises lagoons and marshland with rich birdlife. The inhabitants include whites, mestizos and a strongly independent Indian population mainly from the Cora and Huicholes tribes.

Archaeological Ruins

As well as the pre-Columbian ruined town of Ixlán del Río (see Tepic, Surroundings) there are also a number archaeological ruins which are hardly worth visiting. These include those at Santa Cruz, Chacala, Amapa, Coammiles and Penitas.

History

Nayarit, named after an old-Indian priest king, is generally classed in pre-Columbian archaeology with the neighbouring ruins at Jalisco and Colima under the term Culturas del Occidente (Cultures of the West). They began without doubt in the pre-Classic period and reached their heyday in the Classical (about A.D. 200–850). The Nayarit-style finds, predominantly clay statues, are, like those of Colima and Jalisco, depictions of daily life. In contrast to Colima's extremely finely-worked figures they are cruder but have features of caricature. Very little is known of the people who created this culture. During the post-Classic period Indian tribes, such as the Tepehuano, Totorano, Huicholes and Cora, migrated in phases into the region. They were driven back in the late post-Classical phase (1250–1521) by the Indian state of Xalisco which belonged to Chimalhuacán Confederation.

The Spanish who penetrated here in 1526 under Francisco Cortés Buenaventura and later under Nuño Beltrán de Guzman drove the

Indians into the mountains, but did not entirely succeed in subjugating them. The Coras and the Huicholes continually rebelled, first against the Spanish and subsequently against the Mexican rulers. One of the bloodiest and longest uprisings was that led by "Mariano" which lasted throughout the first 20 years of the 19th c. In 1854 the tribes under the leadership of Manuel Lozada ("Tiger of Alica") rose up against the Mexican government, later supported Emperor Maximilian and finally gave way when their leader was executed in 1873. Other rebellions, mainly led by the Huicholes, continued, however, until the 20th c. Separated from Jalisco in 1889 and raised to the independent territory of Tepic, Nayarit did not become a state of the Republic of Mexico until 1917.

Agriculture

Nayarit is predominantly an agricultural area, where farming and forestry mainly produce corn, tobacco, sugar-cane, beans, coffee, fruit and various timbers. Tourism and the sale of local artwork have developed recently.

Huicholes

Approximately 9000 Huicholes who live in and around Nayarit have been able to retain many of their traditions because of the remoteness of their territory. The tribe belongs to the large Uto-aztec language family but its exact origins are obscure. The Huicholes probably migrated from the north of the present state of San Luis Potosí, a region which they consider as their sacred land of Wirikuta.

Religion

Each year between October and February the Huicholes travel 500km/311 miles into this desert area to obtain the Peyotl (also Peyote or Hikuri) cactus which represents for them the body of the deer god. A cult has grown up around this sacred plant which causes a feeling of euphoria. The Indians "hunt" (pierce with arrows) the cactus in complicated ceremonies. They then languish intoxicated with mescalin, the hallucinogenic active substance found in the Peyotl, believing they are receiving messages from their gods.

Although mainly converted to Christianity, the Huicholes are polygamous and usually pray to deities of nature, such as the sun, fire, water and fertility. Their celebrations include the local change of headman around January 1st, Carnival, Holy Week and various festivals connected with the harvest. They are all linked by special rituals, including particular foods, drinks, music, dances, sacrifices, etc.

Area of Settlement

Today these people are settled in the east of Nayarit beween La Yesca and Guadalupe de Ocotán; in the north of Jalisco in, among other places, Santa Catarina, Mexquitic, San Andrés Cohamiapa, San Sebastián and Tuxpan de Bolañas; in Zacatecas in Colotlán and in Durango in Huazamote.

Within their five politico-geographical districts the Huicholes practise extensive self-administration.

Costumes and Handicrafts

Although costumes vary from village to village, the Huicholes typically wear cotton shirts colourfully embroidered with cross-stitch with geometric and stylised patterns. Over these they wear a row of brightly-embroidered belts and bags hanging on colourful ribbons. The broad-brimmed hats, woven from palm fibres, are decorated with bright felt and wool.

Handicraft produced by the women usually comprises embroidered blouses, bags, belts, skirts and ribbons; for their religious ceremonies they make paper flowers, symbolic arrows, pockets, pearl-decorated pumpkins, miniature reproductions of objects used in their everyday lives or of animals or ritual objects in numerous shapes and colours. Of most interest are undoubtedly the "thread paintings", created by sticking multi-coloured threads on to a piece of wood smeared with beeswax. These thread pictures depict deer, Peyotl, corn and other religious and symbolic motifs.

Cora Indians

The Cora tribe, which presently comprises approximately 8000 people, lives along a coastal stretch in the state of Nayarit and in settlements in the Sierra Nayar, e.g. in Dolores, Santa Teresa, Mesa del Nayar, Jesús Maria, San Francisco and Corepán. Their self-administration extensively evades the influence of the state. Their origins are unknown, but it is assumed that they migrated from the south-west of the present USA into the the Mexican central plateau and were later driven to the west coast.

Religion

Although converted to Christianity, Cora Indians continue to practise many pagan rites. They pray to the Catholic saints as well as to their old idols which represent the sun, the stars, and the water. An important Coran ceromony is the driving out of angry spirits from the bodies of the dead. Their cult rituals also include a number of dances, whose origins are pre-Christian, but which have also adopted Catholic features. The main festivals, which follow the Christian calendar, are February 2nd (Candlemas), Holy Week, October 15th (Santa Teresa) and November 2nd (All Saints' Day).

Costumes and Handicrafts

The festive costume worn by the Cora resembles that of the Huicholes, although it has its own patterns.

By way of handicrafts the Cora produce handbags made from Maguey fibres with geometric flower and bird patterns, decorated woollen bags, colourful belts and embroidered shirts.

Nogales

See Sonora

Nuevo Laredo

See Tamaulipas

Nuevo León (State)

Abbreviation: N. L.
Capital: Monterrey
Area: 65,103sq.km/25,136sq. miles
Official population 1990: 3,098,700 (1994 estimate: 4,200,000)

Landscape and Topography

The state of Nuevo León shares a short border in the north with the USA, and is surrounded on the west by Coahuila, on the south by San Luis Potosí, and on the east and north-east by Tamaulipas. While the north of Nuevo León is barren and dry, the east has sub-tropical vegetation, and the mountain chains of the south and west are forested. The state has won a leading role for itself as a centre of industry and trade within Mexico. Nuevo León is mainly inhabited by mestizos and Criollos (descendants of Spaniards).

The state has no pre-Columbian archaeological sites of any consequence.

History

In the pre-Columbian period no Indian culture developed here; the region's barren territory being inhabited only by nomads. The Spanish,

led by Luis Carvajal y de la Cueva, began to colonise the area in 1582/83. Towards the end of the 16th c. the Reino de Nuevo León incorporated the present-day states of Tamaulipas, Coahuila, Zacatecas, Durango and parts of San Luis Potosí, Texas and New Mexico. The present state evolved after independence. In the War of Independence (1810–21), the US–Mexican War (1846–48) and during the French Intervention (1862–66) there were frequent military conflicts in the region. Towards the end of the Mexican Revolution (1917–19) violent battles took place between supporters of Venustiano Carranza and Francisco "Pancho" Villa. The state's economic upswing during this century is directly linked to that of its capital Monterrey.

Economy

A well-developed system of communications and the generation of hydro-electric power and gas form the basis of the state's strong industrialisation which is mainly concentrated around Monterrey. The most important branches of industry are steel production and metal processing, as well as the production of synthetic materials, glass, textiles, ceramics, cement, food and beer. The cultivation of cotton, sugar-cane, oranges and agaves plays a role in agriculture. Cattle breeding, tourism, and silver and lead mining are also of importance.

Important Towns

Besides the economic metropolis of Monterrey (see entry), the principal towns are Linares (population 130,000), Montemorelos (populaton 54,000), Sabinas Hidalgo (population 49,000) and Cerralvo (28,000).

Oaxaca (State)

Abbreviation: Oax.
Capital: Oaxaca
Area: 94,211sq.km/36,375sq. miles
Official population 1990: 3,019,600 (1994 estimate: 3,100,000)

Location and Topography

Oaxaca, Mexico's fifth-largest state, borders the states of Puebla and Veracruz in the north, Guerrero in the west, the Pacific Ocean in the south, and Chiapas in the east. Its landscape is one of the country's most richly varied, comprising long sandy beaches, the rugged mountain chains of the Sierra Madre with forests and deep valleys, as well as the savannas covered with scrub and cacti. Oaxaca's highest mountain is Cempoaltépetl (3400m/11,159ft). Together with Chiapas, Oaxaca is the republic of Mexico's most "Indian" state.

Indian Natives

The descendants of the Zapotecs and the Mixtecs, who once created large pre-Spanish civilisations, and no fewer than fifteen other Indian tribes populate many of Oaxaca's settlements, which remain fairly undisturbed by modern development. It is estimated that, in addition to the lesser tribes, there are now still around 300,000 Zapotecs, 200,000 Mixtecs, 100,000 Mazatecs, 60,000 Mixes, 55,000 Chinantecs, 25,000 Amuzgos and 20,000 Triques.

Archaeological Sites

Among the many old-Indian ruins are the following: Monte Albán (see entry), Dainzú, Lambityeco, Zaachila, San José Mogote, Huijazoo, Cuilapan (for all of these see Oaxaca City, Surroundings), Yagul (see entry), Mitla (see entry) and Guiengola (see Tehuantepec, Surroundings).

History

Traces of settlements found in 1200sq.km/463sq. mile Oaxaca Valley indicate that the region was inhabited as early as the seventh century B.C. Around 1500 B.C. San José Mogote developed into the valley's most important settlement and maintained this position until 600 B.C. when it was replaced as the main centre by Monte Albán, which was

Mexico
United Mexican States
Estados Unidos Mexicanos

Oaxaca

initially under the influence of the Olmecs, as were Huijazoo and Dainzú. The origins of the Zapotecs are uncertain; they possibly migrated from the gulf coast, the home of the Olmecs. Even before the Christian era the influence of the Maya from Guatemala and later the culture of Teotihuacán from the high-lying valley of Mexico became evident. From very early times Oaxaca found itself at a crossroads of human migration and changing cultural influences. During the 7th c. the Mixtecs migrated into the north-west of the state and founded their first dynasty in Tilantongo at Monte Negro. In the 9th and 10th c. they spread further and further out, driving the Zapotecs from Monte Albán and other cult sites. The decline of the Zapotecs began, although they have survived, like the Mixtecs, as a people until the present day. While the Zapotecs left immense artistic constructions and large ceramics as memorials, the Mixtecs were masters at producing fine ceramics, jewellery and codices. During the second half of the 15th c. both these peoples were attacked by the Aztecs and partially subjugated. The Spanish conquered part of the region by 1521, skilfully utilising the conflict existing between Zapotecs, Mixtecs and Aztecs. Hernán Cortés was given large estates here as well as the title of Marqués del Valle de Oaxaca. After the end of the War of Independence Oaxaca became a Mexican state in 1824. Two of Mexico's most famous presidents, Benito Juárez a pure-blooded Zapotec, and the mestizo Porfirio Díaz, came from Oaxaca.

Economy

Although rich in mineral resources such as silver, gold, coal, uranium and onyx, and with fertile soil, Oaxaca's unfavourable economic and social structure makes it one of Mexico's poorest states. An upswing is hoped for by working its reserves of minerals, oil and timber, and by an increase in tourism and the marketing of its popular art. However, the dry climate, over-grazing and some thoughtless deforestation have led to little change in the economic situation.

The Convents of Mixteca Alta

As well as the numerous interesting pre-Columbian and colonial sights both in the capital Oaxaca and in the surrounding area, a visit to the famous 16th c. Dominican convents in the mountainous region of Mixteca Alta is recommended. As these places are on or near the MEX 190 north-west of Oaxaca they are easily accessible. The route leads mainly through high-lying cold valleys. In pre-Columbian times this region formed the centre of the land ruled by the Mixtecs ("those from the land of the clouds") who mainly settled in large towns (Tilantongo, Achiotla, Yanhuitlán, Coixtlahuaca, Tlaxiaco, Zopollán, etc.) between A.D. 1000 and 1521.

The Spanish conquerors, concerned with the quickest possible colonisation and conversion, built a number of splendid Dominican convents, all probably designed by the same architect, with any structural differences attributable to the use of different local craftsmen. For the foundations of their convents the Spanish used material from the ruined Indian temples.

Yanhuitlán

One of these Dominican convents was constructed between 1541 and 1575 in Yanhuitlán (Náhuatl: "new place"), 120km/74 miles north-west of Oaxaca.

The rather simple convent church of Santo Domingo has an original Plateresque main façade which was altered in the 17th c. to incorporate Baroque elements. Its six niches contain statues. The north doorway has a Gothic window with a rose window but is otherwise typical of the Plateresque style. The large nave has complex ribbed vaulting, and the windows are divided by columns in the Gothic style. The Alfarje (a wooden jointed Mudéjar-style roof) in the chancel is particularly beautifully worked.

The "Open Chapel" of Teposcolula

★ Main Altar

The marvellous 17th c. main altar measures 20×10m/66×33ft and is embellished with sculptures and paintings attributed to Andrés de la Concha. Above the altar of the Rosary Chapel there is a unique polychrome marble relief of the Descent from the Cross. To reach the cloister visitors pass through a room containing a number of colourful wooden statues. The stairs are decorated with 16th c. frescos; colonial sculptures and photographs of various local convents are sometimes displayed in the monks' cells.

San Pedro y San Pablo Teposcolula

After a further 15km/9 miles north-west along the MEX 190 a turning on to the MEX 125 is reached; this leads south-west to San Pedro y San Pablo Teposcolula, 13km/8 miles away. This small village, which still depends for its living on the silkworm breeding introduced by the Dominicans, contains the remains of a convent which has been destroyed by both an earthquake and the passage of time.

★ Open Chapel

Although it lies in ruins the Open Chapel is one of the most marvellous examples of 16th c. sacral art in Mexico. With the exception of the centre bays the building is in the purest Renaissance style. In the middle of the double row of arches is a hexagonal chamber, borne by Doric columns which once had a vaulted ceiling; of this little has survived.

Santa Maria Asunción Tlaxiaco

Continue along the MEX 125 for 45km/28 miles beyond San Pedro y San Pablo to reach Santa Maria Asunción Tlaxiaco. The convent here is dedicated to the Assumption of the Virgin Mary and dates from 1550. Of note are the church's plain Plateresque façade and Gothic vault; the altars inside are Neo-Classical.

San Juan Bautista Coixtlahuaca

By turning back along the MEX 190 and continuing north-west for a further 12km/7½ miles in a north-westerly direction we then take a turning to the right which brings us in 24km/15 miles to the settlement of San Juan Bautista Coixtlahuaca. This was once the capital of the Mixteca Alta kingdom and one of the country's important trading centres. In 1458 it was conquered by the Aztecs under their ruler Moctezuma I and made to pay tribute.

★ Convent Church

The Dominican convent has a church dating from 1546 with a remarkable main façade which is predominantly Plateresque. Medallions typical of this style, niches for figures and a Gothic rose-window can be seen above the doorway. It is possible to detect here a trace of the approaching strong Herreriano style. The façade of the side portal is similar in style, without niches. Inside the church there is a large Churrigueresque altar, an interesting arch in the presbytery, an attractive door to the choir and a beautifully carved pulpit. Near the church stand the remains of a once-impressive Gothic open chapel. The convent lies in ruins.

The state of Oaxaca offers further marvellous examples of colonal art, such as in Oaxaca (town, see entry), Tlacolula, Tlacochahuaya and Cuilapan (for all of these see Oaxaca, Surroundings).

Oaxaca (town) — L 9

State: Oaxaca (Oax.)
Altitude: 1545m/5071ft
Population: 400,000
Dialling code: 91 951

Access from Mexico City

By air approximately 50 minutes; by rail about 15 hours; by bus about 10 hours; by car 516km/321 miles on MEX 190.

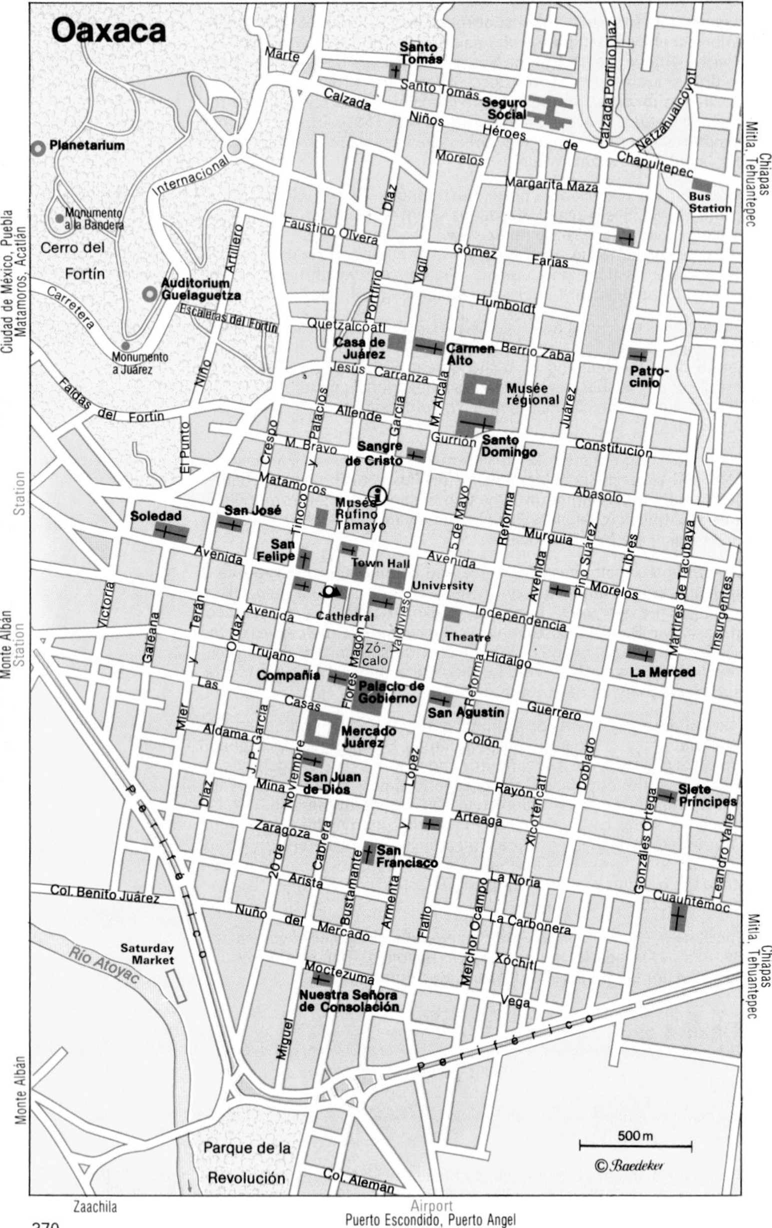
Oaxaca
Planetarium
Monumento a la Bandera
Cerro del Fortín
Auditorium Guelaguetza
Escaleras del Fortín
Monumento a Juárez
Santo Tomás
Seguro Social
Casa de Juárez
Carmen Alto
Musée régional
Santo Domingo
Patrocinio
Bus Station
Sangre de Cristo
Museo Rufino Tamayo
Soledad
San José
San Felipe
Town Hall
University
Cathedral
Theatre
Zócalo
Compañía
Palacio de Gobierno
San Agustín
La Merced
Mercado Juárez
San Juan de Dios
Siete Príncipes
San Francisco
Nuestra Señora de Consolación
Saturday Market
Río Atoyac
Parque de la Revolución
Periférico
Calzada Niños Héroes de Chapultepec
Calzada Porfirio Díaz
Netzahualcóyotl
Internacional
Carretera
Faldas del Fortín
Avenida Independencia
Avenida Morelos
Avenida J. P. García
Las Casas
Col. Benito Juárez
Col. Alemán
500 m
© Baedeker
Ciudad de México, Puebla
Matamoros, Acatlán
Chiapas
Mitla, Tehuantepec
Station
Monte Albán
Zaachila
Airport
Puerto Escondido, Puerto Angel

Location

The charming town of Oaxaca lies almost exactly in the middle of the state of the same name in a valley with subtropical vegetation, surrounded by the high mountains of the southern Sierra Madre.

★Townscape

The town displays an attractive mixture of Indian and Spanish elements. In contrast to other Mexican colonial towns no industrialisation has taken place here as yet and there has also been little growth in population, so that the town has been able to preserve extensively the character of a quiet residential town of New Spain.

History

Oaxaca Valley had already been settled by primitive Indian groups in about 6000 B.C. The beginnings of an independent culture can be dated to San José Mogote (San José phase 1450–1050 B.C.). This was followed by the transitional phase to Monte Albán I between the 8th and 7th c. B.C. This development of the "pre-Zapotecs", who were themselves perhaps Olmecs or were strongly influenced by them, culminated during the following periods in the Zapotec and later Mixtec civilisations. These extended into both the nearby and further surroundings of the town when nothing was known of a settlement on the site of present-day Oaxaca. It was not until 1486 that the invading Aztecs, under their king Ahuítzotl, built their military base Huaxyaca (Náhuatl: "at the acacia grove") here.

In 1521 the Spanish under Francisco de Orozco arrived, laid siege to the Indians and founded a small settlement, christened Antequera, in 1529. By 1532 Emperor Charles V had elevated the settlement to the royal town of Oaxaca, a name which was derived from that of the original Aztec fortress. The town played no part in Mexico's War of Independence (1810–21). In 1830 Porfirio Díaz, the future president of the Republic, was born here as a mestizo of Mixtec origins. The later president and national hero Benito Juárez, a Zapotec Indian, lived in the town when he was governor of the state of Oaxaca from 1847 to 1852.

Sights

★Zócalo

Zócalo (Plaza de Armas or Plaza Central), with its attractive bandstand, beautiful old trees and arcade cafés, is at the centre of Oaxaca's colourful life. The colonial-style Palacio de Gobierno (Government Palace) stands on the south side of the square.

Cathedral

The cathedral, work on which began in the mid-16th c. and lasted for about 200 years, is situated on the north-west side. Its sturdy building style, with two low towers designed to withstand earthquakes, is striking. The original clock, whose mechanism is completely carved from wood, was presented to the church by the King of Spain. The Baroque façade has finely-worked figures and bas-reliefs on its columns. The interior of the church is Neo-Classical; especially noteworthy are the eight engraved glass windows and the various chapels.

★Mercado B. Juárez

Just one block south of Zócalo a daily market (Mercado Benito Juárez) is held in the old market building. Like most of Oaxaca's markets it is very colourful. On Saturdays, when the Indios flock here from all directions, it becomes even livelier; goods on sale include woven articles, earthenware, leatherware, knives and machetes.

The actual large Saturday market was transferred to the Periférico south-west of the town centre.

★★Iglesia de Santo Domingo

The splendid Iglesia de Santo Domingo, a Dominican church founded in 1575, is situated five blocks north of the main square. The church and

Brilliant ceiling relief in the Church of Santo Domingo

the adjoining convent, built with 2m/6½ft-thick walls to make it almost completely earthquake-proof, cover an area of 150m/492ft×150m/492ft. There are numerous niches filled with statues in the impressive Baroque façade.

Interior

The walls and ceiling of the church interior, which dates partly from the 18th c., enjoy a wealth of gilded ornamentation and bright sculptures in high relief, which stand out brilliantly against the white background.

The overall impression is more of a palace than a church. The rustic style of the coloured statues lend the nave, choir arch and chapels a distinctive Mexican note. On the ceiling above the entrance can be seen a vine, from whose golden branches and leaves grow 34 portraits. These depict the family tree of St Domingo de Guzmán, the founder of the Dominican order who died in 1221 and who was related to the royal familes of Spain and Portugal.

Rosary Chapel

Of the eleven different chapels the largest and most beautiful is the Capilla de la Virgen del Rosario (Rosary Chapel). It has its own choir, a sacristy and even a number of towers.

Altar

The lavishly-decorated altar with a figure of the Virgin Mary is considered a jewel of Mexican Rococo.

The majority of the church's original altars and decorations were destroyed in the 1960s when it was temporarily transformed into a stable. Later restoration work was based on the originals.

★Museo Regional de Oaxaca

The Museo Regional de Oaxaca (state-owned regional museum) is housed in the neighbouring convent. Archaeological and ethnological collections of Indian culture, as well as ecclesiastical and secular exhibits from the colonial period, are displayed on two floors.

Gold mask in Oaxaca Regional Museum . . . . . . a turquoise skull from Mixtec Treasure

The ethnological collection includes costumes, masks, jewellery, ceremonial and household implements belonging to the different Indian tribes from the region, together with archaeological finds from the surrounding Zapotec and Mixtec ruins; photographs, charts and maps complete the exhibition.

★★Miztec Treasure

The highlight of the archaeological exhibition is the Mixtec treasure trove of gold, jade, turquoise and other semi-precious stones found in 1932 in Tomb 7 at Monte Albán. Elaborate bracelets, necklaces, ear-rings, breast plates, masks, etc. were produced from these materials. Historical documents and ecclesiastical and secular items from the church and the convent, including an old Spanish kitchen, are to be found here.

Museo de la Ciudad

Contemporary works of art are displayed in the Municipal Museum (Museo de la Ciudad, Alcalá 202), south of Santo Domingo. It is housed in the beautifully restored 16th c. Casa de Cortés, said to have been built on the orders of Hernán Cortés in 1529 after he had been granted the title of Marqués del Valle de Oaxaca. He died without ever seeing it.

★Basílica de Nuestra Señora de la Soledad

Five blocks to the west of Zocalo stands the Basílica de Nuestra Señora de la Soledad (La Soledad Church) which is dedicated to the patron saint of the town. The church was constructed between 1682 and 1690 and has an atrium of limestone blocks surrounded by a covered walk-way at a higher level. The figure of the Virgen de la Soledad wears a black robe of velvet embroidered with gold and other precious stones, and a particularly large pearl on her forehead. Various miracles are attributed to this "royal" saint who is also the patron saint of seafarers.

Other churches

Other notable churches include San Felipe Neri (elaborate altars), San Juan de Dios (Indian depiction of the conquest) and San Agustin (façade reliefs of St Augustine).

★Museo Rufino Tamayo

The Museo de Arte Prehispánico Rufino Tamayo (Rufino Tamayo Museum), a gift to the state from the famous Mexican artist Tamayo, is housed in a palace on the Av. Morelos (no 503), four blocks away from Zócalo. Archaeological objects from the most important Indian cultures are clearly displayed in five rooms.

Museo Casa Juárez

The house at García Vigil 609, where Benito Juárez lived as a servant from 1818 until 1828, has been turned into a museum (Museo Casa Juárez) exhibiting memorabilia concerning the president who was born in 1806 in Guelatao near Oaxaca.

Cerro de Fortín de Zaragoza

A national monument to Benito Juárez, another to the Mexican national flag and an open air theatre are situated on the Cerro de Fortín de Zaragoza, a hill rising about 100m/328ft above the town.

"Guelaguetza"

Every year the country's largest and most colourful fiesta, the "Guelaguetza" (Zapotec: "performance"), takes place here on the two Mondays following July 16th. It includes a mixture of pre-Spanish and Christian dances belonging to the Indian tribes from the state of Oaxaca.

Surroundings

Tree of Tule

The small village of Santa María del Tule lies about 10km/6 miles east on MEX 190. The famous tree of Tule (Arbol del Tule), an impressive example of a species of cypress tree (*Taxodium Mucronatum Ten*), stands in front of a charming little church. It is estimated to be 2000 years old, is 40m/131ft tall and has a circumference of 42m/138ft.

Tlacochahuaya

After a further 10km/6 miles a turning to the left leads to the nearby town of Tlacochahuaya with the 16th c. San Jerónimo Church.

The mighty Tree of Tule

★Indian Paintings

The colourful paintings inside the church are original. Indians portrayed their artistic and religious ideas here in a highly original way by covering the walls with stars, flowers, birds, suns and angels.

Teotitlán del Valle

In another 3km/2 miles a left turn leads to Teotitlán del Valle, 5km/3 miles away. This village with a pre-Spanish past is built around a 17th c. church and is widely known for sarapes (rectangular woollen cloaks with a central hole for the head).

Dainzú

Shortly after Teotitlán del Valle a turning to the left leads to the site of the archaeological ruin Dainzú. Excavation work has revealed that a very old settlement which once existed here was probably inhabited from about 600 B.C. until A.D. 1400, i.e. during the Monte Albán I–V periods. Only a few buildings from this once great Zapotec cult centre have been researched.

Visit to the ruins

One of the most important of these buildings has a pyramid-shaped base and is built in a style similar to that of the north platform at Monte Albán.

★Reliefs

A gallery of highly-interesting flat worked stones was found on the south side of the basement. The reliefs appear, like the "danzantes" in Monte Albán, to have been influenced by the Olmecs. Depictions include people playing the ball game (pelota), and priests or deities with jaguars as patrons of the game. The main staircase in this building was constructed later (about A.D. 700). Similar figures and scenes to those in the wall gallery have been chiselled into the rocks at the summit of the hill. The tomb of a ruler or priest has also been found here. A building in the process of excavation, whose walls and staircases date from the 3rd c. B.C., can be seen in the lower section of the construction. A ball court dating from the 10th or 11th c. A.D. is situated a little to one side.

Lambityeco

A few miles further the archaeological site of Lambityeco lies close to the road. This settlement, which was considerably larger than its present remains suggest, enjoyed its heyday from A.D. 700–900 in line with the decline and abandonment of Monte Albán by the Zapotecs. A small pyramid can be seen, under which an old house was excavated. A total of seven tombs were found here; two heads with names, possibly representing the former owner of the house and his wife, are chiselled into the façade of Tomb 5. Two impressive sculptures of the Zapotec rain god Cocijo were discovered in Lambityeco's second tomb, which was several times built over. A frieze depicting human figures and glyphs, an altar and a tomb, all hewn from stone, are to be found in a patio. It is now assumed that the inhabitants of this unprotected place moved on to settle at Yagul (see entry), an older cult site 5km/3 miles away.

Tlacolula Parish Church

About 2km/1 mile further on a short road on the right leads to the ancient little Zapotec town of Tlacolula, which boasts a parish church built in 1647.

The Baroque façade of the church is in three parts with round-headed arches, columns, niches and a window lighting the choir. The interior is also mainly Baroque with the usual local features. The door to the Capilla del Santo Cristo (Chapel of Christ), the choir screen and the pulpit rails are magnificent examples of the simple wrought ironwork of the colonial period. The fantastic expertly-worked stucco ornamentation of the chapel resembles that of the Santo Domingo Church in Oaxaca, and the Rosary Chapel in Puebla (see entry). Christ, the Virgin of Guadalupe, and martyrs carryng their heads under their arms are portrayed. Also of note are the gold-rimmed mirrors (some embellished with the Habsburg double eagle), the silver chandeliers, the pews and the silver altar. Although Indian influence is occasionally clearly discernible in the ornamentation it is not as evident as in many of the Poblano churches.

A secret passage was discovered in the church which led to a room where valuable silver religious items were discovered. They were hidden here during the Mexican Revolutionary War but are now displayed from time to time.

Sunday market

Tlacolula is also known for its picturesque Sunday market. From Tlacolula it is only 10km/6 miles to Mitla (see entry).

Cuilapan

Cuilapan (Náhautl: "coyote river") lies approximately 12km/7 miles south of Oaxaca and is a centre of the once-important cochineal production. A brilliant scarlet dye is obtained from these insects which live on cacti.

★ Santiago Apóstol

The Church and Convent of Santiago Apóstol, one of the largest of its type in Mexico, is situated on a hill.

Convent Site

Construction of the enormous convent site began in 1555 but remained incomplete. The Renaissance façade of the roofless basilica stands in front of two inner colonnades, part of which collapsed in an earthquake. A stone pulpit, reached by a small flight of steps, can be seen on the left-hand side. The adjoining convent was abandoned in 1663 when the monks moved to Oaxaca. The walls are almost 3m/10ft thick. The murals in the entrance depict the history of the order. The Mexican President Vicente Guerrero was confined in the last room on the main floor before being shot by his enemies in 1831. The terrace on the second floor, where the monks' cells were situated, offers a good panoramic view. On the rear wall a highly interesting stone plaque

Convent of Santiago Apóstol in Cuilapan

bears both the pre-Columbian calendar inscription "10 reeds" and also the Christian year 1555.

Church

The church, the only part of the whole complex still in use, contains the tomb of the last Zapotec princess, the daughter of the ruler Cocijo-eza, who after her baptism was named Juana Donaje.

Museum

A museum of ethnology. and colonial and modern art is housed in the restored part of the convent.

Old-Indian Ruins

Old-Indian ruins discovered near Cuilapan included a remarkable tomb around which a pyramid had been built, an architectural style not typically found in Mexico. An external flight of nine steps leads into an antechamber, from where visitors pass beneath a magnificent stone lintel into the actual tomb. The date-glyphs could not be decoded for a long time. It is assumed that this is a Zapotec tomb from the IV phase (A.D. 800–1200).

Zaachila

The village of Zaachila lies 6km/4 miles further south on the same road as Cuilapan. The last capital of the Zapotec kingdom was once situated here; its remains were only rediscovered in 1962. Up to the present time only the foundations of some of the structures on a hill behind the Church of the Virgen de Juquila have been excavated.

The large central pyramid has hardly been examined. Tombs 1 and 2 were discovered within a patio inside a rectangular platform. Two jaguar heads decorate the façade of Tomb 1; two owls with outspread wings modelled in stucco can be seen in the antechamber. In the burial chamber itself there are stucco figures of two rulers of the underworld with hearts hanging from their shoulders, each accompanied by a priest named "5 Flower" and "9 Flower" with a copal sack. On the back wall an old man is depicted wearing a headdress, with turtle-shell armour on his body and flints in his hands. Tomb 2 was considerably more modestly furnished, although valuable burial objects made of gold, jade and precious stones were found here. These are now kept in the National Museum of Anthropology in Mexico City. As was often the case around Oaxaca, Zapotec graves here were later also used by the Mixtecs as burial chambers. Monoliths, embellished with reliefs, found in the surrounding area are occasionally displayed on the village square.

San José Mogote

The very old ruined site of San José Mogote lies about 10km/6 miles north-west of Oaxaca on the MEX 190 to Guadalupe. Between 1450–1050 B.C. this was the most important of the several settlements in Oaxaca Valley; it was then superseded by Monte Albán between 600 and 500 B.C.

A stone and adobe building dating from the heyday of the site bears reliefs depicting a jaguar's head and vultures, the oldest stone sculptures yet found in Oaxaca. Between 800–600 B.C. a relief slab was made, which served as the threshold of a building, depicting a naked, writhing figure, reminiscent of the later "danzantes" of Monte Albán I.

Reconstructed tombs can be seen with other exhibits in the small museum.

Huijazoo

A further 21km/13 miles north-west along the MEX 190 is the small town of Huijazoo. Shortly behind the town a turning to the left leads over railway lines to the excavation site of Huijazoo (Náhuatl: "in the war fortress") where nine tombs were discovered.

★Tomb 5

The most remarkable of these tombs is Tomb 5 which lies beneath a pyramid not yet examined. A serpent mask forms the entrance to this tomb, whose interior is furnished with sculptured columns and coloured murals. It is thought that these frescos, which depict rulers or priests, date from the 8th to 10th c. A.D. and are of Zapotec origin. The architecture and painting are unique for this part of the country.

Note

The ruins are temporarily closed to visitors.

Orizaba L 8

State: Veracruz (Ver.)
Altitude: 1250m/4102ft
Population: 325,000
Dialling code: 91 272

Access from Mexico City

By rail approximately 8 hours; by bus about 4 hours; by car 275km/171 miles on the MEX 150 D.

Location

Orizaba lies in a fertile valley in the eastern Sierra Madre surrounded by mountains. It experiences heavy rainfall and moderate temperatures. Some 275km/171 miles from Mexico City and 150km/93 miles from Veracruz, the town is both an important centre of communications and one of Mexico's major industrial centres. Despite this it has been able to maintain its colonial character to some extent. Its fertile surroundings and moderate climate have helped the steady development of agriculture and industry within the town. There are coffee and fruit plantations nearby, as well as marble quarries and power stations; the Moctezuma brewery and a cement works, cotton spinning and weaving mills have become established in the town.

History

This once unimportant Indian settlement was conquered by the Aztecs in the mid-15th c. and turned into a military base called Ahuaializapán (Náhuatl: "pleasant waters"). The Spanish occupied this strategic point in the 16th c. Emperor Maximilian and his wife Charlotte enjoyed staying here in their hacienda "Jalapilla" on the outskirts of the town. In 1973 an earthquake destroyed part of the old town, including the bullring.

Sights

San Miguel Parish Church

Massive fortress-like San Miguel Church stands on the north side of the Parque de Castillo. This interesting many-towered church was built between 1620 and 1729. The square bell-tower also serves as a meteorological observatory. One of the church's several towers is Mudéjar in style and covered with tiles. The notable sacristy contains inlay work, as well as murals and pictures by the native artist Gabriel Barranco (19th c.).

Town Hall

The Palacio Municipal (Town Hall) is a curiosity. This green and yellow building, constructed entirely from steel, once served as the Belgian pavilion at the World Exhibition of 1889 in Paris. It was dismantled and transported across the Atlantic to Orizaba and officially opened in 1914.

Museo del Estado de Veracruz

Works by European and Mexican artists are displayed in the Museo del Estado de Veracruz, which is housed in the former church of San Felipe Neri and was opened in 1992.

Surroundings

Presa de Tuxpango

About 6km/4 miles on the MEX 150 a short side road leads to the Presa de Tuxpango (Tuxpango dam and reservoir) on the Rio Blanco. The village of Tuxpango, which lies almost 800m/2625ft below, can be reached by a cableway.

★Pico de Orizaba

Pico de Orizaba (Citlaltépeti), at 5700m/18707ft Mexico's highest mountain, lies on the border with the state of Puebla about 30km/19 miles north of Orizaba. It is best climbed from its west side (see Puebla, Surroundings).

Pachuca de Soto K 7

State: Hidalgo (Hgo.)
Altitude: 2426m/7964ft. Population: 300,000
Dialing code: 91 771

Access from Mexico City

By rail about 2½ hours; by bus about 1½ hours; by car 71km/44 miles on the MEX 85.

Location

Pachuca, the capital of the state of Hidalgo, is surrounded on three sides by mountains and forms the centre of one of Mexico's oldest and richest mining areas. The town, with its steep, crooked alleyways, small squares and beige-painted houses, does not offer many sights. However, the surrounding area enjoys richly varied scenery and towns and villages with interesting early colonial art.

History

The Aztecs are supposed to have founded the settlement of Patlachiucán in about 1490 to mine for the gold and silver located here just below the earth's surface.

Pachuca (Náhuatl: "Pachoa"="narrow place") was established in 1527 by the Spanish conquistador Francisco Téllez. Its first upswing occurred in 1555 when Bartolomé de Medina devised the process of amalgamation, that is separating metals from ores by treating them with mercury. In the mid-18th c. new developments, mainly through the enterprise of Pedro Romero de Terreros, later the Count of Regla, took ore exploitation to a new high point. The considerable number of colonial buildings in the town were also constructed at this time, mainly with his assistance. In 1869 Pachuca became the capital of the Mexican state of Hidalgo.

Sights

Las Cajas

Built in 1670, the fortress-like former treasury Las Cajas in C. Venustiano Carranza 106 is one of the town's most historically-important buildings. The Quinto Real (the King's Fifth), a royal tribute of one fifth of all mineral resources mined in the region given to the Spanish king, was stored here.

Franciscan Convent

The former Franciscan convent, part of an enormous complex, was built at the end of the 16th c. and was renovated and extended several times. The legendary Count of Regla was buried in the church in 1781. An 18th c. impressive Churrigueresque altar forms the centre of the Capilla de la Luz.

★Museo de Fotografia

The convent area also houses the Centro Cultural Hidalgo, the Museum of History (Museo Histórico Regional; archaeological and ethnological collections from the cultures of the Huastecs, Chichimecs, Toltecs, Aztecs and from Teotihuacán, as well as military and religious objects), and the unique Photography Museum (Museo de Fotografia). This museum contains the famous Casasola Collection, with photographs from the late 19th to early 20th c. and, in particular, some portraying the Mexican Revolution.

Torre de Reloj

The Torre de Reloj is a 40m/131ft-tall clock-tower with niches containing four sculptures representing freedom, independence, reform and the republic. The carillon was imported from Austria.

Other noteworthy buildings are Las Casas Coloradas, dating from the end of the 18th c. and now a law court, and the 20th c. Teatro Elfrén Rebolledo.

Surroundings

Venta Prieta

The village of Venta Prieta lies south of the town near the MEX 85. Some of its population, descendants of Spanish Jews and Mexican Indians, form a strict Jewish community. Persecution drove them here from Michoacán at the end of the 19th c.

Mineral del Monte

The important old silver town Mineral del Monte lies within wooded mountains approximately 12km/7½ miles east of Pachuca. Formerly Real del Monte, it was one of the world's richest mines.

★ Mineral del Chico

Picturesque Mineral del Chico, 25km/16 miles to the north and reached by way of El Chico National Park, is another important mining centre.

Huasca de Ocampo

Huasca de Ocampo, San Miguel Regla and San Juan Hueyapan lie in a charming setting approximately 35km/22 miles north-east of Pachuca. The present Hotel Hacienda San Miguel Regla was built in the 18th c.; mined silver ore used to be processed here. Good starting points exist here for excursions into the immediate surroundings, as well as for the Convent Route to the north.

The Convent Route from Pachuca to Huejutla

★ Landscape

A number of interesting 16th c. sacral buildings belonging to the Augustinian order are situated along this stretch (MEX 105), which is characterised by a very richly-varied landscape of mountains, ravines and fertile valleys.

Atotonilco el Grande

From Pachuca it is 34km/21 miles on the MEX 105 to Atotonilco el Grande (Náhuatl: "Place of the Hot Waters"; 2138m/7017ft; population 20,000; market day Thursday) where a mid-16th c. Augustinian convent is situated. The church's Renaissance façade has only been partly preserved and has Plateresque elements with medallions of St Peter and St Paul. The long nave has a very lofty groined vault and the remains of frescos. Murals depicting the great philosophers of antiquity can be seen on the convent staircase.

★ Metztitlán Augustinian Convent

After a further 31km/19 miles a turning to the left leads to Metztitlán (Náhuatl: "Place of the Moon"; 1600m/5251ft; population 20,000) 22km/14 miles away. This was the capital of the like-named independent territory of the Otomí which the Aztecs were never able to subjugate. The 16th c. Augustinian convent has a large atrium with a stone cross, two open chapels and a posa. The plain Renaissance façade of the church has Plateresque features. In the cloister can be seen frescos dating from the 16th c. and later. There is a marvellous view of the valley from the convent ruins.

Metzquititlán

Returning to the main road and continuing northwards the village of Metzquititlán is reached after 10km/6 miles. The 16th c. Augustinian

Church of the Señor de la Salud has a beautiful Indian-Plateresque doorway in the style of Tequitqui stonemason's art.

★ Santa María Xoxoteco

From Metzquititlán a secondary road leads to San Nicolás. After 2.5km/1½ miles a path turns off left across a small river and through fields to Santa María Xoxoteco. In 1974 extremely impressive 16th c. frescos were found in the church. They depict religious themes in a rather morbid interpretation, in the style of the frescos of Actopan (see entry).

Tlahualompa

A road turns off right from the MEX 105 17km/10½ miles north of Metzquititlán to Tlahualompa some 9km/5½ miles away. This is a centre of bellfounding and the work can sometimes be watched here. The Indians living in the area sell copperware. The land between Tlahualompa and the road is rich in obsidian.

Zacualtipán

Returning on the MEX 105 it is 6km/4 miles to Zacualtipán (2020m/6630ft; population 30,000) where a 16th c. Augustinian convent and a church with an Indian-Plateresque façade can be visited.

Molango

The next interesting place is Molango (1650m/5415ft; population 12,000), charmingly situated some 39km/24 miles away and named after the old-Indian god Mola. The convent was founded in 1546 and built on a pre-Columbian cult site. It has an unusual Spanish-Plateresque church façade with a beautifully-made Gothic rose window. Note the rare carved inner side (Alféizar) of the entrance pilasters. The partly-ruined cloister has an impressive harmony.

Espadaña

Remarkable in Molango is the Espadaña, a lengthening of the atrium wall in place of a bell tower.

Laguna Atezca, 6km/4 miles away, offers opportunities for water-sport.

Huejutla de Reyes

The last notable town on this route through the state of Hidalgo is Huejutla de Reyes (population 80,000; fiestas: November 2nd, Dia de los Fieles Difuntos, December 12th, Dia de la Virgen de Guadelupe; Sunday market), approximately 95km/59 miles from Molango. This Huastec town also possesses a mid-16th c. Augustinian convent. Its church has a renovated Plateresque façade and contains a stone font with stylised plant ornamentation. The location of the atrium in the town square is very unusual. Huejutla is also famous for its pottery.

From Huejutla the MEX 105 crosses the state of Veracruz to the port of Tampico (see entry) approximately 165km/103 miles away.

Palenque — N 9

State: Chiapas (Chis.)
Altitude: 150m/492ft
Population: 15,000

Access

By air-taxi from Villahermosa (see entry), San Cristóbal de Las Casas (see entry) and Tuxtla Gutiérrez (see entry); by bus from Villahermosa approximately 2½ hours; by car from Villahermosa 114km/71 miles on the MEX 186 to Cataja, turn off right there on the MEX 199 as far as Palenque (23km/14 miles), continue for another 9km/5½ miles to the ruins; from San Cristóbal de Las Casas via Ocosingo 205km/127 miles on the MEX 199.

Location

Palenque's great Classic Maya site lies at the foot of a chain of low hills covered with tall rain forest, above the green alluvial plain of the Río

Usumacinta. The style of architecture and sculpture which developed locally between A.D. 600 and 800 is unique in its beauty and technical perfection. In contrast to the Mayas of North Yucatán, who liked to locate their imposing buildings around great open squares, the architects of Palenque chose a more enclosed layout which suited the hilly site.

History

It is certain that the ruined site now called by the Spanish name Palenque ("Stockade") already existed in the pre-Classic period (300 B.C.–A.D. 300). At this time the first Mayan culture was already flourishing in the southern region (Pacific coast and highland of Guatemala). It was initially influenced by the culture of the Olmecs and later by Teotihuacán. There is some evidence, however, that the Mayas had undergone their own cultural development long before this.

Present-day historians have established that Palenque first appeared in the Mayan early-Classic period (A.D. 300–600). This religious and political centre experienced its heyday between A.D. 600 and 700. Thanks to recent research into glyphs reconstruction of the genealogy of the kings of Palenque from the accession of Bahlum-kuk ("jaguar quetzal") in A.D. 431 to the death of Cimi-pacal in A.D. 799 has been possible. At this time Palenque was one of the great towns in the central Mayan area, together with Yaxchilán (Chiapas), Tikal, Piedras Negras, Quiriguá, Uaxactún (all in Guatemala) and Copán (Honduras). During this phase basic elements of Mayan culture, including the corbel vault, new hieroglyphic writing, the art of carving stelae and the calendar, were developed to the highest level. This Classical period was earlier called the "Old Empire" to differentiate it from the "New Empire" in northern Yucatán from the 10th c. onwards. As a result of advances in historical knowledge gained in the past two decades this division is no longer tenable.

As with all other Mayan towns in the central region Palenque was abandoned in the 9th c. The last known date discovered is A.D. 799. Twenty years after that Palenque had ceased to exist. Reasons for the sudden desertion of this and other Mayan sites have been puzzled over for many years and it remains unknown what happened at that time. It is most probable that external pressure led to a popular revolt against the caste of priests whose rule was becoming increasingly harsh. The region's great sites deteriorated within a very short time and were swallowed up by primeval forest.

Ordónez y Aguilar, José Antonio Calderón and Antonio Bernanconi were the first to visit the site in 1784. They were followed two years later by the Spanish captain José Antonio del Río, who presented Charles III of Spain with the first report on Palenque. Guillermo Dupaix investigated the site in 1805 and prepared an illustrated report. The controversial Jean Fredéric de Waldeck lived in Palenque from 1832–34. J. L. Stephens and F. Catherwood stayed here in 1841, and their reports and drawings travelled around the world. They were followed by the illustrious researchers Desiré Charnay, Teobert Maler, Alfred Maudslay and, in the 20th c., by Eduard Seler, Sylvanus G. Morley and Frans Blom. During recent decades important research work has been carried out by the Mexican I.N.A.H. (Instituto Nacional de Arqueologia e Historia) under the archaeologists Miguel Angel Hernández and, later, Alberto Ruz l'Huillier and Jorge Acosta. Later excavation work was led by César Sáenz. Arnoldo Gonzáles and Roberto Garcia. UNESCO has declared Palenque a world cultural heritage site.

Visit to the ★ ruins

Archaeological Zone

The archaeological zone being excavated now measures approximately 300m/985ft from east to west and 500m/1641ft from north to

Palenque: view of the Palace and Temple of the Inscriptions

south, and is only a fraction of the entire area of Palenque. It is estimated that this extends for between 8–9km/5–6 miles in an east–west direction. Water from the small river Otulum is channelled underground via an aqueduct, the only one of its kind in Mayan architecture, to the town centre.

After entering the area, the ruins of Temples XII and XIII are seen on the right; both were probably constructed between A.D. 731 and 764.

Temple of Inscriptions
Open from 10am

The next building is the Templo de las Inscripciones (Temple of Inscriptions), begun under the ruler Pacal ("Shield"; A.D. 603–683) and completed in 683. The crypt was built first, followed by the pyramid. This plain classical pyramid with the temple cap measures 20m/66ft in height and comprises nine plinths placed on top of each other.

★Hieroglyphics

Remains of stucco figures can still be recognised on the six pillars framing the five entrances to the temple. A total of 620 glyphs have been chiselled into the walls leading from the main entrance to the chamber at the rear. These inscriptions, from which the building has gained its name, appear mainly to concern the family chronicle of the rulers of Palenque.

★★Crypt

One of the greatest sensations of pre-Columbian archaeology began to emerge when Alberto Ruz l'Huillier discovered an entrance in the middle chamber of the temple in 1949 which led to a flight of steps buried in earth and rubble. It took three years to reveal the secret entrance to the interior of the pyramid. Finally a masonry wall, at the foot of which lay earthenware vessels, shells, pieces of jade and a pearl as votive offerings, was discovered. The wall was torn down and the explorers found themselves standing in front of an upright triangular slab, in front of which were the remains of a tomb with the skeletons

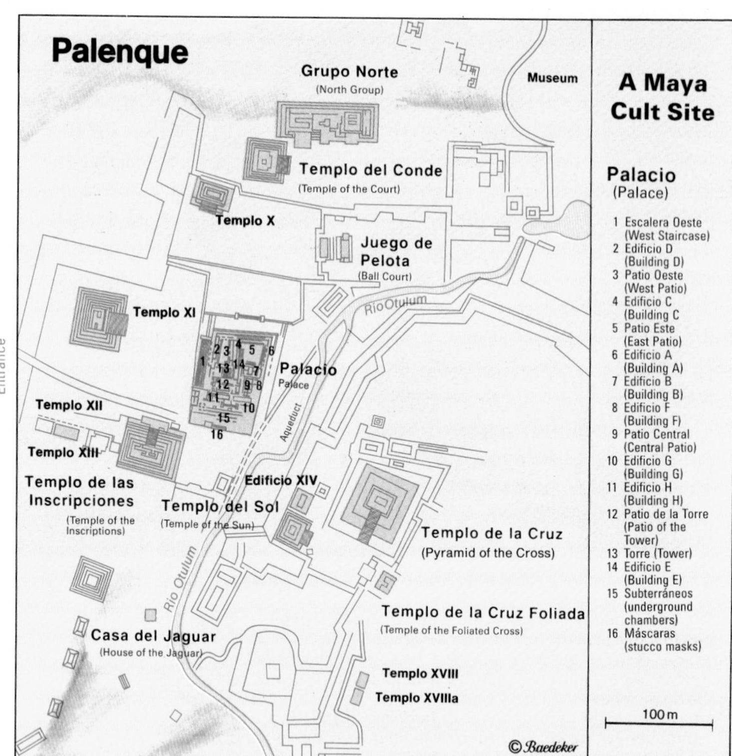

of six youths. The stone slab was turned on its axis to reveal the entrance to a crypt, almost 7m/23ft high, 9m/29½ft long and 4m/13ft wide, situated 27m/89ft below the temple platform. The walls of the chamber, which dripping water had filled with stalagmites and stalactites, display nine stucco reliefs of gods or priests. Two stucco heads, some of the finest of their kind in the world, were found on the floor. The 3.80m/12½ft×2.20m/7¼ft, five-tonne stone slab which sealed the sarcophagus is embellished in low relief. Pacal, the ruler, sits with his knees drawn up and his upper body bent back on a mask which portrays the earth god. A cruciform device, which may represent the "Ceiba", the sacred tree of the Maya, can be seen above this figure and above this again hovers a celestial bird. On the sides of the figure a number of symbolic death signs can be recognised. Chiselled into the sides of the slab are 52 glyphs. It is now known that this is a symbolic representation of the death and rebirth of the ruler Pacal of Palenque, who reigned from A.D. 615–683. Pacal's skeleton lay inside the sarcophagus with a mask made of pieces of jade covering his face. His fingers, throat and arms were also decorated with jade jewellery and he held a piece of jade in each hand and in his mouth.

This discovery in 1952 showed for the first time that a Maya pyramid could also serve as a funerary monument for a ruler, as in Eygpt.

A classical Maya stucco head

Relief in Building E of the Palace

★★ Grave goods

The grave goods and a reconstruction of the crypt of Palenque can be seen in the Museum of Anthropology in Mexico City. Part of this irreplaceable collection, including the aforementioned jade mask, were stolen during a burglary on Christmas night 1985 but happily have since been recovered.

★ **Palace**

The Palacio (Palace) is next encountered on the left-hand side; it is a building untypical of Mayan architecture. It was constructed on an enormous man-made platform, trapezoid in shape, approximately 10m/33ft high, 100m/330ft long and 80m/263ft wide. It is thought that the part of the palace visible today was built in several phases between A.D. 650–770. The irregular site consists essentially of a good dozen buildings arranged around four inner courtyards, Subterráneos (underground passages), and a tower which dominates the whole scene.

It is assumed that the palace served mainly as an administrative building, although part of it was inhabited by the rulers.

Building D

Building D, which has two passages running in parallel, is situated on the west staircase on the left. On the outside there are five doors, the columns of which are decorated with impressive but partly very badly damaged reliefs. These depict, among other things, what are assumed to be a rite of consecration and the dancing ruler Pacal with his wife or mother. The inner side of Building D is bordered by the west courtyard.

★ Tower

The four-storeyed 15m/49ft-tall tower, which rests on an almost square base and was probably used as an observatory, is unique in ancient Indian architecture.

Building E

Building E is reached from the tower courtyard. Its passages and rooms exhibit typical Mayan corbellled vaulting. An oval tablet found here is

Palenque: Temple of the Inscriptions

decorated with a relief of two seated figures, one of whom is handing a headdress to the other, who is seated higher on a double-headed jaguar throne. From the glyphs above it can be inferred that this represents the ruler Zac-kuk and her son Pacal at his accession in A.D. 615. It is remarkable that Zac-kuk is mainly portrayed with her fingers and parts of her head diseased and swollen while Pacal has a club-foot.

East Courtyard

The largest and most interesting patio is the east courtyard, which is enclosed by Building C to the west, Building A to the east and Building B to the south.

Building C

The steps leading to Building C are flanked by stone slabs depicting kneeling figures in obsequious positions. Each of these figures appears to be drawing attention to the glyphs on the steps. As far as these glyphs can be decoded they represent the the name of the ruler Pacal with the dates of his birth (A.D. 603) and accession (A.D. 615). To the right of the steps is a tablet with four enlarged glyphs; these have not yet been deciphered.

Building A

The staircase to Building A, which stands opposite, is framed on both sides by square stone blocks; four on the left and five on the right have massive figures carved into them. As some of the figures are portrayed in obsequious kneeling postures it is believed that they are slaves or prisoners. The columns subdividing the entrances on the exterior eastern façade of the building are decorated with beautiful, but very badly damaged, stucco reliefs. The two outer panels bear glyphs, while the others portray figures of rulers.

Throne

The throne, decorated with hieroglyphics and dated A.D. 662, was once the centre-piece of a cult chamber divided into many parts.

The palace also contains three latrines and a steam bath used for ritual cleansing.

Count's Temple

The path continues past the remains of the ball court (pelota) and on to the Templo del Conde (Count's Temple), which owes its name to the fact that Frédéric de Walbeck once lived here. Constructed between A.D. 640 and 650, it is the oldest building yet excavated.

Mansardes

Typical of the Palenque style are the two parallel passageways, the rear one divided into three chambers. The "mansarde effect", created by the sloping outer walls, is apparent here for the first time. These follow the inner arches which slope in parallel. This is a typical difference between the style of Palenque and that of Puuc in Yucatán, where vertical outer walls are used between the middle and upper tiers. Also Palenque in style are the slanting walls above the middle tier; these are decorated with stucco reliefs of figures and masks, while in the Puuc region stone mosaic decoration dominates. The buildings of Palenque were also often used as burial places; three tombs with burial objects such as jade beads, obsidian knives and shell jewellery were discovered under the floor of the Templo del Conde.

North Group

The Grupo Norte (North Group) adjoins to the north-east. Among this group Temples II, III, IV and V were built between A.D. 695–730.

Museum

The new spacious museum is situated near this group. It exhibits local finds, including: Stela 1 with the figure of a ruler or a priest above a glyph; a tablet with 96 glyphs; a double tablet on which a person and a masked deity are depicted; a limestone sacrificial vessel with a lid; modelled stucco fragments; various ceramics.

★Temple of the Sun

Follow the path towards the palace, past the remains of the aqueduct and across the Otulum to the Templo del Sol (Temple of the Sun). Completed in 692 the temple stands on a four-storeyed pyramid platform and is one of Palenque's most charming buildings.

Roof Combs

The temple has three doorways which lead to two passageways and a rear shrine. The well-retained roof comb, which once embellished most of the buildings of Palenque, is striking. Roof combs served as a decorative function, as well as appearing to increase the height of the buildings and to lengthen the middle supporting wall. The pillars of the doorways are embellished with stucco human figures and glyphs, although only fragments of these remain.

★Bas-relief

A magnificent bas-relief can be seen on the rear wall opposite the central entrance. The middle of the slab is formed by a shield with two crossed lances representing the sun god; beneath this is an altar borne by two seated figures, possibly symbolising gods of the underworld. There are figures to the right and left of this. It is now believed that the left-hand figure is the ruler Pacal (already a deity?) with the right-hand one his son and successor Chan-bahlum ("snakejaguar"; born 635, ruled A.D. 684–702). The inscription above the shield of the sun god shows the date of Chan-bahlum's accession. Both figures are surrounded by glyphs. Chan-bahlum is depicted with six fingers and six toes; this physical abnormality could have brought him special status.

Building XIV

Building XIV, to the north, was probably constructed after the death of Chan-bahlum by his brother and successor Kan-zul ("valuable animal", also called Hok; ruled A.D. 702–722?). The bas-relief dated A.D. 705 shows Chan-bahlum's resurrection from the underworld Xibalba and the homage being paid by his mother Apo-hel. It is assumed that this

Temple of the Foliated Cross

Temple of the Sun

building was created to appease the menacing spirit of the dead ruler, who had the neighbouring temples of the Sun, Cross and Foliated Cross built in his honour.

Temple of the Cross

The Templo de la Cruz (Temple of the Cross) is in the same group. This temple, which resembles the Temple of the Sun, was also built by Chan-bahlum in A.D. 692. It is suspected that the ruler lies buried in this building. The medium-sized relief slab, found in the rear shrine of the temple and now displayed in the National Museum of Anthropology in Mexico City, shows Chan-bahlum on the right, and on the left his father Pacal with a cross-like object ("ceiba", the sacred tree of the Maya?). The temple owes its name to this scene. Carved into the left-hand side panel is a depiction of Chan-bahlum after his accession, while the right-hand one shows the god L, an old god of the underworld who was associated with the ruling house, smoking a cigar. In 1993 Mexican archaeologists discovered four tombs with skeletons and numerous grave goods. The most important tomb was on the south side of the temple, halfway towards the west side. Among other things, it contained some fine jade pieces, including a burial mask, a breastplate and ear adornments, suggesting that the tomb must have been that of a person of high rank.

Temple of the Foliated Cross

The Templo de la Cruz Foliado (Temple of the Foliated Cross) stands opposite the Temple of the Sun, and resembles this and also the two aforementioned buldings and dates from the same decade. The relief here once again concerns the transfer of power between Pacal and Chan-bahlum. The main motif is a cross, which is growing from the head of the sun-god. A sun bird perches on top of the cross. The arms of the cross form the leaves of the maize plant, decorated with human heads. The figure of a ruler again stands on either side; this time it is the dead father who is on the right with his son and successor on the left.

The waterfalls of Agua Azul

There are other buildings near Temples XVIII and XVIII A, while the Casa del Jaguar (House of the Jaguar) stands on the other side of the River Otulum.

Surroundings

Mizol-há

20km/12 miles south-west of Palenque on the road to Ocosingo a turning to the right leads to the Mizol-há (Maya: "waterfall") waterfalls. These beautiful romantically-situated cascades tumble almost 30m/99ft into a large pool in which it is possible to bathe.

★ Agua Azul

Approximatly 45km/28 miles further on a road turns off on the right to the Agua Azul (Spanish: "blue water") waterfalls, 4km/2½ miles away. The water here falls in several wide cascades among tropical vegetation into the Rio Bascan and later into the Rio Tulijá. The unusually clear water in its limestone bed appears blue. Good swimming is possible at certain times of the year in the various natural pools which have been eroded by the action of the water, while other areas are dangerous. Simple restaurants, a camp site and a landing-strip have been recently established here.

Papantla

See El Tajin

Paricutin

See Uruapan

Parral (Hidalgo del Parral)

See Chihuahua (town)

Lago de Pátzcuaro (Patzcuaro Lake) I 8

State: Michoacán (Mich.)

Access from Mexico City

By rail along a beautiful country route in approximately 12 hours; by bus and by car on the MEX 15 about 350km/217 miles via Morelia.

Location

Lago de Pátzcuaro (Pátzcuaro Lake) has a length of 19km/12 miles, an average width of almost 5km/3 miles and lies at a height of 2050m/6725ft.

★Landscape

The lake is surrounded by forested mountains and extinct volcanoes and contains a string of islands, of which Janitzio, Jarácuaro, Tecuén, Yunuén and Pacanda are the most important. Numerous picturesque Indio villages, which have managed to retain to a great extent their old way of life, are situated along the banks of the lake and in the surrounding area. Its location and surroundings make Lago de Pátzcuaro one of Mexico's most popular tourist attractions which can sometimes lead to overcrowding. Pollution, however, has also affected the lake detrimentally during recent years.

★Pátzcuaro

The most important town in the region is Pátzcuaro (Tarascan: "place of the stones for temple building"; 2175m/7138ft; population 90,000; market day: Friday) situated 4km/2½ miles from the lake.

This delightful little town still presents a picture of the past. While the Indian element continues to prevail in the life of this former Tarascan metropolis, its most attractive old buildings date back to 1550 when Pátzcuaro was a Spanish episcopal see. The memory of the Indians' great protector and teacher, Bishop Vasco de Quiroga ("Tata Vasco", 1470–1565), is still very much alive. The history of the town, which received its charter from the Emperor Charles V in 1553, is closely linked to that of Tzintzuntzan and Morelia (see entries).

San Agustin

The former church of San Agustin stands on the colonial-style Plaza de San Agustin (Plaza Chica, Plaza Bocanegra). The church now houses the Biblioteca Gertrudis Bocanegra; inside the building Michoacán's history is portrayed in murals by Juan O'Gorman. An interesting market (Mercado) adjoins the plaza.

★★Plaza Principal

Both the Calle Itturbide and the Calle Zaragoza lead to the Plaza Principal (Plaza Vasco de Quiroga, Plaza Grande), one of the finest and largest of Mexico's squares. The Palacio Municipal (Town Hall), a former 18th c. palace, stands on the right. The Casa del Gigante (House of the Giants), with its beautiful doorway and decorated balcony windows, is situated on the east side of the square.

Fishing with a "butterfly net", now only for tourists

Calle Ponce de León

The old royal customs house is situated in the south-west corner of the square, in the Calle Ponce de León. The Baroque Church of San Francisco stands in the next block. It contains a statue of Christ, credited with miraculous powers.

Cerro del Estribo

By following Calle Ponce de León further to the west, the extinct volcano Cerro del Estribo ("Hill of the Stirrup") is reached after approximately 4km/2½km. From here there is a marvellous view of the town and lake.

Casa de los Once Patios

The Casa de los Once Patios ("House of the Eleven Patios"), a former 17th/18th c. convent of St Catherine stands to the south-east of the Plaza Principal. It contains the Museo de Arte Contemporáneo, which exhibits almost 200 engravings, pictures and sculptures by contemporary Mexican and foreign artists.

La Compañia

Follow Calle Enseñanza north past the Hospital Santa María to the Church of La Compañia which was founded in 1546 by Bishop Quiroga and rebuilt in the 18th c.

★Museo de Artes Populares

The former Colegio de San Nicolás, a school founded in 1540 by Quiroga, occupies the next corner. It houses the notable Museo de Artes Populares with a collection of ethnological exhibits as well as old and new folk art from the region.

La Colegiata

Nearby is the Basilica Nuestra Señora de la Salud (La Colegiata), which was founded as a cathedral by Bishop Quiroga in 1543, but was never completed. It contains a statue of the Virgin of Salud made of thick maize paste (Pasta de Caña), a technique typical of Tarascan sacral art.

El Humilladero

The Calvary chapel of El Humilladero outside the town is reached via the Calle del General Serrato. It has a 17th c. doorway in Renaissance style, showing Indian-influence, an unusual Renaissance doorway, a crucifix dated 1553 and an interesting altar.

★Janitzio Island

From Pátzcuaro town centre it is 4km/2½ miles to Kai (Muelle). Boats can be rented here for trips to the various islands. On and around the lake are some thirty attractive Indian villages. Their inhabitants live predominantly by fishing, mainly using boats hollowed out of tree trunks and a variety of nets to catch delicate whitefish (pescado blanco) as well as various types of perch and trout. The famous "butterfly nets" (Uiripu) are now only used for the benefit of tourists.

Tecuén is the most beautiful island in Lake Pátzcuaro. Janitzio, reached by boat in half an hour, is the most important but most crowded. The picturesque fishing village of Janitzio, with its narrow winding alleyways and tile-roofed houses, is dominated by a grandiose memorial to the Mexican hero of independence José María Morelos. Steps inside the monument lead up to the head of the statue from where a marvellous panoramic view of the lake can be enjoyed. On the walls of the staircase are frescos depicting scenes from the life of Morelos by Ramón Alva de Canal.

★ All Souls' Day Festival

Janitzio is also famed for its All Souls' Day Festival (Spanish: "Dia de los Muertos"; Tarascan "Animecha-Kejtzitakua" = "gifts for the dead"). This very lively celebration takes place on the night of November 1st–2nd and combines Catholic and pagan elements into a particularly impressive religious form. On the morning of October 31st the ceremonial Wild Duck Hunt (Kuirisi-ataku) is held on the lake. Heavy spears (Atlatl) approximately 2.5m/8ft in length, are hurled at the ducks.

Surroundings

★ Erongaricuaro

The pretty Tarascan village of Erongaricuaro (Purépecha: "viewing tower of the lake") lies on the west side of the lake about 18km/11 miles from Pátzcuaro. During the Second World War a group of French Surrealists lived in the village.

Quiroga

Quiroga (1996m/6551ft; population 25,000) is situated on the northern side of the lake, approximately 25km/15½ miles north of Pátzcuaro and 8km/5 miles from Tzintzuntzan (see entry). It boasts a 16th c. Franciscan convent and is well-known as a sales centre for the folk art of the region.

Zacapu

The small lakeside resort of Chupícuaro is reached by following the MEX 15 towards Guadalajara for a few miles. The town of Zacapu (Purépecha: "stone square"; 1980m/6498ft; population 80,000) lies 40km/25km from Quiroga. It is believed that during the 12th or 13th c. it was the first capital of the Tarascans (Purépechas). The 18th c. convent church has a Plateresque façade with Mudéjar elements. Near the town are several excavation sites (Malpais and La Iglesia) in which a large number of tombs were found.

Santa Clara del Cobre

20km/12 miles south of Pátzcuaro is Villa Escalante or Santa Clara del Cobre (2140m/1330ft; population 30,000; fiesta August 15th, Assumption and copperware fair). This little old Tarascan town is widely known for its beautiful beaten copperware. This craft had been well-developed in the pre-Spanish period and was then promoted and encouraged in

The Island of Janitzio, with the monumental Morelos Statue

the 16th c. by Bishop Vasco de Quiroga. The craft museum documents this development.

★ Lake Zirahuén

A road leads west from Villa Escalante for 11km/7 miles to the beautiful Lake Zirahuén (Purépecha: "Tzirahuén" = where it steams), more than 4km/2½ miles long.

★★ Santiago Apóstol de Tupátero (Mon.–Wed. 9am–3pm; Thur.–Sat. noon–6pm; it is best to check in advance at the tourist office in Pátzcuaro)

15km/9 miles from Pátzcuaro in the direction of Tiripetío and Morelia, a right-hand turning to Guanajo leads in 4km/3½miles to the village of Tupátero. Here visitors to the modest adobe Church of Santiago Apóstol are surprised by the altar dedicated to St Jacob and a remarkable Mudéjar-style vault. This is embellished with unique wood carvings which impressively depict the life of Christ and the Madonna as described to the Indians in the 16th c. by missionaries. Comparable religious paintings were found in two churches near Cuzco in Peru.

Paz, La

See La Paz

Pico de Orizaba (Citlaltépetl)

See Puebla (town)

Piedras Negras

See Coahuila de Zaragoza

Popocatépetl/Iztaccíhuatl K 8

State: México (Mex.) and Puebla (Pue.)

Access

From Mexico City via Chalco and Amacameca approximately 86km/53 miles to the mountain hut (albergue) at Tlamacas.

From Puebla to Chalco, from there 43km/27 miles along a poor road via San Nicolas de los Ranchos to the Paso de Cortés. Then turn south to Tlamacas (departure point for Popocatépetl), 5km/3 miles away. Turn north for 7km/4 miles to La Joya (departure point for Iztaccíhuatl).

Location

A volcanic belt, which crosses Mexico from the Pacific to the Atlantic, forms the southern edge of the extensive Mexican highlands. In the early and middle tertiary period enormous lava flows poured over the land. During the second phase of eruptions, which began in Pliozän and still continues, the enormous mountains Popocatépetl (5452m/17,893ft) and Iztaccíhuatl (5286m/17,349) came into being. These two majestic snow-covered peaks of the Sierra Nevada form the mountain ridge separating the high valley of Mexico and the plateau of Puebla.

Advice

An ascent of the two volcanoes does not require any great climbing ability but should not be undertaken without the appropriate equipment (sleeping bag, anorak, climbing boots, rucksack, ice picks and, if necessary, ice spikes, which can be rented). The climb should be made slowly but continuously. Too fast a pace can result in altitude-induced circulation problems. The inexperienced are advised to use the services of a guide (information in Amecameca, Hotel San Carlos, or at the mountain hut (Albergue in Tlamacas; see also Practical Information, Sport, Climbing). It is best to climb the mountains between November and March. According to the wind direction sulphurous vapours can aggravate the ascent.

National Park

The route from Amecameca to Tlamacas passes through Popocatépetl-Iztaccíhuatl National Park, which lies between the two passes and reaches the Paso de Cortés (Cortés Pass).

Paso de Cortés

Hernán Cortés and his conquistadors crossed this pass on November 3rd 1519 on their march from the coast of the Gulf of Mexico to Tenochtitlán.

★★**Popocatépetl**

The mountain hut (Albergue; 3998m/13,121ft), the last departure point for an ascent of Popocatépetl (Náhuatl: "Smoking Mountain"), which can be reached by vehicle, is on the right. From here the summit of the mountain can be reached via two routes. If climbers set off very early (about 3am) they can complete an ascent and descent all in one long day. As the little bivouac shelter Las Cruces burnt down in 1985 and is not yet back in use, it is not at present possible to undertake an ascent over two days. The massive crater at the snow-covered summit measures 826m/2711ft×400m/1313ft, its rocky walls are almost vertical.

Active Volcano

The last great eruption occurred in 1802, since when there have been only minor eruptions; however, a cloud of smoke frequently hovers above the summit. Since the time of the conqueror Cortés great amounts of sulphur, originally used for the manufacture of gunpowder, have been extracted from the crater.

★★**Iztaccíhuatl**

Iztaccíhuatl or Ixtaccíhuatl (Náhuatl: "white woman") Mountain is reached by taking the road from the Paso de Cortés towards La Joya. This craterless mountain, in legend a princess who died from love-sickness and who was united in death with the warrior Popocatépetl,

Popacatépetl: the "smoking mountain"

On the way to the summit of Popocatépetl

Iztacchuatl, the "White Woman"

lies approximately 15km/9 miles from Popocatépetl. Viewed from Mexico City, if visibility permits, the outline of Iztaccíhuatl's three snow-covered peaks resembles the head, chest and knees of a recumbent female figure. Two days should be allowed for the difficult ascent and descent; small bivouac shelters are available. The radio station Torre Retransmisora, at a height of 3950m/12,964ft, offers good and cheap overnight accommodation before and after the ascent.

It is 23km/14 miles from Paso de Cortés to Amecameca (see entry).

Puebla (State)

Abbreviation: Pue.
Capital: Puebla
Area: 33,995sq.km/13,125sq. miles
Official population 1990: 4,126,100 (1994 estimate: 4,400,000)

Location and Topography

The state of Puebla is bounded on the north and east by Veracruz, on the south by Oaxaca and Guerrero, and on the west and north-west by Morelos, the Estado de México, Tlaxcala and Hidalgo. The landscape is characterised by plateaux, mountain ranges with glacial peaks and fertile valleys. Puebla is densely inhabited and is one of Mexico's most important cultural and economic areas. The population includes Criollos (Creoles), descendants of Spaniards, and mestizos, as well as various Indian tribes such as Náhua, Otomí, Totonacs and Mazatecs.

Archaeological Sites

Although Puebla possesses numerous archaeological sites, the only ones likely to appeal to the ordinary visitor are Cholula (see entry) and Yohualichán (see Teziutlán, Surroundings). Las Bocas and Coxcatlán are still under excavation.

Puebla

History

Adjoining the cultural centres of the Anáhuac plateau, the area of the present state of Puebla played a significant role in the pre-Columbian period. The earliest evidence of fruit cultivation (pumpkins, avocados, chillies, cotton), estimated as dating from 7000 B.C., was found in the Tehuacán Valley. Later ancient Indian people, such as the Olmecs, the Zapotecs, the Mixtecs, the Toltecs, the Totonacs and the Aztecs (Mexica), ruled here from 1200 B.C. both after and with each other until the arrival of the Spanish. The most important religious and political centre of the Classic and post-Classic periods was without doubt Cholula, which continued to exert strong influence through many centuries until the Conquista.

The Spanish under Hernán Cortés arrived in the area of the present state in 1519 on their way from the Gulf Coast to Tenochtitlán. The conquerors colonised the land very quickly, and Puebla's ensuing history is bound up with that of its capital which bears the same name.

Economy

Soon after the Conquista the state became, and has remained, of major importance for its communications and its agricultural products such as grain, maize, coffee, sugar-cane and Maguey agaves. The principal minerals worked here were gold, copper, coal, onyx and marble. Also of importance is hydro-electric power, which is partly responsible for the rapid development of industry in the state. Ceramics (mainly tiles), textiles, glass, soap, leatherware and, not least, vehicles are manufactured in the state. Local craft products, tourism and mineral water bottling (Tehuacán) all contibute to the economy.

Places of Interest

As well as the well-known tourist centres and their surroundings, including Puebla, Acatepec, Cholula, Huejotzingo and Teziutlán (see entries), the following places in the state of Puebla are worth mentioning:

Tehuacán

Tehuacán (1670m/5481ft; population 160,000; Harvest Festival in June; Saturday market) lies in the south-west of the state and is a quiet little spa with the churches of San Francisco (17th and 18th c.) and El Carmen (18th c.), as well as the Tehuacán Valley Archaeological Museum and the Dr Miguel Romero Mineral Collection. The thermal baths here are well-known, as is the water which has become the best-known mineral water in Mexico.

Izcuar de Matamoros

Situated approximately 80km/50 miles south of Puebla (see entry), Izcuar de Matamoros (1300m/4267ft; population 70,000; Fiesta: July 25th, Dia de Santiago; Monday market) possesses a beautiful 16th c. fountain, a 16th c. Dominican convent with ruined posas (processional chapels), and the 18th Church of Santiago.

San Martin Texmelucan

Visitors to this small town (2270m/7450ft; population 68,000; Fiesta: November 11th, Día de San Martín; Tuesday market) on the border with the state of Tlaxcala should see the 16th/17th c. Franciscan convent and Church of San Martín.

Huauchinango

Huauchinango (1500m/4923ft; population 60,000; Flower Festival, March 10th–20th; Saturday market), to the north, is a small pleasant Indian town in an attractive location.

Acatlán de Osorio

Acatlán de Osorio (1213m/3981ft; population 20,000; Fiesta: October 24th, Día de San Rafael Arcángel; Sunday market) is a picturesque little Mixtec town famous for its ceramics, particularly painted pottery.

Piedras Encimadas

Visitors to the north-west of the state of Puebla are advised to make a detour to the curious rock formations known as Piedras Encimadas (stepped rocks) which can be found in a valley near Zacatlán.

Puebla de Zaragoza — K 8

State: Puebla (Pue.)
Altitude: 2162m/7096ft. Population: 2,000,000
Dialling code: 91 22

Access from Mexico City

By rail about 5 hours; by bus about 2½ hours; by car 126km/78 miles on the MEX 150.

Location

Puebla, the capital of the state of the same name, lies in a fertile high valley surrounded by mainly volcanic mountains such as Popocatépetl (5452m/17,893ft), Iztaccíhuatl (5286m/17,349ft) and La Malinche (4461m/14,641ft).

★Townscape

History and colonial architecture characterise this old town which boasts sixty churches and has become famed for the manufacture and use of brightly-coloured tiles. During the last decade Puebla has developed into an important industrial centre, but has managed to retain the character of a town from the Colonial period.

History

As far as is known Puebla has no pre-Hispanic period. The settlement was founded by Franciscan monks in 1521 as Ciudad de los Angeles on the orders of Bishop Julián Garcés of Tlaxcala. By 1537 it already had a university, in 1539 it became the see of a bishop and from then on was called Puebla de los Angeles. The town quickly developed into a centre

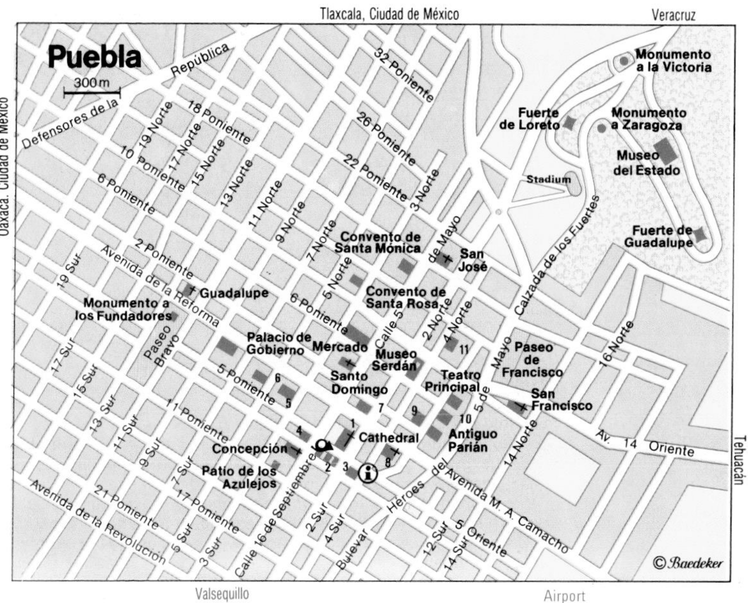

1 Zócalo (Plaza de la Constitución)
2 Biblioteca Palafoxiana
3 Palacio de Justicia
4 Casa del Dean
5 Museo Bello
6 San Agustin
7 Town Hall
8 Compañía
9 Casa del Alfeñique (Museo Regional)
10 Barrio del Artista
11 Bus Station

for the surrounding agricultural area as well as an important traffic junction on the road between the Gulf of Mexico and the Pacific. The manufacture of azulejos (tiles) had already started in the 16th c. following the Spanish example, especially that of Talavera de la Reina. Of Spanish foundation and mainly of European character, Puebla stands in natural contrast to the neighbouring Indian city of Cholula, which it began to overshadow during the 17th c.

During the US–Mexican War (1846–48) bitter conflicts broke out between the troops of General Winfield Scott and of Antonio Lopéz de Santa Ana, which led to the temporary occupation of Puebla by US troops. During the French Intervention, Mexicans led by General Ignacio Zaragoza beat the French back in a battle on May 5th 1862. Since then this day has been celebrated as a national holiday throughout Mexico. One year later the French finally conquered the town, which then remained in the sphere of control of the Emperor Maximilian until April 1867 when General Porfirio Díaz managed to drive the imperial troops from the town. During the Mexican Revolution (1910–20) Puebla was also the scene of violent battles.

Sights

Orientation

The Avenida de la Reforma leads from Zócalo westwards, the Avenida Avila Camacho extends east from the main square; they separate the

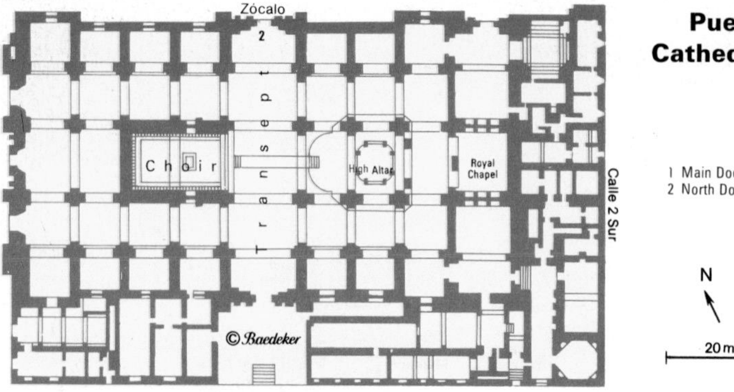

Puebla Cathedral

1 Main Doorway
2 North Doorway

N

20 m

town into northern (Norte) and southern (Sur) areas. The Calle 16 de Septiembre south of Zócalo and the Calle del 5 de Mayo north of it divide the town into western (Poniente) and eastern (Oriente) zones.

All roads following an east–west direction are called Avenidas; those in the northern half of the town bear even numbers, those in the southern half odd numbers. All roads extending from north to south are Calles; in the eastern half they have even numbers, in the western half odd numbers.

★ Zócalo

The magnificent main square (Zócalo, Plaza de la Constitución), with its tall trees, flower beds and fountains, is lined with arcades (Portales) and forms the busy centre of the town.

★ **Cathedral**

On the south side of Zócalo stands the cathedral, the country's second largest after that of Mexico City. Work began on this impressive, predominantly Renaissance-style, construction in about 1575, but it was not officially opened until 1649. The north portal on the main square is decorated with high reliefs of the four Spanish kings from the Habsburg line (Charles V, Philip II, Philip III, and Philip IV); under the arched border the Spanish royal coat of arms. The main façade and its doorway are completely plain and uniform and show signs of the approaching Baroque style. The two towers are unusually tall and slender; one dates from 1678, the other was completed ninety years later. The enormous cupola, covered with Azulejos typical of Puebla, is noteworthy.

Interior

The impressive interior of the cathedral measures 90m/295ft×47m/154ft, is 25m/82ft tall and has three naves and a large transept. Of particular note are Manuel Tolsa's Neo-Classical high altar (about 1800), Mateo de la Cruz's wrought-iron choir screen (1679), the carved wooden choir stalls (1719–22), the work of Pedro Muñoz, and the two impressive organs dating from the same time. Also worth mentioning are the Baroque altar in the Royal Chapel and the Baroque retablo by the Flemish artist Diego de Borgraf in the San José Chapel, as well as a number of 17th and 18th c. paintings attributed to Pedro Garcia Ferrer and Miguel Cabrera.

★ Choir stalls

★ Biblioteca Palafoxiana

The Biblioteca Palafoxiana, founded in 1646 by Bishop Juan Palafox, is housed on the first floor of the beautiful old Archbishop's Palace, now

Puebla: the Casa del Alfeñique, a typical "wedding-cake" style building ▶

the Casa de la Cultura, south of the cathedral. It houses a large collection of rare and valuable books and old maps; the impressive Baroque reading room is worth seeing.

Museo Amparo

Also south of the cathedral in Calle 2 Sur is the Museo Amparo, opened in 1991. This museum houses the magnificent pre-Columbian collection of Josué and Jaqueline Sáenz, one of the largest private collections of its kind. It includes the well-known Maya altar of the "Lords of Yaxchilán".

West of Zócalo

Casa del Dean

One block west of the Archbishop's Palace stands the Casa del Dean (Deanery; C. 16 de Septiembro 505), an attractive old Renaissance-style town house dating from 1580. Inside there are impressive murals interpreting Petrarch's poem "I trionfi" of the triumph of love, death, chastity, glory, time and eternity, with Indian symbols.

Museo Bello

The magnificent Poblano-style house in Av. 3 Pte. 302, west of the Deanery, contains the beautiful collection of Chinese porcelain, Talavera ceramics, wrought iron, etc. belonging to José Luis Bello.

Santo Domingo

The Church of Santo Domingo, opened in 1611 and with a Baroque façade, stands two blocks from the main square in Calle del 5 de Mayo.

★ Rosary Chapel

The Capilla del Rosario (Rosary Chapel) was built in 1690 and is a brilliant achievement of Mexican Baroque art. Every inch of the walls, ceiling, pillars and portals is covered with tiles, gold leaf, sculptures and carving. Of note is an orchestra of cherubs surrounded by a riot of arabesques from the middle of which God the Father appears to be floating down.

★ Convent of Santa Monica

Continue along the 5 de Mayo to the Convent of Santa Monica (Av. 18 Pte. 103), founded in 1609 and renovated in 1680. Although it was closed by the Reform Laws of 1857 the nuns continued to run it secretly until they were discovered in 1934. The former secret chambers and the furnishings unfortunately were lost during a conversion. However, two cells with plank beds and instruments for self-flagellation, and an old kitchen with an adjoining dining hall are among areas that can be visited. The convent now houses the Museum of Religious Art.

Santa Rosa Convent

The former Santa Rosa Convent is situated on Calle 3 Norte 1203 two blocks south-west. It now contains the Museo de Arte Popular (Museum of Popular Art), a library, shops, and a model of the original fully-tiled convent kitchen with old utensils, where in 1680 a nun is supposed to have invented the famous *Mole Poblano*, a dish prepared with numerous spices and chocolate (see Practical Information, Food and Drink).

East of Zócalo

La Compañía

Two blocks east of the main square stands the Jesuit church La Compañía, opened in 1767, which has a Churrigueresque façade and a blue and white tiled cupola. In the year of its opening the Jesuit order was expelled from Mexico. In the sacristy can be seen the tomb of a supposed Chinese princess who was sold by pirates as a slave and brought to Mexico before gaining her freedom in Puebla at the end of the 17th c. She is said to have been the instigator of the picturesque China-Poblana costume which later spread throughout Mexico. The adjoining former Jesuit grammar school is now occupied by the university.

Casa de los Muñecos

The Casa de los Muñecos (House of the Puppets), an attractive house in the "wedding cake style", is situated at the beginning of Cale 2 Nte.

Casa Arquiles Serdan

Continue along Calle 2 Nte. to the Casa Arquiles Serdan, a museum dedicated to the Revolution. It commemorates the leader of the opposition opposing the re-electon of Porfirio Díaz in 1910 in the town of Puebla.

★ Casa del Alfeñique

The original Casa del Alfeñique (Almond Cake House; 4 Ote. 16) is in Av. 4 Ote. 416, a right-hand turning off Calle 2 Nte. This guest-house, thought to have been built built at the end of the 18th c. by Antonio de Santa Maria Incháurregui, boasts coloured tiles, red brick and white stucco, and is one of the best examples of the Poblano style, the local version of Baroque. Today this building is the Museo Regional, in which the principal exhibits are ceramics, weapons, paintings, costumes and furniture.

Antigua Parian

Originally set up in the 18th century in order to entice back the tradesmen of Zócalo who had fled, it is now devoted to arts and crafts in little shops. Especially worth-while purchases include examples of onyx. In the adjoining "Barrio del Artista" artists can be seen at work.

Teatro Principal

To the north lies the Teatro Principal (6 Nte., 8 Ote.). It was built between 1756 and 1769 and is one of the oldest theatres in Latin America.

San Francisco Convent

A short diversion leads to this convent in Av. 14 Oriente. It dates from 1551 and has a beautiful tiled façade. Of interest are the Churrigueresque doorway and the carved 18th c. choir stalls. In about 1800 the convent was rebuilt in the Neo-Classical style.

Fort Loreto

Crowning a fortified hill in the north-east of the town stands Fort Loreto (Fuerte de Loreto), built in 1816 and now a military museum. It is dedicated to the struggle against the French which took place on this hill. From the fort a fine view of the town can be enjoyed. On the southern side of the hill is Fort Guadalupe (Fuerte Guadalupe).

Centro Civico

Between the two forts, Loreto and Guadalupe, extends the Centro Civico de 5 de Mayo where, as well as a planetarium, an open-air theatre and exhibitions of arts and crafts, can be also found the Museo del Estado de Puebla (the state museum) in which interesting archaeological finds (Olmec, Toltec and Aztec) and ethnological exhibits from the region are on show.

Museo Nacional del Ferocarril

In the north-west of the town, in the old railway station (corner of 12 Pte. and 11 Norte) an original Railway Museum has been installed. It consists of almost 200 old locomotives, coaches and other material from the heyday of Mexican railways.

Surroundings

Dam

Valsequillo Dam (Presa Manuel Avila Camacho) is situated approximately 15km/9 miles south of Puebla and offers opportunities for water sports.

Africam

Nearby lies Africam, an open-air enclosure with many species of exotic animals.

By following the MEX 190 for 6km/4 miles in the direction of Oaxaca, we come to Tlaxcalancingo (see Acatepec, Surroundings). Next comes Acatepec (see entry) after 17km/10½ miles, and, after turning right one mile further on, Tonantzintla (see Acatepec, Surroundings).

★ Atlixco

Continuing along the MEX 190 brings the visitor to Atlixco (Náhuatl: "Place Above the Water"; 1885m/6187ft; population 160,000), some 31km/19 miles from Puebla. The town has a number of Poblano-style buildings. The parish church (16th c., built over in the 19th c.) in the main square, the stucco façade of the earlier La Merced Church, and the Franciscan fortress-like convent church (16th c.) on the the Cerrito de San Miguel (San Miguel Hill) with a sober colonial-Plateresque façade are all worth seeing.

"Atlixcáyoti" Fiesta

During the last week in September Indian groups hold the colourful "Atlixcáyoti" festival, which features dancing.

★ Tepeaca

36km/22 miles along the MEX 150 towards Tehuacán is Tepeaca (Náhuatl: "Tepeyacac" = Nose of the Hill; 2257m/7407ft; population 40,000; Friday market). Cortés founded this town in 1520 as a second settlement after Veracruz. A watch-tower ("Rollo") with Moorish and Renaissance features stands in the main square of this former post station. The Spanish are said to have chained Indian prisoners to this tower and whipped them. Cortés had the house with the red façade opposite built and is said to have lived in it after his defeat at Tenochtitlán ("Noche Triste", June 30th 1520).

★ Franciscan Convent

The solid, defensive construction of the 16th c. Franciscan convent is one of the country's earliest and most impressive. Of note are the walkway around the battlements which surround the church, the colonial-Plateresque façade, and the architectural quality of the entrance hall of the convent.

Tecali

Tecali (Náhuatl: "alabaster") lies about 10km/6 miles south of Tepeaca, a centre of the processing and marketing of onyx and marble objects.

Pico de Orizaba (Citlaltépetl), Mexico's highest mountain

Acatzingo

A few miles behind Tepeaca on the MEX 150 a turning leads left to Acatzingo (2160m/7089ft; population 24,000; Tuesday market), 11km/7 miles away. The 16th c. Franciscan convent is a smaller copy of that at Tepeaca and has an attractive Indian-style font.

★Pico de Orizaba

From Acatzingo there are two ways of reaching the foot of 5700m/18,707ft-high Pico de Orizaba or Citlaltépetl (Náhuatl: "Mountain of the Stars"), Mexico's highest mountain. To reach the south side travel first in a north-westerly direction along the MEX 140 as far as El Seco, then follow the MEX 144 for a further 25km/15 miles to El Serdán, the starting-off point.

The north side is best reached from Tlachichuca. To get there drive via El Seco, turn off right after 9km/5½ miles and continue for 21km/13 miles to Tlachichuca. Here climbers can either rent a four-wheel drive vehicle (difficult stretches) or be driven 32km/20 miles to the inn at the Piedra Grande (overnight stays possible) at 4260m/2647ft. From here an ascent of this magnificent glaciated volcano can be undertaken by experienced mountaineers in one day. Information about the route to be followed should be obtained in advance from the appropriate places (see Practical Information, Sport, Climbing).

From Puebla it is approximately 120km/26 miles to Tehuacán (see Puebla, State) and 180km/112 miles to Teziutlán (see entry).

Puerto Escondido L 10

State: Oaxaca (Oax.). Altitude: at sea-level
Population: 15,000. Dialling code: 91 958

Access

By air from Oaxaca (see entry) and Mexico City (1 hour); by bus from Oaxaca 10–18 hours, from Acapulco (see entry) 7½ hours; by car from Oaxaca approximately 265km/165 miles along the MEX 131 (numerous bends) via Miahuatlan and Pochutla, or about 310km/193 miles on the MEX 175 and MEX 200 (better roads), from Acapulco about 420km/261 miles on the MEX 200.

Location

The fishing port of Puerto Escondido lies in a sheltered bay in the Pacific Ocean and is surrounded by hills with luxuriant vegetation. Magnificent long beaches extend on both sides of the town. In places the surf is very high. Until recently Puerto Escondido was recommended to holiday-makers looking for a quiet life by the sea away from great hordes of tourists. However, the building of a new airport has made this seaside resort considerably more popular.

★★Seaside Resort

The resort mainly comprises small restaurants and bars along the main street Pérez Gazga. The long beaches and the lagoons lying in small bays (Puerto Angelito, Carizalillo, Manzanillo Bacocho) are rich in waterfowl. Some stretches of the coast are particularly suitable for swimming despite the heavy surf. The undertow at other points makes them dangerous. Its breakers have established Puerto Escondido as a popular venue for surfing (competitions at Playa Zicatela).

Surroundings

San Pedro Tututepec

75km/47 miles west along the MEX 200 a road turns off to San Pedro Tututepec, 10km/6 miles further on. In this Chatino Indian mountain village a number of pre-Columbian sculptures (atlases, snakes, jaguars) can be viewed behind the church.

★Lagunas de Chacahua

Continue along the MEX 200 for a few more miles to a left-hand turning to Lagunas de Chacahua National Park, which comprises three lagoons and several islands with numerous birds and amphibians.

Puerto Angel

Puerto Angel (population 9000), an attractive fishing port with two beautiful beaches (Puerto Angel and Pantéon), lies 84km/52 miles from Puerto Escondido. Playa Zipolite, 10km/6 miles west, is popular with young campers. Puerto Angel and its surroundings have only been discovered by tourists during the last decade.

Huatulco

Huatulco's nine picturesque bays extend 40km/25 miles east of Puerto Angel over more than 30km/18½ miles. The Mexican government and private investors have recently created a 20,000ha/49,420 acre tourist centre around Santa María Huatulco, modelled on the one at Cancún (see entry). An international airport has already been built; large hotels belonging to international chains are also either complete or in the process of being constructed. One hundred thousand tourists are expected annually, and by the year 2000 there will be 9000 hotel rooms ready to cater for 800,000 guests every year.

This project has not been without its disputes after the building land was obtained using some questionable methods. In May 1984, for example, the community of Santa María Huatulco was granted 51,000ha/126,021 acres of land by decree of the president; the next day 21,000ha/51,891 acres were immediately expropriated for the tourism project. Some landowners only received 10,000 pesos compensation. It appears that this is to be a similar development to the one at Cancún, at which Mexican tourists can barely afford to stay.

Puerto Vallarta — G 7

State: Jalisco (Jal.)
Altitude: at sea-level
Population: 280,000
Dialling code: 91 322

Access

By air from Mexico City about 2 hours, additional connections with other Mexican and North American towns; by bus from Guadalajara (see entry) about 7 hours; by car from Tepic (see entry) about 170km/106 miles on the MEX 200, from Guadalajara about 320km/199 miles on the MEX 15 and the MEX 200; ferry links from Cabo San Lucas (see entry).

Location

Puerto Vallarta, one of Mexico's most popular seaside resorts, lies in a wide bay backed by luxuriantly wooded hills. Only three decades ago an unknown remote fishing village, it is now one of the country's best-known holiday centres.

History

The settlement was first founded in 1851 and was given its present name in 1918 in honour of the state's then governor, Ignacio Luis Vallarta. The sleepy fishing village first came to notice in the 1960s when the neighbouring village of Mismaloya was used as a location for the film "The Night of the Iguana" starring Richard Burton and Elizabeth Taylor, who began their much publicised affair here. In 1968 the town gained a road link with Tepic and since then has developed rapidly.

Coastal Resort

Although Puerto Vallarta's cobbled alleys and white houses roofed with red tiles make it an attractive town, visitors are mainly drawn here

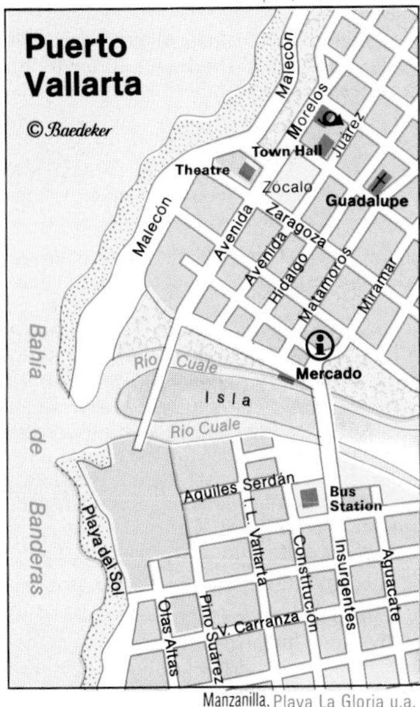

The beach at Puerto Vallarta

by its expansive beaches, opportunities for water-sports, and tropical scenery. As well as its sea-front promenade (the Malecón) and its numerous hotels, restaurants, night-spots and gift shops, Puerto Vallarta also has a small museum in Escuela 15 de Mayo and Guadalupe Church featuring a curious crown-shaped tower.

★Bahía de Banderas

The Bahía de Banderas (Bay of Flags), on which Puerto Vallarta lies, boasts a good two dozen beaches extending north and south of the Rio Cuale which divides the town. The most famous beaches north of the river include Playa de las Glorias, Las Palmas (or Las Cruces; palm grove), Oro (palm-fringed; near the marina) and Chino (lying in the state of Nayarit; popular for picnics).

South of the river are the beaches Playa del Sol (or de los Muertos, popular), Las Amapas and Conchas Chinas (below the cliffs), Las Estacas, Punta Negra, Palo María and Gemelas (all with attractive bays). Mismaloya Beach lies 12km/7½ miles south, features the Los Arcos rock formation and offers canoe excursions to the diving area of the nearby lagoon.

★Yelapa

Yelapa ("place of reunion") is an especially picturesque beach with a freshwater lagoon and waterfall; it is also a good place for diving.

The new Marina Vallarta development, just north of the town, has an extensive marina, luxury hotels, villas and an 18-hole golf course.

Surroundings of Puerto Vallarta

15km/9 miles further north of the town along the MEX 200 we reach the holiday centre of Nuevo Vallarta in the state of Nayarit and the adjoining fishing village of Bucerias. Nuevo Vallarta boasts one of Mexico's largest yacht marinas. After a further 15km/9 miles the resorts of Rineón de Guayabitas and Peñita de Jaltemba (see Tepic, Surroundings) are reached.

Costa Alegre

To the south, along the MEX 200, stretches the Costa Alegre, with some magnificent beaches and rich flora and fauna. The Bel Air/El Tamarindo hotel and resort complex provides for ecologically-conscious tourists.

Querétaro (State)

Abbreviation: Qro.
Capital: Querétaro
Area: 11,769sq.km/4544sq. miles
Official population 1990: 1,051,200 (1994 estimate: 1,300,000)

Location and Topography

The state of Querétaro lies almost exactly in the middle of Mexico. Together with the state of Guanajuato it is known as the Bajío, the granary of Mexico. The altitude of this fertile plateau, situated between the eastern and western mountain chains of the Sierra Madre, ranges from 1500m/4923ft to 2000m/6564ft. On the south Querétaro borders the Estado de México and the state of Michoacán, on the west Guanajuato, on the north San Luis Potosí and on the east Hidalgo. The state is made up of a mountainous region, rich in minerals, and plains and valleys used for agriculture. At 3350m/1082ft, Cerro El Gallo is its highest point. The population of the state comprises Mestizos, Otomí Indians and Criollos.

History

The area of the present-day state of Querétaro (Tarascan: "place of the ball game") was once ruled by Otomí Indians. In the mid-15th c. they were conquered by the Aztecs. Evidence of the pre-Columbian period is still being found in the archaeological ruined sites of Las Ranas, Toluquilla, Neblinas, El Lobo and Villa Corregidora.

The Spanish first appeared here in 1531 and settled the area within a quarter of a century. During the Colonial period and after the winning of

independence the history of the state was primarily tied to the development of its capital.

Economy

Agriculture, mainly the production of maize, clover, fruit and vegetables, plays an important role. Cattle-rearing is also of great importance. Mining is mainly for mercury and opals, but also for silver, lead and copper. Various industries, producing such items as agricultural machinery, motors, glass and vehicles, have recently settled around the capital.

Otomí Indians

Area of settlement

Querétaro, like the states of Hidalgo, Guanajuato, San Luis Potosí, northern Veracruz, north-western Puebla, Tlaxcala and Estado de México, was an area settled by the Otomí. These relatively widely distributed Indian people, whose numbers are estimated at 300,000, speak a language of their own. Little is known of their origins; they probably lived in the Mexican highlands and were forced into the surrounding regions during the 8th and 9th c. In the 14th and 15th c. they were subjugated or driven into inaccessible areas by the Mexica (Aztecs).

During the Conquista most of the Otomí sided with the Spanish in the fight against their Aztec oppressors.

Religion

The Otomí practise a mixture of the Catholic and the old-Indian religion. They make sacrifices mainly to the earth goddess and believe in the return of the souls of their dead, whom they fear and therefore try to appease.

Costume and Handicrafts

When the Otomí are not seen in the normal clothing worn by country folk, the women usually wear colourful embroidered costumes. The artistic and valuable craft products of these people include wickerwork articles, ceramics, woollen materials and wooden furniture.

Querétaro (Town) — I 7

State: Querétaro (Qro.)
Altitude: 1836m/6026ft
Population: 780,000
Dialling code: 91 42

Access from Mexico City

By rail about 5 hours; by bus approximately 2½ hours; by car 225km/140 miles on the MEX 57D.

Location

Querétaro, the capital of the state of the same name, lies surrounded by rounded mountain tops in a valley in the Mexican highlands at the foot of the Cerro de las Campanas ("Hill of the Bells").

★Townscape

The town is known for its attractive houses, churches and squares dating from the Colonial period, and for its well-tended parks and fountains. Although industry has recently settled in the surrounding area, the town centre has managed to preserve much of its tranquil character.

History

The town was founded by the Otomí Indians long before Mexico was discovered. In the mid-15th c. it was taken by the Aztecs.

The Spanish brought the area under their control between 1531 and 1570. They used it as their supply centre for the rich mines in Guanajuata and Zacatecas. In 1699 Querétaro was awarded civic status. Later

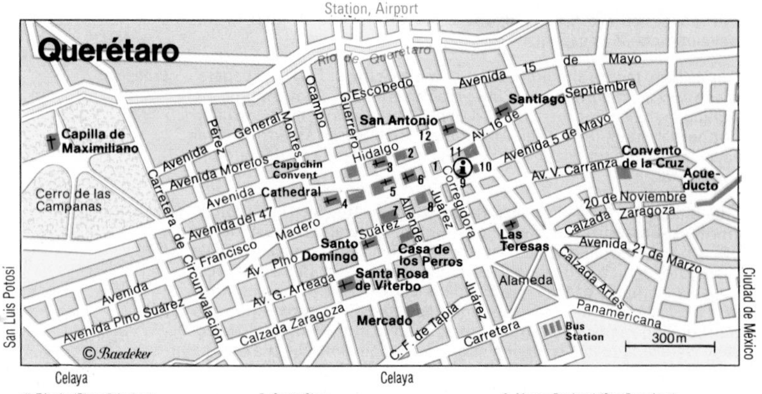

1 Zócalo (Plaza Principal)
2 Casa del Marqués
3 El Carmen
4 Palacio Municipal (Town Hall)
5 Santa Clara
6 San José de Gracia
7 Palacio Federal (San Agustín)
8 Hostería de la Marquesa
9 Museo Regional (San Francisco)
10 Casa de Escala
11 Palacio de Gobierno (Casa de la Corregidora)
12 Teatro de la República

Querétaro became historically significant above all other Mexican towns. This was where, in 1810, the conspiracy around Father Hidalgo began, which led to the War of Independence and ultimately to the independence of Mexico from Spain. In 1848 the Treaty of Guadalupe Hidalgo, which ended the war between the United States and Mexico, was signed in Querétaro. The last encounter between the troops of President Benito Juárez and those of the Habsburg Emperor Maximilian of Mexico was fought here in 1867. After Maximilian and his two generals Miramón and Mejía were captured and convicted they were shot on July 19th 1867 on the Cerro de las Campanas.

Mexico's present constitution was drafted in Querétaro in 1917.

Sights

Aqueduct

The townscape is particularly characterised by an aqueduct east of the city centre. Still functioning, the aqueduct was built between 1726 and 1738 on the orders of the Marqués de la Villa del Villar del Aguiler. This interesting construction is almost 9km/6 miles long with 74 arches up to 29m/95ft high.

Convento San Francisco

South of the main square (Plaza Principal or Jardin Obregón) lies the old Convent of San Francisco, founded in the mid-16th c. A century later the church was renovated and subsequently the convent as well. It now houses the interesting Museo Regional, with works by the great artists of the Colonial period from the 17th to the 19th c., as well as a collection of historical weapons, documents and other items.

Teatro de la República

Maximilian and his two generals, Mejía and Miramón, were tried and sentenced to death in the Teatro de la República north of the main square. The Federal constitution was proclaimed here in 1917.

Plaza de la Independencia

The peaceful Plaza de la Independencia (Plaza de Armas) has retained its Colonial character.

Aguila Memorial

A memorial to the architect of the aqueduct, the Marquis de la Villa del Villar del Aguila, stands in the middle of the plaza.

Querétaro: the Aqueduct which is still functioning

Casa de la Corregidora

The Palacio de Gobierno or Casa de la Corregidora (Government Palace), an attractive building dating from 1770 with wrought-iron balconies, is situated on the Avenida 5 de Mayo and the Plaza de la Independencia. Here Josefa Ortíz de Domínguez, the wife of the mayor ("Corregidor"), warned the conspirators in the 1810 independence movement of the discovery of their plans, which led to the premature outbreak of the War of Independence.

Casa de Escala

The Casa de Escala (Casa Municipal de la Cultura) also stands in the plaza. It is a beautiful building decorated with sculptures and wrought-iron balconies.

Convento de la Cruz

Further east along the Avenida Venustiano Carranza is the Convento de la Cruz (Convent of the Cross). Its original 16th c. building was replaced by a Baroque one about a century later. In 1867 Emperor Maximilian established his headquarters in the convent and was later held here for a time after his capture. Note the tree with cross-shaped needles in the convent garden.

Capilla del Calvarito

The Capilla del Calvarito (mid-17th c.) lies opposite on the site where the Spanish are said to have celebrated their first Mass after conquering the settlement in 1531. According to legend, at the height of the battle the sky darkened to reveal both the Apostle Jacob on horseback and a shining cross – and the Spanish were victorious. The founding of the Convento de La Cruz dates back to this legend.

Going south-west from the main square along Avenida Francisco Madero in a south-westerly direction, the Hosteria de la Marquesa (mid-18th c.) is passed on the left and the church of San José de Allende (late 17th c.) on the right. The Fuente de Neptuno (Neptune Fountain), a

Neo-Classical work by the sculptor Francisco Eduardo Tresguerras dating from 1797, stands in the small park on the corner of Madero and Allende.

★ Santa Clara

The adjoining church of Santa Clara, which once belonged to a powerful convent, has a simple 17th c. façade.

Interior

In contrast the interior of the church is a particularly fine example of the Churrigueresque style of the 18th c. with lavishly carved and gilded retablos. Sculptures of apostles, saints, cherubs, flowers and other ornaments decorate the altarpiece. Especially remarkable is the intricately carved wooden choir screen with the figure of Christ in the middle and the painted draperies on each side. The wrought-iron grille above the sacristy doorway and the altar inlaid with silver and shells is impressive. The Av. Madero continues to the Plaza de Guerrero, the site of the Neo-Classical Palacio Municipal (Town Hall).

★Augustinian convent

Before reaching the Plaza de Guerrero, the Calle Allende Sur turns off left and leads to the Palacio Federal, a former Augustinian convent dating from the first half of the 18th c. This building, thought to have been designed by Ignacio Mariano de Las Casas, is one of the most attractive in the town. The tripartite Baroque façade with statues in the niches, and the magnificently carved arches and pillars in the cloister are a notable feature.

The Museo del Arte Querétaro, with its extensive collection of 16th and 17th c. Mexican and European paintings, can also be found in this complex.

Santo Domingo Rosary Chapel

Diagonally opposite, on the Avenida Pino Suárez and Calle Guerrero Sur, can be seen the plain façade of the Santo Domingo Church (end

A secluded square in Querétaro

17th c.) and the Rosary Chapel, the work of Mariano de Las Casas and dating from 1760.

Casa de los Perros

The Casa de los Perros (House of the Dogs), the former home of Mariano de Las Casas, stands near Calle Allende Sur 16. This small 18th c. palace owes its name to the gargoyles on the exterior and in the beautiful patio, decorated with an unusual fountain.

★ Santa Rosa de Viterbo

Turn the next corner into Avenida General de Arteaga and follow this to the right to the Plaza Ignacio Mariano de Las Casas to reach the church of Santa Rosa de Viterbo, one of the most interesting churches in the town. Another of Ignacio Mariano de Las Casas' works, it was completed in 1752, but was later altered by Tresguerras. The two flying buttresses in the form of heavy volutes are striking. The clock is reputed to be the first repeating striking clock in America.

Interior

The retablos inside the church are richly decorated in the Churrigueresque style. The church also contains valuable paintings in the Colonial period. As in many churches belonging to convents there is a fine wrought-iron choir screen, behind which the nuns could take part in the Mass. Of note are the superbly carved confessional, the high Baroque organ and in the sacristy the life-sized statues of the twelve Apostles at the Last Supper; behind these is a painting by Tresguerras, covering the whole wall, which depicts St Rosa surrounded by her nuns.

Other buildings

Other buildings in Querétaro worthy of mention include the 18th c. Cathedral of Felipe Neri, the 17th/18th c. church of El Carmen, the 18th c. church of San Antonio and the 17th/18th c. church of Santiago with its convent cloister lined with arcades and its Neo-Mudéjar portals. The Capuchin convent, dating from the early 18th c., was Emperor Maximilian's last place of confinement before he was shot. The Casa de la Marquésa (Casa de Cultura) dates from the first half of the 18th c. and possesses a highly-imaginative patio with Neo-Mudéjar elements.

Cerro de las Campanas

The Capilla de Maximiliano stands on the Cerro de las Campanas ("Hill of the Bells") on the western edge of the town. This chapel was endowed by the Austrian emperor Franz Joseph in memory of his brother, the Emperor Maximilian of Mexico, who was executed on this spot. The enormous statue of his victorious opponent, the Mexican president Benito Juárez, towers over the chapel.

Opal Mining

The area around Querétaro is a centre of opal mining. Opals and other semi-precious stones, including topaz, aquamarine and amethyst, are mined here and sold in speciality shops.

Surroundings

San Juan del Río

San Juan del Río (1980m/6498ft; population 100,000), a centre of wickerwork and wooden furniture-making, lies 55km/34 miles south-east on the MEX 57D.

Tequisquiapan

About 20km/12½ miles north-west of San Juan del Río on the MEX 120 lies the charming seaside resort of Tequisquiapan (1700m/5579ft; population 30,000). Its hotels and thermal baths (radioactive springs), and its facilities for riding and fishing attract visitors, particularly from Mexico City.

Bernal

A turning in Ezequiel Montes, 17km/10½ miles north of Tequisquiapan, leads to Bernal. The inhabitants of this town, situated at the foot of a spectacularly rocky hill shaped like a hat, are renowned for the production of heavy woollen sarapes.

Cadereyta de Montes

The MEX 120 continues from Tequisquiapan to Cadereyta de Montes (2070m/6794ft; population 30,000). This former mining town contains the large cactus farm "Quinta Federico Schmoll", which sends its products all over the world.

Toluquilla and Las Ranas

A good but winding road leads off to the right 33km/20½ miles north of Cadereyta to San Joaquín (2550m/8396ft) 24km/15 miles away. The archaeological sites of Toluquilla and Las Ranas are open to visitors. The partially-restored Las Ranas ("The Frogs") can also be reached by car. Little is known of the builders of this late-Classic (A.D. 600–900) site. They were probably influenced by the cultures of the Toltecs and that of Xochichalco, and possibly also by the Huastecs. Las Ranas consists of four levels, of which the two upper ones each have five buildings. The sloping and steep faces and the rounded-off steps, which suggests the Tablud-Tablero style, are striking.

Jalpan

The MEX 120 leads from the turning to San Joaquín through the magnificent scenery of the Sierra Gorda to Jalpan (770m/2527ft; population 15,000), approximately 95km/59 miles distant. This small town is situated in an area of sugar-cane and coffee production.

★Baroque Church

It is worth visiting the Indian-style Baroque church, which is dedicated to St Jacob and was built between 1751 and 1758. In the lower part of the façade the imperial double eagle is combined with the eagle of the Aztecs, which is eating a snake.

Part of the façade of the church at Jalpan

The legendary Franciscan Father Junipero Serra was responsible for the construction of the church. He was commissioned with the conversion of the Indians in the area and later founded several missions in California, which developed into San Diego, San Francisco and Santa Clara in the present-day USA. Serra and his brothers founded four more missions in the vicinity of Jalpan, whose churches are worth viewing for their striking Baroque façades: Concá (38km/23½ miles), Landa (22km/13½ miles), Tilaco (49km/30½ miles) and Tancoyol (60km/37 miles).

★ Jungle Castle Rancho Conchita

Xilitla, in the State of San Luis Potosí, is situated some 84km/52 miles from Jalpan. From here it is another 4km/2½ miles along the road to Ciudad Valles where a path turns off to the left across fields to Rancho Conchita. Edward James' jungle castle, never completed, can be visited here. This eccentric English millionaire and art collector, who died in 1984, built his bizarre refuge in a luxuriant tropical setting. Since his death the castle has remained uninhabited and has become dilapidated; the jungle is steadily regaining the upper hand and vegetation is slowly enveloping the building.

Quintana Roo (State)

Abbreviation: Q.R. Capital: Cheturnal
Area: 50,350sq.km/19,440sq. miles
Official population 1990: 493,300 (1994 estimate: 600,000)

Location and Topography

The state of Quintana Roo, which includes the eastern and southern parts of the Yucatán peninsula, borders the Mexican states of Campeche and Yucatán, as well as Belize (formally British Honduras) in the south and Guatemala. The predominantly flat land is overgrown with tropical jungle and savannahs and has an extensive coastline along the Caribbean Sea with magnificent beaches, lagoons, coral reefs and islands. There are a number of pre-Columbian sites both on the coast and inland in this hot and damp region. Only a fraction of these have so far been recorded or examined, and it is hoped that future excavations will produce important finds. The state is mainly populated by Maya Indians and Mestizos.

Maya Sites

Quintana Roo's most important sites include Tulum (see entry), Cobá (see entry), Kohunlich (see entry) and Xel-há (see entry), as well as El Rey (see Cancún), Xcaret (see Akumal), Tancah (see Xel-há) and Chunyaxché.

History

As can be concluded from the archaeological finds, the area of present-day Quintana Roo was densely populated during both the Maya Classic period (A.D. 300–900) and also during post-Classic period until the Conquista. Spanish seafarers had already made contact here by 1512. Later, the Spanish conquerors settled at only a few coastal places where they had to protect their forts against constant attacks by Indians and pirates. The greater part of the land was left to the Mayas. The first Spanish settlement, Salamanca Bacalar, was founded in 1544, but destroyed by pirates in 1652. The later settlement of Bacalar played a major role as a fortress and trading centre until the mid-19th c. It was destroyed in 1858 during the Caste War (from 1847) by the insurgent Mayas, who found support in the British colony of Honduras. It was not until 1901 that the Mexican army was finally able to suppress the Maya rebellion. Until 1910 this region housed a penal colony for political and criminal prisoners including rebellious Yaqui Indians from Sonora. The

territory of Quintana Roo was created in 1902 from parts of the states of Campeche and Yucatán, and named after the Mexican poet and leader of the 19th c. independence movement, Andrés Quintana Roo. In 1974 the territory became incorporated as the 30th of the United Mexican States. In September 1988 Hurricane Gilbert inflicted severe damage, mainly to the tourist centres of Cancún and Cozumel.

Communications

As well as regular flights to Isla Mujeres, Cancún, Cozumel and Chetumal (see entries), an efficient road network has recently been created. The MEX 180 leads from Mérida via Chichén Itzá (see entry) and Valladolid to Cancún, Puerto Juárez and Punta Sam (ferries to Isla Mujeres). From here the new coastal road, the MEX 307, passes through Puerto Morelos (ferry to Cozumel), Playa del Carmen (ferry to Cozumel) and Akumal to Tulum and then inland via the intersection at Felipe Carillo Puerto and Bacalar to the capital Chetumal. Good roads now lead from Tumul to the Maya site of Cobá (see entry), from where there is a road link along the MEX 180 to Nuevo Xcan, 70km/43½ miles east of Valladolid. The MEX 295 connects Valladolid directly with Felipe Carillo Puerto. In addition there is a southern route along the MEX 184 from Mérida (see entry) via Muna and Oxkutcab to Felipe Carillo Puerto and then to Tulum (see entry) on the coast or directly south to Chetumal (see entry). From there a road connection exists to Belize City, the largest town in the state of Belize. The MEX 186 crosses the southern part of the Yucatán peninsula westwards to the intersection at Francisco Escárcega, where the road forks south to Palenque and Villahermosa (see entries) and north to Champotõn and Campeche.

Economy

Until recently the economy of this isolated territory, far from the centre of the country, was mainly based on hardwoods, chicle, sisal fibres, coconuts and fishing. Improvement of its holiday resorts and its road network, and the construction of free trade areas, have made tourism

Coastal scenery in Quintana Roo

by far the most important branch of the economy in the state of Quintana Roo.

Sian Ka'an Nature Reserve

In 1986 an area of more than 485,000ha/1198,435 acres was declared the Sian Ka'an (Maya: "beginning of the sky"; Reservacióonde la Biósfera Sian Ka'an) Nature Reserve. This almost undisturbed and unpopulated region of lagoons, tropical forest, mangrove swamps, palm groves, marsh and coral reefs is bordered on the north by Tulum, on the west by Felipe Carillo Puerto, on the south by Punta Herrero and on the east by a coral reef. The reserve is not only intended to protect flora and fauna but should also guarantee a balanced use of nature in harmony with its inhabitants. Countless fish, crustaceans and bivalves live in the reserve, as do crocodiles, turtles, manatees, tapirs, monkeys, small deer, jaguars, ocelots, pumas and many species of birds, including parrots, pelicans and flamingos.

Salamanca 17

State: Guanajuato (Gto.)
Altitude: 1760m/5776ft
Population: 170,000
Dialling code: 91 464

Access from Mexico City

By rail about 7½ hours; by bus or car a total of approximately 300km/186 miles on the MEX 57 D to Querétaro and from there via Celaya on the MEX 45 D or the MEX 45.

Location

The town of Salamanca lies on the north bank of the Río Lerma in the middle of the Bajío, a fertile plateau extending over parts of the states of

Guanajuato and Querétaro. Although famed for its large petroleum refinery, the town in fact contains one of the country's most richly-decorated churches.

History

In the pre-Spanish period the Otomí settlement of Xidoo was situated here. After the Spanish influx the brothers Juan and Sancho Barahoma, the owners of a hacienda, gave the settlement the name Salamanca. The official foundation date of the town is given as 1603. During the 17th and 18th c. there was much building activity here by the Church. Like all settlements in Mexico's heartland, Salamanca also played a part in the Mexican War of Independence (1810–21). The Revolution in the 20th c. and the ensuing epidemics caused relapses in the development of the region. In the last 40 years there has been considerable agricultural and industrial growth from which the town of Salamanca has also profited.

Sights

★ San Agustín

The most splendid historical monument to the Colonial period of Salamanca is the church of San Agustín, work on which began in 1615. This tall and relatively narrow building, inconspicuously situated, has a simple façade. Severe columns, embellished with hollow spiral mouldings, flank the entrance. The positioning of the crucifix on the top of the façade beneath a conche is unusual.

Interior

The interior of the church is almost completely covered with painted and gilded panelling. Strong Moorish influence (Mudéjar) is apparent in the gilded wooden ornamentation of the dome and the wooden choir railings. The side altar of San Nicolás de Tolentino artistically portrays the life story of this 14th c. friar; the form of the net-shaped background is masterly. The high altar was replaced in 1832 by a Neo-Classical work.

Side Altars

Two further magnificent side altars, dedicated to St Joseph and St Anne, have been preserved unaltered. These two altars are magnificent examples of the Churrigueresque style. In contrast to the relatively flat moulding of the altars in the nave, the emphasis here is on a particularly vivid portrayal of the almost life-size figures of the saints.

San Bartolo

The old parish church of San Bartolo has a "rural" Baroque façade. The typically Churrigueresque estipites (pyramidal pilasters with the pointed end downward) are complemented by sculptures by local masters which incorporate old-Indian motifs such as the snake.

Surroundings

Irapuato

20km/12½ miles north-west on the MEX 45D is Irapuato (1795m/5891ft; population 327,000; fiestas: February 15th, Foundation Day; April 2nd, Strawberry Mass). This rapidly-growing town is a centre of agriculture and of probably the largest strawberry-growing region in the world. It also has a number of interesting buildings including the beautiful Neo-Classical Palacio Municipal (Town Hall) with its enormous patio, the church of El Hospital (Churrigueresque façade, early 18th c.) and the mid-18th c. La Parroquia (parish church) with its richly-embellished doorway. The church of San Francisco houses two notable paintings: "Virgin of Guadelupe" by Cabrera, and "Virgin of the Apocalypse" by Tresguerras.

Saltillo

See Coahuila de Zaragoza

San Blas

See Tepic

San Cristóbal de Las Casas N 9

State: Chiapas (Chis.)
Altitude: 2200m/7220ft. Population: 125,000
Dialling code: 91 967

Access

By bus from Mexico City about 18 hours, from Tuxtla Gutiérrez (see entry) about 2 hours; by car from Tuxtla Gutiérrez (see entry) 83km/52 miles on the MEX 190 (Panaméricana) from Mexico City.

Location

San Cristóbal de Las Casas, the oldest Spanish settlement in Chiapas, lies in the Jovel Valley surrounded by forest-clad mountains, of which the highest are Tzontehuitz (2858m/9380ft) and Huetepec (2717m/8917ft). Although a typical Colonial town with many churches and low houses with tiled roofs and barred windows, considerable Indian influence is evident, creating an unusual atmosphere. San Cristóbal and its surroundings are some of the most interesting places to visit in Mexico. Despite its southern location the high altitude of the town affords it a cool climate, a fact particularly apparent after sunset. The area also experiences a considerable amount of precipitation, with rain falling even during the dry period (November–May).

Until 20 years ago the town was completely cut off from and unaffected by tourism, which has since expanded greatly and led to changes. On New Year's Day 1994 the town was temporarily occupied by members of the Zapatist Army of Liberation (EZLN). Negotiations between the insurgents and the government took place in the cathedral.

Advice

When visiting Indian villages it should be remembered that their inhabitants strongly dislike being photographed; pictures should only be taken from a distance or permission requested beforehand. The easiest way to avoid difficulties is not to take a camera on such trips. Note also that very casual dress and inconsiderate "tourist behaviour" can also cause bad feeling.

Sights

Cathedral and San Nicolás Parish Church

San Cristóbal has many churches, of which only a few are of importance however. Building of the Cathedral of Nuestra Señora de la Asunción on the Zócalo (Plaza 31 de Marzo) began in 1528 and it has since been altered and redecorated several times. Inside there are several 17th–19th c. Baroque altars, paintings and sculptures, including a picture of Mary Magdalene by Miguel Cabrera, and the principal picture of the Altar del Perdón by Juan Correa. Also noteworthy are the wood carvings; particularly attractive ones decorate the pulpit.

The parish church of San Nicolás stands next to the cathedral. It was built between 1613 and 1620 and restored in 1815.

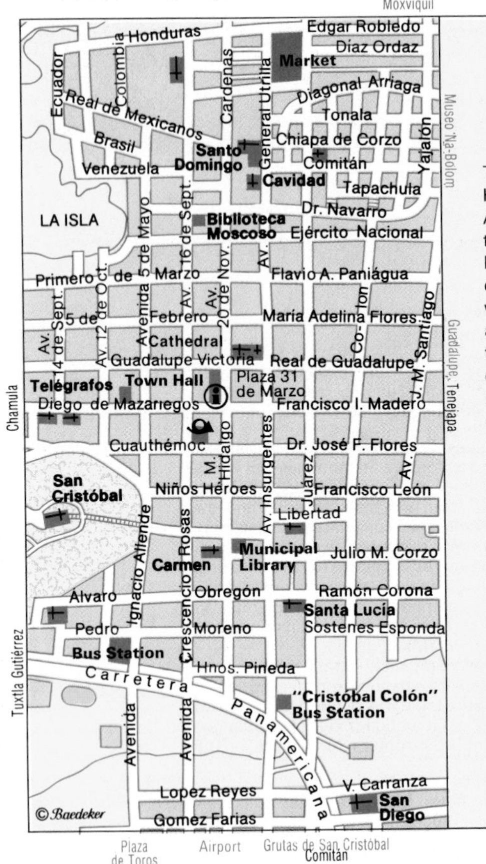

San Cristóbal de Las Casas

The Maya settlement of Huezecatlán came under Aztec control at the end of the 15th c. The Spaniards had great difficulty in subduing the Maya tribes and were able to make advances only after bitter fighting. In 1528 the conquistador Diego de Mazariegas founded the town of Villa Real, which was later renamed Cristóbal de las Casas in honour of its patron saint St Christopher and the great patron of the Indians Bartolomé de las Casas who was bishop of the town. Together with the rest of Chipas it was governed by the Spanish authorities in Guatemala until Mexico became independent. San Cristobal was the capital of Chipas until 1892, when it lost that status to Tuxtla Gutiérrez.

Casa de Mazariegos

The house of the founder of the town, now a hotel, lies opposite the cathedral on the corner of Av. Insurgentes. Stone heads of Castillian lions can be seen on the doorway.

★Santo Domingo

Going north from the Zócalo along Avenida General Utrilla we come to the most important sacral building, the church of Santo Domingo. Built between 1547 and 1560 on the orders of Bishop Francisco de Marroquin of Guatemala, its present 17th c. façade is typically Mexican-Baroque and is one of the largest in surface area of its kind in Mexico. The imperial double eagle, the coat of arms of the Emperor Charles V, can be seen above the barred central opening and on the sides. The interior is over-lavishly decorated and contains a number of sculptures and wooden altars covered with gold leaf. The particularly richly and artistically carved pulpit dates from the 19th c., its plinth is carved from a single piece of wood and is one of the most remarkable examples of Baroque in the western hemisphere.

An Indian market

The Church of Santo Domingo

The adjoining convent was built at the same time. It served as a prison in the 19th c. and is now used by an Indian textile co-operative (Tianguis Jolobil). A museum of religion stands next to it.

★Market

The Mercado (market) lies near the church of San Domingo. Indios from the nearby villages gather here daily. Some years ago part of the market was replaced by a modern market hall. This has resulted in the loss of much of the character of San Cristóbal's original unique market. Members of the two peoples of the Maya group can be seen here: the Tzotzil (about 110,000 members; Chamula, Zinacantán, Larrainzar, Huixtán and Chenal-hó) and the Tzeltal (approximately 100,000 members; Tenejapa, Carranza, Amatenango del Valle, Oxchuc and Cancuc). They wear costumes which vary from village to village. The most striking are those of the Chamula and of the Indians from Tenejapa and Zinacantán.

★Museo Na-Bolom

It is worth visiting the archaeological and ethnological museum and library housed in Na-Bolom Inn (Maya: "house of the jaguar"; Av. Vicente Guerrero 33). Both were established by the Danish archaeologist Frans Blom, who died in 1963, and are dedicated to the Indians of Chiapas and their cultural inheritance, above all to the Lacandons whose declining culture is recorded in the marvellous photography of Gertrude Duby-Blom, wife of the researcher, who died in 1993. Since her death a board of directors has run the house, opening it to visitors from 4pm.

Casa Sergio Castro

This house in Av. 16 de Septiembre 32 contains a famous private collection of Indian costumes.

Museo Moscoso

Professor Prudencio Moscoso's private library is kept in house number 29 on the opposite side of the street. This can be visited; it also exhibits old-Indian finds from Chiapas.

Other Churches

The following churches are also worth mentioning: Caridad, Merced, San Francisco, Carmen, which burned down in 1993 and has been rebuilt (with the Arco del Carmen), Guadalupe and San Cristóbal, on the hill of the same name to the west of the town, which offers an excellent view.

Surroundings

Advice

Many of these places can only be reached by cross-country vehicles. "Colectivos" (buses) depart from the Zócalo in San Cristóbal for the villages. Market days, with the exception of special holidays, are usually on Sundays.

Grutas de San Cristóbal

Follow the MEX 190 for 10km/6 miles towards Comitán until reaching a right-hand turning to the nearby Grutas de San Cristóbal (San Cristóbal grottoes). The part of these now open constitutes only a fraction of the extensive dripstone caves.

★Huixtán

A few miles further on the road bends left to Ocosingo (about 90km/56 miles) and Palenque (see entry). The village of Huixtán lies approximately 20km/12½ miles along this road. As in other mountain villages, only a small number of the Tzotzil Indians now live here in accordance with old Mayan traditions. The village contains only a church, an administrative building and a few shops. The majority of the population live in the surrounding hills.

Most of the men continue to wear their traditional wide white cotton trousers, held up with a broad red sash. Their white shirts are mainly embroidered on the collars and sleeves. A black or brown woollen cape is worn over these. A red band decorates the flat hats, made by the Indians themselves. The women wear long dark blue skirts with a red belt with yellow stripes. The collars of their cotton blouses are embroidered in blue and their white scarves are colourfully embroidered with animals and flowers. Of the approximately 12,000 Huixtecos of the Tzotzil tribe, only about 10% live in Huixtán (fiestas: May 14th–16th, San Isidro; June 27th–30th, San Pedro and September 28th and 29th, San Miguel Arcángel).

Ocosingo

Ocosingo, until recently a completely isolated small town in the middle of the Tzeltal Indians' settlement area, is reached after a further 50km/31 miles. It still retains a certain importance as a centre for lumberjacks, chicle gatherers and hunters. The magnificent scenery of the surrounding area, parts of which are difficult to reach, contains unspoiled Indian settlements and haciendas (El Real, Australia, etc.), as well as the picturesquely situated village of Altamirano.

★Toniná

The excavation site of Toniná lies 14km/9 miles east of Ocosingo. This Maya site experienced its heyday during Maya Classic period in the 8th and 9th c. From inscriptions on stelae it has been established that Ruler 3 of Toniná took Kan-zul (Maya: "precious animal"), the ruler of Palenque, prisoner in A.D. 711. Kan-zul is supposed to have been ritually sacrificed by his enemies in Toniná in A.D. 722.

The site extends over seven terraces on a hill, at the foot of which are two ball game courts. A large number of stelae dated from between A.D. 495 and 909, round calendar stones and human sculptures without heads were found in the excavation area. Particularly noteworthy finds are an underground chamber with a typical overhanging arch and a wooden door lintel, a tomb with a sarcophagus, large stone masks and stucco figures, probably depicting prisoners. Finds made in the early

1990s – including the Palace of the Underworld, built from a kind of stone previously completely unknown in this region, and with Maya motifs and Toltec memorials and the large stucco mural with the Fourth Sun – lead experts to think that Toniná survived the end of the Maya Classic period and came under Toltec influence.

★Tenejapa

Tenejapa, an Indian village, lies about 28km/17 miles north-east of San Cristóbal de Las Casas. Only a few hundred of the total of approximately 15,000 Tzeltal-speaking Indians living in the surrounding area actually inhabit the village.

The men's costume comprises a black woollen tunic worn over short white trousers embroidered on the legs, and a pointed straw hat with wide, coloured ribbons. The women of Tenejapa, who are particularly good at weaving and embroiderery, wear richly-embroidered blouses, dark blue skirts with narrow vertical stripes. They also wear a wide red and black belt and over this a narrow white one (fiestas: January 23rd, San Ildefonso and July 22nd–24th, Santiago Apóstol).

★Zinacantán

Zinacantán lies about 7½ miles west of San Cristóbal de Las Casas. This village, populated by only a few hundred people, is the religious and political centre of approximately 14,000 Tzotzil-speaking Zinacantecos who live in the area.

Striking features of the men's costumes are their grey-checked shawls worn over short white trousers, and their flat straw hats decorated with multi-coloured ribbons. The way in which the ribbons are worn (tied or untied) shows whether the man is married or not. The women's costume compares very unfavourably with that of the men. Brilliant scarlet also features in the garments worn by men and women. Fiestas: January 18th, San Sebastián; August 8th–11th, San Lorenzo; September 8th, Virgen de la Navidad.

★San Juan Chamula

San Juan Chamula, about 11km/7 miles north-west of San Cristóbal, is the ceremonial centre of the Chamula Indians, the largest Tzotzil-speaking group. A large number of the more than 40,000 Chamulas live in surrounding small settlements. As is often the case in the mountain villages of the Mayå tribe, three large crosses, symbolising the tree of life, can be seen in the village and on the hills. It is worth visiting the small church in which people burn candles in memory of their dead. Catholic rites and old Mayan myths blend intensely here. A nominal fee is charged to enter the church (tickets are obtained from a small office, nearby, on the square).

Over their white cotton trousers and shirts the Chamulas wear woollen capes, often with an orange belt. On special days they wear straw hats with coloured ribbons hanging behind them. Men holding official posts in the community wear black capes. The women wear mid-calf length black wrap-around skirts with orange, red and green striped belts. Their blouses used to be white, but they now prefer blue cotton or dark wool. Fiestas: January 16th–22nd, San Sebastián, Carnival; Easter Week; May 3rd, Santa Cruz; June 22nd–25th, San Juan Bautista; August 30th, Santa Rosa.

Advice

It must be pointed out that people gathered in the village for religious services react extremely sensitively to tourists with loaded cameras. Photography is strictly forbidden in the church and visitors are strongly advised to abide by this prohibition.

Less well-known, but certainly equally impressive, especially during the fiestas, are other Indian villages, e.g San Andrés Larainzar, San Pedro Chenal-ho and Amatenango del Valle.

A little church in San Juan Chamula

Comitán

From San Cristóbal de Las Casas it is 57km/35 miles south-east on the MEX 190 (Panaméricana) to reach Comitán (1630m/5350ft; population 63,000), a pleasant Colonial town in a garden-like setting (orchid growing). There is a small museum in the Casa Dr Belisario Dominguez. The speciality of the town is *comiteco*, a famous type of tequila.

Montebello Lakes

A further 16km/10 miles along the MEX 190 a left-hand turning leads in 40km/25 miles to the Lagunas de Montebello (Montebello Lakes; see entry).

Mexican–Guatemalan Border

From Comitán it is about 80km/50 miles along the MEX 190 to Ciudad Cuauhtémoc, on the Guatemala frontier. A new tourism region is due to be developed in the area around the Mexican–Guatemalan border, which is characterised by magnificent scenery, a pleasant climate, many lakes and Maya ruins. The civil war in Guatemala has driven many refugees across the border into Mexico, resulting in this project being at present unfeasible.

San Cristóbal de Las Casas is a good base from which to take air taxis to the Mayan ruined sites of Palenque, Bonampak and Yaxchilán (see entries), which all lie in the rain forest of the Selva Lacandona.

San Luis Potosí (State)

Contraction: S.L.P.
Capital: San Luis Potosí
Area: 63,231sq.km/24,091sq. miles
Official population 1990: 2,003,200 (1994 estimate: 2,100,000)

Location and Topography

The centrally-situated state of San Luis Potosí borders the states of Zacatecas, Nuevo León, Tamaulipas, Veracruz, Hidalgo, Querétaro and

Mexico
United Mexican States
Estados Unidos Mexicanos

San Luis Potosí

Guanajuato. The eastern part of the state is crossed by mountain chains of the Sierra Madre Oriental, while the centre and the west consists of a dry plateau. The inhabitants are mainly Criollos, mestizos and Indios from the Otomí, Nahua, Huastec and Pame tribes.

Archaeological Sites

El Tamuin and El Ebano (see Tampico, Surroundings) are among the state's most important archaeological sites.

History

The east of the state was influenced by the important Huastec culture during the pre-Columbian period; in the second half of the 16th c. the Huastecs were made to pay tribute to the Aztecs. The remaining parts of the state were populated by semi-nomadic tribes such as the Cuachichiles, the Pames, the Guamares, the Copucas, the Nahuas and the Otomí, of which only a few have survived.

The Spanish, under Hernán Cortés, had reached the east of the present state by 1522. Some 70 years later precious metals were discovered in the region and mined with the help of the Tlaxcaltecs who had migrated here. People from the state played very important roles during the War of Independence (1810–21). In 1824 the period of Intendancy (Spanish government rule) which had existed until then, was abolished and various states evolved, among them the present San Luis Potosí.

Economy

The state is rich in salt and minerals, chiefly gold, silver, copper, lead, mercury and zinc. As well as the important contribution made by cattle breeding, its agricultural economy also relies on sugar-cane, coffee, tobacco, grain, corn, beans and cotton produced in the tropical lowlands and irrigated areas. Industry is chiefly located in the main town and comprises tanning, founding, milling and brewing, as well as textile and furniture factories.

In the ghost town of Real de Catorce

Places of Interest

In addition to the capital San Luis Potosí (see entry) and its surroundings, the state's archaeological sites and Ciudad Valles and Tamanzunchale (see Tampico, Surroundings), the following places are worth mentioning:

Matehuala

Matehuala ("place of the green water"; 1614m/5264ft; population 75,000; fiestas: January 8th, Fiesta del Cristo de Matehuala; June 13th, Día de San Antonio), 130km/81 miles north of San Luis Potosí, has little of interest but is a convenient place to stay overnight.

★Real de Catorce

The impressive ghost town Real de Catorce lies approximately 30km/18½ miles north-west of Matehuala and is reached along a mountain road and through a 2.5km/1½ mile-long tunnel. Supposedly named after fourteen soldiers who were murdered here by Indians in about 1700, this was an important mining town, especially at the end of the 19th c. when the population stood at about 45,000 (it is now approximately 800) and it boasted a theatre, a mint and an electric mining railway. A visit to the church of San Francisco, the destination every year on October 4th of thousands of pilgrims, is highly recommended. The pilgrims leave numerous votive tablets in thanks for their prayers for health, prosperity and protection against bad luck being answered.

"Wirikuta" Holy Land

The Peyoti cactus grows around Real de Catorce and is considered sacred by some Indian peoples such as the Huiholes and the Tarahumara. They believe that while experiencing mescaline-induced hallucinations they receive messengers from their gods. As the Peyoti does not grow in the area where the Huicholes are at present settled, they undertake pilgrimages every winter of up to 500km/311 miles into this region, which they consider to be their sacred land of "Wirikuta". This pilgrimage involves complicated ceremonies and ends with the picking of the cactus, which has previously been pierced by an arrow.

San Luis Potosí (Town) I 6

State: San Luis Potosí (S.L.P.)
Altitude: 1877m/6160ft. Population: 950,000. Dialling code: 91 48

Access from Mexico City

By rail about 10 hours; by bus approximately 6 hours; by car about 425km/264 miles on the MEX 57.

Location

San Luis Potosí, the capital of the state of the same name, lies on a steppe-like plateau and is important as a traffic junction and a trade centre. Despite increasing modernisation, the town with its beautiful old buildings and parks has preserved much of the character of the colonial period.

★Townscape

History

Little is known of the town's pre-Spanish history. Tanjamanja, a settlement founded by the Cuachichil Indians, was once supposed to have been situated here.

The first Spaniards, led initially by Miguel Caldera and soon after by Franciscan friars, arrived in the area between 1585 and 1590. At the same time considerable quantities of silver and gold were discovered, and the settlement of Real de Minas de San Luis Potosí was founded, taking the name Potosí (Quechua: "place of great wealth") from the silver town of the same name in Bolivia. In 1658 the settlement received its municipal charter from Philipp IV. Until 1824 San Luis Potosí was the principal town of an extensive *intendencia*, to which Texas also belonged. During the French War of Intervention (1862–66) and for a short time afterwards San Luis Potosí served as the seat of Benito Juárez's government which had been expelled from Mexico City.

Sights

Palacio de Gobierno

In the town centre is the Plaza de Armas with the Jardin Hidalgo. The Palacio de Gobierno (Government Palace), a massive, Neo-Classical building dating from the end of the 18th c., stands on the west side. Inside, the Sala Juárez contains life-size wax figures depicting, among other scenes, the meeting between Benito Juárez and Princess Salm-Salm on June 18th 1867. The princess asked the Mexican president to spare the life of Emperor Maximilian who was, however, executed the following day in Querétaro.

★Cathedral

The Baroque Cathedral, constructed between 1670 and 1740, is also in the main square. The façade of the unusual hexagonal porch is

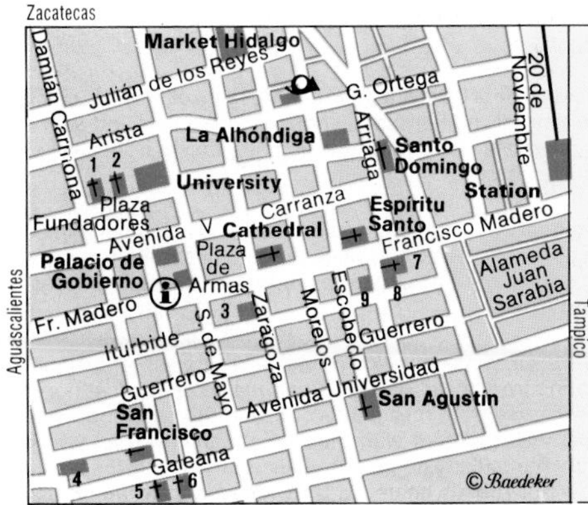

San Luis Potosí: the Cathedral in the Plaza de Armas

decorated with statues of the twelve Apostles standing in niches. The over-ornate decoration of the interior reveals a mixture of styles.

★El Carmen

The church of El Carmen is situated in the Plaza del Carmen, east of the cathedral. Dating from the 18th c., its façade is a magnificent example of Mexican Baroque. The church contains a Neo-Classical high altar, several Churrigueresque side altars and a particularly attractive shell-shaped Camarin.

Teatro La Paz

The Teatro La Paz stands next to El Carmen. Built at the end of the 19th c. from pink Cantera stone, its interior is decorated with murals by Fernando Leal.

★Mask Museum

The Museo Nacional de la Mascara (National Museum of Masks), which dates from the time of the Porfiriat, is housed in the Palacio Federal opposite. A once private collection of old and new masks from all over Mexico is displayed here.

Museo Regional

The Museo Regional Potosino (Regional Museum) is to be found in an old Franciscan convent in the Calle Galeana south of the main square. Its exhibits are principally archaeological finds from the region (Huastec, Totonac and Aztec).

★Capilla Aránzazu

The Capilla Aránzazu, a masterpiece of the New Spanish Churrigueresque style dating from the early 18th c., is situated on the first floor; the door lintels, carved from mesquite wood, and the enormous Estípites (pyramidal wall pilasters with their points downwards) which bear the vault are particularly noteworthy. Also of interest is the statue of Christ, made from reeds coated with a resinous mixture, which stands in the entrance hall, and the paintings in the chapel and in the adjoining rooms.

San Francisco

The 17th c. convent church of San Francisco on the Jardín Guerrero has a marvellous Baroque façade. Inside can be seen a crystal chandelier in the shape of a ship, and beautifully carved figures of saints.

Other sights in the town include the church of San Agustín (17th/18th c.), which has a simple Baroque façade, a beautiful tower and a Neo-Classical interior, Loreto, a Jesuit church, and the adjoining Sagrario. The Museo Regional de Arte Popular (House of Folk Art), the Casa de la Cultura (House of Culture) and Hidalgo market (rebozos, sarapes, wicker and cane work, ceramics, etc.), situated north of the main square, are recommended for shopping. Finally, the Museo Taurino (Bullfighting Museum) should also be mentioned.

Surroundings

Cerro de San Pedro

The ghost town Cerro de San Pedro is situated approximately 20km/12½ miles east in the direction of Río Verde. The silver and gold found here at the end of the 16th c. formed the basis of the wealth of San Luis Potosí.

Laguna de Media Luna

5km/3 miles before reaching Río Verde a road branches off to the Laguna Media Luna ("Half Moon"); its warm and clear waters make it popular with amateur divers; many archaeological objects have been found here.

Santa María del Rio

The attractive little town of Santa María del Rio, famous for the fine rebozos made here, lies about 50km/31 miles south of San Luis Potosí. Nearby are the radioactive thermal baths at Gogorrón, Lourdes and Ojo Caliente.

San Miguel de Allende — I 7

State: Guanajuato (Gto.)
Altitude: 1910m/6150ft. Population: 85,000
Dialling Code: 91 465

Access from Mexico City

By bus about 4 hours; by car approximately 280km/174 miles on the MEX 57D via Querétaro (see entry).

Location
★Townscape

The town of San Miguel de Allende nestles on a hill and extends down into a valley. It is one of the few places in the country designated as a national monument and has thus been able to preserve almost entirely its character as a colonial town.

Hidden behind often simple façades are some particularly attractive houses with patios and gardens. The charming townscape, the attractive surroundings and the pleasant climate have attracted many foreigners to San Miguel de Allende, either as visitors or as permament residents. The town has consequently become a centre of intellectual and artistic life, predominantly in the spheres of painting, sculpture, pottery, music, literature and drama.

History

During the pre-Columbian period there were several Tarascan and Chichimecan settlements in the area around San Miguel de Allende. Juan de San Miguel, the Franciscan friar who became famous in Michoacán for his beneficent work among the Indians, founded an Indian mission here in 1542. He named it after the saint whose name he bore and the San Miguel de los Chichimeca Indians who resided here. A little later Indians from Tlaxcala settled here, having to defend themselves against attacks by warlike Chichimecs. In 1555 the settlement

1 Town Hall 2 Casa del Mayorazgo de Canal 3 Birthplace of Ignacio de Allende 4 San Rafael 5 Nuestra Señora de la Salud 6 San Felipe Neri

became the provincial town and was soon renamed San Miguel el Grande. During the Colonial period rich owners of mines and land from Guanajuato and Zacatecas settled here. Some of their mansions and houses are among the town's finest.

Ignacio de Allende, born here in 1779, took up the fight for Mexican independence in 1810 together with Juan Aldama and Father Miguel Hidalgo. In recognition of the deeds carried out by Allende, who was later executed by the Spanish, the town was given the epithet "de Allende" in 1862.

During the past decades the town has developed into one of the country's important cultural centres, without losing much of its traditional charm.

Sights

★ Parroquia

A symbol of the town is the Parroquia, the parish church situated in the attractive main square (El Jardin, Plaza de Allende). This unusual Neo-Gothic building, constructed in about 1880 on the site of an older more modest church, is the work of the Indian architect Ceferino Gutiérrez, who used as his models a number of European cathedrals.

Inside on the left is the chapel of the Señor de la Conquista with the figure of the Cristo de la Conquista. This highly-revered 16th c. statue was made by Indians in Pátzcuaro following a traditional technique; it is constructed of a paste of maize stalks stuck together with a gum made from orchid tubers and coated with chalk (*de cana*). Fragments of Federico Cantu's murals can still be seen in the chapel; upon completion they were considered too radical by a priest who partially destroyed them. The remains of the former Mexican president, General Anastasio Bustamante (1770–1833), who died in San Miguel, are interred in the crypt. The Neo-Classical Camarín behind the main altar is the work of the versatile artist Tresguerras.

San Miguel de Allende ▶

San Rafael

The church of San Rafael (18th c.) adjoins the Parroquia on the right-hand corner. It contains simple sculptures.

Museo Allende

A Baroque-style corner house, the birthplace of Ignacio de Allende, stands on the west side of the main square. It now houses a museum exhibiting archaeological and historical finds and examples of handicrafts.

Casa del Mayorazgo de Canal

The north-west corner of the Plaza on Calle Canal is occupied by the imposing Casa del Mayorazgo de Canal, which displays Baroque and Neo-Classical elements; it has an attractive inner courtyard.

Handsome 18th c. colonial buildings, including the Palacio Municipal (Town Hall), stand along the north side of the square.

Convento La Concepción

By following Calle Canal westwards, past the Casa de Canal with its marvellously carved door, we come to the church and convent of La Concepción (Las Monjas). Building started on these in the mid-18th c. but was not completed until the end of the last century. Of note is the church's splendid twelve-sided cupola completed in 1891 and also the work of the architect Ceferino Gutiérrez. Inside the church are pictures attributed to the artists Miguel Cabrera and Juan Rodríguez Juárez. The convent possesses a beautiful inner courtyard lined with old trees and two-storeyed arcades. It now houses the Centro Cultural Ignacio Ramírez. Diagonally opposite stands the Teatro Angela Peralta. It was founded as an opera house and enjoyed its heyday in 1873, when the "Mexican Nightingale", Angela Peralta, appeared here.

In Calle Hernandez Macías, which runs south alongside the convent, are the former prison building and the headquarters of the Inquisition (Cuadrante 18) standing opposite one another.

Instituto Allende

Don Manuel Tomás de la Canal's beautiful 18th c. former manor house stands on the left-hand side of the Calzada Ancha de San Antonio when following it out of the town. It now houses the Instituto Allende, one of the town's two important art schools. The Parque Juárez lies to the east behind the grounds of the institute.

★ San Francisco

★ Façade

The church of San Francisco, built at the end of the 18th c., can be found one block north-east of the main square. It has a beautiful Churrigueresque façade with a tall Neo-Classical tower, believed to be the work of Francisco Eduardo Tresguerras. The influence of Tresguerras is just as strongly evident in the Neo-Classical interior. In front of the church lies a small park containing a monument to Christopher Columbus, and on its west side stands the 18th c. Church of the Third Order.

★ San Felipe Neri

The church of El Oratorio de San Felipe Neri, further north on the other side of Calle Mesones, was founded in 1712; it replaced the former "Mulato" church of Ecce Homo. Indian features are clearly evident on the pink stone façade, particularly on the five statues of saints standing in niches. On the Neo-Classical altar can be seen various pictures on oval mirrors, and on the altar in the right transept a painting of the Virgin of Guadalupe by Miguel Cabrera. The 33 pictures detailing the life of St Felipe Neri are also attributed to Miguel Cabrera.

Santa Casa de Loreto

★ Camarin

The Santa Casa de Loreto, a copy of the Santa Casa in Italy with a statue of the Virgin Mary, was built at the expense of Manuel Tomás de la Canal in 1735. Paths on both sides lead to the Camarin, an octagonal room with six altars, one in the Neo-Classical style, the others Baroque.

The Baroque retablos, with their carved and gilded wooden and stucco ornamentation, are marvellous examples of Mexican Churrigueresque. The benefactor and his wife are buried in the chapel.

Nuestra Señora de la Salud

Nuestra Señora de la Salud Church (mid-18th c.) stands to the east of San Felipe Neri. A large conch containing the "Eye of God" forms the upper part of the early Churrigueresque façade. The interior has Neo-Classical altars and some old paintings, including works by Miguel Cabrera, Antonio Torres and Tomás Xavier de Peralta. Behind it lies the covered market and the adjoining craft market.

Indian Chapels

In San Miguel de Allende and in neighbouring villages and Ranchos there are still isolated notable Indian chapels, whose simple buildings contain strange portrayals of saints, crosses and religious themes, all created in very individual styles. The Indians could hold prayer meetings in these chapels with their mixture of Indian and Catholic styles, free from the Spanish gaze.

Orchid Growing

Interested tourists can visit the firm of Stirling Dickinson at Sto. Domingo 34, one of the leading orchid-growers.

Viewpoint

Above the town when leaving in the direction of Querétaro, El Mirador viewpoint offers an impressive panorama of San Miguel de Allende and its surroundings. Above the road stands the equestrian memorial to Ignacio de Allende.

Capilla de Casqueros

In the midst of fields, 5km/3 miles on the far side of the railway line, stands the town's oldest church, probably dating from the middle of the 15th c.

Surroundings

Thermal Baths

Very close to the town, mainly in the direction of Dolores Hidalgo, are a number of thermal baths.

Atotonilco

Atotonilco (Náhuatl: "place of the hot waters"), a convent founded by Father Felipe Neri de Alfaro in 1740, is a popular place of pilgrimage with a much-revered statue of the Redeemer. It lies approximately 15km/9 miles north of the town and about 3km/2 miles from the road. After the proclamation of Mexico's independence from Spain the priest Miguel Hidalgo interrupted his march at the head of his hastily-assembled army here. Taking the painting of the Virgin of Guadelupe from the church, he fixed it to his banner. In this way the Madonna became the patroness of the Mexican freedom movement.

★Santuario de Jesús Nazareno

The interior of the convent church of Santuario de Jesús Nazereno and the various chapels are decorated with frescos, mainly by Miguel Antonio Martínez de Pocasangre, depicting attractive traditional themes. Behind the high altar, in the Camarín, there are sculptures of the Virgin Mary and the Apostles. The Rosary Chapel on the right has frescos of the Battle of Lepanto and leads to a Camarín with a ceiling in the form of a shell.

Place of Pilgrimage

Every year the town is the destination of pilgrims from all over Mexico. Two weeks before Easter Sunday the statue of the Christ of Señor de la Columna is carried in a grand nocturnal procession into the church of San Juan de Dios in San Miguel de Allende. On the third Sunday in July a local religious festival with Indian dances takes place in Atotonilco.

Dolores Hidalgo

The little town of Dolores Hidalgo (1990m/6531ft; population 41,000) lies about 28km/17 miles north-west of Atotonilco. With Father Miguel Hidalgo y Costilla's "Cry of Dolores" ("Grito de Dolores") from the parish church early on the morning of September 16th 1810, after the conspiracy was threatened with discovery, Mexico's War of Independence began.

★ Parish Church

The parish church, built between 1712 and 1778, has a beautiful Churrigueresque façade. The two retablos on the left and right are similarly impressive; the former, which is gilded, contains the famous image of the Virgin of Guadelupe.

Casa de Don Miguel de Hidalgo

The Casa de Don Miguel de Hidalgo houses a historical museum, mainly displaying memorabilia concerning the heroes of the freedom movement. Dolores Hidalgo is also known for the colourful tiles (Azulejos) produced here.

★ Mineral de Pozos

Follow the MEX 110 north-west from Dolores Hidalgo and cross the MEX 57 to reach the pretty little town of San Luis de la Paz (2020m/6630ft; population 31,000), some 8km/5 miles away. From here it is a further 10km/6 miles south to the town of Mineral de Pozos. Once a prosperous mining town with 60,000 inhabitants, it is now mainly deserted and has the atmosphere of a ghost town.

San Miguel de Cozumel

See Cozumel

San Miguel Regla

See Pachuca

Sayil P 7

State: Yucatán (Yuc.)
Altitude: 28m/92ft

Access

By bus (only as far as the Puuc Road turn-off) or by car from Mérida (see entry) southwards on the MEX 261 as far as Kabah (see entry) (about 100km/62 miles), then another 5km/3 miles on the same road until a turning to the left leads after 4km/2½ miles to Sayil.

Location

The archaeological site of Sayil, with Xlapak (see below) and Labná (see entry), forms a group of Maya centres, all with buildings in the pure Puuc style, which have been left largely unexplored and unvisited, despite the existence of a new road now for a number of years which has made them much more accessible.

History

As no definite dating has been possible in Sayil (Maya: "ants' place") up to now, people have had to determine the age of the site by the style of its buildings. This has led experts to claim that the two main buildings date from the 9th c. A.D., i.e. the Maya Late Classic period. Clearly all building activity must have ceased by the year 1000.

Visiting the ★ ruins

★ Palace

Dominating the site is the partially restored Palace (Palacio), with its several storeys of terracing, which represents one of the most perfect of all architectural creations in the Mayas' Classical Puuc style. Every floor of the 80×40m/260×130ft building is set back slightly from the one immediately below with the result that the roof of the lower storey

The Palace at Sayil

Western range of the Palace

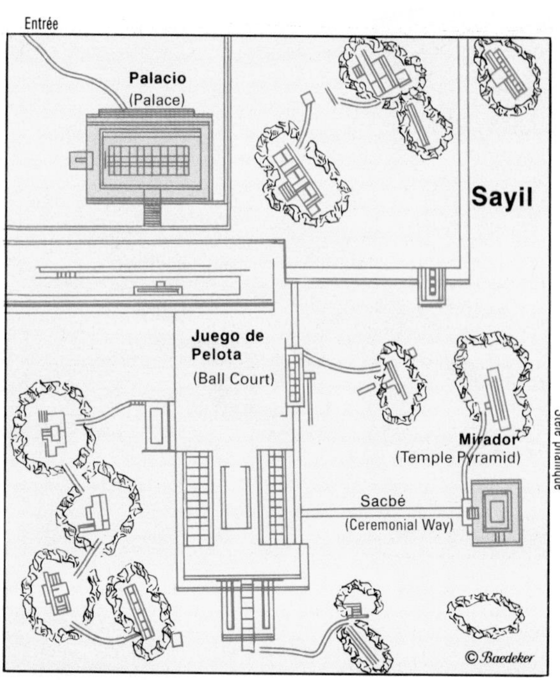

is also part of the balcony of the upper storey. This means that the third storey of this gradually tapering building is the highest one and on the south side there is an enormous flight of steps leading up to it.

★West section

The most interesting part of the building is the west section of the middle storey, which has two doors and four openings, each of which has a pair of stone pillars crowned by a square capital. In between these, there are linked columns, modelled on the wooden posts of the Maya huts, which contribute to the harmonious overall impression. In the centre of the frieze running along the top, there is an enormous mask of the rain-god Chac, which is flanked by ornamental glyphs. The frieze also contains tiny rounded columns in rows and, over the doors, the stylised motif of "the falling god" with open snakes' mouths turned away on either side.

At the north-west corner of the palace there was once a large "chultún" or cistern.

Mirador

Apart from the remains of the Ball Court (Juego de Pelota) and a small temple, the other thing to see at Sayil is the famous temple, now heavily weathered, known as the Mirador. At one time it was linked to the palace by a sacbé (ceremonial road). The temple rests on a platform and is notable for the crest of its roof, which was probably originally decorated with stucco ornaments, something quite unusual in the Puuc region as limestone was generally used here for mosaic work.

A path some 100m/110yd in length leads from this building to a large stela, something rather strange for the Mayas, which has a sculpted figure with an exaggerated phallus.

Phallic stela

Surroundings

Following the road eastwards in the direction of Labná for about 6km/4 miles, the excavation site of Xlapak is reached. The most important of the buildings which have been restored here is also called the Palace (Palacio) and it is in the characteristic Puuc style. Above the simple ground-level section of the main façade an interesting frieze can be seen underneath a ledge which is decorated with pillared embellishments. Over the middle of the three doors there is a tower-like section, which displays a complicated mask-like ornamentation. On either side there are panels with geometric adornments which turn into a broad ledge further up. The corners, which have been preserved, are formed by sections composed of elaborate Chac masks overlapping one another.

Xlapah

Sinaloa (State)

Abbreviation: Sin.
Capital: Culiacán
Area: 58,488sq.km/22,582sq. miles
Official population 1990: 2,204,000 (1994 estimate: 2,500,000)

This narrow state, which runs along the coast of the Mar de Cortés (Gulf of California), is bounded on the north by Sonora, on the south by Nayarit, and on the east by Durango and Chihuahua. This arid tropical coastal region merges in the east with the foothills of the Sierra Madre Occidental. The five rivers which flow down from the mountains into the Gulf support an extensive irrigation system by means of dams. Most of the population is either half-caste or creole; there are also pockets of Indians, principally of Mayo stock.

Location and topography

Of the small number of archaeological sites in the state, most of which consist of burial grounds or cave paintings, mention should be made of Camanito, Majada de Abajo, La Nanchita, Majada de Arriba, Imalá, Chametia and Guasave.

Archaeological sites

In the pre-Hispanic period Sinaloa was subject to heavy influxes of people from the central Mexican region. The remains left by these population movements have become referred to by the names of archaeological sites such as Chametia, Aztatlán, Culiacán and Guasave. Most of the finds so named are vessels made of alabaster and onyx or glazed coloured ceramics. They have now been classified as belonging to the period A.D. 400–1400 and have been attributed to the influences of the civilisations of Teotihuacán, Tula (Toltecs) and Mixteca-Puebla. In the 200 years before the Conquista the people living here were driven out in large numbers by nomadic tribes coming down from the north. A further influence at this time was exerted by the confederation of Chimalhuacán further to the south.

History

The first Spaniard to venture into the region now known as Sinaloa was probably Nuño Beltrán de Guzmán in 1531. Most of the settlements founded here during the 16th c. were destroyed by Indians and it was not until the second half of the 17th c. that a peace was reached with the help of Jesuit missionaries including Juan Padilla, Juan de la Cruz and Eusebio Francisco Kino. Together with Sonora, Sinaloa

formed part of the relatively independent western province within the Spanish viceroyship. After the War of Independence (1810–21) Sinaloa was finally separated from Sonora in 1830, thereby becoming a federal state of the Mexican Republic in its own right.

Economy

In recent years artificial irrigation has enabled Sinaloa to develop into an important agricultural area. Its products include wheat, cotton, tobacco, sugar cane, winter vegetables and fruit. As one would expect, fishing and its allied processing industries are also important. Sinaloa's industries include beer, tobacco products, edible oil, soap, textiles and ironmongery, while its mines produce salt, graphite, manganese ore and certain precious metals. Tourism is also an increasingly important source of income. In terms of transport, it is the railway lines which have most of all contributed to Sinaloa's development.

Places of Interest

Besides the important port and resort of Mazatlán (see entry) the following places in Sinaloa deserve mention:

Culiacán

The capital of the state of Sinaloa is Culiacán (Náhuatl for "place where the god Coltzin is worshipped" or "where two waters meet"; 65m/213ft; population 700,000). The settlement of San Miguel de Navito was founded here in 1533 by Nuño Beltrán de Guzmán on the site of a pre-Columbian Nahua village. After later becoming a mining settlement, Culiacán, by the use of irrigation, developed into the centre of an extensive agricultural region (cotton, sugar cane, winter vegetables, etc.). The surrounding area is known for its legal cultivation of the poppy (source of opiates) and its illicit cultivation of the cannabis plant, marihuana.

Culiacán has few noteworthy buildings apart from the 19th c. cathedral, the enormous modern building housing the social centre (Centro-Cívico Constitución) and the museum, with its archaeological pieces and exhibits of the flora and fauna of the region.

"Bandas Sinaloenses"

The "bandas sinaloenses", which play military music with Dixieland jazz and Cuban rhythms, are very popular both in Culiacán and in the state as a whole.

Thermal baths, artificial lakes and beaches

On the edge of Culiacán and in the immediate surroundings of the city can be found the thermal baths of Carrizalejo, Macurimi and Imalá on the Río Tamazula; nearby there are Indian cave paintings. Anglers can take advantage of the artificial lakes of Sanalona and Adolfo López Mateos (perch, catfish, trout, etc.), while on the coast of the Gulf of California there are the beautiful beaches of Altata, Campo Aníbal and El Dorado.

Guasave

In Guasave (38m/125ft; population 140,000; fiesta: first Sunday in October, Día de la Virgen del Rosario), Mayo dancing can be seen; nearby there is an archaeological burial area.

Los Mochis

Los Mochis (73m/239ft; population 180,000) is situated at a major railway junction and is an important centre for the surrounding agricultural area, which is notable for the cultivation of sugar cane, rice, vegetables and flowers – in particular, globe flowers, which, when fed to hens, give their yolks a better colour. The town is also the starting-point for the spectacular railway journey up the Barranca del Cobre (see entry).

San Miguel de Zapotitlán

About 20km/12 miles north of Los Mochis is the town of San Miguel de Zapotitlán where there are demonstrations of Mayo dancing on local saints' days, Holy Week (Semana Santa) and at Christmas time.

Topolobampo

Topolobampo (population 30,000; fiesta: June 1st, Día de la Marina), 24km/15 miles south-west of Los Mochis, is the terminus of the Chihuahua Pacific railway line and also has ferry connections with La Paz in Lower California. This fishing village, principally involved in prawn-catching, lies on the large Bay of Ohuira, known for its curious rock formations. Some of the nearby islands are breeding-grounds for sea-lions.

★Bay of Ohuira

Sonora (State)

Abbreviation: Son.
Capital: Hermosillo
Area: 182,553sq.km/70,484sq. miles
Official population 1990: 1,823,600 (1994 estimate: 2,050,000)

Location and topography

Sonora, the second largest state in Mexico, is bounded on the north by the USA (Arizona), on the west by Lower California and the Gulf of California (Mar de Cortés), on the south by Sinaloa and on the east by Chihuahua. The landscape consists of desert and semi-desert rich in cacti, wooded mountain chains forming part of the Sierra Madre Occidental, artificially irrigated valleys and the coastline, which is both rocky and sandy. The largest island in Mexico, the Isla del Tiburón, lies off the coast of Sonora. The state is populated by a majority of whites and mestizos, but there are also still some of the original Indian tribes such as the Pápagos, Opatas, Pima, Seri, Yaqui and Mayo.

Archaeological sites

Of the few archaeological sites in Sonora, such as Caborca, Sahuaripa, La Pintada and Yécora, only those with cave paintings are really worth visiting.

History

In pre-Columbian times Sonora (Spanish for "resonant", named after the sound of marble being hewn here) was the home of a number of both nomadic and settled Indian tribes, whose descendants are still living here in certain defined areas.

The first Europeans to reach the region were Spanish conquistadores, including Francisco Vázquez de Coronado, Álvaro Núñez Cabeza de Vaca and Pedro Almindes Chirinos, who arrived in 1531 and 1533 and met powerful resistance from the Indians. An expedition led by Francisco de Ibarra discovered the first valuable treasures in 1567. A number of Spanish settlements over the next 100 years all fell victim to attacks by Indians, notably by the Yaqui tribe. It was not until the great explorer Pater Eusebio Francisco Kino arrived in 1687 and established a network of Jesuit missions across the country that a short-lived peace occurred. After the expulsion of the Jesuits from New Spain in 1767 Indian rebellions flared up again.

At the beginning of the 19th c., Sonora with Sinaloa became part of the western province within the Spanish viceroyship. In 1830, after the War of Independence (1810–21), in which José María González Hermosillo played a prominent part, Sonora was made a state in its own right, separate from Sinaloa. There were large Indian uprisings among the Yaqui and Mayo tribes in 1825, 1875 and 1886. Towards the end of the 19th c., during the period in which Porfirio Díaz was in power, the transport system and mining industry were dramatically extended, while at the same time rebellious Yaqui Indians were deported to Yucatán, later to return and stage their final uprising in Sonora in 1927. The sons of Sonora played an important part in the War of Revolution (1911–20), some of them later becoming presidents of Mexico, including Álvaro Obregón, Adolfo de la Huerta, Plutarco Elías Calles and Abelardo Rodríguez.

Economy

Until the Second World War Sonora, with its rich mineral deposits, was important merely as a supplier of precious metals (gold, silver, copper, lead and tin). Today, besides fishing and cattle-rearing, artificially irrigated areas of cultivation are of considerable importance and cotton, fruit, vegetables, wheat, soya beans, maize, sugar cane and tobacco are all grown. The metal-refining and tourist industries have also enjoyed a continuous upward trend in recent years. The state is fortunate in having good rail and road connections.

Places of Interest

Apart from the capital Hermosillo (see entry), the port of Guaymas (see entry), Álamos (see Guaymas) and their surrounding areas, the following places in Sonora deserve mention:

Nogales

Nogales (1179m/3868ft; population 180,000; fiesta: May 5th, Battle of Puebla). Although undoubtedly important as a frontier town, adjoining the US state of Arizona and facing the American town with the identical name on the other side of the border, Nogales does not really have any noteworthy places of interest.

Magdalena de Kino

Magdalena de Kino (893m/2930ft; population 40,000; fiesta: October 4th, Día de San Francisco Xavier), another frontier town about 90km/56 miles to the south of Nogales, is noteworthy for the Church of San Francisco Xavier, in which Pater Kino's grave was discovered as late as 1966.

Other well-known mission stations which go back to Pater Kino's time are those of Cocospera, Caborca, Pitiquito, Sonoita, Oquitoa and Tubutama.

Puerto Peñasco

The fishing town of Puerto Peñasco (sea-level; population 40,000), which is situated in the northern part of the Gulf of California on the Guaymas–Mexicali–Tijuana railway line, has in the last few years developed into a fast-growing seaside resort owing to its close proximity to the USA.

Pápago Indians

Several hundred Indians of the Pápago tribe still live in Sonora. This tribe, which is closely related to the Pima, also has about 12,000 members in South Arizona. In 1950 there were still 15,000 Pápagos in Mexico but the majority of these subsequently emigrated to the United States. It is believed that the Pima-Pápagos are descendants of the Hohokam people, whose civilisation flourished in the south-west of the USA from about A.D. 700 to 1400 (Pima: "the people who have gone"). This half-nomadic tribe, which has constantly feuded with the Apaches, became partially converted to Christianity at the end of the 18th c. by the Jesuits. In the middle of the 19th c. there were large rebellions which were however put down by the Mexican government. The Pápagos today live as farmers, hunters and gatherers. Their religion, which exhibits only certain Christian characteristics, embraces a belief in the immortality of the soul and includes the sun and stars among its deities. Its festivals, which have a strong dance element, generally take place in connection with harvesting and hunting. Their main Catholic feast day is October 4th (Día de San Francisco).

Sumidero, El

See Tuxtla Gutiérrez

Tabasco (State)

Abbreviation: Tab.
Capital: Villahermosa
Area: 25,337sq.km/9783sq. miles
Official population 1990: 1,501,700 (1994 estimate: 1,650,000)

Location and topography

The federal state of Tabasco, which is situated on the southern edge of the Gulf of Mexico, is bounded on the east by the state of Campeche and Guatemala, on the south by the state of Chiapas and on the west by Veracruz. The state is for the most part flat, with large numbers of lakes, rivers and swamps and in places covered with dense rain-forest. Two navigable rivers, the Usumacinta and the Grijalva, traverse the region before emptying into the Gulf. Tabasco is principally populated with mestizos and Chontal Indians. Many species of tropical animals inhabit the forest, savannas and inland waters.

Archaeological sites

The most important of the pre-Columbian sites belonging to the Olmecs are La Venta (see Catemaco Lake) and San Miguel, while those of the Mayas include Comalcalco (see Villahermosa), El Bellote, Jonuta and Balancán. Today the most important towns, apart from the capital Villahermosa (see entry), are Frontera, Emiliano Zapata, Tenosique, Huimanguillo and Teapa.

History

In the distant past Tabasco ("moist earth") and Veracruz formed the original home of the mysterious Olmecs. Later Tabasco was settled by

the Chontal Indians, who played an important part in the population movements which took place between central and southern Mexico and Yucatán in the pre-Hispanic Spanish period.

Juan de Grijalva (1518) and Hernán Cortés (1519) were the first Europeans to land here although they were soon driven out again. It was not until 1540 that Francisco de Montejo successfully conquered part of the territory. In 1824 Tabasco became a federal state within the Republic of Mexico, while in the 1860s it became an arena for revolutionary battles and skirmishes with French troops who intermittently occupied parts of Mexico with the aim of propping up the Emperor Maximilian. In the 1920s and 1930s the radical governor Tomás Garrido Canabal waged a bitter struggle against the Church. Most of the churches were destroyed, the priests expelled, and worship at church was forbidden. It was these events which Graham Greene used as the backcloth to his novel "The Power and the Glory".

Economy

In this hot damp climate bananas, coconut palms, cacao, coffee and sugar cane are all crops which flourish and have an important part to play in the economy, as well as hard and precious woods and chicle. Cattle-rearing and fishing are also significant. But it is the abundant oil-wells which have had the greatest influence on the development of Tabasco's economy, albeit at the price of increasing pollution along the coast.

Tajín, El

See El Tajín

Tamaulipas (State)

Abbreviation: Tamps.
Capital: Ciudad Victoria
Area: 79,602sq.km/30,734sq. miles
Official population 1990: 2,249,600 (1994 estimate: 2,600,000)

Location and topography

The state of Tamaulipas is bounded on the north by the USA (Texas), on the west by Nuevo León and on the south by San Luis Potosí and Veracruz. The eastern edge of the state is the Gulf of Mexico with its wide beaches and many lagoons, while the western part is characterised by mountain ranges belonging to the eastern Sierra Madre and tropical valleys. The northern part of the state consists mainly of broad arid plains. Today the southern part of Tamaulipas is still populated predominantly by Huastec Indians.

History

In the very early history of the present-day state of Tamaulipas ("High Mountain") there were only nomads crossing through the territory. Later individual tribes settled here and as early as 1100 B.C. a ceramics-based civilisation had developed here, which is generally supposed to be that of the Huastecs. The first phases of this formative period have been called Pavón, Ponce and Aguilar (up to 350 B.C.) and the later pre-Classic, Classic and post-Classic Pánuco I to V. Whence and when the Huastecs really arrived in the area is not known with any certainty. It is thought that they migrated from the southern Gulf coast, which was probably the cradle of Meso-American civilisation. The fact that their language belongs to the Maya group, and that other external similarities are apparent, has led experts to conclude that they are in fact a

Maya tribe which had wandered a long way from its original home. The tribe inhabits an area extending from Tamaulipas across parts of San Luis Potosí, Hidalgo, Querétaro and the north of Veracruz.

Huastecs

The Huastecs have had a considerable influence on the civilisations of the Mexican highlands and the whole of the north of the country during the course of their long history. Early on, there were cultural exchanges with Teotihuacán which persisted for many years. According to a chronicle the Huastecs are later supposed to have taken part in the dynastic struggles in Tula (Tollán), which finally led to the downfall of the Toltec empire. It is thought that the Huastecs' influence in the north even extended as far as the Mississippi and Ohio valleys. In the end the Aztecs forced them to pay tribute at the end of the 15th c., although they were not subjugated. Other peoples, including eventually the Aztecs (Mexica), adopted some of the Huastecs' gods, such as Quetzalcóatl as the wind god Ehécatl, Xipe Tótec, the "broken god" as a symbol of renewal and Xochiquétzal, the goddess of love and flowers. Although their cultural achievements cannot compare with those of the Mayas to the south, they have bequeathed much of interest to posterity. A high level of invention and artistry is apparent not only in their fine clay figures and large stone statues of priests and noblemen but also their metalwork, and craftwork involving shells and semi-precious stones. Huastec architecture is characterised by circular and conical buildings.

When the Spanish arrived in the region they found no united Huastec empire but instead a large number of small "domains" which defended themselves implacably against the invaders. Hernández de Córdoba and Juan Grijalva arrived first in 1518, but it was Francisco da Garay, Hernán Cortés and Gonzalo de Sandoval who succeeded in subduing the area between 1521 and 1526. The province was then administered by Nuño Beltrán de Guzmán, under whose harsh rule a lucrative slave trade was set up between Huasteca and the West Indies. In more recent times the fortunes of the region have tended to follow those of its largest port, Tampico (see entry).

Economy

The ports on the Gulf coast and the border with the United States (Texas) have made the state one of the most economically vibrant in Mexico. Oil and its exploitation are at the main focus of this activity, followed by the farming of cotton, maize and sorghum (a kind of cereal). Cattle-rearing and fishing are also important. Recently, processing industries in the frontier areas have developed at a staggering rate.

Important towns

The following large towns are important as ports, trans-shipment centres, or new industrial and agricultural centres: Tampico (see entry), Matamoros (12m/39ft; population 500,000), Reynosa (37m/121ft; population 450,000), Nuevo Laredo (171m/561ft; population 350,000) and the state capital, Ciudad Victoria (altitude: 321m/1053ft; population 300,000).

Tampico L 6

State: Tamaulipas (Tamps.)
Altitude: 12m/39ft
Population: 600,000
Telephone code: 91 12

Access from Mexico City

By air about ¾ hour; by rail via San Luis Potosí; by bus about 10 hours.

Location and topography

The city of Tampico lies on the north bank of the Río Pánuco and, after Veracruz, is the most important port on the coast of the Gulf of Mexico. It originally grew up as an oil and cotton port but today it is a well-equipped and busy trans-shipment port for goods from all over the USA, Europe and South America. The overall appearance of the city and its surroundings is determined by its oil tanks and refineries, bustling port, river estuaries, lagoons and beaches.

History

The area around Tampico was probably settled very early on by the Huastecs, a people speaking a Maya tongue. Evidence of their ceramics, which date back to before 1000 B.C., supports this assertion. In the second half of the 15th c. the Aztecs succeeded in making the Huastecs tributary to them.

A river expedition led the first Spaniards here under Alonso Alvárez de Pineda as early as 1519. Within the next ten years the Huastecs were subdued. The Franciscan padre Andrés de Olmos founded a monastery on the ruins of an Aztec settlement in 1532 and it was from here that the city later developed. The monastic settlement, which was called San Luis de Tampico was granted the title "villa" (township) in 1560. During the next hundred years the harbour was the object of many attacks by incursive Indian tribes, such as the Apaches, sweeping down from the north, and pirates coming in from the sea. In 1683 Tampico was destroyed and it was not until 1823, after the War of Independence, that it was rebuilt. In 1829 the town was occupied by the Spanish, who were finally defeated by the Mexican general, later president, Antonio López de Santa Ana. During the Mexican-American War (1846–48) the town was for a time occupied by US troops under General Zachary Taylor. Even French soldiers gained a foothold in Tampico during their country's intervention in Mexico. The discovery of oil near the town at the beginning of the 20th c. under the presidency of Porfirio Díaz brought

Turn-of-the-century warehouses in the port of Tampico

an influx of US and British capital, and the subsequent boom made Tampico for a time the biggest oil port in the world. Following the nationalisation of the oil companies in 1938 the prosperity of the port temporarily went into a massive decline.

Sights

Tampico is not really a rewarding place for the tourist to visit. The Plaza de Armas (Zócalo) is a good vantage point for the city's night life and is also the location of the cathedral and city hall (Palacio Municipal).

Huastec Museum

About 7km/4 miles north of the Plaza, in the satellite town of Ciudad Madero, is the Huastec museum (Museo de la Cultura Huasteca), which is housed in the Instituto Tecnológico. Its principal contents include stone sculptures, terracotta figurines, clay dishes, articles of jewellery made out of gold, silver, copper, shells and semi-precious stones, ritual objects made of stone, as well as weapons and costumes belonging to this fascinating people.

Beaches

The most popular beaches near the town are those of Miramar and Altamira.

Surroundings

Ebano

About 60km/37 miles to the west on the MEX 70 is the town of Ebano (S.L.P.). A Huastec archaeological site was discovered near here which reveals an interesting early building from the epochs of Pánuco I to II (350 B.C.–A.D. 200 – in other words from the pre-Classic period. It is a dome-shaped building almost 30m/98ft in diameter and 3m/10ft high, the rounded shape of which is characteristic of Huastec architecture. This temple is thought to have been consecrated to the wind god Ehécatl. Access to the excavation site, however, is not easy.

El Tamuín

After a further 44km/27 miles (6km/4 miles before the town of Tamuín) there is a left turning in the direction of San Vicente Tancualayab which leads after 6km/4 miles to the Huastec excavation village of El Tamuín. The site was one of the most important towns in the Huastec empire, but unfortunately the ruins are neither spectacular nor well preserved.

Along the Río Tamuín there is an area covering some 17ha/40 acres which consists of platforms, altars, patios and earth mounds. The finds on this site included a 3m/10ft high platform with a large open flight of steps which was once covered in painted stucco. A low temple platform connected to a conical altar has also been uncovered and reveals wall-paintings which are still visible today. It is believed that this site dates from the 8th or 9th c. and therefore belongs to the Classic period. One of the finest and most famous of Huastec sculptures was also discovered at El Tamuín, the 1·45m/4½ft high statue of a youth with symbols of the wind god Ehécatl. A copy is in the museum in Tampico/Ciudad Madero, while the original can be seen in the National Museum of Anthropology in Mexico City.

Ciudad Valles

Continuing westwards on the MEX 70, about 30km after Tamuín, the town of Ciudad Valles (90m/295ft; population 195,000) is reached. Situated in the state of San Luis Potosí, it is an agricultural centre with a small archaeological museum and a series of attractive thermal baths, caves and waterfalls close by.

Tamazunchale

Following the MEX 85 southwards, the town of Tamazunchale (206m/676ft; population 31,000; fiesta: June 24th, San Juan Bautista) is reached after 107km/66 miles. This Huastec settlement is situated in the midst of luxuriant tropical vegetation and the surrounding area is a paradise for ornithologists and lepidopterists. The road, fringed by orange-groves, winds its way southwards through the magnificent wild scenery of the eastern Sierra Madre into the state of Hidalgo.

Tapachula

See Chiapas

Taxco de Alarcón K 8

State: Guerrero (Gro.)
Altitude: 1670m/5479ft
Population: 125,000
Telephone code: 91 732

Access from Mexico City

By bus about 3 hours; by car about 170km/106 miles on the MEX 95 and 95D, turning off in Amacuzac.

Location and ★★ townscape

Taxco, spectacularly situated on the side of a series of hilltops, is one of the most famous and most popular tourist destinations in Mexico by virtue of its harmonious townscape dating back to the colonial period, with low tiled houses, tiny squares, alleyways and secluded corners.

History

In pre-Columbian times the area was inhabited by the Tlahuicas, one of the Nahua tribes. About 10km/6 miles from present-day Taxco stood

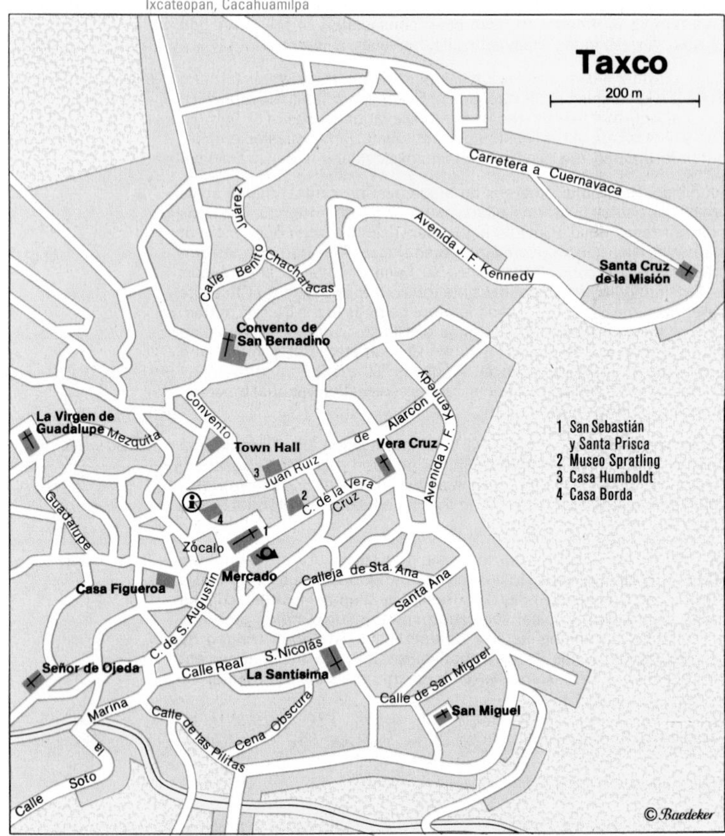

the Indian town of Tlachco (Náhuatl: "where ball was played"). The Aztecs under their rulers Itzcóatl and Moctezuma I invaded the area and finally annexed it in the middle of the 15th c.

The Spanish arrived here in 1522 in search of tin and silver. In 1529 they founded the settlement of El Real de Tetzelcingo, from which the town of Taxco was finally to emerge in 1581. Large deposits of silver were not found until the middle of the 18th c. when José de la Borda discovered and exploited the large mine of San Ignacio. In gratitude for the riches he had acquired, Borda had the church of Santa Prisca built. After the Revolutionary War (1910–20) the region became increasingly impoverished until the American William Spratling (1900–67) settled there in 1930. He was successful in reviving the old artisan skills by bringing in silversmiths from Iguala and getting them to produce jewellery using the traditional Indian models. Today Taxco lives almost exclusively from tourism and the silversmiths' trade, the latter employ-

Panorama of Taxco

ing over 1500 craftsmen in several hundred tiny workshops scattered throughout the town. The silver used for this work is in fact an alloy made up of 950–980 grams of silver to 20–50 grams of copper.

Sights

★★ San Sebastián y Santa Prisca

The small square or "zócalo" (Plaza de la Borda), in which stands the church of San Sebastián y Santa Prisca, is undoubtedly picturesque. The church, a masterpiece of Churrigueresque architecture, was commissioned by the silver king, José de la Borda, and built by the architects, Diego Durán and Juan Caballero. The portal is flanked on each side by a pair of Corinthian columns, which enclose a row of sculptures. In the upper part of the façade over the pope's triple crown can be seen, instead of a central window, a large medallion depicting the baptism of Christ. Above this is the chancel window, which is topped by a rounded gable. The elaborate ornamentation, which includes statues, weapons, foliage, shells, ribbons and cherubims, is particularly finely wrought. The uniformity of the side walls is broken on either side of the portal by ornately framed windows. The towers above the façade are richly decorated with felicitously embellished columns and grotesque sculpted faces. The magnificent picture presented by the church is completed by the dome which is covered with blue and yellow azulejos (tiles).

Interior

Inside the church there are superbly carved, painted and gilded retablos which show many figures of apostles, angels and saints in the middle of richly fashioned motives of flowers, fruits and birds. Above the entrance to the chapel of the Indians (Capilla de los Indios) there is a painting by Miguel Cabrera depicting the martyrdom of the church's

Silver jewellery from Taxco

patron saint, Santa Prisca. There are other noteworthy paintings by the same artist hanging in the chapel and in the sacristy.

South of the Zócalo

The Calle del Arco leads from the Zócalo to the Market (Mercado), which is well worth seeing. Further to the south-east is the Baroque Santísima Church dating from 1713, from which the Calles Real de San Nicolás and Progreso lead westwards to the Iglesia Ojeda (finished in 1822), which stands on a hill.

Casa Figueroa

Going through the Calle de San Agustín from the church back towards the main square, the visitor will pass the Plaza de los Gallos, which is still suffused with the atmosphere of old Spain, and the Casa Figueroa (Calle Guadalupe 2). This building dating from the middle of the 18th c. was originally called "Casa de las Lágrimas" ("House of Tears"), because the nobleman who commissioned it, Conde de Cadena, had it built by Indians under conditions of slave labour, many of whom were literally worked to death. The artist Fidel Figueroa acquired it in 1943 and the house is now a museum which is looked after by his widow.

North of the Zócalo

The Casa Borda not far from the main square is the former home of the silver baron José de la Borda. The Silver Museum (Museo de la Platería) on the Plaza Borda is open to visitors.

William Spratling Museum

Situated in Porfirio Delgado I, behind Santa Prisca, is the William Spratling Museum (Museo Guillermo Spratling), in which archaeological pieces from the western cultures and objects from Taxco's heyday as a silver town are on display.

Casa Humboldt

On the Calle Juan Ruiz de Alarcón stands the Casa Humboldt, a magnificent building with a beautiful mudéjar gateway, which Juan de Villa-nueva had built in the 18th c. The name of the house is derived from the fact that in April 1803 the German naturalist and geographer Alexander von Humboldt spent the night here during his travels through the Spanish West Indian colonies which lasted several years. He recorded his impressions in 35 volumes and on 1300 copper-plates. Today silver-work is displayed in the Casa Humboldt.

Convento de San Bernardino

The Calle Convento leads past the town hall to the former Convent of San Bernardino. The convent was originally a Franciscan foundation dating from the 16th c., but was burnt down during the 19th c. and then rebuilt in the Neo-Classical style.

Iglesia de la Virgen de Guadalupe

On a hill, looking in a south-westerly direction, is the church of the Holy Virgin of Guadalupe. This church, which has a lovely view of the Zócalo and Santa Prisca, dates from the 18th c. and was restored in 1877.

Lomas de Taxco

Minibuses and taxis travel from the Zócalo to the base station of the cableway, which is in the north of the town near the Hacienda del Chorillo. The railway soars up to the 240m/787ft high chain of hills called Lomas de Taxco. The view during the ascent and from the plateau is exceptional.

★ Processions

Every year during Holy Week a unique series of processions takes place in Taxco. They begin on Palm Sunday and reach their high point on Maundy Thursday and Good Friday, when "penitentes" (penitents who wear foot chains), "encruzados" (faithful who drag heavy thorn bushes on their bare shoulders) and "flagelentes" (penitents whipping themselves with thin scourges) make their way through the streets and hope thereby to gain redemption for their sins.

Surroundings

★★ Grutas de Cacahuamilpa (Map pp. 452/53)

31km/19 miles to the north-east of Taxco and situated in the national park of the same name are the 1100m/3609ft high dripstone caves Grutas de Cacahuamilpa (Náhuatl: "in the cacao fields"). Since their discovery in 1835 tunnels have been driven into the caves to a depth of over 16km/10 miles without yet arriving at the limits of the cave system.

All kinds of different dripstone formations extending through 16 chambers, some of which are as much as 80m/262ft wide and 77m/253ft high, make these caves some of the largest and most interesting in Mexico.

Grutas de la Estrella

26km/16 miles north of Cacahuamilpa are the Grutas de la Estrella. Open to visitors since 1976 they can be reached on foot comfortably in 15 minutes.

This cave, which is about 1km/½ mile long and has an almost continuous series of stalactites, is probably connected with the caves of Cacahuamilpa, although a definite link has yet to be established.

Ixcateopan

The little town of Ixcateopan (Náhuatl: "cotton temple"); population 8000) is situated 40km/25 miles west of Taxco in magnificent mountain country. It is said that underneath the altar of the 16th c. church of Santa María de la Asunción, which today houses a museum, the mortal remains were found of the last Aztec ruler Cuauhtémoc, whom Cortés ordered to be put to death in Honduras in 1525.

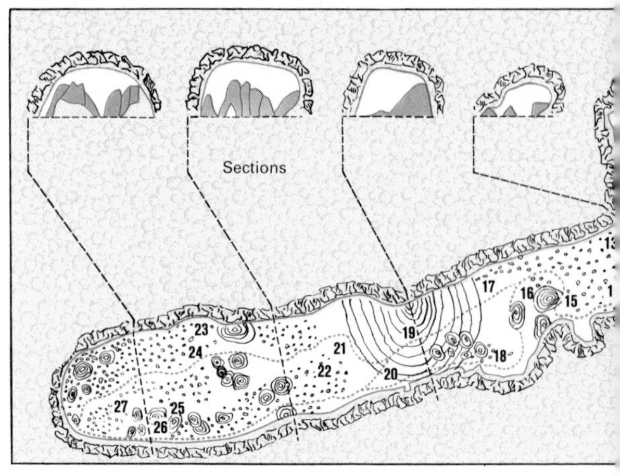

INTERESTING FORMATIONS

1 Chivo
2 Fuentes
3 Canastas
4 Confites
5 Aurora
6 Tronos
7 Portada de los Querubines
8 Panteón
9 Relicario
10 Plaza de Armas
11 Hornos

Tehuacán

See Puebla (State)

Tehuantepec M 9

State: Oaxaca (Oax.)
Altitude: 110m/361ft. Population: 90,000
Telephone code: 91 971

Access from Mexico City

By rail about 23 hours; by bus via Oaxaca (see entry) about 12 hours; by car on the Panaméricana (MEX 190).

Location

The town of Tehuantepec, which is an important road and rail junction, has given its name not only to the Gulf along the Pacific coast but also to the isthmus where Mexico is at its narrowest (only 200km/125 miles wide). This tropical town, with its humid climate and lush vegetation, is situated in a valley surrounded by low hills and the broad sweep of the Río Tehuantepec. The population consists of Zapotecs and Mestizos.

History

Tehuantepec (Náhuatl: "mountain of the jaguar") almost certainly had a long history prior to the arrival of the Spanish for it was a centre of the Zapotecs. Around A.D. 1470 the town was occupied by an army led by Axayácatl, the ruler of the Aztecs.

At the time of the arrival of the Spanish in 1521–22 the town was ruled by Prince Cocijo-pii, who was the son of the Zapotec king Cocijo-eza and an Aztec princess. The prince allied himself with the Spanish

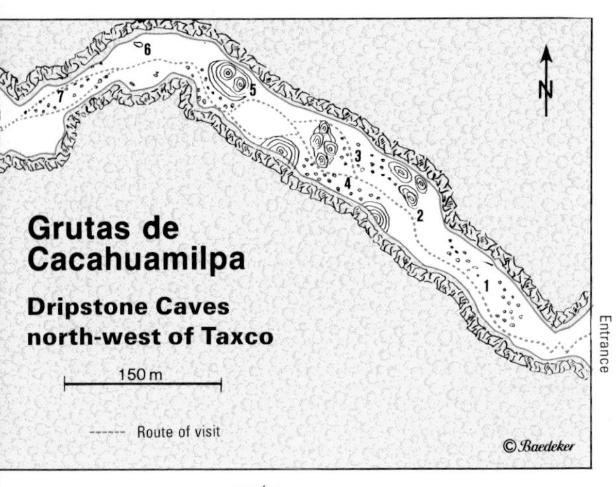

12 Volcán
13 Pedregal del Muerto
14 Virginias
15 Nacimiento
16 Campanario
17 Ánimas
18 Ágna Bendita
19 Puerto del Aire
20 Bautisterio
21 Lagunillas
22 Torres Palmares
23 Gloria
24 Canastillas
25 Emperatriz
26 Infiernillo
27 Órganos

against the Aztecs. At the beginning of the colonial period Tehuantepec was one of the possessions of Hernán Cortés.

This strategically important town, situated on the shortest land connection in Mexico between the Atlantic and Pacific, set Cortés and then later the Spanish viceroy and the Mexican government thinking about communication routes in this area of the continent. Roads were built, and also a railway line, but the plans to dig a canal never came to fruition. Tehuantepec's importance plummeted when the Panama Canal was opened in 1914 and it is only since the oil boom in Mexico over the last few years and the laying of a pipeline from Teapa in the state of Veracruz that the port of Salina Cruz and with it Tehuantepec have acquired a more significant role.

Sights

The town has only a few old buildings of any interest. The former Dominican church dating from 1544, now the cathedral, has been rebuilt on several occasions but still retains its old arches and domes. The colourful town hall, supported on pillars, is very striking.

Surroundings

Salina Cruz

17km/10½ miles to the south lies the port of Salina Cruz (70m/230ft; population 75,000), which has recently enjoyed a big upsurge in activity as a trans-shipment and processing centre for oil. The town is only really worth a visit, however, for those also wishing to go to the long beach of La Ventosa (Posada Rustrian), which is 7km/4 miles away.

Juchitán de Zaragoza

Taking the MEX 190 from Tehuantepec in an easterly direction, the visitor comes after 26km/16 miles to Juchitán de Zaragoza (38m/125ft; population 100,000; fiestas: May 15th, San Isidro Labrador; August 13th, Vela de Agosto; September 3rd, Vela Pineda). The town is important as a trading centre for the surrounding region. Of interest to the visitor are the market and the attractive folk costumes which are mainly worn for the fiestas.

Guiengola

About 15km/9 miles west of Tehuantepec a country track branches off from the MEX 190 to the right and leads to the ruins of Guiengola. At the end of the 6km/4 mile long track a path leads up the mountain slope through a picturesque landscape of rocks, bushes and cacti to a summit (ascent about one hour). Here, about 400m/1312ft above the valley and situated on the mountain of Guiengola, are the ruins of the Zapotecs' last great fortress.

The remains of a 3m/10ft high and 2m/6½ft wide wall, which once encircled the whole mountain, have been preserved. On the great square stand the remains of a large pyramid-shaped temple on four levels, three smaller cult buildings and a ball court. On the slope there once stood the palace of the Zapotec king, Cocijo-eza, who successfully defended this fortress in 1496 against the attacks of Aztec invaders. From the cliffs there is a wonderful view across the valley of Tehuantepec.

Tenayuca K 8

State: México (Mex.)

Access from Mexico City

Metro line 5 as far as the Estación de Autobuses del Norte, from there continue by bus; by car or taxi along the Insurgentes Norte as far as the crossroads with the Río Consulado and the Calzada Vallejo, then north-west on the Calzada Vallejo to the village of San Bartolo.

Location

12km/7½ miles north of the centre of Mexico City near Tlalnepantla stands the impressive pyramid of Tenayuca, which was extended upwards on seven occasions between the 13th and 16th c. As a product of the clash between the advanced civilisation of the Toltecs and the up-and-coming Chichimec empire, the serpent-shaped pyramid of Tenayuca is a classic example of the architectural styles that the Aztecs employed in constructing their temple pyramids.

History

According to tradition Tenayuca (Náhuatl: "walled square") was where Chichimecs who had taken part in the destruction of Tula settled under their leader Xólotl ("immense") in A.D. 1224. In 1246 Xólotl and his followers Nepaltzin ("honoured cactus fruit") and Tlotzin ("falcon") succeeded in conquering the Toltecs who had recently settled in Culhuacán. At the beginning of the 14th c. the Chichimecs, who had already been heavily influenced by the Toltecs, moved their capital to Texcoco. From that point on Tenayuca came increasingly under the influence of other peoples such as the Tepanecs, Tlahuicas and the Mexica and from the middle of the 15th c. onwards the inhabitants of this region were to a large extent ruled by neighbouring Tenochtitlán. After the conquest the Spanish destroyed the temples on the pyramid and installed Rodrigo de Paz Moctezuma, a son of the Aztec ruler, Moctezuma II, as governor of Tenayuca. Initial archaeological explorations of the area were undertaken in 1900 by Leopoldo Batres, the work being continued in 1931 and 1957 by Ignacio Marquina.

★Serpent pyramid

It is thought that the serpent pyramid, which was dedicated to the sun cult, used to be given a new casing every 52 years, in keeping with the Aztec calendar cycle. The last occasions on which this happened under

An Aztec "turquoise serpent" in Tenayuca

predominantly Aztec influence were in 1351, 1403, 1455 and 1507. The two previous occasions, which makes a total of seven in all, could well have been in 1247 and 1299 under Chichimec-Toltec influence.

The core of the building measures 31×12m/102×39ft and has a height of 8m/26ft, the final casing structure measuring 66×62m/217×203ft with a height of 19m/62ft. Although no actual observatory-type buildings have been found, it is assumed, on the basis of various indicators, that this site was also used for star-gazing and that the building was aligned with heavenly bodies. A pointer to this is the existence of posts in the pyramid walls at the exact spot where the sun goes down on March 21st and September 23rd, in other words at the vernal and autumnal equinoxes. As at Chichén-Itzá (see entry) and Teotihuacán (see entry) the north–south axis here at Tenayuca has also as a result been shifted 17 degrees to the east.

The main part of what is visible today of the pyramid derives from the last three casing structures to be added. The final appearance of the site is in its essential features very similar to the main temple (Templo Mayor) of Tenochtitlán (see Mexico City), which was almost completely destroyed, its remains having only been discovered in the last few years. The pyramid is surrounded on three sides by a platform which is decorated by the bodies of recumbent serpents. This "serpent wall" (Coatepantli) today comprises 138 serpent sculptures. Originally the pyramid is thought to have been embellished with a total of 800 stone serpents. The rolled-up fire or turquoise serpents (Xiuhcóatl) next to the small platforms (two on the north and one on the south side), which presumably served as symbols of the sun's authority, date from the time that the fifth casing structure was added. A vault decorated with skulls and skeletons, to the right of the pyramid, probably symbolises the setting of the sun. Two wide parallel flights of steps used to lead across the four-storey pyramid to the double temple.

Surroundings

★Temple pyramid of Santa Cecilia Acatitlán

About 3km/2 miles north of the serpent pyramid is the 10m/33ft high temple pyramid of Santa Cecilia Acatitlán, which has been completely restored. This is thought to have been used for worshipping the sun and the rain-god Tláloc. Of special interest is the temple building on the pyramid; this is still the original one, although restored. The museum adjoining the pyramid is in a house with an attractive patio.

Tenochtitlán

See Introduction, pre-Columbian Civilisations: Life in the Aztec Empire; see Distrito Federal; see Mexico City

Teotihuacán K 8

State: México (Mex.)
Altitude: 2281m/7484ft

Access from Mexico City

By metro line 5 to Autobuses del Norte, from there continuing by bus (Counter 8, Bay 6) or line 3 to Indios Verdes, from there also by bus; by car about 50km/31 miles on Insurgentes Norte, which turns into the MEX 85.

Location

Teotihuacán, to date the largest pre-Columbian site so far excavated in Meso-America, is situated in an area devoid of all trees, on the edge of the high-lying valley of Anáhuac. Both the symmetry of the enormous site and the unity of its architectural style make it one of the most impressive ruined cities in the world. In the first 600 years A.D. Teotihuacán was the most influential political, religious and cultural power in Central America.

History

Nothing is known of the original architects of Teotihuacán (Náhuatl: "place where man becomes God"), their language and more detailed history. It was once thought that the town had been inhabited by the Toltecs and it was only during the excavations at Tula that the discovery was made that Teotihuacán had already been abandoned or destroyed 200 years before the Toltecs came to power. The names which the city and its individual buildings are known by are either derived from Náhuatl or are of recent origin and therefore linguistically have nothing to do with their original creators.

Proto-Teotihuacán

During the period defined as Proto-Teotihuacán (600–200 B.C.) village communities formed in the area and, towards the end of the period, a much larger village grew up in what became the north-west part of the later city. The earliest obsidian workshops also started at this time. The glasslike, mainly grey and green, obsidian stone was an essential material for many precision tools and important as a commodity in its own right.

Teotihuacán I

The actual emergence of the city itself occurred in the epoch known as Teotihuacán I (200 B.C.–0), with the north–south axis, the "Street of the Dead" and the main buildings, the sun and moon pyramids, already in place at the end of this period. Influences from Oaxaca are also detectable, as can be deduced from finds from the epoch of Monte Albán II.

Teotihuacán II

In the succeeding period, Teotihuacán II (A.D. 0–350), the city reached its greatest extent at an estimated 20sq.km/8sq. miles and indeed exceeded the area of the city of Rome as it then was. At this time the sun and moon pyramids were completed and the Quetzalcoátl temple and the citadel were built. In the area of fine arts important "thin orange"

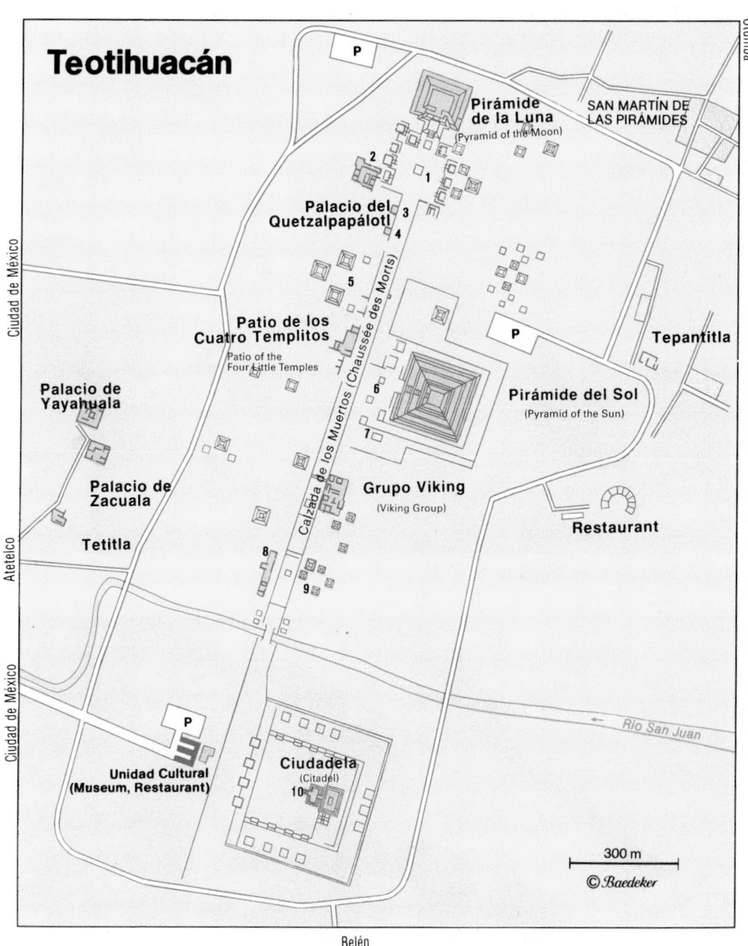

1 Plaza de la Pirámide de la Luna (Piaza of the Pyramid of the Moon)
2 Palacio de los Jaguares (Palace of the Jaguars)
3 Templo de la Agricultura (Temple of Agriculture)
4 Templo de los Animales Mitológicos (Temple of the Mythological Animals)
5 Pillared Plaza
6 Plaza de la Pirámide del Sol (Plaza of the Pyramid of the Sun)
7 Casa de los Sacerdotes (Priests' House)
8 Edificios Superpuestos (Two-storey buildings)
9 1917 excavations
10 Templo de Quetzalcóatl (Temple of Quetzalcóatl)

ceramics, three-footed cylindrical vessels with lids and monumental sculptures were all created.

Teotihuacán III

The next period, Teotihuacán III (A.D. 350–650), can be considered the city's heyday, when it probably had as many as 200,000 inhabitants. It is in this period that most of the additions were made to the buildings,

The Sun Pyramid of Teotihuacán

Teotihuacán: sculptures on the Temple of Quetzacótal

principally the Quetzalcóatl temple and the moon pyramid. The Quetzalpapálotl palace was built and most of the wall paintings date from this period. The cultural cross-fertilisation which occurred reciprocally between Teotihuacán and Monte Albán, El Tajín, Panuco, Cholula, Guerrero and the Maya territory to the south reached incredible proportions. During the 5th and 6th c. the city of Teotihuacán exerted its strongest influence on the cultures and civilisations of Meso-America. It is not clear whether this occurred as a result of military conquests or through the peaceful means of politics, trade and religion. In any event there is definite evidence of the dominance which existed in this period in places as far removed from Teotihuacán as Xochichalco (Mor.), Cacaxtla (Tlax.), Kaminaljuyú (Guatemala) and in Petén (Guatemala, especially in Tikal).

Teotihuacán IV

It was during the last period, Teotihuacán IV (A.D. 650–750), which began with further additions to the "Street of the Dead" and the creation of superlative wall paintings and ceramics, that the city came to a sudden and violent end, similar to that which befell the other classic advanced civilisations of Meso-America, albeit 200 years earlier. Although the causes are still not known even today, the fact that the ceremonial centre of the city was systematically destroyed suggests that the priests destroyed their temples themselves while under the sway of some external enemy (probably barbaric tribes from the northwest). It is also possible that uprisings challenging the rule of the priests or an economic crisis may have contributed to the city's downfall. The former metropolis was reduced to a mere regional centre, its 30,000 inhabitants living among the ruins alongside the foreign invaders.

There is no doubt that the collapse of Teotihuacán sent shock waves throughout the whole of Meso-America, with centres of power going into decline and trading routes becoming severed. As a result an overall economic decline set in. For the civilisations which followed, such as the Toltecs and the Aztecs, the abandoned city of Teotihuacán was a ghost-town of mythical origin.

After the Conquista

When the Spanish came here in 1519 after their defeat at Tenochtitlán (Noche triste), the old city was completely covered over with earth. The first excavations were undertaken in 1864 by Almaraz and these were followed in the 1880s by those of Désiré Charnay and Leopoldo Batres. Reconstructions carried out at the beginning of the 20th c. partially destroyed and falsified the original outlines of some of the main buildings. Further excavations and restorations carried out under Manuel Gamio and Ignacio Marquina in the 1920s, and other work started in 1962 by the Instituto Nacional de Arqueología e Historia, all resulted in outstanding achievements. This work has been continued by the Arizona State University. In 1988 UNESCO declared these ruins of Teotihuacán to be cultural heritage sites.

Visit to the ★★ruins

The site has only been partially uncovered. The archaeological zone extends over an area of more than 20sq.km/8sq. miles, while the actual ceremonial centre occupies a mere 4·2sq.km/1½sq. miles. When seeing the rather uniform-looking architecture, the observer would do well to remember that originally all the façades of the buildings would have been covered in a multi-coloured layer of stucco and were partly decorated with sculptures.

Unidad Cultural

Beyond the entrance there is a museum housed in the Unidad Cultural. With its displays reinforced by chronological tables and a large model of the site it gives the visitor a good overview of the history of Teotihuacán. The museum was once the site of Teotihuacán's enormous market place.

★ "Street of the Dead"

Beyond the Unidad Cultural is the 4km/2½ mile long and 45m/148ft wide main street "Miccaotli", erroneously called the "Street of the Dead" (Calle de los Muertos), which runs in a north–south direction from the moon pyramid. On crossing the street an impressive rectangular site is reached, surrounded by four platforms, known as the citadel (ciudadela). It is assumed that this was a place of worship and a dwelling-place for the priests and rulers. The ciudadela is a fine example of what is for Teotihuacán a style which recurs again and again, the talud-tablero style (sloping wall/sheer wall), with in this case the sheer part with its framed panels predominating. Frames and panels used to be covered with a thick layer of stucco, which was itself covered with colourful frescos. The talud-tablero style of building was borrowed in other pre-Columbian places (Monte Albán, Xochicalco, Kaminaljuyú, Tula, etc.), usually in a slightly altered form.

Citadel

★ Temple of Quetzalcóatl

In the middle of the ciudadela stands the temple of Quetzalcóatl. This pyramid, which was twice extended upwards, is principally distinguished by its original 366 sculptures, a rarity in a city in which very few stone sculptures have been found. To whom this shrine was actually consecrated is not known, except that it has some connection with rain and maize. One of the two alternating types of sculptures is that of a serpent; its head is framed with blossom leaves or feathers, its body surrounded by shell and snail motives representing water. The other type of sculpture is a stylised mask, possibly that of the rain god Tláloc or a maize god, represented by large round eyes and a pair of fangs. The remains of paint can still be seen on the stone figures, which once must have been covered with stucco. In 1986 a burial chamber was discovered with the skeletons of 18 priests who, it would appear, underwent ritual sacrifice around A.D. 150. This sensational find offered proof that it was not just slaves and prisoners who were put to death in this way, but also high-ranking personages. The victims, whose hands had been tied behind their backs, had teeth inlaid with jade and other precious stones and were surrounded by shells, arrowheads and small clay figures.

Superimposed buildings

Going on down the "Street of the Dead" in the direction of the moon pyramid, after some 400m/440yd we come to the remains of the Superimposed Buildings (Edificios Superpuestos) on our left. These once included an antechamber with six columns, a large courtyard with a staircase, a small temple, arcades and various other rooms. On some of the walls it is still possible to see the remains of frescos which to some extent recall similar paintings in El Tajín (see entry).

Opposite there is a group of buildings which is known as Excavations of 1917 (Excavaciones de 1917).

Viking Group

A little further to the north we come to the Viking Group (Grupo Viking), which is named after an American foundation which has been active here. On this site, which includes two inner courtyards, two slabs of mica, each 6cm/2in. thick, were found in one of the courtyards. The purpose of these pieces of mica has given rise to much speculation.

★★ Sun Pyramid

Going past the House of the Priests (Casa de los Sacerdotes) on the right-hand side, we come up a broad flight of steps to the square of the Sun Pyramid (Plaza de la Pirámide del Sol), which is some 70m/77 yd wide. In the middle there is an altar, while at the corners there are the remains of temples and other buildings.

At the eastern end of the square we see the largest building in Teotihuacán towering up, the Sun Pyramid (Pirámide del Sol). This gigantic structure, which in the whole of Meso-America is only surpassed in size by the Pyramid of Cholula, is laid out in such a way that on the day of the summer solstice the sun sets exactly opposite its front side. The base area (220×225m/722×738ft) is almost as big as the Egyptian pyramid of Cheops, its height (63m/207ft, with the former temple 74m/243ft) is however less by 70m/230ft. The capacity of its interior, which for the most part is filled with adobe bricks, has been estimated as being a million cubic metres (1,308,000cu.yd). In the course of ill-fated restoration work at the beginning of this century a layer of stucco and stone not less than 7m/23ft thick was lost from the original covering of the pyramid.

Two rows of steps lead across the entrance building, which is divided into three parts, up to the first level section of the pyramid. From here a wide staircase goes up past several intermediate storeys to the top of the building, which is where the temple once stood. From the top the visitor has a magnificent view of the whole of the archaeological site. In 1971 a shaft 7m/23ft deep was discovered by chance at the foot of the main flight of steps. From it a 103m/117yd long passageway leads to a group of four cloverleaf-shaped rooms. Inside these chambers, which until today have not been open to the public, the remains of ceramic objects and slates (mirrors?) have been discovered, presumably left behind after acts of plunder. The most wide-ranging speculative theories have been advanced as to the purpose of this cave system, which was probably laid out around A.D. 250 – these extend from a place of sacrifice or a tomb to a cult chamber dedicated to the rain or maize gods.

Along the "Street of the Dead"

Returning along the "Street of the Dead", on the left on a terrace we see the remains of four temples, which have been called the Patio of the Four Small Temples (Patio de los Cuatro Templitos). Further on, on the right-hand side, we see a long primitive wall said to have been built by the Chichimecs. Behind it, underneath a protective roof, there are interesting wall paintings depicting a jaguar of about 2m/6½ft in length. Before the street opens out into the Square of the Moon Pyramid (Plaza de la Pirámide de la Luna), we see on the left the Temple of the Mythological Animals (Templo de los Animales Mitológicos), in which the remains of frescos of animal figures have been found, and the Temple of Agriculture (Templo de la Agricultura), the original frescos of which, depicting plants, cannot be viewed – only copies of them.

★ Square of the Moon Pyramid

The symmetry and layout of the site makes the Square of the Moon Pyramid (Plaza de la Pirámide de la Luna) at the end of the street one of the most impressive examples of architectural planning in the whole of Teotihuacán. This ceremonial area consists of steps and pyramid-like platforms, mostly of four storeys, which originally were crowned, like the main pyramid, with temples. In the middle there is a large rectangular altar.

Palace of the Quetzal Butterfly

On the left-hand side stands the Palace of the Quetzal Butterfly (Palacio del Quetzalpapálotl). This palace, which was probably used as living quarters by the high priests, is possibly the finest and most important dwelling-place in the city. It is richly decorated and boasts well-preserved frescos. A staircase, which is embellished by an enormous serpent's head, leads to an antechamber decorated with wall-paintings. This leads into a small arched courtyard with square columns which are covered with interesting bas-reliefs depicting the mythological figure of the Quetzal butterfly as well as symbols of birds and water. The reliefs were originally painted and inlaid with layers of obsidian which have been partially preserved. Equally remarkable are

Remains of former domestic area

the heavily stylised figures painted on a red background and the roof edges decorated with symbols connected with the different parts of the year.

Palace of the Jaguars

The adjoining Palace of the Jaguars (Palacio de los Jaguares) has many remarkable early wall-paintings, which include depictions of predatory cats with human heads and jaguars blowing into shells. On a frieze symbols of the rain god and the year can still be made out.

★ Substructure of the Feathered Snails

A tunnel leads to part of what is probably the oldest building in Teotihuacán. Known as the Subestructura de los Caracoles Emplumados (Substructure of the Feathered Snails), it lies hidden away beneath the Palace of the Quetzal Butterfly. The largest of the remaining façades, which once belonged to a temple, is decorated with superb reliefs. Snails decorated with colourful feathers (musical instruments?), green birds (parrots?) and four-leaved flowers are all visible.

★ Moon Pyramid

At the north end of the square stands the imposing Pirámide de la Luna (Moon Pyramid). Its front-facing side is made up of a five-storey pyramidal building in the talud-tablero style. The wide flight of steps leads to the actual pyramid itself, which consists of four staggered storeys. The ground area measures 140×150m/460×490ft, while the height reaches 46m/151ft. Although 17m/56ft lower than the Sun Pyramid, its summit is on the same level thanks to the higher terrain. The steps merely lead up to the third level. From the summit of the Moon Pyramid there is also a fine view across the whole of the site.

During the dry season a son et lumière performance takes place six times a week.

Front of the Pyramid of the Moon, in talud-tablero style

Beyond the ceremonial centre

At some distance from the ceremonial centre there are ruins of dwelling-places which are well worth seeing, although they are best reached by car.

★ Tepantitla

Situated 500m/540yd to the east of the Sun Pyramid, the site of Tepantitla (Náhuatl: "Place of the thick walls") has several very fine wall-paintings; their subject-matter includes richly-decorated priests, the god Tláloc rising from the ocean and distributing rain, and the paradise of the rain god.

Tetitla

Situated about 1·5km/1 mile from the Sun Pyramid, on the west side of the "Street of the Dead", is the site of Tetitla (Náhuatl: "Place with stones"), where magnificent frescos from two different architectural periods can be seen. The subjects include jaguars with head decorations made of feathers, richly dressed priests, the rain god Tláloc, the Quetzal bird and symbolic hands. 100m/110yd away lie the Zacuala Palace (Palacio de Zacuala) and the Yayahuala Palace (Palacio de Yayahuala).

★ Atetelco

About 400m/440yd to the west of Tetitla are the interesting ruins of Atetelco (Náhuatl: "on the stone wall next to the water"). The two patios belong to two different architectural periods. Of considerable interest on this site is the patio incorporated into the building, which has superb frescos of priest figures, coyotes and birds' heads. In the White Patio, the older of the two, with its three magnificent pillared walkways, the frescos depict jaguars and coyotes with feathered head decorations, as well as Tláloc symbols.

Tepic G 7

State: Nayarit (Nay.)
Altitude: 915m/3002ft. Population: 280,000
Telephone code: 91 321

Access from Mexico City

By rail via Guadalajara about 19 hours; by bus about 14 hours.

Location

Tepic, capital of the state of Nayarit, is situated at the foot of the extinct volcano of Sanganguey (2360m/7743ft), in the middle of green wooded hills about 50km/31 miles east of the Pacific coast. To the east of the town there is a wide plain with tobacco and sugar cane plantations. Until the beginning of the 20th c. Tepic led the peaceful existence of a provincial town far removed from the centre of the country; today, however, the town offers plenty of evidence that it has joined the modern age.

History

The settlement of Tepic (Náhuatl: "hard stone") was founded in 1531 by Nuño Beltrán de Guzmán near the old Indian town of Nayarit. In 1711 Philip V gave Tepic its town charter. During the colonial period and the first century of Mexican independence Tepic was to a large degree isolated from the actual heart of the country, a fact which can be put down in no small measure to continued attacks by the rebellious Indians (Cora and Huicholes). It was not until the railway connection was built in 1912 that the modern development of the town and its surrounding area was able to get underway.

Sights

The town does not have very much to offer in the way of historical buildings, but it is well placed as a starting-point for excursions to the beaches along the coast and to the Indian villages in the surrounding area, the inhabitants of which can also be seen in Tepic on their visits to the town.

The cathedral, which stands in the Plaza Principal and has two Neo-Gothic towers, dates from the middle of the 18th c. Also worthy of mention is the church of La Cruz de Zacate, likewise dating from the middle of the 18th c., which derives its name from a cross from Zacategras which grows in a courtyard and is revered by the Indians.

Museums

★ Regional Museum

The Museo Amado Nervo (Zacatecas 284) is devoted to the famous Mexican poet, who was born here. Of interest is the Regional Museum, the Museo Regional de Antropologia e Historia, which has on display archaeological finds from the area, paintings from the colonial period and exhibits connected with the life of the Cora and Huichol Indians.

Surroundings

Ixtlán del Río

70km/43 miles along the MEX 15 in the direction of Guadalajara, the road passes through some strange countryside covered by lava from the volcano Ceboruco and shortly afterwards the little town of Ixtlán del Río is reached (Náhuatl: "obsidian place"; 1024m/3360ft; population 40,000; fiestas: last Sunday in October, Día de Cristo Rey and December 8th–12th, Virgen de Guadalupe). 3km/2 miles beyond the town on the left-hand side is one of the few archaeological sites in western Mexico not consisting entirely of burial grounds, the "Centro Ceremonial Rincón de Ixtlán y Los Toriles".

This area, which has been partially excavated, must have been inhabited as long ago as the 6th and 7th c. The buildings visible today probably date from the Early post-Classic period (A.D. 900–1250), when the influence of the Toltecs was unquestionably felt here. The most interesting of the buildings include an L-shaped building on a low platform and a round building with conical windows and two altar platforms which were probably consecrated to Quetzalcóatl in his capacity as wind god. Nearby can be seen dwelling-places, platforms, altars and buildings still waiting to be uncovered.

Compostela

About 40km/25 miles south of Tepic lies Compostela (1020m/3346ft; population 55,000; fiestas: first Friday in December, Día del Señor de la Misericordia and July 25th, Día de Santiago Apóstol). This old mining town possesses an interesting parish church dating from the 16th c. and is situated in a tobacco-growing region.

Some of the fishing villages lying to the south-west of Compostela have become popular seaside resorts during the last few years.

San Blas

Along the MEX 15 in the direction of Mazatlán, a road turns off after 34km/21 miles to the seaside resort of San Blas, 36km/22 miles distant, which has become very popular during the last ten years (population 6000; fiesta: February 3rd, Día de San Blas). The little town can also be reached from Tepic via Santa Cruz (51km/32 miles) and then 25km/16 miles along the beaches. In the colonial period San Blas was an important trading port boasting shipping connections with eastern Asia. Testimony to this link is provided by the remains of the old Spanish fort of Fuerte San Basilio. Using San Blas as a picturesque base, it is possible to make attractive boating trips through tropical river and lagoon landscapes, which are chiefly distinguished by their rich bird life. The miles of superb beaches include the Playa El Borrego in the south and in the south-east the Playas Las Islitas (9km/5½ miles), Matanchén (11km/7 miles), Los Limones, de los Cocos and Miramar (23km/14 miles).

Playas Los Corchos

The popular beach area of Playa Los Corchos can be reached by travelling north-west from Tepic on the MEX 15 to Santiago Ixcuintla and from there turning off west to the sea (entire length of route: about 100km/62 miles).

Laguna Mexcaltitán

From Santiago Ixcuintla a detour is worth making, leaving the road to Playa Los Corchos and branching off to the 25km/16 mile distant Laguna Mexcaltitán. The village of Mexcaltitán (fiesta: June 28th/29th Peter and Paul and start of the fishing season), a kind of tiny Venice, is situated on a circular island in the middle of the lagoon, which is rich in fish and bird-life. Many historians believe this island to be the legendary Aztlán, the original home of the Nahua people and therefore of the Aztecs.

Tepotzotlán — K 8

State: México (Mex.)
Altitude: 2270m/7447ft
Population: 40,000

Access from Mexico City

By metro line 2 to Tacuba, and from there by bus in about one hour; by car on the MEX 57 northwards, after about 42km/26 miles turn off to Tepotzotlán (2km/1 mile).

Location

Tepotzotlán is a pretty little town dating from the colonial period, situated not far from Mexico City. It was once a centre for spiritual instruction in New Spain. Today its convent houses a highly interesting museum of religious art, while the well-restored church is one of the jewels of Mexican Baroque architecture.

History

The Jesuit college of San Martín was founded in 1582 in Tepotzotlán (Náhuatl: "place of the hunch-back"), an old Otomí settlement, and built with the support of Indian caciques, using native labour. It was used for the instruction of the Spanish in the Indian languages of Náhuatl and Otomí and for the religious education of the sons of the Indian élite. In the 17th and 18th c. the convent was considerably enlarged. One of the most important patrons was Pedro Ruiz de Ahumada, who made possible the rebuilding of the church, which was named after Saint Francisco Xavier. It was newly consecrated in 1682, but not completed until 1762. With the expulsion of the Jesuits from New Spain in 1767, the college and its church passed into other hands. After Mexico gained its independence, the Jesuits returned to Tepotzotlán, though with less influence, and they remained there until the secularisation of the convents in 1859. In more recent times the convent and church were placed under the control of the Instituto Nacional de Antropología e Historia. Since 1964 a musuem of religious art has been housed in the former convent and in the church.

★★Convent site

Convent church

The façade of the convent church, which was basically built between 1628 and 1762, is, with La Valenciana at Guanajuato (see entry) and Santa Prisca in Taxco (see entry), among the most outstanding examples of Churrigueresque style in Mexico. It was crafted by various artists between 1760 and 1762 and its harmonious arrangement of figures includes "estípites" (Eng. stipites = pilasters in the shape of a pyramid with the point downwards) at the top, niches with plinths and sculptures and medaillons with reliefs. The statue of San Francisco Xavier can be seen over the window while in the side niches there are statues of the saints Ignacio de Loyola, Francisco de Borja, Luis Gonzaga and Estanislao de Kotska, the most important personalities in the Jesuit order. The two-storey tower is also decorated with "estípites". The small tower set back to the left belongs to the Casa de Loreto.

Interior

Passing through the convent the interior of the church is reached, its broad nave containing seven magnificent altars, predominantly carved in wood and painted in gold, displaying the typical Churrigueresque style. The high altar is in three sections and in its design is similar to the façade of the church. In the middle there is a statue of San Francisco Xavier while higher up in the centre there are especially expressive sculptures of the Immaculate Conception (high up in the middle) and John the Baptist (left-hand niche). The right-hand top part of the altar is dedicated to Luis Gonzaga, the left-hand part to San Estanislao de Kotska. The other altars, dating from between 1733 and 1758, are also remarkable, as are the chapels of San Ignacio de Loyola with sculptures of the order's founder, Nuestra Señora de Guadalupe with a painting and frescos of Mexico's patron saint by Miguel Cabrera, Nuestra Señora de la Luz with a fine statue, and Nuestra Señora de Loreto, which contains a copy of the house of the Virgin Mary in Nazareth and a reredos with an early Italian statue.

Camarín

Adjoining the last-named chapel is an octagonal room, the Camarín, which ranks as one finest examples of Mexican High Baroque art. The hand of Indian artists can be detected in the shapes and composition of the retablos and of the ceiling. The figures of the archangels and the

Tepotzotlán: San Francisco Xavier

Netzahualcóyotl Monument in Texcoco

black oxidised representations in silver are remarkable. The early ribbed vaulting in the Camarín shows Mudéjar influence. The light entering through the alabaster windows contributes to the magnificent overall impression.

Returning to the nave of the church we see on the right-hand side the chapel of Relicario de San José, which contains a painting of José Ibarra and an especially fine small reredos.

Museo Nacional del Virreinato

The building of the former Jesuit college today houses the National Museum of the Viceroyship (Museo Nacional del Virreinato). The Claustro de los Aljibes (Cloister of the Fountains) mainly contains oil paintings of Cristóbal de Villalpando.

Capilla Doméstica

This leads to the Capilla Doméstica (domestic chapel), in the gateway (portería) of which paintings by Miguel Cabrera can be seen. The chapel, dating from the middle of the 17th c., which was later restored, has vaulting with decorations showing the coats of arms of the six most important orders in New Spain. The altar with its sculptures, mirrors and pictures of Jesuit saints, is particularly interesting. To the left is the kneeling figures of the patron Pedro Ruiz de Ahumada.

In the many rooms and corridors of the museum there is a varied sequence of mainly ecclesiastical treasures from the 16th to 19th c. They come from all over the former viceroyship of new Spain and include sculptures, altar panels, and paintings by the most significant artists of the period, as well as furniture, porcelain, weapons and church implements of all kinds. Part of the premises is used regularly for concerts and theatrical performances.

Surroundings

Los Arcos del Sitio

About 27km/17 miles in a south-westerly direction via San Miguel Cañadas, we reach Los Arcos del Sitio, an aqueduct on several levels erected in the 18th c. by the Jesuits for the water supply of Tepotzotlán. At 60m/197ft it is the highest in Mexico.

If we go from Tepotzotlán back on to the MEX 57 and continue in the direction of Querétaro as far as the turning for Tepeji del Río (27km/17 miles), it is from there another 20km/12 miles to the great Toltec archaeological site of Tula (see entry).

Tepoztlán

See Morelos

Tequila

See Jalisco

Texcoco de Mora K 8

State: México (Mex.)
Altitude: 2278m/7474ft
Population: 95,000
Telephone code: 91 595

Access from Mexico City

By bus (departure from Terminal del Oriente near the metro station Candelaría); by car 20km/12 miles past the airport on the road leading across the dried-up Texcoco Lake or 44km/27 miles on the MEX 190 and 136 via Los Reyes.

Location

From the 14th to the 16th c. Texcoco had a historically important role. Founded on the edge of the lake of the same name (today dried-up), the town rivalled Tenochtitlán, the Aztec metropolis which had been built on an island in what was then a lake. Today Texcoco, conveniently situated not far to the north-west of Mexico City, is a trading centre for woollen clothing, ceramics and glass with a surrounding area which boasts many archaeological sites and artistic treasures from the colonial period.

History

The Chichimecs, who under their leader Xólotl had founded Tenayuca in the 13th c., under Quinatzin moved their capital city at the beginning of the 14th c. to Texcoco (Náhuatl: "place of the large rocks"), which had already been founded in the Toltec period. In the second half of the 14th c. the town came under the ruling influence of the Tepanecs of Atzcapotzalco (Náhuatl: "anthill of men"). Finally in 1428 the Tepanecs were defeated by an alliance between the Mexica and Texcoco and the kingdom of Texcoco was restored in 1431. Its benevolent ruler Netzahualcóyotl ("hungry coyote"; 1418–72), who became legendary as a poet and warrior, concluded a tripartite alliance with Tenochtitlán and Tlacopán (Tacuba) and in so doing ushered in Texcoco's golden age. Politically the city state, which developed a reputation as a spiritual and artistic centre, was under the dominance of the warlike Mexica. After the death of Netzahualcóyotl's son and successor Netzahualpilli (1472–1515) there were disputes about the succession which were exploited by the Mexica to the disadvantage of Texcoco. After the town was occupied by the Spanish in 1521 without any great resistance, Texcoco became the launching-place for the ships built in Tlaxcala, which played a decisive role in defeating the lakeside town of Tenochtitlán. It is estimated that the population of Texcoco grew to as much as 150,000 after the Spanish conquest. Soon after their arrival the Franciscans built a school for the Indians. Hernán Cortés, who lived in Texcoco intermittently, is supposed to have buried his first wife there in 1530, then later his mother and in 1536 a son. The plague epidemic of 1575–76 decimated the population and a century later Texcoco was no more than an insignificant small town.

Sights

The old splendours of the town are scarcely noticeable any longer. Of the Franciscan convent built next to the Palace of Netzahualpilli the entrance hall with the Open Chapel and a Renaissance cloister are all that remain. The beautiful Spanish-Plateresque north doorway in the parish church is notable, while the portal of the Capilla de la Concepción ("La Conchita") is a particularly fine example of the 16th c. Indian stonemason's craft known as "Tequitqui".

Surroundings

Chiconcuac

Papalotla Santo Toribio

About 7km/4 miles to the north lies the village of Chiconcuac, which is known for its woollen goods (sarapes, rebozos, etc.). Not far away is the village of Papalotla, whose pretty little church of Santo Toribio has carved Baroque retablos and an atrium entrance with a beautifully crafted arch dating from the 18th c.

Tepetlaoxtoc

About 20km/12 miles north-east of Texcoco in the village of Tepetlaoxtoc there is a Dominican convent dating from 1529, the cloister of which still has remains of frescos. An attractive fountain and an 18th c. church are also worth seeing there.

Molino de las Flores

The Hacienda Molino de las Flores ("mill of flowers"), situated 7km/4 miles east of Texcoco, which was founded in 1616, is today completely dilapidated. The small Baroque chapels and the beautiful gardens are especially noteworthy. Nearby, at the Cerro de Texcotzingo, there are the remains of the magnificent former summer residence of Netzahualcóyotl with baths and "hanging gardens".

Chapingo

3km/2 miles south of Texcoco in the main building of the agricultural college (Escuela Nacional de la Agricultura) of Chapingo can be found some of the best frescos of Diego Riveras, in which he depicts the agrarian revolution, the earth's prolificity and a better future for mankind.

★ Huexotla

Just a few kilometres/miles from Chapingo is the village of Huexotla (Náhuatl: "place of the willows"), formerly an important town, although under the hegemony of Texcoco. The fortified walls, which originally surrounded the central shrine of Teocalli, can still be seen today. The whole area consists of an extended archaeological site, of which, however, only a fraction has been investigated.

At the small unassuming Franciscan convent of 1541 the stone crosses on the two ledges in the atrium are noteworthy. The unconventional, richly decorated Churrigueresque façade of the church of San Luis Obispo, which dates from the 17th and 18th c., with its pronounced Indian elements, is in complete contrast. Its interior contains a remarkable 16th c. stone pulpit.

San Miguel Coatlinchán

Further south lies the village of San Miguel Coatlinchán (Náhuatl: "house of the snake") with a pretty church consecrated to Saint Michael, a fortified building with a Baroque façade and tiled tower. The stone sculpture weighing 167t/164 tons of the water goddess Chalchiuhtlicue, the sister and wife of the rain god Tláloc, was found nearby. Today it stands at the entrance to the National Museum of Anthropology in Mexico City.

From Texcoco it is 25km/15½ miles to the famous convent of Acolman (see entry) and 35km/22 miles to the ruined city of Teotihuacán.

Teziutlán L 8

State: Puebla (Pue.)
Altitude: 1990m/6529ft
Population: 105,000
Telephone code: 91 231

Access

By car from Jalapa about 110km/68 miles via Perote and Altotonga.

Location

The pleasant colonial town of Teziutlán lies along a winding road carved out of the rocks in the middle of wooded mountains. Although Teziutlán itself does not have anything of special interest for the visitor, its position – conveniently situated as it is on one of the roads linking Mexico City with the coast of the Gulf of Mexico – makes it a good base for excursions into the interesting mountain areas surrounding the town.

Sights

Founded as long ago as 1520, the town still possesses many reminders of the colonial period, which is everywhere visible in its beautiful imposing buildings. The pretty main square and the church of El Carmen deserve mention.

Surroundings

Zacapoaxtla

After travelling 15km/9 miles in a westerly direction the visitor passes the springs of Chignautla. 46km/29 miles from Teziutlán in the same direction, just past Zaragoza, a road branches off to the town of Zacapoaxtla 17km/11 miles to the north (1800m/5905ft; population 31,000; fiesta: beginning of May and June 29th, San Pedro; Wednesday market). The town lies in magnificent mountain countryside, often shrouded in mist, and is distinguished by its varied and unspoilt scenery and the customs of its different Indian tribes. Its festivals, handed down through generations by the Nahua, Otomí and Totonac Indians, are among the most colourful and fascinating in the whole country. In the town the church of Guadalupe de Libres and the parish church of San Pedro should be seen.

★Cuetzalán

From Zacapoaxtla there is a magnificent mountain route leading northwards 35km/22 miles to Cuetzalán (Náhuatl: "Place of the Quetzal"; 1200m/3937ft; fiestas: July 15th–18th, town festival; October 2nd–6th, San Francisco and Coffee Mass; December 12th, Guadalupe; Sunday market). This picturesque little town, in the middle of the Sierra Norte in the state of Puebla, is a centre for various Indians groups which enliven the scene on market and feast days with their attractive traditional costumes. The annual festivals, at which selected folk groups from the region (Quetzales, Negritos, Santiagos and Voladores) perform their characteristic dances, are especially famous. Cuetzalán's sights include the town hall (Palacio Municipal) with its European-style architecture, the Parroquia with its unusual Torre de los Jarritos and, some way out of the town, the church of Guadalupe with its beautifully decorated graves in front. The most important business in the town and its surroundings is the cultivation and processing of coffee.

★Yohualichán

For those interested in archaeology a visit to the excavation site of Yohualichán (Náhuatl: "house of night") is recommended. It can be reached in about 50 minutes from Cuetzalán using a cross-country vehicle. This cult centre constructed on four different levels has up to now been the only famous place outside El Tajín (see entry) to have been built in the same style. Today there are in total five buildings visible. The most worth seeing are the pyramids, decorated with niche friezes, one of them a seven-storey pyramic, and the ball court which, at 90m/295ft in length, is one of the largest in Meso-America. Since this place was, like El Tajín, inhabited by Totonacs when the Spanish arrived, the large buildings were for a long time assumed to be the work of this people. Today, however, we still do not know for sure who the builders were of these sites, which date from the Classic period (A.D. 300–900). The finds made so far have not indicated that Yohualichán approached the same cultural level as El Tajín and this has led many people to assume that it was founded much earlier.

Tijuana A 1

State: Baja California Norte (B.C.)
Altitude: 152m/499ft
Population: 1,300,000
Telephone code: 91 66

Access

Many air connections with Mexican and United States airports; by bus from the USA (Greyhound terminus on the US side); by car from the USA or even crossing the border on foot.

Location

Tijuana is the most important Mexican frontier city along the border with the United States of America (California), and of all the cities in Mexico it is the one most heavily influenced by the United States. Its main industries are tourism and the servicing and processing sectors and some 50 million commuters and visitors cross the border here, making it the largest such crossing place between Mexico and California. Tijuana is the starting-point of the Carretera Transpeninsular (MEX 1) which runs the full length of Lower California.

History

Tijuana (Cochimi: "Ticuán" = "close water") has a relatively short history. The large city which exists today developed from a cattle hacienda called Tía Juana ("Aunt Joan"), which was founded in 1829 by José María Echandi. Its rapid period of growth began during the Prohibition period (1920–33) when the consumption of alcohol was banned in the United States and thousands of thirsty Americans used to cross the frontier to indulge their craving.

Frontier city

One of the few noteworthy buildings in the city is the 20th c. cathedral which is consecrated to the Virgin of Guadalupe. Visitors coming to Mexico who begin their trip in Tijuana can also get an initial impression of the country from the multi-media show and museum which can be visited in the architecturally interesting Centro Cultural FONART (Plaza de los Héroes e Independencia). Tijuana's importance lies in its large range of duty-free goods from all over the world as well as local Mexican folk art and souvenirs, its many different types of entertainment (bull-fights, horse and dog races, jai alai, frontón, baseball) and its night life. The focal point of all this activity, especially at weekends, is the main square, the Parque Municipal Guerrero, the shopping quarter situated around the Avenida Revolución and the Bulevar Agua Caliente with its many hotels, restaurants, shops and sports arenas.

Surroundings

Tecate

Driving eastwards from Tijuana on the MEX 2, the town of Tecate (480m/1575ft; population 110,000; fiestas: first Sunday in July and December 12th, Día de Nuestra Señora de Guadalupe) is reached after about 50km/31 miles. It is a border crossing-point as well as an agricultural and industrial centre with a large brewery.

★ La Rumorosa

Continuing eastwards the MEX 2 leads to La Rumorosa, where there are weird rock formations from which spectacular panoramic views across the desert can be enjoyed.

Laguna Salada

After another 30km/19 miles the visitor comes to the start of the Laguna Salada, a shallow lake stretching southwards, which can suddenly dry up over night.

Mexicali

From Tecate it is 140km/87 miles to Mexicali (3m/10ft; population 880,000). The name is formed from the first syllables of "Mexico" and "California". As recently as 1898 a Cucupá Indian village stood here with the name Laguna del Alamo. Today it is the dynamic capital of Baja California Norte, a centre for the high quality processing and service industries and agriculture (cotton, fruit, vegetables), as well as being a border crossing-point connecting with its sister town of Calexico in the USA. In the University Museum there are facilities for studying palaeontology, archaeology, ethnography and the history of missionary work in Lower California.

Cerro Prieto

24km/15 miles south of Mexicali a road leads off from the MEX 5 to the geothermic zone of Cerro Prieto. This volcanic area is the second largest geothermic generator on earth and provides a good part of the electricity for the valley of Mexicali.

San Felipe

The fishing village of San Felipe (population 30,000), situated 193km/120 miles south of Mexicali on the Sea of Cortés, is a very popular seaside resort as well attracting many deep-sea anglers. The Mexican government is planning a large tourist centre here.

Tlacolula

See Oaxaca (town)

Tlaquepaque

See Guadalajara

Tlaxcala (State)

Abbreviation: Tlax.
Capital: Tlaxcala
Area: 4027sq.km/1555sq. miles
Population: 655,000

Location and topography

Tlaxcala is the smallest, but also one of the most densely populated states of Mexico. It is surrounded on three sides by the state of Puebla, on the west by the Estado de México and on the north by Hidalgo. This high-lying countryside, covered in forests and fields, has a pleasantly cool climate. The 4461m/14,636ft high mountain of La Malinche (Malantzín) is the fifth highest peak in Mexico. Tlaxcala is mainly inhabited by Otomí Indians.

Archaeological sites

Among the relatively few pre-Hispanic sites those of Tizatlán, Cacaxtla (see entry) and Xochitécatl should be mentioned.

History

Very little is known of the early history of what is now the state of Tlaxcala. It is possible that it was people from the Gulf coast (Olmecs?) who first settled here between 1000 and 500 B.C. Between A.D. 650 and 800 the Olmeca-Xicalanca brought their culture to present-day Tlaxcala. Around the middle of the 14th c. Nahua Indians from the tribe of Tlatepotzca came from Texcoco and interbred with the Otomí Indians living here. From this developed Tlaxcala, a kind of republic, which consisted of four autonomous ruling entities. Tlaxcala played an important part in the struggle against the Aztecs (Mexica) who ruled in Tenochtitlán. After a temporary expansion as far as the Gulf coast the Tlaxcaltecs were pushed back into their tribal area by the Aztecs during the second half of the 15th c. and besieged there for decades. At the beginning of the 16th c. the Aztecs concluded a treaty with the undefeated Tlaxcaltecs which limited hostilities to the occasional skirmish, the aim of which was merely to take prisoners for religious sacrifices ("flower battle" = Xochiyáoyotl).

The Spanish who invaded in 1519 were initially met with fierce resistance by the Tlaxcaltecs, but the latter soon formed an alliance with Cortés against the hated Aztecs. Only Xicoténcatl the Younger, a son of one of the four rulers, turned down this alliance and as a result

was executed two years later by the Spanish. Even after the first unsuccessful attempt by the Spanish to conquer Tenochtitlán, the Aztec capital ("Noche Triste" = sad night), the Tlaxcaltecs maintained their support. Cortés and his troops prepared themselves in Tlaxcala for the final siege of Tenochtitlán. Thus it was here that the first brigantines were built which were to make possible the decisive attack from Lake Texcoco against the Aztec capital. These, coupled with the help that he received from thousands of Tlaxcaltecs, enabled Cortés and his conquistadors to succeed in taking the Aztec capital in 1521 and destroying it. In gratitude for its help the Spanish crown conferred various privileges on Tlaxcala and these offered some relief to the lives of the Indian inhabitants. Later on the ties of friendship between Tlaxcala and Spain proved to be so strong, that there was opposition here to the movement towards independence, which broke out in 1810. At the time of the French invasion and the battle between the conservatives and liberals (Guerra de Reforma) there were several pitched battles on Tlaxcaltec soil between 1862 and 1864. A peasant revolt, which broke out in 1910 against the president Porfirio Díaz, led to the revolution of the following years.

Economy

The rural economy of the region is concentrated mainly on cereal-growing, the cultivation of maguey agaves and cattle-rearing. The skilled and technical production of woollen fabrics and clothing also plays an important role, along with pottery manufacture.

Tlaxcala (Town) K 8

State: Tlaxcala
Altitude: 2255m/7400ft
Population: 100,000
Telephone code: 91 246

Access from Mexico City

By bus about 2 hours; by car 113km/70 miles along the MEX 150 and MEX 119.

★Location

Tlaxcala is situated in the Mexican highlands on the slopes of the eastern Sierra Madre and is the capital of the state of the same name. The town was once a focal point in the process of integration between Spaniards and Indians and also in the Christianisation of Mexico. Today only a few old buildings in the town's sleepy little centre remain as evidence of its long and important history.

History

Tlaxcala (Náhuatl: "place of maize") was given its later name "de Xicoténcatl" from a ruler at the time of the Conquista, who opposed any alliance with the Spanish. The town was founded in the middle of the 14th c. by a Nahua tribe called the Tlatepotzca, which had migrated from Texcoco, and for almost 200 years its played an important role as capital of a republic seeking to assert itself against the surrounding Aztec empire. The town's history prior to the arrival of the Spanish is closely connected with the Tlaxcaltec state.

The Spanish arrived as early as 1519 on their way to Tenochtitlán and after initial hostilities the Tlaxcaltecs forged an alliance with them against the Aztecs. After their withdrawal from Tenochtitlán ("Noche Triste") the Spanish were able to gather here and rearm with the support of the indigenous population. Without the help of Tlaxcala, which provided Cortés with protection as well as materials and warriors, the Spanish conquest of Tenochtitlán would possibly never have succeeded. In 1524 Franciscans were involved in building new additions to the town and giving the first Christian baptisms to Indians in Mexico. In 1535 Emperor Charles V granted the town its charter as well as special privileges in recognition of the support which the Tlaxcaltecs had given to the Spanish. The populous town, which at that time was one of the largest in Mexico, lost a large proportion of its inhabitants between 1544 and 1546 owing to a plague outbreak. Tlaxcala was never really able to recover from this setback and as a result the part it has played in the later history of Mexico has been relatively modest.

Sights

Palacio Municipal

The Palacio Municipal (town hall) stands in the Plaza de la Constitución and was built in 1550. Its second-storey window arches are fashioned in the unusual and arresting Indian-Moorish style.

Palacio de Gobierno

Next to the town hall stands the Palacio de Gobierno (government palace), which was begun in 1545. Its passageways are decorated with modern frescos, depicting the history of the town, by the Tlaxcaltec painter Desiderio Hernández Xochitiotzin.

Palacio de Justicia

The present-day palace of justice (Palacio de Justicia), which is on the site of the old royal chapel (Capilla Real), was begun in 1528. Towards the end of the 18th c. it was partially destroyed by a fire, and then in 1800 by an earthquake. The bas-reliefs on the entrance frieze, which show the coats of arms of Castile and León and the House of Hapsburg, are a survival from the original chapel. The church, which was consecrated to Charles V, was once a place of prayer for baptised noblemen.

Parish Church of San José

The parish church of San José, with its brick façade clad in brightly-coloured tiles, stands in the street connecting the main square with the market.

★San Francisco

Near the Plaza in a south-easterly direction are the convent and church of San Francisco, founded in 1526 and thereby becoming the first monastic foundation in Mexico. The main complex of buildings on the

Tlaxcala: Palacio Municipal

Regional Museum

convent site was erected between 1537 and 1540 and this is where the regional museum (Museo Regional) is housed.

Iglesia de la Asunción

The Iglesia (church) de la Asunción, today Tlaxcala's cathedral, is worth seeing for its magnificent Moorish-style cedarwood ceiling decorated with stars and also for the font in the Chapel of the Third Order where the four rulers of Tlaxcala are supposed to have been baptised.

On a lower level, reached by two flights of steps, is the Gothic "Open Chapel" (Capilla Abierta or Capilla de Indios), which was one of the first of its kind in Mexico. In the atrium can be seen the remains of two of the original four Capillas Posas (processional chapels).

Museo de Artes y Tradiciones Populares

In this museum (C. Emilio Sánchez) local people display examples of weaving and carpet-knotting work. The production of *pulque* (Mexican fermented drink) is also explained.

★Basilica of the Virgin of Ocotlán

Outside the town, about 1·5km/1 mile distant, stands one of the most beautiful religious buildings in Mexico, the Basilica of the Virgin of Ocotlán (Náhuatl: "place of the pine"). It was conceived by the Indian Francisco Miguel in the middle of the 18th c. The white stucco ornaments in the inner part of the Churrigueresque façade and in the towers stand out brilliantly against the curved exterior with its facing of hexagonal red tiles. This combination and the sculptured "shell arches" everywhere contribute to the exceptionally graceful impression created by this Baroque building. The doorway is crowned by the figure of Saint Francis, who supports the three worlds which symbolise his order. The crowned Virgin soars above him. The stuccowork and the tiles used in this building were produced in Puebla.

Interior

★★Camarín

The interior of the basilica was completed around the middle of the 19th c. and partially restored during the 1930s. No alterations however have been made to the high altar or the two side altars, nor to the octagonal Camarín (niche or chamber, containing an image of the Holy Virgin), a small chapel behind the high altar with multicoloured stucco decorations showing the Indian influence. The dome of this richly fitted chapel has a representation of Mary and the apostles in the middle of a golden ring, with the Holy Ghost hovering over their heads. The Camarín table, which dates from 1761, stands on eight legs in the shape of a monkey (ozomatli), the old Indian symbol for joy.

Today Ocotlán is still a very popular place of pilgrimage.

Surroundings

San Esteban Tizatlán

About 5km/3 miles north of the town, on the road to Apizaco, is the village of San Esteban Tizatlán, once one of the four ruling powers of the Tlaxcala republic. The remains of the palace of Xicoténcatl and two altars with interesting pre-Columbian wall-paintings can be seen here. These frescos conceived in the style of Mixtec pictographic writings depict mythological figures such as Xochiquétzal, the tutelary goddess of Tlaxcala, Tezcatlipoca ("smoking mirror"), the god of war of the north, Mictlantecuhtli, the prince of the underworld and Tlahuizcalpantecuhtli, the ruler of the morning star. In the ruins there is a church with an open chapel dating from the 16th c.

Huamantla de Juárez

Following the MEX 119 the town of Azipaco (2408m/7900ft; population 45,000) is reached after about 20km/12 miles. From here the MEX 136 proceeds in a south-easterly direction, arriving after 27km/17 miles at

Basilica of the Virgin of Octolán ▶

San Francisco Church: cedar-wood ceiling

Baptistery in the Basilica of Octolán

the town of Huamnatla de Juárez (2560m/8399ft; population 90,000). The 16th c. Franciscan convent, the Baroque church (restored in the 18th c.) and the bull-fighting museum (Museo Taurino) are all worth seeing.

Festival

The town is widely known for its colourful festival which takes place in August. On the 15th of the month (Assumption) bulls are driven through the streets as in Pamplona in Spain and mosaic-like carpets of flowers ("xochipetate") in honour of the Virgin of Charity (Virgen de Caridad) are spread out in the streets. At the same time a cattle market and craftwork fair are held.

★La Malinche Volcano

Returning from Huamantla to Apizaco on the MEX 136, a new road turns off after about 13km/8 miles. It leads to the "Centro Vacacional Malintzín", situated 14km/9 miles away at an altitude of 3000m/9800ft. The centre is an ideal starting-point for the ascent of the extinct volcano of La Malinche (4461m/14,636ft), which is named after the Indian lover and interpreter of Cortés. For the ascent about three to four hours is needed, for the descent about two hours. A second route up the volcano from San Miguel Canoa (north-east of Puebla, see entry) is considerably longer and should only be attempted by experienced mountaineers.

Tollán

See Tula

Toluca de Lerdo K 9

State: México (Mex.)
Altitude: 2680m/8793ft. Population: 700,000
Telephone code: 91 721

Access from Mexico City

By rail about 2 hours; by bus about 1 hour; by car 67km/42 miles on the MEX 15.

Location

Toluca, the capital of the Estado de México, is situated in the mountain valley of the same name to the west of Mexico City. It is the highest large city in Mexico and has become increasingly important in the last few years both as a communications and trading centre and as an industrial base. From the visitor's point of view the city has less to offer than the surrounding area.

History

The area around Toluca (Náhuatl: "Tollucán" = "place of the reeds") was probably under the dominance of Teotihuacán during the Classic period. The Matlatzinca (Náhuatl: "the people with small nets"), a Nahua tribe with linguistic links with the Otomí, who took on pronounced Toltec characteristics, probably settled here in the middle of the 13th c. In the 14th c. they came under the rule of the princes who reigned in the valley of Anáhuac. At the beginning of the 15th c. they were still allied to the Aztecs but were finally subjugated by them and expelled into part of what is today the region of Michoacán. The Matlatzinca had to pay the price of several rebellions against their Aztec rulers with large numbers of human sacrifices. They gave the Spanish limited assistance in the conquest of Tenochtitlán. In 1521 the Spanish under Gonzalo de Umbria explored the valley of Toluca, in 1529 the Franciscans founded their first convent there and in 1667 Toluca de San José was granted its town charter. In 1830 it became the capital of the Estado de México and at the end of the 19th c. the town received its secondary name of de Lerdo in memory of Sebastián Lerdo de Tejada.

Sights

The attractive main square (Zócalo, Plaza de los Mártires) is dominated by the cathedral, a Neo-Classical building dating from the 19th c. The government palace (Palacio de Gobierno) dating from 1872 adjoins it to the north. A long shopping street with 120 archways (portales) stretches the length of one block to the right of the main square. Not far away stands the 18th c. Baroque church of El Carmen; in its convent is the Museo de las Bellas Artes (Museum of Fine Art).

Botanic Garden

The Botanic Garden (Jardin Botánico; Juárez/Lerdo) is housed in an Art Nouveau style building with some wonderful stained glass windows.

Market

The giant market (Mercado Juárez), one of Mexico's most colourful markets, will be found on the road to Mexico City. The best day to visit it is Friday.

Museums

Other museums include the Museo de Arte Popular (exhibitions and sale of handicrafts); four more museums were opened in 1992 – Museo José Maria Velasco (19th/20th c. landscape artists), Musep Gutiérrez (19th c. portrait painters), Museo Nishizawa (Japano–Mexican artists), and the Water Colour Museum. There are also four museums in the Centro Cultural Mexiquense (10km/6 miles to the south-east on the Hacienda de la Pila): Museo de la Charrería (riding), and museums of modern art, folk art and anthropology and history.

Surroundings

Calixtlahuaca

The MEX 55 leaves Toluca in a northerly direction and after 8km/5 miles a road branches off to the left and leads to the ruined site of Calixtlahuaca (Náhuatl: "place with houses on the plain") 2·5km/1½ miles away. The early history of this religious site is largely unclear. Remains of buildings which have been discovered can be traced back to the Teotihuacán civilisation and in the post-Classic period to Xochicalco and the Toltecs. They were followed by the Matlatzinca, who ruled here until they were subdued by invaders from the valley of Anáhuac. The Aztecs occupied the town for the first time in 1474 and exerted a significant influence on the later building activity which took place there. A number of unsuccessful uprisings by the Matlatzinca against the Aztecs ended in the destruction of the Matlatzinca temple.

Temple of Quetzalcóatl

The most important building on the site, the Temple of Quetzalcóatl, situated on a large enclosed terrace, has been built over on several occasions (Estructura 3). The rounded pyramid on four levels has a wide staircase and an altar. The temple was consecrated to the wind god Ehécatl who was taken over by the Huastecs and then embodied by Quetzalcóatl. The Museum of Teotenango (see below) contains a statue of the god which was found here.

On a higher level, not readily visible from below, is a complex of buildings consisting of the Temple of Tláloc (Estructura 4) and a pyramid platform (Estructura 7) with a broad flight of steps. On the small plaza stands the T-shaped altar of the skulls ("Tzompantli"), so named because of the cones and skulls towering up from its tablero.

Altar of the skulls

A third, even higher level has the partially overgrown remains of two platforms (Estructura 5 and 6) and two carved stone slabs.

Temple of Quetzalcoátl in Calixlahuaca

Calmecac

Leaving the site in the direction of the crossroads, a little further to the left is the fourth group of Calixtlahuaca, which has been named Calmecac after the elite school of the Aztecs (Estructura 17). This site consists of several rooms and platforms which are grouped around a large quadrangle.

Metepec

About 8km/5 miles south-east of Toluca is the little town of Metepec (2060m/6761ft; population 50,000; Monday market) with its 16th/17th c. Franciscan convent of San Juan Bautista and the pretty church, the Iglesia del Calvario, with its large atrium. The town is known for the green stoneware and multicoloured clay figures which are produced here.

7km/4½ miles south-west, near the old Hacienda Zacango, is a Zoological Garden.

Teotenango

About 25km/16 miles south of Toluca on the MEX 55 lies the village of Tenango del Valle (or de Arista) .The archaeological site of Teotenango (Náhuatl: "place of the divine wall"), which is situated close by, is an extensive site, unified in its conception, its beginnings dating back at least to the 7th c. A.D. The heyday of the site occurred between the 10th and 12th c., but the cultural influences of late Teotihuacán, the Toltecs, the Matlatzinca and the Aztecs tended to merge with one another. A large part of this once highly important Indian cultural centre, which was based in the Toluca valley and strongly influenced by the Matlatzinca, was only uncovered during the last twenty years. The heart of the site has been called the Sistema Norte (north system) and is divided into six connecting sections (conjuntos). The site is distinguished by its pyramid platforms with their three or four staggered levels, on which the temple buildings once rested, access to which was gained by sometimes massive stairways.

On entering the site, the visitor will first of all come to the A Complex, situated at the Plaza del Jaguar. On the second level of the supporting wall there is the relief of a jaguar with the motive of "2 rabbit" ("2 tochtli") carved on the left-hand side and on the right the symbol of "9 house" ("9 calli").

Behind this is the E complex with its ball court (23×10m/75×33ft) and steam bath. The building of the ball court necessitated the pulling down of some dwelling-houses, the remains of which can still be seen.

The most extensive area of the Sistema Norte is the D complex. As well as platforms, dwelling-places and patios, a building 120×40m/472×131ft in area was discovered, the so-called "Serpent Base" (Basamento de la Serpiente). In front of this the Plaza de la Serpiente (Square of the Serpent), probably once the market place, stretches out. It is bounded on the west by the Calle de la Rana (Street of the Frog) and on the north by the Plaza del Durazno (Square of the Peach). The Plaza de la Serpiente and the Calle de la Rana take their names from a snake-shaped relief and a sculpture of a frog, both of which were discovered here.

Museum

The museum houses remarkable archaeological finds from the Estado de México, mainly from Teotenango, Malinalco (see entry) and Calixtlahuaca. The statue of Ehécatl from Calixtlahuaca and the carved wooden drum (Panhuéhuetl) from Malinalco are particularly worth seeing.

★Nevado de Toluca

A trip from Toluca which is well worth making is to take the roads nos. 103, 134 and 3 to the extinct volcano, Nevado de Toluca or Xinantécatl (Náhuatl: "undressed man"; 4575m/15,010ft; hostel at 3750m/

On an extinct volcano, the Nevado de Tolcada

12,303ft), which is situated about 50km/31 miles to the south-west and is often covered with snow. The road goes up to the Laguna del Sol (Sun Lagoon; 4200m/13,779ft) and the Laguna de la Luna (Moon Lagoon). From the summits around the edge of the crater there is a glorious view of the valley of Toluca, the mountain scenery around Guerrero, the forested region of Michoacán and the peaks of the Sierra Nevada, Popocatépetl and Iztaccíhuatl.

★ Valle de Bravo

About 80km/50 miles to the west of Toluca is the pretty holiday town of Valle de Bravo (1800m/5905ft; population 35,000). It is situated by a reservoir (Presa de Valle de Bravo or Presa Miguel Alemán) in the middle of lush vegetation and mountainous scenery. The nearby rock formations of La Peña and waterfall of Salto de Ferrería can be visited.

Tonantzintla

See Acatepec

Topolobampo

See Sinaloa

Torreón

See Coahuila de Zaragoza

Tula (Tollán)

State: Hidalgo (Hgo.)
Altitude: 2030m/6660ft
Population: 40,000 (Tula de Allende)
Telephone code: 91 773 (Tula de Allende)

Access from Mexico City

By bus (Terminal del Norte) about 1½ hours; by car on the MEX 57D in the direction of Querétaro, turning off after 68km/42 miles to Tepejí del Río, and then a further 20km/12 miles to Tula de Allende and 3km/2 miles to the ruins.

Location

The remains of Tollán, the Toltec capital, lie on a hill, separated from the present-day township of Tula de Allende by a river. The Toltecs not only presided over the development of the Early post-Classic period in Central Mexico but also, by some interaction which has still not been properly explained, influenced the Maya civilisation 1200km/750 miles away in Yucatán.

History

The area around present-day Tula was initially inhabited by Otomí Indians who interbred with the Chichimecs – Náhuatl-speaking nomads who arrived from the north-west between the 7th and 9th c. It is quite likely that around the same time another tribal group, the Nonoalca (Náhuatl: "where the language changes") came to Tollán from Tabasco on the southern Gulf coast. According to the latest findings a cultural centre already existed in Tula Chico as early as A.D. 650.

The account which follows mixes myth with historical reality to such an extent that the traditional version of events can only have a limited validity. The leader of the Nonoalcos and founder of the Toltec dynasty, the legendary figure Mixcóatl ("cloud snake"), settled in the valley of Anáhuac. He married Chimalma ("reclining shield"), a princess from Tepoztlán, who in A.D. 947 gave birth to Ce Acatl-Topiltzín ("1 reed our prince"). After studying in the cultural centre of Xochicalco, which was dedicated to the god Quetzalcóatl, the young prince took over the leadership of the Toltecs and in A.D. 958 founded the new capital of Tollán ("place of the reed"). He encouraged the peace-loving members of the Quetzalcóatl cult to be teachers of the arts and sciences and also as a priest king took the name of this god. About 20 years later he found himself in conflict with his mythical rival Tezcatlipoca ("smoking mirror"), the warlike god of the night and champion of evil spirits. Vanquished in this struggle, Topiltzín was forced to leave Tollán in 987 and went to Cholula where he is said to have stayed for a long time. He then went to Veracruz and from there to Yucatán, taking Toltec culture to the Mayas and bringing about a renaissance in their civilisation in his role as the god king Kukulcán. According to another version Quetzalcóatl is supposed to have left the country by boat, promising that he would return one day, and even to have been burned and transformed into the morning star.

It is thought that the Nonoalca-Toltecs returned to their original homeland of Tabasco in the second half of the 10th c., subsequently moving on to Chichén Itzá which they finally subdued. The result of this fusion of Toltec militarism with the artistic skill of the Mayas was the post-Classic renaissance of Maya art. With the victory of the warring faction in Tollán a militaristic empire developed which was based on the elite warrior orders of the eagles and the jaguars. It is also assumed that it was the Toltecs who instituted mass sacrifices of humans in order to appease the gods. In A.D. 1125 the decline of Tollán was apparently set in train by a struggle between the Chichimecs and the Nonoalcas, which led to the first emigration to Cholula and its conquest. The great fire of Tollán followed and then the arrival of other Chichimec groups who took part in the struggle for Cholula. The end of the Toltec domination of Tollán finally occurred in 1175 under the rulers Topiltzín (Quetzalcóatl, a descendant of the legendary founder) and Huémac. Both of them fled southwards. The majority of the inhabitants of Tollán settled elsewhere in the valley of Anáhuac or migrated to the coast of the Gulf of Mexico or to Chiapas, Guatemala and Nicaragua. The Pipil Indians who still live in these areas and speak a Náhuatl tongue are probably the survivors of this wave of emigration. The Aztecs who later ruled over the region felt themselves to be the successors of the Toltecs and adopted aspects of their culture, in particular their religion.

The writings of the 16th c., above all those of Bernardino de Sahagún and Fernando de Alba Ixtlilxóchitl, are the first written reports of the mysterious city of Tollán, which however was not actually discovered for another four hundred years. Thus, right up to the end of the 1930s it was erroneously believed that Teotihuacán had been the Toltecs' capital. Admittedly Antonio García Cubas in 1873 and Désiré Charnay in 1880 had stumbled across remains of an archaeological site at Tula, but it was not until 1938 that Wigberto Jiménez Moreno discovered the old city. Systematic excavations of the site were begun in the 1940s under Jorge R. Acosta and these finally led to its being identified beyond all doubt as the former Toltec metropolis. Further excavations under the direction of Eduardo Matos Moctezuma revealed that the central area of Tollán in its heyday extended to 12sq.km/5sq. miles and supported a population of some 60,000 people.

Visit to the ★Ruins

Ball court

On entering the site the visitor comes to the small Plazuela Norte (northern square) with its ball court (Juego de Pelota No. 1), which measures 67m by 12·50m (220ft by 41ft).

Serpent wall

The so-called "Serpent Wall" (Coatepantli; 2·20m/7ft high and 40m/131ft long), which runs along the south side of the small square, encloses the Temple of the Morning Star. Underneath shell patterns and geometric ornaments can be seen reliefs of snakes devouring human skeletons.

★Temple of the Morning Star

After passing Edificio 1 (Building no. 1), a palace which has been built over on several occasions and probably served as a dwelling-place for priests, the visitor comes to the main square of the site. On this square stands the Temple of the Morning Star (Templo de Tlahuizcalpantecuhtli), also known as the Pyramid of Quetzalcóatl or Edificio B (Building B). From the main square a stairway leads up to the five-storey 10m/33ft high stepped pyramid (40m/131ft square), on which the temple once stood.

★Atlantes

Columns which have been found on the site, as well as the colossal statues known as the Atlantes (the left one and also the upper part of the right one are reproductions: originals in the National Museum of Anthropology in Mexico City) have been assembled on the platform of the temple pyramid. The superb 4·60m/15ft high statues, which once supported the roof of the temple, symbolise the god Quetzalcóatl in his guise of the morning star. In their right hand the statues each hold a sling for hurling spears (atlatl), while in their left hand they hold a bundle of arrows, a pouch of incense and a small sword. On their breast they carry a shield in the shape of a butterfly. The rear belt-buckle is in the form of a setting sun. The square columns display reliefs with the

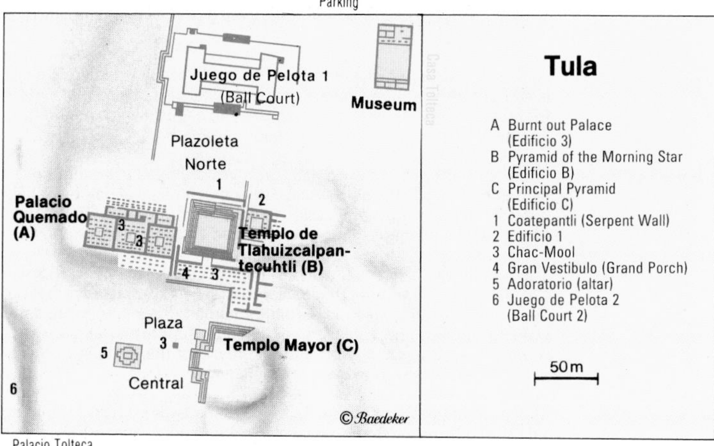

symbol of the earth (a crocodile's head) and pictures of warriors and weapons; the column which is incomplete has the face of Quetzalcóatl depicted on it. The round columns are decorated with finely-carved reliefs made up of feather patterns, as they were originally columns in the shape of serpents, whose heads formed the base. During the destruction of Tollán the temple was torn down and the great Atlantes,

Tula: Temple of the Morning Star

together with the shattered columns, were hurled over a ramp into the depths below.

Side walls

On the side walls, which are formed in a modified talud-tablero style, it is still possible in many places on the vertical sections to make out a frieze with impressive reliefs of jaguars and eagles, which are holding human hearts in their claws and devouring them.

Entrance hall

In the former great entrance hall (Gran Vestíbulo) all the columns are reconstructions. In the north-west corner the remains of painted reliefs are visible, depicting a procession of warriors and priests. To the right of the ascending steps the statue of a headless Chac-mool stands.

The whole site is in many ways similar to the palace of warriors in Chichén Itzá (see entry). These characteristic "exported" symbols of Toltec architecture, such as serpent columns, friezes with reliefs of striding jaguars and eagles, small atlantes supporting altars, Chac-mools, etc., can certainly be found in many of the regions of Meso-America, especially, however, in Chichén Itzá.

Burnt-down Palace

To the left of the Temple of the Morning Star stands Edificio 3 (Building no. 3), the Burnt-down Palace (Palacio Quemado). This building was formerly composed of several large rooms, columned halls (largely reconstructed) and courtyards. In the central quadrangle there are two Chac-mool sculptures and in the north-west corner there is a wall with painted reliefs depicting a procession of richly adorned noblemen.

To the south of the palace, in the middle of the Plaza Central, a small altar (adoratorio) stands on a square platform. At the east end of the square is Edificio C (Building C), the Main Temple (Templo Mayor). On

The Atlas figures on the Temple of the Morning Star

the steps leading up to the upper platform there is a Chac-mool. On a stone slab to the right of the steps it is possible to make out the motive of Venus, one of the symbols of Quetzalcóatl.

Museum

The Jorge R. Acosta Museum, in which Toltec stone sculptures and ceramics are displayed, is to be found at the entrance to the site.

Surroundings

El Corral

About 1·5km/1 mile to the north of the ruins a strange monument, known as El Corral, is to be found. The central section is round, while two rectangular structures on the east and west sides have been added. An interesting altar which formerly used to stand here is now on display in the museum.

El Cielito

On a hill 6km/4 miles to the south-east of Tula, known as El Cielito (the "Little Heaven"), the ruins of an Aztec palace have been found, standing on the site of an older Toltec palace. The palace was actually still inhabited in the early years of the viceroyship of New Spain and historians have been able to establish that it was the residence of Pedro Moctezuma, the son of the Aztec ruler Moctezuma II. This Aztec prince, a brilliant pupil at the first Franciscan school for the Indian elite, was appointed Cacique of Tula by the Spanish.

Cerro de la Malinche

The Cerro de la Malinche, a hill on the other side of the Río Tula to the west of the town of Tula de Allende, is where, chiselled into the smooth rock-face, the calendar motive of "1 reed 8 flint" (A.D. 980) was found. This suggests the period of Ce Acatl Topiltzín's regency, although it was probably added later by the Aztecs.

Tula de Allende

In the little town of Tula de Allende (2030m/6660ft; population 40,000), 3km/2 miles away, which was founded in 1529 by Franciscans, stands the massive fortified church of San José, built between 1550 and 1553. Its façade is in a pure Renaissance style; the interior has some remarkable ribbed vaulting in the choir and side chapels.

Tepejí del Río

About 20km/12 miles from Tula, near the MEX 57D, lies the town of Tepejí del Río (2175m/7136ft; population 50,000; fiesta Good Friday). The impressive convent church of San Francisco, which was completed in 1586, has a fine colonial-Plateresque façade. There is a memorial in honour of the scientist and Mexican foreign minister Melchor Ocampo, who was shot dead on his hacienda in 1861.

Tulum

P 7

State: Quintana Roo (Q.R.)
Altitude: 14m/46ft

Access

By bus from Cancún (see entry) about 2 hours, from Chetumal (see entry) about 4 hours; by car from Cancún 131km/81 miles on the MEX 307, from Chetumal 250km/155 miles on the MEX 307, from Mérida (see entry) 315km/196 miles on the MEX 180 and then the turning from Nuevo Xcan via Cobá (see entry).

★Location

Tulum is the only well-known fortified Maya town to be situated by the sea. The site, which is bounded on the landward side by a wall, is visible for miles around by virtue of its dominating position on top of 12m/39ft high cliffs overlooking the white sandy beaches of the Caribbean Sea.

Estructuras 57,59

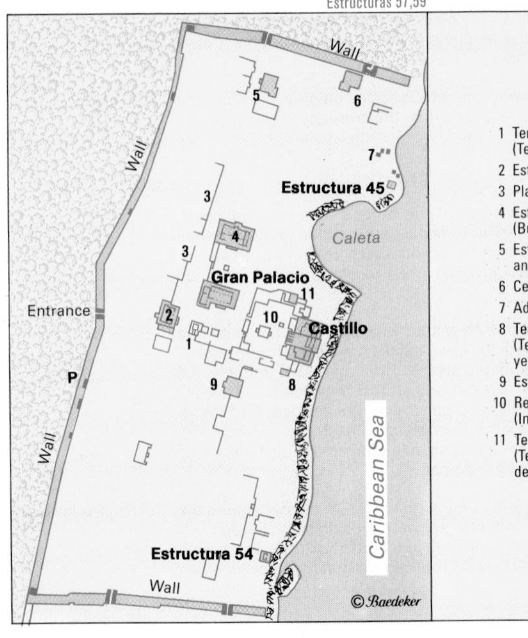

Although in comparison with other Maya sites, it has no special architectural importance, Tulum is nevertheless, thanks to its unique position and its wall paintings, one of the most fascinating ruined towns on the Yucatán Peninsula.

History

Not very much is known about the past history of Tulum (Maya: "fortification"). The original name of the town is thought to have been Zamá (Maya: "dawn"). The site today is ascribed to the Maya Late post-Classic period (after A.D. 1200), in other words the period of the "May-anised" Toltecs. The most important buildings were probably not erected until 1450. It is true that a stela with the date A.D. 564 has been found in Tulum, but it is now thought that this calendar stone must have come from some other place, probably nearby Tancah.

Members of a Spanish expedition under Juan de Grijalva were sailing along the coast of Yucatán and became the first Europeans to come across the fortification when they arrived here in 1518. The town appears to have been inhabited until 1544 when the Spanish conquered the north-east of Yucatán. Towards the end of the last century, during the "Caste War", Maya Indians barricaded themselves once more at Tulum. The first accurately illustrated description of the archaeological site came about as a result of the efforts of the American Stephens and his British draughtsman Catherwood, who explored Tulum in 1842. During this century, archaeologists who have been active here have included the Americans Morley and Howe from the Carnegie Institute and later the Mexican Angel Fernández as well as various other Mexican organisations.

Tulum, on the Caribbean

Visit to the ★Ruins

Fortifications

The relatively small area occupied by the ruins of Tulum is, like the later post-Classic Toltec-influenced Maya towns of Mayapán and Ichpaatún, surrounded on the landward side by a fortified wall. This enclosed area measures from north to south 380m/416yd and from east to west 165m/181yd. The stone wall was originally 3 to 5m (10 to 16ft) high and on average 7m/23ft wide and contained five exit points provided with stone slabs. These features lead to the conclusion that Tulum was not only a religious site but also included a dwelling area. A circular walkway protected by a parapet led along the length of the wall. At each of the two inner corners there was a small temple which was also used as a watchtower.

★Temple of the Frescos

The most important building at Tulum from an archaeological point of view is the Temple of the Frescos (Templo de los Frescos; Edificio 16). It stands more or less in the middle of the walled area and on the east–west axis. The essential parts of the building were probably constructed about the year 1450. As with so many of the Maya religious buildings, in the course of time the temple was built over on several occasions.

Ground floor

The only room on the ground floor has an entrance on the west side which is divided up by four columns. Above this there is a double ledge which is sectioned off by three niches. In the central niche there is a stucco sculpture of the God Descending. The side niches are decorated with other reliefs modelled in stucco which depict seated figures with elaborate head-dresses. The corners of the ledges consist of large bas-relief masks; they were once painted over and are thought to have depicted Itzamná, the old Sky God revered by the Yucatán Mayas.

In the Temple of the Frescos at Tulum

Upper floor

Over the door of the upper floor there is a niche with the remains of a stucco relief which originally is likely to have represented the God Descending. The wall of the interior room is decorated by interesting codex-like paintings which in terms of their content are Maya, while in terms of their style they are Mixtec. They mainly depict figures from the world of the Maya gods. In the upper section two representations of the Sky God, Itzamná, face one another, flanked on the right by the rain god Chac. The central part of the frescos depicts the moon and fertility goddess Ixchel alongside two unknown figures. In the upper part on the right-hand side a picture of the goddess Ixchel is again recognisable, its base comprising a sea scene with stylised fishes.

Stela 2

In front of the temple on an altar stands the 1·30m/4ft high stela no. 2, which bears a post-Classic Maya calendar date which has been deciphered as A.D. 1261.

Castillo

The largest and most striking building on the site is called the Castillo (Edificio/Building no. 1). It is situated at the eastern end on the cliff-edge overlooking the sea. As far as can be ascertained, it was built during three separate periods. A broad flight of steps leads to a terrace on which the two-roomed temple stands. In front of the temple there is a stone which was probably used as an altar for human sacrifices. The entrance to the temple is subdivided by two serpent columns. In the niche above the central door a stone figure can be seen which represents the God Descending.

Temple of the God Descending

Directly to the north of the Castillo is the Temple of the God Descending (Templo del Dios Descendente); Building/Edificio no. 5). The temple

Sumidero Canyon near Tuxtla Gutiérrez ▶

was erected on top of an older structure; it is striking because its walls taper downwards, a method of building which was supposed to provide a special stability. The Temple of the God Descending only possesses one single room; the niche over the entrance contains a stucco sculpture of the God Descending (flying, diving downwards). This deity, which occurs over and over again in Tulum, has wings on its arms and shoulders, as well as a bird's tail. This figure has given rise to various interpretations: the swooping bee, the evening star going down, the setting sun or lightning. Today hardly anything can be seen of the earlier paintwork on the main façade and the east wall inside the temple.

Temple of the Initial Series

The Temple of the Initial Series (Templo de la Serie Inicial, Building 9) lies to the south of the castle. This temple was named after the Stela 1 which Stephens found here on his visit of exploration through Yucatán and which was dated as A.D. 564. It is now in the British Museum in London.

Other buildings

Also noteworthy are Building 25, with its multicoloured God Descending, Building 35, which was built over a "cenote" or underground water deposit, and Building 45, with its round platform and superb view of the sea and the Castillo. Outside the walls are Buildings 57 and 59, the latter being the only building in Tulum to have a pointed roof.

Surroundings

Chunyaxché

After travelling southwards for 26km/16 miles on the MEX 307, Chunyaxché is reached, or Muyil as it is also known in archaeological circles. The site is not far from the road and comprises a 2·5sq.km/1sq. mile area with pyramids, temples and palaces dating from the Late Classic and post-Classic Periods. The highest building is a 19m/62ft high pyramid. The ruins of this largely unexplored site are, however, for the most part covered in vegetation. A pathway leads to the lagoon of Chunyaxché, where it is possible to swim and fish.

Other Maya sites

Both along the coast to the north of Tulum as well as in the southern part of Quintana Roo there are a large number of Maya sites which predate the arrival of the Spanish. Of these mention need only be made of Las Milpas, San Miguel de Ruz, Chamax, Chacmool (Santa Rosa) and Tupak.

Tuxpan

See El Tajín

Tuxtla Gutiérrez N 9

State: Chiapas (Chis.)
Altitude: 530m/1739ft
Population: 450,000
Telephone code: 91 961

Access

By air from Mexico City (1¼ hours) and other Mexican airports; by bus from Mexico City about 16 hours, from Oaxaca (see entry) in 7 hours.

Location

Tuxtla Gutiérrez, the capital of the state of Chiapas, lies on the Carretera Panaméricana in a fertile subtropical valley. With its central position and the oil finds in Chiapas, Tuxtla Gutiérrez has developed into a modern progressive town.

History

The region around present-day Tuxtla was inhabited by members of the Maya tribe called Zoque, who named the place Coyactocmo (Zoque: "place of the rabbits"), and it was from this that the later name Tuxtlán (Náhuatl: "place of the rabbits") derives.

The first Spanish monks who arrived here in the 16th c. were followed by Spanish settlers. The latter frequently had to ward off attacks from Zoque Indians who constituted the majority of the population in the region. At the beginning of the 19th c. Tuxtla was still an unimportant township. In 1848 it received the additional name of Gutiérrez and in 1892 it replaced San Cristóbal de Las Casas as the capital of Chiapas. Today it has acquired considerable importance as an administrative and cultural centre and as a centre for the handling and transfer of commercial goods.

Sights

The town does not possess many old buildings. The cathedral, which has been rebuilt several times, should be mentioned, and also the Palacio de Gobierno (government palace) with its white and red colours.

★Regional museum

The regional museum of anthropology and history (Museo Regional de Antropología e Historia) is in the Parque Francisco Madero in the north-east of the town. The museum has archaeological finds from the time of the Olmecs and the Mayas and ethnological objects from the surrounding area. The park is also the location of the Teatro Emilio Rabasa and the Botanic Garden.

★Zoological Garden

The zoological gardens of Miguel Alvarez del Toro, which specialises exclusively in animals from Chiapas, are to be found in the south-east of the town in the woodland area of El Zapotal and cover an area of 100ha/250 acres.

Surroundings

★★El Sumidero

About 22km/14 miles north of the town the look-out point (mirador) known as Los Chiapas offers a good view down into the highly impressive Cañón (canyon) del Sumidero. The distance from the edge of the ravine down to the river winding along at the bottom, the Río Grijalva (Río Grande de Chiapa), is a good 1000m/3281ft. This is where the Chipanecs from Chiapa are supposed to have plunged to their deaths in 1528 in the face of the advancing Spaniards. Dramatic boat trips through the gorge are organised from Chiapa de Corzo.

Chiapa de Corzo

About 18km/11 miles east of Tuxtla Gutiérrez, on the Carretera Panaméricana, is the little town of Chiapa de Corzo (415m/1362ft; population 40,000). Even from the main road-junction a one-storey restored pyramid can be seen, inside which a tomb has been discovered.

The excavations undertaken by the New World Archaeological Foundation have demonstrated that the area around Chiapa del Corzo, like that around Izapa (see Chiapas), was one of the oldest pre-Columbian sites in Meso-America. The ceramics which have been found here suggest that the region was settled from 1400 B.C. until A.D. 950, in other words from early formative times up to the Classic period. The oldest date inscription so far found in the archaeology of America was uncovered here on the Stela 2 and this corresponds to the date of December 8th 36 B.C. The stela is today housed in the Museo Regional

Fountain in Chiapa de Corzo

in Tuxtla Gutiérrez. The identity of the builders of this religious site is not known; a transitional period between the Olmecs and the Mayas or a proto-Maya civilisation are possibilities which have been mentioned.

The present-day town was founded in 1528 by the conquistador Diego de Mazariagos around an enormous ceiba tree (ceiba pendantra), which was worshipped by the Indians. The tree is today known as "La Pochota" (Náhuatl: "póchotl" = "the hunchback"). The Church of Santo Domingo is worth visiting. Built in the middle of the 16th c., it has undergone several alterations since then. The octagonal fountain in the Zócalo is curious: begun by Pater Rodrigo de León in 1552 and completed 10 years later, it is conceived in the Moorish style and in its construction resembles the Spanish royal crown. The tiny lacquer museum (Museo de Laca), which presents a comparison of local with Chinese lacquerwork in a vivid way, is also to be found on the Zócalo.

★Zócalo fountain

Reservoirs

Several large reservoirs, which offer good facilities for water sports, can be reached from Tuxtla Gutiérrez. About 35km/22 miles north of the town is the reservoir Presa Chicoasén with one of the largest hydroelectric power stations in Latin America; 88km/55 miles to the north-west, beyond Ocotzocuatla, is the reservoir of Netzahualcóyotl or Mal Paso while 68km/42 miles to the south-east, beyond Las Limas, is the reservoir Presa de la Angostura.

Tzintzuntzan I 8

State: Michoacán (Mich.). Altitude: 2100m/6890ft

Access

By bus from Pátzcuaro or Quiroga (for both see Pátzcuaro Lake); by car from Pátzuaro 18km/11 miles to the north, from Morelia (see entry) 53km/33 miles to the west via Quiroga.

Location

The Tarascan ruins of Tzintzuntzan lie above the village of the same name on a hill with a superb view across the nearby lake of Pátzcuaro. The site with its unusual building styles was formerly the most important cultural centre of the Tarascans.

History

Tzintzuntzan (Tarascan: "place of the humming-birds") building may well have started in the 12th c. A.D. Together with Pátzcuaro and Ihuatzio it was later to form the tripartite power base of the Tarascan kingdom. It is not known where the Tarascans (tarascue = stepson) came from, although they called themselves Purépechas. The most likely thing is that in the 10th and 11th c. during the Toltec epoch, in common with the Aztecs, they came in from the north-west, but, unlike other tribes, did not carry on into the highlands of Mexico and instead settled in the lake district of present-day Michoacán. Their original capital appears to have been Zacapu, until, under Hireticátame ("portly king"), in the Late post-Classic period of the 14th and 15th c., they extended their influence over the whole of Michoacán and large parts of Jalisco and Colima. Tariácuri, who succeeded in uniting the various tribes in the region, must, however, count as the true founder of the Tarascan kingdom, which in effect was a tripartite federation. With an area of almost 7sq.km/3sq. miles and a population of some 40,000, Tzintzuntzan was the ruling town of the Tarascans, who continued to develop into most formidable warriors. Thus in 1748, under Tzitzipandácuri, they managed, not least thanks to their copper weapons, to defeat the Aztecs, who, after their successful conquest of Toluca, invaded under their ruler Axayácatl. Later attempts by the Aztec king Ahuízotl to subdue the Tarascan realm also came to grief.

The Spanish under Cristóbal de Olid reached Tzintzuntzan in 1522 and secured a bloodless agreement with the Tarascans which involved a recognition of Spanish supremacy. In 1529 the notorious conquistador Nuño Beltrán de Guzmán appeared and killed the Tarascan ruler Tangáxoan II, which led to rebellions against the Spanish. The Spanish monarchs sent out the priest and jurist Vasco de Quiroga (1470–1565) who succeeded in restoring peace. Vasco de Quiroga was appointed Bishop of Michoacán in 1537 with a provisional seat in Tzintzuntzan; later the bishopric was moved to Pátzcuaro. The bishop promoted the Indians' skills and capabilities as artisans and craftsmen in the widest possible way and thereby initiated the development of the wide variety of trades and crafts which to this day are practised by the inhabitants of this region. Detailed descriptions of Tzintzuntzan were already being included in old Spanish chronicles. A thorough exploration of the site and its partial excavation, however, had to wait until the efforts of Charles Hartfort in 1878, Carl Lumholtz around the turn of the century, and Alfonso Caso, Daniel Rubín de la Borbolla and Jorge Acosta in the 1930s and 1940s.

The Tarascans

The Tarascans, who today still number some 95,000, basically lived from fishing, hunting and the cultivation of maize. The people were divided into two main classes, one comprising the military elite and the priests, the other made up of the fishermen, farmers and slaves. At the head of the divine world stood the fire god Curicaveri, with next to him Cuerauáperi ("earth mother"), Tata Uriata ("father sun") and Nata Cutzi ("mother moon"). Although primarily warriors, the Tarascans were superior to most of the other peoples of Meso-America in the fashioning of metals – copperwork as well gold and silver. The fact that so little copperwork seems to have taken place in Mexico suggests that this skill was brought in from Peru or Colombia. But the quality of Tarascan featherwork, ceramics, textiles and obsidian work was also famed throughout Meso-America. The roughly-hewn, archaic-looking stone sculptures, some of which are identical with the Toltec Chac-mool figures, are especially striking. In their relatively simple, but utterly original style of architecture it is the "yácatas" which predominate – temple platforms with rounded tops, which can still be seen today in Tzintzuntzan.

Visit to the ruins

Great platform

The old site, of which only parts are still extant, is interesting more for its architectural style and as a totality than for its execution. The enormous platform (425×250m/465×274yd) supported five flat T-shaped temple buildings (yácatas; Náhuatl: "nose"), the rectangular foundations of which end in oval platforms. The latter, which originally were capped with a round top section with a roof, apparently served as graves, while the actual yácatas were used as places of worship for the fire god Curicáveri. Excavations at the circular building of Temple V brought to light tombs of Tarascan rulers and their families with many burial gifts laid alongside.

On the east side of the fortress-like site a monumental flight of steps some 30m/98ft wide led on to the terrace.

Yácatas

The yácatas, which are numbered from I to V (beginning with one's back to the lake on the right) each had 12 ledges of about 0·90m/3ft and could be reached by steps. These temples were built using flat stones laid one upon another which were held together by walls of varying sizes. For the outer covering the volcanic stone "xanamu" was used, combined in regular pieces with a mixture of clay and pebblestone.

Museum

Finds from the site are displayed in the museum which was opened in 1992.

Tzintzuntzan Town

On the opposite side of the road to Quiroga is the present-day town of Tzintzuntzan (2050m/6726ft; population 22,000; fiestas: February 1st to 7th, Día de Nuestro Señor del Rescate; Holy Week; Corpus Christi). The Franciscan monastery, which was rebuilt in 1570 is noteworthy, with its large atrium and its old olive trees – a rarity in Mexico, as the Spanish had forbidden them to be grown in their American colonies. Connected

The ruins of Tzintzuntzan

to the monastery is the Church of San Francisco (16th c.) with its "open chapel", which was damaged by fire in 1944 and has a colonial-plateresque façade. Next to it stands the Church of the Third Order. The town is well-known for the painted ceramics which are manufactured here, as well as wood-carvings, stone sculptures and basketwork.

Surroundings

Ihuatzio

From the road to Pátzcuaro, on the lake of the same name, a side road leads off to the right to the village of Ihuatzio (Purépecha: "place of the coyotes") 5km/3 miles distant. 2km/1 mile up a farm track the ruined site of the former Tarascan capital is reached. It was some 1·3sq.km/½sq. mile in area and would have had about 5000 inhabitants. On a large ceremonial square surrounded by high walls the partly restored remains of two pyramids can be seen, and, just to one side, three yåcatas which have still not been excavated. Because of the poor access road a visit to the site can really only be recommended to those particularly interested in archaeology.

Uruapan de Progreso H 8

State: Michoacán (Mich.)
Altitude: 1610m/5282ft
Population: 350,000
Telephone code: 91 452

Access from Mexico City

By rail about 13 hours; by bus about 9½ hours; by car on the MEX 15 via Toluca (see entry), Morelia (see entry) and Pátzcuaro (see Pátzcuaro Lake).

Location

Uruapan is a town relatively untouched by tourism. It lies on the Río Cupatitzio in the middle of a wooded area and its chief assets are its mild climate, lush vegetation and its beautiful parks.

History

The town of Uruapan (Tarascan: "where the flowers bloom") was founded in 1532 by the Franciscan Pater Juan de San Miguel and given the name San Francisco de Uruapan. It was laid out in a chessboard pattern and divided up into nine districts (barrios) which even to this day have retained their own individual character.

Sights

Hospital chapel of Guatápara
Museum of Folk Art

The focal point of the town is the Plaza Principal (Jardín Morelos) which was designed as a market place in the early colonial period. On the square stands the former Hospital Chapel of Guatápara or Huatápera, which goes back to Juan de San Miguel. It is also known as Santo Sepulcro and has a beautiful plateresque doorway with the statue of the founder "Santo de Uruapan" or "Tata Juanito". The hospital, which has a fine patio, today houses the Museum of Folk Art (Museo de Artes Populares), which mainly displays the lacquerwork which has been so closely associated with the town since the 16th c.

Markets

The market, which is held daily, is well worth seeing. As well as lacquer-work, handwoven cloths and traditional garments are sold. Behind the Hospital Chapel is the Mercado de Antojitos, a "snack market", where it is possible to sample Mexican cooking.

Parks

Among the fine parks, pride of place must go to the Jardín de los Mártires ("Garden of the Martyrs") and the national park of Eduardo

Ruiz at the gorge of the Río Cupatitzio (Purépecha: "where the waters meet"). Here there are beautiful walks leading through lush vegetation past waterfalls, rock formations and springs.

Surroundings

★ La Tzaráracua

The waterfall of La Tzaráracua (Tarascan: "the sieve") is situated on the MEX 37 roughly 12km/7 miles to the south. One of the most beautiful waterfalls in the whole of Mexico, it is surrounded by attractive woodland near the Laguna Cupatitzio.

El Infiernillo

About another 70km/43 miles along the MEX 37 lies the reservoir El Infiernillo ("Little Hell"). This artificial lake over 100km/62 miles long with a dam 175m/574ft high is fed by the rivers Tepalcatepec and Balsas.

Tingambato

About 30km/19 miles west of Uruapan in the direction of Pátzcuaro on the MEX 14 is the little town of Tingambato (Purépacha: "place of the warm water"). There is a noteworthy excavation site which has been established as dating back to between A.D. 500 and 1000. Large pyramid platforms in the tablud-tablero style, which suggest the influence of Teotihuacán, were found next to a ball court.

Angahuan

18km/11 miles to the north of Uruapan a road turns left off the MEX 37 and leads to the town of Angahuan (population 26,000) 21km/13 miles away. The parish church of Santiago has a particularly impressive "mudéjar-plateresque" doorway which dates back to 1562. It is executed in "tequitqui", the Indian art of stonemasonry, lavishly decorated and resembles the doorway of the Guatápara chapel in Uruapan.

Paricutin and the Church of San Juan Parangaricutirorícuaro, half-buried

★★Paricutín

From Angahuan it is a 50 minute trip with hired mules or horses, or 5km/3 miles on foot, to the unique lava field of Paricutín (Tarascan: "what lies in front"). The volcano of Paricutín (2575m/8449ft) became famous throughout the world when it erupted on February 20th 1943 and several settlements were buried under the masses of lava which it emitted. The eruptions lasted for almost three years and more than 5000 people had to leave their homes. The top of the village church of San Juan Parangaricútiro protrudes from the midst of the lava field in splendid isolation. If contemplating an ascent of the volcano, it is recommended to engage the services of a local guide.

Paracho de Verduzco

The MEX 37 continues for another 20km/12 miles after the turning to Angahuan and leads to Paracho de Verduzco (1567m/5141ft; population 27,000; fiestas: August 8th, village festival; November 16th to 26th, arts and crafts fair). The town is famous for its woodcraft, in particular guitars, violins, toys and furniture.

Uxmal P 7

State: Yucatán (Yuc.)
Altitude: 12m/39ft

Access

By bus from Mérida (see entry) ("Via Ruinas") about 1½ hours or from Campeche (see entry); by car from Mérida 80km/50 miles on the MEX 261, from Campeche 152km/94 miles on the MEX 261.

Location

The famous Maya site of Uxmal is situated on a plain covered with thick scrub 80km/50 miles south of Mérida in the north-west of the Yucatán Peninsula. Although in terms of surface area it is not one of the largest excavation sites in Mexico, Uxmal, with its preponderance of classical Maya-Puuc architecture, lays claim to being one of the most unified and beautiful pre-Columbian sites in the whole country.

History

It is thought that Uxmal (Maya: "thrice built") was founded by a tribe which had wandered northwards from the area of Petén (in present-day Guatemala) during the 6th c. A.D., which falls in the Maya Classic period. The existence of an earlier settlement, possibly in the pre-Classic period, can not be ruled out. The most brilliant architectural period in Uxmal occurred in the 9th and 10th c. Although the Indian chronicles assert that the Xiú, a highland tribe, founded Uxmal around the end of the millennium, the zenith of the settlement's development was by this time already over. It is more likely that the Xiú only settled in or around the deserted settlement of Uxmal in the 13th or 14th c. and, after the destruction of Mayapán in the middle of the 15th c., moved on to Maní, which was their last bulwark against the advance of the invading Spanish.

Fray Alonso Ponce was the first Spaniard to write about Uxmal, which he visited in 1586. In 1836 Jean Frédéric de Waldeck carried out explorations in Uxmal and in 1841 John L. Stephens and Frederick Catherwood spent some time in the ruined town. The first systematic excavations were undertaken by Frans Blom in 1929. He was followed by Silvanus Morley from the Carnegie Institute in 1941, José Erosa Peniche, and later a whole series of Mexican research initiatives which were conducted by Jorge Acosta, César Saenz and Rubén Maldonado Cárdenas at the end of the 1970s.

Visit to the ★★ruins

Puuc style

In contrast to Chichén Itzá there is an almost complete absence of Mexican (Toltec) stylistic elements in the architecture in Uxmal, with

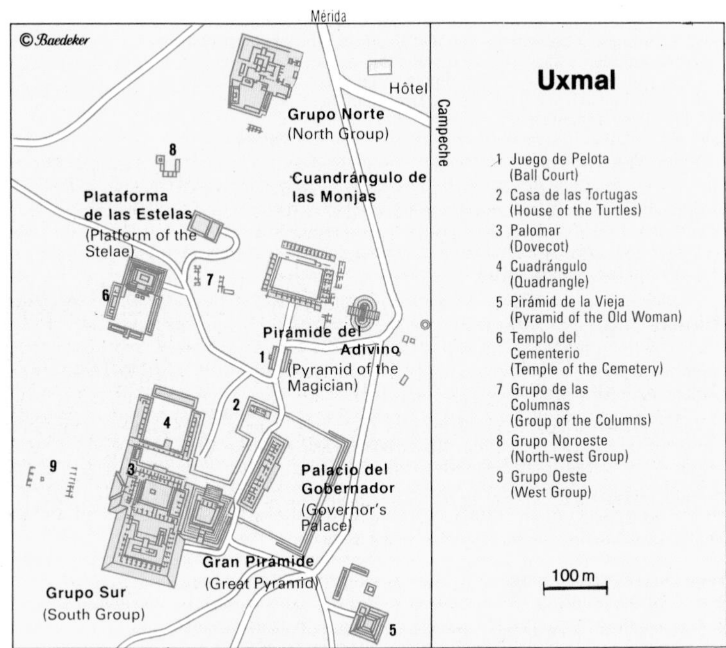

the result that in Uxmal the Classic Maya architecture in the Puuc style (so named after the chain of hills in the north-west of Yucatán; A.D. 700–1000) was preserved. This style is characterised by thin limestone cladding in a square or lattice-style pattern on top of smooth walls, a device that replaces the stucco decorations of the Maya Classic period. This ornamentation, which is used to decorate almost exclusively the upper part of a building, is supplemented with panels of Chac masks (the rain god) with long curved noses and snakes with stiff bodies. The picture is completed by rounded stone columns in the entrances and covered columns in long rows.

That part of the Maya town which has been uncovered covers an area of 700×800m (766×875yd). As with many other pre-Hispanic sites only a tiny part of the original site has so far been excavated. Uxmal was not, as in the case of other towns in Yucatán, laid out around one or more "cenotes" (underground water deposits), as this type of natural water pool does not exist in this area. The people used to manage with "aguadas" and "chultunes", places where the earth had caved in and then become sealed, or artificially created cisterns, in which rain water was collected. This lack of ground water enabled the rain god Chac to assume his pre-eminent position, evidence of which is provided by the decorations on the buildings.

Museum

Among the exhibits displayed in the museum at the entrance to the site are four stone heads of the rain-god Chac, panels with hieroglyphics, a phallic sculpture and a stone turtle.

Nunnery Quadrangle and Pyramid of the Soothsayer

★Pyramid of the Soothsayer

Opposite the entrance to the site is the highest building in Uxmal, the 35m/115ft high Pyramid of the Soothsayer or Sorcerer (Pirámide de Adivino). Legend has it that this pyramid was built by a dwarf in one night with the help of his mother, a witch. In fact it consists of five buildings lying on top of one another, which were erected over a period of more than three centuries and which are all quite clearly distinct from each another. Instead of the usual rectangular ground-plan which was customary elsewhere, the base of this building is oval.

Temple I

On the west side at the base of the pyramid it is possible to see the foundations of Temple I, the oldest of the buildings. A date chiselled into a door lintel reveals the building's inception to have been A.D. 569. The façade, richly decorated mainly with masks of Chac, the Maya rain god, also has the famous sculpture known as the "Queen of Uxmal". This figure, which depicts a tattooed priest's head caught in the jaws of a snake, is now to be found in the National Museum of Anthropology in Mexico City.

Temples II and III

Temple II (Templo Interior Oriente), which has a central interior supported by pillars, is reached through an opening in the upper middle part of the east steps. Temple III (Templo Interior Poniente) is not visible from the outside. It adjoins the rear part of Temple II and consists of a small shrine and an antechamber. The steps on the west side, which have a gradient of 60°, do not possess a balustrade in the traditional sense. The parapet is set back and formed by stylised Chac masks which frame the steps.

Temple IV

These steps lead to Temple IV (Templo Chenes), the entrance to which is formed by the open jaws of a stylised mask. In contrast to the Puuc style which is elsewhere the norm in Uxmal, this temple is conceived in

Pyramid of the Soothsayer, reputed to have been built by a dwarf

the pure Chenes style, as evidenced by the entrance. The façade of this cube-shaped building is completely covered with Chac masks and lattice-style ornamentation.

Temple V

Temple V, also called the House of the Soothsayer, belongs to the last wave of building which took place in Uxmal (about A.D. 1000). It can be reached either directly from the steps on the east side or by two narrow lateral flights of steps situated along the west side of the Templo Chenes (Temple IV). The rectangular building appears to date from the late 9th c. and to be a smaller-scale reproduction of the governor's palace. Part of the façade of the temple, which consists of three interior rooms, is decorated with lattice-style ornamentation.

From the summit of the Pyramid of the Soothsayer there is a marvellous view of the other buildings on the site and the countryside surrounding Uxmal.

★ **Nuns' Quadrangle**

Directly to the north-west of the Pyramid of the Soothsayer stands the magnificent Nuns' Quadrangle (Cuadrángulo de las Monjas; A.D. 900–1000) which was given its name by the Spanish because of the large number of "cells" which the building possesses. The four long buildings, which enclose the 64×46m/210×151ft trapeziform inner quadrangle, stand on terraces of varying heights and were erected at different times.

South building

The inner quadrangle is entered by the large arched entrance in the south building, which is the second oldest building on the site. The arch lies on an axis with the ball court which is situated in front of the quadrangle and is largely in ruins. There are eight rooms both to the right and left of the central walkway, of which one half face outwards, while the other half face north into the inner quadrangle. The frieze over

Nunnery Quadrangle

the doors has sculptures of Maya huts which stand out above panels of latticework.

North building

Opposite, and standing on a platform almost 7m/23ft high, is the oldest and most important building of the Nuns' Quadrangle, the north building, which is almost 100m/328ft in length. The 30m/98ft wide stairway is flanked by two small temples. The left one (to the west) is called the Venus Temple, because a motive in the frieze has been connected with the planet Venus. The temple rests on four columns which form a hall. It is the only building in Uxmal which has such columns. The north building comprises 26 chambers and eleven entrances on to the inner quadrangle. As is usual with buildings in the Puuc style the basement level has no ornamentation. Over the ledge there are four "mask" towers, each with four Chac masks placed above one another. Next to them there are pictures of thatched houses and reliefs of monkeys and snakes.

East building

The third oldest structure is the east building with its five entrances. The ledge consists of an ornamental serpent, its heads looking out on the north side. The frieze is quite stark in its conception and consists principally of latticework. On top there are trapeziums in which owls' heads are inserted.

West building

The newest section, the west building, has seven entrances. Its frieze is considered to be the most ornate in all Puuc architecture. Above the main entrance there is a throne with a baldachin, on which a seated figure, half man, half turtle, can be seen. The magnificent panel displays alternating sculptures of two Maya huts, rows of masks, geometrical ornaments and meandering coiled snakes. The last-named belong to the few Toltec stylistic elements to be found in Uxmal and were only added as an afterthought. Each of the edges of the building have three masks of the rain god Chac placed one above another.

Ball court

To the south of the Nuns' Quadrangle is the ball court which measures 31×10m/102×33ft. The two mortised stone rings bear the calendar date A.D. 649.

House of the Turtles

Further to the south is the House of the Turtles (Casa de las Tortugas; A.D. 800–900). Measuring almost 7m/23ft high, 29m/95ft long and 11m/36ft wide it is one of the most symmetrically proportioned buildings in Uxmal. Three entrances lead from the east side through the unadorned basement into the interior of the house. The frieze running above the central ledge consists of a row of pillars standing close to one another. The building gets its name from the stylised turtles which decorate the upper ledge.

★★ Governor's Palace

Immediately to the south is the Governor's Palace (Palacio del Gobernador), possibly architecturally the most perfect building in prehispanic America. The palace stands on an enormous platform and a terrace and is 98m/322ft long, 12m/39ft wide and 8m/26ft high. The building comprises a main building and two side wings which open on to two vaulted passages. These were later closed in by cross walls.

In the basement with its plain façade there are eleven entrances on the front wall and one on each of the sides; they lead to 24 chambers which all have the typical arched vault. Along the central ledge there is a 3m/10ft high frieze which in its upper section consists of an almost uninterrupted row of 103 Chac masks. Alongside it there is a host of geometric shapes. The lower part has a row of S-shaped decorations which form a serpent which once almost encircled the whole building like a necklace. The sculpture over the middle entrance has been

Jaguar altar, Governor's Palace

Chac masks, Nunnery Quadrangle

restored; with its headdress of quetzal feathers it could be a former ruler of Uxmal. It is estimated that some 20,000 hewn stones with an individual weight of 20 to 80kg (44 to 176lb) were used to make this enormous mosaic frieze.

Jaguar altar

In front of the palace stands an altar with a two-headed jaguar in the middle. This figure could be a symbol of power and have been used as a throne; it is hewn out of a single block of stone and was discovered by Stephens in 1841.

Great Pyramid

To the south-west of the Governor's Palace stands the Great Pyramid (Gran Pirámide), which has been partially restored. This building, which once had nine storeys, is 30m/98ft high and was levelled off at the top. It did not have a temple, but merely small palace-like buildings on its four sides. The top storey had ornamentation in the Puuc style, including masks, parrots, latticework, flowers and meanders. One of the masks is fashioned in such a way that the nose forms a step or a throne, similar to the Codz-poop mask in Kabah (see entry).

Dovecot

To the west is the Dovecot (palomar) which has been only partially restored; its buildings surround a central courtyard (60×40m/190×130ft) similar to the Nuns' Quadrangle. It derives its name from the novel design of its serrated roof-crest. On a row of columns there are nine triangular constructions with window-like openings which give the appearance of a dovecot. It is thought that this interesting building is as much as 200 years older than the Nuns' Quadrangle or the Governor's Palace, and was therefore probably built between A.D. 700 and 800.

South Group and Quadrangle

The buildings to the south and north, the South Group (Grupo Sur) and the Quadrangle (Cuadrángulo), which have not yet been restored, have a similar ground-plan to the Dovecot.

Pyramid of the Old Woman

One of the oldest remains in Uxmal is probably the Pyramid of the Old Woman (Pirámide de la Vieja; *c.* A.D. 670–770), which lies to the south-east and still awaits excavation. From the top of this pyramid it is possible to take excellent photographs of the Governor's Palace.

Temple of the Phalluses

From the Pyramid of the Old Woman a path leads to the remains of some buildings, 400m/438yd away, which have been given the name Temple of the Phalluses (Templo de los Falos). There is a row of stone sculptures in the shape of phalluses, which were probably used as fountains.

Temple of the Cemetery

To the east of the Nuns' Quadrangle is the group of buildings which includes the Temple of the Cemetery (Templo del Cementerio). The square inner courtyard is surrounded by buildings in varying states of dilapidation which include on the north side a pyramid on top of which stands an almost completely destroyed temple. Only on the west side is there a relatively well-preserved building, into which three doors lead. The roof-crest of the temple is built in a very similar way to that of the dovecot. This leads to the conclusion that this building is also of an older date. The whole group of buildings gets its name from the four small platforms, probably altars, which are covered with pictures of skulls with eyes and crossbones and hieroglyphics.

Platform of the Stelae

Not far from the Temple of the Cemetery is the Platform of the Stelae (Plataforma de las Estelas). This is where originally 16 stelae and 15 altars stood, of which only a few in poor condition have survived.

Son et lumière

Every evening in the Nuns' Quadrangle a spectacular son et lumière show is held, in which various places are lit up to the accompaniment of drum and flute music, while a speaker recounts the history of Uxmal. The 45 min. long performance is given at 7pm in Spanish and 9pm in English.

Surroundings

Oxkintok

16km/10 miles from Uxmal on the MEX 261 is the town of Muna, where a road goes off to the west in the direction of Maxcanú. After 25km/16 miles on this road the village of Calzehtoc is reached. From here an unmade-up road leads to the caves of Calzehtoc 3km/2 miles away. Just before the caves a track goes off for another 4km/2½ miles to the large Maya site of Oxkintok, which is one of the oldest known Maya centres in Yucatán. It is probable that Oxkintok dominated this part of Yucatán from A.D. 400 to 800, until it was superseded by Uxmal. Excavations have brought to light 22 sizeable buildings and a number of stelae. Most of the finds can be seen in the Museum of Archaeology and History in Mérida (see entry). A stone door-lintel has been found, dated A.D. 475 and therefore from the Early Classic period, while the most recent date, found on a stela, is A.D. 849. The architecture of the buildings corresponds in the Early Classic period to the Petén style, in the Late Classic section to the Puuc style. Calzehtoc and Oxkintok can also both be reached from Mérida and Campeche on the MEX 180 via Maxcanú.

Valle de Bravo

See Toluca

Venta, La

See Catemaco Lake

Veracruz (State)

Abbreviation: Ver.
Capital: Jalapa
Area: 71,896sq.km/27,759sq. miles
Official population 1990: 6,228,200 (1994 estimate: 6,600,000)

Location and topography

Veracruz, one of the most populous states in Mexico, is bounded on the north by Tamaulipas, on the west by San Luis Potosí, Hidalgo, Puebla and Oaxaca and to the south-east by Chiapas and Tabasco. The scenery is full of contrasts. Between the rugged peaks of the Sierra Madre Oriental with the snow-covered Pico de Orizaba and the wide beaches on the coast of the Gulf of Mexico, coffee plantations alternate with maize fields, industrial towns with vanilla plantations, and oil fields with tropical rain forests. Once inhabited by the legendary Olmecs, the state is today occupied primarily by mestizos, although there are also descendants of slaves, as well as Totonacs, Huastecs and Nahuas.

Archaeological sites

The main sites belonging to the Olmecs are Cerro de las Mesas, Tres Zapotes and San Lorenzo Tenochtitlán (see Catemaco Lake for all of these). The Huastecs, Totonacs and other tribes have left traces in El Zapotal (see Catemaco Lake) Zempoala, El Pital, Quiahuitzián (see

Mexico
United Mexican States
Estados Unidos Mexicanos

Veracruz

Surroundings of Veracruz for all these), Castillo de Teayo (see Surroundings of El Tajín) and El Tajín (see entry).

History

The earliest civilisation was probably that of the Huastecs and, most importantly, the Olmecs (around 1200–1400 B.C.), whose influence extended over a sizable area of Mexico. Until the arrival of the Totonacs foreign tribes mixed with the indigenous people (e.g. Remojadas culture). In the 15th c. the Aztecs subdued a large part of the country.

In 1519 the conquest of Mexico began with the landing of the Spanish under Hernán Cortés near the present-day town of Veracruz. The first Spanish settlement was founded not far from Quiahuiztlán but then moved to La Antigua in 1524. In both the Spanish and Mexican periods the history of the state was closely bound up with that of its most important city, the port of Veracruz.

Economy

As well as the many kinds of tropical and subtropical products associated with the plantation economy, Veracruz's industrial goods include beer, spirits, tobacco, soap, cement, chemicals, glass and leather. Freight traffic, cattle rearing, fishing, and, to an increasing extent, tourism also play an important part in the state's economy. The oil refinement industry is concentrated in the south of the country around Minatitlán and Coatzocoalcos. Veracruz is therefore without question a prosperous state, although there exists a significant gap between the industrialised south and the impoverished, largely agricultural, north.

Veracruz (City) L 8

State: Veracruz (Ver.)
Altitude: 3m/10ft. Population: 700,000
Telephone: 91 29

Access from Mexico City

By air about ¾ hour; by rail about 10 hours; by bus about 6 hours; by car 424km/263 miles on the MEX 150 or MEX 190 via Puebla (see entry) and Córdoba (see entry).

Location

The old city of Veracruz is situated in a hot humid climatic zone and was built on a sandy beach only a few metres/feet above sea level. Mexico's most important port is connected to the state capital Jalapa by two railway lines and several cross-country roads. Given its importance over several centuries as a customs port and centre for the coastal

regions of the Gulf of Mexico and the tropical hinterland, it comes as no surprise that Veracruz should have had a varied history. Despite its climate, Veracruz is a vibrant city, much favoured by domestic tourists, with a sympathetic mixture of colonial buildings and modern architecture.

History

In the period before Christ the area around Veracruz (Spanish: "true cross") was probably inhabited by the mysterious people called the Olmecs and then later by the Totonacs. The capital of their empire was Zempoala, about 40km/25 miles away from the present-day city of Veracruz.

On April 22nd 1519, Good Friday, Hernán Cortés landed with his Spanish soldiers on the coast near La Antigua and shortly afterwards received a delegation from the Aztec ruler Moctezuma. The latter assumed that Cortés must be Quetzalcóatl returned – the legendary ruling figure who had been driven out of the Toltec capital of Tula (Tollán) some 530 years previously and disappeared with the promise that he would return from across the sea. Cortés made the symbolic gesture of founding the town of Villa Rica de la Vera Cruz ("rich town of the true cross"), before the Spanish settled shortly afterwards near the Totonac town of Quiahuiztlán. Five years later the settlement was transferred to what is present-day La Antigua, 30km/19 miles distant. In the years following the Spanish in fact moved their headquarters a number of times, until they finally built La Nueva Veracruz on the site of the present-day city in 1599. Although at first the town itself did not develop to any extent, the harbour was of paramount importance for the maritime traffic between Mexico on this side of the Atlantic and Cádiz and Seville in Spain on the other. As early as the 16th c., and to a greater degree in the 17th c., Veracruz was the target of attacks by British, French and Dutch pirates. In 1821, towards the end of the War of Independence, the Mexican General Agustín de Iturbide defeated the last viceroy of New Spain, Juan O'Donojú, who subsequently recognised Mexico's independence in the Treaty of Córdoba after a ten-year struggle.

In 1838 the port was occupied by French troops, empowered to secure compensation for their government; in 1847 it was Americans who occupied Veracruz intermittently during the war between Mexico and the USA. The interference of the Spanish, French and British in the clash between Liberals and Conservatives in Mexico ended with the occupation of the port by a French expeditionary corps. Maximilian von Hapsburg, who was appointed Emperor of Mexico with the support of the French, landed here in 1864 on his way to Mexico City. His hapless fate was sealed when in 1867 the French who had come to support him took to their ships in Veracruz, thereby abandoning Mexico for good. An intervention corps of the US army occupied the port once again for a short time in 1914. The frequent occupation of Veracruz by foreign troops can principally be put down to the fact that the duty collected by the customs authorities at the port constituted a major source of income for the Mexican state. Accordingly the customs dues were kept back by foreign governments as security for sums that they were owed by Mexico.

Sights

★Plaza de Armas

Although the city is one of the oldest in Mexico, it possesses hardly any important buildings in the colonial style. The 17th c. city hall (Palacio Municipal) with an interesting façade and a beautiful patio and the Catedral de Nuestra Señora de la Asunción, consecrated in 1734 and formerly the parish church (La Parroquia), are situated on the Plaza de

The harbour promenade and Customs Office

Armas (Plaza de la Constitución; Zócalo). In the evenings this attractive square, framed by palm-trees, tropical plants and arcades, is the centre of activity of this peaceful city.

Santo Cristo del Buen Viaje

The church of Santo Cristo del Buen Viaje, which stands on the Plaza Gutiérrez Zamora, dates from 1610 and is thus the oldest church in the city.

Museums

The Museo de la Ciudad (Calle Zaragoza no. 397) displays archaeological finds and art from the Indian civilisations which have dominated the history of Veracruz – the Olmecs, Totonacs and Huastecs – as well as paintings, craftwork and photographs of the history of the city. In the lighthouse, the Faro Carranza (Figueroa y Arista), from where the revolutionary general Venustiano Carranza directed government business in 1914/15, this period of history is today commemorated by the Museo de la Revolución which has furniture and documents connected with the revolutionary hero. The Baluarte de Santiago is the only part of the old 18th c. city walls which remains. It houses an historical museum with the "Fisherman's Jewels", 35 pieces of pre-Columbian jewellery found by a fisherman in 1976 and which lead experts to wonder whether they could possibly form part of the lost treasure of Moctezuma.

Port

Castillo de San Juan de Ulúa

It is worth visiting the port, where a walk along the quayside (Malecón) enables the visitor to observe the harbour activities. There is also the opportunity to take a boat trip to the great island fortress, the Castillo de San Juan de Ulúa, which is a landmark and symbol for the whole city. In 1528 the Spanish began to build the fort, which was intended to protect the coast from pirate attacks, in which aim it was, however, not always successful. In the 19th c. the fortress became a notorious prison with cells which would often be under water at high tides. The island is also connected to the city by a road.

Beaches

The beaches closest to the city are Playa de Hornos and Playa Villa del Mar. To the south the beach of Mocambo is 8km/5 miles distant. This is followed by the fishing village of Boca del Río and somewhat further on the village of Mandinga with its beaches. The sea at the beaches close to the city is heavily polluted in places, so it is best to go further afield if at all possible.

Surroundings

La Antigua

Proceeding northwards along the coast road, there is a turning after 25km/17 miles to the little town of La Antigua. Today merely a fishing village, it is historically important because it was here that Cortés landed in 1519 and established his provisional headquarters. He set fire to his ships in the Bay of Antigua so that there was no possibility of the planned campaign of conquest being revoked. In 1524 the main Spanish administration was set up here, although it was subsequently transferred to Veracruz; it is still possible to see the remains of the fort, now overrun with tree roots, and the church, the first to be erected on Mexican soil.

★Zempoala

Following the coast road another 10km/6 miles past José Cardel, there is a turning to the left which leads to Zempoala or Cempoala (Náhuatl: "Cempoatl" = "20 water") 3km/2 miles away. From the 13th c. to the Spanish conquest this was the last capital of the Totonacs. In the second half of the 15th c. the Aztecs conquered the Totonacs and made them tributary. 23 days after his landing in Mexico, on May 15th 1519, Cortés met the Totonac king Chicomacatl, called "Cacique Gordo" (fat king) by the Spanish, in Zempoala. The conquistador succeeded in making allies of the Totonacs, who were hostile towards the Aztecs.

Visit to the ruins

The site at Zempoala (Cempoala) covers 5sq.km/2sq. miles in all and comprises ten groups of buildings, although today only a few which have been restored can be visited. They date from the last 300 years before the arrival of the Spanish. Certain of the buildings display quite pronounced Aztec stylistic elements. Some of the finds, however, lead to the conclusion that Zempoala was probably already settled in the first millennium A.D.

Main Temple

On the north side of the principal square is the Main Temple (Templo Mayor) or Temple of the Thirteen Steps. The pyramid is 11m/36ft high;

Templo Mayor in Zempoala

thus the height of each of the thirteen steps is 85cm/33in. The platform on which the building was constructed measures 67×40m/220×131ft. At the top of the pyramid it is possible to make out the remains of a rectangular temple.

Temple of the Chimneys

At the east end of the square is the Temple of the Chimneys (Templo de las Chimeneas). A broad flight of steps leads up to the top of the six-storey building. On the upper platform there are the remains of some columns which gave the building its name.

Great Pyramid

A building of later construction is the Great Pyramid (Gran Pirámide) at the west end of the square. In reality it is a row of platforms placed one on top of another, which taper as they go upwards.

Temple of the Little Heads

To the east of the square is the interesting Temple of the Little Heads (Templo de las Caritas) which in terms of its construction resembles the Great Pyramid. The niches set into the walls once contained a total of 360 earthenware heads, from which the building derives its name.

Museum

At the entrance to the archaeological zone there is a small museum with finds from the site.

Villahermosa N 9

State: Tabasco (Tab.)
Altitude: 11m/36ft
Population: 640,000
Telephone code: 91 931

Access from Mexico City

By air about 1¼ hours; by bus about 15 hours; by car 863km/536 miles.

Location

Villahermosa, the capital of the state of Tabasco, was until a few years ago a sleepy town on the Río Grijalva surrounded by tropical countryside. New roads as well as the rich oil finds in Tabasco and Chiapas have turned Villahermosa into a fast-growing, modern city. This important commercial and trading centre is situated in a low-lying area intersected by waterways and has a hot humid climate with heavy rainfall.

History

Whether the history of the settlement goes back to Old Indian times is not known with any certainty. The modern town was founded by the Spanish in 1598 under the name Villa Felipe II and later renamed Villahermosa (Spanish: "beautiful village"). In the course of time it developed into the largest town in the state of Tabasco.

Sights

There are only a few historic buildings in Villahermosa apart from the cathedral which dates from 1614. On the other hand it has two of the most interesting museums in Mexico.

★Regional Museum of Anthropology (Museo Carlos Pellicer)

The CICOM (Centro de Investigaciones de las Culturas Maya y Olmeca) was opened in 1980 on the west bank of the Río Grijalva and is home to the Regional Museum of Anthropology (Museo Regional de Antropología Carlos Pellicer Cámara), named after the famous poet, collector and museum founder Carlos Pellicer (1897–1977).

Circular tour

The circular tour of the museum begins on the second floor with an overview of the civilisations of the pre-Columbian period, illustrated by individual pieces, including stone masks and ceramics from Teotihuacán, ceramic urns and heads made by the Zapotecs and Totonacs, and Aztec stone sculptures. The first floor is concerned with the Olmecs and Mayas and has on display extraordinary clay sculptures made by the Maya in Jaina and Olmec jade from La Venta. On the raised ground floor selected finds belonging to both these civilisations can be seen. Objects on show include the "Teyapa Urn" with the figure of a seated Maya priest, a delicately painted Maya drinking vessel and a jade dagger from La Venta with the engraving of a jaguar warrior.

The CICOM complex also includes an auditorium, the state theatre "Esperanza Iris", a library, exhibition and sales rooms for craft products, restaurants, shops and an arts hall with a garden situated inside the building.

Tabasco 2000

Adjoining the centre to the west is the new complex known as "Tabasco 2000", which includes a planetarium, a conference centre, department stores and the city hall.

★★Parque-Museo de La Venta

The archaeological open-air museum, the Parque-Museo de La Venta, is situated on the south-west shore of the Laguna de las Ilusiones. In this tropical park, monumental finds from the Olmec civilisation (golden period 1200–400 B.C.), such as altars, stelae and animal sculptures are displayed, and, most significantly of all, the famous colossal heads from La Venta. A start has been made to produce reproductions of the original pieces out of synthetic materials. These will probably replace the originals in order to protect these from the unavoidable processes of weathering. The Tabasco-born anthropologist Carlos Pellicer has here managed in a highly impressive fashion to present to the general public the relics of a great civilisation in an appropriate environment. The places where the finds were originally made are located in inaccessible marshland areas in the states of Tabasco and Veracruz.

A Small human head (basalt)
B Relief of a human
C Stone spigot
D Container and fragment of drain
1 Feline head
2 Column with monkey
3 Human jaguar figure
4 Whale
5 Animal in human form
6 Altar with royal figure
7 Serpent stone (reproduction)
8 Jaguar Mosaic
9 Human figure with cloak
10 Stele of the King
11 Colossal head
12 Stele of the bearded man
13 Acrobat
14 Cleft human head
15 Altar with seated figure
16 Silhouette
17 Fragment of sculpture with linear engraving
18 Stele with female sculpture
19 Stone seat
20 Grandmother
21 Ceremonial figures
22 Monument with striding figure
23 Jaguar masks
24 Tomb with basalt columns
25 Colossal head
26 Altar with seated figure
27 Colossal head
28 Unfinished head
29 Figure with child
30 Altar with niches

Olmecs

There are many archaeologists who consider that all the civilisations of Meso-America originate in the Olmecs. What is certain is that this mysterious people represents the oldest known civilisation in Mexico, and one which exerted a powerful influence over large parts of the country. As far as we know, the Olmecs were the first people, apart from the proto-Zapotecs, to develop glyphic script and to use numbers; in this respect they can be viewed as precursors of the Mayas. Their oldest known dating up to the present time (31 B.C.) is to be found on stela C in Tres Zapotes. They did not just create magnificent large sculptures but were also true masters in the fine art of modelling clay figures and the elaborate crafting of jade. Besides La Venta, mention should be made of San Lorenzo Tenochtitlán, Tres Zapotes and Cerro

Museo de la Venta, Olmec head . . .

. . . and altar with figure of ruler

de las Mesas as being important places in the Olmec region where finds have been made.

Colossal heads

To this day it is still unexplained how these people managed to move these colossal heads shaped out of basalt, which could weigh anything up to 20 tons and were up to 3m/10ft high. The quarry which was used is actually some 120km/75 miles from La Venta. Some of the faces chiselled out of the stone have negroid features, while in other examples human characteristics are mixed with those of the jaguar. The appearance of these faces, which seem so un-Indian, has led to the wildest theories. Thus there are many people who maintain that these colossal faces are actually representations of Nubian princes who were sent westwards by Ramses III of Egypt in search of the underworld and ended up by landing here. Others on the other hand seek to see in them the depiction of rulers from the prehistoric megalith civilisations of southern England and northern France. It has to be said, however, that there is not the slightest evidence for any of these hypotheses.

Monkeys, deer, jaguars (including two magnificennt black specimens), crocodiles and snakes can be seen in the small zoo within the park.

Other museums

In the "Casa de los Azulejos", the Tabasco Historical Museum exhibits documents, cards and photographs illustrating the history of the state. Regional costumes and dress can be seen in the Museum of Folk Culture.

Surroundings

★**Comalcalco**

From Villahermosa it is 52km/32 miles via Nacajuca or 82km/51 miles on the MEX 180 and 187 via Cárdenas to the town of Comalcalco

(Náhuatl: "in the house of the Comales"; "comalli" = "tortilla pan"; population 31,000). 5km/3 miles north-east of the town is the archaeological site of Comalcalco, the most westerly of all the more important Maya sites. It dates from the Maya Late Classic period (A.D. 600–900) and most probably had its heyday in the 8th c. The site of the temples, the type of stucco decoration and the way it is used, as well as the ornamentation of a gravestone which has been found, all have a certain similarity with the art of Palenque. It is striking that, in the absence of stone and because of the proximity of the sea, levelled burnt bricks and mortar made out of crushed shells were used, something which is unique in the Maya Classic period.

North square

Temple I, a large multi-storey pyramid with the remains of a temple on its summit, stands on the west side of the vast North Square (Plaza Norte). On the left-hand side of the pyramid, at the foot of the wide flight of steps, damaged stucco figures can be seen. On the north side of the square Temple II stands on an eminence. Other buildings are in the process of being uncovered.

Acropolis

In the south part of the site there is a large artificial platform, the Acropolis, which encloses the square of the same name (Plaza de la Acrópolis). On the platform stand two small temples and a building referred to as a palace (palacio). The Tomb of the Nine Lords of the Night (Tumba de los Nueve Señores de la Noche) was discovered not far away. Nine stucco reliefs, three on each side of the tomb walls, presumably represent the nine rulers of the underworld. The figures were once painted red and only to a limited extent display Classic Maya characteristics. The sarcophagus was at some stage plundered by grave robbers.

Further down, on a terraced platform, are Temple VI, with an impressive stucco mask, and Temple VII, also with stucco ornamentation, including a seated figure in profile.

Museum

The new museum at the excavation site displays evidence which has been found in Tabasco of the pre-Columbian settlement.

Teapa

Going southwards from Villahermosa on the MEX 195, the town of Teapa (72m/236ft; population 50,000) which has the heaviest rainfall of any in Mexico, is reached; there is also a small Museum of Anthropology and History. The town is a starting-point for a visit to the remarkable caves Grutas de Coconá (Maya: "water which falls from the sky"), which are situated nearby and were once used as a pirates' hiding-place. The sulphur springs of El Azufre are also worth seeing.

Xel-há P 7

State: Quintana Roo (Q.R.)

Access

The Caleta (bay) of Xel-há is 1km/½ mile from the MEX 307. It can be reached from Cancún (see entry) by travelling 116km/72 miles southwards (10km/6 miles south of Akumal (see entry)), and from Chetumal (see entry) by travelling 263km/163 miles northwards (15km/9 miles from Tulum (see entry)).

Location

The interesting national park of Xel-há contains within a relatively small area a freshwater lake, a sea bay and Maya ruins. This most attractive area offers walkers, swimmers and snorkellers the opportunity to observe the rich flora and fauna both above and below the water. At the lagoon it is also possible to rent diving equipment. It becomes very crowded at weekends, however, and is best avoided at that time.

Ruins

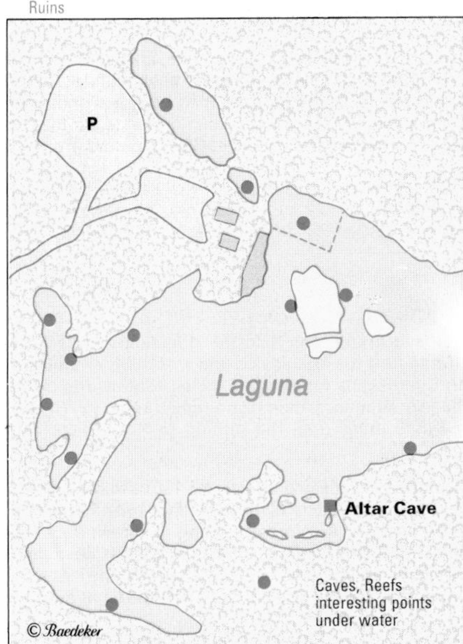

Xel-há

The mixture of fresh and salt water which is regularly found in the bays (*caletas*) of Quintana Roo produces a rich and varied underwater life. The shores of the lagoon, with their alternation of caves, inlets and backwaters and their exotic plants, form a picturesque frame for the colourful underwater world. Xel-há offers every facility for swimmers and snorkellers.

★ National park

This area, which is now a popular destination with visitors, was not discovered and made accessible to the general public until 1959 during a coastal expedition organised by the Club de Exploraciones y Deportes Acuáticos de México (CEDAM). To a greater degree than other places in this region which lie along coastal bays, Xel-há (Maya: "where the waters were born") appears to have been an important Maya cult site even in the Classic period. This emerges from the archaeological finds which have been made along the edge of the water.

Maya finds

These finds include parts of a fortified wall which was built in the post-Classic period as well as several altars lying under water, including a chapel-like cave which appears to have served as a shrine. The remains of two chimneys were found here, which supports the theory that this might have been a crematorium used by the Mayas. Unfortunately, during the last few years and apparently even before this, parts of the altars have been removed.

This cave, which lies on the south side of the lagoon not far from the exit to the open sea, can be easily reached by a good swimmer, although at times it is only possible by diving.

In more recent times the Maya ruins lying inland near the MEX 307 have also been excavated and partially restored. It is worth visiting the three groups of remains – mercado, palacio and jaguar with their pyramids, palace and temple buildings – as well as a romantically situated cenote (underground water source).

Surroundings

Tancah

About 10km/6 miles to the south, inside a hacienda, are the Maya ruins of Tancah with a cenote. The temples which have been found resemble those at Tulum, although in part they appear to be of a significantly earlier date. It is thought that Tancah was a kind of satellite town to nearby Tulum (see entry) during the Late post-Classic period (from A.D. 1200).

Xochicalco K 8

State: Morelos (Mor.)
Altitude: 1525m/5003ft

Access

By bus from Cuernavaca (see entry) in the direction of Miacatlán, alighting at the turning off for Xochicalco and then 4km/2½ miles on foot; by car from Cuernavaca for 28km/17 miles southwards on the MEX 95 to the village of Alpuyeca, then take a right turning to "Grutas" and proceed for 8km/5 miles until the turning to Xochicalco (4km/2 miles).

Location

The fortress-like ruins of Xochicalco stretch for 130m/142yd across a wide mountain plateau, on which platforms have been created by deposits of soil and erosion. As almost nothing is known about the people who built this site, and the finds which have so far been made point to the influence of several advanced civilisations, the history of Xochicalco remains one of the great mysteries of archaeology of Meso-America.

History

Xochicalco (Náhuatl: "in the house of the flowers") was probably settled around 500 B.C. It is unlikely that the site attained any importance until the 7th and 8th c. when it developed into an important trading centre in the wake of the decline of Teotihuacán. Here, at the point of intersection of both northern and southern civilisations, there are influences of Teotihuacán as well as the culture groups of the Mayas, Zapotecs, Mixtecs and Toltecs. Later Xochicalco became an important centre of learning, in which apparently Ce Acatl Topiltzín is supposed to have received his education about the middle of the 10th c., before going on to become the legendary creator of the Toltecs' advanced civilisation in Tula and their god king, with the epithet Quetzalcóatl. Xochicalco is not thought to have been developed as a fortress until the 9th c. But as early as A.D. 900 the town started to forfeit its importance and only a short time later the end came, with the town either being conquered by other tribes or being abandoned for economic reasons. The population was absorbed by Toltecs, Tlahuicas and Aztecs in the course of time.

The first Spanish description of Xochicalco dates from the 16th c. and was written by Pater Bernardino de Sahagún. The first excavations were carried out by Pater José Antonio Alzate in 1777. At the beginning of the 19th c. Alexander von Humboldt spent some time here. In 1877 exploration and restoration work was carried out by A. Peñafiel and in 1910 by Leopoldo Batres. Since the 1960s the Instituto Nacional de Arqueología e Historia has been working in Xochicalco under the direction of the Mexican archaeologists Eduardo Noguera and César A. Sáenz.

Stylistic trends

In Xochicalco there is evidence of the influence of various Mexican civilisations:

Maya: ball court, reliefs of seated persons, beams and marks as numbers, steam bath.

Pyramid of the Feathered Serpents

Teotihuacán: modified talud-tablero style, glyphs, figurines, ceramics.
Zapotecs: beams and marks as numbers.
Toltecs: names of warriors and priests, ceramics.
Mixtecs: ceramics.

Visit to the ★ ruins

Site area

The total area of the former religious and military metropolis covers more than 12sq.km/5sq. miles, while the actual religious centre extends over about 1200m/1313yd from north to south and over about 700m/766yd from east to west. From the highest point there is a splendid view of mountains, plains and lakes.

Plaza Inferior

If beginning the visit at the entrance square (Plaza Inferior), the first thing the visitor will see are two restored pyramid buildings with stepped levels, referred to as Buildings C and D. Between them is the Altar of the Stela of the Glyphs (Adoratorio de la Estela de los Glifos), where a large stela with hieroglyphs, almost 3m/10ft high and 6 tons in weight, was excavated

Pyramid of the Stelae

Beyond the poorly preserved Building A stands the Pyramid of the Stelae (Pirámide de las Estelas), on the highest level area of the site, with a 15m/49ft wide stairway leading up to its temple. Three 1·80m/6ft high stelae with reliefs of Tláloc, the sun god, and his wife, the moon goddess, were found here. These sculptures, dating back to A.D. 600 and 700, probably represent an agricultural cycle expressing the wish for an abundant harvest. The symbolism calls to mind El Tajín, but also the central area of the Mayas. The three stelae are on display in the Anthropological Museum in Mexico City.

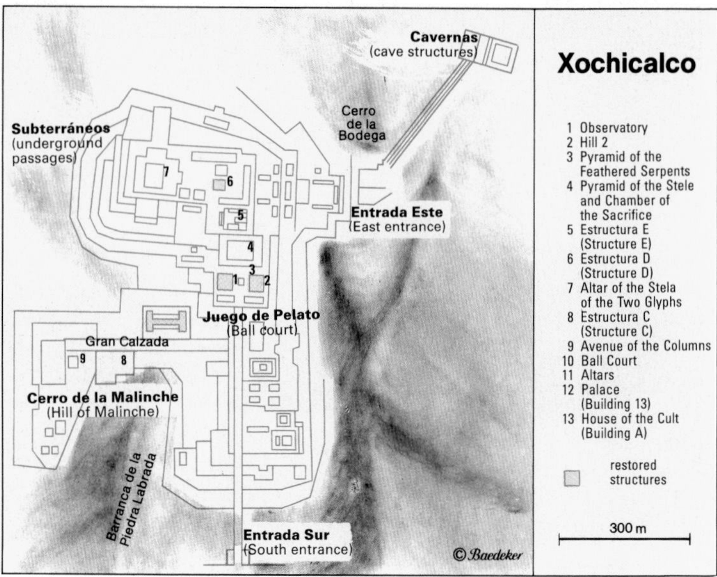

Sacrifice chamber

To the right, at the foot of the steps, there was once the shrine of the sacrifice chamber (Cámara de las Ofrendas), in which sacrificial offerings such as stone figurines, a jade head, obsidian arrowheads and human bones have been found.

★ Pyramid of the Feathered Serpents

A little further to the north is the most important building in Xochicalco, the Pyramid of the Feathered Serpents (Pirámide de las Serpientes Emplumadas), which has also been called the Uncovered Monument (Monumento Descubierto). It is thought that this building (base 21×18·60m/69×61ft) may have been erected to commemorate an important gathering of priest-astronomers.

Lower section

The building consists of two levels, of which only the lower section has been preserved in its entirety. It is built in the talud-tablero style, although here, in contrast to the building methods customarily employed in Teotihuacán, the sloping wall predominates. On this wall superb bas-reliefs can be seen, depicting eight feathered serpents encircling glyphs and seated human figures. They were once coloured white, red, black, blue and yellow, but were finally painted over completely in red, the colour of death, probably as a sign of imminent destruction. The glyphs on either side of the steps (three symbols of day) possibly indicate an amendment to the sacred calendar. On the sides of the steep face of the building it is possible to distinguish illustrations in relief of seated figures, stylised serpents and calendar glyphs now in poor condition. Above the ledge which juts out over the steep wall of the first storey there is a frieze made up of patterns of stylised shells, which have been connected with the god Quetzalcóatl.

Upper section

The sloping wall, which is partially covered with poorly preserved reliefs, is the only remaining part of the upper section of the building.

Relief of serpents

The outer wall encloses an almost square temple hall (11×10·50m/36×33ft), which is thought by some researchers, although this theory is disputed, to have been open to the elements, hence the building's name of "Monumento Descubierto". On the right-angled walls on either side of the entrance it is possible to make out the delineation of a coyote and symbols for fire.

Subterranean passages and chambers and observatory

Proceeding westwards from the Pyramid of the Feathered Serpents to Hill A and from there down the northern slope, the visitor will come to the underground passages and chambers (Subterráneos) to the left of the entrance. From a large hall a wide flight of steps leads across three ledges to a passageway. Another path leading from the entrance hall ends in a higher room (19m/62ft long, 12m/39ft wide and 3·50m/115ft high), in which there are three square columns (4×2m/13×7ft). In the corner there is an air shaft which was probably used for astronomical observations. At the time of the solstice on June 21st the sun shines down the shaft and illuminates the chamber. In this area there are still a number of known and unknown underground passages which are gradually being opened up. The Subterráneos are from time to time closed to visitors.

Ball court

The ball court (juego de pelota), the only one of several in Xochicalco to have been restored, is roughly in the middle of the cultural centre of the site. From east to west it measures 69m/226ft and is bounded at the sides and ends by sloping walls. The stone rings which served as marker posts for the ritual game of "tlachtli" were set into the side walls. In its layout and equipment the court shows similarities with those in the Maya area, but also with the one at Tula.

Other buildings

From the ball court a 20m/66ft wide road (Gran Calzada) leads westwards to a series of buildings, while parallel to the Gran Calzada there is a row of low circular platforms, which were possibly altars. The first building in the series is Building B (Edificio B), also called a palace, with priests' dwelling-rooms, steam bath and patios; the next one is Building A (Edificio A), a religious building, and finally the Cerro de la Malinche, a raised-up area of ground with a terrace in the form of a flattened pyramid, from which there is a fine view.

Surroundings

Cuahtetelco

About 20km/12 miles to the south-west (4km/2 miles from Mazatepec) lies the township of Coatetelco (Náhuatl: "hill of the snakes") on the lake of the same name. In a small archaeological zone the visitor will find the partially excavated site of Cuahtetelco with an archaeological museum in which stone sculptures, ceramics and other artistic relics of the various civilisations (Teotihuacán, Tlahuicas and Aztecs, etc.) can be seen.

Xochimilco

See Mexico City

Yagul L 9

State: Oaxaca (Oax.)
Altitude: 1650m/5413ft

Access

By bus from Oaxaca (town) in the direction of Mitla (see entry), alighting at the turning for Yagul and then proceeding on foot for 2km/1 mile; by car from Oaxaca on the MEX 190 in the direction of Tehuantepec, after 34km/21 miles turning off left to the excavation site 2km/1 mile away.

Location

Yagul, once an important secular and religious centre of the Zapotecs and Mixtecs, lies on the slope of a hill in the north-east of Tlacolula in the middle of countryside covered with high-growing cacti. The temples and palaces, which are built on three levels, are dominated by a fortress situated on the summit, from which there is a view across the valley of Oaxaca.

History

Yagul (Zapotec: "old village") was already settled in the pre-Classic period in the phases of Monte Albán I and II (600 B.C.–A.D. 100). More than 30 graves, often arranged in pairs, have been discovered. This building activity reached its peak between A.D. 800 and 1200 (phase of Monte Albán IV), when, with the surrender of Monte Albán, the fall of the Zapotec empire began. At the same time the influence of the Mixtecs increased, and it is thought that Mitla, some 15km/9 miles away, underwent a similar development. In spite of this it is still not really known for certain who actually built the pre-Columbian sites around Yagul.

At the end of the 1950s the site was rediscovered and excavated and restored by the University of the Americas and the Instituto Nacional de Arqueología e Historia under the direction of Ignacio Bernal. Part of the site has still not been excavated.

Visit to the ★ ruins

Patio of the Triple Tomb

The lower, mainly excavated part of the site is the Patio of the Triple Tomb (Patio de la Triple Tumba), which comprises four temples and in

Panorama of the ruins of Yagul

the middle a sacrificial square. On the left-hand side of the square there is the sculpture of a seated toad which symbolises the rain god.

From a platform in the middle of the patio it is possible to go down through the left opening into a tomb which consists of three chambers. These have elaborate façades with human heads made of stone and contained the skeletons of dignitaries and rich burial offerings. Both sides of the memorial slab are decorated with finely-worked hieroglyphs.

★ Ball court

In the second row of buildings stands the ball court (juego de pelota), one of the largest and architecturally most perfect examples among those so far found in Meso-America. In common with all the other ball courts in Oaxaca, it lacks the heavy stone rings on the side walls which were normal elsewhere. In contrast to Monte Albán, however, there are no niches or marker stone here.

Patio I

The large Patio I, surrounded by low terraces, adjoins to the west. The courtyard, which measures 30×36m/98×118ft and contains several tombs with decorated façades, is bounded on the north by the Council Hall (Sala del Consejo).

Palace of the Six Patios

The last row of buildings is known as the Palace of the Six Patios (Palacio de los Seis Patios); here Zapotec buildings were also built over by the Mixtecs. In this sprawling labyrinth, which possibly served as living quarters for the elite, the rooms have between one and three entrances, leading to the patios. In a long narrow passageway, stone mosaic patterns in the style characteristic of Mitla can be seen.

Fortress

The ascent to the fortress, which is surrounded by a massive defensive wall, is rather difficult, but worth the effort because of the unusual

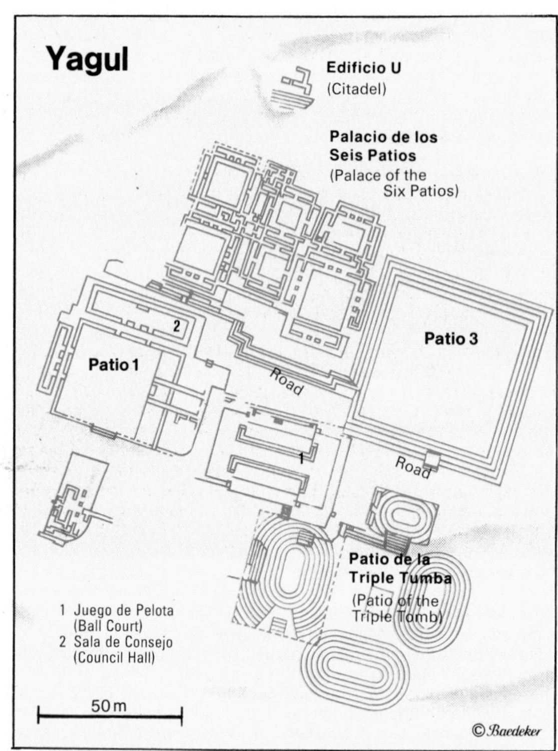

architectural style and the superb view. Tombs which have been found here date back to the epoch of Monte Albán I (600–200 B.C.).

Surroundings

Caballito Blanco

Just before the turning for Yagul a track leads off to the right to the historically interesting Caballito Blanco. Here the remains of white drawings of stylised human figures can be seen on a stone wall. A stepped path leads up to the sparse remains of a building which resembles Building J of Monte Albán. Dating carried out here has produced the year 240 B.C., towards the end of the Monte Albán II phase.

Yanhuitlán

See Oaxaca (state)

Yaxchilán O 9

State: Chiapas (Chis.). Altitude: 320m/1050ft

Access

By light plane from Tuxtla Gutiérrez (see entry), San Cristóbal de las Casas (see entry), Palenque (see entry) or Tenosique; also by light plane to Agua Azul on the Río Usumacinta and from there by boat along the river to Yaxchilán. Alternatively it is possible to drive – preferably in a cross-country vehicle – from Palenque (see entry) to the border town of Frontera Echeverria, and then continue by boat from there 20km/13½ miles upriver to Yaxchilán.

Location

The great Maya site of Yaxchilán in the east of the state of Chiapas is almost completely surrounded by a loop in the Río Usumacinta, which forms the border with Guatemala and is here 200m/219yd wide. The excavation site is barely visible from the river because it is for the most part covered by the thick vegetation of the rain forest. The town, which extends along the river for a distance of almost 1·5km/1 mile and also inland across a number of high terraced hills, is among the most fascinating archaeological sites in Mexico.

History

During the Maya Classic period (A.D. 300–900), Yachilán was, together with Palenque (Chiapas), Piedras Negras 60km/37 miles downstream, Tikal and Quirigua (all in Guatemala) and Copán (Honduras), one of the great religious and political centres of the central lowland area of the Maya empire. At the time of its greatest flowering in the 8th c., Yaxchilán seems, as far as can be gathered from glyphs which have been deciphered, to have ruled a number of other places in the surrounding area, e.g. Bonampak. Recently it has been possible to decipher glyphs which outline the chronicle of a dynasty, the legendary founder of which, "Jaguar penis" (Yat Balam), is thought to have ruled in A.D. 320. Some 130 monuments have been dated between A.D. 514 (stela 27) and A.D. 808 (lintel 10), three quarters of which fall within the reigns of "Shield Jaguar" (A.D. 647–742, from 681 regent) and "Bird Jaguar" (A.D. 709–786, from 752 regent), who apparently exerted a far-reaching influence in the region. In common with all other sites in the Maya

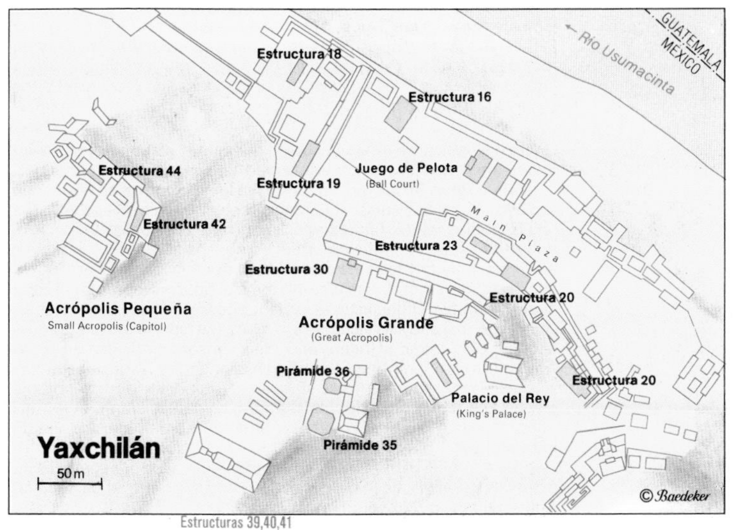

central region, Yaxchilán was abandoned, for reasons unknown, in the 9th c. A.D. Until a few years ago nomadic Lacandon Indians still celebrated their ancient rites in the ruins of the temple palaces here.

Edwin Rockstroh was the first person to reach Yaxchilán from Guatemala in 1881; however, it was left to the Englishman Alfred P. Maudslay to discover the site for science one year later. He named the place Menché (Maya: "green tree"). With the approval of the Guatemalan government, which at that time was considered responsible for this area, Maudslay had seven door-lintels removed and these are now on display in the British Museum in London. Soon afterwards the Frenchman Désiré Charnay arrived, but it was the Austrian Teobert Maler, who worked here between 1897 and 1900, who gave the site its present name of Yaxchilán (Maya: "place of the green stones") which he took from the nearby river of the same name. At the beginning of the 20th c. the American archaeologists A. M. Tozzer, S. G. Morley and H. Spinden carried out scientific work here, while in the last few years valuable restoration work has been undertaken by the Mexican I.N.A.H. under the direction of Roberto García Moll.

Visit to the ★ ruins

Before visiting the site it is essential to consult the local tourist offices in order to ascertain conditions at the site and its accessibility. It is advisable to engage the services of a knowledgeable guide on the spot and to take appropriate equipment.

Overview

Only a very small proportion of the buildings, which are scattered along the Río Usumacinta and on the surrounding hills, have been excavated and restored. Most are still overgrown or, having been cleared, are now the property of the jungle again, so that access is very difficult. The groups of buildings are set out stepwise in four rows which stretch out from the river bank over the hilly ground to the west. The buildings display no particular architectural features; there are fewer pyramid temples than palaces, most of which have three entrances and two parallel passages. The upper parts of the façades and the protruding roof-crests (cresterías) were once decorated with stucco and stone figures. As with the large Maya site of Palenque the roofs exhibit the so-called "mansard effect", with the roof combs rising in the middle.

★ Reliefs

Of great significance in Yaxchilán are the unique elaborate yet powerfully crafted reliefs which were carved into the stelae, altars, door-lintels and steps. So far, inscriptions have been found on no fewer than 125 of these stone panels. Their dates range from A.D. 454 to 807. The reliefs often show two figures, which apparently symbolise a change of power. The greater, more important personage has his face in profile, while his body and legs are represented frontally and his feet turned outwards. The second, considerably smaller figure is represented completely in profile. Other pictures in stone show prisoners, battle scenes, consecrational and sacrificial rites. Among the latter there is a preponderance of pictures of rulers and their consorts with barbed cords cutting through their tongues and genitalia. In the last few years the scientist T. Proskouriakoff has succeeded in partially deciphering the glyphs and thereby confirming the long-held suspicion that, in this unique way, historical events and personalities are being immortalised.

Quite a number of the stelae and altars are damaged or, together with many of the reliefs, have been transferred to the National Museum of Anthropology in Mexico City or abroad.

First row of buildings

The first row of buildings by the river bank include Building (Estructura) 18 with a stela, Building 16 with two door-lintels, the ball court with five sculptures and Building 5 with a hieroglyph staircase.

Stela 11

Stela 11, which stands on the main square, was to have been taken to Mexico City in 1966, but proved too heavy for the available means of transport and so remained in Yaxchilán. This stone sculpture dates from between A.D. 743 and 755 and on the front-facing side shows the ruler "Bird Jaguar" ascending the throne, with a holy banner being exchanged between him (on the right) and his predecessor "Shield Jaguar". On the rear side of the stela "Bird Jaguar" can be seen standing over prisoners in chains. This picture underlines the fact that success at waging war was the foundation of the dynasty.

Second row of buildings

To the south of the main square lies the second row of buildings, of which Building 19 or the "Labyrinth" with its two altars is the most remarkable. The building has several entrances, with rooms on two levels linked to one another, and the remains of a roof-comb (crestería). Building 22 is also known as the Temple of the Inscriptions and has an unusual door-lintel and two altars. Building 20 or the Temple of the Bird Sacrifices possesses three entrances, but only one of these is intact. It is crowned by an elaborate lintel which depicts three elevated persons in rich apparel.

Great Acropolis

On a solitary hill stands a group of buildings, accessible by steps, which is known as the Great Acropolis (La Acrópolis Grande).

★Palace of the King

Its most significant building is Building 33 or the Palace of the King (Edificio 33, Palacio del Rey), which probably dates from A.D. 757. This imposing building measures about 22×5m/72×16ft with a height of

Palacio del Rey (Building 23)

7m/23ft, with the roof comb protruding another 6m/20ft. The hieroglyph staircase discovered in 1974 has thirteen panels which show "Bird Jaguar" ascending the throne in A.D. 752. Eleven of the panels have scenes of ball-games, in which the ruler is beating people whose broken bodies are transformed into balls. Possibly a ball-game is being described here, which may have taken place in A.D. 744 between "Bird Jaguar" and his important prisoner "Jewel Head". The three entrances are decorated with door-beams which show scenes from the life of the ruler; there are also niches above them in which stone figures once sat. The frieze also shows remains of earlier embellishments. The double roof comb, which is especially beautiful, contains rectangular concavities which form eight horizontal rows. In the middle there once sat the 2·50m/8ft high statue of a ruler with a magnificent head-dress. In front of the building stands the torso of a figure which was discovered inside the building, which has been called the "King" (Rey); the head of this statue lies a little to one side. Until a few years ago the Lacandon-Maya Indians worshipped their god Hachakyum, who they believed dwelt in this figure.

Fourth row of buildings

Further upwards the fourth row of buildings is reached (Buildings 39 to 41). This elevated site was once linked by a large flight of steps to a platform lying 100m/110yd further down.

Small Acropolis

To the north-west of the Palace of the King is the group of buildings known as the Small Acropolis (Acrópolis Pequeña), which is made up of Buildings 49 to 52.

Yucatán (State)

Abbreviation: Yuc.
Capital: Mérida
Area: 38,508sq.km/14,868sq. miles
Official population 1990: 1,363,000 (1994 estimate: 1,450,000)

Location and topography

The state of Yucatán is only a part of the larger peninsula with the same name, which also includes the Mexican states of Campeche and Quintana Roo, as well as the northern part of Guatemala (Petén) and Belize (formerly British Honduras). The Yucatán Peninsula is bounded on the west and north by the Gulf of Mexico and on the east by the Caribbean Sea. The coastline in the west and north consists of sandbanks, lagoons and mangrove swamps, while along the eastern side it is characterised by coral-reefs and islands (Cozumel, Islas Mujeres). Yucatán is essentially an enormous flat chalkland tilted gently to the south, which has a typical karst landscape with savannah and scrubland. The rainfall, which increases the further south one goes, quickly seeps through the thin layer of earth and the chalk, thereby forming underground rivers and lakes. When the roofs of these caves collapse, circular spring-like water-holes of varying size are formed, called "cenotes" (from the Maya word "dzonot"). Before the Spanish conquest the Mayas built their cult centres around these cenotes, which even today are important for the supply of water.

Flora and fauna

Jaguars and ocelots can still be found in the thick scrubland of Yucatán, although in the course of time they have retreated more and more into inaccessible areas. The alligator was also hunted mercilessly and now hardly exists here any more. On the other hand there are roedeer, wild boars, pheasants, wild ducks, wild turkeys and monkeys. Iguanas are still to be found, as well as the boa constrictor and other snakes. A large number of tropical birds, including parrots, toucans, flamingos and humming-birds, are native to the peninsula.

The abundant stocks of palm-trees on the peninsula have been severely affected by a disease which also appeared in previous centuries. An attempt is being made to re-establish a belt of palms along the beaches by planting a resistant strain of south-east Asian trees.

Economy

One of the main branches of the economy is the cultivation and processing of sisal-hemp (henequén), which is obtained from agaves, although its importance has undergone a sharp decline with the development of artificial fibres. Timber production and fishing also play a significant role. Until the 20th c. Yucatán looked more to Europe and had few links with the centre of Mexico, road and rail connections with the rest of the country having only been established since the 1950s. The most important seaport is Progreso on the Gulf of Mexico, which deals with a large part of the trade of the state. In the last few years the number of tourists coming to the archaeological sites of the Mayas and to the beaches has increased considerably.

History

With its large number of finds from the Classic period (A.D. 300–900) of the Maya civilisation Yucatán plays a key role in the field of archaeology.

In more recent history the period between 1512 and 1519 marks the first contacts between the Spanish conquerors and the original inhabitants of Yucatán. At this time the classic Maya sites had already with few exceptions been abandoned. It was only after 20 years of hard struggle that the conquistadores were able, under the leadership of the two Montejos, to establish Spanish rule over almost half the peninsula. In the colonial period Yucatán remained quite an unimportant part of the viceroyship on account of its isolated position. Rebellious Maya tribes tried again and again to win back parts of the country. In the second half of the 19th c., in particular, this resulted in bitter struggles which at times led to independence from the Mexican central state ("Caste

War"). It was only at the beginning of the 20th c. that the Mexican state succeeded in achieving full sovereignty over Yucatán. Many of the vanquished Indians retreated into the wilds of Quintana Roo. Apart from a number of Spaniards, mainly in and around Mérida, the population of the state of Yucatán consists mainly of Maya Indians and mestizos. In some areas the Maya language is spoken exclusively.

Mayas

Scarcely any other area of Mexico can boast as many archaeological sites as Yucatán. The post-Classic period of the Mayas (A.D. 900–1450) was sustained by the activities of Maya tribes, both those who had always lived there and those who had migrated there from elsewhere, as well as Toltecs who had come there from their homes in the Mexican highlands. It led to magnificent architecture, in which early Maya elements became mixed with the style of the Toltecs. Nevertheless, the art of ceramics and stone sculpture no longer reached the high quality of the Early and Late Classic Periods (A.D. 300–900), which were primarily associated with south Campeche, Chiapas, Guatemala, Belize and Honduras.

Calendar

The "Long Count" is the historic calendar of the Mayas, which counts every day from when they began to record time, and which uses as its base day our date August 13th 3114 B.C. This began to be used only in an abbreviated form in the post-Classic period, whereas the original Maya calendar is considered one of the most detailed and exact of its time. The Mayas were also the first people to use the number zero, which enabled them to calculate dates which involved very long periods of time. The oldest definite Maya calendar date so far found is A.D. 292 on Stela 29 in Tikal, Guatemala (the origin of the "Hauberg Stela" with the date A.D. 199 is unsure).

Hieroglyphic script

The Mayas possess the only hieroglyphic script which was fully developed both from a logographic and phonetic aspect. The 800 or so glyphs so far identified can stand for both a syllable and a word. Today we are able to read and pronounce 25 to 35% of the glyphs, with at least an idea of the meaning of the remainder. The breakthrough in deciphering it occurred in 1958 when a German living in Mexico, Heinrich Berlin, found what became known as the "weapon glyphs". He discovered that certain signs always only appeared in particular places. This enabled the glyphs of the eight classical Maya towns of Palenque, Yaxchilán (Mexico), Tikal, Piedras Negras, Quiriguá, Seibal, Naranjo (Guatemala) and Copán (Honduras) to be deciphered. From this Berlin was able to deduce that the writings on the stelae and other monuments were in fact the history of those places. Tatjana Proskouriakoff from the Carnegie Institute was then able to establish that the datings on special groups of stelae recorded the dates of a ruler's reign and the dates of his birth and marriage. At the same time it also became possible to find out from the glyphs the names of particular rulers and members of their families. In the 1950s and 1960s Jurij Knorosow did some important work, and in the 1970s Linda Schele, Peter Mathews and Floyd Lounsbury of the University of Texas documented the genealogy of the ruling dynasty of Palenque until practically the end of these sites around 800. In the 1980s the German Berthold Riese and the Frenchman Claude F. Baudez made significant further achievements in deciphering (see Baedeker special, pages 84/85).

Similar to the Maya "books" are the codices made from plaster-lined paper manufactured from bark and folded in a special way. Those which were not destroyed by the Spaniards or disappeared were for the most part sent to Europe as a gift to Charles V and are today to be found in Dresden, Madrid and Paris. The "Grolier Codex", first brought to light in 1917 and the validity of which was initially questioned, is at present in Mexico City.

Places to visit

Maya sites

The most important Maya sites in Yucatán include Chichén Itzá, Yaxuna (see Cobá), Izamal, Dzibilchaltún, Uxmal, Kabah, Sayil, Labná (see entries), Chacmultún (see Surroundings of Labná), Xlapak (see Surroundings of Sayil) and Mayapán (see Surroundings of Mérida). The other important sites on the peninsula are to be found in the states of Campeche and Quintana Roo. Almost all the Maya sites have been adversely affected by acid rain to an increasing extent over the last few years.

Ruta Maya

The Ruta Maya, created in the late 1980s, comprises the archaeological zones and colonial towns of Mexico, Guatemala, Belize and El Salvador. The programme includes the modernisation of roads, restoration of the sites and creation of additionnal accommodation for visitors. The region extends eastwards from the Isthmus of Tehuanntepec via the whole of the Yucatán Penninsula to Belize and El Salvador.

Colonial art

As in Mérida (see entry), Izamál, Valladolid (see Surroundings of Chichén Itzá), Motul and Tikul (town, see Campeche), there are examples of colonial art in almost all the towns in Yucatán, especially in the Franciscan churches and convents built in the 16th and 17th c. These are generally still situated in unspoilt scenery and are worth visiting for their atmosphere alone. These places to the south-east and south-west of Mérida include:

Kanasín

Iglesia de San José; also well-known for its special Yucatán dishes;

Acanceh

Iglesia de Nuestra Señora de la Natividad on the main square next to a Maya pyramid;

Tecoh

Iglesia y Convento de La Asunción; situated in a sisal-hemp growing area; numerous cenotes nearby;

Tekit

Iglesia de San Antonio de Padua;

Mama

Iglesia y Convento La Asunción with fine espadaña (belfry) and old well-wheel in the monastery;

Chumayel

Iglesia de la Purísima Concepción with a black Christ over the altar; the place is well-known because of the discovery of one of the "Books of Chilam Balam", the great Maya chronicle;

Teabo

Iglesia San Pedro y San Pablo;

Tipical

Iglesia de La Magdalena on a hill;

Maní

Iglesia y Convento de San Miguel (see Surroundings of Labná);

Oxkutzcab

Iglesia y Convento San Francisco de Asís; citrus-fruit plantations; nearby system of caves similar to those at Kukikán and Lol-tún (see Surroundings of Labná);

Tikul

Iglesia de San Antonio; reproductions of Maya sculptures and ceramics;

Muná

Iglesia y Convento de La Asunción; in a tobacco-growing area; cenotes nearby;

Uman

Iglesia y Convento de San Francisco de Asís; in a sisal-growing area.

Yuriria

See Celaya

Zacatecas (State)

Abbreviation: Zac.
Capital: Zacatecas
Area: 73,454sq.km/28,361sq. miles
Official population 1990: 1,276,300 (1994 estimate: 1,350,000)

Location and topography

The high-lying state of Zacatecas, because of its very low rainfall, has only a few rivers with constantly flowing water. It is bounded on the north by Coahuila, on the west by Durango, to the south by Jalisco and Aguascalientes and in the east by San Luis Potosí. The landscape of the state is characterised by rugged mountain ranges and sandy plateaux and the area is well-known for its rich mineral deposits. Zacatecas is inhabited predominantly by criollos (descendants of the Spanish) and mestizos, while in the area around Colotlán there are Huichol Indians. In addition there are two firmly established colonies of Mennonites who migrated from Canada in 1923, La Batea and La Honda.

Archaeological sites

Besides such well-known archaeological sites as La Quemada (Chicomóztoc) and Chalchihuites there are also a number of smaller places of which Teul de González Ortega and Estación Canutillo deserve mention.

History

Zacatecas (Náhuatl: "country where zacate grass grows") was inhabited in pre-Hispanic times by various Indian tribes including the Cax-

canes, Tecuexes, Hachichiles, Huicholes, Coras and Tepehuano, of whom all except the last three have disappeared. What is certain is that in the post-Classic period the area came under the cultural domination of Chalchihuites, which in turn was presumably influenced by the Toltecs. The Aztecs, who were later to rule in central Mexico, came southwards from the north-west and therefore probably never reached this region.

The Spanish, led by Pedro Almíndez Chirinos, who arrived after the Conquista in search of precious metals, soon found themselves locked in conflict with the Indians. With the help of tribes who were later pacified, the first rich silver mines were discovered around the present state capital. The exploitation of the mines brought prosperity to the state and this expressed itself in the construction and lavish fitting-out of both sacred and secular buildings. During the Reform War (1858–61) and the Revolutionary War (1910–20) the whole of the state, and above all certain of its towns, were the scene of bloody fighting.

Economy

Zacatecas is one of the richest states in Mexico for minerals; the most significant deposits are those of gold, silver, copper, zinc, mercury and lead. Industry in the state is limited to the smelting of ores and the processing of sugar-cane, agaves, wool and cotton. Compared with cattle-rearing, which is of considerable importance, agriculture plays a lesser role, cereals, sugar-cane and maguey-agaves being the main crops. Tourism is steadily growing.

Places to visit

As well as the state capital, Zacatecas (see entry), and nearby places such as La Quemada (Chicomóztoc), Jérez García de Salinas and Fresnillo, the following places deserve mention:

Sombrerete

This picturesque little town (2351m/7713ft; population 34,000; fiesta: February 2nd–10th, La Candelaria = Candlemas) is in the west of the state on the border with Durango. The churches of San Francisco (16th c.), Santo Domingo (18th c.; Churrigueresque façade) and San Juan Bautista (18th c.) are worth seeing.

Chalchihuites

51km/32 miles south-west of Sombrerete is the little township of Chalchihuites (Náhuatl: "chalchihuitl = "green stone") and from there it is another 7km/4 miles to the extensive archaeological site of Chalchihuites, which is also known by the name Alta Vista. Very little is known about the people who built the site, which stretches across the haciendas of Alta Vista, El Vergel and El Chapín. It was already settled at the time of Christ, although the heyday of the site would probably have been between the 5th and 7th c. It was not until the 11th c. that the town declined in importance and it is thought that it was abandoned about 1400. The location of the site, directly on the Tropic of Cancer, appears to have been due to astronomical calculations. It attained far-reaching importance both as a cult centre and as a trading-place in a mining region where dealings were conducted in flint, jade and turquoise.

Visit to the ruins

This level site has an unwalled pathway which, from its position and construction, must have been used as an observatory. Next to it there is a curving snake-like wall with appropriate markings, the Hall of Columns (Salón de las Columnas) with 28 pillars and priest-alcoves with sacrificial and fire altars. Symbols of crosses carved into the rocks of Cerro El Chapín were, like almost all the buildings, created according to astronomical rules.

Zacatecas: archaeological zone of Chalchihuites

Zacatecas (Town) H 6

State: Zacatecas (Zac.)
Altitude: 2496m/8189ft
Population: 220,000
Telephonne code: 91 492

Access from Mexico City

By air about 1 hour; by rail about 17 hours; by bus about 8 hours; by car 613km/381 miles on the MEX 75D and MEX 45 via León (see entry), Querétaro (see entry) and Aguascalientes (see entry).

Location

The attractive colonial town of Zacatecas, capital of the state of the same name, is situated in a narrow gorge, dominated by the hills of La Bufa, Mala Noche and El Padre and surrounded by a plateau with mountainous outcrops. For centuries the town was an important centre for silver mining. Today Zacatecas is one of the most beautiful colonial towns in the country with its attractive old buildings and cobbled streets.

History

The region around Zacatecas (Náhuatl: "land where zacate grass grows") was inhabited by various Indian tribes in pre-Hispanic times. Very little is known about them although they may well have at times come under the influence of the culture centres of Chalchihuites and La Quemada (Chicomóztoc).

A group of Conquistadores led by Juan de Tolosa, who were searching for silver, founded the town in 1546. The settlement quickly became rich through silver mining and in 1585 received its charter from Philip II. During the Revolutionary War there was a bitter struggle here between troops of the dictator Victoriano Huerta and Francisco ("Pancho") Villa, in which the latter was the victor. In 1993 UNESCO declared this historical town a world cultural heritage centre.

Sights

Cathedral

The magnificent cathedral, which stands on the Plaza Hidalgo, is for many people the most perfect example of the Mexican Churrigueresque style. The building was begun in 1612 on the site of an earlier church, but the form it has today is primarily the result of additions dating from the period 1730–60.

★★ Façade

The façade, with its exceptionally elaborate decorative work which is typical of the richness of form of Spanish-Mexican Baroque, has illustrations of Christ with the twelve apostles, four Church Fathers around the chancel window, and in the uppermost section God the Father surrounded by eight angels making music. These images are fashioned with a mixture of Romanesque elements and motives derived from the Indian philosophy of life. The dome was rebuilt in 1836.

The austere interior, mainly decorated in the Neo-Classical style, is disappointing; the exceptionally rich fittings (gold and silver objects, European paintings, etc.) which were once there disappeared during the Reform War and the turmoil of the Revolution.

Palacio de Gobierno

The government palace (Palacio de Gobierno), which is also situated in the Plaza Hidalgo, dates from the 18th c. and has attractive wrought-iron balconies.

Santo Domingo

Across the Callejón de Veyna, which begins at the government palace, we come to the church of Santo Domingo, a sober Baroque building dating from the middle of the 18th c. The façade is in the form of a "Spanish wall". Inside along the sides there are beautifully carved Churrigueresque retablos and a Neo-Classical main altar. The 18th c. paintings in the sacristy are noteworthy.

The church is adjoined by the old Jesuit college with a lovely cloister.

Panorama of Zacatecas

Zacatecas: the façade of the Cathedral

San Agustín

This, once the most magnificent religious building in Zacatecas, still captivates – although for the most part in ruins – by its Plateresque side door which has decorations depicting the conversion of Saint Augustine which must rank among the most beautiful in the country.

Cerro de la Bufa

A symbol of the city is the Cerro de la Bufa (2700m/8858ft), situated 4km/2 miles from the city centre. The Capilla de los Remedios or Virgen del Patrocinio Señora de los Zacatecos, which was built at the end of the 18th c., is situated on top of the mountain. There is a beautiful view of the city from here and it is also the starting-point of the cable-car which goes up to the Cerro El Grillo (650m/½ mile away).

El Edén

To the north-west of the city centre (C. Antonio Doval), a visit to the El Edén mine, which can include a trip on the mine railway, gives a good insight into the harsh and often inhuman work of the silver mines.

Museo Goitia

It is well worth visiting the Museo Francisco Goitia which is housed in the former Casa del Pueblo, a Neo-Classical building not far from the aqueduct. There are works on display by contemporary Mexican painters including the important expressionist painter Francisco Goitia (1884–1960), who was born in Fresnillo and chronicled the Revolutionary War in his paintings.

Coronel Museum

The Museo Rafael Coronel is housed in the former San Francisco convent. Its exhibits include 4000 masks, mainly pre-Spanish, from all over Mexico, drawings by Coronel and a puppet collection. Displayed in the Colegio de San Luis Gonzaga on the Plaza de Santa Domingo are works by Rafael's elder brother, Pedro Coronel, as well as pre-Columbian, European, African and Asian art.

Other sights

Other sights include the strange metal construction of the Jesús Gonzáles Ortega market from the end of the 19th c., the church and convent of San Francisco with its Gothic cloister (16th/17th c.), the Teatro Calderón (end of the 19th c.), the folk museum of the Huichol Indians (Museo Arte Huichol) and the aqueduct (18th/19th c.) at the southern end of the city.

Events and festivals

An international week of culture is held during Easter week. On September 8th, the annniversary of the founding of Zacatecas, a two-week fair, begins together with bull and cock-fights, sports meetings and concerts.

Surroundings

Casco de la Hacienda Bernardez

At the km 2·5 marker on the MEX 45 road stands the mansion owned by Don Ignacio de Bernardez, where visitors can now see silversmiths at work and purchase their products.

★Nuestra Señora de Guadalupe

The little town of Guadalupe, famous for its convent, is situated about 7km/4 miles to the east on the MEX 45. The convent of Nuestra Señora de Guadalupe was founded by the Franciscans in 1707 and has today been converted into an extensive museum (Museo Regional de Guadalupe). It contains a library (not open to the public) and a collection of valuable paintings from the colonial period, which can be visited. This collection includes works by the painters Cristóbal de Villalpando, Rodríguez Juárez, Miguel Cabrera, Antonio Torres and Antonio Oliva.

The convent church was consecrated in 1721 and has an interesting Baroque façade. On either side of the entrance gate can be seen a pair of columns flanking niches containing statues. In common with the columns in the upper part, they are decorated in three sections with figures, spirals and interlacing. Above the door there is an alto-rilievo composed of the Virgin of Guadalupe being painted by the apostle Luke. The upper part of the façade is in the style of local Mexican masters and recalls the design of the cathedral at Zacatecas. The total effect of the façade is seriously weakened by the left-hand tower which was added in the late 19th c.

The beautiful Neo-Classical Capilla de la Purísima (Capilla de Nápoles; 19th c.) inside the church is richly decorated with gold leaf and has some old paintings. The parquet flooring is unique: it is made of mesquite wood into which an elaborately worked and imaginative combination of anenomes, zodiac signs and scriptures is inlaid.

Jerez de García Salinas

From Zacatecas on the MEX 45, with a turning off right after 23km/14 miles, it is 56km/35 miles in all to the town of Jerez de García Salinas (2190m/7185ft; population 42,000; fiestas: January 23rd, Día de San Ildefonso; Easter Saturday; September 8th, Día de la Virgen de la Soledad); this town has an Andalusian atmosphere.

Fresnillo

About 60km/37 miles north-west of Zacatecas on the MEX 45 is the old silver town of Fresnillo (2250m/7382ft; population 140,000; fiestas: August 23rd, foundation day; in Plateros (7km/4 miles away) June 15th, Día del Santo Niño). There are thermal baths nearby.

La Quemada

The pre-Columbian archaeological site of La Quemada or Chicomóztoc (Náhuatl: "seven caves") is situated about 53km/33 miles south of Zacatecas on the MEX 54. This cult centre, which stretches across a large hill, probably had its beginnings as long ago as the Early Classic period. It is highly doubtful, however, whether it is identical with the legendary place of Chicomóztoc from which, according to the saga, the seven Nahua tribes are supposed to have set off on their migration to the south. What is certain is that La Quemada, together with Chalchihuites (see Zacatecas (State)) and other places in Zacatecas and

Durango, lies in an area which represented the northern boundary of Meso-American civilisation.

History

This fortress-like site, probably the most important in the northern area, had its heyday in the Early post-Classic period in the 10th and 11th c. and must have gone into a serious decline at the beginning of the 13th c. A legend of the Huichol Indians mentions the destruction of a town in this region after it had tried to seize Peyotl trade for itself.

As early as 1650 the site was described by Pater Antonio Tello, who named it Tuitlán. The earliest scientific description dates from 1826 and is by G. F. Lyon. In 1903 excavations were begun under the direction of Leopoldo Batres and continued in the fifties and sixties by José Corona Nuñez and Pedro Armillas.

Description of the site

In spite of the clear Meso-American influence demonstrated by its stepped pyramid, ball court, circular columns and embankments, the site can in no way be compared with the architecture of the archaeological sites situated further to the south. The buildings, which are scattered across a mountain ridge, are constructed mainly of small stone slabs and adobe bricks.

King's Palace

The first buildings on the left-hand side form a complex known as the King's Palace or the Cathedral (Palacio del Rey; Catedral). An extensive terrace has been preserved, surrounded by walls and measuring 67×64m/220×210ft.

Hall of columns

On the east side there is an entrance to the 40×31m/131×102ft large Hall of Columns (Salón de las Columnas). The eleven stone pillars are up to 5m/16ft high but it is not known whether they also supported a roof.

Ball court

Not far from the palace, looking in a northerly direction, there is a small platform from which a 10m/33ft wide street leads to the ball court (juego de pelota), something which is most unusual for this region.

★ Votive Pyramid

Adjoining the ball court is the impressive Votive Pyramid (Pirámide Votiva or Pirámide del Sol). This 11m/36ft high restored pyramid consists of two storeys.

The buildings known as the Citadel or Acropolis (Ciudadela or Acrópolis) extend to the west.

"Second Section"

On the level area known as the "Second Section" (Segundo Cuerpo) there is a large courtyard which is surrounded on all sides by platforms. A flight of steps leading to the north, which is flanked by walls almost 7m/23ft high, opens out into another courtyard in which a heavily damaged pyramid stands.

"Third Section"

The "Third Section" (Tercer Piso) is reached by a flight of steps supported by a supporting wall as much as 10m/33ft high. On an open sunken courtyard stands the Sacrificial Temple (Templo de los Sacrificios), a beautiful five-storey pyramid. Its southern steps lead to a small rectangular altar (Altar de los Sacrificios), which it is assumed was used as a place of sacrifice. Along the well-preserved east wing of the courtyard extends a hall measuring 22×30m/72×98ft with an oriel.

La Terraza

A staircase and a narrow passage lead to the highest level, where a row of ruined buildings with terraces and galleries is to be found. From the building known as La Terraza, which can be ascended by a steep flight of steps on its southern side, there is a fine view of the whole of the archaeological zone and its surroundings.

Zihuatanejo-Ixtapa

I 9

State: Guerrero (Gro.)
Altitude: sea level
Population: 60,000
Telephone code: 91 753

Access

By air daily from Mexico City and from other Mexican and American airports; by bus from Mexico City about 9 hours, from Acapulco (see entry) about 2 hours; by car from Mexico City on the well-constructed Autopista del Sol (MEX 95) and MEX 200 in about 7½ hours, from Acapulco 240km/150 miles on the MEX 200. The road via Toluca and Ciudad Altamirano should be avoided because of road conditions and risk of accident.

Location

The former fishing port of Zihuatanejo, situated on a sheltered bay, is surrounded by beautiful beaches, wooded hills and rocks. Together with the smart resort of Ixtapa, which was not founded until 1975, it is one of the most relaxing seaside resorts along the Mexican Pacific coast.

★ Resort

History

In pre-Hispanic times Zihuatanejo (Náhuatl: "dark woman") is supposed to have been a winter seaside retreat of the last king of the Purépecha (Tarascans), Tangáxoan II Caltzontzin. In the colonial period the place was important for a time as a trading port. It was not until the 1960s that the sleepy fishing port was discovered by tourists who preferred beaches in more remote areas. With the establishment of the neighbouring town of Ixtapa (Náhuatl: "where it is white high up")

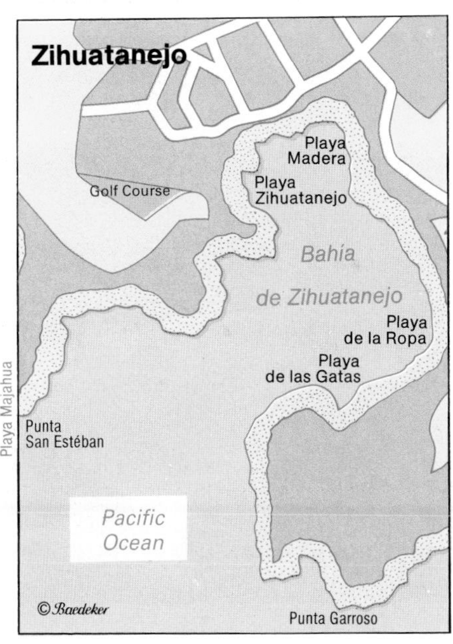

A bay near the old village of Zihuatanejo

Playa La Ropa at Zihuatenejo

some 10km/6 miles away, Zihuatanejo has also enjoyed a boom, which has led to the town being modernised, but has also taken away much of its charm.

Zihuatanejo

The fishing port of Zihuatanejo offers hardly anything of interest, although recently a pedestrian zone with shops and restaurants has been opened. The main beaches on the road from the airport to Ixtapa are:

Playa de las Gatas, which can only be reached by boat or over a stony path, has a stone wall, not far from the shore, which according to legend goes back to the Tarascan king Tangáxoan II, who desired to bathe here completely undisturbed; Playa de la Ropa; Playa de la Madera; Playa del Malecón and the beach between Zihuatanejo and Ixtapa, Playa de Majahua.

Ixtapa

Just under 10km/6 miles before the modern resort of Ixtapa lies the Playa Hermosa.

It is followed by the attractive beaches of Don Juan, San Juan de Dios, Rodrigo, Las Cuatas, Quieta and Linda.

The offshore islands, with their pretty beaches, often good snorkelling opportunities and varied flora and fauna, include Isla Ixtapa (Isla Grande), Isla de la Pie and Morro de los Pericos. In Ixtapa there is also a pretty tropical lagoon surrounded by lush vegetation. A large marina is in course of construction.

Interesting excursions can be made into the areas surrounding Zihuatanejo and Ixtapa with their fishing villages, coconut, banana and coffee plantations.

Practical Information

Air Travel

The great distances between different parts of the country make air travel an important means of travel in Mexico, bringing the larger towns and vacation centres within easy reach. The fares are now fairly high. New domestic services are contributing to more reasonable fares and reduced fares are on offer.

Airports

Mexico has 59 national and international airports. The principal one is the Aeropuerto Internacional Benito Juárez in Mexico City, to which there are flights from the principal airports in North and South America, the UK and many other countries. 24 million passengers passed through the airport in 1986. Mexico City airport is also the main centre for transferring to flights to other parts of the country. There is an airport departure tax of 12 US$ (1996) however this may be included in the ticket price.

Airlines

Aeroméxico, a private air line formed in 1988, is owned by Aerovias de Mexico; in March 1993 it obtained a controlling interest in Mexicana, another private line. Together they control 85% of the Mexican market.

In addition to domestic services Aeroméxico now flies daily to New York, Miami, Houston, Los Angeles, Tucson, San Diego and New Orleans, three times a week to Paris, five times to Madrid and twice to Frankfurt and Rome.

In addition to flights to the USA the private airline Mexicana (Compañia Mexicana de Aviación) provides a network of domestic services. Towns not at present served are gradually being included in the itineraries of regional airlines.

Aeroméxico

Paseo de la Reforma 445, Torre A, planta baja
Col. Cuahtémoc
06500 México, D.F.;
tel. (915) 228 9910

aeromexico

Mexicana

215 Chalk Farm Road, Camden Town
London NW1 8AF
tel. (0181) 284 2550

MEXICANA

Av Xola No 535, Col del Valle
México, D.F.;
tel. (915) 325 0990

Aero California

Paseo de la Reforma 332
06 500 México, D.F.;
tel. (915) 207 1392

AVIASCA

Homero No 1406, Col. Polanco
11560 México D.F.;
tel. (915) 395 5278, 580 4614

TAESA

Paseo de la Reforma 30
México D.F.;
tel. (915) 705 6164

◀ *All ready for a holiday in Cancún*

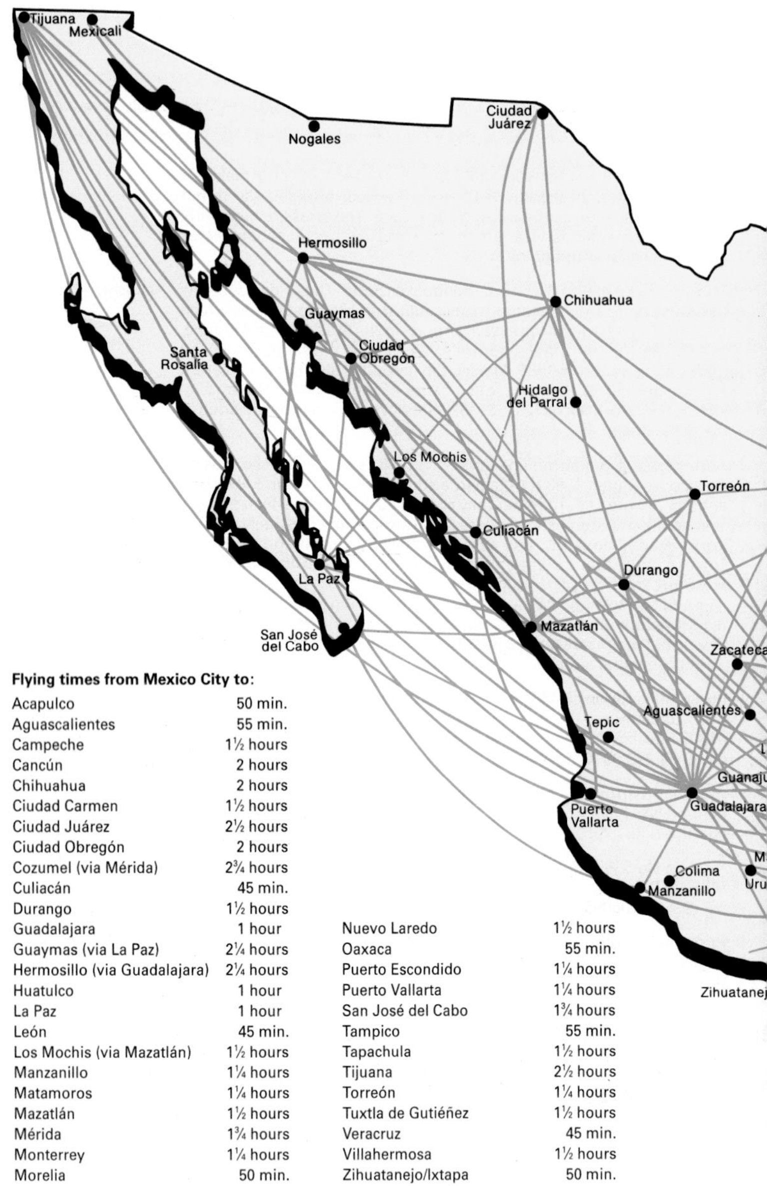

Flying times from Mexico City to:

Acapulco	50 min.
Aguascalientes	55 min.
Campeche	1½ hours
Cancún	2 hours
Chihuahua	2 hours
Ciudad Carmen	1½ hours
Ciudad Juárez	2½ hours
Ciudad Obregón	2 hours
Cozumel (via Mérida)	2¾ hours
Culiacán	45 min.
Durango	1½ hours
Guadalajara	1 hour
Guaymas (via La Paz)	2¼ hours
Hermosillo (via Guadalajara)	2¼ hours
Huatulco	1 hour
La Paz	1 hour
León	45 min.
Los Mochis (via Mazatlán)	1½ hours
Manzanillo	1¼ hours
Matamoros	1¼ hours
Mazatlán	1½ hours
Mérida	1¾ hours
Monterrey	1¼ hours
Morelia	50 min.
Nuevo Laredo	1½ hours
Oaxaca	55 min.
Puerto Escondido	1¼ hours
Puerto Vallarta	1¼ hours
San José del Cabo	1¾ hours
Tampico	55 min.
Tapachula	1½ hours
Tijuana	2½ hours
Torreón	1¼ hours
Tuxtla de Gutiéñez	1½ hours
Veracruz	45 min.
Villahermosa	1½ hours
Zihuatanejo/Ixtapa	50 min.

Air Services in Mexico

Aeroméxico and Mexicana

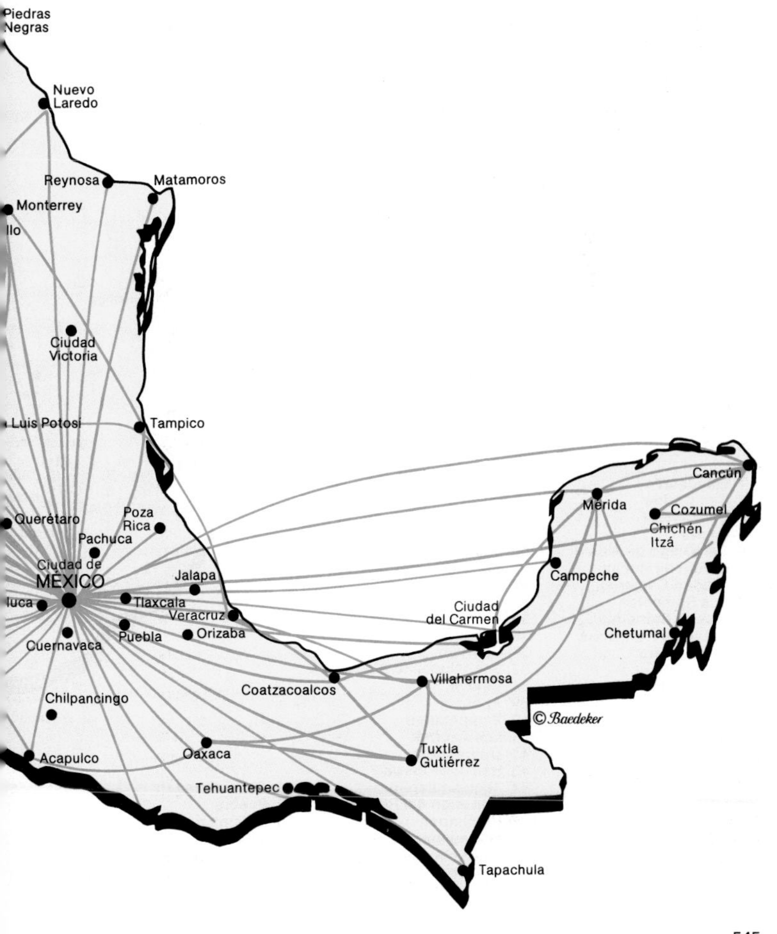

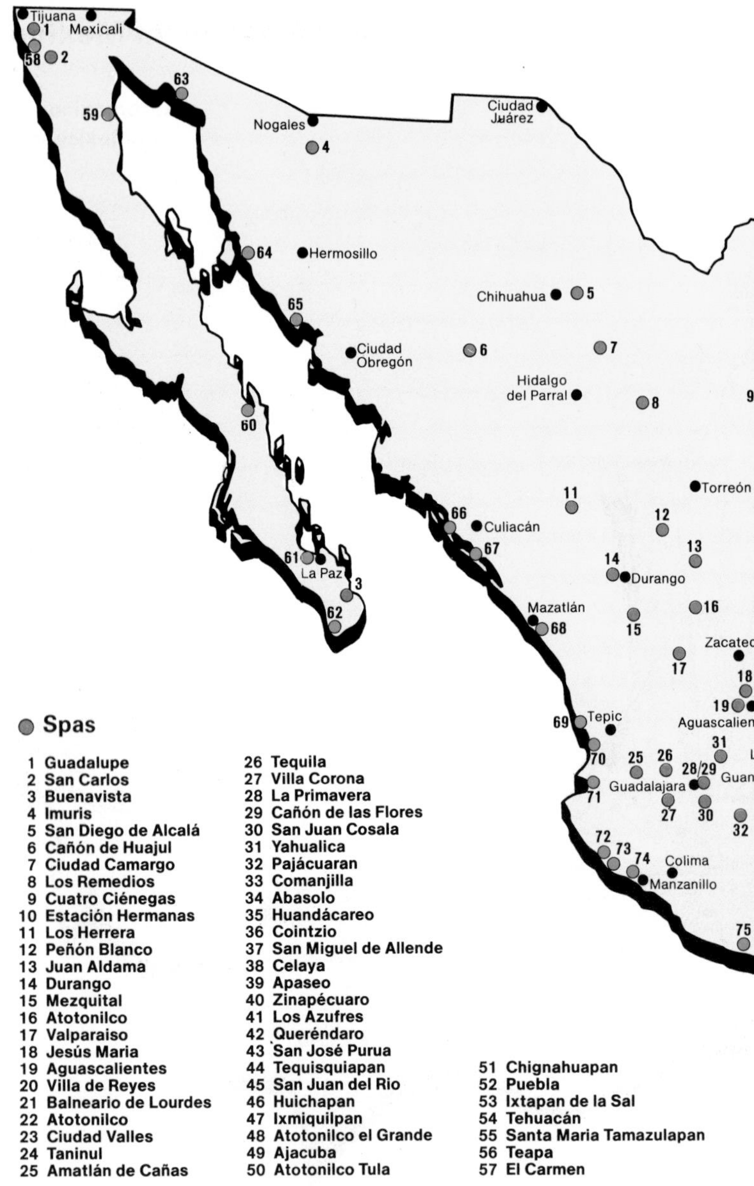
Tijuana
Mexicali
Nogales
Ciudad Juárez
Hermosillo
Chihuahua
Ciudad Obregón
Hidalgo del Parral
Torreón
Culiacán
La Paz
Durango
Mazatlán
Tepic
Guadalajara
Colima
Manzanillo
Spas
1 Guadalupe
2 San Carlos
3 Buenavista
4 Imuris
5 San Diego de Alcalá
6 Cañón de Huajul
7 Ciudad Camargo
8 Los Remedios
9 Cuatro Ciénegas
10 Estación Hermanas
11 Los Herrera
12 Peñón Blanco
13 Juan Aldama
14 Durango
15 Mezquital
16 Atotonilco
17 Valparaiso
18 Jesús Maria
19 Aguascalientes
20 Villa de Reyes
21 Balneario de Lourdes
22 Atotonilco
23 Ciudad Valles
24 Taninul
25 Amatlán de Cañas
26 Tequila
27 Villa Corona
28 La Primavera
29 Cañón de las Flores
30 San Juan Cosala
31 Yahualica
32 Pajácuaran
33 Comanjilla
34 Abasolo
35 Huandácareo
36 Cointzio
37 San Miguel de Allende
38 Celaya
39 Apaseo
40 Zinapécuaro
41 Los Azufres
42 Queréndaro
43 San José Purua
44 Tequisquiapan
45 San Juan del Rio
46 Huichapan
47 Ixmiquilpan
48 Atotonilco el Grande
49 Ajacuba
50 Atotonilco Tula
51 Chignahuapan
52 Puebla
53 Ixtapan de la Sal
54 Tehuacán
55 Santa Maria Tamazulapan
56 Teapa
57 El Carmen

Spas and Bathing Beaches in Mexico

Beaches

58 Ensenada
59 San Felipe
60 Bahia Concepción
61 La Paz
62 Cabo San Lucas
63 Puerto Peñasco
64 Bahia Kino
65 San Carlos
66 Altata
67 El Dorado
68 Mazatlán
69 San Blas
70 Rincón de Guayabitos
71 Puerto Vallarta
72 Tenacatita
73 Barra de Navidad
74 Manzanillo
75 Playa Azul
76 Zihuatanejo/Ixtapa
77 Acapulco
78 Puerto Escondido
79 Puerto Ángel
80 Huatulco
81 Puerto Madero
82 Tulum
83 Isla Cozumel
84 Isla Cancún
85 Isla Mujeres
86 Progreso
87 Celestún
88 Ciudad del Carmen
89 Veracruz
90 Nautla
91 Tecolutla
92 Tuxpan

This is only a selection of the most easily accessible and best equipped of Mexico's many beaches.

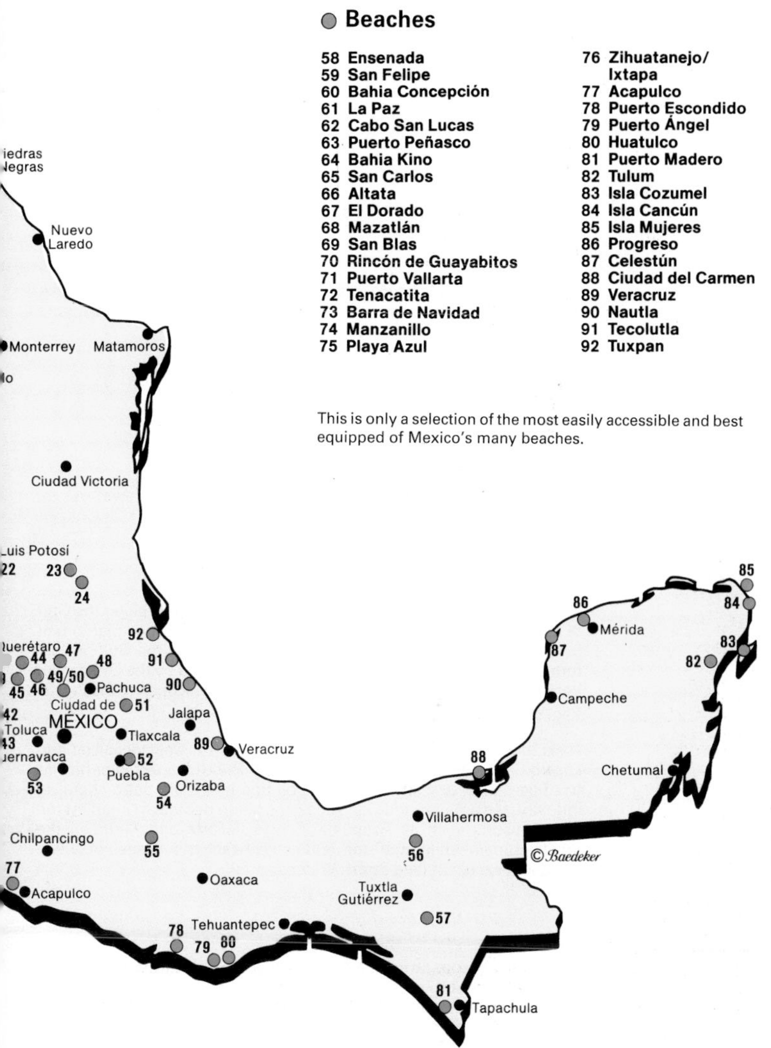

Aeromar

Sevilla 4 esq. P. de la Reforma
06 600 México, D.F.;
tel. (915) 627 0205

Lufthansa

Av. Paseo de las Palmas 239
Col. Lomas de Chapultepec
06 600 México, D.F.;
tel. (915) 202 8866

Iberia

Paeo de la Reforma 24
México, D.F.;
tel. (915) 705 0716/2565

Air France

Paseo de la Reforma 404–15
México, D.F.;
tel. (915) 627 6060

KLM

Avenida de las Palmas 735, piso 7
México, D.F.;
tel. (915) 202 4444

Flight passes

Aeroméxico and Mexicana offer visitors from Europe and the USA reasonably-priced passes ("Mexi Pass" and "Maya Pass") for flights within Mexico (see Getting There).

Banks

See Currency

Beaches and Spas (Map pages 546/547)

Beaches

With a coastline measuring some 10,000km/6000 miles along the Gulf of Mexico and the Pacific Ocean, Mexico can offer a varied plethora of beaches (*playas*). On the Gulf coast (Atlantic) and in the Gulf of California (Pacific) which is protected from the open sea by the Californian Peninsula, the sea is normally calm, but on the coast open to the Pacific heavy waves and strong currents are the norm.

Water quality

Near the large ports such as Tampico, Veracruz, Coatzocoalcos and Lázaro Cárdenas the water quality is poor. The Gulf coast in particular has been adversely affected by the oil boom and the petro-chemical industry, the area around Coatzocoalcos being particularly bad. At the larger resorts such as Acapulco, Puerto Vallarta and Mazatlán the quality varies, while at all the remaining beaches it ranges between good and excellent (see Sport, Water sports).

Spas

Most Mexican spas lie in the southern part of the Sierra Madre Occidental and in the south of the Central Highlands.

Properly organised spa centres with sophisticated infrastructures will be found only in the major resorts of Aguascalientes, Ixtapán de la Sal, Rio Caliente, Comanjilla and Tehuacán, where the famous Mexican mineral water known as "Agua Tehuacán" comes from. At other resorts the baths are very simple; many places have some rather crude mineral springs used only by the local folk.

Bus Travel

Buses (camiones, autobuses) are the most popular form of public transport in Mexico, and most towns can be reached in reasonable comfort by this means. Buses run several times a day – in some cases every hour or so – between the major towns inland, along the frontiers and on the coast. As well as local services there are first and second class buses on the main highways.

First class

First and luxury class travel (*primero* and *de lujo ejecutivo*) is to be recommended for long-distance journeys, the fares being only 10% to 20% more than those for second class. The buses are often air-conditioned and the seats are very comfortable. It is necessary to book in good time, preferably the day before, to avoid having to wait for the next departure if all the seats are taken.

Second class

Second class buses are often quite old and therefore slower. They stop frequently for refreshments and fresh passengers are always getting on resulting in overcrowding; nevertheless, this is a good way of coming into contact with local people.

Tip

Generally speaking it is advisable to enquire in good time about departure times, tickets, connections and reservations. Buses tend to get particularly crowded during the school holidays at Easter, in August and at Christmas and the New Year, so if possible it is best to avoid using them at those times or at least book several weeks in advance.

Information

Information and tickets can be obtained from bus terminals (*camionera*) found mainly around the outskirts of towns. In some towns there are separate bus stations for each class of bus and the company concerned.

Bus stations in Mexico City

Mexico City has five large stations situated in the outskirts from which buses travel to various parts of the country. These are:

Terminal Central Indios Verdes
Metro station: Indios Verdes (Line 3)
Buses to Teotihuacán and the northern suburbs.

Terminal Central del Norte (T.A.N.)
Av. de los Cien Metros 4907, Col Magdalena
tel. (915) 5 87 15 52
Metro station: Terminal del Norte (Line 5)
Buses to Tula, Querétaro, Guanajuato, San Luis Potosí, northern Mexico and the USA.

Terminal Central del Oriente (T.A.P.O.)
Calz. Ignacio Zaragoza 200, Col. 1er de Mayo
tel. (915) 7 62 59 77, 542 7156–8
Metro station: San Lázaro (Line 1)
Buses to Puebla, Oaxaca, Mérida and Yucatán

Bus Travel

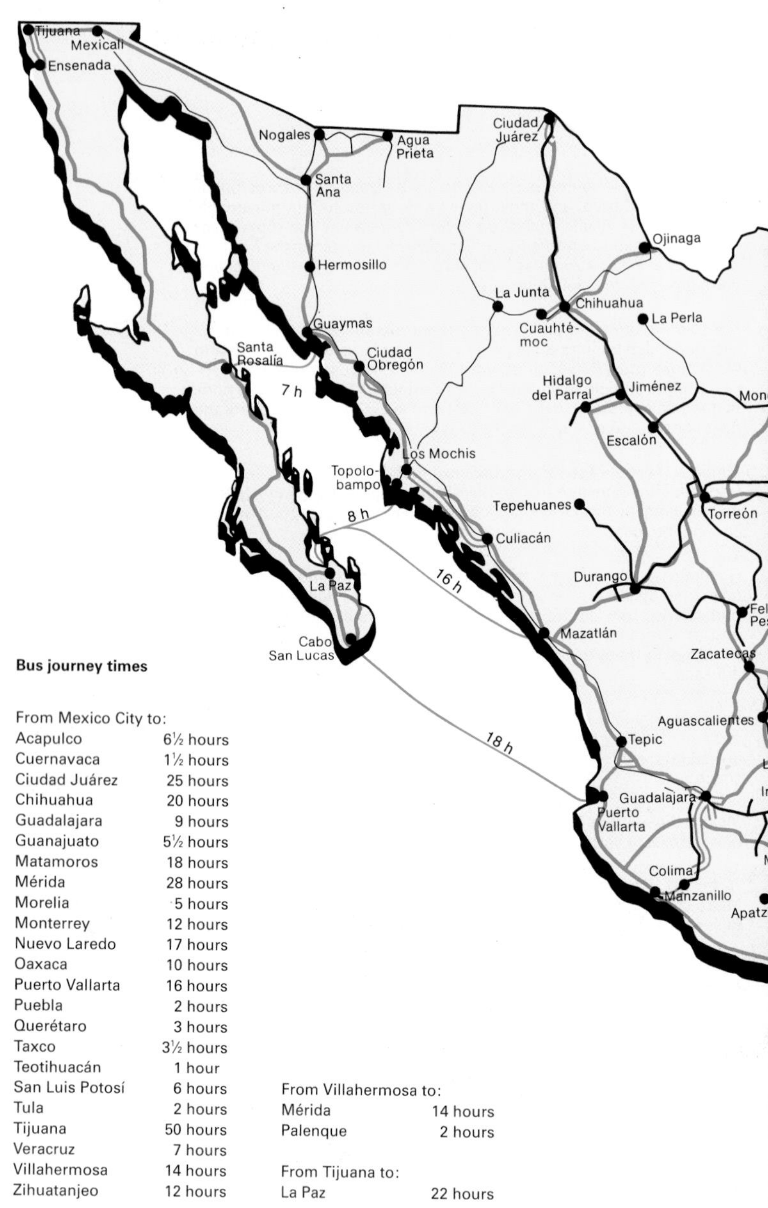

Bus journey times

From Mexico City to:	
Acapulco	6½ hours
Cuernavaca	1½ hours
Ciudad Juárez	25 hours
Chihuahua	20 hours
Guadalajara	9 hours
Guanajuato	5½ hours
Matamoros	18 hours
Mérida	28 hours
Morelia	5 hours
Monterrey	12 hours
Nuevo Laredo	17 hours
Oaxaca	10 hours
Puerto Vallarta	16 hours
Puebla	2 hours
Querétaro	3 hours
Taxco	3½ hours
Teotihuacán	1 hour
San Luis Potosí	6 hours
Tula	2 hours
Tijuana	50 hours
Veracruz	7 hours
Villahermosa	14 hours
Zihuatanjeo	12 hours

From Villahermosa to:	
Mérida	14 hours
Palenque	2 hours

From Tijuana to:	
La Paz	22 hours

Long-distance Routes in Mexico

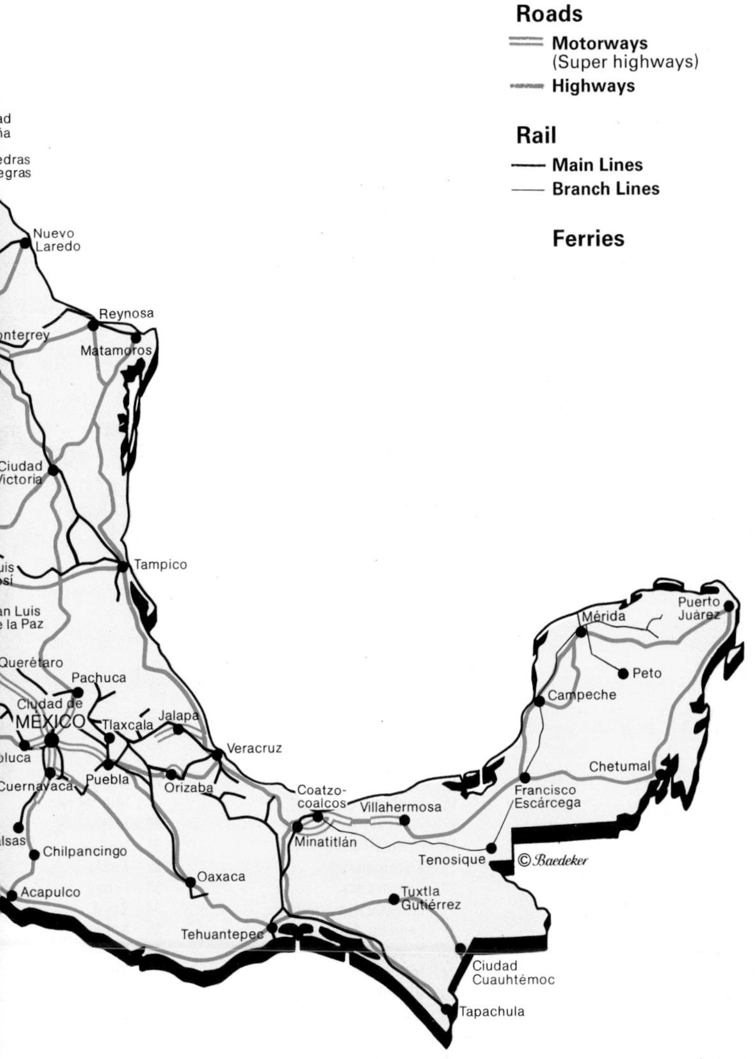

Principal Tourist Sights in Mexico

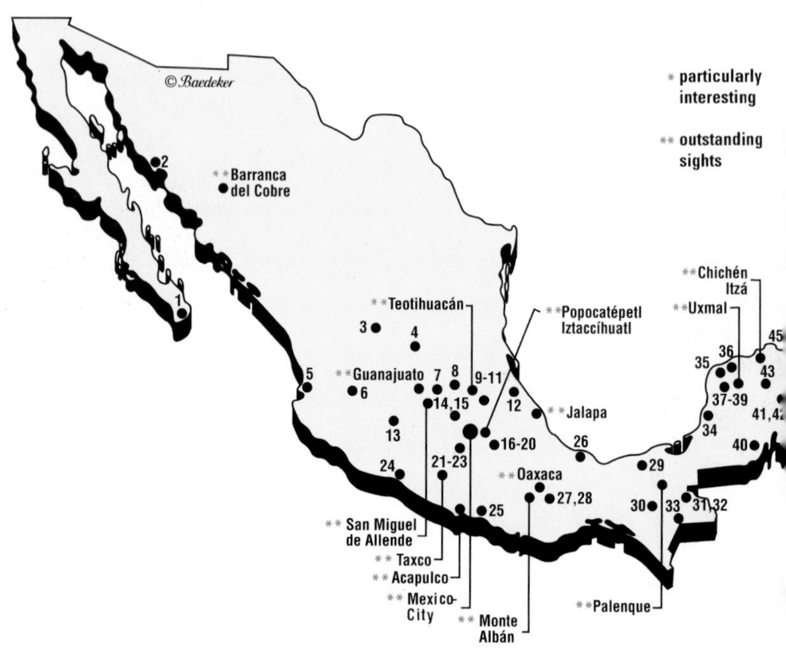

1 * Guaymas
2 * Zacatecas
3 * San Luis Potosí (Town)
4 * Puerto Vallarta
5 * Guadalajara
6 * Querétaro (Town)
7 * Tula
8 * Actopan
9 * El Tajín
10 * Lago de Pátzcuaro
11 * Tenayuca
12 * Tepotzotlán
13 * Acatepec
14 * Cholula
15 * Huejotzingo
16 * Puebla (Town)
17 * Tlaxcala
18 * Malinalco
19 * Xochicalco
20 * Cuernavaca
21 * Zihuatanejo-Ixtapa
22 * Lago de Catemaco
23 * Yagul
24 * Mitla
25 * Villahermosa
26 * San Cristóbal de Las Casas
27 * Yaxchilán
28 * Bonampak
29 * Lagunas de Montebello
30 * Mérida
31 * Izamal
32 * Kabán
33 * Labuá
34 * Sayil
35 * Kohunlich
36 * Tulum
37 * Xel-há
38 * Cobá
39 * Cozumel
40 * Cancún
41 * Isla Mujeres

A country bus-station

Terminal Central del Sur (T.A.S.)
Av. Taxqueña 1320, Col Campestre Curubusco,
tel. (915) 6 89 80 00
Metro station: Taxqueña (Line 2)
Buses to Cuernavaca, Taxco, Acapulco and the south

Terminal Central del Poniente (T.A.P.)
Av. Sur 122, Esq. Río Tacubaya, Col. Real del Monte,
tel. (915) 2 71 04 81
Metro station: Observatorio (Line 1)
Buses to Toluca, Morelia and the west coast.

Camping and Caravanning

Mainly owned by US firms, "trailer parks" (*campos para remolques*) are to be found almost everywhere; tent sites (*campamentos*), on the other hand, are less common. A list of cheap accommodation, which includes a list of camp sites (*Directorio de albuerges, cabañas, campamentos, campos para remolques*) can be obtained from the Mexican Tourist Ministry (see Information). Travellers entering Mexico from the USA can obtain brochures and information from the AAA (American Automobile Association) or from a Mexican insurance company at the border.

Although not prohibited, camping away from recognised sites is not advised, even though some isolated beaches and other beautiful spots may appear tempting.

Car Rental (coches de alquiler)

Car rental is not cheap in Mexico. Rental firms can be found in all the major towns and holiday resorts. Vehicles provided by international rental companies are usually in good condition while those from smaller local firms should be carefully checked over first.

Conditions

Although the driver's national driving licence is normally sufficient to be able to rent a car it is best to be able to produce an international driving licence as well. The minimum age is usually 25. Most rental firms ask for a credit card; customers paying in cash are required to put down a sizeable security deposit. 15% VAT will be added to the bill; this may be less in some places. The car must be handed back in Mexico, and if left at a branch other than that from which it was hired a repatriation fee will usually be charged.

AVIS

Paseo de la Reforma 308
México D.F.; tel. (915) 207 7777

Budget

Atenas No. 40
06 600 México D.F.; tel. (915) 5 35 69 27, 533 0450

Dollar

Paseo de la Reforma 157–B
México D.F.; tel. (915) 207 3838/9285

Europcar/Interrent

Marsella 48, Col. Juárez
06 600 México D.F.; tel. (915) 533 0375–79

Hertz

Versalles No. 6, Col. Juárez
México D.F.; tel. (915) 5 66 00 99, 592 6082/8343

Chemists

See Health

Consulates

See Diplomatic Representation

Currency

The unit of currency is the Mexican peso ($, normally with one vertical bar, and not to be confused with the sign for the US dollar, normally shown with two vertical bars).

In January 1993 the Mexican government introduced a new peso to simplify calculations. Unnder the new system 1000 old pesos equals one new peso. There are banknotes for 10, 20, 50 and 100 pesos and coins for 5, 10, 20 and 50 centavos and 1, 2, 5 and 10 pesos.

Exchange rates

The rate of exchange is based on the US dollar and fluctuates accordingly vis-à-vis European currencies. For tourists there exists a special peso rate which varies according to supply and demand; in mid-1994 the tourist rate was between N$ (*nuevos pesos*) 3·20 and 3·35 to one US dollar.

Mexican currency

Currency regulations

The import and export of Mexican or foreign currency in excess of US$10,000 must be declared.

Exchange of money

Money can be exchanged in banks, bureaux de change (*casas de cambio*) and in many hotels. It is preferable to take travellers' cheques in US dollars and a few dollars in cash (small notes). There could be problems in exchanging sterling.

Credit cards

Hotels, car rental firms and large shops accept the standard credit cards, but these will probably be viewed with suspicion outside the main tourist centres.

Banks

The major Mexican banks are Banco Nacional de México (BANAMEX), Bancomer, Banco Internacional, Banco del Atlántico and Serfin.

Business hours: normally Mon.–Fri. 9am–1.30 or 2.30pm, in some cases as late as 5pm in large towns; many branches of large banks also open Sat. 9am–noon.

Customs Regulations

On entry

Personal effects and holiday equipment may be taken into Mexico without payment of duty. There are also duty-free allowances for each adult over 18 years of age of 20 packets of cigarettes or 50 cigars or 250g of tobacco and 3 litres of spirits, one camera or video-recorder with twelve rolls of film or cassettes, gifts of a value up to 100 US dollars and three items of used sports equipment.

Harpoons and spears for underwater hunting, weapons, plants, fruit and pornographic material may NOT be brought in.

Incoming visitors must complete a customs Declaration Form and baggage is subject to spot checks.

On leaving — The export from Mexico of gold, antiquities and archaeological items is prohibited. Visitors are also warned against carrying even the smallest amounts of drugs.

Return to the UK or any EU country — The duty-free allowances for British subjects returning to the UK or any EU country are as follows: 200 cigarettes or 100 cigarillos or 50 cigars or 250g of tobacco, two litres of still table wine, one litre of spirits or strong liqueurs over 22% volume or two litres of fortified or sparkling wine or other liqueurs or a further two litres of still table wine, 60cc of perfume, 250cc of toilet water and £145 worth of all other goods, including gifts.

Return to the USA — US citizens may take in 200 cigarettes, 100 cigars and one litre of alcohol, plus $400 worth of other purchases (with a 10% tax on the next $1000 worth).

Return to Canada — Canadian citizens may take in 200 cigarettes, 50 cigars and 40 ounces of alcohol, plus $150 worth of other purchases ($300 worth if they have been out of Canada for a week or more).

Protected species — See entry

Drugs — See entry

Diplomatic Representation

In Mexico

United Kingdom
Rio Lerma 71
México D.F.;
tel. Chancellery (915) 207 2069/2449

USA
Paseo de la Reforma 305
06 500 México, D.F.;
tel. (915) 211 00 42

Canada
Schiller 529
11 560 México D.F.;
tel. (915) 724 7900

Australia
Jaime Balmes 11, Pza. Polanco, Torre B, piso 10
11 510 México D.F.;
tel. (915) 395 9988

Note — In emergencies, if the consul for the visitor's country of origin is unavailable, that of another country forming part of the Commonwealth or of an EU country will usually be able to assist.

Mexican Embassies Abroad

United Kingdom
42 Hertford Street
London WY1 7TF;
tel. (0171) 499 8586

USA
2828 16th Street NW
Washington DC 20009;
tel. (202) 234 6000–6003

Australia

14 Perth Avenue
Yarralumla
Canberra ACT 2600;
tel. (06) 273 905/47/63

Drugs

Mexico is one of the main suppliers of marijuana and heroin to the US market and also one of the chief countries involved in the transit of cocaine. Opium poppies, which provide the raw material for heroin, are grown in particular in the state of Sinaloa, on the US border, as well as in Chihuahua and Durango.

The illegal use of drugs is strictly prohibited in Mexico. Under pressure from the USA the police prosecute and punish heavily anyone found cultivating, smuggling or possessing even small quantities of drugs. Luggage is searched thoroughly at borders and surprise raids anywhere can catch visitors unaware, especially young people travelling alone, so the message is clear – do not attempt to carry drugs!

Electricity

In Mexico the electricity supply is usually 110 volts, but occasionally 126 or 220 volts. Power sockets normally take the US flat-prong type of plug, so Europeans should purchase a plug adaptor in advance if they wish to use their own electrical appliances.

Emergency Calls

Emergency telephone numbers in Mexico City are:
Ambulance/accident rescue (Cruz Verde): 06
Red Cross (Cruz Roja): 5 57 57 57–60
Police (Policía Judicial): 08
Police (Distrite Federal): 588 5100
Police (major highways): 6 84 21 42
Breakdown/towing service (Patrullas de auxilio turístico): 2 50 82 21
Missing Persons Service (LOCATEL): 6 58 11 11

Ferries

In the Pacific

Car ferries operate between the Mexican mainland and Baja California (Southern California), and are a worthwhile alternative to the tiring and time-consuming journey round the Gulf of California. Details of times of departure can be obtained at the individual ports concerned. Early reservation of seats is advisable, either at the main office in Mexico City or at one of the offices at the ports of departure.

Baja Express
Paseo de la Reforma 359 6th floor;
tel. (915) 525 7204

Sematur de California
Paseo de la Reforma 509, 4th floor;
tel. (915) 286 1267

Mazatlán – La Paz

Return trip daily.
Takes 17 hours (Sematur)

Guaymas – Santa Rosalia

Outward trip Wed. and Sun., return Tues. and Thur;
Takes 6½ hours (Sematur)

Topolobampo – La Paz

Timetable information from Baja Express offices;
Takes 8 hours

In the Caribbean

There are ferries several times a day between the mainland and the islands of Cozumel and Isla Mujeres. No reservations are necessary. Tickets are on sale at the landing stages.

Playa del Carmen – Cozumel

Passenger ferry: daily ten outward (7.30am–9pm) and return (6.30am–8pm) trips; car ferry: daily six outward (6.30am–8pm) and return (7.30am–9pm) trips;
Takes about one hour

Puerto Aventuras–Cozumel

Car ferry: daily 9.30am and 5.30pm outward, 8.30am and 4.30pm return
Takes about 2 hours

Cancún–Isla Mujeres

Passenger ferry: daily four outward (9am–7pm) and return (10am–8pm) trips;
Takes about 30 minutes

Food and Drink

The culinary traditions of the Indian population, combined with influences brought in by Spaniards and other incomers, produce a distinctively Mexican cuisine, with local variations in different parts of the country. The large hotels also, of course, serve the usual international dishes.

An almost ubiquitous item in a Mexican meal is the *tortilla*, a maize pancake which is served either as an accompaniment to the main dish or on its own with a filling of meat, vegetables, spices, cheese, etc. Also very popular are the various species of peppers (chillies) and a range of sauces. Poultry appears frequently on the menu, and in the coastal regions there is excellent seafood, though surprisingly few kinds of fish. Popular side dishes are *frijoles refritos* (beans fried in oil with various spices) and rice. Potatoes and pasta are rarely served.

Mole poblano

A popular dish for festive occasions is *mole poblano*, an elaborate sauce made according to an Indian recipe with numerous ingredients, including several kinds of pepper, bitter chocolate, etc.

Reading a Mexican menu (*lista de comidas*)

Table utensils

Tablesetting *cubierto*; spoon *cuchara*; teaspoon *cucharita*; knife *cuchillo*; fork *tenedor*; plate *plato*; glass *vaso*; cup *taza*; napkin *servilleta*; corkscrew *saca corchos*.

Meals

Breakfast *desayuno*; continental breakfast *desayuno continental* or *café con pan*; "elevenses" *almuerzo*; lunch *comida*; dinner *cena*.

Those who prefer their food not too highly seasoned should order it *sin picante*.

Hors d'œuvres (*antojitos*)

Guacamole avocado salad; *tacos* stuffed rolled tortillas; *frijoles refritos* fried beans; *ostiones* oysters; *coctel de camarones* prawn cocktail; *ceviche* fish or seafood marinated in lemon juice.

Soups (*sopas*)

Pozole veracruzano maize soup with chopped vegetables, spices, etc. served separately; *cocido* thick soup; *gazpacho* cold vegetable soup; *menudo* soup made with offal of veal, pork or poultry.

Egg dishes (*platos de huevos*)

Huevo egg (*crudo* raw, *fresco* fresh, *duro* hardboiled, *tibio* softboiled); *huevos revueltos* scrambled eggs; *huevos rancheros* fried eggs with highly seasoned sauce.

Fish and seafood (*pescado y mariscos*)

Pescado fish (*frito* fried, *asado* roasted, *a la parilla* grilled, *cocido* boiled, *ahumado* smoked).
Trucha trout; *carpa* carp; *anguila* eel; *bagre* catfish.

Atún tuna; *bonito* bonito, white tuna; *corvina* sea raven; *jurel* yellow-tail; *lisa* mullet; *mero* sea bass; *lenguado* sole; *sardina* sardine; *sierra* mackerel pike; *pez espada* swordfish; *marlin* fanfish; *bacalao* dried cod; *tiburón, cazón* shark.

Mariscos seafood; *camerón* shrimp; *langosta* crayfish; *langostino* crab; *jaibo, cangrejo* shrimp; *pulpo, calamar* octopus; *ostión* oyster; *abalone* abalone, ear-shell; *tortuga* turtle.

Meat (*carnes*)

Asado roast; *pierna* leg; *chuleta* chop, cutlet; *gordo, graso* fat; *carnero* mutton; *cerdo* pork; *cochinillo, lechón* sucking pig; *cordero* lamb; *ternera* veal; *vaca* beef; *bisteck* steak; *rosbif* roast beef; *carne estofada* meat stew; *carnitas* roast pork; *chicharrón* crackling, pork scratchings; *carne salada* salt meat; *carne ahumada* smoked meat; *tocino* bacon; *jamón* ham; *chorizo* highly seasoned sausage; *longaniza* spiced pork sausage; *tamales* minced meat with crushed maize and seasoning.

Poultry (*aves*)

Pavo, guajalote turkey; *faisán* pheasant; *ganso* goose; *pato* duck; *perdiz* partridge; *pichón* pigeon; *pollo* chicken.

Game (*caza*)

Venado venison; *jabali* wild pig; *liebre* hare; *conejo* rabbit; *cabrito* kid.

Sauces (*salsas*)

Mole poblano a sharp sauce made with bitter chocolate; *salasa verde, pipián verde* sauce made with herbs, peppers and green tomatoes; *salsa roja* made with tomatoes, chillies and herbs; *salsa borracha* made with pulque and herbs.

Vegetables (*verduras*)

Aguacate avocado; *alcachofas* artichokes; *calabacitas* courgettes; *flor de calabaza* pumpkin flowers; *col* cabbage; *col lombarda* red cabbage; *col de Bruselas* Brussels sprouts; *coliflor* cauliflower; *repello* white cabbage; *acelgas* chards; *cebollas* onions; *espárragos* asparagus; *espinacas* spinach; *guisantes* peas; *garbanzos* chick peas; *frijoles* kidney beans; *jitomates* tomatoes; *zanahorias* carrots.

Salads (*ensalada, lechuga*)

pepino cucumber; *apio* celery; *escarola* endive; *vinagre* vinegar; *aceite* oil; *pimienta* pepper (*molida* ground); *sal* salt (*salado* salted, salty); *Mostaza* mustard; *guacamole* avocado salad with onions, tomatoes, chilli and coriander.

Tortillas

Chilaquiles tortillas with meat and cheese; *tacos* stuffed rolled tortillas fried in oil; *enchiladas* tortillas with sharp chilli sauce and meat; *chapulas* tortillas with upturned edges fried in oil with meat, sausage and salad; *tamales* filled with minced meat and wrapped in maize husks.

Desserts (*postres*)
Helado ice; *budin, flan* pudding.

Fruit (*frutas*)
Cerezas cherries; *higos* figs; *tunas* prickly pears; *fresas* strawberries; *manzanas* apples; *duraznos* peaches; *chabacanos* apricots; *melones* melons; *naranjas* oranges; *peras* pears; *piñas* pineapples; *plátanos* bananas; *uvas* grapes. There are also various tropical fruits like paw-paws, mangoes, guavas and zapotes.

Drinks (*bebidas*)

Beer (*cerveza*)
Beer is increasingly displacing the old national drink, pulque. Excellent light-coloured (*clara*), semi-dark (*semioscura*) and dark (*oscura*) beers are brewed in Mexico. The largest breweries are Cuauhtémoc in Monterey, Moctezuma in Veracruz and Modelo in Mexico City/Toluca. Mexicans often drink their beer with some salt and lime; those who like something even stronger drink a *calichal*, a mixture of pulque and beer, or a *submarino*, beer with tequila.

Wine (*vino*)
Wine is being increasingly produced and some of it is of good quality but not cheap. The chief wine-producing regions are in Baja California and around Aguascalientes.

Spirits and liqueurs
Pulque, a milky, cloudy drink which has an alcohol content of about 3%, is made from the juice of the maguey agave. Pulque is drunk in *pulquerías*, which are open only to men – foreigners are unlikely to get in unless accompanied by a male Mexican friend. Maguey juice (*agua miel* or "honey water") is also distilled to produce a strong spirit, tequila, the best quality brand of which is known as Mezcal. As proof of its quality good Mezcal contains a small maguey worm, which connoisseurs bite and drink down with the last swallow. Tequila is normally drunk with some salt and lime sprinkled on the back of the hand. Aguardiente, a colourless brandy, and rum (*ron*) are distilled from sugar-cane.

Coffee (*café*)
Coffee is a popular drink. The beans are roasted to a very dark colour. Black coffee (*café solo*) is preferred in the Mexican highlands, coffee with milk (*café con leche*) on the coast.

Chocolate, cocoa (*chocolate*)
Mexico is the homeland of chocolate which – whipped into a froth and flavoured with vanilla – is a regular feature of the Mexican breakfast.

Soft drinks (*refrescos*)
Widely available, soft drinks include pure fruit juices (*jugos*), some of exotic tastes, fruit juices diluted with water (*agua fresca*), milk-shakes (e.g. *leche de mango*) and mineral water (*agua mineral*, Tehuacán: *con gas* carbonated, *sin gas* non-carbonated).

Coconut milk is also very popular. Whole coconuts are sold especially at beach-stalls.

Getting to Mexico

By air
The limited time available means that most holidaymakers will choose to fly to Mexico. Mexico City International Airport can be reached in about 11 hours from the UK (see Air Travel).

Airlines
British Airways (0181–897 4000) now fly direct non-stop to Mexico City from Heathrow. In addition flights are available from all the large European cities, for example, KLM from Amsterdam, Sabena from Brussels to Atlanta and then by Eastern Airlines, Air France from Paris, Iberia from Madrid, etc.

Aeroméxico, Mexicana and US airlines fly to Mexico from many towns and cities in the USA. Such flights are especially recommended for anyone wishing to combine a trip to Mexico with a holiday in the USA.

From South America Ecuatoriana flies to Mexico City from Quito, Aerolineas Argentinas from Buenos Aires and AeroPeru from Lima.

Mexi Pass Vimex
Mexi Pass
Maya Pass Vimex
Maya Pass

For onward connections Aeroméxico offers reasonably priced flight passes to 30 destinations within Mexico. Travellers from Europe flying direct with Aeroméxico, or with Mexicana via the USA, can apply for the Mexi Pass Vimex; passengers with other airlines can purchase the (somewhat more expensive) Mexi Pass. For 27 routes in the south and south-east of Mexico there is the corresponding Maya Pass Vimex or Maya Pass.

By sea

Those with an additional two or three weeks to spare may prefer to travel by sea. It is also possible to book trips taking in, say, the east coast of the USA and the Gulf of Mexico. Freighters from ports on the east and west coasts of the USA will also carry passengers to Mexico.

Passenger ships on Caribbean cruises often make brief calls at Mexican ports, especially Cancún and Cozumel.

By land

Those travelling to Mexico by road will usually do so from the USA. The major border crossings are San Diego (California)–Tijuana (B.C.N.), Calexico (California)–Mexicali (B.C.N.), Nogales (Arizona)–Nogales (Son.), El Paso (Texas)–Ciudad Juárez (Chih.), Presidio (Texas)–Ojinaga (Chih.), Del Rio (Texas)–Ciudad Acuña (Coah.), Eagle Pass (Texas)–Piedras Negras (Coah.), Laredo (Texas)–Nuevo Laredo (N.L.), McAllen (Texas)–Reynosa (N.L.) and Brownsville (Texas)–Matamoros (Tamps.)

By car

It is only worth buying a car if you intend to stay in Mexico for a considerable period. The car should preferably be purchased in the USA; the purchase will be recorded in your pasport and the vehicle may be kept in Mexico for a maximum of 180 days, at the end of which it must be returned to the USA. Failure to observe this time-limit will result in a heavy fine.

An insurance policy taken out in the USA will not be valid in Mexico. Although Third Party insurance is not obligatory in Mexico it is strongly recommended.

The firm of Sarnborn's has proved to be reliable; they have offices in all the major border towns.

See Safety and Road Transport.

By bus

US buses serve the major border towns, from where the cheaper Mexican buses can be taken to Mexico City and other towns. (See Bus Travel.)

By rail

Travellers can transfer from US to Mexican trains at the border termini of Calexico (California; by bus from Phoenix or San Diego), Nogales (Arizona: by bus from Tucson), El Paso (Texas), Presidio (Texas; by bus), Del Rio (Texas), Eagle Pass (Texas), McAllen (Texas; by bus) and Nuevo Laredo (Texas).

Travellers should bear in mind that rail travel is by far the slowest means of transport in Mexico. See Rail Travel.

Health

Vaccinations
innoculations

Visitors entering Mexico from a country where yellow fever exists will be required to produce a relevant vaccination certificate; otherwise there are no vaccination or innoculation regulations. Nevertheless, the prudent traveller will ensure he is fully protected against typhoid, tetanus, poliomyelitis and hepatitis. For those travelling to the tropical lowlands vaccination against malaria is strongly recommended.

Climate

The Mexican climate can have adverse effects on health unless certain safeguards are taken. The high altitude can cause circulatory problems for Europeans who are not accustomed to it especially if, during the first few days they indulge in too much physical activity or eat and drink too much. The same precautions are necessary in the hot and humid lowland regions. The time difference, too, is a good reason for taking it easy for a day or two in order to adjust. Protection against strong light and sunburn is essential, and it is advisable to carry an insect-repellant. The tropical climate means that food does not keep well and micro-organisms flourish, so that stomach and intestinal disorders ("Moctezuma's revenge") are common.

Preventive measures

Never drink plain tap water, and do not even use it when cleaning your teeth. Most restaurants provide *agua purificado* (filtered bottled water). To be absolutely safe insist on mineral water (*agua mineral*) straight from the bottle. It is best to avoid drinks with ice, and vegetables and salads should be washed in *agua purificado*. Fruit should be washed and peeled. Be very careful when consuming food and drinks from market stalls and the like.

Remedies

In spite of all precautions, "Moctezuma's revenge" can still strike all too readily! Rest and plenty of (safe!) drinks to counteract dehydration are the best thing. A good medicine obtainable in Mexico is Lomotil; European remedies seem to have little effect. If the infection gets worse and fever sets in consult a doctor.

Medical help

Most hotels will be able to suggest a doctor, but if they cannot do so contact the local tourist office or your own embassy (see Diplomatic Representation) who will give the names of English-speaking doctors. It is best to take a dictionary when visiting a physician.

Doctor's bills have to be paid on the spot – remember to ask for a receipt.

Hospitals

Hospitals with English-speaking staff can be found in Mexico City and Guadalajara, as well as other towns.

Hospital Inglés (American-British Cowdray)
Calle Sur 136, Col. Americas
01 120 México 18 D.F.; tel. (915) 277 5000

Hospital México-Americano
Colomos 2110
Guadalajara (Jal.); tel. (9136) 41 31 41

Chemist's shops (*farmacias*)

Chemists often sell other things besides medicines, and a good many medicaments are obtainable without prescription. The best chemists are managed by doctors.

See Safety

Hotels (Hoteles; a selection)

The more sophisticated hotels in the larger towns and holiday centres meet European standards and are equipped to suit American tastes. Those under Mexican management are more individual in atmosphere and appearance. There are also hotels under German and Swiss management which are pleasant and comfortable. Away from the main tourist centres visitors may not find the degree of comfort they would normally expect.

Hotel categories

Hotels are at present classified under a system ranging from GT (Gran Turismo, luxury class) and five-star down to one star establishments. A tourism law was introduced in 1993 which ended price fixing for hotels so that prices vary according to supply and demand. The prices indicated below can therefore only be very approximate. They will also vary according to the local economic situation and may be open to negotiation. Some higher category hotels in Mexico City offer reduced rates. Many hotels quote in US$. The following table is taken from the current Mexican Travellers' Guide.

Categories of hotel		Double room per night	
official	in this guide	(in £)	(US$)
GT	L	90–200	above 200
★★★★★	L	55–110	above 150
★★★★	A	35–70	100–150
★★★	A, B	32–45	60–100
★★	B, C	20–32	under 60
★	D	15–20	under 30

Tip

"Moteles de Paso" are hotels renting rooms by the hour, and should be avoided.

Abbreviations

SP = swimming pool; T = tennis; G = golf; LS = landing strip; F = fishing; S = sailing; R = riding; SD = skin diving; WS = water skiing.

Acapulco

L ★ Acapulco Princess, Playa Revolcadero (SP, T, G); L ★ Hyatt Regency, Costera Miguel Alemán 1 (SP, T); L★ Las Brisas, Carr. Escénica Clemente Mejía 5255 (SB, T, WS, F); L ★ Pierre Marquez, Playa Revolcadero (SP, T, F, WS); L Acapulco Ritz, Av. Costera Alemán 159 (SP, F, WS); L Fiesta Americana Condesa, Av. Costera M. Alemán 1220 (SP, T. WS, F); L Mayan Palace, Acapulco Diamante (SP, T, G); L Paraíso Radisson, Costera M. Alemán 163 (SP, T); L El Presidente, Av. Costera M. Alemán 89 (SP, F, WS); L Sheraton Acapulco, Costera Guitarrón 110 (SP, T); L Villa Vera Raquet Club, Lomas del Mar 35 (SP, T); A Calinda Beach Acapulco, Costera M. Alemán 1260 (SP); A★ Plaza Las Glorias, Quebrada 74 (SP) (Quebrada Springer); A Acapulco Imperial, Av. Costera Alemán 251 (SP, T); A Arabela del Pacífico, Av. Costera M. Alemán 55 (SP); A Club Majestic Acapulco, Av. Pozo del Rey 73 (S); B De La Costera, Costera M. Alemán 139 (SP); B Caribe, Av. López Mateos 10; B Oviedo, Costero M. Alemean 207; B Villa Rica, Universidad esq. I. Chávez (SP); C California, La Paz 12; C Don Quijote, Av. Insurgentes 70; C Villa Roma, Morro 22

Actopan

B Rirra, Lerdo de Tejada 50; C Del Convento, Plaza Juárez 15

Aguascalientes (Town)

A Las Trojes, Blvd. Norte y Campestre (SP, T); A Francia, Plaza Principal 113; A Motel Medrano, Blvd. José María Chávez 904 (SP); B Colonial, 5 de Mayo 552; C Roble, 5 de Mayo 502; C San José, Hidalgo 207; D Bahía Guadalupe 144

Akumal

A Las Casitas Akumal (SP, T); A Club Akumal Caribe Villas Maya (SP. T); A Ina Yana Kin Akumal Caribe (SP, T)

Hotels

Amecameca de Juárez	B San Carlos
Bahía Concepción	D Playa Santispac; Posada Concepción; Recreo Playa Cocos
Barra de Navidad	A Cabo Blanco, Pueblo Nuevo (SP, T, F, WS); B Barra de Navidad, Av. López de Legazpi; B El Marqués, Filipinas (S); C Delfin, Morelos 23; D San Lorenzo, Av. Sinaloa 9
Buenavista	A Club Spa Buenavista (SP, T, spa); ★Rancho Buenavista (SP)
Barranca del Cobre	In Creel: B Cabaña Cañon del Combre (22km/14 miles outside the town; no electricity); B Motel Prador de la Montaña; C Casa de Huespedes Margarita; Korachi; Nuevo; in Cerocahui: D Misión (Bahuichivo rail station); in Cuiteco: B Cuiteco; in Divisadero: B Cabañas Divisaderos Barrancas; in Areponapuchic: A Cascada Inn
Cabo San Lucas	L★Cabo San Lucas, Bahia Chileno (SP, T, LS, F, R); L Rancho El Tule (SP, T, LS, F, R); L Clarion Cabo San Lucas, Carr. Transpeninsular km 4·5 marker (SP, F); L★Finisterra, Bahia Cabo San Lucas (SP, F); L★Hacienda, Bahia Cabo San Lucas (SP, T, F, R, SD, WS); L Melia San Lucas, Playa El Médano (SP, T, F); L★Twin Dolphin, Bahia Santa Marta (SP, T, F, R); A★Solmar, Bahi Cabo San Lucas (south end: SP, F); A Bahía, Playa El Médano (SP, F); B Mar de Cortés, Av. L. Cardenas y U. Guerrero (SP); B Marina Cabo San Lucas, Blvd. de La Marina y Guerrero (SP); C Casa Blanca, Av. Morelos y Revolucíon
Campeche (Town)	A Ramada Inn, Av. Ruiz Cortines 51 (SP); A Alhambra, Resurgimiento 85 (SP); A Baluartes, Av. Ruiz Cortines (SP); A Mision Si-ho-Playa, 40km/25 miles along the MEX 180 towards Champotón (by the sea; SP); B López, Calle 12 No. 189; C Central, Gobernadores 462
Cancún In the tourist area	L★Presidente Intercontinental, Blvd. Kukulkan, km 7.5 marker; L★Camino Real, Punta Cancún 14 (SP, T); L★Casa Turquesa, Blvd. Kukulkán, km 13·5 marker (SP, T): L Continental Villas Plaza, Blvd. Kukulkán, km 11 marker (SP, T); L★Hyatt Cancún Caribe, Blvd. Kukulkán, km 10·5 marker (SP, T); L Mariott Casamagna, Blvd. Kukulkán, Retorno Chac L–41 (SP, T); L Miramar Mision Cancún, Blvd. Kukulkán 400 (SP, T); L Paraíso Radisson Cancún, Blvd. Kukulkán, Lote 18 (SP, T); L Sheraton Cancún, Blvd. Kukulkán (SP, T); A★Club Méditerranée, Punta Nizuc (SP, T, SD, S); A Club Las Velas y Marina, Blvd. Kukulkán, esq. Calle Galeón (SP, F); A Fiesta Inn Golf Cancún, Lotes 21 y 22, Paseo Pok Ta Poc (SP, G); A Girasol, Blvd. Kukulkán, km 9 marker (SP); B Cancún Clipper, Blvd. Kukulkán, km 9 marker (SP); B Club Las Perlas, Blvd. Kukulkán, km 2·5 marker (SP); B Dos Playas, Blvd. Kukulkán, km 6·5 marker (SP)
In the town	A América Cancún, Av. Tulum y Brisa (SP); A Mariá de Lourdes, Av. Yaxchilán 80 (SP); B Novotel, Av. Tulum 75 (SP); B Hacienda, Av. Sunyaxchén 39 (SP); B Kokai Suites, Av. Cobá 82; C Canto, Av. Yaxchilán S.M. 22; C Kaché, P. Juárez 15; D Colonial, Tulipanes 22; D Canto, Av. Yaxchilán
Careyes	L Bel-Air, km 53·5, Puerto Vallarta, Barra de Navidad highway (SP, R) L★Las Alamandas, 15km/9 miles north of Chamela (SP, T, R, WS); A★Club Méditerranée, Playa Blanca Cihuatlán (SP, S, SD, R)
Catemaco Lake By the lake	A La Finca, Carr. Costera del Golfo 147 (SP); B Playa Azul, Carr. a Sontecomapán, km 2 marker (SP); C Del Lago, Paseo del Malecón
In the town	B Catemaco, Venustiano Carranza 8 (SP); C Berthangel, Madero 1

Celaya

A Celaya Plaza, Blvd. López Mateos y Carr. Panaméricana (SP); B Mary, Blvd. López Mateos y Zaragoza 1; B Motel El Cid, Blvd. López Mateos 1548 Pte.: C Roble, Av. B. Juárez 106

Champotón

C De Venecia, Calle 38; C Snook Inn, Calle 30 No. 1 con Av. Revolución (F)

Chapala Lake
From east to west along the north bank

A Brisas de Chapala, km 39 marker on the Carr. Guadalajara–Chapala (SP); A Danza del Sol, Zaragoza 165, Ajijic (SP); B Chapala Haciendas, km 40 marker on the Carr. Guadalajara–Chapala; B El Nido, Av. F. Madero (SP); B Nueva Posada, Donato Guerra 9; B Villas Buenaventura, Carr. Chapala–Jocotopec, (SP); C Posada del Pescador, Jocotepec (SP)

Chetumal

A Best Western Continental Caribe, Av. de los Héroes 171 (SP); A Los Cocos Chetumal, Av. de los Héroes 134 y Chapultepec (SP); B El Marqués, Av. Lázaro Cárdenas 121 (SP); B Caribe Princess, Av. Alvaro Obregón 168; D El Rey, Leona Vicario 346

Chichén Itzá

A Hacienda Chichén (SP); ★ Mayaland (SP); ★ Villas Arqueológicas (SP); in Pisté: A Mision Chichén Itzá (SP); B Pirámide Inn (SP); Posada Novelo; C Cunanchén; D Dolores Alba, Carr. 180, km 122 marker (SP)

Chihuahua

L★ Palacio Del Sol, Independencia 500 (SP); L★ San Francisco Park, Plaza International, Victoria 409; L★ Sicomoro, Blvd. Ortiz Mena 411 (SP); A Mirador, Av. de Universidad 1309; A Parador San Miguel, Av. Technológico 7901; B Del Pacifico, Calle Aldama 1911; C El Capitán, Av. Technológico 2300

Chilpancingo
de los Bravos

A Jacarandas, Rufo Figueroa (SP); B Posada Meléndez, Av. Juárez 50 (SP); C Laura Elena, Francisco Madero 1

Cholula

A★ Club Med Villas Arqueológicas (SP); B Calli Quetzalcóatl, Portal Guerrero 11 (SP); B Campestre los Sauces, km 122 marker on the Carr. México–Puebla; Calli Quetzalcóatl, Portal Guerrero 11

Ciudad Juárez

L Chula Vista, Paseo T. de la Républica 3555 Ote. (SP); Plaza Juárez, Av. Lincoln y Coyoacán (SP); B Impala, Av. Lerdo 670 Nte.; C Manport, Altamirano 103; D Asturias, Vicente Guerrero 102

Ciudad del Carmen

L Eurohotel, Calle 22 No. 208 (SP); A Del Parque, Calle 33 entre 20 y 22 (SP); B Isla del Carmen, Calle 20–A, No. 9; C Acuario, Calle 51 No. 60

Cobá

L★ Club Med Villas Arqueológicas (by Lago Cobá; SP, T)

Colima

A America, Av. Morelos 162 (SP); A María Isabel, Blvd. Camino Real km 1 marker, (SP); B Villa del Rey, Blvd. Camino Real km 1 marker (SP); C Ceballos, Torres Quintero 16; D El Tapatío, Medellín 651

Córdoba

A Palacio, Av. 3 y Calle 2 (SP); A Real Villa Florida, Av. 1 No. 3002 (SP); B Marina, Av. y Calle 11; C Virrereynal, Av. 1 No. 309

Cozumel
On the beach

L★ Coral Princess, Zona Hotelera Nte., km 2·5 marker (SP, SD, F, WS); L★ El Cozumeleño, Playa Santa Pilar (SP, T, F, WS, SD); L Holiday Inn Cozumel Reef, Carr, Chankanab, km 7·5 marker (SP, F, T, WS, SD); L Presidente Intercontinental, Carr. Chankanab, km 6·5 marker (SP, T, WS, SD, F); A Fiesta Inn, Costera Sur, at km 1·7 marker (SP, SD, WS, F); A Sol Cabañas del Caribe, Carr. Santa Pilar, km 4·5 marker (SP, SD, WS, F); B Casa del Mar, Costera Sur, km 4 marker (SP, WS, SD); B La Perla, Carr. Chankanab, km 2·2 marker (SP, SD, WS)

Hotels

In the town	B Barracuda, Av. R. Melgar Prol. Sur 628 (SP); B Colonial 5a Av. Sur 9; B Mesón San Miguel, Av. Juárez 2 (SP); C El Marqués, 5a Av. Sur 8; D Flores, Calle Adolfo R. Salas 72
Cuauhtémoc	A Posada del Sol, Calz. Belisario Chávez (SP); B Tarahumara Inn, Allende y 5a Av. (SP); C Granada, V. Guerrero y A. Melgar (SP)
Cuautla	L ★ Hacienda Cocoyoc – see under Hacienda hotels; A El Varadero, Carr. México–Oaxaca 468 (SP); B Méson del Rey, Progreso 505
Cuernavaca	L ★ Calinda Racquet Club, Francisco Villa 100 (SP, T); L ★ Camino Réal Sumiya, Fracc. Sumiya, Col. José Parres; L ★ Hacienda de Cortes, Plaza Kennedy 90, Col. Atlacomulco; L ★ Hosteria Las Quintas, Av. Díaz Ordaz 107 (SP, T); A ★ Las Mañanitas, R. Linares 107 (SP); A llebal, Chula Vista 7 (SP); B Mariaba, Sonora 1000; C España, Av. Morelos 200; C 20 de Julio, Cuauhtémoc 22; D Gaby, Carr. Cuernavaca–Cuautla, km 2·5 marker;
Culiacán	A Executivo, Av. A. Obregón y Blvd. Madero (SP); B Lord, M. Hidalgo 552 Ote.; C Valle Bonito, Blvd. Solano y J. Carranza
Durango (Town)	L Gobernador, Av. 20 de Noviembre 257 Ote. (SP); A Fiesta Mexicana, Av. de 20 de Noviembre e Independencia (SP); B Los Arcos, Heróico Colegio Militar 2204 Ote; C Prince, Juárez 502 Sur
Ensenada	A Ensanada TraveLodge, Av. Blancarte 130 (SP, T); A Estero Beach Resort, Playa Estero (SP, T); A La Pinta Prado Inn, 1a y Bucaneros (SP); B Colonial, Av. Miramar 120; C Anaya, Gastelum 127
Fortin de las Flores	A Fortín de las Flores, Av. 2 entre 5 y 7; B El Pueblito, Av. 2 Ote. No. 505
Gómez Palacio	A Posada del Rio, Madero y Juárez (SP); B Motel La Siesta, F. I. Madero 320 Nte.; C Motel Monarrez, Madero y Centennario 301 Nte.
Guadalajara	L ★ Camino Real, Av. Vallarta 5005 (SP, T); L ★ Fiesta Americana, Guadalajara, Aurelio Aceves 225 (SP, T); L ★ Hyatt Regency, López Mateos Sur y Av. Moctezuma (SP); L ★ Quinta Real, Av. México 2727 (SP); L ★ Carlton Hotel Guadalajara, Av. Niños Héroes y 16 de Septiembre (SP); A Calinda Roma, Av. Juárez 170 (SP); A De Mendoza, V. Carranza 16 (SP); A Fénix, Av. Corona 160; A Francés, Maestranza 35; B Colón, Revolución Pte. 12; B Del Parque, Juárez 845; B Isabel, Gpe. Montenegro 1572 (SP); C Campo Bello, Av. López Mateos Sur 1599; C Estación, Calz. Independencia Sur 1297; C San Jose, 5 de Febrero 166
Guanajuato (Town)	A ★ Castillo de Santa Cecilia, Carr. a Dolores Hidalgo, km 1 marker (SP); A ★ Parador San Javier, Plaza Aldama 92 (SP); A ★ Real de Minas, Nejayote 17; A ★ San Gabriel Barrera, Camino Viejo a Marfil km 2 marker (SP, T); B Hacienda de Cobos, Calle Hidalgo 3; B San Diego, Jardin Union 1; C Alhóndiga, Insurgencia 49; (outside): ★ A Comanjilla, Carr. Panaméricana, km 385 marker Comanjilla, Gto. (SP, T)
Guaymas In the town	A Armida, Blvd. García López (SP); B Ana, Calle 5, No. 135; B Impala Calle 21 No. 40
On Carr. Internacional	B Casa Blanca, Carr. International 129 (SP)
On Bahia Baccochibampo	A ★ Playa de Cortés (SP, T); Leo's Inn, Norte de Miramar (SP, T)
On the Bahia; San Carlos	L Howard Johnson, Creston Nte. Lote 367 (SP, T, SD, F, WS); A ★ Club Méditerranée, Playa de los Algodones (SP, T, WS, SD); B Fiesta San Carlos, Carr. a San Carlos km 8.5 marker

Hermosillo

L Holiday Inn, Blvd. Eusebio Kino 369 (SP); A Bugambilia Valle Grande, Blvd. Eusebio Kino 712 (SP); B Gándara, Blvd. Eusebio Kino 1000 (SP)

Huatulco

L ★Sheraton Huatulco, Bahía de Tagolunda (SP, T, F, WS, SD); L Club Plaza Huatulco, Bahía de Tagolunda (SP, T, WS, SD, F); A ★Club Méditerranée, Bahía de Tagolunda (SP, T, SD, F, WS); A Posada Flamboyant, Bahía de Santa Cruz (SP, F); B Suites Bugambilias, Bugambilias esq. Flamboyant (SP); C Grifer, Av. Guamúchil esq. Garrizal (SP)

Isla Mujeres

A Cabañas Maria del Mar, Carlos Lazo 1 (SP); A Na Balam, Calle Zazil-ha 118 (SP); B Berny, Juárez y Abasolo (SP); B Perla del Caribe, Av. Fco. I Madero 2; B Rocamar, Av. Nicolás Bravo y Zona Marítima; C Caracol, Av. Matamoros 5; D Osorio, Av. Madero

Ixmiquilpan

B Avenida, Insurgentes 89; B Club Alcantara, Peña y Ramírez

Ixtapa

L ★Westin Ixtapa Resort, Playa Vista Hermosa (SP, T, WS); L Dorado Pacífico, Blvd. Ixtapa (SP, T, G, WS); L Krystal Ixtapa, Blvd. Ixtapa (SP, T, WS); L Omni Ixtapa, Blvd. Ixtapa Lote 5A (SP, T, G, SD, WS); L Puerta del Mar, Paseo de las Gaviotas esq. Agua de Correa (SP, T, W); L Presidente Intercontinental Ixtapa, Blvd. Ixtapa (SP, T, WS); A Villa del Lago, Retorno Alondras (SP, T, WS)

Ixtapán de la Sal

A Ixtapán, Plaza San Gaspar (SP, T); A Villa Vergel,, Blvd. San Román y Av. Juárez (SP); B Sara Isabel, Blvd. Arturo San Román (SP)

Jalapa (Xalapa)

L Xalapa, Victoria y Bustamante (SP); A María Victoria, Zaragoza 6 (SP); B Posada del Virrey, Dr. Lucio 142; C Limón, Av. Revolución 8

Lago de Pátzcuaro

See Pátzcuaro Lake

Laguna de Catemoco

See Catemoco Lake

Laguna de Chapala

See Chapala Lake

Lagunas de Montebello

See Montebello Lakes

La Paz

L Gran Baja, Calle Rangel (SP, T); L Palmira, Blvd. Alberto Arámburu (SP, T); A La Concha, Carr. Pichelingue, km 5 marker (SP, T); A Los Arcos, A. Obregon 498 (SP, F, SD); B Perla, Av. A. Obregón 1570 (SP); C La Purísima, 16 de Septiembre 408; D San Bernardino, Abasolo 436

León de los Aldamas

L Estancia del León, Blvd. López Mateos 1311 Ote. (SP); L Fiesta Americana León, Blvd. López Mateos 1102 (SP); A Condesa, Portal Bravo 14; B El Dorado, B. Domínquez 320; B Rex, 5 de Febrero y Pino Suárez; C Fénix, I. Comonfort 338

Loreto

L Presidente Intercontinental, Blvd. Misión de Loreto; A La Pinta Prado Inn, Prol. Fco. Madero (SP); B Misión de Loreto, Blvd. López Mateos 1 (SP); C Oasis, Baja California

Los Bariles

A Palmas de Cortés (SP, T); Playa Hermosa (SP, T); ★Punta Pescadora (SP, T, L; 15km/9 miles north).

Los Mochis

A El Dorado, Gabriel Levya 525 (SP); A Santa Anita, Leyva y Hidalgo (SP); B Del Sol, Blvd. M. Gaxiola y 10 de Mayo; B Posada Real, Levya y Buelna; C Fénix, Av. Flores 3652; C Montecarlo, Angel Flores 322 Sur

Manzanillo In town centre

B Colonial, Av. México 100 (SP); C Miramar, Juárez 122; D Flamingos, Madero y 10 de Mayo

Hotels

Peninsula de Santiago	L ★ Las Hadas Resort (SP, T, G, R, F); L Puerto Las Hadas (SP, T, G, WS, F); L Sierra Manzanillo (SP, T, F, WS); A Club Maeva Manzanillo (SP, T, WS, G, R, F); A Plaza Las Glorias (SP); B Playa Santiago (SP)
Playa Azul	A Brisamar (SP); A Martha's Custom Suites (SP); B Suites New York; B Suites Rosa Mar
Playa La Audencia	B Orduña (SP)
Playa Las Brisas	A Club Vacacional Las Brisas (SP); La Posada (SP)
Matamoros	L Gran Hotel Residencial, Av. A. Obregon 249 (SP); A Minerva Paula, 11A y Matamoros (SP); B Ritz, Matamoros 6
Matehuala	A Motel Las Palmas, Carr. Central km 617 marker; B Motel Oasis, Carr. Central, km 617 marker; C Motel El Pedregal, Carr. Central, km 618 marker (SP)
Mazatlán In the town	B Central, B. Dominguez y A. Flores; C Papagayo, Papagayo 712
From south to north along the bank	L ★ Camino Real, Punta de Sábalo (SP, T, F, WS, SD); L ★ El Cid Mega Resort, Calz. Camarón Sábalo (SP, T, WS, F, SD); L El Rancho, Av. Sábalo–Cerritos 3000 (SP, F, SD, WS); L Holiday Inn Mazatlán, Calz. Camarón Sábalo 696 (SP, T, F, WS); L Los Sábalos, T. Loaiza 100 (SP, T, F, WS); L Playa Mazatlán, T. Loaiza 202 (SP, T, SD, F, WS); A Aguamarina Best Western, Av. del Mar 110; L Balboa Towers, Av. Camarón Sábalo y Callejón Guerrero (SP, F, WS, SD); A Costa de Oro, Calz. Camarón Sábalo (SP, T, F, WS); A De Cima, Av. del Mar (SP); A Las Jacarandas, Av. del Mar 2500 SP); B Azteca Inn, T. Loaiza 307 (SP); B Motel del Sol, Av. del Mar 800 (SP); B Posada de Don Pelayo, Av. del Mar 1111 (SP)
Mérida	L ★ Casa del Balam, Calle 60 N0. 488 (SP); L ★ Holiday Inn Mérida, Av. Colón No. 498 y Calle 60 (SP); L Fiesta Americana, Av, Colón 451, Esq. Paeso Montejo (SP, T); L Hyatt Regency Mérida, Av. Colón, Esq. Calle 60 (SP, T); A Colonial, Calle 62 No. 476 x 57 (SP); A D'Champs, Calle 70 No. 543 x 67 Centro (SP); A El Castellano, Calle 57 No. 513 (SP); B Colón, Calle 62 No. 483; B Gran Hotel, Calle 60 No. 496; B Paseo de Montejo, Paseo de Montejo 482 (SP); C El Caminante, Calle 64 No. 539; C Flamingo, Calle 57 No. 485; C México, Calle 60 No. 525; D América, Calle 67 No. 500
Mexicali	L Holiday Inn Crowne Plaza, Blvd. de los Héroes 501 (SP); L Holiday Inn Mexicali, Blvd. b Juárez 2220 (SP); A Calafia, Calz. Justo Sierra 1495 (SP); B La Siesta, Calz. Justo. Sierra 899 (SP)
Mexico City (Ciudad de México) Paseo de la Reforma and surroundings and other parts of the city centre	L ★ Camino Real: Mariano Escobedo 700 (SP, T); L ★ Nikko México, Campos Elíseos 204 (SP); L ★ Presidente Intercontinental, Campos Elíseos 218 (SP); L ★ Four Seasons Hotel, P. de la Reforma 500; L Crowne Plaza, Reforma 1; L Fontan, Colón esq. con Reforma (SP); L Holiday Inn Crowne Plaza, Reforma 80 (SP); L Imperial, Paseo de la Reforma 64 (SP); L Marco Polo, Ambéres 27 (SP); L Marquis Reforma, Paseo de la Reforma 465 (SP); L Sheraton María Isabel, Paseo de la Reforma 325 (SP); L Westin Galería Plaza, Hamburgo 195 (SP); L Fiesta Americana, P. de la Reforma 80 (SP); A Calinda Genève, Londres 130 (SP); A Clarion Reforma, Paseo de la Reforma 373; A ★ De Cortez, Av. Hidalgo 85; A ★ Majestic, Av. F. I. Madero 73; A ★ Ritz, Av. F. I. Madero 30; B Del Angel, Río Lerma 154; B Lepanto, Guerrero 90; B Maria

Cristina, Río Lerma 31; B Misión México, Napoles 62; C Isabel, Isabel La Catolica 63; C Londres, Plaza Buena Vista 5; B Viena, Marsella 28

In the outskirts

L Fiesta Americana, Aeropuerto (SP); L Holiday Inn, Aeropuerto (SP); L Real del Sur, Av. Divisón del Norte 3640; A Brasilia, Av. Cien Metros 4823; A Cibeles, Calz. de Tlalpan 1507; B Cien Metros, Av. Cien Metros 1191; B Oslo, L. Cardenas 337

Mitla

B Posada La Sorpresa

Montebello Lakes

D Albergue by Tziscao Lake

Monterrey

L ★Ambassador, Hidalgo 310 Ote. (SP, T); L ★Gran Hotel Ancira, Hidalgo y Escobedo (SP); L Fiesta Americana Mty., Av. Vasconcelos 300 Ote (SP, T); L Holiday Inn Crowne Plaza, Av. Constitución 300 (SP, T); A Antaris, Río Danubio 400 Ote. (SP); A Fastos, Av. Colón y Villagrán; A Holiday Inn Express, Av. Eugenio Garza Sada Sur 3680 (SP); B Jandal, Cuauhtémoc 825 Nte.; B Quinta Avenida, Madero 243 Ote.; B Soles, Jiménez 1120 Nte.; C Los Reyes, Hidalgo Pte. 543C Nuevo León, Amado Nervo 1007 Nte.; D Parador Granada, Washington 209 Pte.

In San Nicolás de los Garza

L Days Inn–Granada Monterrey, Av. Jorge de Moral (SP, T); A Dorado, Carr. a Laredo 901 Nte. (SP); B Palmas, Carr. a Laredo, km 14·5 marker (SP)

Morelia

L ★Calinda Morelia Quality Inn, Av. Camelinas 3466 (SP, T); L Comfort Morelia, Av. Camelinas 500 (SP, T); L Gran Hotel Centro, Av. V. Puenta/ Camelinas; A ★De La Soledad, Ignacio Zaragoza 90 (SP); A Mansión de la Calle Real, Av. Madero 766 Ote. (SP); A Marco Polo Bugambilias, Av. Camelinas 3325 (SP); A ★Virey de Mendoza, Portal Matamoros 16; B Catedral, Zaragoza 37; B Las Américas, Av. Camelinas 2783; C Posada de Don Vasco, Vasco de Quiroga 232

Outside

A ★Villa Montana, Patzimba (SP, T)

Nogales

A Fray Marcos Niza, Obregón y Campillo (SP); A Granada, Av. Lopez Mateos y González (SP); B Imperial, Av. Obregón 19; C Regis, Av. Juárez 34

Nuevo Casas Grandes

A Hacienda, Av. Juárez 2603 Norte (SP, T); B Pinon, Av. Juárez 605 (SP)

Nuevo Laredo

A Hacienda Motor Hotel, Prolongación Av. Reforma 5530 (SP); A Villa Real, C. López de Lara 2412 (SP); B Cazadores, Ocampo 2502; C Don Antonio, González 2437; D Dos Laredos, Matamoros 108

Oaxaca

L ★Presidente Intercontinental, Calle 5 de Mayo 300 (SP); L San Felipe de Oaxaca, Av. Jalisco 15 Sur (SP); L Victoria, Lomas del Fortín 1 (SP, T); A Hostal de la Noria, Av. Hidalgo 918 (SP); A Misión de los Angeles, Calz. Porfirio Díaz 102 (SP, T); B Hacienda La Noria, Periférico Esq. La Costa (SP); B Margarita, Calz. Madero 1254; B Marqués del Valle, Portal de Clavería; B Parador Plaza Hotel, Murguía 104; B Señorial, Portal de Flores 6; C Las Golandrinas, Palacios 411; C Mesón del Rey, Trujano 212; C Monte Alban, Alameda de León 1

Orizaba

A ★Fiesta Cascada, Carr. Puebla–Córdoba, km 275 marker (SP, T, G); A L'Orbe, Poniente 5 No. 33 (SP); B Aries, Oriente 6 No. 263; B Plaza Palacio, Poniente 2 esq. Norte 1

Pachuca de Soto

A Country Club Calinda, Carr. México–Pachuca, km 855 marker (SP, T, G); B Ciro's, Plaza Independencia 110; B La Paz, Carr. Cubitos–La Paz, km 2 marker (SP); C Noriega, Matamoros 305; D Grenfel, Plaza Independencia 116

Palenque
In the town

B Casa de Pakal, Juárez 10; La Cañada, Calle Merle Green 13; B Maya Tulipanes, Cañada 6; C Misol-há, Av. Juárez 14; C Palenque, Av. 5 de Mayo 15 (SP); C Vaca Vieja, Av. 5 de Mayo 42; D Avenida, Av. Juárez 173

Outside

A Misión Palenque, Rancho San Martín de Porres (SP); A Best Western Plaza Palenque, Playas de Catazajá–Palenque, km 27 marker (SP, T); B Chan-Kah, Carr. a las Ruinas, km 31 marker; B Nututún Palenque, Carr. Palenque–Ocosingo, km 3·5 marker (open-air swimming pool); B Tulija, Carr. Zona Arqueológica, km 27.5 marker

Papantla

B Totonacapán, Olivo y 20 de Noviembre; C Arenas, Victoria 1; C El Tajín, Núñez Domíngez 104; D Papantla, Enríquez 103

Pátzcuaro Lake
In Pátzcuaro

B Fiesta Plaza, G. Bacanegra 24; B Los Escudos, Portal Hidalgo 73; B Mansión Iturbe, Portal Morelos 59; B Mesón de Gallo, Dr. Coss 20 (SP); C Posada de la Salud, Av. Serrato 9; C Posada la Basílica, Av. Arciga 6; C Val-Men, Lloreda 34

Outside

A Posada de Don Vasco, Av. Lázaro Cárdenas 450 (SP); B Mesón de Cortijo, Av. Alvaro Obregón y Glorieta Tanganyuan; B Villa Pátzcuaro, Av. Lázaro Cárdenas 506; C La Basílica, Av. Lázaro Cárdenas 500

In Tzintzuntzan

B Cabañas Tzintzuntzan, Carr. Piroga–Pátzcuaro, at km 6 marker

Playa del Carmen

L Continental Plaza, Bahía del Espíritu Santo (SP); A Diamond; B The Blue Parrot Inn; D Lily

Puebla
de Zaragoza

L ★El Mesón del Angel, Av. Hermanos Serdán 807 (SP, T); L ★Gran Hotel del Alba, Hermanos Serdán 141 (SP); L Aristos Puebla, Av. Reforma 533 (SP); L Condado Plaza, Priv. 6-B Sur 3106 (SP, T); L Misión Puebla, Calle 5 Poniente 2522 (SP); A Lastra, Calz. de los Fuertes 2633 (SP); A Posada San Pedro, Av. 2 Oriente 202 (SP); B Colonial, 4 Sur 105; B Royalty, Portal Hidalgo 8; B Señorial, Calle 4 Norte 602; C Imperial, 4 Oriente 212; C San Sebastián, 8 Oriente 403

Puerto Angel

B Angel del Mar, Playa del Pantéon; B La Posada Cañon Devata; C Soraya, Calle Virgilio Uribe; D Casa de Huéspedes Gundi y Tomás

Puerto Escondido
In the town

A Santa Fé, Calle del Morro (SP); B Arco Iris, Calle del Morro; B Nayar, Av. A. Pérez Gasca 407; B Paraíso Escondido, Calle Union 10; C Las Palmas, Av. A Pérez Gasca; C Rincón del Pacífico, Av. A Pérez Gasca 503

Outside

A Fiesta Mexicana, Blvd. B. Juárez (SP); A Posada Real, Blvd. B. Juárez Lote 11 (SP); A Suites Villasol, Loma Bonita 2 (SP); B Camino del Sol, Carr. Costera, km 1·5 marker (SP); B El Mirador, Carr. Costera del Pacífico 113 (SP)

Puerto Morelos

L Maroma, Highway 307, km 51 marker, Costa Maya (SP); B La Ceiba; C Playa Ojo de Agua

Punta Beté

B Camptel Kai Luum; B El Marlín Azul; B La Posada de Capitán Lafitte (SP, SD, F)

Puerto Vallarta
In the town

A Buenaventura, Av. México 1301; A Descanso del Sol, Pino Suárez 583 (SP); A Oro Verde, Rodolfo Gómez 111 (SP); B Nuevo Hotel Rosita, Paseo Díaz Ordaz 901; B Tropicana, Amapas 274A (SP); C Océano, Galeana 103; D Río , Morelos 170

North of Rio Cuale on the Bahia de Banderas

L Bel Air Resort Vallarta, Pelicanos 311, (SP, T, G);L ★Krystal Puerto Vallarta, Av. de las Garzas (SP, T, WS, F); L ★Sheraton Bugambilias, Carr. al Aeropuerto 999 (SP, T, G); L Marriott Casamagna, Paseo de la Marina 5 (SP, T, F, WS); L Los Tules, Carr. al Aeropuerto km 2.5 marker (SP); L Plaza Las Glorias, Av. de las Garzas (SP, T, F, WS); L Quinta Real, Pelícanos 311 (SP. T, G); A Las Palmas, Paseo de las Palmas km 2·5 marker (SP, F, WS); A Pelícanos, Carr. al Aeropuerto km 2·5 marker

South of Rio Cuale

L ★Camino Real, Playa Las Estacas (SP, T); L Hyatt Coral Grand, Carr. a Barra de Navidad, km 8·5 marker (SP, T, F); A Conchas Chinas, Carr. a Barra de Navidad, km 2·5 marker (SP); A Playa Los Arcos, Olas Altas 380 (SP, F, SD, WS)

Querétaro (Town)

L ★Meson de Santa Rosa, Pasteur Sur 17; L Holiday Inn, Av. 5 de Febrero 110; L Plaza Camelinas, Av. de 5 de Febrero 28; A Casablanca, Av. Constituyentes 69 Pte. (SP, T); A Mirabel, Constituyentes 2 Ote; A Torre Blanca, Av. Constituyentes 67; B Amberes, Corregidora Sur 188; B Impala, Colón y Corregidora; C Del Marquez, Juárez 104

Outside

A ★Hacienda Jurica, Carr. a San Luis Potosi, km 229 marker (SP, T, R); B Azteca Hotel Motor Inn, Carr. a San Luis Potosí, km 15·5 marker

Salamanca

A Suites Aliana, Paseo de los Prados 129; B El Monte, Juárez T. Estévez; B Trevi, Hidalgo 221

Saltillo

L ★Camino Real Saltillo, Blvd. Los Fundadores 2000 (SP, T); L La Quinta Inns, Blvd. Echeverría y La Fragua (SP); A Motel La Fuente, Blvd. Los Fundadores, km 3 marker (SP, T); B Saade, Aldama 397 Pte

San Andrés Tuxtla

B Del Parque, F Madero 5; B Posada San José, Belisario Domínquez 10

San Cristobal de las Casas

A Flamboyant Español, Calle 1 de Marzo 15; A Casa Mexicana, 28 de Agosto 1 (T); A Hotel Diego de Mazariegos, Maria Adelina Flores 2; A, B Rincón del Arco, Ejercito Nacional 66; B Bonampak, Calz. México 5; B Ciudad Real, Plaza 31 de Marzo 10; B ★Na Bolom, Av. V. Guerrero 33 (with museum and library); C Fray Bartolomé de las Casas, Niños Heroes 2; C San Martin, Real de Guadelupe 34

San José del Cabo

L Calinda San José del Cabo (SP, T, F); L Howard Johnson (SP, T, F); L Presidente Intercontinental (SP, T, F); Westin Regina, Carr. San José del Cabo – Cabo San Lucaskm 22.6 marker; A Fiesta Inn (SP, F)

In the town

B Tropicana Inn, Blvd. Mijares 30; C Colli, Calle Hidalgo; C Posada Terranova, Calle Degollado y Zaragoza (SP); D San José Inn, Calle Degollado

San Juan del Río

L ★Antigua Hacienda de Galindo, Carr. Amealco–Querétaro, km 5 marker (SP, T); A ★La Estancia de San Juan, Carr. México a Querétaro, km 172 marker (SP, T, R)

San Luis Potosi

A Panorama, Av. Carranza 315 (SP); B Filher, Av. Universidad 375; B Maria Cristina, Juan Sarabia 110; C Plaza, Jardin Hidalgo 22

Outside

L Maria Dolores, Carr. San Luis Potosí a México, km 1 marker (SP); L Motel Hostal del Quijote, Carr. 57, km 420 marker (SP); L Real de Minas, Carr. 57, km 426·6 marker (SP); B Colonial, Diagonal Sur 340

San Miguel de Allende

L ★Casas de Sierra Nevada, Hospico 35 (SP, T); A ★La Puertecita Boutique Hotel, Santo Domingo 75 (SP); A ★ Hacienda Taboada, Carr. a Dolores Hidalgo, km 8 marker (SP; out of town); A ★Villa Santa

Mónica, Baeza 22 (SP); A Aristos de San Miguel, Calle Ancha de San Antonio 30 (SP, T); A Villa Jacaranda, Aldama 53 (SP); B Hacienda de las Flores, Hospicio 16 (SP); B Mansión del Bosque, Aldama 65; C Hotel Central, Canal 19; C Posada Carmina, Cuna de Allende 7; C Sautto, Hernandez Macías 59; D Parador San Sebastián, Mesones 7

San Quintin B La Pinta (SP); C Cielito Lindo Motel; D Molino Viejo; D Motel Chávez

Santa Rosalia B El Morro, Carr. Transpeninsular Sur, km 1·5 marker (SP); B Francés, Av. 11 Julio 30; D Blanco y Negro, Av. Sarabia 1 y Calle 3

Tampico L Camino Real, Av. Hidalgo 2000 (SP); L Inglaterra, Salvador Díaz Mirón 116 Ote (SP); L Posada de Tampico, Prol. Av. Hidalgo 2200 (SP, T); A Colonial de Tampico, F. I. Madero 210 Ote; B Costa Brava, Calz. San Pedro 111; C Galería, Alameda esq. F. I. Madero; D Imperial, López de Lara 101 Sur

Tapachula A Loma Real, Carr. Costera 200, km 244 marker (SP, T); B Don Miguel, 1a Calle Pte. 18; C Fénix, 4a Av. Nte. 19

Taxco de Alarcón L ★Monte Taxco, Lomas de Taxco (by way of the "Teleférico" cable railway; SP, T, G, R); A ★Hacienda del Solar, Pareje del Solar (SP, T, G, R); A De La Borda, Cerro del Pedregal 2 (SP); B ★Rancho Taxco Victoria, Carlos J. Nibbi 14 (SP); B Agua Escondida, G. Spratling 4 (SP); B Loma Linda, Av. Kennedy 52; B Los Arcos, J. Ruiz de Alarcón 12 (SP); C Posada de los Castillos, J. Ruiz de Alarcón

Tehuacán A Villablanca, Calz. A. López Mateos 1800 (SP); C Acuario, Lerdo 327

Tehuantepec A Calli, Carr. Crisóbal Colón, km 790 marker (SP); B Donaji, Juárez 10

Teotihuacán A ★Club Med Villa Teotihuacán, Zona Arqueológica (SP, T); D La Cascada, Carr. México–Tulancinquo, km 12·5 marker

Tepic A Fray Junipero Serra, Lerdo y México (SP); B Ibarra, Durango 297 Nte.

Tepotzotlán A Tepoztián (SP); B Posada de Teporzteco

Tepoztlán A Tepoztlán (SP); B Posada de Tepozteco

Tequisquiapán L Sol y Fiesta, Av. Heróico Colegio Militar 4 (SP, T); A Las Cavas, Paseo de la Media Luna 8 (SP, T); B El Relox, Morelos 8 (SP)

Tequesquitengo L ★Hacienda Vista Hermosa, Carr. Alpuyeca–Tequesquitengo, km 7 marker (SP, T, R); A Tamay, Lago de Tequesquitengo (SP, WS)

Texcoco de Mora D Castillo, M. González y Juárez Nte.; D Colón, Colón 218

Teziutlán A Mesón de San Luis, Barrio de Aguateno Camino a Toluca

Tijuana L ★Gran Hotel Americana Tijuana, Blvd. Agua Caliente 4500 (SP, T); L Lucerna Tijuana, Paseo de los Héroes 10902 (SP); L Paraíso Radissón Tijuana, Blvd. Aguacaliente 1 (SP, G); A Country Club, Blvd. Aguacaliente esq. con Tapachula (SP); B Alfredos, Bugambilias 50; B Padre Kino, Aguacaliente 3; B Riviera, Margaritas 6; C Leyva, Constitución 236; C Plaza, Quinta 2019; D Coliseo, Mutualismo 629

Tlaxcala (Town) L ★Posada de San Francisco, Plaza de la Constitución 17 (SP, T); A Chalets Tlaxcala, Blvd. Revolución 6 (SP); B Jeroc's, Blvd. Revolución 4B

A Marquis Paseo Tollocan 1056 Ote.; B Tollocan, Paseo Tollocan 806; C Colonial, Av. Hidalgo Ote. 103	**Toluca** de Lerdo
L Holiday Inn Toluca, Carr. México–Toluca, km 63.5 marker (SP, T)	Outside
L Del Prado, Paseo de la Rosita 910 (SP); L Paraiso del Desierto, Blvd. de la Independencia 101 Ote (SP, T); A Calvete, Ramón Corona Sur 320 (SP); B Posada del Rey, V. Carillo 333 Sur	**Torreón**
A La Joya, Carr. Pirámides–Tulancingo, km 92 marker; B Genisa, Zaragoza 100	**Tulancingo**
C El Faisán y El Venado, on the turn-off from the MEX 307; C Maya Tulum, 4km/2½ miles before reaching the ruins; D Crucero, 1km/½ mile before reaching the ruins on the turn-off from the MEX 307	**Tulum**
A Boca Paila Fishing Lodge (22km/14 miles; SP, F); A Qualton Club Pez Maya Fishing and Beach Resort (25·5km/16 miles; F); C Cabañas Chac-Mool (5·5km/3½ miles); D Cabañas de Tulum (7·5km/5 miles); D Los Arrecifes (7km/4½ miles)	Coast road to the south
L Flamboyant Blvd. Dr. Belisario Dominguez, km 1081 marker (SP); A Real de Tuxtla, Carr. Panaméricana 1088 (SP); B Alberto, 1a Pte. Sur 537; C Avenida, Central Norte 224; Camino Real, Blvd. Dr Belisario Dominguez 1195 (SP, T)	**Tuxtla Gutiérrez**
A ★ Mansión de Cupatitzio, Parque Nacional (SP); A ★ Real de Uruapan, Nicolas Bravo 110; A Plaza Uruapan, Ocampo 64; B Concordia, Portal Carillo 8; B Nuevo Hotel Alameda, 5 de Febrero 11	**Uruapan** de Progreso
A ★ Hacienda Uxmal, Carr. Mérida a Campeche, km 78 marker (SP); A ★ Club Med Villa Uxmal, Carr. Muna Sta. Elena (SP); B Misión Uxmal, Carr. Mérida–Campeche, km 78 marker (SP)	**Uxmal**
B El Mesón del Marqués, Calle 39 No. 203 (SP); C Don Luis, Calle 329 no. 191	**Vallodolid**
A Fontanarica, Calle Fontana 16 (SP); A Los Arcos, F. González Bocanegra 310 (SP)	**Valle de Bravo**
L ★ Avándero Golf and Spa, Fracc. Avándero (SP, T, G, R); B Parador Avándero, Vega del Campo 19 (SP, R)	In Avándero
L Emporio, Insurgentes Veracruzanas 210 (SP); L Howard Johnson, Blvd. A. Camacho 1263 (SP); B Colonial, Miguel Lerdo 117; B Gran Hotel Diligencias, Av Independencia 1115 (SP); C Guadalajara, Mina 1053	**Veracruz** (Town)
L ★ Torremar Resort, Av. A Ruiz Cortines 4300 (SP, T); A Playa Paraíso, Blvd. Ruiz Cortines 3500 (SP); A Villa del Mar, Blvd. A. Camacho (SP, T): B Posada de Cortés, M. Suárez 1314	South by the lakeside
L ★ Hyatt Villahermosa, Av. Juárez 106 (SP, T); L Holiday Inn Tabasco Plaza, Paseo Tabasco 1407 (SP, T); A Cancali, Juárez y Paseo Tabasco (SP);A Maya Tabasco, A. R. Ruiz Cortinez 907 (SP, T); B Don Carlos, Av. Madero 418; C Laguna, Sindicato de Economía 212; D Madero, Madero 301	**Villahermosa**
L Aristos Zacatecas, Lomas de Soledad (SP, T); L Gallery Best Western, Blvd. L Mateos y Callejón del Barro (SP); L ★ Quinta Real, Av. Rayón	**Zacatecas** (Town)

434; A★ Paraíso Radisson, Av. Hidalgo 703; A Misión del Real, Blvd. L. Portillo 12; B Posada de los Condes, Av. Juárez 107; C Condesa, Av. Juárez 5

Zihuatanejo (Town)

A Puerto Mío, Paseo del Morro 5; B Zihuatanejo Centro, A. Ramírez 2; B Zihuatanejo Inn, Av. de los Mangos y Calle Las Palapas (SP); C Tres Marías, Calle Juan Alvarez 52

Playa de la Madera

A Irma (SP); B Posada Caracol; B Villas Miramar; C Palacios

Playa de la Ropa

L★ Villa del Sol; A Fiesta Mexicana (SP); A★ La Casa que Canta (SP); B Bungalows Palacios; B Sotavento; C Catalina

Zimapán

D Posada del Rey, Carr. 85 México–Laredo, km 206 marker

Hacienda hotels

Haciendas are large estates which were given as rewards to Spanish conquerors. In some of these luxurious hotels have now been installed. Some of the best known are:

★ Hacienda Cocoyoc (SP, T, G)
Carr. Cuernavaca–Cuautla, km 32·5 marker
Reservations in Coyococ: tel. (91735) 6 15 61; in México City: tel. (915) 550 73 31

★ Hacienda Vista Hermosa by Tequesquitengo Lake (SP, T, R)
Carr. Alpuyeca–Tequesquitengo, km 7 marker
Reservations in Tequesquitengo: tel. (91734) 7 04 92; in México City: tel. (915) 566 77 00
This hacienda was built by Hernán Cortés in 1529.

★ Antigua Hacienda de Galindo near San Juan del Rio, Qto. (SP, T, R)
Carr. Amealco–Querétaro, km 5 marker
Reservations in San Juan: tel. (91467) 2 00 50; in México City: tel. (915) 533 35 50
This hacienda was a gift from Cortés to his Indian interpreter and lover Malinche.

Guest-houses and family accommodation

For those with simple tastes there are a large number of *casas de huespedes* (guest-houses) and *posadas familiares* (family "pensions"), where bed and breakfast accommodation is very cheap.

Information

In the UK

Mexican Government Tourist Office
60–61 Trafalgar Square, London WC2N 5DS
tel. (0171) 734 1058

In the USA

Mexican Government Tourist Office
405 Park Avenue, New York NY 10022
tel. (212) 755 7261

In Canada

Mexican Government Tourist Office
2 Bloor Street West, Suite 1801,
Toronto, Ontario M4W 3E2
tel. (416) 925 0704

Information in Mexico

Tourist Ministry

Secretaria de Turismo
Av. Presidente Masaryk 172
México 11587, D.F.
tel. (915) 25 08 555

Sub Secretaria de Promocióny Fomento
M. Escobedo 726
Delegación Miguel Hidalgo
México 11590, D.F.
tel. (915) 254 89 67

Hotline

Tel. (915) 25 00 123, 25 00 589, 25 00 151; 91 800 903 92 (toll free)
This bi-lingual (Spanish and English) telephone service by the Tourist Ministry provides information twenty-four hours a day.

Legal advice for tourists

Calle Florencia 20, Zona Rosa
tel. (915) 6 25 87 61

Calle Argentina y Ildefonso, Centro
tel. (915) 78 90 133

Tourist offices in the various Mexican states

Listed below are the individual state tourist offices (Oficinas Estatales de Turismo) situated in the capital or chief town of the state concerned. They will provide information on the places of interest and sights to be found in their particular region. On a local level, there are tourist offices (Delegación/Subdelegación de Turismo) in the larger towns and resorts.

Aguascalientes

Oficina Estatal de Turismo
Av. Universidad no. 1001, Edif. Torre Plaza Bosques 8 piso, Aguascalientes, Ags.
tel. (91 49) 12 19 00

Baja California

Oficina Estatal de Turismo
Blvd. Díaz Ordaz, Edif. Plaza Patria Nivel 3, Tijuana, B.C.N.
tel. (91 66) 11 52 66, 81 94 92

Baja California Sur

Oficina Estatal de Turismo
Ca. al Norte Fracc Fidepaz. km 5·5, La Paz, B.C.S.
tel. (91 112) 4 01 00

Campeche

Oficina Estatal de Turismo
Calle 12 No. 153 entre 53 y 55, Campeche, Camp.
tel. (91 981) 6 67 67

Chiapas

Oficina Estatal de Turismo
Blvd. Belisario Domínquez 950, Tuxtia Gutiérrez, Chis.
tel. (91 961) 33 028, 25 509

Chihuahua

Oficina Estatal de Turismo
Libertad y Calle 13, Chihuahua, Chih.
tel. (91 14) 29 34 21

Coahuila de Zaragosa

Oficina Estatal de Turismo
Blvd. Los Fundadores, km 6·5, Centro de Convenciones Planta Alta, Saltillo, Coah
tel. (91 84) 30 05 10, 30 06 95

Colima

Oficina Estatal de Turismo
Portal Hidalgo No. 20, Colima, Col
tel. (91 331) 2 43 60

Distrito Federal

Secretario de Turismo
Amberes No. 54
México D.F.
tel. (915) 525 93 81–86

Durango	Oficina Estatal de Turismo Hidalgo 408 Sur, Durango, Dgo. tel. (91 18) 11 31 60, 11 11 07
Estado de México	Oficina Estatal de Turismo Lerdo Poniente No. 101–1 Piso, Toluca, Edo. de México tel. (91 71) 14 13 42
Guanajuato	Oficina Estatal de Turismo Plaza de la Paz 14, Guanajuato, Gto. tel. (91 473) 2 15 74, 2 00 86
Guerrero	Oficina Estatal de Turismo Costera Miguel Aleman No. 187, Fracc. Hornos, Acapulco, Gro. tel. (91 74) 84 31 40
Hidalgo	Oficina Estatal de Turismo Ca. México–Pachuca km 93·5, Blvd, Felipe Angeles s/n, Centrp Minero, Pachuca, Hg. tel. (91 771) 1 38 06
Jalisco	Oficina Estatal de Turismo Morelos 102, Plaza Tapatía, Guadalajara, Jal. tel. (913) 613 11 96, 614 01 23
Michoacán	Oficina Estatal de Turismo Nigromante 79, Palacio Clavijero, Morelia, Mich. tel. (91 43) 12 52 44, 12 37 10
Morelos	Oficina Estatal de Turismo Av. Morelos Sur 802, Cuernavaca, Mor. tel. (91 73) 14 38 60, 14 37 90
Nayarit	Av. México Sur 34, Tepic, Nay. tel. (91 321) 29 546, 29 547
Nuevo Léon	Oficina Estatal de Turismo Zaragoza No. 1300, Edif. Kalos Nivel A–I, Desp. 137, Monterrey, N.L. tel. (918) 344 43 43, 340 10 80
Oaxaca	Oficina Estatal de Turismo Independencia No. 607 Esq. García Vigil, Oaxaca, Oax. tel. (91 951) 67 700, 60 717
Puebla	Oficina Estatal de Turismo 5 Oriente No. 3, Puebla, Pue. tel. (91 22) 46 12 85, 32 48 59
Querétaro	Oficina Estatal de Turismo Constituyentes Ote. 102, Querérara, Oro. tel. (91 42) 13 85 12, 13 84 43
Quintana Roo	Oficina Estatal de Turismo Av, Miguel Hidalgo No. 22, 2 Piso, Chetumal, Q.Roo. tel. (91 983) 20 855, 20 266
San Luis Potosí	Oficina Estatal de Turismo Venustiano Carranza 325, San Luis Potosí, S.L.P. tel. (91 48) 12 99 43, 19 99 06

Sinaloa
Oficina Estatal de Turismo
Paseo Olsa Altas 1300, Mazatián, Sin.
tel. (91 69) 85 18 47, 85 12 20

Sonora
Oficina Estatal de Turismo
Comonfort entre Av. Cultura y Paseo Canal 3 Piso, Hermosillo, Son.
tel. (91 62) 17 00 76, 17 00 44

Tabasco
Oficina Estatal de Turismo
Tabasco 1504, Tabasco 2000, Villahermosa, Tab.
tel. (91 93) 16 36 33, 16 28 89

Tamaulipas
Oficina Estatal de Turismo
Rosales 2162, Ciudad Victoria, Tamps.
tel. (91 131) 21 057, 27 002

Tlaxcala
Oficina Estatal de Turismo
Juárez 18, Palacio Legislativo, Tiaxcala, Tlax.
tel. (91 241) 20 027, 22 787

Veracruz
Oficina Estatal de Turismo
Av. Manuel Avila Camacho 191, Jalapa, Ver.
tel. (91 28) 18 70 97 ext 128, 129

Yucatán
Oficina Estatal de Turismo
Calle 50 No. 514 entre 62 y 64, Mérida, Yuc.
tel. (91 99) 24 80 13

Zacatecas
Oficina Estatal de Turismo
Prol. González Ortega y Estaban Castorena s/n,
Edif. Marzes, Zacatecas, Zac.
tel. (91 492) 40 552, 40 393

In addition to the tourist offices in each state the following are some of the more important local information offices:

Mexico City
Secretaria de Turismo
Av. Presidente Masaryk 172
11587 México, D.F.
tel. (915) 25 08 555, 25 00 123 (Hotline)

Tijuana
Coordinación de Turismo
Puerta Mexico, P.A.
Linea Internacional, Tijuana, B.C.N.
tel. (91 66) 82 3387, 82 3347, 82 3348

Barranca del Cobre
Oficina Auxiliar de Turismo
Av. Technológico 7901, Chihuahua, Chih.
tel. (91 14) 17 8972

Cancún
Coordinación de Turismo
Av. Tulum 81, Edif. Fira, Cancún, Q.Roo.
tel. (91 988) 43 238, 43 438

Insurance

It is essential to take out short-term health and accident insurance when visiting Mexico, since the cost of treatment can be high. It is also advisable to have baggage insurance and cover for personal valuables, as well as cancellation insurance, particularly if you have booked a package holiday. Arrangements can be made through a travel agent or insurance company. Many firms organising package holidays now include insurance cover in the total price.

Ladies

Unfortunately, ladies travelling alone must expect to be regarded by some Mexican men as fair game for their suggestive remarks and amorous overtures. Failure to eradicate ideas they have about the supposed sexual freedom enjoyed by European and American females, together with the "machismo" of the Mexican male, leads them to think that all lady tourists are looking for a romantic liaison. How each lady deals with the situation is up to her, but if possible all those travelling alone should avoid going for walks on their own, especially at night, watch how they dress especially in rural areas, and not go into inns and bars which are frequented mainly by men.

Information and assistance

In Mexico City:
Protectur; tel. (915) 5 16 04 90

Difusión Cultural Feminista
Av. Universidad 1855, 4° Piso, Colonia Oxtopulco
CP 04 310 México D.F.; tel. (915) 5 50 73 06

Language

The official language of Mexico is Spanish, but the colloquial idiom is interspersed with many words taken from the language of the Náhuatl Indians.

As the mother tongue of over 320 million people Spanish is the most widely spoken of the Romance languages and, after English, the world's most important commercial language. It incorporates many words of Arabic origin.

It adds greatly to the pleasure of a visit to Mexico, and may avoid some problems, to have at least some acquaintance with the language. The large numbers of tourists from the USA and Canada has meant that English is widely understood in the popular tourist centres and larger towns, but nevertheless English-speaking travellers who want to get off the beaten track of tourism will find it a great help to have some idea of the pronunciation of Spanish, the basic rules of grammar and a few everyday expressions.

Pronunciation

Vowels are pronounced in the "continental" fashion, without the diphthongisation normal in English. The consonants *f, k, l, m, n, p, t* are normally pronounced much as in English; *b* has a softer pronunciation than in English, often approximating to *v* when it occurs between vowels; *c* before *e* or *i* is pronounced like *th* in "thin", otherwise like *k; ch* as in English; *d* at the end of a word or between vowels is softened into the sound of *th* in "that"; *g* before *e* or *i* is like the Scottish *ch* in "loch", otherwise hard as in "go"; *h* is silent; *j* is the Scottish *ch; ll* is pronounced like *l* followed by a consonantal *y*, i.e. like *lli* in "million" (in many cases like *y* without the *l); ñ* like *n* followed by a consonantal *y*, i.e. like *ni* in "onion"; *qu* like *k; r* is strongly rolled; *z* is like *th* in "thin".

Stress

The general rule is multisyllabic words ending in a vowel or in *n* or *s* have the stress on the penultimate syllable; words ending in any other consonant have the stress on the last syllable. Any departure from this rule is indicated by an acute accent on the stressed vowel. Thus Tampico and Esteban, with the stress on the penultimate syllable, and Cozumel, Veracruz, with the stress on the last syllable, are spelt without the acute accent; contrast México, Tonalá, Yucatán, Juárez, etc. For this purpose the vowel combinations *ae, ao, eo, oa* and *oe* are regarded as constituting two syllables, all other combinations as monosyllabic: thus *paseo* has the stress on *e, patio* on *a,* without the need of an acute accent to indicate this. The accent is, however, required when the first vowel in the combinations *ia, io, iu, ua, ue, ui, uo* and *uy* is to be stressed (e.g. *sillería, río),* and when the second vowel in the combinations *ai, au, ay, ei, eu, ey, oi, ou* and *oy* is to be stressed (e.g. *paraíso, baúl).*

Grammar summary

In Spanish *all* nouns (and not simply persons and animals) are considered to be either masculine, feminine or neuter in gender. The definite article is *el* for masculine nouns, *la* for feminine and *lo* for neuter. The preposition *de* is used with the definite article to denote possession in the widest sense (in the "genitive " case) and *a* with an indirect object (in the "dative" case); these combinations are contracted to *del* and *al* in the masculine singular. The direct object in a sentence (the "accusative" case) is usually spelt the same as the subject, or "nominative case".

Everyday Expressions

Good morning!	¡Buenos dias!
Good afternoon	¡Buenas tardas!
Good evening, good night	¡Buenas noches!
Goodbye!	¡Adios! ¡Hasta Luego!
Yes, no	Si, no (señor, señora, etc)
Please	Por favor
Thank you (very much)	(Muchas gracias)
Not at all! (You're welcome!)	¡De nada ¡No hay de qué!
Excuse me! (*e.g. for a mistake*)	¡Perdon!
Excuse me! (*e.g. when passing in front of someone*)	¡Con permiso!
Do you speak English?	¿Habla Usted inglés?
A little, not much	Un poco, no mucho
I do not understand	No entiendo
What is the Spanish for . . .?	¿Cómo se dice en español . . .?
What is the name of this church?	¿Cómo se llama esta iglesia?
The Cathedral (of St John)	La catedral (San Juan)
Where is Calle (street) . . .?	¿Dónde está la calle . . .?
Where is the road to . . .?	¿Dónde está el camino para . . .?
To the right, left	A la derecha, izquierda
Straight ahead	Siempre derecho
Above, up	Arriba
Below, down	Abajo
When is it open?	¿A qué horas está abierto?
How far	¿Qué distancia?
Today	Hoy
Yesterday	Ayer
The day before yesterday	Anteayer
Tomorrow	Mañana
Have you any rooms?	¿Hay habitaciones libres?
I should like . . .	Quisiera . . .
A room with private bath	Una habitación con baño

With full board	Con pension completa
What does it cost?	¿Cuánto vale?
Everything included	Todo incluído
That is too dear	Es demasiado caro
Bill, please! (*to a waiter*)	Mesero, la cuenta, por favor!
Where is the lavatory?	¿Donde está el retrete (el baño)?
Wake me at six	Llámeme Usted a las seis
Where is there a doctor?	¿Dónde hay un médico?
a dentist	un dentista?
a chemist	una farmacia?
Help!	¡Socorro!
I have a pain here	Siento dolores aquí
I am suffering from . . .	Padezco de . . .
I need medecine for . . .	Necesito un medicamento contra . . .
How often must I take it?	¿Cuántas veces tengo que tomar esta medicina?

Road Signs

Aduana	Customs
¡Alto!	Halt!
¡Atención!	Caution!
Aparcamiento	Car park
Autopista	Motorway – always toll-roads, but not always dual carriageways
Bifurcación	Road-fork
Cañada	Track for livestock
¡Ceda el paso!	Give way!
¡Cuidado!	Caution
Desvío	Diversion
Dirección única	One way only
Grúa	tow-away service
¡Conserva su deucha, la izquierada!	Keep to the right/left
Niebla	Fog
¡Obras!	Road works
¡Al paso!	Dead slow
Paso a nivel	Level crosing
Paso prohibido	No entry
Peaje	Toll (*on motorway, etc.*)
Peatones	Pedestrians
¡Peligro!	Danger
Playa	Beach
Prohibido estacionar	No parking
Prohibido rebasar	No overtaking
Sentido único	One-way street
Viraje peligroso	Dangerous bend

Travelling by Train and Bus/Coach

All aboard!	¡Viajeros al tren! ¡Subir!
All change!	¡Cambiar de . . .!
Arrival	Llegada
Bus, coach	Camión, autobus
Departure	Salida
Fare	Precio, importe
First class	Primera clase
Halt	Apeadero

Junction	Empalme
Luggage, baggage	Equipaje
Non-smoking compartment	No fumadores
Platform	Andén
Second class	Segunda clase
Smoking compartment	Fumadores
Station	Estación
Stop	Parada
Ticket	Billete
Ticket-collector, conductor	Revisor
Ticket-window	Taquilla de billetes
Timetable	Horario de trenos
Train	tren
Waiting room	Sala de espera

Points of the Compass

Norte (Nte.)	North
Sur (S.)	South
Oeste, Poniente (Pte.) Occidente	West
Este, Oriente (Ote.)	East

At the Post Office

Address	Direcciön
Air mail	Por avión
Express	Por correo urgente
Letter	Carta
Letter-box, post-box	Buzón
Postage	Porte, franqueo
Postcard	Tarjeta postal
Poste restante	Lista de correos
Postman	Cartero
Post office	Correo
Printed matter	Impreso
Registered letter	Carta certificada
Stamp	Sello
Telegram	Telegrama
Telephone	Teléfono

Geographical, Architectural, etc. terms

Adobe	air-dried mud bricks
Alfiz	Surround to Moorish arch
Arco	Arch
Arrabal	outlying district of a town
Artesania	handicrafts
Artesonada	panelling. coffered ceiling
Ayuntamiento	Town hall
Azulejos	Glazed tiles (originally blue – *azul*)
Bahía	Bay
Barranca	gorge, ravine
Barrio	District, quarter (of a town)
Cabo	Cape
Calle	Street
Camino	Road, track, path

Cantina	bar, public house
Capilla	Chapel
Capilla abierta	open chapel
Capilla mayor	Principal chapel with high altar
Carretera	(Main) road
Casa	House
Castillo	Castle
Cementerio, panteón	Cemetery, churchyard
Churrigerismo	Cluttered Baroque style (after the Spanish architect José de Churriguera)
Ciudad	City, town
Claustro	Cloister
Colegio	College, seminary
Concepción	Conception
Convento	Monastery, convent
Coro	Choir
Costa	Coast
Cuesta	Slope, hill
Cueva	Cave
Cumbre	Summit
Custodia	Monstrance
Ermita	Chapel, small church
Estrella	Rose window
Faro	Lighthouse
Fuente	Fountain, spring
Huerta	Fertile irrigated area
Iglesia	Church
Indigena	Native, Indian
Jardin	Garden
Mar	Sea
Mirador	Viewpoint, roof terrace
Monasterio	Monastery, convent
Montaña	Mountain, hill
Mudéjar style	Moorish style
Muralismo	Large mural
Palacio	Palace
Palacio Arzobispal	Archbishop's Palace
Palacio Episcopal (Obispal)	Bishop's Palace
Parque	Park
Parroquia	Parish church
Paseo	Avenue, promenade
Paso	Figure, group of saints, etc. carried in Easter procession
Patio	Courtyard
Pico	Peak, summit
Picota	Pillory
Playa	Beach
Plateresque	Filigree style of ornamentation
Plaza	Square
Poblano	Popular Baroque style in and around Puebla
Porteria	Foyer
Posa	Processionary chapel
Pueblo	Village
Puente	Bridge
Puerta	Door
Puerta del Perdón	Name of main door of many cathedrals

Puerto	Port, harbour, pass
Quinta	Country house
Rambla	Watercourse (which dries up in summer; avenue, boulevard
Reja	Grille, grating
Retablo	Reredos, altarpiece
Ría	Tidal estuary of a river
Riera	Brook, stream
Río	River
Roque	Rock
Sagrario	Sacristy, chapel
Sala capitular	Chapterhouse
Selva	Wood, forest
Serpiente	Snake, serpent
Serrania	Range of hills
Sierra	Mountain range
Sillería	Choir-stalls
Tianguis	Market
Tiburón	Shark
Torrente	Mountain stream
Tumba	Grave
Urbanización	Housing development
Valle	Valley

Numbers

Cardinal numbers

0	cero
1	uno, una
2	dos
3	tres
4	cuatro
5	cinco
6	seis
7	siete
8	ocho
9	nueve
10	diez
11	once
12	doce
13	trece
14	catorce
15	quince
16	dieciséis
17	diecisiete
18	dieciocho
19	diecinueve
20	veinte
21	veintiuno
22	veintidós
30	treinta
31	treinta y uno
40	cuarenta
50	cincuenta
60	sesenta
70	setenta
80	ochenta

90	noventa
100	ciento (cien)
101	ciento uno
153	ciento cincuenta y tres
200	doscientos
300	trescientos
400	cuatrocientos
500	quinientos
600	seiscientos
700	setecientos
800	ochocientos
900	novecientos
1000	mil
1,000,000	un million

Ordinal numbers

1st	primero (primera)
2nd	segundo
3rd	tercero
4th	cuarto
5th	quinto
6th	sexto
7th	sétimo/séptimo
8th	octavo
9th	nono/novena
10th	décimo
20th	vigésimo
100th	centésimo

Fractions

$\frac{1}{2}$	medio (media)
$\frac{1}{3}$	un tercio
$\frac{1}{4}$	un cuarto
$\frac{1}{10}$	un décimo

Months

January	enero
February	febrero
March	marzo
April	abril
May	mayo
June	junio
July	julio
August	agosto
September	setiembre
October	octubre
November	noviembre
December	diciembre

Days of the Week

Sunday	domingo
Monday	lunes
Tuesday	martes
Wednesday	miércoles

Thursday	jueves
Friday	viernes
Saturday	sábado

Times of day

Morning	mañana
Midday	mediodía
Evening	tarde
Night	noche

Indian languages

Náhuatl

Most of the major pre-Columbian inhabitants of Mexico spoke one of the Náhuatl tongues, a sub-group of the Uto-Aztec group of languages. Náhuatl comprises several dialects and is still spoken today by nearly a million people.

The grammatical structure of Náhuatl is basically different from that of the Indo-European languages. It is one of the polysynthetic languages, in that a whole sentence can be condensed into a single word. The basic phonetic element of Náhuatl, the "tl", has over the centuries been rounded off to a simple "t", so that now it is pronounced as "Náhuatl" or "Náhua". Until the time of the Spanish conquest Náhuatl was recorded only in the form of sculptured symbols, and was only really written down after the Spaniards introduced the Latin script into Mexico; as Náhuatl has only about twenty different sounds this did not present any great difficulties. Words taken from Náhuatl are today found especially in the names of plants and animals.

Our everyday words "cocoa" and "chocolate" are in fact derived from the Náhuatl.

Other Indian languages

Other Indian languages still spoken in parts of Mexico today include Otomí, Maya, Tarask (Purépecha), Zapotek, Mixtek, Totonak and Mazatek, all of which differ one from the other and from Náhuatl. The one factor common to most of the Indian languages of Mexico is that at one time they were spoken by a highly cultured class of people but after this nobility disappeared they have now become just colloquial dialects spoken by country people. It is estimated that about 1·5% of all Mexicans speak only Indian languages.

Manners and Local Customs

In Mexico even more than in Spain much emphasis is placed on politeness, a trend which has sometimes led to the development of overly formal levels of etiquette. Arrogant or inconsiderate behaviour is poorly received in Mexico, and tact is of the very essence in social intercourse. Impatience is an emotion the Mexicans do not seem to feel themselves or appreciate in others, and in general punctuality – as that term is understood in northern Europe or North America – is not a Mexican habit. Visitors should therefore be ready to allow at least half an hour's grace in relation to appointments, opening times, etc.

Siesta

The afternoon *siesta* between 2 and 5pm is a sacred insitution, and should not be interrupted without very good reason indeed.

Invitations

Mexicans tend to issue invitations rather freely; unless the offer is then later repeated and a definite date and time quoted it should be regarded merely as an expression of politeness and not something to be taken literally and acted upon. If a definite rendezvous is arranged it will probably be in a restaurant or café. To be invited to your host's house indicates a high degree of confidence and trust and is a real honour. If the visitor admires an article in the host's home the latter will often appear to offer it as a gift; once again, this is merely done out of politeness and should not be taken literally!

"La mordida"

In certain circumstances the offer of an appropriate sum of money can work wonders. Thus public officials, who tend to be poorly paid, will expect some pecuniary recognition – a *mordida,* the Spanish word for "a bite" – even for services (e.g. customs clearance) which are part of their official duties. To Mexicans this seems perfectly in order as a means of speeding things up, and is not seen as implying bribery or corruption. A government-led campaign against "la mordida" in 1990 enjoyed a degree of success.

Shopping

Shops in Mexico have fixed prices, but in the markets bargaining is normal – if only as a means of engaging the other party in conversation. In places with a large tourist trade the original prices asked are likely to be set very high and the buyer should counter with a far lower offer and then be prepared to haggle.

Indian population

One or two points should be emphasised regarding relations with the Indian population. These people, who for centuries have lived in the shadow of the European incomers to their country, appreciate it when visitors show respect for their customs and way of life and avoid patronising them.

In recent years there has been an increasing reluctance on the part of Indians to be photographed by tourists, most noticeably in Chiapas state with its colourful religious ceremonies. In some case this has even led to violence, so it is a matter of tact, at least, to respect the wishes of any Indians who object to being photographed.

Anyone who – whilst regretting the way in which Indian culture has been corrupted through tourism – nevertheless wishes to make a trip to some outlying Indian villages (such as those of the last of the Lacandons in Chiapas) may like to make his or her own arrangements accordingly. This Guide has deliberately refrained from attempting to give details of how to reach such tribes.

Clothing

For the most part, Mexicans dress very correctly, and tourists would do well to remember this. Away from the main tourist centres it is best not to be seen out in shorts or bathing costumes. Suitable dress should be worn when visiting the better class restaurants. Anyone wearing shorts or with their shoulders bare will probably be refused entry to churches.

See Photography and Ladies

Maps and Plans

Most US road atlases contain good general maps of Mexico.

The Mexican Tourist Office (see Information) supplies free of charge a road map, the *mapa turístico de carreteras.*

Road atlases (*atlas de carreteras*) are published by PEMEX, the state oil company, by the motoring clubs (see Road Transport) and by Guia Roji. The latter firm of publishers also produce good maps of the individual

Mexican states and these can be purchased in most bookshops in Mexico. Maps are also obtainable from the insurance firm of Sanborn's.

Opening Times

Shops

Mexican shops have no standard opening and closing times, and usually remain open into the evening and also open on Sundays in some cases. In the hotter parts of the country there is a lunch break between 2pm and 5pm.

Banks

Mon.–Fri. 9am–1.30 or 2.30pm; in some larger towns and resorts until 3 or 5pm.

Post offices

Mon.–Fri. 8am–6pm, Sat. 9am–1pm

Government offices

These are normally open to the public in the mornings only, until 2pm.

Museums

Museums are normally open 9am–6pm daily except Monday, when they are closed.

Photography

Visitors to Mexico may bring in a camera and a cine-camera, each with 12 films. It is best to buy films at home, because they are very expensive in Mexico.

In museums and at archaeological sites photography using a tripod is allowed only with an official permit. This can be obtained from the:

Instituto Nacional de Antropologia e Historia (INAH)
Tonalá 10, Col. Roma
México City
tel. (915) 208 65 02 or 208 35 65
or
Córdoba 42, Col Roma
México City
tel. (915) 533 20 15 or 533 22 63

Light conditions

Visitors from more northerly latitudes should remember that as Mexico lies closer to the Equator the length of the day varies less over the year than it does at home. In northern Mexico the longest summer day lasts only 13 hours and the shortest day in winter lasts 11 hours; in southern Mexico the difference between the length of day in summer and winter is even less. The period of twilight is also shorter. It rapidly becomes light enough to take photographs in the morning, and darkness falls with corresponding speed in the evening. The middle of the day is less suitable for taking colour photographs than in more northerly countries, since the sun stands high in the sky; both light and shade are hard, and the gentler side lighting required for some subjects is lacking.

Tip

Visitors should respect any reluctance on the part of the Indian population to be photographed, especially at solemn religious celebrations. It is best to refrain from any surreptitious use of cameras and flash in churches. Generally speaking it is advisable to get permission from the village headman before trying to take any photographs. See also Manners and Local Customs.

Post

Letter post (*correo*)

The postage on postcards (*tarjeta postal*) and letters (*cartas*) by air mail (*correo aéreo, por avión*) to Europe is charged at different rates. As a rule, they may take up to two or three weeks to arrive. As the postal rates change several times a year there is little to be gained by attempting to quote them here. Current rates will be displayed in post offices. It is wise to post letters and cards in a post office rather than in a pillar box (*buzón*) in the street.

Parcels (*paquetes*)

Anyone thinking of sending parcels home by sea should bear in mind that these may take three to five months to arrive. It is expensive to send parcels by air mail.

Poste restante (*lista de correos*)

Anything sent poste restante to Mexico must be addressed to a definite post office and clearly marked *lista de correos.* The item will be held for ten days only.

Protected Species

Anyone in sympathy with the Washington Convention on International Trade in Endangered Species of Wild Fauna and Flora can assist in safeguarding endangered species by refusing to buy "souvenirs" in the form of wild animals and plants. In Mexico these will include cacti, tortoiseshell, turtleshell, black coral, lizard-skin, live or stuffed crocodile, parrots, tortoises and giant spiders. Objects made from protected animals and plants also fall under the scope of the above mentioned Convention. Visitors should also refrain from catching animals or digging up plants.

See Customs Regulations

Public Holidays

Every town and village in Mexico has a fiesta in honour of the local saint or patron; details of fiestas held in some of the smaller places can be found in the A to Z section of this guide under Surroundings.

There are also numerous other reasons for celebration, including the main church festivals and national holidays. In the fiestas old Indian rituals, Christian practices and the Mexicans' natural *joie de vivre* combine to produce a lively and colourful pageant which may last several days. Mexicans of all social classes are prepared to go to considerable expense to play their part in these celebrations.

Particularly important fiestas are the *Dia de los Reyes* (Day of the Kings, i.e. Twelfth Night) on January 6th, when children are given presents; *Candlemas* (Día de la Candelaria, February 2nd); *Carnival,* which incorporates both European and Indian features; *Holy Week* (Semana Santa), strongly influenced by Spanish practice; *Corpus Christi* (Jueves de Corpus), with a strong Indian element; *Independence Day* (Día de la Independencia, September 15th), when the celebrations last several days; *All Saints* and *All Souls* (Todos los Santos, Día de los Muertos, November 1st–2nd), when the dead are remembered and a symbolic family meal is eaten at the graveside; *Revolution Day* (Día de la Revolución, November 20th); the fiesta of the *Virgin of Guadalupe* (December 12th), with an Indian pilgrimage to Mexico City; the *Posadas* (nine days beginning December 16th), symbolising Mary and Joseph's journey to Bethlehem; and finally *Christmas* (Navidad), an occasion for gay and noisy celebrations.

Public and Religious Holidays

Año Nuevo (New Year's Day)	January 1st
Día de los Reyes (Twelfth Night)	January 6th
Día de la Constitución (Constitution Day)	February 5th
Birthday of Benito Juárez (b. 1806) – a national hero and President 1858–72	March 21st
Día del Trabajo (Labour Day)	May 1st
Anniversary of Battle of Pueblo (1862)	May 5th
Día de la Nación (National Day)	September 1st
Día de la Independencia (Independence Day: 1810)	September 16th
Día de la Raza (Day of the Race, Columbus Day)	October 12th
Todos los Santos, Día de los Muertos (All Saints, All Souls)	November 1st and 2nd
Día de la Revolución (Revolution Day: 1910)	November 20th
Día de la Virgen de Guadalupe (Feast of the Virgin of Guadalupe: 1531)	December 12th

A procession in Zacatecas

Public Holidays

December 25th	*Navidad* (Christmas)
Movable festivals	*Semana Santa* (Holy Week) *Jueves de Corpus* (Corpus Christi)

Fiestas

January 1st	Throughout Mexico: *New Year's Day*, with feasts, processions, horse-races, cock-fights, dancing and music.
January 6th	Throughout Mexico: *Twelfth Night* (Día de los Reyes). The children leave their shoes in front of the door to be filled with sweets.
January 17th	Throughout Mexico: *San Antonio Abad*, when all domestic animals are blessed and adorned with garlands of flowers. This fiesta is particularly impressive in Taxco, Tlalpan and in Mexico City, in the church of San Juan Bautista in Coyoacán, on the Plaza de las Tres Culturas in the church of Santiago, and in the suburb of Xochimilco in the "Floating Gardens".
January 18th	Taxco: *Festival of Patronage* at the church of Santa Prisca.
January 20th	Chiapa de Corzo (Chis.): naval battle re-enacted on the Río Grijalva. Guanajuato: *Town Festival* (until January 22nd).
January 31st	Morelia (Mich.): *Feast of the Immaculate Conception* (Día de la Inmaculada Concepción). The town is decorated with flowers and lanterns.
February 2nd	Throughout Mexico: *Candlemas* (Día de la Candelariea), particularly colourful in Cholula, Taxco and Tlacotalpan (Ver.)
February 5th	Throughout Mexico: *Constitution Day* (Día de la Constitución) with parades on horseback and bull-fights. Colima: *Fiesta Brava*
Mid/end of February	Throughout Mexico: ★ *Carnival*. The Carnival in Veracruz is famous, but those held in Mazatlán, Villahermosa and Mérida are also glittering events.
Ash Wednesday	Amecameca de Juárez (Mex.): pilgrimage to church of Señor de Sacromente
Holy Week/ Easter	Processions and pilgrimages throughout Mexico. Particulary interesting are the portrayal of the *Suffering of Christ* in Mexico City (Ixtapalapa district) and the *Passion Plays* at the church of Santa Prisca in Taxco.
April 3rd	Izamal (Yuc.): *Feast of San Ildefonso*
April 5th	Ticul (Yuc.): *Tobacco Festival*
Mid-April	Hopelchén (Camp.): *Feast of Corn and Honey*
April 25th ★ *Fería de San Marcos*	Aguascalientes (town): *Fería de San Marcos* in honour of the patron saint of the town, with bull and cock-fights, singing and dancing. This fiesta has been celebrated since 1604 and is one of the liveliest and most beautiful in all Mexico. It starts a week before the official date and lasts for three weeks.
May 3rd	Throughout Mexico: *Day of the Holy Cross* (Día de la Santa Cruz). Buildings are decorated and there are fireworks and dancing. Particularly beautiful in Tepotzotlán and Valle de Bravo (both in Mex. state).

Throughout Mexico: *Fería de San Isidro*, patron saint of land-workers; animals are adorned and the fields are blessed. In Huistan (Chis.) the Tzotzil Indians dance on stilts.	May 15th
Tecoh (Yuc.): start of the *Hammock Festival*	May 20th
Throughout Mexico: dancing, singing by children in peasant costume, with toy donkeys made from corn. in Papantla (Ver.) the "Flying Men" (*voladores*) appear for eight days.	*Feast of Corpus Christi*
Guanajuato: *Fiesta de la Olla*	June 23rd
Throughout Mexico: *Feast of St John* (Día de San Juan Bautista), with fairs and markets and diving in the rivers. In San Juan Chamula (Chis.) there are flag-bearing processions by the Indians from the southern highlands.	June 24th
Throughout Mexico: *Day of Our Lady of Carmel* (Día de Nuestra Señora del Carmen). In the San Angel district of Mexico City there is a market and flower show.	July 16th
Cuetzalán (Pue.): folklorists (Quetzales, Negritos, Santiagos and Voladores) selected from the surrounding areas perform traditional dances.	July 15th/18th ★*Dance festival in Cuetzalán*
Oaxaca (town): The *Guelaguetza* perform a mixture of pre-Spanish and Christian traditional dances by Indians from the state of Oaxaca in original costumes. The dances are in honour of the Corn Goddess.	Last two Mondays in July ★*Guelaguetza*
Guanajuato: *Fiesta de la Bufa*	July 31st
Juchitán (Oax.): local *Dance Festival* lasting four days. Mexico City: on the Square of the Three Cultures Indian dances are performed in memory of the battle around Tenochtitlán.	August 13th
Huamantla (Tlax.): to celebrate the Assumption of the Virgin Mary mosaic-like carpets of flowers (*xocipecate*) are laid down. Dances, pilgrimages and fairs throughout Mexico.	August 15th
Tapachula (Chis.): commencement of the ten-day *Feast of St Augustine* (San Augustin).	August 20th
San Luis Potosí (town): *Feast of the Patron Saint*, with dancing by Matachines and Malinches.	August 25th
San Juan Chamula: *Feast of St Rose* (Día de la Santa Rosa).	August 30th
Juchitán (Oax.): *Vela Pineda* (Festival of the Candles)	September 3rd/5th
Tepozteco (Mor.): old Indian plays acted in the ruins. Tepotzlán (Mor.): legends acted out in the market place (Sept. 8th).	September 7th/8th
Throughout Mexico: *Independence Day* (Día de la Independencia); in Mexico City there are military parades and patriotic performances on the Zócalo.	September 16th
Huejotzingo (Pue.): commencement of the *Apple Juice Festival* which lasts for a week.	September 23rd
San Miguel de Allende (Gto.): *Día de San Miguel Arcángel* with big town party.	September 29th

October 2nd — Cuetzalan (Pue.): *Coffee Festival*

October 4th — Cuetzalán (Pue.): *San Francisco*

October 12th — Guadalajara (Jal.): *Fiesta de la Virgen de Zapopán*, with processions, dancing, bull and cock-fights. The statue of the Virgin is carried in procession through the streets from the cathedral to her church in Zapopán.

October 24th — Uruapan (Mich.): *Dance Festival* with singing competitions.

November 1st/2nd
★*All Saints* and *All Souls*

Throughout Mexico: *All Saints* and *All Souls* (Todos los Santos, Día de los Muertos). Relatives visit graves and bring gifts, food and drink with them or build a table for gifts at home which also contains some personal effects of the deceased. Everywhere brightly-painted death's heads made of icing sugar and death loaves (*pan de muertos*) decorated with bones made of icing sugar or dough are offered up. This feast is celebrated particularly on the island of Janitzio in Lake Peatzcuaro.

November 22nd — Zapotitlán (Jal.): *Feast of Mariachis*

First Sunday in December — Coyutla (Ver.): *Feast of St Andrew* (Día de San Andrés) with a procession carrying the Cross.

December 8th — Pátzcuaro (Mich.): *Feast of Our Lady the Redeemer* (Día de Nuestra Señora de la Salud) with market and fair.

December 12th
★*Feast of the Virgin of Guadalupe*

Throughout Mexico: *Feast of the Virgin of Guadalupe* (Día de la Virgen de Guadalupe), the national saint of Mexico. This is the main religious festival in Mexico. Huge crowds gather in front of the Basilica of the Virgin in Mexico City to watch folk-plays and religious performances.

December 16th/24th — Throughout Mexico: *Posadas*, nine days symbolising Mary and Joseph's journey to Bethlehem. Processions.

December 28th — Throughout Mexico: *Day of the Innocents* (Día de los Niños Inocentes), when "All Fools' Day" jokes are played.

Rail Travel

Rail network

The network of Mexican railways (*ferrocarriles*, or FFCC for short) covers a total length of some 26,000km/16,000 miles and is thinly spread except in the area between Manzanillo on the Pacific and Veracruz on the Gulf of Mexico. There are no lines in Baja California Sur and Quintana Roo. Most of the main lines are state-owned by the *Ferrocarriles Nacionales de México* (National Railways of Mexico). Other lines are served by private companies such as Ferrocaril del Pacifico, Ferrocarril de Chihuahua al Pacifico and Ferrocarril Sonora–Baja California. Tickets are valid on all lines, no matter where they were issued.

Rail is by far the cheapest mode of travel in Mexico, but standards of comfort and punctuality are not high and the journeys are long and slow.

Mexican trains have first and second class coaches. Sleeping cars are available to first class passengers only. Some of the rolling stock is up to fifty years old and a lot of it is in poor condition, so visitors should

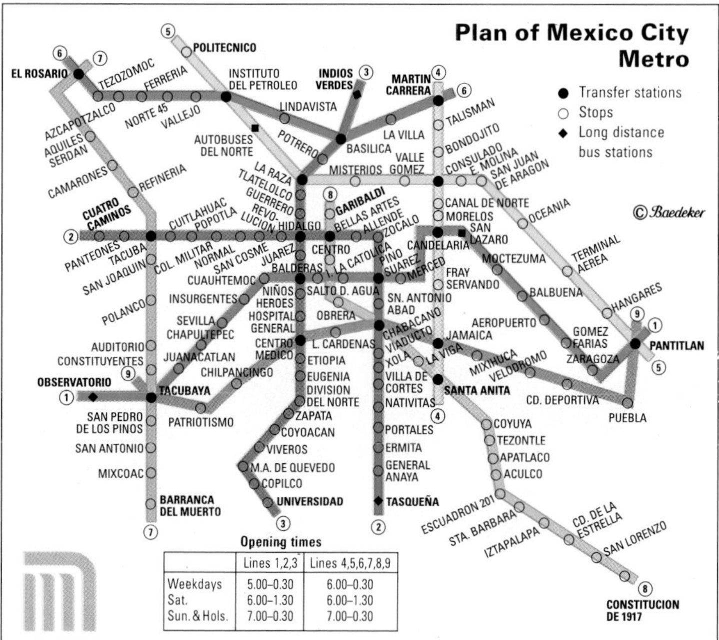

	Lines 1,2,3	Lines 4,5,6,7,8,9
Weekdays	5.00–0.30	6.00–0.30
Sat.	6.00–1.30	6.00–1.30
Sun. & Hols.	7.00–0.30	7.00–0.30

always travel first class, especially for overnight journeys; reclining seats and simply equipped sleeping compartments are available at extra charge. Take precautions against theft. It is advisable to book well in advance if possible.

In spite of its many disadvantages a train journey can be an experience for those who have the time to spare. The routes often lead through parts of the countryside which would not otherwise be seen, a coach on a train is a good place to mix with Mexican people going about their everyday business, and at the stations *campesinos* provide refreshments and other facilities.

A most rewarding experience is a journey on the *Espreso Cañon del Cobre*, belonging to the *Ferrocarril de Chihuahua al Pacifico*, along the line from Chihuahua to Los Mochis through the rugged range of mountains known as "Copper Canyon" in the northern Sierra Madre Occidental (see A to Z, Barranca del Cobre).

Information

Ferrocarriles Nacionales de México
Estación Buenavista (main station in Mexico City)
Departamento de Tráfico de Pasajeros
Av. Insurgentes Norte 140, Colonia Buena Vista,
06 358 México 3, D.F.;
tel. (915) 547–6593

Ferrocarril de Chihuahua al Pacifico, S.A. de C.V.
Apartado Postal 46, Chuhuahua, Chih., México;
tel. (91161) 12 22 84

Guard's van of the Ferrocarril de Chihuahua al Pacifico

or in Mexico City:
Ferrocarril de Chihuahua al Pacifico, S.A. de C.V.
Av. Central 140, Piso 6, ALA "C", 06 538 México, D.F.;
tel. (915) 547–85 45, 547–69 39

Restaurants

Mexican cuisine ranges from top-quality restaurants to small fast-food stores and street-stalls; the latter, however, should be treated with caution. The *fonds*, tiled food-counters found in the market halls, provide genuine Mexican fare at bargain prices.

In restaurants meals are mainly substantial and consist of several courses. They usually offer a lunchtime menu, the *comida corrida*, which is often considerably cheaper than eating à la carte. Don't be afraid to ask for this menu. Lunch is normally served between 2 and 4pm, dinner not before 8pm.

There are restaurants in most of the hotels named in this guide (see Hotels), as well as those listed alphabetically below.

Acapulco

Beto, Costera M. Alemán 99; Carlos'n Charlie's, Costera M. Alemán 999; Chulavista, Costera M. Alemán 1229; Cocula, A. Costera Alemán y El Patio; ★Coyuca 22, Coyuca St. 22; El Corralón, Playa Icacos; El Costeño, Playa Caletilla; El Torito, Av. Costera Alemán 36; Hard Rock Café, Costera M. Alemán 37; Hard Times, Av. Costera Alemán 400; Huachinango Charlie's, Costera M. Alemán 115; La Mansion, Costera M. Alemán 81B; ★Madeiras, Carr. Escnica 39; Mariscos Pipo, Almirante Bretón 3; Miramar, in the "La Vista" shopping centre, Carretera Escénica; Normandie, Costera Alemán y Capitán Alejandro Malespina;

Paraíso, Playa Condesa; Pepe & Co., Av. Costera Alemán 777; Pinzona, Pinzona 65; Raffaello, Costera M. Alemán 1221; Raul y Tony, Av. López Mateos 57; ★Senor Frogs, Vista Mall, Las Brisas Carr. Escénica; ★Suntory, Costera Alemán y Maury

Aguascalientes
(Town)

Agua's 'n Charlie's, Blvd. José María Chávez 904–906; Atardecer Zapatio, Av. Circunvalación Sur 1109; Caballo Loco, V. Carranza 310; Cenaduria San Antonio, Chávez 507; El Cabrito, Circunvalación Nte. 704; Mitla, Madero 320; El Campeador, 5 de Mayo 517

Cabo San Lucas

Carlos & Charlie's, Marina 20; Kankún, Marina El Galeón; Alfonso's

Campeche
(Town)

Campeche, Calle 57 between 8 y 10; Kalua, Calle 12 No. 150; La Perla, Calle 10 No. 189; Miramar, Calle 8 y Calle 61; Restaurant Bar Marganza, Calle 8, No. 268

Cancún

El Pescador, Tulipanes 5; El Potrero, Av. Yaxchilán 50; El Tacolote, Cobá 19; La Habichuela, Margaritas 27; Los Almendros, Av. Bonampak; Pizza Rolandi, Av. Cobá 12

In the town

★Chac-Mool, Playa Chac-Mool; ★Mauna Loa, opposite the Centro de Convenciones

Celaya

La Cueva del Perico, Tabachines y Puerta de Oro del Bajío; La Perla, Cuauhtémoc 201 C; Terranova, Blvd. A. López Mateos 1104

Chapala Lake
In Ajijic

El Mesón; La Huerta; Los Naranjitos; La Posada Ajijic; La Rusa; ★Los Telares, Morelos 6

An open-air restaurant

Mariachi musicians entertain customers

In Chapala — Beer Garden; Café Paris; Café Superior; La Viuda

In Jocotepec — La Carreta

Chetumal — Buffalo Steak, Av. A. Obregón 208; Campeche, Av. A. Obregón y Héroes; Caribe, 22 de Enero y Esmeralda; Chez Farouk, Av. Belice 186; Los Pozos, Av. E. Aguilar, corner of Calle Revolución; Sergios Pizza, Av. A. Obregón 182

Chihuahua (Town) — Casa de Nutrición Naturaleza, Libertad 1910a; El Castellano, Cuathemoc 2002; Hostería 1900; Independencia 903; La Hacienda, Reforma/Calle 20; La Olla de Chihuahua, Av. Juárez 3331; Los Parados de Tony Vega, Av. Juárez 3316; Salignac

Colima (Town) — El Faisán, Madero 66; Grotto's, Galván 207; Los Naranjos, G. Barreda 34

Córdoba — La Palma, Av. 3, 210

Cozumel — Café del Puerto, Av. Melgar 3; Carlos'n Charlie's; Casa Denis; ★ El Acuario; El Portal; La Laguna (Chankanab National Park); La Misión, Av. Juárez 23; Las Palmeras, at the landing-stage, Av. R. Melgar; Las Tortugas, 10 Av. Norte 82; ★ Morgan's; Pepe's; Pepe's Grill, Av. R. Melgar; Ranchito; San Francisco, Playa San Francisco; Soberanis, Av. R. Melgar 471

La Pizzeria Esgiro, Conspiradores 6; Onis, Carr. México–Oaxaca 31	**Cuautla**
Café Viena, Guerrero 104; Casa de Campo, Abasolo 101; Château René, Atzingo 11; El Faisán, E. Zapata 1233; ★Hacienda de Cortés, at northern entrance to the town; Harry's Grill, Gutenberg 3; India Bonita, D. Morrow 9; Los Arcos, opposite the post office; ★Maximilian's, Galeana 125; Vienes, Lerdo de Tejada No. 4	**Cuernavaca**
Sumiya, Jiutepec	Outside the town
El Plaza, Calle Negrete 1003, Pte.; La Bohemia, 20 de Noviembre 907, Pte.; La Majada, 20 de Noviembre Ote.; Mansión, Juárez 315 Sur	**Durango**
Brazz, Plaza del Sol; ★Cazadores, Av. López Mateos Sur and Av. Américas 759; Cazuela Grill, Av. L. Mateos Sur 3755; Copenhagen, López Cotilla y Marcos Castellanos; El Delfín Sonriente, Niños Héroes 2229; El Mesón de Sancho Panza, Marcos Castellanos 114; El Tirol, Tomás V. Gómez 25; Guadalajara Grill, Av. L. Mateos 3771; Hacienda de la Flor, Aurelio Ortega 764; Hongkong, Corona, opposite Fenix Hotel; La Vianda, Av. Chapalita 120; Luscherly, General San Martin 525; Piaf, Marsella 126; Sanborns, Vallarta 1600; Suehiro, Av. de la Paz 1701; Zanahoria (vegetarian), Las Américas 538	**Guadalajara**
Casa Valadéz, Jardin de la Unión 3; Centro Nutricional Vegetariano, Aguilar 45; El Retiro, Sopeña 12; Escalanita, Lascurain de R. 4.; L'Antorcha, Carretera Panorámica y Callejón Guadalupe; La Manzana, Plazuela San Fernando 27; La Tasca de los Santos, Plaza de la Paz 28	**Guanajuato** (Town)
Del Mar, Av. A. Serdán 206; El Paraíso, Av. Rodriguez 20; Los Charros Grill, Av. A. Rodríguez 166; Mandarin, Calle 21 No. 40; Pako's, A. Serdán 80; Tecate, A. Serdán 219	**Guaymas**
Country Club: El Yate; Shangri-La	In the Bahía de San Carlos
Chez Megaley, Av. Rueda Medina; El Sombrero de Gomar, Av. Hidalgo 35; La Pena, Guerrero 5	**Isla Mujeres** In the centre
El Garrafón de Castilla; María's; Villa del Mar, 5km/3 miles outside, by the sea	Outside
La Casa de Mamá, Av. A. Camacho 113; La Parroquia, Av. Zaragoza 18; La Pergola, Lomas de Estadio; Terraza Jardín, Edificio Nachito	**Jalapa**
Bismarck, 16 de Septiembre y A. Serdán; Dino's, Bravo 601/2; El Qunito Sol, Independencia y Domínquez; La Arboleda, Ocampo y Revolución; La terraza, Paseo Obregón 1570; La Venta Internacional, Colima y Ramirez; Lamarck y Peña, 16 Septiembre 1365	**La Paz**
Jaime Nunó 503; Los Delfines, M. Alemán 1308; Mesón de los Coras, Paseos de los Insurgentes	**León** de los Aldamas
Belén, Independencia 18; Los Girasoles, Av. México 79; Savoy 2, Plaza Santiago	**Manzanillo** In the town
Chivi's, Carr. al Aeropuerto, km 8·5 marker: Coco's, Playa Salahua; El Vaquero, Crucero Las Brisas; Las Margaritas, Carr. al Aeropuerto, km 10 marker; Manolo's, Playa Salahua; Osteria Bugatti, Crucero Las Brisas	Outside
El Dorado, Playa Olas Altas; ★El Terral; ★Legazpi; ★L'Recif, Peninsula de Juluapán; Oasis, Playa Miramar	In the Las Hadas Holiday Centre

Restaurants

Mazatlán

★Casa Loma, Las Gaviotas 104; El Marinero, 5 de Mayo y Paseo Claussen; Doney, Mariano Escobedo y 5 de Mayo; La Parillada, Av. del Mar 1004; Larios, R. Loaiza 14; Lobster Trap, Calz. Camarón-Sábalo; Los Arcos, Calz. Camarón-Sábalo; Mamucas, S. Bolivar 73 Pte.; Pepe Toro, Av. Garzas 18; Puerto Azul, Av. del Mar y Playa/Playa Norte; Señor Frogs, Av. del Mar 225; Señor Pepper, Av. Camarón-Sábalo Norte; ★The Shrimp Bucket, Olas Altas 11; Tony's, Mariano Escobedo 1111; Tres Islas, Calz. Camarón-Sábalo

Mérida

★Alberto's Continental Patio, Calle 64 y 57; Amarantus, Prol. Paseo de Montejo 250; Café Pop, Calle 57 between 60 and 62; ★Château Valentin, Calle 58 No. 499D; El Louvre, Calle 61 y Calle 62, by the Zócalo; El Patio de las Fajitas, Calle 60 No. 467; La Casona, Calle 60 No. 434; ★Le Gourmet, Av. Pérez Ponce 109A; Los Almendros, Calle 59 No. 434; Muelle, Calle 21 No. 142; Pancho's, Calle 59 y Calle 60; Portico del Peregrino, Calle 57 y Calle 60; Siqueff, Calle 59 No. 553

Mexico City (Ciudad de México)

Andrea, Amberes 12, Zona Rosa; Antigua Hacienda de Tlalpan, Calz. de Tlalpan 4619; Arroyo, Insurgentes Sur 4003; Bar la Opera, city centre, 5 de Mayo/Filomena Mata; Bellinghausen, Londres 35; Café de Paris, Plaza Melchor Ocampo 14; Café de Tacuba, Tacuba 28; Café la Blanca, 5 de Mayo 40; Café la Habana, Bucareli/Morelos 62; Casa de los Azulejos, Madera 4; Châlet Suizo, Zona Rosa, Niza 37; Casa del Campo, Masaryk/Calderón de la Barco Polanco; ★Champs Elysées, Reforma y Amberes; Churchill's, Avila Camacho 67; Da Raffaelo, Londres 165; ★Del Lago, Nuevo Bosque de Chapultepec, Lago Mayor; Delmonico's, Londres 78; Don Chon, Calle Regina; El Buen Comer, E. A. Poe 50, Polanco (lunchtimes only); El Colonial Loredo, Hamburgo 29; El Danubio, Uruguay 3; ★Fonda del Refugio, Liverpool 166; Fonda Santa Anita, Humboldt 48; Fuji, Río Pánuco 128; Gatolete, Estrasburgo 31, Zona Rosa; ★Hacienda de los Morales, Vázquez de Mella 525; Hasti Bhawan, Plaza San Jacinto 9; ★Honfleur, Amberes 14A, Zona Rosa; Isadora, Molière 50; La Calesa de Londres, Zona Roas, Londres 102; La Faena, city centre, Venustiano Carranza 49; La Fonda del Recuerdo, Bahía de Palmas; La Galvia, Campos Elíseos 247, Polanco; La Marinera, Liverpool 183; La Petite France, Presidente Masaryk 360–10; La Troje, Insurgentes Sur 1217; Las Delicias, Venezuela 41; Les Moustaches, Río Sena 88; ★L'Estoril, Génova 75; Loma Linda, Reforma Lomas 1105; Loredo, Hamburgo 29; Loredo, Homero y Suderman, Polanco; Los Girasoles, Calle de Tacuba entre 8 y 10; Los Guajolotes, Insurgentes Sur, corner of San Antonio; Mazurka, Nueva York 150, Nápoles; Pabellón Suizo, Plaza Villa de Madrid 17; Paraiso de Oriente, Amsterdam 1, Col. Hipódromo; Pomodoro, Paseo de la Reforma 264, esq. Niza; Rincón Argentino, Lope de Vega 338, Polanco; Rincón Gaucho, Insurgentes Sur 1622, Del Valle; Riscal, Insurgentes Sur 1618; ★San Angel Inn, Palmas 50; ★Suntory , Montes Urales 537

Monterrey

Das Bierhaus (The Beerhouse), Av. Revolución y Jardin Sur; El Gaucho, Arroyo Seco 100; El Granero, Calzada del Valle 333 Ote; El Pastor, Madero Pte. 1067; El Tío, Hidalgo y México; Galería del Gourmet, Calzada San Pedro 117 Ote; ★Henry VIII, Hidalgo 2726 Pte.; Las Pampas, Av. E. Garza Sada 2401; ★Luisiana, Hidalgo 530 Sur; Regio, Av. Gonzalitos y Vancouver

Morelia

El Pastra Nostra, Leazaro Cárdenas 2276; Janitzio, Ruiz 521; La Cueva de Chucho, Eduardo Ruíz 620; La Fuente, Madero Ote 493; La Huacana, Garcia Obeso y Aldama; La Posta de Gallo, Garcia de León 1035; Las Bugambilias, Av. de las Camelinas 514; ★Las Mercedes, León Guzmán 47; Las Morelianas, El Retajo 90; Los Comensales, Zaragoza 148;

Michoacano, Portal Galeana 149a; Solar de Villagrán, Rincón de las Comadres 7

Oaxaca

Ajos y Cebollas, Juárez 605; Alfredo da Roma, Alcala 400; Del Jardín, Portal de Flores 10; Doña Elpidia, Miguel Cabrera 413; El Asador Vasco, Portal de Flores 11; El Sol y la Luna, Murgia 105; Guelatao, Portal Benito Juárez 102; La Coronita, Díaz Ordaz 208; Mi Casita, Hidalgo 616; Santa Fé, 5 de Mayo 103

Pachuca

El Fogón de Pakal, Calle Merle Green; La Canada, Calle Merle Green; La Selva, Carr. Palenque; Maya, Av. Independencia

Palenque

Ciro's, Plaza Independencia 110; De Antaño, Leandro Valle 200; La Parroquia, Guanajuato 20; Pasquinelle, Revolución 1104

Pátzcuaro Lake
In Pátzcuaro

El Patio, Plaza Vasco de Quiroga; Los Escudos, Portal Hidalgo 74; Posada la Basílica, Arciga 6

Outside

El Faro, Muelle 2; El Gordo, Av. de las Américas 2; Fonda del Sol, Av. de las Américas 157

Puebla
de Zaragoza

Bavaria, Av. Juárez 2713; Charlie's China Poblana, Av. Juárez 1918; Chesa Veglia, 2 Oriente 202; D'Armando's, Av. Juárez 2105; Del Parian, Av. 2 Ote No. 415; El Cortijo, 16 de Septiembre 506; El Vegetariano, Av. 3 Pte. No, 525; ★La Fonda de Santa Clara, 3 Poniente 307; La Princesa, Portal Juárez 101; Sanborns, 2 Oriente 6

Puerto Escondido
In the town

Bananas, Av. Gasga; Bucanero, Av. Gasga; La Palapa, in town centre, Av, Gasga; La Posada, Av. Gasga; Nautilus, Av. Gasga; Papayago; Perla Flameante, Av. Gasga; Spaghetti House, Playa Principal

Outside

La Sardina de Plata, Playa Bacocho; Puerto Angelito, Playa Puerto Angelito

Puerto Vallarta
In the town

Balam, Basilio Badillo 425; Brazz, Morelos y Galeana; Café des Artistes, Guadalupe Sánchez 740; Captain Morgan's, Puesta del Sol, Club de Tenis; Carlos O'Brian Bar & Grill, Diaz Ordaz 786; Chez Elena, Matamoros 520; ★Daiquiri Dick's, Olas Altas 246; El Patio, Encino 287; Franzi Café, Isla Río Cuale; La Cebolla Roja, Díaz Ordaz 822; ★Le Bistro, Isla Río Cuale; ★Manantial, Allende 168; Moby Dick, 31 Octubre 128; Ostión Feliz, Libertad 177; Roberto's Puerto Nuevo, Basilo Badillo 284

Outside

Chico's Paradise, Carr. y Navidad at km 20 marker; El Rinconcito, Playa de Mismaloya; ★Le Kliff, Carr. a Barra de Navidad, at km 17 marker; Miramar, 20km/12½ miles north in La Cruz de Huanacaxtle

Querétaro
(Town)

El Arcángel, Guerrero y Madero; El Cortijo de Don Juan, Jardín Corregidora 1416; Fonda San Antonio, in town centre, Corregidora 144; Josecho, Dalia 1; Fonda Santa María, Morelos 160; La Fonda del Refugio, Jardin Corregidora 26; La Mariposa, Angel Peralta 7; Museo, Prol. Corregidora Sur 25

Salamanca

Boca del Río, Abasolo 207; Bugambilias, Juárez 125; Camino Real, Morelos 203; El Cascabel, Aldam 1010

San Cristóbal de las Casas

El Faisán, Madero, near the Zócalo; El Fogón de Jovel, 16 Septiembre 11; Lacanjá, Lacanjá, 10 de Marzo 13; La Galería, Hidalgo 3, near the Zócalo; La Hostería del Virrey, Diego de Mazariegos 56; La Langosta, Madero 9; Los Arcos, F. Madero 6; Madre Tierra, Insurgentes 19; Normita, Juárez y F. Flores; Tuluc, Av. F. Madero y B. Juárez

Restaurants

San Luis Potosí	El Ejecutivo, Av. Carranza 749; El Faisán, Carranza 410; El Muelle 3, Arista 1210; La Gran Vía, Av. V. Carranza 560; La Parroquia, Carranza 950; ★La Virreina, Av. V. Carranza 830; Villa Fontana, 5 de Mayo 455
San Miguel de Allende	Antigua Trattoria Italiana, Codo/Zacateros; Bugambilia, Hidalgo 42; Carmina, Cuna Allende 7; Casa de Janos, Callejón de la Palma 13; Fonda Mesón de San José, Mesones 38; Hobo's, Calle Ancha de San Antonio 31; La Princesa, Recreo 5; Mama Mia, Umarán 8; Rincón Español, Correo 10; Vendemia, Hidalgo 12;
Tampico	Chinatown, Av. Hidalgo y Av. Real; Del Mar, Aduana Sur 309; Diligencias, Calle Tampico Ote. 415; Flamingo, Av. Hidalgo y Nayarit; Jardín, Corona, Av. M. Hidalgo 1915; La Mansión Loredo, Fresno 101
Taxco de Alarcón	Cielito Lindo, Plaza Borda 14; La Taberna, B. Juárez 8; Los Balcones, Plazuela de los Gallos; Los Reyes, Juárez 9; Pagaduría del Rey, Calle H. Colegio Militar; Señor Costilla, Plaza Borda 1
Outside	★La Ventana de Taxco, Carr. a Acapulco
Teotihuacan	★La Gruta; museum and restaurant; Piramid Charlies, Unidad Cultural
Tepic	Chante Clair, Laureles y Góngora; El Farallón, Insurgentes 276 Pte.; La Tarraza, Insurgentes 98 Pte.; Los Jazmines, Léon 118 Nte.
Tijuana	Bol Corona, Av. Revolución 520; Cilantro's, Paseo Tijuana 406; La Costa, Galeana 150; Pedrin's, Av. Revolución 1115; Tía Juana Tilly's, Av. Revolución 701
Tlaxcala (Town)	Los Molcajetes, Juárez 29; Mesón Taurino, Independencia 12
Toluca de Lerdo	Alexander's Steakhouse, Paseo Tollocán 1214; Concorde, Aquiles Serdán 111; El Mesón de las Ramblas, Matamoros 107; Fonda San Felipe, Hidalgo 8; La Gamba, Fabela Norte 105; Luigis, López Mateos 143; La Cabaña Suiza, Carr. México–Toluca, km 63 marker
Tuxtla Gutierrez	Cafetería San Marcos, Plaza Crystal 2d; Chung Shan, 1 Nte. Pte. 217; Flamingo, 1 Pte. Sur 168; La Selva, Dominguez 1360, west of town centre; Las Pichanchas, Av. Central Ote. 837; London, 2 Nte, y 4 Pte
Uruapan de Progreso	Antojitos Yucatecos "Cox Hanal", Emilio Carranza 37; El Rincón del Burrito, Matamoros 7; Las Palmas, Donato Guerra 2; Mansión Cupatitzio, Parque Nacional; Parrilla Tarasca, A. Obregón 4;
Veracruz (Town)	★Café La Parroquia, Independencia 105; La Bamba, A. Camacho y E. Zapata; Las Brisas del Mar, Blvd. A. Camacho 3797; Marthita, Trigueros 43; ★Prendes, Zócalo; Salón Familiar Tiburón, Landero y Coss/Aquiles Serdán
Outside	Pardiños, in Boca del Río (10km/6 miles south)
Villahermosa	Club de Pesca, 27 Febrero 812; El Ganadero, 27 Febrero 1618; El Guaraguaya, 27 Febrero 927/Mina (town centre); El Mesón de Castilla, Pagés Llergo 125; El Mesón del Duende, Av. Gregorio Méndez 1703; Galerías Madan, Av. F. Madero 408; Leo, Paseo Tabasco 429; Los Tulipanes, Carlos Pellicer 511 (near museum)
Zacatecas (Town)	La Cantera Musical Fonda y Bar, Tacuba 2 (Mercado); La Cuija, Tacuba 5; Las Pampas, Regeneración/López Mateos; Mesón de la Mina, Av. Juárez 15; Villa del Mar, Ventura Salazar 338 y 340

Zihuatanejo
In the town of Zihuatanejo

Casa Elvira, Paseo del Pescador; Coconuts, Guerrero 4; El Castillo, Ejido 25; Garrobos, Juan Alvarez 52; La Mesa del Capitán, Nicolás Bravo 18; Peppers Garden, Ignacio Altamirano 46

On the beach

Kon-Tiki, Carr. Playa de la Ropa; La Gaviota, Playa de la Ropa; La Perla, Playa de la Ropa

In Ixtapa

Carlos'n Charlie's, Playa del Palmar; El Faro, Playa Vista Hermosa; Mama Norma, La Puerta Center; ★ Villa de la Selva, Paseo de la Roca

See also Food and Drink.

Road Transport

Road network

The 235,000km/146,000 miles of roads in Mexico vary according to the density of population in the various states. Thus, in the north – Baja California Norte and Sur, Sonora, Chihuahua and Coahuila – the network is relatively thin, the best developed part of the system being the important north–south connections; the central and southern parts of the country – broadly between a line from Mazatlán via Monterrey to Matamoros and the frontiers with Guatemala and Honduras – are much better served.

Motorways (*autopistas*, most of which, like bridges, are subject to tolls) are practically confined to the vicinity of large towns and traffic centres (Mexico City, Guadalajra, Monterrey, Saltillo, Coatzacoalcos, Villahermosa, Veracruz, Hermosillo, Mazatlán, Tijuana, Chihuahua, Puebla, Querétaro, Colima). Since 1990 the government has been granting 30 year-long franchises to private companies to build several thousand kilometres of four-lane motorways. Compared with Europe and the USA the tolls are very high. The backbone of the road system is formed by the federal highways (*rutas federales*), which are marked by signs with "Mex" and a serial number (e.g. MEX 180). Other major roads are state highways (*rutas estatales*), also numbered, which are maintained by the individual states (e.g. GTO 49). Secondary roads, often unsurfaced, serve the smaller towns and villages and the more remote areas of the country. At night the traveller needs to watch out for unlit vehicles or cattle on such roads.

Warning

In the rainy season most unsurfaced roads become impassable for normal vehicles, and even four-wheel drive cross-country vehicles find them difficult. The Tourist Ministry (see Information) issues a monthly bulletin (*Boletin de condiciones de carreteras*) giving the latest situation on the roads. However, bus drivers are the most reliable source of information for long journeys.

Traffic regulations

Vehicles travel on the right in Mexico. At junctions and intersections between roads of equal status vehicles coming from the right have priority. Traffic on a roundabout has right of way. Road signs and markings are mainly in accordance with international standards.

The maximum speed limit is 40kph/25mph in built-up areas, 80kph/50mph on major trunk roads and 110kph/68mph on motorways. Many roads through towns and villages have "sleeping policemen" (*topes*), bumps built in the road at intervals to slow down the traffic. Often there is no warning of these.

Tip

It should not be assumed that local drivers, particularly in the large towns, will strictly observe traffic regulations. Visiting drivers should

A police motor-cycle in Mexico City

therefore be constantly on their guard; driving in the busy traffic of Mexico City – or, for that matter, in rural areas where animals, pedestrians and cyclists share the roads – is an experience which calls for steady nerves and quick reactions. There is one rule that must be strictly obeyed – that of "no parking". Mexican traffic police have developed a clever way of tracing those who breach parking regulations – they unscrew their number plates, which can be retrieved only on payment of a "fee" which goes into the pockets of the police.

Breakdowns
"Angeles Verdes"

The main highways are patrolled by the green vehicles (*angeles verdes*, or "green angels") of the road emergency sevice run by the Ministry of Tourism. They will carry out repairs, give first aid and provide information. Only the costs of spares and petrol have to be paid for. The Mexican Automobile Association also runs a breakdown service; its service vehicles are painted yellow and bear the letters "AMA".

There is no general telephone number for the "green angels", so all one can do is wait by the side of the road with the bonnet up to show that help is needed. In the more remote areas, however, the driver is really on his own. However, it is usually possible to find someone at a petrol station or in villages who can carry out repairs. Drivers are recommended to equip themselves with a kit of useful spares before undertaking longish journeys, especially in rural areas.

Petrol stations

The state PEMEX petrol stations tend to be rather few and far between, and drivers are advised to fill up at every opportunity. Petrol stations are marked on the PEMEX Road Atlas. Lead-free petrol *magna sin* is also now obtainable at most filling stations.

Distances en km	Acapulco	Chetumal	Chihuahua	Ciudad Juárez	Durange	Guadalajara	Guanajuato	Hermosillo	La Paz	Manzanillo	Metamoros	Mérida	Mexico City	Nogales	Nuevo Laredo	Oaxaca	Piedras Negras	Puebla	Querétaro	San Luis Potosi	Tampico	Tapachula	Tijuana	Veracruz	Villahermosa
Acapulco		1849	1852	2227	1300	949	762	2372	4700	1195	1334	1946	397	2677	1588	656	1714	497	619	821	869	1326	3283	821	1278
Chetumal	1849		2832	3308	2352	1984	1804	3407	5781	2292	2078	446	1449	3684	2346	1275	2558	1323	1671	1873	1556	1256	4290	1054	571
Chihuahua	1852	2832		375	709	1144	1161	1921	4221	1469	1141	2960	1455	2198	1048	1971	1036	1581	1233	1031	1276	2630	2804	1869	2308
Ciudad Juárez	2227	3308	375		1084	1519	1536	2297	4596	1844	1516	3350	1830	2573	1423	2346	1411	1956	1608	1406	1723	3076	3179	2255	2737
Durange	1300	2352	709	1084		600	609	1212	3512	925	938	2408	903	1489	825	1419	833	1029	681	479	871	2088	2095	1327	1766
Guadalajara	949	1984	1144	1519	600		301	1423	3723	325	1010	2040	535	1700	998	1051	1124	706	348	354	746	1720	2306	1004	1398
Guanajuato	762	1804	1161	1536	609	301		1724	4031	626	866	1860	355	2001	977	881	1103	491	133	210	602	1540	2607	789	1218
Hermosillo	2372	3407	1921	2297	1212	1423	1724		2300	1634	2150	3463	1958	277	2057	2519	2045	2129	1781	1691	2083	3143	883	2427	2821
La Paz	4700	5781	4221	4596	3512	3723	4031	2300		3934	3450	5852	4303	2293	3357	4819	4345	4429	4081	3991	4383	5549	1457	4727	5210
Manzanillo	1195	2292	1469	1844	925	325	626	1634	3934		1335	2348	843	1911	1323	1274	1449	969	667	679	1071	2004	2517	1267	1706
Metamoros	1334	2078	1141	1516	938	1010	866	2150	3450	1335		2149	960	2427	348	1445	765	1024	858	656	492	1892	3033	1024	1507
Mérida	1946	446	2960	3350	2408	2040	1860	3463	5852	2348	2149		1505	3740	2409	1346	2599	1379	1227	1929	1627	1327	4346	1125	642
Mexico City	397	1449	1455	1830	903	535	355	1958	4303	843	960	1505		2280	1191	516	1317	126	222	424	468	1185	2841	424	863
Nogales	2677	3684	2198	2573	1489	1700	2001	277	2239	1911	2427	3740	2280		2334	2796	2322	2406	2058	1968	2360	3465	822	2704	3143
Nuevo Laredo	1588	2346	1048	1423	825	998	977	2057	3357	1323	348	2409	1191	2334		1652	756	1284	969	767	752	2152	2940	1284	1767
Oaxaca	656	1275	1971	2346	1419	1051	881	2519	4819	1274	1445	1346	516	2796	1652		1833	408	738	940	953	669	3402	421	704
Piedras Negras	1714	2558	1036	1411	833	1124	1103	2045	4345	1449	765	2599	1317	2322	756	1833		1443	1095	893	972	2372	2928	1504	1987
Puebla	497	1323	1581	1956	1029	706	491	2129	4429	969	1024	1379	126	2406	1284	408	1443		348	550	532	1077	3012	298	737
Querétaro	619	1671	1233	1608	681	348	133	1781	4081	667	858	1727	222	2058	969	738	1095	348		202	539	1407	2664	646	1085
San Luis Potosi	821	1873	1031	1406	479	354	210	1691	3991	679	656	1929	422	1968	767	940	893	550	202		392	1609	2574	848	1287
Tampico	869	1556	1276	1723	871	746	602	2083	4383	1071	492	1627	468	2360	752	953	972	532	539	392		1370	2966	502	982
Tapachula	1326	1256	2630	3076	2088	1720	1540	3143	5549	2004	1892	1327	1185	3465	2152	669	2372	1077	1407	1609	1370		4026	868	685
Tijuana	3283	4290	2804	3179	2095	2306	2607	883	1457	2517	3033	4346	2841	822	2940	3402	2928	3012	2664	2574	2966	4026		3310	3704
Veracruz	821	1054	1869	2255	1327	1004	789	2427	4727	1267	1024	1125	424	2704	1284	421	1504	298	646	848	502	868	3310		480
Villahermosa	1278	571	2308	2737	1766	1398	1218	2821	5210	1706	1507	642	863	3143	1767	704	1987	737	1085	1287	982	685	3704	480	

Automobile club

Asociación Mexicana Automovilistica (AMA)
Orizaba 7, Colonia Roma
06700 México D.F.;
tel. (915) 5 11 68 73

There are branches of the Automobile Club in all the larger Mexican towns.

See Getting to Mexico, Car Rental and Language, Road Signs

Safety

A Safe Journey

Insurance

Most long-term insurance policies, i.e. Life assurance, Personal Accident and Personal Liability covers will apply world-wide and thus offer protection during trips abroad; however, it might be best to check in advance that this is so.

See under Insurance for details of additional recommended holiday insurances.

On a federal highway

Important documents

A valid passport. All British travellers must be in possession of a valid 10-year British passport, valid for at least 6 months beyond the intended return date. Visas are not normally required.

At the time of going to press it is not a legal requirement for UK citizens to be in possession of a valid certificate of vaccination, but certain precautions are nevertheless advisable; see Health.

Driving certificate. Motoring organisation certificate. All tickets. Photocopies of all important papers. Traveller's cheques, credit cards. Maps of Mexico.

See Travel Documents

Medicaments

In addition to a first-aid kit visitors should ensure they have an adequate supply of all the medicines they regularly take. When travelling to warmer climes it should be borne in mind that the local chemists may not stock the same medical preparations which are obtainable at home, and that equally those you bring with you may not be effective against certain local ailments. If in doubt, check with your doctor before leaving.

Also bear in mind that certain medicaments can affect reactions and ability to drive.

Safe Driving

Car rental

When hiring a car go only to firms with an international name in order to be sure that steering, chassis, engine, brakes, lights and bodywork are up the standard expected. If necessary, take out additional Motor and Personal Insurances. Many car rental firms will give a discount to members of motoring clubs, such as the RAC, AA, etc. Paying by credit card can avoid the need to leave a deposit. See Car Rental.

Seat-belts

Always wear seat-belts and ensure that your passengers do the same, whether they are in the front or the back. The straps should be taut and not twisted; badly-fitted seat-belts can result in further injuries in the event off an accident.

Belts can work properly only when used in conjunction with correctly adjusted head-restraints. The upper edge of the restraint must be at or higher than eye-level; only then is the spine fully protected.

Safety for spectacle wearers

Wearers of spectacles can drive more safely at night with non-reflective lenses. Some forms of tinted glasses should not be worn during twilight or hours of darkness. Because glass reflects part of the light falling on it even a perfectly clear windscreen only allows 90% of the light outside to reach the driver's eyes. Tinted or dirty windscreens and tinted spectacles combine to reduce this figure to only 50%, with a considerable effect on driving safety.

What To Do in the Event of an Acccident

Immediate measures

Even if angry, try to keep calm and polite. Keep a clear head and complete the following steps in order:

Safety measures

1. Make the scene of the accident safe by switching on warning lights and setting up flashing lights and/or warning triangles at a safe distance.

Injured persons

2. Attend to any injured persons. Send for an ambulance if necessary.

Police

3. Inform the police if necessary.

Notes

4. Make notes of the names and addresses of the other parties involved and of their insurance particulars, together with the registration numbers and makes of their vehicles.

   It is also important to note the time and place and the address of any police unit involved.

Evidence

5. Obtain evidence. Write down names and addresses of any independent witnesses if possible. Makes sketches of what happened at the scene; better still, take photos from various angles.

Signatures

Do not admit liability (even if you feel you were in the wrong) and do not sign anything acknowledging responsibility or indeed any document written in a language you do not understand!

Other legal rulings

Claim settling procedures and legal rulings applying may differ considerably from those the driver is familiar with at home. The law of the land will, of course, apply and claims may well take a long time to settle and then perhaps not in full!

See Road Transport

Shopping and Souvenirs

Mexican hand-made goods are popular with souvenir-hunters. They are best bought direct from the place where they are made or from the local market. Never buy silver or gold items from street traders; these, too, should come from the manufacturer (mainly in Taxco) or from reputable shops. Genuine silver has to be marked "Sterling" or "925".

Antiques	Visitors are advised against buying antiques, as there is an embargo on taking them out of the country. Excellent reproductions are on sale in the National Anthropological Museum in Mexico City. Almost without exception, the larger "archaeological finds" frequently offered for sale at the sites of such digs are fakes which have only recently been buried; techniques in reproducing "old" ceramics are now so sophisticated that even experts find it hard to tell them from the originals.

Handiwork and Local Crafts

Mexico has few equals as regards the quality and variety of its local handicrafts. In spite of increased mass production in recent years there is still an ample supply of good and imaginative hand-made goods on offer. Like many other things here, local products present a charming mixture of Spanish and Mexican forms and designs. Many rural areas have developed their own artistic styles to suit all tastes and purses.

Ceramics (*cerámica*)	Michoacán: Pátzcuaro, Tzintzuntzan, San José de Gracia Jalisco: Tonalá, Tlaquepaque, Tateposco México: Texcoco, Metepec Guanajuato: Dolores Hidalgo, Guanajuato Oaxaca: San Bartolo Coyotepec Chiapas: Amantenango Puebla: Puebla, Acatlán
Basket and wickerwork (*cestería*)	Querétaro: Tequisquiapan, San Juan del Rio Michoacán: Pátzcuaro México: Toluca, Lerma
Sarapes (Shawls of wool or cotton, for men)	Querétaro: Bernal Tlaxcala: Santa Ana Chiantempan, Tlaxcala México: Toluca, Tenancingo, Texcoco, Coatepec Harinas Guanajuato: San Miguel de Allende Jalisco: Jocotepec Oaxaca: Teotitlán del Valle
Embroidered blouses (*blusas bordas*)	Distrito Federal: Mexico City México: Tenancingo Michoacán: Pátzcuaro, Morelia
Silverware (*objetos de plata*)	Distrito Federal: Mexico City Guerrero: Taxco Jalisco: Guadalajara
Copper and brass (*Objetos de cobre, láton*)	Guanajuato: San Miguel de Allende Michoacán: Santa Clara del Cobre (Villa Escalante)
Gold filigree work (*filigrana de oro*)	Oaxaca: Oaxaca, Tehuantepec Yucatán: Mérida
Semi-precious stones	Querétaro: Querétaro San Juan del Río, Tequisquipan
Hand-blown glass (*vidrio soplado*)	Nuevo León: Monterrey Puebla: Puebla Guanajuato: San Miguel de Allende

Handcrafted copper-ware from central Mexico

Lacquerwork (*lacas*)

Michoacán: Uruapan, Pátzcuaro, Quiroga
Guerrero: Olinalá
Oaxaca: Oaxaca
Chiapas: Chiapa de Corzo

Woodcarvings (*labrados de madera*)

Michoacán: Paracho, Quiroga
Guanajuato: Apaseo el Alto

Leather goods (*objetos de cuero*)

Guanajuato: León
Zacatecas: Jerez de García Salinas
Chiapas: San Cristóbal de Las Casas
Oaxaca: Oaxaca

Hammocks (*hamacas*)

Veracruz, Tabasco, Campeche, Yucatán and Chiapas

Hats (*sombreros*)

Particularly good quality in Michoacán, Campeche and Yucatán

Market

The market (*mercado*) plays a central role in Mexican life. When the Spaniards first arrived in the country they were astonished by the size of the market-places, the range of goods on sale and the excellent organisation; the markets of Mexico are still conducted with much less noise and bustle than in other southern countries. Bargaining over prices is normal, and indeed is expected. The abundance and variety of the wares on sale – local craft products, folk art, flowers, fruit, vegetables and much else – make a fascinating scene. The travelling Indian markets are known as *tianguis*.

See Protected Species and Customs Regulations

Markets are found everywhere and at all hours of the day

Sport

Crowd sports

The most popular crowd sport in Mexico is bull-fighting, although perhaps the word sport is something of a misnomer.

Charreadas

Somewhat less bloody are the *charreadas*, rodeo-like games in which the riders display their skill (see Art and Culture, Folklore). In Mexico City *charreadas* can be watched in the Hipódromo de las Américas, Blvd. A. M. Camacho e Industria Militar, from the middle of October to the middle of September (Tues., Thur., Sat. from 2pm).

Jai Alai (*Frontón*)

Jai alai is an extremely exciting but dangerous sport in which the players have on their right hand a long scoop-like basketwork "glove" with which they drive a hard ball against the wall at great speed (see Art and Culture, Folklore). In Mexico City games of *jai alai* are played every evening except Mondays and Fridays in the Frontón México on the Plaza de la Revolución.

Participant sports

Water-sports

The man-made lakes and reservoirs in the interior of the country provide an opportunity for enjoying almost all water-sports (*deportes acuáticos*) such as boating, sailing, wind-surfing, water-skiing, etc.

On the coasts open to the Pacific – the west coast of Baja California and the mainland coast south of Mazatlán – the heavy swell coming in from the sea affords excellent surfing.

Diving (*buceo*) enthusiasts are also well catered for. Snorkellers and scuba divers will find plenty of scope, especially off the east coast of Yucatán (Cancún, Cozumel, Isla Mujeres). The plant and animal life of the coral reefs in this area provide magnificent subjects for underwater photography.

See Beaches and Spas

Surfing in Baja California

Tennis

Once restricted to a few fashionable private clubs, tennis (*tenis*) has now developed on a considerable scale to meet the needs of tourists. Many large hotels have their own tennis-courts, and most clubs welcome visitors.

Riding

The Mexicans are great horse-lovers. A number of hotels offer facilities for riding (*equitación*), and on a visit to a hacienda a ride can usually be arranged.

Golf

Golf-courses, most of them managed by local clubs or hotels, will be found near the larger towns and at tourist centres.

Climbing

Mexico offers only limited scope for real mountaineering (*alpinismo*), but there is excellent walking to be had in the main ranges, the Eastern, Western and Southern Sierra Madre. Since the tree-line lies at about 4000m/13,000ft the mountain ranges do not have the Alpine character of European peaks. There is little in the way of overnight accommodation facilities, so climbers must confine themselves to day trips unless they are prepared to spend the night in an Indian village. The landscape pattern is often masked by the dense vegetation, and it is therefore necessary to be prepared to deviate from the direct route and negotiate gorges which cannot be seen from a distance.

Three peaks of genuine Alpine character are the snow-capped volcanoes *Popocatépetl* (5452m/17,888ft), *Iztaccíhuatl* (5286m/17,343ft) and *Citlaltépetl* (Pico de Orizba, 5700m/18,700ft); but even for these stamina, rather than high mountaineering skill, is required. Rock-climbing is possible at heights of up to 4000m/13,000ft, but the rock is often weathered and crumbling. At higher altitudes there are great expanses of volcanic ash and isolated pinnacles of rock.

Information can be obtained from the following climbing clubs:

Club Alpino Comolumno
Calle Lago Superior 188, Col. Torre Blanca
México D.F. 11280
Tel. (915) 5 27 14 17

Associación Mexicana de Alpinismo
Calle Huertas 93C
Colonia del valle
México D.F.
Tel. (915) 5 24 97 20

Fishing

The coastal waters and continental shelf of Mexico are abundantly stocked with fish and attract large numbers of coastal and deep-sea fishermen. Boat trips in search of the larger fish are popular.

There is relatively little fresh-water fishing in Mexico, since there are few rivers with a flow of water throughout the year. Many lakes and reservoirs do, however, offer good sport.

For rod-fishing (*pesca con caña*) a fishing permit (*permiso de pesca*) is required. In the inland regions this is usually issued by the local authority, on the coast by the local harbourmaster or branch office of the Ministry of Industry and Commerce. Information is obtainable from:

Departamento de Pesca
Av. Alvaro Obregón 269
México 7, D.F. 06700
Tel. (915) 2 86 74 08

Telephone

Local calls

Local calls made from telephone boxes cost 10 pesos for three minutes. When the tone is heard dial the number required and wait for the other party to speak before inserting coins.

Information

For Mexico City dial 04

Long distance (*larga distancia*)

Long-distance calls cannot be made from a telephone box; these must be made from a post office or a *Oficina de Larga Distancia*, which will be found in most large towns. In such offices both long-distance and local calls are made through the operator. The caller has to complete a form with the requisite details and then, when the connection has been made, he or she will be asked to enter a kiosk to make the call. In many shops and chemists' there are *casetas de larga distancia*, with blue telephones, which can also be used to make long-distance calls.

Overseas calls are very expensive; they are always based on units of three minutes, even if the actual duration of the call happens to be less than that, and are subject to a tax of 10%. Hotels impose a further heavy surcharge. The operator will be able to tell you how much it will cost.

Automatic dialling

Only private telephones can be used for automatic dialling.

Dialling codes

For calls within Mexico dial 91

For calls to:
Europe dial 98 plus country code
UK dial 98 44
USA or Canada dial 95

Australia dial 98 61
New Zealand dial 98 64
– followed by the number required, omitting the zero of any area code

From the UK dial 00 52
From the USA or Canada dial 011 52

Enquiries:

Local operator dial 02
International operator (*operador internacional*, English-speaking) dial 09

Telegrams

Telegram services are not provided in post offices. Telegrams must be sent from special offices, *oficinas de telégrafos*, and are charged according to whether they are to rank as *extra urgente*, *urgente* or *ordinario*.

Time

Mexico is on Central Standard Time year round. but there are some exceptions. The state of Baja California is on Pacific Daylight or Pacific Standard Time. the following states stay on Pacific Standard time year round: Baja California Sur, Sinaloa, Sonora and Nayarit. From spring 1994 Mexico adopted a "Daylight Saving Time" schedule.

Tipping

In hotels and restaurants tips are not included in the bill and it is customary to add between 10% and 15%. Taxi-drivers do not usually expect a tip, but the amount on the meter should be rounded up at your discretion.

Travel Documents

All British travellers must be in possession of a 10-year British passport, valid for at leat six months beyond the planned return date. A married woman whose passport is still in her maiden name must travel with her marriage certificate.

For entry into Mexico beyond the border towns a Tourist Card is required. This can be obtained in duplicate from a Mexican consulate, a travel agent or on the aircraft. The original covers entry into Mexico and the duplicate should be kept safely for the return journey.

A Tourist Card is normally issued for a period of 30 days, but can be extended to cover 90 or 180 days if required. Within Mexico such an extension can be obtained from the Secretaría de Gobernación, Av. Chapultepec 284, Mexico City, on production of proof of adequate financial means. Any lost cards can also be replaced there.

Driving licence

Those travelling to Mexico by car legally require only their national driving licence, but nevertheless an international driving licence is advisable. A credit card is very useful, sometimes essential, when hiring a vehicle in Mexico.

Animals

Animals need a certificate of innoculation against rabies which is not more than six months old and has been certified by a Mexican consulate.

Value-added Tax

A general Value-added Tax of 15% is charged on consumer goods and in hotels and restaurants. Basic foodstuffs are exempt, and for regular border trade 6% is charged.

Weather

See Facts and Figures, Climate

Weights and Measures

The metric system is in use in Mexico.

Youth Hostels

In Mexico there are youth hostels (*villas juveniles*) in Aguascalientes, Cabo San Lucas, Campeche, Cancún, Ciudad Obregón, Cuautia, Durango, Guadalajara (2), La Paz, Mexicali, Monterrey, Morelia, Oaxaca, Playa del Carmen, Querérato, San Luis Potosi, Tijuana, Tuxtia Gutierrez, Veracruz, Villahermosa, Zacatecas (2) and Zihuatanejo. There is no age limit. Guests must register by 8pm; stays of up to 15 days are permitted in the same hostel.

Information

Dirección General de Atención a la Juventud
Calz. de Tlalpan 583, Col. Alamo, México D.F. Tel. (915) 519 4029

Coordinación Nacional de Turismo
Glorieta Metro Insurgentes, Local CC-11, Col. Juárez, 06 600 México D.F. Tel. (915) 525 2548 and 525 2974

Index

Principal Places of Tourist Interest at a Glance

Note: The above list includes only the more important places of touristic interest in Mexico which are worth seeing either for themselves or for other attractions in the vicinity. In addition there are many other notable sights which are designated by one or two asterisks within the text of each entry.

Imprint

246 colour photographs, 31 ground plans, 20 town plans, 8 drawings, 1 large map at end of book

Original German text: Anita and Karl von Bleyleben
Additional text: Vera Beck, Rainer Eisenschmid, Prof. Dr Hans-Dieter Haas, Prof. Dr Wolfgang Hassenpflug, Frank J. Klug, Peter M. Nahm
Editorial work: Baedeker-Redaktion (Rainer Eisenschmid)
General direction: Dr Peter Baumgarten, Baedeker Stuttgart

English Translation:
Wendy Bell, Julie Bullock, David Cocking, Brenda Ferris, Crispin Warren
Editorial work: Alec Court

Cartography:.Gert Oberländer, Munich; Christoph Gallus, Hohberg-Niederschopfheim; Mairs Geographischer Verlag, Ostfildern (large map)

Source of photographs: Anton (5), Bächle (1), Baedeker-Archiv (3), Beyerle (4), Bildagentur Schapowalow (1), Bildagentur Schuster (5), von Bleyleben (24), Braunstein (11), Consejo Nacional de Turismo México (4), Eid (6), Gauss: (16), Gormsen (9), Granthwohl (4), HB-Verlag, Hamburg (4), Historia-Photo (4), Imago Mexiko (2), Internationaler Sortenerkennungsdienst (1), Kober (4), Lufthansa-Bildarchiv (2), México Desconocido (4), Mexican National Tourist Office (18), Möhle (47), Rode (11), Sacher (1), Schütz-Gormsen (2), Schmid (1), Smettan (2), Sprattler (19), Ullstein (7), Verplanken (1), Wüttemberg Provincial Library (2), ZEFA (3)

2nd English edition 1996

Published in the United States by:
Macmillan Travel
A Simon & Schuster Macmillan Company
1633 Broadway
New York, NY 10019–6785

Macmillan is a registered trademark of Macmillan, Inc.

Distributed in the United Kingdom by the Publishing Division of the Automobile Association, Fanum House, Basingstoke, Hampshire RG21 2EA

A CIP catalogue record of this book is available from the British Library

Licensed user:
Mairs Geographischer Verlag GmbH & Co.,
Ostfildern-Kemnat bei Stuttgart

Printed in Italy by G. Canale & C.S.p.A – Borgaro T.se –Turin

ISBN 0–02–861359–7 USA and Canada
0 7495 1418 3 UK

Notes

Notes

Notes

Notes

Notes